THE INTERNATIONAL SURVEY OF FAMILY LAW

1994

PUBLISHED ON BEHALF OF
THE INTERNATIONAL SOCIETY OF FAMILY LAW

THE INTERNATIONAL SURVEY OF FAMILY LAW

1994

Edited by

Andrew Bainham

Fellow of Christ's College, Cambridge
Lecturer in Law, University of Cambridge, U.K.

MARTINUS NIJHOFF PUBLISHERS
THE HAGUE / BOSTON / LONDON

A C.I.P. Catalogue record for this book is available from the Library of Congress.

ISSN 1384-623X
ISBN 90-411-0218-3

Published by Kluwer Law International,
P.O. Box 85889, 2508 CN The Hague, The Netherlands.

Sold and distributed in the U.S.A. and Canada
by Kluwer Law International,
675 Massachusetts Avenue, Cambridge, MA 02139, U.S.A.

In all other countries, sold and distributed
by Kluwer Law International,
P.O. Box 85889, 2508 CN The Hague, The Netherlands.

Layout and camera-ready copy:
Anne-Marie Krens, Oegstgeest, The Netherlands

Printed on acid-free paper

INTERNATIONAL SURVEY OF FAMILY LAW

PUBLISHED ON BEHALF OF
THE INTERNATIONAL SOCIETY OF FAMILY LAW

A   THE HISTORY OF THE SOCIETY

On the initiative of Professor Zeev Falk, the Society was launched at the University of Birmingham, UK in April 1973. The Society's first international conference was held in West Berlin in April 1975 on the theme *The Child and the Law*. There were over 200 participants, including representatives of governments and international organizations. The second international conference was held in Montreal in June 1977 on the subject *Violence in the Family*. There were over 300 participants from over 20 countries. A third world conference on the theme *Family Living in a Changing Society* was held in Uppsala, Sweden in June 1979. There were over 270 participants from 26 countries. The fourth world conference was held in June 1982 at Harvard Law School, U.S.A. There were over 180 participants from 23 countries. The fifth world conference was held in July 1985 in Brussels, Belgium on the theme *The Family, The State and Individual Security*, under the patronage of Her Majesty Queen Fabiola of Belgium, the Director-General of UNESCO, the Secretary-General of the Council of Europe and the President of the Commission of the European Communities. The sixth world conference on *Issues of the Aging in Modern Society* was held in 1988 in Tokyo, Japan under the patronage of H.I.H. Prince Takahito Mikasa. There were over 450 participants. The seventh world conference was held in May 1991 in Croatia on the theme, *Parenthood: The Legal Significance of Motherhood and Fatherhood in a Changing Society*. There were 187 participants from 37 countries. The eighth world conference took place in Cardiff, Wales in June/July 1994 on the theme *Families Across Frontiers*. The Society has also increasingly held regional conferences including recently Lyon (1995), Quebec City (1996), and Seoul (1996). The Ninth World Conference of the Society will be held from 26-31 July 1997 in Durban, South Africa on the theme *Family Disintegration and Re-integration: African Themes and World Issues*.

B   ITS NATURE AND OBJECTIVES

The following principles were adopted at the first Annual General Meeting of the Society held in the Knogresshalle of West Berlin on the afternoon of Saturday 12 April 1975.

1 The Society's objectives are the study and discussion of problems of family law. To this end the Society sponsors and promotes:
   a International co-operation in research on family law subjects of world-wide interest.
   b Periodic international conferences on family law subjects of world-wide interest.
   c Collection and dissemination of information in the field of family law by the publication of a survey concerning developments in family law throughout the world, and by publication of relevant materials in family law, including papers presented at conferences of the Society.
   d Co-operation with other international, regional or national associations having the same or similar objectives.
   e Interdisciplinary contact and research.
   f The advancement of legal education in family law by all practical means including furtherance of exchanges of teachers, students, judges and practising lawyers.
   g Other objectives in furtherance of or connected with the above objectives.

C   MEMBERSHIP AND DUES

In 1994 the Society had approximately 500 members in some 49 countries.
a Membership:
   · Ordinary Membership, which is open to any member of the legal or a related profes-
     sion. The Council may defer or decline any application for membership.
   · Institutional Membership, which is open to interested organisations at the discretion
     of, and on terms approved by, the Council.
   · Student Membership, which is open to interested students of law and related dis-
     ciplines at the discretion of, and on terms approved by, the Council.
   · Honorary Membership, which may be offered to distinguished persons by decision
     of the Executive Council.
b Each member shall pay such annual dues as may be established from time to time
   by the Council. At present, dues are U.S. $35 (or equivalent) for ordinary membership
   payable annually, or $80 for three years.

D   DIRECTORY OF MEMBERS

A Directory of Members of the Society is available to all Members.

E   BOOKS

The proceedings of the First World Conference were published as *The Child and the
Law* (F. Bates, ed. Oceana 1976); the proceedings of the second as *Family Violence* (J.
Eekelaar & S. Katz, eds. Butterworths, Canada 1978); the proceedings of the third as
Marriage and Cohabitation (J. Eekelaar & S. Katz, eds. Butterworths, Canada 1980);
the fourth, *The Resolution of Family Conflict* (J. Eekelaar & S. Katz, eds. Butterworths,
Canada 1984); the fifth, *Family, State and Individual Economic Security* (Vol. I & II)
(M.T. Meulders-Klein & J. Eekelaar, eds. Story Scientia and Kluwer 1988); the sixth
An Aging World: Dilemmas and Challenges for Law and Social Policy (J. Eekelaar &
D. Pearl eds. Clarendon Press 1989) and the seventh conference *Parenthood in Modern
Society* (J. Eekelaar and P. Sarcevic, eds. Martinus Nijhoff 1993). These are commer-
cially marketed but are available to Society members at reduced prices.

F   THE SOCIETY'S PUBLICATIONS

The Society regularly publishes a newsletter, *The Family Letter,* which appears twice
a year and which is circulated to the members of the Society and reports on its activities
and other matters of interest. *The International Survey of Family Law* provides information on current developments in family law throughout the world and is received
free of charge by members of the Society. The editor is currently Andrew Bainham,
Christ's College, Cambridge, CB2 3BU. The Survey is circulated to members or may
be obtained on application to the Editor.

TABLE OF CONTENTS

CONTRIBUTORS

ALGERIA

Professor M.N. Mahieddin
c/o Professor Jacqueline Rubellin-Devichi
L'Universite Jean Moulin
40 Quai Gailleton
69002 Lyon
France

ANGOLA

Professor Maria do Carmo Medina
Caixa Postal 963
Luanda

ARGENTINA

Dra Cecilia P. Grosman
Corrientes 1515
PISO 6° "B"
1042 Buenos Aires

AUSTRALIA

Professor Frank Bates
Faculty of Law
The University of Newcastle
University Drive
Callaghan
Newcastle 2308

AUSTRIA

Professor Erwin Bernat
Institut Fur Bergerliches Recht
Heinrichstrasse 22 A-8010
Graz

BULGARIA

Dr Anna Staneva
8 Elin Pelin Str.
Sofia 1421

CAMEROON

Professor Ephraim Ngwafor
Faculty of Law
University of Yaounde II
B.P. 1365
Yaounde

CANADA   *Professor Nicholas Bala*
                          Faculty of Law
                          Queen's University
                          Kingston

CHILE   *Professor Inés Pardo de Carvallo*
                          Catholic University of Valparaiso
                          Fundacion Isabel Caces de Brown
                          Avenida Brazil 2950
                          Casilla 4059
                          Valparaiso

CHINA   *Michael Palmer*
                          School of Oriental and African Studies
                          Department of Law
                          Thornhaugh Street, Russell Square
                          WC1H OXG London
                          England

CZECH REPUBLIC   *Professor Judge Jiri Haderka*
                          Jan Werich Street 2a
                          CZ 736 01 Havirov

ENGLAND   *Professor Michael Freeman*
                          Faculty of Laws
                          University College, London
                          Bentham House
                          Endsleigh Gardens
                          WC1H OEG London

FINLAND   *Mr Matti Savolainen*
                          Ministry of Justice
                          Helsinki
                          Fin-00130

FRANCE   *Professor Jacqueline Rubellin-Devichi*
                          L'Universite Jean Moulin
                          40 Quai Gailleton
                          69002 Lyon

GERMANY

Professor Dr Rainer Frank
Direktor des Institus für ausländisches und internationales
Privatrecht Abt. II
Europlatz 1
D-7800 Freiburg 1

REPUBLIC OF IRELAND

Professor Paul O'Connor
Dean of the Faculty of Law
University College Dublin
Dublin

ITALY

Anna Galizia Danovi
c/o Prof Avv. Raffaella Lanzillo
Ord. nell' Università de Pavia
20122 Milano-Via Podgora 15

JAPAN

Professor Yukiko Matsushima
Dokkyo University
Law Faculty
1-9-2 Shakujii-cho
Nerima-Ku
Tokyo 177

Professor Satoshi Minamikata
Faculty of Law
Niigata University
8050 Ikarashi 2-nocho
Niigata 950-21

MALAWI

Garton Kamchedzera
Clare Hall
Herschel Road
CB3 9AL Cambridge
England

MALTA

Dr Ruth Farrugia
Faculty of Law
University of Malta
Valletta

also at: Casa Giarda
Tal-Balal
BKR 14

THE NETHERLANDS *Ms Caroline Forder*
Rijksuniversiteit Limburg
Faculteit der Rechtsgeleerdheid
Vakgroep Privaatrecht
Postbus 616
Maastricht 6200 MD

NEW ZEALAND *William R. Atkin*
Reader in Law
Faculty of Law
Victoria University
PO Box 600
Wellington

NORWAY *Professor Peter Lødrup*
Universitetet i Oslo
Faculty of Law
Karl Johansgt. 47
0162 Oslo

RUSSIA *Dr Olga Khazova*
Institute of State and Law
Russian Academy of Sciences
Znamenka IO
Moscow 119841

SINGAPORE *Professor Peter de Cruz*
School of Law
University of Staffordshire
College Road
ST4 2DE Stoke-on-Trent
England

SOUTH AFRICA *Professor R.T. Nhlapo*
Department of Private Law
University of Cape Town
Faculty of Law
Private Bag Rondebosch 7700
Cape

SPAIN

Professor Gabriel Garcia Cantero
Catedratico de Derecho Civil
Facultad de Derecho
Pedro Cerbuna 12
50009 Zaragoza

SWEDEN

Professor Åke Saldeen
Uppsala Universitet
Juridisk Institutionen
PO Box 512
Uppsala 75120

TURKEY

Professor Esin Örücü
School of Law
Stair Building
The University
G12 8QQ Glasgow
Scotland

UKRAINE

Professor Irina V. Zhilinkova
Ukrainian Law Academy
Civil Law Department
77 Pushkinskaya Str.
310018 Kharkiv

U.S.A.

Professor Marygold S. Melli
University of Wisconsin
Law School
Madison WI 53597

PREFACE

This is the first *International Survey of Family Law* to be published on behalf of the International Society of Family Law. For many years the Society collaborated with the University of Louisville's Journal of Family Law in producing the *Annual Survey of Family Law*. Then in 1994 the Executive Council of the Society, while expressing its appreciation of the long and successful association with Louisville, felt that the time had come to establish the Survey as the Society's own independent publication. It also decided that the Survey should be renamed to reflect its truly international character. The Society was delighted to reach agreement with Martinus Nijhoff for publication of a hardback and paperback version of the new International Survey.

The objectives of the Survey, as I see them, remain much the same. The intention is to provide information, analysis and comment on recent developments in Family Law across the world on a country by country basis. The Survey will continue to be published annually and its title will reflect the calendar year surveyed. Where a country has been regularly surveyed each year, the developments discussed correspond more or less precisely to the year in question. In the current volume this is true, for example, of the articles from Australia, England, New Zealand and Sweden. Some countries, however, will not have been surveyed for a few years and here the contributions will usually attempt to cover the time period since the last article appeared. This applies, for example, in the present volume to the contributions relating to China and Turkey. Yet other countries will be covered for the first time and in this case it is appropriate for the article to provide more background information about the state of family law in the country in question while at the same time concentrating on recent developments. Examples in this volume are the contributions from Bulgaria and Malta.

The Society and I owe a considerable debt of gratitude to all those who have assisted me with the editorial work. Carol Dowling of the secretarial staff of the Faculty of Law at the University of Cambridge spent countless hours producing the manuscript and sending correspondence to contributors. Without her cheerful assistance and meticulous attention to detail my task would have been infinitely more difficult. Alison Careless, also of the secretarial staff, kindly assisted with proof-reading. I am also most grateful to several of my colleagues at Christ's College, Cambridge. Steve Hedley's computing expertise proved priceless when it came to the conversion of disks and I received valuable help from Virginia Cox and Serafina Cuomo in the translation of one contribution. While on the subject of translation, the Society is very fortunate to have the continued assistance of my former colleague Peter Schofield. I would like to thank him for all his work on the French and Spanish texts, some of which had to be done under severe constraints of time. Last, but certainly not least, I would like to pay tribute to my predecessor Michael Freeman without whose efforts there would in my view be no Survey – at least not one recognisable as the one we see today. During his ten years as editor, a staggering eighty countries were surveyed worldwide. As incoming editor I have profited immeasurably from his advice and from the many contacts established by him. In short I have been able to take over the editorship of a publication already in excellent shape. I was therefore delighted when Michael Freeman agreed to continue his association with the Survey by writing the contribution on England for 1994. Regular readers will, I can confidently predict, quickly recognise his inimitable style!

My task as editor is now to build on these sure foundations laid by Michael Freeman. The principal objectives are to increase the core of countries regularly surveyed and, perhaps more importantly, to extend coverage of the Survey to parts of the world never previously covered. There is a pressing need to extend the reach of the Survey further into the countries of Central and South America, North Africa, the Middle East and other parts of Asia. I would be glad to hear from anyone interested in writing on family law developments in those parts of the world or who can suggest anyone who might be able and willing to contribute. And I would like to conclude by thanking all those who have contributed to the present volume.

Andrew Bainham

ALGERIA

MARRIAGE: ITS FORMATION AND EFFECTS IN ALGERIAN SUBSTANTIVE LAW

M.N. Mahieddin*

I   INTRODUCTION

To understand islamic jurisprudence we must realise that law is, to its theologian-jurists, only part of a wider whole (fiqh) covering ritual and even morality as well as strictly legal norms.

Secondly, muslim jurists have worked out a theory (ilm usûl al-fiqh) of the "sources of law". The origin of the legal rule lies in the Qur'an, the tradition of the prophet (Sunna), the consensus of doctors of law (Ijmâ') and argument by analogy (qiyâs). Other, more controversial sources have been suggested.

Finally, islamic law contains several "schools", named after their founder or after a disciple of his who took on himself to set out formally the master's teaching. There are today four major schools of law, formed between the 6th and 9th centuries, among the (majority) Sunni muslims: Maliki, Hanafi, Shafi'i and Hanbali. In Algeria, the dominant school is Maliki, but there are also 'Ibadites following a school formed after a split with the Shi'ites. For details of this, we would refer, among other works to

· Louis Milliot and François-Paul Blanc, *Introduction à l'étude du droit musulman*, Paris, Sirey, (1987).
· Henri de Waël, *Le droit musulman*, CHEAM, Paris, (1989).
· Noël J. Coulson, *A History of Islamic Law*, Edinburgh University Press (1964) (translated into French by D. Amlar, PUF Paris, 1995).

The first Algerian Code of Family Law[1], promulgated on June 9, 1984, ended at least twenty years of legal uncertainty. After independence, a law of December 31, 1962[2] had kept the pre-independence law in force; the

---

*   Nahas M Mahieddin, Professeur à l'Université d'Oran. Translated by Peter Schofield.
1   Law n° 84.11 of June 9, 1984, codifying the law of the family, OJ n° 24 of June 12, 1984 p. 612.
2   By Ordonnance of July 5, 1973.

1

A. Bainham (ed.), The International Survey of Family Law 1994, 1–28.
© 1996 *The International Society of Family Law. Printed in the Netherlands.*

abrogation of this law[3] had left what some had regarded as a "legal vacuum" prejudicial to justice, from July 1975 (when the ordonnance of July 5, 1973 took effect) until the adoption of the Family Law Code. The Civil Code of 1975 has few provisions on family law and does not seek to be comprehensive. Like almost every other country of islamic tradition, Algeria has chosen to have a separate family Code. In it the Algerian Legislature[4] seeks to reach a compromise between the rules of "classical" islamic law and those of a system less bound to its historical and doctrinal sources, particularly as those appear in works of writers of the Maliki school.

The Algerian Family Code is arranged in four books, covering marriage and its dissolution, legal representation, succession and provisions relating to wills, legacies, gifts and assets held in trust (waqf).

II   MARRIAGE

The Code is based on islamic law, but takes account of the development of Algerian society, especially in the last hundred years, under the pressure of so-called "modernist" ideas held by the elite of some countries of islamic civilisation[5], and also the direct and indirect influence of French colonial rule in Algeria (1830-1962).[6] Marriage is not defined simply by its object, but is more broadly presented as a contract formed between a man and a woman, in legal form. It has, among other aims, the founding of a family based on affection (mawada), domestic tranquility (rahma) and mutual assistance and the moral protection of the spouses for the preservation of family ties (article 4). While the Algerian code does not classify marriage as a covenant or vow (mithâq, the only term by which the Qur'an classifies

---

3   On the effects of the ordonnance of July 5, 1973, see our study "De la reconduction légale à la reconduction coutoumière ou des effets transitoires de l'ordonnance du 5 juillet 1973 en matière de statut personnel", (From renewal by legislation to renewal by custom or the transitional effects of the ordonnance of July 5, 1973 concerning personal status) in *Cahiers du CRIDSSH,* Oran, n° 8, 1984.

4   See *Official Journal of the debates in the Assemblée Populaire Nationale,* n° 46, (1984), p. 14.

5   See Maurice Borrmans, *Statut personnel et famille au Maghreb de 1940 à nos jours* (Personal status and family in the Maghreb from 1940 to the present day), Paris, La Haye-Mouton, (1977).

6   M.N. Mahieddin, "Les facteurs historiques de l'évolution récente du droit de la famille en Algérie" (to be published in *Cahier des droits maghrébins,* Casablanca).

marriage), but only as a contract (âqd), the terms in which it defines the relation between spouses (mawada, rahma) are Qur'anic in origin (Sura "Al-Rum", verse 21).

The Family Code specifies the substantive and formal conditions for a valid marriage, reserving first of all two articles for the betrothal.

The betrothal "Khitba"

Here, following the example of some other islamic systems, the Algerian Legislature modifies the definition of the engagement to marry as it existed in classical islamic law. For the islamic jurist, the "Khitba" forms a prelude to the marriage, essentially composed of approaches made by the man (or by his family) to the woman (or to her family), asking for her hand in marriage if the proposed union is legally possible. Terms and conditions are negotiated at this stage, which may end in mutual promises of marriage with a number of effects. Although highly recommended (mustahabha)[7], the "khitba" is not an obligatory step to render the marriage valid.[8]

Formally there is a "khitba" as soon as words are spoken which express a request for marriage. They may be followed by agreement on the woman's part or, more commonly, by her representative, father, brother, even her son, or any other male person, related or not, acting as "wali" (matrimonial guardian). The request may be explicit (tasrihan) or implicit (taridan). This is a distinction made by jurists, and is linked to the permissibility or otherwise of requesting a woman in marriage, depending on whether she is free, divorced or a widow.

The main effects that follow are: the right of the parties to meet each other, but never alone; and the relative prohibition against a third party making a request for the girl in marriage now she has become "engaged".

---

7   Ibn Djuzzay, Al qawânin al fiqhiyya, p. 147 (Ibn Juzzay is a jurist of 14th century Andalucia.)

8   This optional nature is referred to in Egyptian court decisions, Shari'a Court of Karmuz, August 7, 1932, in Al Muhâmât, n° 13, p.4, cited by Abd-Al-Aziz Ameur, Al Ahwâl al-Shaksiyya fi-sharia al-islâmiyya, Ed Dar al-Fikr al Arabi, Cairo, 1st edition, (1984), p. 18.

Algerian substantive law does not lay down the conditions and effects of the "khitba" and treats it as "a promise of marriage" (article 5, para. 1).[9] However, "either party may revoke the promise" (article 5, para. 1).[10] So it is a means of becoming better acquainted so as to reach an informed decision on eventual marriage – the objective of the khitba according to works on islamic law[11]. It cannot of itself constitute a marriage, however, and legislation is quite explicit on this point.[12] Article 6 (para. 1) says specifically: "Betrothal may take place at the same time as the fatiha, or at any time before it." This has been confirmed in the courts[13]; marriages conducted in customary form – though valid under islamic law – cannot be entered on the civil status register.

Although the promise is revocable the law does take account of damage which can arise on the breaking-off of an engagement. It will not compel performance, but it may be necessary and equitable to restore the equilibrium disrupted by the attitude of one of the couple. This affects engagement gifts and compensation for damage, material or mental, caused by the breach.

Dowry paid has to be returned, as it is conditional on the marriage (whether cohabitation follows or not). As to gifts, paragraphs 3 and 4 of article 5 of the Family Code make a distinction between revocation from the man's side and from the woman's. In the latter case, she returns whatever

---

9   Old decisions of French courts in Algeria had so defined the "khitba" (see judgments cited by G. Bennelha, *Le droit algérien de la famille*, OPU Algiers, (1993), p. 39-40) and regarded it as having no legal effect (Cour d'Alger, 4th Ch. September 12, 1919 and 1st Ch. May 6, 1920, note L. Milliot, *Revue Algérienne* 1921, part 2, p. 47). A recent Algerian decision reaffirms this view (Cour de Mostaganem, ch.civ. November 3, 1966, *Revue Algérienne* 1968, p 1200).

10 Cour Suprême, December 25, 1989, in Al majalla al-qadâ'iyya, n° 4,1991, p.102.

11 Which is why these works emphasise the principal effect of the "khitba", namely the right of the future spouses to meet each other, see Hussein Mohamed Yussef, Ikhtiyâr al-zawjaïn fi-l-Islâm wa adab al-Khitba, Cairo, (1979), particularly p. 25.

12 Particularly if the agreement is concluded orally between parties, with the recitation of the "Fatiha" (the first Sura of the Qur'an) without entry on the register of civil status. In the course of the debates leading to the Code's adoption, some deputies laid stress on the fact that it is the "fatiha" that gives validity to the marriage (*Official Journal of debates in the Assemblée Populaire Nationale*, n° 46, (1984), p. 20).

13 Cour Suprême, February 29, 1988 in Al majalla al-qadâiyya, n° 1, 1991, p. 49. In a case where "khitba" had been followed by cohabitation, the Court refused to recognise the existence of a valid marriage, for want of witnesses, despite the fact that the applicant had given birth to a child, and her partner had promised to marry her as soon as pregnancy was confirmed.

remains unconsumed. This is in contrast to the Maliki interpretation of islamic law[14], whereby, if she revokes her engagement, she has to restore all the presents given to her, whether or not consumed (or to pay the value of what has been consumed and so cannot be restored). If the man revokes, in accordance with classical islamic law, he cannot claim the return of anything.[15]

Article 5, para. 2, provides: "if, as a result of such revocation, either party suffers harm, mental or physical, damages can be awarded." (In classical islamic law, as the "khitba" did not create a legal obligation to marry neither could claim damages on revocation by the other.) Legal opinion on this has not been consistent. Based on identical principles of islamic law, some would allow compensation[16], others refuse it[17], but most see that while revocation cannot of itself give a right to damages, the circumstances must be taken into account and may justify liability on the basis of the quasi-delictual responsibility of the party concerned.[18]

Article 5, para. 2, follows the then existing judicial view[19] and has since been judicially reaffirmed.[20] Thus compensation may be awarded if: the breach is wrongful; and it gives rise to physical or mental damage; and there is a causal link between the two.[21] However the way it is drafted does not mean this article "presumes that every revocation is abusive in nature" for it is not clear that the Legislature intended such a presumption on the basis of a desire to "discourage the examination of evidence which might disturb relations between families", as certain writers suggest.[22]

---

14 But, to an extent, it is consistent with Hanafi law.
15 Cour Suprême, April 23, 1991, File n° 73919 in Al-majalla al qadâ'iyya n° 2, (1993), p. 58.
16 Mustafa al-Sibâ'i, Sharh qânûun al-ahwâl al-shakhsiyya, Damascus (1957) p. 41.
17 Muhamad Abû-Zahra, 'Aqd al-zawâj wa atâruhu, Cairo, (1971), p. 70.
18 A Sanhury, Al wasît fi-sharh al-qânûn al madani, Nazariyat al iltizâm p. 827 ff.; Tawfiq Hasan Faraj, Al-Tabi'a al qânûniyya li-l- khitba wa asâs al- Tawîd fi halat al-'udûl minha, in Majallat al huqûq, Univ. of Alexandria n° 3-4, p. 50.
19 Cour de Mostaganem, ch. civ., November 3, 1966, in *Revue Algérienne* n° 4, 1968, p.1200.
20 Cour Suprême, December 25, 1989, in Al majalla al qadaiyya, n° 4 1991, p. 102; Cour Suprème, April 23, 1991, in Al majalla al qadaiyya, n° 2, 1993, p.58.
21 G. Benmelha, op. cit., p. 45.
22 M.C. Salah-Bey in Jurisclasseur Legislation Comparée, s.v. Algeria, 2. (1988), p. 5.

III THE FORMATION OF THE MARRIAGE CONTRACT

The Legislature has essentially kept faith with ancient doctrine, while introducing certain adjustments. The Algerian Family Code distinguishes the elements of a valid marriage and the means of proving one exists.

A   *Conditions of substance*

In islamic law, as in the enacted law, marriage is formed by the giving of mutual consents by the two parties, in the presence of two witnesses and of a matrimonial guardian (wali) representing the wife who is to receive a dowry (article 9). It can neither be formed for a fixed term as is allowed in Shi'a law[23] nor, unless and until the reason for the prohibition ceases to exist, with a "forbidden" woman. We examine these conditions in turn.

1   Consent
Both the man and the woman must clearly and unequivocally express their consent to the marriage. Exchange of consent takes place in a "contractual meeting" (majlis), by way of a request (ijab) and an acceptance (qabûl) on the part of the man and the woman respectively (article 10, para. 1).

The minimum age for valid consent is 21 years for the man, 18 for the woman (article 7, para. 1)[24]. In this, the law continues a development begun in Algeria by a law of May 2, 1930 (then in force only in Kabylia) fixing the minimum age of marriage at 15; then by the ordonnance of February 4, 1959 (affecting only the people of M'zab), fixing it at 18 for the man and 15 for the woman (article 5 of the ordonnance); and last by the law of June 29, 1963, which kept the age for men at 18 while raising to 16 that for the woman (article 5 of that law).[25]

---

23   Iranian law, following Shi'a doctrine, allows temporary marriage (zawaj al-mut'a).

24   The Civil Code makes 19 the age of majority (C. civ. article 40).

25   The Family Code of 1984, unlike the law of June 29, 1963, imposes no sanctions in case of non-age marriage, whether against the validity of the marriage itself (article 3. paras. 1 and 2 of the law of 1963), or against the parties to it or the Registrar (article 2 of the law of 1963); sanctions which were sometimes judicially enforced (Cour de Mostaganem, ch. correct. May 31, 1967, in *Revue Algérienne* n° 4, 1968, p. 1205; Court d'Oran, ch. correct. December 1, 1967 in *Revue Algérienne* n° 4, 1968, p. 1207, cited by G. Benmelha, op. cit., p. 51).

This is a change in relation to islamic law[26], which does not fix a minimum age for marriage, but determines the age at which the union can be consummated by reference to the age of puberty (bulûgh).[27] A judge, "for important reasons or in case of necessity" (article 7, para. 2)[28], may dispense with the age requirement. However, we must note that the question of consent is not entirely simple under the law now in force: the woman cannot express her consent to the marriage in person, but must always be represented by a matrimonial "guardian" (wali), unlike the man, except where he is under incapacity by reason of his age or mental condition. This is not based on incapacity, but on customs and practices under which modesty requires that the woman cannot consent to her own marriage in front of a group of men she does not know.[29] This raises the question whether the bride's consent is genuine, or whether she may be forced into marriage. See below.

2 *Matrimonal guardianship (wilâya)*
Islamic law distinguishes between guardianship over assets (wilâya âlâ- al-mâl) and that over the person (wilâya âlâ-al-nafs). Usually the guardian is the father as holder of the patria potestas over his minor children. For the

---

26   Such legislative intervention is not new in countries of islamic tradition. As early as 1917, the Ottoman Family Code had set a minimum age for marriage.

27   This is why, for example in Moroccan case-law, we find decisions to the effect that this minimum age is required at the time of the making of the marriage contract, not that of consummation (Cour Suprème Marocaine, November 15, 1968, in Majallat al qada' wa-l-qanun, 1969, n°97, p. 418).

28   Which was already provided for under the law of May 2, 1930, but the dispensation was then granted by the Governor General for "weighty reasons", after hearing the opinion of a commission nominated by him, comprising two judges and a doctor. The ordonnance of 1959, for its part, gave this discretion to the President of the Tribunal de Grande Instance and the law of June 29, 1963, maintaining the discretion of the President of the Tribunal, added a requirement of hearing the opinion of the Procurator of the Republic.

29   One appreciates the rule thus in the socio-cultural context of the time (7th Century). "Society in Medina, for instance, remained faithful to the concepts of Arabian tribal law, under which the arranging of marriage alliances was the prerogative of the male members of the family. No woman, therefore, could contract a marriage on her own account, but must be given in marriage by her guardian. In Kufa, on the other hand, a town in Iraq [where the hanafi school of law was to develop]... women occupied a less inferior position and in particular the right to conclude her own marriage contract without the intervention of her guardian" (N.J. Coulson, *A History of Islamic Law*, (1964), Edinburgh University Press, p. 30).

latter, males or females, marriage requires his authorisation or that of a guardian (wali). He can even compel sons or daughters to marry (right of "jerbr"). This matrimonial guardianship cannot be exercised over a male who has reached the age of puberty, but it applies to women regardless of age or physical or mental capacity. However, the schools diverge, there being no clear and unequivocal authority in the Qur'an or in the tradition of the Prophet – the two fundamental sources of islamic law.[30] The Maliki school, in opposition to Hanafi opinion, regards the intervention of the wali as a condition of the validity of the marriage (Shart sihha) of the woman, even after puberty; although, if she has attained puberty (a "major"), the authors agree that it is not "wilâyat ijbâr", but "wilâyat ishtihbâb", which does not give the one who exercises it the power to compel her to conclude a marriage. The wali acts as agent of the woman, who authorises him to conclude her marriage for her. While Maliki law allows the father, but only the father, to compel his daughter to a marriage, if it is her first[31], many traditions (hadith) and a number of islamic jurists say it is preferable that the woman be consulted over her marriage.

In Algeria, before the adoption of the texts, French court decisions, headed by the Chambre de Révision Musulmane, saw matrimonial guardianship not as an absolute right exercised by the father. Rather it "should [exclusively] be linked, in every case, to the consent of his virgin daughter, failing which the marriage is void"[32], confirming that this right was becoming less rigid as earlier decisions[33], all of which stressed the vital role of the consent of the spouses or of their representatives[34], had indicated.

The marriage ordonnance of February 4, 1959 does not recognise the wali, declaring that marriage can only be concluded by the consent of both spouses (article 2, para. 1) and judicial opinion at the time considered that the text ended the requirement that he be present at the wedding (except in the case of minors or those judicially declared incompetent, articles 2

---

30 Lakhal Ben Hawa, Nazariyat al-wilâya fi-zawâj fi-l-fiqh al-islâmî wa-l-qawânin al'arabiya, SNED, Algiers, (1982).

31 Ibn Juzzay, Al qawânîn al-fiqhiyya: "Le droit de contraindre au mariage s'exerce par le père sur la jeune fille 'bikr'." p. 150.

32 Ch. Rév. Mus. March 16, 1950, cited by G. Benmelha op. cit. p. 56.

33 Ch. Rév. Mus. April 11, 1922 in *Revue Algérienne*, 1922-23, part 2, p. 183; June 30, 1928 in *Revue Algérienne*, 1929, part 2, p. 156.

34 Ch. Rév. Mus. June 18, 1946, cited by G. Bemelha, op. cit., p. 57.

and 3). After independence in 1962, Algerian judges went on applying this rule[35], but then the Supreme Court restored the rule of islamic law that the absence of the wali invalidated the marriage.[36] The strictest interpretation of Maliki law was thus restored.

The Family Code of 1984 partially clarifies the matter, making it the rule that "marriage is contracted by the consent of the future spouses (and) the presence of the matrimonial guardian" (article 9), who "is responsible for concluding the marriage" (article 12) although "the wali, whether he is or is not the father, may not force the person whose guardian he is to marry, so that he cannot give her in marriage without her consent" (article 13).

The power to force into marriage (ijbâr) is thus formally abrogated, the matrimonial guardian is no more than the representative of the woman, who is presumed to authorise him to conclude the marriage which she wishes and agrees to contract. Thus the Legislature has chosen the Hanafi doctrine in the matter, itself based on the Qur'an (Sura "The Heifer", verse 232) and on various traditions of the Prophet (hadith).

Unable to force the woman under his guardianship into marriage, a father can still exercise his paternal authority to prevent the marriage of his daughter if he considers her interest so requires (article 12, para. 2) and she has never been married.[37] No other guardian shares this power with him[38], but does even a father have an absolute right to oppose his daughter's marriage? Answering this question, we note that, under the wording of the text

---

35 Trib. d'Alger, 1ere ch. civ., July 23, 1965, in *Revue Algérienne* n° 4, 1968, p. 1194; Cour de Mostaganem ch. civ., November 3, 1966, in *Revue Algérienne* n° 4 1968, p. 1200; Cour d'Alger, ch. d'accus., April 21, 1966 in *Revue Algérienne* n° 4 1968, p. 1195.

36 Cour Suprème, December 7, 1966, "Le consentement du tuteur matrimonial est nécessaire sans quoi le mariage contracté est entaché de nullité absolue que le juge doit prononcer d'office." (The matrimonial guardian's consent is essential, failing which the marriage is absolutely void and the judge can only pronounce its nullity.) (cited by G. Benmelha, op. cit., p. 58.)

37 The opposite rule applies in islamic law (Ibn Juzzay op. cit p. 150). The rule as formulated by the Legislature is unclear unless it concerns a minor (the term formerly used to translate "bikr"), but two successive amendments (OJ n° 31 of July 31, 1984) translating "bikr" as "virgin" and (OJ n° 41 of September 19, 1984) giving the Arabic word in Roman characters, not translated, leave the matter uncertain pending interpretation in the courts.

38 Any other guardian's opposition to a marriage is judicially evaluated and the judge can authorise the marriage (article 12, end of para. 1).

itself, opposition is possible only if the woman is a spinster (bikr). Thus it does not apply to a second marriage. Secondly, even if it is a first marriage, the islamic law rule applies.[39] This allows submission of the case to a judge, who may order the father to permit his daughter to marry, if such is her wish and if there is no obstacle which could be the basis of the refusal. If the father persists in his refusal, the judge can authorise the marriage.[40]

Any marriage concluded without the formal consent of the woman[41] is ineffective, with the legal consequences this entails, particularly nullity. Algerian substantive law thus follows the spirit of islamic law[42] and the judicial trend of the 1950s[43] has been followed in Algerian courts after independence.[44]

The Family Code also lets a man marry by proxy (article 20) so giving effect to a classical islamic law rule.[45]

3   The Dowry

In islamic law, the formation of marriage requires delivery of a dowry (sadâq) by the man to his wife. This requirement rests on the Qur'an (Sura "The Women" verses 4 and 24) as explained by the tradition of the Prophet, commented and developed by the classical jurists. It expresses the sincere, serious and true intention of the man to establish a joint household with the woman (the term "sadâq" used in the Qur'an for dowry, has the root s-d-q, which connotes both to give alms and also to be true and sincere).

The Algerian Family Code, includes "the establishing of a dowry" as one of the constitutive elements of marriage (arkâ al-zawâj) (article 9), defining it as "that which is paid to the future wife in money or in any other assets legally permitted" (article 14). In this the Algerian Legislature follows

---

39   Because the Family Code makes it applicable if there is a lacuna in the law.

40   Ibn Djuzzay (op. cit. p. 151) envisages the intervention of authority (the Sultan).

41   Note that the marriage is celebrated before the officer of the civil status register, in the presence of the bride and bridegroom, who must sign the register in person, after having established their identity.

42   It follows it to the letter, since tradition has it that the Prophet, on the request of a woman, annulled a marriage to which she had not consented.

43   Ch. rév. mus. March 16, 1950, cited by G. Benmelha, op. cit. p. 61.

44   Cour de Mostaganem, ch. civ. November 3, 1966; Cour Suprême ch. dr. privé February 9, 1966, in *Revue Algérienne*, n° 4, 1968, p. 1220.

45   Ibn Juzzay, op cit. p. 152.

Maliki doctrine; as opposed to Hanafi teaching, in which dowry is an effect of marriage[46]; so following a long standing and consistent judicial trend.[47]

The dowry becomes the property of the wife to use at her discretion (end of article 14) in conformity with islamic law. Maliki authors say she is expected to use all or part of it to pay for her trousseau, however, the Algerian Family Code leaves the wife free to use it as she wishes.[48] Neither her father nor any other wali has any right over this dowry.[49] Islamic law allows the dowry to be paid as a lump sum or by instalments and the Code, article 15, follows this principle. It must always be quantified (al-sadâq al-musammâ); the parties must have defined it by common consent; it must also be real and serious.[50]

The woman's right to the dowry arises as soon as the union has been consummated following celebration of the marriage (article 16). If it has not been quantified in the course of negotiations the wife has the right to a suitable dowry, which can be determined by the judge.

To the Maliki school, a year of cohabitation counts as consummation, with or without sexual intercourse between spouses. The Algerian Code is silent, but judicial decisions have held the marriage consummated as soon as the spouses are alone together (khalwa), whereupon the wife becomes entitled to her dowry in full.[51] On divorce or on repudiation before consummation, the wife receives only half of the agreed dowry (article 16) (Qur'an, Sura "The Heifer", verse 235) but classical islamic law imposes conditions that Algerian law does not mention. It remains for the courts to interpret the text more or less widely by reference to islamic law.

---

46 Mohamed Abû-Zahra, 'aqd al-zawâj wa atâruhu, Cairo, (1971), p. 20.
47 See cases cited by G, Benmelha, op. cit. p 83, note 60.
48 Judicial decisions have always applied the classical islamic law rule. The wife's purchases made from the dowry remain hers exclusively.
49 This applies even if she is a minor in terms of proprietary capacity. Where this applies, she receives the dowry on attaining majority (cases cited by G. Benmelha, op. cit. p. 87).
50 This is why, despite its in some ways symbolic nature, jurists have fixed a minimum, but not a maximum, advising against excess as to the amount. Such a minimum serves as a yardstick in case of litigation, but not so as to invalidate the payment of a lesser dowry (see Afif Tabara, Rûh al-din al- islâmî, Beirut, (1980) p. 366).
51 Cour suprême, October 2, 1989, in Al majalla al qadâ'iyya, n° 1, 1991, p. 34; Cour suprême, June 18, 1991, file n° 74375, in Al-majalla-al-qadâ'iyya n° 1, 1993, p. 61. Case law does not follow the islamic law rule, which requires cohabitation to last for a year.

Finally, litigation over the dowry between the spouses, in the absence of evidence from either side, if it is begun before consummation, is decided by oath-taking on the affirmation of the wife; if after, by oath-taking on the statements of the spouses (article 17) following the Maliki interpretation of the rule. Article 17 of the Code extends the provisions to the couple's heirs under the same conditions. The judges have had occasion to apply these principles.[52]

4   *The Witnesses*

Some schools treat this as substance, others as form. So, in the Maliki school, witnesses are only the means of publicity required at the moment when the bride takes up residence in the matrimonial home (dukhûl)[53], while, for the Hanafi, witnesses must be present when the marriage contract is concluded.[54] Their role is to ensure publicity for the marriage, or to provide the judge with evidence should there be any dispute, but muslim authors often classify the presence of the witnesses as "rukn", that is an essential element of marriage. It gives solemnity to the marriage.

Algerian law has chosen the Hanafi doctrine, placing the presence of witnesses among the essential elements (article 9) and allowing annulment of a marriage without witnesses, unless it has been consummated (article 33). In this, the Code follows the judicial trend of the colonial period[55] and of the ordonnance of February 4, 1959 (article 2, para. 2). So current case law rests on established precedent.[56]

The Code is silent as to the qualifications of witnesses except that there must be two of them (the islamic law rule). So we go back to the teachings of classical jurists: they must have reached majority (puberty) and be of sound mind, muslims[57], honourable ('adl)[58] and male[59], they must per-

---

52   Cour suprême, June 5, 1989, in Al majala al-qadâ'iyya, n° 4, 1990, p. 80.

53   Ibn Djuzzay, op. cit., p. 48.

54   Ali Hasb Allah, Al-zawâj fi-shari'a al-islamiyya, Ed. Dâr al-ma'ârif (s.d.) p. 68.

55   Ch, rev. mus. June 18, 1946 (cited by G. Benmelha, op. cit. p. 103).

56   Cour suprême, February 29, 1988, in Al-majalla al-qadâiyya, n° 1, 1991, p. 49.

57   The Hanafi school allows christians and jews when a muslim man marries a christian or a jew (see Badrân Abû-l-Aïnaïn Badrân, Al 'Alâqât al-ijtimâ'iyya bayn al-Muslimin wa ghayr al-Muslimin, Beirut, 1983, p. 226).

58   A requirement not made by the Hanafi (see Badran Abu-l-Aïnaïn Badran, Al fiqh al-muqâran li-l-Ahwâl al-Shaksiyya, Beirut, 1967, vol 1, p. 66; Mustafa Shalabi, Ahkâm al-usra fi-l-islâm, Beirut, 1977, p. 115).

sonally attend the marriage ceremony (they must give proof of identity to the civil status registration officer and sign the record of the marriage), and be able (in particular before a judge) to state clearly the place, the time, and the amount of the dowry. They must also (if required) bear witness to the facts that the consents were genuine and that the wife had been taken to the matrimonial home.[60]

5 Prohibited marriages
Islamic authors list forty-eight categories of women whom one may not marry, twenty-five absolutely and permanently, the rest only temporarily prohibited.[61] The details do not appear in the Algerian Family Code, which simply lays out principles, listing categories, cutting out anachronisms[62] and staying silent on some points.[63] Otherwise, modern law distinguishes in the same way as classical law between permanent and temporary impediments.

a Permanent impediments[64]
Article 24 of the Family Code defines the impediments arising out of relationship by consanguinity (al-qarâba), by affinity (al-musâhara) and by breast feeding (al-ridâ').

i Consanguinity
Along with Judaism and Christianity[65], Islam and islamic law forbid the marriage of close relatives. The categories of women with whom marriage is permanently forbidden are listed in the Qur'an (Sura "The Women", verse 23).

---

59 The Hanafi school allows one man and two women, if two men cannot be found, relying on the Qur'an (Sura "The Heifer", verse 28). Algerian case-law has ruled that a woman cannot be a witness to a marriage (Cour suprème, February 29, 1988, in Al-majalla al-Qadâ'iyya, n° 1, 1991, p. 49; Cour suprème, December 15, 1986, file n° 43889 in Al-majalla al-qadâ'iyya, n° 2, 1993, p. 37.

60 Cour suprème, March 27, 1989, file n° 53272, in Al-majalla al-qadâ'iyya n° 3, 1990, p. 82.

61 Ibn Djuzzay, op. cit. pp. 155. ff.

62 Thus modern Codes no longer refer to wives of the Prophet, or to certain slaves...

63 For instance marriage with a woman who is sick.

64 The Arabic text of the Code uses "mu' abbada" meaning permanent, the official French version refers to "empêchements 'absolus'." (Irremovable impediments).

65 Kupferu, Les interdictions à mariage dans la Bible et le Talmud, D.E.S., Paris, (1978).

Article 25 picks up the list set out in verse 23, forbidding marriage with mother, daughter, sister, paternal or maternal aunt, and the daughter of a brother or sister. Cousins may marry (Sura "Al-Ahzâb", verse 50).[66]

ii Affinity

Relationship through marriage makes some marriages legally impossible. Again the Qur'an sets out the prohibition (Sura "The Women", verses 22-23) so equating this form of kinship to consanguinity. Thus, from the completion of the marriage record, one may not marry one's wife's ascendants, from its consummation, her descendants; nor can one marry widows or divorcees of one's own ascendants, nor descendants of one's spouse, without limit.

iii Breast-feeding

The Qur'an forbids the marriage of persons who have been breast fed by the same wet nurse (Sura "The Women", verse 23) treating such foster feeding as equivalent to a blood relationship. This prohibition is the same as that which results from consanguinity or affinity affecting relatives of the wet nurse and of her husband and article 27 of the Code enshrines this principle, declaring the rule applicable to the child in relation to his wet nurse, her spouse, and their children. The prohibition extends to the descendants of any child who has been so foster fed.

Verse 231 of Sura "The Heifer" of the Qur'an is interpreted as meaning that, to have this effect, the feeding must have taken place in the first two years of the child's life, and article 29 of the Family Code follows this, adding that the weaning period can also be taken into account, so following the opinion of many islamic jurists.[67]

Feeding must have been genuine and a minimum quantity is needed[68], but the Code (end of article 29) specifies no quantity, relying on the teaching of the Maliki school.[69] Proof of foster feeding can be by witnesses or by

---

66 This verse is addressed to the Prophet, who is thereby authorised to marry cousins who followed him to Medina, but commentators consider that this dispensation applies equally to all muslims (Zaki-al-Din Sha'bân, Al-Ahkâm al-Shar'iyya li-l Ahwâl al Shakhsiyya, Cairo, (1969), p. 14.

67 Ibn Djuzzay (op. cit., p. 156) adds a margin of 1 to 3 months after the two years.

68 Shafai proposes at least five breastfuls.

69 Al-Qayrâwâni, Risâla, ed. de Rabat, (1984) p. 88.

admission.[70] Finally we note that this form of relationship gives rise to no rights between persons, in particular in relation to succession.

b Temporary impediments

In contrast to the permanent impediments which arise independently of any voluntary act in relation to status on the part of the person affected, temporary impediments cease to exist when their cause disappears, whether or not as a result of such a person's voluntary act.

The Code, in article 30, lists the categories of women with whom, for the time being, marriage is forbidden: the married woman (muhsina)[71], the woman in legal seclusion ('idda) following divorce or widowhood, one may not directly remarry a woman one has thrice divorced (Sura "The Heifer", verse 227), nor exceed the legally permitted number of wives.

On the ending of her marriage by divorce or the death of her husband, a woman must observe a period of seclusion ('idda), three menstrual periods for the divorcee (Sura "The Heifer" verse 226), four months and ten days for the widow (Sura "The Heifer", verse 232), during which she may not remarry. Authors explain this as being partly to prevent confusion of paternity and partly to enable the divorcing husband to take back his wife, if he wishes, without having to go through a fresh marriage, since during 'idda the marriage tie continues to exist.

The Algerian Code keeps this rule (articles 58 and 59), but 'idda lasts until delivery if the woman is pregnant (article 60).

Following a third repudiation, the couple can only remarry each other after the wife has been married to another man and this union has been properly dissolved (by repudiation, divorce or death) (Qur'an, Sura "The Heifer", verse 228). Article 29,3 of the Code reproduces this rule. Relying on a tradition of the Prophet, authors state that this marriage must be concluded validly and seriously, not merely to satisfy formally the rule of the Qur'an.[72] In theory, therefore, a marriage of convenience does not legally enable the husband to remarry his wife after the third repudiation.

---

70   There is a divergence as to the conditions of witnesses. See Ibn Djuzzay, op. cit., p. 157; Ali Hasb Allah, Al-zawâj fi-shari'a al-islamiyya, Ed. Dâr al-Mâarif, p. 94; Zaki-al-Din Shâbân, Ahkâm al-Shari'a li-l Shwâl al- Shaksiyya, Cairo, (1969) p. 169.

71   Because polyandry is forbidden.

72   Ibn Djuzzay, op. cit. p. 158.

i   Polygamy

Islamic law, reproduced by the Family Code, allows a man to take up to
four wives (Qur'an, Sura "The Women", verse 3), but we should note that
this provision is not listed among the rights of men (quâ husbands) but in
that concerning impediments to marriage[73] for, in origin the rule was imposed to limit pre-islamic practices which let men take as many wives as
they wished.[74] Islamic law adds a number of conditions, in particularly
the duty to treat all one's wives equally, aimed at discouraging polygamy.
In effect, the rule is monogamy, polygamy being the exception (note islamic
reformers led by the Egyptian Mohamed 'Abduh, in 1897, proposed legislation forbidding polygamy except in case of "absolute necessity" – limited
to sterility on the part of the wife).[75] For "modernists", the way to women's
"liberation" is through the prohibition of polygamy[76], relying particularly
on an interpretation of verse 128 of Sura "The Women".[77] De facto,
polygamy is still tolerated, but is increasingly uncommon in Algeria.

In Algerian law, article 8 of the Family Code provoked long debates,
marked often by strong conservatism[78] and permits "marriage to be
concluded with more than one wife within the limits of the Shari'a", that
is with up to four wives. The Algerian Legislature thus abstains from innovation and stays faithful to the contents of the Qur'anic verses we have
mentioned (Sura "The Women" verse 3), reproducing the equality condition,
but not specifying who monitors it – or the penalties for its breach – so
apparently leaving it a matter solely for the husband's spiritual conscience.[79]
Of course it is hard in practice to go beyond the material aspects of equality.

If this first classical condition is satisfied, the Code requires good cause
for polygamy. One government draft rejected by the National Assembly in
the debates, would have allowed "marriage with more than one wife" only

---

73   See, for instance, Ibn Djuzzay, op. cit., p. 158.
74   Abd al-Salâm al-Tarmânînî, Al-zawâj 'inda al-'arab fi-l-djahiliyya wa-l- islâm, Kuwait,
     (1984) p. 228.
75   Mohamed 'Amâra, Al-Islâm wa-l-mar'a fi ra'y al-Imâm Muhammad 'Abduh, Beirut,
     1981, p. 80.
76   Qâsim Amîn, Al-mar'a al-jadîda, Cairo, (s. d.).
77   The polygamist is in effect required to treat each of his wives equally, but the Qur'an
     declares "you cannot be fair to all your wives, even if you wish to".
78   See *Official Journal of Debates in the Assemblée Populaire Nationale*, n° 52 (1984),
     p. 18 ff.
79   Apparently, so far as the emotional content of equality is concerned, all that is required
     of him is the intention of fairness (niyat al'adl).

after judicial approval "pronounced after a waiting period of three months from the receipt of the husband's application for it, and after inquiry into and establishing of the grounds and of the ability to give equal support and housing and after informing the current and future wives.[80]" A circular from the Ministry of Justice (n° 102/84 of September 23, 1984) sets out the meaning of good cause (motif jusitifié)[81] in article 8. The only ground on which polygamy can be authorised is "extreme necessity", consisting of the wife's sterility or illness preventing normal married life, supported by a doctor's certificate. Apart from this, the officer of the register of civil status cannot receive the couple or draw up a record of their marriage.

Finally, the current and future wives must be told of their husband's intention to conclude a polygamous marriage. The Code allows either wife to bring an action in case of fraud, or to demand divorce, particularly if she did not consent. No other penalty attaches to remarriage which does not meet the legal conditions. The second marriage is valid in law for all purposes.

ii Differences of religion

The prohibition on marrying a non-muslim applies only to women. Men can validly marry "people of the Book" – christian or jewish women (Qur'an, Sura "The Table", verse 6). The Qur'anic rule forbids putting pressure on the wife to convert to islam (Sura "The Heifer", verse 225).

Islamic jurists draw from the Qur'an (Sura "The Heifer", verse 219 and Sura "The Woman to be Examined", verse 10) the rule forbidding women to marry non-muslims. In their view, the man is head of the household, putting the muslim wife in a position of inferiority in relation to him, and the children would not be brought up as muslims, which is contrary to Qur'anic teaching (Sura IV, "The Women", verse 140) and would weaken the muslim community. Most countries of the islamic area keep this rule

---

80 See *Official Journal of debates in the Assemblée Populaire Nationale* n° 52 (1984), p. 20.

81 Note that polygamy is relatively rare in Algeria. Statistics for 1977 show 70,000 cases of polygamy in nearly 2,400,000 families (a third of wives of polygamous husbands were separated from them de facto).

in force[82] and article 31 of the Algerian Family Code likewise forbids such a marriage, but the prohibition is lifted if the suitor converts to islam.

Having referred to these rules, we must note that islamic jurists from classical times never encouraged such marriages, wishing to avoid possible pressures and harm as much to the couple themselves as to the children.[83]

Note, finally, that in Algerian substantive law, apart from religious affiliation, "marriage between Algerians of either sex and foreigners must comply with the regulations" (article 31, para. 2). So marriage between an Algerian of either sex and a foreigner (even a muslim) cannot be concluded without administrative authorisation.[84]

B   Formal conditions

In islamic law, the distinction betwen conditions of substance and of form was not established along the lines of modern legal theory. Thus the presence of witnesses and of the matrimonial guardian (wali) can be classed as conditions of form as certain authors do[85], or as conditions of substance.

We need not return to the question of the "wali" or of witnesses, and can restrict ourselves to matters of form in the strict sense in which the Family and Civil Status Codes interpret the term in their provisions as to the recording and proof of marriage.

In classical islamic law, marriage is not conducted before a particular authority and the presence of witnesses serves the purposes of ensuring its publicity[86], and of providing proof of its existence[87], as well as being a

---

82   Syrian Code, article 48; Iraqi Code, article 17; Iranian Code, article 1059; Jordanian Code, article 339; Kuwaiti Code, article 18; Moroccan Code, article 29 ...

83   There are no succession rights between spouses if either is a non-muslim. Children do not inherit from a non-muslim mother.

84   This regulation antedates the Family Code, being contained in an order of the Minister of the Interior dated February 11, 1981, and in a Circular, n° 2/DRAGS/DRO of the same date.

85   G, Benmelha, *Le droit algérien de la famille*, OPU. Algiers, (1933), pp. 97 and 102; M.C. Salah Bey, Algérie (Législation comparée, 2, 1988) considers only the presence of two witnesses to be a condition as to form.

86   Ali Hasb Allah, Al-zawâj fi-shari'a al-islâmiyya, Ed. Dâr al-Ma'ârif (s. d.) p. 68. Marriage can neither be celebrated in secret nor kept secret in islamic law. Clandestine marriage is void.

condition of the validity of the union itself according to the Hanafi rule adopted by the Algerian Legislature. Writing was (and still is, as article 19 of the Family Code allows) much more used to record the conditions agreed between the parties (constitution or amount of dowry, husband's promise to stay monogamous[88]...) rather than to record or register a union official-ly.[89]

In Algerian substantive law, marriage cannot be contracted outside the control of the State authorities; "the act of marriage is concluded before a notary or an authorised official" says article 18 of the Family Code, thus enabling the office of civil status, set up in 1882[90], to register marriages as provided in article 21 of the Family Code. Thus the only way to prove a marriage now is by an extract of the register of civil status (article 22 of the Family Code), but conclusion of marriage before an authorised official (article 18) is not a condition sine qua non of validity. Marriage is given existence and validity by the fulfilment of the conditions listed in article 9 of the Family Code[91], and this right of either spouse to have a declaration of validity of the union, even after the death of one of them, is not barred by lapse of time.[92] The registration is "relegated to a purely evidentiary role[93]" which is why article 22 of the Family Code adds that "failing [civil status] registration it [the marriage] is validated by court order ... [and thereafter] recorded in the civil status register". The Legislature thus tries to take account of social reality as found in country districts of the Maghreb in general[94], where so-called "customary marriages" or marriages "à la Fatiha" – conforming to the rules of islamic law – persist, despite numerous

---

87   Proof by witnesses is regarded as the best evidence by islamic jurists even though marriage can be proved by writing or public notoriety also.
88   The husband's undertakings which derogate from his personal freedom are not enforceable against him (Cour suprême, June 20, 1988, in Al-majalla al- qadâ'iyya, n° 2, 1991, p. 54).
89   Ibn Djuzzay, op. cit., p. 150.
90   The law of 1882 on civil status was amended in 1930, 1957 and 1959. Since independence, an ordonnance promulgated in 1970 organises civil status.
91   Cour suprême, December 7, 1987, file n° 45658 in Al-majalla al-qadâ'iyya, n° 4, 1990, p. 61; December 25, 1989, in Al-majalla al-qadâ'iyya, n° 4, 1991, p. 110.
92   Cour suprême, April 23, 1991, file n° 71732 in Al majalla al qadâ'iyya, n° 2, 1993, p. 51.
93   M.C. Salah Bey, Jurisclasseur législation comparée, s.v. Algérie, 2, p. 7.
94   For Morocco, for instance, see Hamad al'Araki, Sharh qânûn al-zawâj al- maghribi, Casablanca, (1965) p. 64.

provisions enacted by the Algerian Legislature, even before the promulgation of the Family Code.[95]

Some authors have seen behind these provisions a traditionalist view which refuses to regard the official recording of the marriage (acte) as an essential element in the formation of marriage.[96] In fact what motivated the Legislature was realism. It is not, as some would have it, a question of whether to treat marriage as a religious or as a secular matter. In islamic law, marriage is not "'ibadât" (cultural practices) but "mu'amâlât" (civil relations in general). It is neither celebrated in a place of worship nor before a representative of the faith. Sunni islam in any case lacks the equivalent of a "clergy". Although customarily blessed by the recitation of verses from the Qur'an, this is in no way a condition of its validity. Thus marriage retains, from the point of view of islamic law, and in current law, a strictly civil law nature.

Further, as we have seen, marriage with foreigners – irrespective of their sex or religion – is subject to administrative control (article 31, para. 2). By order dated February 11, 1980, the Minister of the Interior gave the Préfets power to authorise such marriages. Authorisation must be given within three weeks, but if there is an imminent danger that one party may die, authorisation will be given at once on the application of the civil status registration officer (circular n° 2/DRAGS/DRO, of February 2, 1980).

Similarly, members of the national security services may only marry with the approval of the guardianship authority. Women members of the national police force may not marry before they have become established (Decree of August 13, 1983). The marriage of servicemen in the armed forces is also subject to approval of the Ministry of National Defence (circulars of 13 June, 1967 and 25 June, 1968).

---

95   The first legislative text on these lines is the law of June 29, 1963, which declares in article 5: "No one may claim the status or the effects of marriage, unless he presents an act of marriage drawn up or transcribed into the civil status register." Despite a transitional period of three years, celebration of traditional marriages went on without registration. So the delay was prolonged by ordonnances of June 23, 1966, September 16, 1969 and September 22, 1971.

96   M.C. Salah Bey, Jurisclasseur législation comparée s.v. Algérie, 2, p. 7.

IV THE EFFECTS OF MARRIAGE

Islamic jurists class some of the effects of marriage as reciprocal rights and duties, because they concern the two spouses at the same time (Algerian Family Code article 36), others concern one only of the couple (articles 37 to 39).

A *Rights and duties common to both spouses*

As one author has pointed out[97], "relations between spouses are regulated on the basis of the traditional patriarchal model of the family ... which is why, rather than set out mutual duties of succour and help, it deals with the moral duties which are imposed on the spouses." While his first proposition remains true of what article 36 of the Code has to say about: "– preserving conjugal relations and the duties of their shared life; – joint contribution to preserving the interests of the family, the protection of children and their healthy upbringing; – preserving the bonds of family relationships and understanding among relatives", the second requires qualification. Moral imperatives can merge into legal duties and article 4 of the Family Code, in defining marriage states that the objectives of the contract which unites husband and wife include: "founding a family based on affection, domestic tranquillity and mutual assistance". This implies fidelity, succour and assistance, which can be applied by the judge, since islamic legal doctrine, on which the Legslature drew, is not short of detailed statements of their content.

It must be noted first of all that the husband is the head of the household (article 39), which imposes on him a duty of support towards his wife (article 74), which means the selection of a home suitable to receive her. We find this rule in the Qur'an (Sura "Al Talâq", verse 6); and the wife can only refuse to join her husband there if she or her children would be in physical or moral danger. However, she cannot be obliged to live with in-laws, or with co-wives of a polygamous husband, each wife being entitled to in-dividual accommodation.[98]

---

97 M.C. Salah Bey, article cited above, p. 8.
98 Cour de Tlemen, ch. civ. March 16, 1967 in *Revue Algérienne* n° 4, 1968, part 2, p. 1221 (cited by G. Benmelha, op. cit. p. 129, note 149).

The wife's failure to live with her husband in the matrimonial home amounts to misconduct justifying him in withdrawing support (article 37, para. 1). Desertion of the matrimonial home would give rise to a claim for divorce and for damages (article 55); as also does absence of the husband for over a year unless he pays his wife maintenance (article 53, para. 5).[99]

Spouses are required to live together in a spirit of mutual tolerance and respect, and to do all in their power to maintain their married happiness, security and tranquillity – obligations set out in article 36 of the Family Code, and based on the Qur'an (Sura "The Heifer", verse 186, Sura "Al-Nissâ", verse 19 and Sura "Al-Rum", verse 21).

While these provisions may seem moral rather than legal in nature (but remembering that the "fiqh" goes beyond the merely legal), this is not the case with succession rights between spouses. Consistently with another Qur'anic rule (Sura "Al-Nissâ", verse 12), found in the Family Code (article 130), the couple linked by the bond of marriage have reciprocal succession rights. This right rests on marriage, consummated or not (article 130), and ends, in case of divorce, only with the end of the period of 'idda (article 132). The husband inherits half his wife's assets if she leaves no child (article 144, para. 1), otherwise only a quarter (article 145, para. 1). The wife succeeds to a quarter of her husband's assets if he leaves no child (article 145, para. 2), otherwise only one eighth (article 146).[100]

As to succession rights between spouses whose religion is different, the Code is silent. In classical islamic law, no succession rights exist here[101], but a husband may lawfully leave up to a third of his assets to his jewish or christian wife.

---

99 Note that his failure to pay maintenance also renders the husband liable to penal sanctions, once two months have elapsed.

100 In case of a polygamous husband, the co-wives share equally the quarter or the eighth of his assets, according to whether he left any child surviving (on all these questions see Shawqi Abdallah al-Sâmâ, Mawsu'at Ahkâm al- Mawârith, Beirut, (1988)).

101 Case law has clarified the point, reaffirming the applicability of islamic law although the principles set out in the matter in the Code could be interpreted, in the light of the Constitution, as permitting the wife who is not a muslim to be a legal heir, but, interpreted in the light of what has been called "islamic public order", the non-muslim wife is not an heir. Before the Cour d'appel of Oran, in an actual case, the question was not debated and the judges decided on the basis that it was not proved that the wife was not a muslim, despite her European name (Cour d'appel d'Oran, January 21, 1987, case n° 577/84 unreported).

Finally note, in Maliki law, if a man suffering from a fatal illness repudiates his wife, she does not lose her succession rights, even if he survives the period of 'idda, nor even after remarriage to a new husband.[102]

B The duties of the husband

Article 37 of the Family Code defines the husband's obligations, which consist essentially in a duty to maintain (nafaqa) and this is explained in article 78 of the Code as involving "food, clothes, medical care, housing or rent and all that is considered necessary in custom and practice". These duties conform to the principles of the Qur'an (Sura "Al Baqara", verse 231, and Sura "Al-Talâq", verse 7) and numerous traditions of the Prophet notably reported by Moslem and Bokhâri.[103]

In Algerian law "the husband is required to contribute to his wife's maintenance of his spouse" (article 74), even if she deserts him without justification (article 37. para. 1), until the marriage is dissolved. After repudiation or divorce, the husband's maintenance liability continues until expiry of the period of "'idda" (end of article 61), or until delivery of her child if the marriage is dissolved during her pregnancy (Qur'an, Sura "Al Talâq", verse 6). As to her right to live in the matrimonial home, we must distinguish the cases of repudiation, divorce and death of the husband.

In case of repudiation or divorce, the wife does not have to leave the matrimonial home throughout the period of "'idda" (article 61 and Qur'an, Sura "Al Talâq", verse 1). Thereafter her right to a tenancy is less certain. She has the benefit of the right to look after her children, and must not be forced to return to her father or other guardian, but the husband must still have a home available to him (article 52, paras. 2 and 3 of the Family Code). In contrast, on the husband's death, the provisions of the Civil Code apply,

---

102 Abd al-Salâm Fifu, Ahkâm tasarrufât al marîd mardalmawt, Thesis, Faculty of Law, Casablanca, (1992).

103 Moslem and Bokhâri are two famous authors of collections of traditions considered by Muslims to be authentic. The first was born at Nishapur in 817 and died there in 875, the second was born at Bokhara in 810 and died there in 870. (See Henri de Waël, *Le droit musulman*, CHEAM Paris 1989, p. 34; Nabhani Koribaa, *Les Sounnites*, Publisud, (1994) p. 21.)

giving the widow the right to have the tenancy transferred into her own
name.

C   *The rights and duties of the wife*

Articles 38 and 39 of the Family Code set out the rights and duties of the
wife, and it is important to specify their nature and extent, for this is a matter
frequently presented on the basis of assumptions which fit neither the spirit
nor the letter of the texts which govern them.

In the first place, because of the way law is conceived of in the islamic
tradition, we must not be surprised to find among these rights and duties
matters not in the western legal ambit. Thus works on classical islamic law
("fiqh"), and substantive law as now codified, set out that the wife's right
to visit and receive visits from her relatives in accordance with "custom and
practice" (article 38, para. 1). She has the duty "to breast feed her children
if she is able to do so and to bring them up" and "to respect her husband's
parents and family" (article 39, paras. 2 and 3).

Finally, the Code requires the wife to "obey her husband and to pay
respect to him as head of the family" (article 39, para. 1). This last rule is
justified by classical jurists on the basis of a wish to maintain family stability
but in the context of a good understanding and of mutual respect between
spouses. Their teaching insists that this prerogative of the husband must not
be exercised in an arbitrary manner. He must decide after consulting his
wife, and in the interest of the whole family. The wife's duty to obey extends
only to decisions which are lawful (mashrû'a) and not humiliating (idlâl)
to her.[104]

The other duties are similarly in the spirit of islamic law based on the
principles of the Qur'an which bind men and women alike, for instance the
duty to safeguard "blood relationship" (Sura "Al Nissâ", verse 1 and Sura
"Al Anfâl", verse 75). On this basis we find a number of rules, some of
which we have already elaborated. Thus the wife is always allowed to
maintain contact with her family of origin, that is to say her husband is
forbidden to obstruct her visiting her relatives, since he would himself

---

104 Mohamed Fârûq Al-Nabahân, Ahamniyat murâ'at al-qiyam al-islâmiyya fi qawânin al
Ahwâl al-shaksiyya, in Majallat al mayâdin, Oujda n°3, 1988, p. 71.

thereby be in breach of the duty to respect these relatives (Qur'an, Sura "Al Asrâ", verse 23). This provision must be understood in the context of the spirit of a bedouin society, where marriage could mean remoteness from family, who could be living in another tribe, so creating practical difficulties for a woman to visit them. Today, the rule may seem obsolete, but one can see a certain benefit in its retention when spouses come from different countries.

As to the wife's obligation to feed her children, this rests on the child's rights which must be respected by both parents who must collaborate to protect them.[105] The rule rests on a provision in the Qur'an advising mothers to breast feed their child up to the age of two, if possible (Sura "Al Baqara", verse 231) but it is quite possible to entrust the feeding to another person (Sura "Al Baqara", verse 233) if both spouses so agree.

The mother can, on dissolution of the marriage, obtain certain rights as a result of this duty. As long as the mother is breast feeding, her husband is bound to pay her maintenance, until the child is weaned.

Further, para. 2 of article 38 of the Family Code gives the wife the right "to dispose of her assets in full freedom". This provision, taken from classical islamic law, is explained by the possibility of polygamous marriage, and the need to avoid having a regime of matrimonial property which would incorporate in his assets those of a spouse, which would then fall into his estate and could be inherited by a co-wife, whereas, despite allowing of polygamy, islamic law prefers above all the idea of the married couple.[106] Therefore quite logically islamic law imposes strict separation of property between spouses, permitting a wife freely to manage her own assets (Qur'an, Sura "Al Baqara", verse 227 and Sura "Al Nissâ", verses 20 and 21).

The rule applies regardless of the nature of the assets (movable or immovable), and of whether they were obtained by the wife on her own account (inherited, professional earnings...) or as gifts from the husband. The husband has no right to manage her assets[107], but islamic jurists have ques-

---

105 Ibrahim Al-Dasûqî, Al-Tufûla fi-l-Islam, Cairo, (1979), p. 32; Al-Ghazâli Mohamed Amîn, Huqûq al-awlâd. Institut dIEtudes islamiques, Cairo, (1971) p. 23.

106 Another example of this is seen when we see that "modern" islamic law forbids enabling one wife to become pregnant using a donated ovum from a co- wife ("Fetwa" - response - of a theological commission in Saudi Arabia).

107 A wife can obviously, should she so wish, let her husband dispose of her assets or manage them, but he may in no case do so against her wishes or without her knowledge (Qur'an, Sura "Al Nissâ", verse 4).

tioned whether this freedom granted to a married woman could be total or whether the husband could have some control over her transactions. The Hanafi school does not let the husband intervene in the wife's management of her own assets. On the other hand, the Maliki school does not allow her to make gifts to third parties without his authorisation. They justify this on the ground that she must be protected lest she act against her own interests, and dissipate her assets of which she could later be in need, if, say, the husband disappeared, but others advance another explanation, based on the husband's fear of finding her estate devoid of assets, on her death.[108]

V   LEGAL CONSEQUENCES OF SUBSTANTIVE AND FORMAL REQUIREMENTS

In islamic law, failure to fulfil one or more of the conditions for the formation of marriage can lead to dissolution or annulment of the union that is irregularly contracted. Depending on the importance of the unfulfilled condition, the marriage may even be considered not to exist at all. But it is possible for it to have certain effects even if it is annulled. On the other hand taking up living together without the intention of marriage is no marriage and in no way can the effects of marriage be applied to concubinage.

Failing one of the conditions precedent for its formation, for instance consent, the marriage is void (bâtil). In the absence of the consent of the bride, the contract of marriage is "voidable" (mardûd)[109], to take the term used in classical legal writing. Conversely marriage is "defective" (fâsid) if the condition is one that can be remedied. Then it can be regularised, particularly if not yet consummated. On failure to agree the dowry, for instance, the judge can fix a suitable dowry payable to the party entitled to it.

So nullities of marriage are classified as absolute and as relative. Algerian family law has stayed faithful to this doctrine.

---

108 Mohamed AlMahdî al-Hajwî, Al mar'a bayn al-shar' wa-l-qânûn, Casablanca, (1967) p. 28.

109 Judicial decisions have annulled marriages concluded without the bride's consent: Cour de Mostaganem, ch. civ. November 3, 1966, in *Revue Algérienne* n° 4, 1968, Part 2, p. 1200.

A Absolute nullity

Article 32 of the Family Code provides that "the marriage defective in relation to one of the conditions for it to be concluded is declared void, likewise if there is an impediment, or a clause repugnant to the object of the contract of marriage, or on proof of the spouse's apostacy." This is the sanction for non fulfilment of a condition so fundamental that the institution of marriage itself is gravely impugned and regularisation is impossible. Such a union is considered contrary to *ordre public*. Nullity may be pleaded at any time, and may even be automatic.[110] This applies to marriage to a woman forbidden because of relationship or foster-feeding[111], of marriage to two sisters at the same time, or to a woman and her paternal or maternal aunt[112], to a fifth wife[113], for a woman, to a non muslim man[114], for a man, to a wife who is an unbeliever or a polytheist, to a woman during her period of 'idda[115], or to a woman the man has three times repudiated, until she has concluded and had dissolved a marriage to a third party.[116]

In all these cases the marriage is deemed never to have existed, but the wife must observe celibate seclusion (end of article 34) if there has been cohabitation, and in that case she retains her dowry.

Apart from this, a child born of such a union is considered legitimate (article 34) with all the legal consequences of such recognition (particularly the right to take the father's name, and to inherit).

B Relative nullity

Article 33 applies relative nullity to marriages in the absence of the marriage guardian (wali), of the two witnesses or of the dowry. Here the parties may

---

110 G. Benmelha, op. cit. p. 113.
111 Breach of articles 23 ff. of the Family Code.
112 Breach of article 30, para. 2.
113 Breach of article 30, para. 1 (4th).
114 Breach of article 31, para. 1.
115 Breach of article 30, para. 1 (2nd).
116 This concerns marriage with the same husband who has repudiated her (article 30, para 1 (3rd)). Judicial decisions have sometimes allowed such a remarriage without insisting on application of the islamic law rule (Cour d'Alger, February 17, 1968, cited by G. Benmelha, op cit. p. 116 note 125).

choose to treat the marriage as valid; note, however, that this is not so "if the marriage is defective in respect of several of the elements essential for its conclusion".[117]

Two situations are envisaged by the Legislature: if unconsummated, the marriage is voidable; if consummated, it can be validated "by means of the payment of a fair dowry if it is defective in one of the elements for its conclusion."

These, then, are the sanctions provided by the law, consistently with islamic law, when the fundamental conditions are not fulfilled. If a marriage is dissolved as affected by absolute nullity, and it is not possible for the parties to go through a new marriage ceremony, the same consequences apply as in the case of divorce.

---

117 This last provision has been applied judicially: Cour Suprème, February 29, 1968, in Al majalla al-qadâ'iyya, n° 1, 1991, p. 49.

ANGOLA

AFFILIATION IN THE NEW ANGOLAN FAMILY CODE

Maria do Carmo Medina[*]

I   INTRODUCTION

The new family code was approved by Act Nr. 1/88 of February 20 and entered into force on the same day. The People's Assembly in 1982 had committed to its Commission of Legal and Constitutional Affairs the task of preparing a draft for a new Code and in 1984 the first draft was presented to the Assembly. In view of the social importance of this law it was decided that the draft should be exposed to public discussion all over the country. This took place for more than two years. In August 1987 an amended draft was presented to the People's Assembly and this was approved subject to small modifications.

Some years after publication of the Family Code the benefits of the new law had become clear. It not only brought about the complete reform of all familial institutions but also made important innovations in the law governing civil proceedings. During the colonial period there were two different legal regimes applying to the family: one that was applied to citizens with all political and civil rights and another that was applied to the indigenous population which was generally customary law. The Family Code is the first law affecting the family which applies to all Angolan citizens.

In Angola customary law is applied directly by the courts where two conditions are satisfied. First, it must be accepted by the parties concerned and secondly it must not conflict with fundamental legal principles. The Family Code has adopted some of the principles of customary law but others have been rejected. As long as customary law does not violate the fundamental rules enshrined in the Family Code, and it is accepted by the parties, it can go on being applied. Customary law is a social reality that cannot be ignored and it will survive to an extent commensurate with economic development. The new law is therefore essentially neutral on the application of customary law.

*   *Professor, Faculty of Law, University Agostinho Neto, Luanda.*

A. Bainham (ed.), The International Survey of Family Law 1994, 29–35.

On the subject of affiliation, the Family Code adopts the principles already embodied in Law Nr. 10/77 of April 15 which removed all discrimination between legitimate and illegitimate children and preserves the use of the word "incognito" in the Civil Registry which is applied to any unknown parent of a child.

The Family Code is divided into eight sections. Section I refers to "Fundamental Principles" and provides in Article 4 that children deserve special care from the Family which, in collaboration with the State, may grant to them the widest protection and equality and provide for their education. The other Sections refer respectively to Family Constitution, Marriage, De Facto Unions, Parents and Children Relations, Adoption, Guardianship and Alimony.

II   THE AFFILIATION LINK

The affiliation link between the child and his parents is considered fundamental to the family structure. The Family Code acknowledges that parenthood can be established both by consanguinity and by adoption.

Section V of the Family Code entitled "Parents and Children Relations" consists of Articles 127-196 inclusive and is sub-divided into three chapters dealing respectively with Powers and Duties, Exercise of Parental Authority and Establishment of Affiliation.

Under Article 127, the father and mother have equal powers and duties towards their children and these duties must be carried out for the benefit of the child and society. Under Article 128, children have reciprocal rights and duties towards their parents whether or not their parents are married. This principle is of first importance since it abolished legal discrimination between children born in or out of wedlock.

Where parents are married this, of course, has some legal relevance since affiliation in relation to the mother and her husband is then established by the fact of birth. In other cases, the law provides different mechanisms for establishing affiliation. Under Article 168, there will be a presumption of parenthood where a couple are living in a "de facto union" or where the child is in the possession, or "possession d'état", of the person claiming to be the parent.

Affiliation can also be established by making a statement at the Civil Registry. Under some circumstances, the statement of motherhood can be made by a third person and a statement as to fatherhood can be made by the child's mother for up to one year after the birth. These statements can be refuted by the person named as parent. Where affiliation has not been established by any of these means it can always be determined judicially.

The State itself is interested in facilitating the establishment of the affiliation link in order to determine legally for every citizen who is his father and mother and, also, in trying to ensure that the legal link accords with the biological reality. The principle is reinforced by the range of mechanisms for establishing filiation, described above, and also by the provisions which allow the Public Attorney to bring proceedings on behalf of the child within three years of the birth and the child himself to bring proceedings as of right and without time limit. The right of affiliation is thus considered a fundamental right and is legally protected as such. The law no longer classifies children as illegitimate, or adulterous or natural. Rather, the legal concept of affiliation is a unitary one giving rise to a whole range of rights and duties as between the child and his parents without discrimination and reflecting the fact that there is a single status of childhood.

III PARENTAL AUTHORITY

Parents have specific rights and duties in relation to their minor children. These exist to enable them to raise and educate them. Under Article 127, these powers and duties must be used for the best interests and benefit of the children and society itself. Parental authority is thus not in the nature of a private right. To achieve the equality of both parents the Family Code replaced the legal expression "paternal power", used in the Civil Code, to "parental authority".

Parents must exercise their parental authority by "consensus" and the father's opinion no longer prevails over the mother's view. The child's name must be chosen by both parents, but the child takes his surname from the father and from the mother as a personal right granted automatically by law. Other important issues, such as choice of career, travel abroad etc., must be decided by both parents. Where the parents fail to agree the conflict must be resolved by the court. In all matters affecting a child the court must hear the Public Attorney.

Parental authority can be exercised in three different ways – jointly by both parents (Article 139), by one parent acting alone (Article 147) or separately by each parent (Article 148). The manner of exercise depends on whether the parents are living together or apart and it is irrelevant whether or not they are married to one another. Where parents are cohabiting both must discharge all the powers and duties which go with parental authority and each parent may represent the minor child. Where the child is the child of only one partner in a cohabiting couple, the other partner must cooperate over the upbringing of the child. Exclusive exercise of parental authority arises on the death of one parent, where one parent is absent or in cases of legal incapacity or impossibility. Separate exercise arises where there is a de facto separation or where the parents' marriage is dissolved or annulled.

Parental agreements on custody must be ratified by the court. Where parents disagree the court must decide which of them is to be given the child's custody (Article 48). The custodial parent has custody, care and control (Article 149) but the non-custodial parent retains personal relations with the child and must cooperate with the custodial parent on the child's upbringing and education. Maintenance of children is a duty of both parents and alimony is determined by order of the court. Exceptionally, parental authority may be exercised by a third person in specified cases (Article 151).

In disputed cases the court must act solely in the best interests of the minor excluding considerations relating to the behaviour of the spouses or partners towards one another. The aim of the Family Code, in the case of separated parents, is to preserve a normal relationship between the child and the non-custodial parent. It attempts to achieve this not only through contact between parent and child but also through communication and cooperation between the two parents in order to preserve the child's well-being. The Court's underlying objective is to avoid more suffering to the child than that which arises by virtue of the parents' separation itself. Loss of involvement between the child and the non-custodial parent is resisted by appealing to both parents to participate in his upbringing.

IV ADOPTION

Adoption Act Nr. 7 of 1980, had already revoked the provisions of the Civil Code on this important matter. The new country felt that it was necessary to have a new law on adoption which brought a solution to the situation of the thousands of children who had lost their parents during the fight for national liberation and decolonization. The Family Code reiterated part of this legislation but broadened the legal effects of adoption.

Under Article 197 the scope of adoption is the social, moral and effective protection of the minor child and it creates a legal relationship similar to that which arises between the child and his natural parents. An adoption order can only be made in special proceedings in the Family Court. By Article 200 only a person under the age of 18 and unmarried may be adopted. The applicant for an adoption order must satisfy several conditions. He or she must be at least 25 years of age, of good moral character and must have the economic standing to provide for the maintenance and upbringing of the child.

Where the child is abandoned, or orphaned, no consent is required. Otherwise consent must be given by the child's parents. Consent is mandatory for adoption and, in the absence of parents, must be given by other relatives such as grandparents or adult collateral members of the family. The court can dispense with consent in the interests of the child or where there is great difficulty in finding relatives. Where the minor is over 10 years old, he or she must also consent to the adoption.

Applicants for adoption fall into one of the following two categories:
· married, not being separated, or living in a "de facto union" which is legally recognised.
· a sole unmarried applicant.

The adoption application must be made jointly, by a married or "de facto" couple. A sole application may however be made if the child is the natural child of one of the spouses or de facto partners.

Adoption extinguishes any parental link between the child and the natural parents. Its legal effects are extensive and the adoptive child is placed in the same position as a natural child with similar legal rights and duties. The Family code specifically gives the adopted child the right to take the surname of both adoptive parents. The child's own name can be changed under special circumstances. The adopted child is thus totally integrated into the adoptive family and is considered a relative of the wider family members.

In cases of sole adoption applications there are two possible situations:
· where the applicant adopts the child of his spouse or partner, parental authority is shared between the two of them.
· where the child is adopted by a single individual parental authority is granted exclusively to him.

One consequence of adoption is the duty of the adoptive parents to maintain the minor child. On attaining majority, the adult adopted child will have a reciprocal duty to maintain his adoptive parents (Article 249).

Adoption of an Angolan child by a foreigner must be authorised by the National Assembly, the Parliament (Article 204). The Court must stay the proceedings until such permission is given. Adoption orders must be registered in the Civil Registry Board. Angola is not a State party to the Hague Convention of 1993 relating to Intercountry Adoption.

An adoption order can be annulled by the court in cases specified by law (Article 216), which relate to essential errors concerning the person of the adopted child or lack of consent. An order may be revoked by the court (Article 218) where, for example, there has been wilful abandonment of the adopted child or ill-treatment not compatible with the care owed to a natural child. Adoption cannot be revoked by agreement between the adoptive parents and the child, but only by court order. The court must decide in accordance with the best interests of the child in the circumstances.

V   THE FAMILY COUNCIL

The Family Code introduced an enlarged concept of Family Council different from that used in the Civil Code. The Family Council is an organ composed of four members. These members are chosen, according to the type of case, from members of the family of each spouse or "de facto" partner and, in the case of the child, two from the father's family and two from the mother's.

The advice of the Family Council is not mandatory, but the court must take it into consideration. The Family Council is an institution derived from Angolan customary law which generally subjected family conflicts to the decisions of family meetings. Discussion within the family was the preferred course with the aim of arriving at harmonious solutions and obviating the necessity of resorting to the court.

In cases relating to the establishment of affiliation (Article 195) and the exercise of parental authority (Article 159), the court can hear the Family Council of its own volition or at the request of the litigants whenever it considers it convenient in assisting it to arrive at its decision. The court can hear the Family Council, under similar conditions, in Adoption cases.

VI CONCLUSION

The new Family Code brought about fundamental changes to the establishment of affiliation, the exercise of parental authority, the rights of children
and adoption. The emergence of the Family Code has been a positive
development in spite of the many difficulties which Angola has endured
through war and distress of the civilian population.

ARGENTINA

EFFECTS OF THE RECENT CONSTITUTIONAL REFORM ON FAMILY LAW

*Cecilia P. Grosman**

I CONSTITUTIONAL REFORM

The reform of the Argentine Constitution in 1994 has greatly affected family law, because of the constitutional primacy given to international human rights treaties to which this country has subscribed (National Constitution Article 75, sub. 22). We should mention, as having most relevance to family law, the American Declaration on Human Rights and Duties, the International Treaty on Civil and Political Rights, the International Treaty on Economic, Social and Cultural Rights, the Convention on the Elimination of Discrimination Against Women, the Convention on the Rights of the Child, and the American Convention on Human Rights (Treaty of San José de Costa Rica).

Guarantees of many of the rights covered by these treaties were already to be found in our family law, on the basis of legislative changes over the past decade, notably equality of the sexes in family relations, and the equal rights of all children, whether born in or out of wedlock (see commentary in Annual Survey of Family Law, 1990, v. 14). All the same, some provisions remain which do not respect the notion of equality, or breach other human rights which now enjoy constitutional status. Such provisions must be considered abrogated by implication, and could be declared unconstitutional.

Likewise the reformed constitution allows, in the absence of any more appropriate remedy, an action against any act or omission of public authorities or private individuals which damages or is imminently likely to damage, restrain, derogate from, harm or threaten, in a manifestly arbitrary or illegal way, rights and guarantees recognised by the Constitution, by a Treaty, or by Legislation. In such a case, the judge can also declare the legal basis of such act or omission unconstitutional (National Constitution, Article 75, sub. 23).

---

* Researcher of the National Council of Scientific and Technical Research. Professor of family and succession law, University of Buenos Aires. Translated by Peter Schofield.

A. Bainham (ed.), The International Survey of Family Law 1994, 37–51.
© 1996 *The International Society of Family Law. Printed in the Netherlands.*

Under this rubric of constitutional reform, we focus on the effects on the situation of children in family relations.

II   DETERMINATION OF FILIATION

A   *The principle of equality, the right to personal identity and the principle of biological truth*

Our law establishes that filiation has identical effects, whether in or out of wedlock, or by adoption (Civil Code, Article 240). This principle of equality governs the determination of filiation. Maternity is always established by the fact of birth (Civil Code, Article 242), whether in or out of wedlock. Regarding paternity, advances have been made in procedures, but there are still normative, social and economic obstacles to be cleared before genuine equality is realised. This is a serious infringement of the child's right to know his parents and his right to personal identity (Convention on the Rights of the Child, Articles 7 and 8, included in the National Constitution, Article 75, sub. 22).

1   *Refusal of biological tests by putative father*

Our law enshrines the principle of freedom of proof of filiation, including the right to have biological tests (Civil Code, Article 253). The Act establishing the National Genetic Database (Law 23.511), the object of which is to obtain and preserve genetic information which facilitates the determination and clarification of filiation disputes, supports the validity of biological tests. Similarly, doctrine and judicial decision alike hold that these are overwhelming evidence of affiliation. All the same, many men against whom filiation is claimed refuse to submit to such tests. In the face of this, doctrine and judicial decision, by a majority and based on the principles of personal inviolability and autonomy in law, maintain that it is not acceptable to compel a person to submit to a blood test, while at the same time holding that his behaviour gives rise to a strong presumption against the man who refuses. In this line of authority, a recent decision attaches very great significance to refusal to submit to expert examination biological samples in a paternity case, in which not only individual interests are at stake, but also those of society as a whole.[1]

All the same, judicial authority does not consider that refusal of biological tests is alone sufficient to determine a paternity suit, and holds that other corroborating evidence is necessary. Other decisions have gone further, maintaining that, in the face of a refusal, it does not require much additional evidence to prove the case. A much stronger position was taken by the National Chamber of Appeals in Civil Matters, allowing an extramarital paternity action, and basing its judgment solely on the putative father's refusal, without good cause, to submit to blood tests. The Court held that the weight to be given to a party's refusal should be determined in the context of the instant case, but that a presumption of paternity should be drawn from it, rebuttable only by the defendant producing some evidence that he is not the father. This means the burden of proof is reversed. This criterion, says the judgment, "will have repercussions on future cases and act to deter behaviour which unjustifiably obstructs the provision of overwhelming evidence such as this in affiliation cases".

2 The right to exhumation of the putative father's corpse for the purpose of biological tests.

The court, in an extramarital paternity suit held that the family of the deceased cannot oppose the taking of samples from the corpse for molecular analysis to obtain the DNA sequence in order to establish the biological link between the dead man and the woman claiming recognition as his daughter. The judgment held that, as between the family's right to protect the mortal remains from disturbance and that of the child under the Convention on the Rights of the Child, that of the child to have paternity established must be accorded priority as this is a matter of personal identity rights. It adds that determining filial status is a question of public order,[2] notwithstanding the fact that the filiation suit is private litigation, because society has an interest in securing assumption of responsibility for procreation (C.N. Civil, Sala A, 28/2/94, ED, 158-462). The decision, besides settling the conflict of rights

---

1   Cla. CC San Isidro, Sala I. 28/4/94, ED, 22/9/94.
2   CNC Sala M, 8/6/93; LL, 1994-A-77; C Grosman and C Ariana, Los efectos de la negativa a someterse a los exámenes biológicos en los juicios de filiación paterna extramatrimonial (The effects of refusal to submit to biological tests in extramarital filiation actions), LL, May 20 1992.

in favour of the interests of the child, lines up decidedly in a judicial attitude allowing the exhumation of the corpse, in contrast to older decisions refusing to allow this.

3   The right of the Ministerio Público de Menores to bring an extramarital paternity suit

Where children are registered without paternal filiation, our law (Civil Code, Article 255) permits the Ministerio Público de Menores to take steps to secure recognition by the putative father. If this is not given, the Ministerio brings an extramarital paternity action, provided the mother consents. Doctrinal writing holds that constitutional reform has abrogated by implication the requirement of the mother's consent. The consequence of this would be that her consent would no longer be needed for the Ministerio to bring the action.[3]

4   The action to deny the husband's paternity

The affirmation of the principle of non-discrimination goes along with that of biological truth, that is the child's right to the truth of his parentage. This right was much restricted in the case of the child of a married woman. Modern law has adopted an open system (Civil Code, Article 258), facilitating the declaration of the true relationship, whereas the old rules only allowed the presumption of paternity to be displaced on specific grounds provided by legislation. Not only does the reform let the husband dispute his paternity; the child can also do so. Under the former system, the husband during his lifetime could alone bring the action. However, it is not open to the mother, nor to the man claiming to be the putative father, to impugn the husband's paternity, and this is supported by judicial authority.[4] For some writers, this infringes the principle of sexual equality in family relations, provided in human rights treaties, now ranked on the constitutional level (Convention on the Elimination of Discrimination Against Women,

---

3   XII National Conference of Judges and officers of justice for minors; Mariá Josefa Mendez Costa, Encuaqre legal del derecho a la identidad (Legal framework of the right to identity), p. 1128; Grosman-Ariana, Hacia una mayor efectividad del Article 255 del Código Civil (Towards a greater effectiveness for article 255 of the Civil Code), JA. 1992-II-892.

4   SC Buenos Aires, 5/10/93, ED. 12/4/94.

and Treaty of San José de Costa Rica).[5] The restriction is also seen as infringing the child's right to the truth of his parentage, an integral part of his right to identity, and consequently, from this point of view also the legal limitation would be unconstitutional.[6] Other authors, however, believe the right to identity is a qualified one, on which limits can in particular cases be placed, in the interest of "family peace", so as to override the protection of biological truth.[7]

III THE CHILD'S RIGHT TO PRESERVATION OF HIS FAMILY RELATIONSHIPS

The child's right to identity does not stop at that of knowing his parents; rather courts have recognised other aspects which would form part of his right to individual personality. Consistent with this trend, one decision holds that the right to identity also extends to the ability to maintain the links that are part of his life history, such as contact with grandparents or siblings.[8]

Likewise, in another decision, regarded as pivotal to the "child's interest" principle, it was said that the exercise of parental authority should be seen in the light of the interest of children in keeping up emotional ties and contact with all close family members, and even with persons outside the family where it is established that such communication would be good for the child. The focus of attention, said the court, is the interest of the child, which must be the judge's aim when conflict is unleashed. It underlined the child's right to keep contact and communication with all those with whom there is a legitimate interest, based on family relationships, or even with other non-relatives with whom the child has an emotional tie.[9]

---

5   Florencio Varela, Inconstitucionalidad de la discriminación de la mujer en el articulo 259 del Código Civil (Unconstitutionality of discrimination against women in Article 259 of the Civil Code); Cecilia P Grosman and Irene Martinez Alcorta, La filiación matrimonial. Su reforma según la ley 23.264, LL, t. 1986-D, p. 924.

6   German J. Bidart Campos, Las realidades biológicas y la normas jurídicas, ED, diary of 8/6/94; LL, diary 30/9/94; Cecilia P Grosman and Irene Martinez Alcorta, La filiación matrimonial. Su reforma según la ley 23.264, LL, t.1986-D, p. 924.

7   Augusto C Belluscio, Incidencia de la reforma constitucional sobre el derecho de familia (Effects of constitutional reform on family law), LL, issue 24/2/95; Mendez Costa, op. cit. p. 1126.

8   CNC, Sala A, 22/3/94, ED, 1/7/94: CNC, Sala L, 10/3/93.

9   CNC, Sala F, 18/5/93, 11 1994-B-240.

IV   RESPONSIBILITY OF BOTH PARENTS FOR THE UPBRINGING AND DEVELOP-
MENT OF THE CHILD AND THE MAINTENANCE OBLIGATION

A   *Maintenance of the as yet unrecognised extramarital child*

With the aim of securing the support of the extramarital child, and of affir-
ming the principle of responsibility of both progenitors in his upbringing,
doctrinal and judicial opinion allow for the granting of provisional maintenance even before a declaration on the substantive issue, provided the
relationship relied on is established in summary form.[10] This criterion forms
part of a legislative project approved by the Chamber of Deputies on November 3 1993, now under consideration by the National Senate. Article 273
provides that "for the sole purpose of providing provisional maintenance,
the court is to proceed to summary investigation of the probability of paternity or of maternity."[11]

B   *Measures against failure to maintain and fraudulent insolvency.*

In most cases of divorce or separation, child custody, by consent or by
judicial order, goes to the mother, the father's right to contact with the child
or adolescent being preserved. Despite the end of consortium, both parents
are responsible for maintenance and education of their children, even though
day to day control vests in one alone (Civil Code, Article 271).

All the same, social practice shows a gradual detachment of the father
from the child's life, and failure to fulfil his role of assistance properly, thus
infringing not only the national law, but also international treaties which
rank on a level with the Constitution and which impose family responsibilities on both parents equally (Articles 18 and 27 of the Convention on
the Rights of the Child; Article 23.4 of the Treaty on Civil and Political

---

10   Borda Guillermo, Tratado de Derecho Civil Argentino. Familia No. 1244-3, 9th ed.,
Buenos Aires (1993); G Bossert op. cit. No. 210, p. 190; Cecilia P Grosman, Acción
alimentaria de los hijos extramatrimoniales no reconocidos o no declarados como tales
(The claim for maintenance of extramarital children neither recognised nor judicially
declared as such). Buenos Aires, Ed. Perrot, p. 54 ff.; CNC Sala E, 19/12/88, LL,
1989-C-384; CNC Sala H, 28/2/92, ED, 148-435.
11   Augusto C Belluscio, La reforma del derecho de familia sancionada por la Cámara de
Diputados (The reform of family law passed by the Chamber of Deputies) LL, 23/3/94.

Rights; Article 16,c of the Convention on Elimination of Discrimination Against Women).

Legislation and judicial interpretation have developed various means of giving effect to the maintenance duty, such as: 1) The classic methods of taking security for payment, including guarantees of future contributions, in case of persistent failure to maintain, or of well founded suspicion that the liable party intends to declare insolvency or to flee the jurisdiction;[12] 2) Judicial order against an employer for maintenance payment by attachment of earnings. In such a case criminal sanctions are available to compel the employer to comply with the order (Procedure Code, Article 239), and damages can be awarded to the recipient to compensate for any loss,[13] which will consist of making good the payment of sums the employer failed to retain. The legislative project approved by the Chamber of Deputies mentioned above provides, "Anyone failing to comply immediately with the judicial order to retain the sum corresponding to an obligation of maintenance to a dependant or creditor incurs joint liability on the obligation" (Article 324). The project, which is currently being considered, establishes a prohibition on leaving the jurisdiction against anyone ordered to pay maintenance, unless he first gives proper guarantees for fulfilment of his obligation (Article 328).

Despite the range of civil remedies, to which we should add the penal sanctions provided in Law 13.944 by which breach of the duty of family assistance is made an offence, in many cases a father evades his role of support, by manoeuvres of all kinds, for example by transfer of assets to a nominee, claiming to be a mere employee in a concern in which he is really a partner, or vesting all his assets in a limited company.

Law 24.029 created a penal measure to stop the device of fraudulent insolvency. It punishes with imprisonment of from one to six years any one who, with the intention of evading fulfilment of his support obligations, maliciously destroys, renders useless, hides, damages or causes to disappear

---

12 G Bossert op. cit. and decisions there referred to; CNC Sala A, 10/8/89, R.49.890; CNC Sala F, 26/2/87, R.27.078.
13 Gustavo A Bossert, Régimen jurídico de los alimentos (The law of maintenance), Astrea, Buenos Aires (1993), p. 518.

any of his assets, or fraudulently reduces their value in such a way as to frustrate wholly or in part the fulfilment of the duty of support.[14]

V   THE RIGHT OF THE CHILD OF SEPARATED PARENTS TO KEEP REGULAR PERSONAL RELATIONS AND CONTACT WITH BOTH PARENTS

A   *Obstruction by the non-custodial parent*

Our law, regardless of how care and control of children is organised, requires an award to one person, with preference for the mother if the children are under five years old. Above this age, failing agreement of the spouses, they are placed in the custody of whichever the judge considers more suitable for this role (Civil Code, Article 206), All the same, in judicial practice we find that custody, be it by consent or by court order, is generally given to the mother. Argentine courts have traditionally rejected agreements to share custody, above all if this is with alternating care and control, which they regarded as harmful to the minor's upbringing and development. All the same, lately, and with increasing frequency, judges have recognised the right of parents to come to such agreements. Picking out one judgment, we find it said that shared exercise of patria potestas (parental authority) benefits the interest of children, because "parents remain mindful of the responsibility they share in relation to the care and education of children, in spite of the breakdown of consortium." Further, the judgment adds, it maintains "the objective of the law that not one alone, but both parents should take the decisions, express or tacit, touching the life and property of their child."[15]

In cases of informal or formal separation, divorce or nullity of marriage, exercise of patria potestas is ascribed to the custodial parent, the other having the right to sufficient communication with the child or adolescent, and to control over his or her education (Article 264, sub. 2).

Quite often, however, a father stops seeing his children, so infringing the child's right to be brought up and trained by both parents, as well as

---

14   Guillermo Pablo Desimone and Luis A Caimmi, Incumplimiento de los deberes de asistencia familiar e insolvencia alimentaria fraudulenta (Failure to fulfil the duties of family support and fraudulent maintenance insolvency), LL, January 5 1995.

15   CNC, Sala F, October 23 1987, LL, 1989-A-95; likewise such agreements have been accepted in: CNC, Sala B, LL, t. 1990-B-171.

the right of the mother, normally the custodial parent, who is made to assume sole responsibility for upbringing and education.

At the same time, mothers often obstruct relations between fathers and children. To infringe the right of contact with the absent parent in this way attracts civil and penal sanctions. One decision goes so far as to take custody away from the parent obstructing contact with the other, handing it to the latter.[16] Family courts have also, in awarding custody, considered that the more suitable parent to exercise it is the one who is most likely to maintain the child's links with the other parent.[17]

On the basis of these situations, which occur very often, a penal law has been passed (No. 24.470) providing for the punishment of imprisonment for from one to twelve months of a parent or other person who illegally obstructs or impedes contact between minors and their absent parents (Article 1). The penalty rises to from six months to three years in the case of a child under 10 or subject to disability. Similar penalties fall on any one who, in order to impede contact with the absent parent, moves house without judicial authorization. Likewise penalties are imposed if, with the same intention, the parent emigrates without judicial authorization, or exceeds the limits of such an authorization (Article 2). Last, the criminal court must, within 10 days, take the necessary measures to restore contact with the minor.

One reason for the mother's refusal to let the father see the children is his failure to pay maintenance. While, in the past, judges on the application of the mother would suspend the father's visitation rights on that ground, the modern tendency is to maintain communication with the father since it is a matter of an essential right of the child, and to remove it is to impose a double punishment on the child; besides not getting support, he loses contact with his father.[18]

Often the child or adolescent himself expresses his own unwillingness to meet the absent parent. In such a case, the court looks into whether the rejection is spontaneous or induced, and into its justification.[19] It considers whether it is the mother's duty to secure compliance on the children's part

---

16 Advice of the assessor of Minors of the Chamber, CNC, Sala I, September 12 1991, LL 1991-E, p. 503; CNC Sala C, November 1 1990, ED, 141, p. 795.
17 CNC Sala L, 12/2/91, LL, t. 1991-E-503; CNC Sala B, 22/11/89, LL 1990-E-170.
18 CNC, Sala C, 26/12/85, LL., 1986-B-333.
19 CNC Sala B, August 3 1989, ED. 137, p. 561.

with the visitation regime on the basis of which custody was awarded to her.[20] Judges give great value to communication between children and their father, emphasising in some decisions that breaking the tie between father and child can lead to behavioral disturbance, and commonly produces harm which is hard to remedy in adult life.[21]

Despite all the means and sanctions created to ensure contact between the child and the non-custodial parent, Argentine judges, at increasing levels of seniority, recognise that these conflicts cannot be resolved exclusively by penal sanctions which benefit neither the child nor the family as a whole. Therefore attempts have been made to correct such resistance and disagreements by making the parents undergo therapy, with sanctions in case of non-compliance. It has been held that, for the sake of the child, the courts cannot stand by indifferent, but must seek suitable ways to resolve family conflict.[22]

B   Foreign travel of the custodial parent

In accordance with Argentine law, both parents must consent if the child is to leave the country. If either refuses, or it is impossible for him to consent, the judge decides what is in the interest of the family (Article 264, quater).

Lately in Argentina, there have been certain cases where a custodial parent wishes to go abroad with the children. In these circumstances there is an obvious conflict between the right of a parent to achieve his life ambitions and that of a child to keep direct contact with both parents on a regular basis (Convention on the Rights of the Child, Article 9).

The tendency of our law is to grant authorization to the custodial parent to move to another country so long as he gives valid reasons for the move and provides adequate guarantees of the right of communication between the child and the other parent. In a recent case, a couple were divorced, custody of their daughters being granted to the mother. She later lived with a Peruvian, by whom she had a child. In this situation, she applied to the judge for authority to take the daughters to Peru, where the whole family

---

20   CNC Sala C. 1/11/90, LL, t. 1992-B-1.
21   CNC Sala B, 3/8/89, LL, 1990-A-109; CNC Sala C, 1/11/90, LL, 1992-B-2.
22   CNC, Sala E, February 20 1989, ED 136, p. 685; CNC Sala E, 31/5/88, LL, 14/12/89; CNC, Sala E, 26/5/86 LL, t. 1986-E-437.

group wished to settle, including her new partner and his children. The former husband opposed the application, and the court did not grant authorization, on the ground of the possibility that "a change of cultural context appears as a dangerous experiment for the physical integrity of the minors, especially as the formation of the new relationship requires of them a new adaptation." The court held that such a move abroad should only be authorised if it gave the children "so many benefits as to greatly exceed the detriments the move would imply." It is to be noted that, in that case, both parents had in fact agreed that the girls should go with their mother to Peru, and that a generous arrangement should be made for visits to their father. The judgment indicates a dangerous attitude, since it fails to have regard for parental autonomy in authorising their children's departure from the country, which is recognised specifically in the law (Article 264 quater). As we have noted, in an earlier paper,[23] children have the right to live in a place which is not the residence of one of their parents, and this does not infringe the right of contact, which right must be adjusted to circumstances. The judicial decision placed the mother in the position of choosing whether to renounce custody of the daughters and travel to Peru with her intended husband and their son, or to abandon the intention of forming a new family group and stay in Argentina with the daughters of her first marriage. Thus the court infringed the mother's freedom and her right to a family life in which the girls from the former union would live and be educated with their new brother. We note, in that paper, that the State has no right to break these ties, separate siblings, and obstruct family life. The duty of the judge, in such cases, must be restricted to ensuring that, in spite of the move, the children remain in contact with both parents. Fortunately the Supreme Court reversed the decision, in the light of the parties' agreement, on the ground of their private autonomy in reaching a solution to family conflict which was not contrary to any public order family law interest.[24]

---

23 Cecilia P Grosman and Marta Poinkiewicz, La autonomia de los padres para decidir el traslado y lugar de residencia de sus hijos (The autonomy of parents to decide on the movement and place of residence of their children), LL, 2/2/94.

24 Corte Suprema, 22/12/89; ED, 5/5/94.

C The child's views on matters affecting his person (Convention on the Rights of the Child, art. 12)

At present in our law there are provisions for the child to be heard in proceedings which may affect his person. For instance, in case of dispute between the parents over the exercise of parental authority, the judge, to determine what is in the child's interest, can hear the minor if he has enough understanding and the circumstances make it desirable (Civil Code, Article 264 ter). In adoption cases, the judge may hear the person being adopted if he thinks this necessary, so long as the person is over 10 (Law 19,134, Article 10, sub. c). Where the adopter has children biologically related to him, they too may be heard, if over 8 years, where the judge considers this necessary (Law 19.134, Article 4). In some Provinces, the judge is expressly required to hear the minor (Provinces of Mendoza and of Buenos Aires).

At present, in accordance with Article 12 of the Convention on the Rights of the Child, incorporated in Article 75, sub. 22 of the National Constitution, judges are required to make the children or adolescents parties to the case so they may express their opinions in all litigation relating to their persons, subject to their age and maturity.

VI ILLICIT REMOVAL OF MINORS

With the number of Argentines now travelling abroad for work or study, there have recently been cases which have considerable public repercussions, in which application has been made to Argentine courts to return children illegally brought to Argentina. These applications have been based on the Convention on Civil Aspects of the International Abduction of Children concluded at the Hague in 1980, and accepted by our country in Law 23.857 of 1990.

In one such case, the mother had been granted provisional custody of a girl in Spain, but the judge had ordered that the girl should not leave that country without express judicial authorization. The Spanish court set up a regime of contact with the father and required both parents to surrender their passports to the court, to prevent either of them leaving its jurisdiction. Contrary to that decision, the mother moved with the child to Argentina. The father claimed the return of the girl, and after a contest which continued several years, the Chamber of Appeals in Civil matters granted his request, since, although more than a year had passed since the move, the girl had not settled in her new environment (Hague Convention, Article 12). This decision was based on inadequate performance of the girl in school, on the mother's proved intention to exclude the father from playing any part in his daughter's life, which the court held to be contrary to her psycho-social development. Another reason was that the mother had made unproven accusations of sexual abuse against the father, so forcing the girl to be subjected to gynaecological examination. The court held this conduct of the mother, who subsequently withdrew the criminal case, was a form of maltreatment of the girl. The resulting decision was that she should be returned, as requested by the Spanish court, since she had not settled in Argentina, and, to the contrary, the move had shown scant respect for her individual rights.[25]

VII DOMESTIC VIOLENCE AND MISTREATMENT OF CHILDREN

International human rights treaties, which in our country rank at the level of constitutional provisions, guarantee the right of all persons to life and to psychological and physical integrity. To guarantee enjoyment of these rights, a Law on protection against domestic violence has recently been passed, No.24.417; now in force in the Federal Capital; Provinces are invited to enact their own similar laws (Article 9).

According to this legislative text, whoever suffers physical or psychological mistreatment at the hands of another member of the family group can complain about it to the family court judge claiming protective measures, without prejudice to any criminal proceedings that may arise. The married woman and the concubine are alike protected, even after separation, that is when the spouses, or unmarried former partners now no longer live in the same household.[26]

Where children or persons under incapacity are concerned, their legal representatives (mother, father, tutor, curator) must lay the complaint, or the Ministerio Público does so. This means that if the father or mother strikes

---

25 CNC Sala G, case no. 144.845, March 1995.
26 Cecilia Grosman and Alcorta Irene Martinez, *Una ley a mitad del camino, la ley de protección contra la violencia familiar* (A law half-way down the road; the law of protection against domestic violence), LL, March 27 1995.

the child, the other parent is obliged to report the facts to the family judge. Likewise denunciation is obligatory for the caring services, social or educational, public or private, health professionals and any other person in the public service who comes to know of such aggression in the course of his work (Article 2). Although the law provides no sanction for non-performance of the duty to report, the normal liability in damages applies, and public servants can suffer the normal consequences of a breach of their duty. The minor, or person under incapacity can report the facts to the Ministerio Público de menores, which in turn reports to the family judge.

According to Article 3, the judge seised of the case calls for certain expert witness reports, a) a medical examination, aimed at establishing the truth of the allegations of violence and the extent of any physical or psychological injuries suffered by the victim; b) a social background report; and c) a diagnosis of family interaction.

The judge can take various precautionary measures (Article 4), including: a) exclusion of the perpetrator (whether he is the husband or the concubine) from the family home for so long as the judge deems necessary; b) prohibition by court order against his coming near the family home, work place, or place of study of the victim; c) ordering that any person driven from the family home by mistreatment be enabled to return, and that the aggressor be excluded; d) in the same proceedings, the judge can order maintenance payments, child custody and the terms on which communication with children may take place (Article 4). It is important for the same judge to have power to resolve all these problems, since research findings show that often the woman puts up with the mistreatment for want of means, or fear of losing the children.

Last, the family judge calls parties to a hearing to get the perpetrator, or the family group as a whole, according to the diagnosis of family interaction, to undergo a programme of therapy or education (Article 5).

The law as passed is positive in that it opens a new field of reporting and increases the visibility of the facts of family violence, which usually remain hidden in domestic privacy. On the other hand it extends the rules of protection and pushes the perpetrator in the direction of therapy. All the same, unlike the earlier projects which served as models for it, it imposes no sanctions on perpetrators who disobey protective orders, fail to attend therapy, abandon therapy, or re-offend while in therapy.

After this summary of the latest advances in the field of family law, we conclude that the changes introduced by legislation and by judicial interpretation in relation to the situation of the child in family relations are evidence of concern to extend the effectiveness of human rights in the domestic setting, so as to reinforce the fundamental rights of family members.

AUSTRALIA

"...BEAUTIFUL AND IDEAL OR THE REVERSE..."[1] AUSTRALIAN FAMILY LAW IN 1994

Frank Bates[*]

I   SOME INTRODUCTORY CONSIDERATIONS

Although 1994 has, in Australian family law, been instantly characterised by the threat of, yet again, significant amendment to the *Family Law Act* 1975,[2] that has not meant that there have not been significant and interesting developments during the year. Development has touched on all major areas of family law and contiguous areas.

Given Australia's demographic and geographical situation, it would have been surprising had there not been important decisions with an international aspect. The most significant of these decisions has been the decision of the High Court of Australia in *Z.P.* v *P.S.*[3] The essence of that decision is that the highest appellate Court in Australia has refused to apply its own earlier decision in *Voth v Manildra Four Mills*[4] to cases involving children. In *Voth,* the High Court decided that, when an issue arose as to whether a foreign forum, as opposed to an Australian court, was the most convenient forum to determine a dispute, then the Australian Court should hear the matter unless it was satisfied that it was a clearly inappropriate forum. In a variety of subsequent cases[5], the Family Court of Australia had decided that Australian courts were clearly inappropriate.

---

*   Professor of Law, University of Newcastle (N.S.W.).
1   Havelock Ellis, *Little Essays of Lust and Virtue* (1992) Chapter 1, "The family only represents one aspect, however important an aspect, of a human being's activities and functions ... A life is beautiful and ideal or the reverse only when we have taken into consideration the social as well as the family relationship".
2   For comment, see below text at note 86.
3   (1994) FLC 92-480.
4   (1990) 171 CLR 538. For comment on this case in the context of family law, see PE Nygh, "*Voth* in the Family Court: Forum Conveniens in Property and Custody Litigation". (1993) 7 *Aust. J. Fam. L.* 260.
5   See *In the Marriage of Scott* (1991) FCL 92-241; *In the Marriage of Erdal* (1992) FLC 92-292; *In the Marriage of Van Rensburg and Pacquay* (1993) FLC 92-391; *In the Marriage of Gilmore* (1993) FLC 92-353.

A. Bainham (ed.), The International Survey of Family Law 1994, 53–74.
© *1996 The International Society of Family Law. Printed in the Netherlands.*

Z.P. v *P.S.* involved the custody and welfare of a seven-year-old child who had been born and brought up in Greece until his mother brought him to Australia in breach of a custody order made, paradoxically in her favour, by a Greek court. The mother was an Australian citizen of Greek origin, as was the father and the child. The wife applied to the Family Court of Australia to have custody of the child and obtained an interim order to that effect. At the same time, the Greek Court had revoked its initial order and awarded custody to the husband.

The Family Court also made a number of orders, the most important of which was that parties were to submit themselves to a Greek Court for the determination of all issues relevant to the child. In the Family Court, the wife had intimated that she was prepared to return to Greece in the event that the determination was to be made in that country. She later, though, said that she no longer intended to return there. The first issue in the appeal was whether the Family Court of Australia was entitled to make a summary order that the custody of a child could be determined by a foreign court. If that question was determined in the affirmative, the second issue was whether, in making the order, the Family Court was required to, and did, have regard to the welfare of the child.

Although the appeal was allowed by a majority, all of the seven judges of the High Court took a similar approach regarding the *Voth* decision[6]. The decision was made easier on the facts of the case, because, at the relevant time, Greece was not a party to the *Hague Convention on the Civil Aspects of International Child Abduction*; though there is a serious matter of principle involved as one of Australia's nearest neighbours (Malaysia) is unlikely ever to be a party to the Convention[7]. The major issue was, thus, how far the doctrine of *forum non conveniens* was applicable to cases involving children and s64 (1)(a) of the *Family Law Act* 1975, which requires Courts to regard the welfare of the child as the paramount consideration. "It follows", as Mason CJ., and Toohey and McHugh JJ., put

---

6   The majority – Brennan, Deane, Dawson and Gaudron JJ. – took the view that the Full
     Court of the Family Court had erred in principle in making their decision. The remainder
     – Mason CJ., Toohey and McHugh JJ. – did not.
7   See *In the Marriage of B (Child Abduction)* (1986) FLC 91-749. For comment on various
     aspects of this case, see F. Bates, "Child Abduction: Australian Law in International
     Context" (1988) 37 ICLQ 945, "The Story of *B* : Australian Family Law in an Asian
     Context" (1994) 3 *Asia Pacific L.R.* 33.

the matter,[8] "that when a child is within the jurisdiction of the Family Court, the Doctrine of *forum non conveniens* has no application to a dispute concerning the custody of a child. Injustice to one or other of the parties, expense, inconvenience and legitimate advantage, which are always relevant issues in a *forum non conveniens* case, are not relevant issues in a custody application ... When the Family Court is seized of jurisdiction in relation to the custody of a child, its duty is to exercise its jurisdiction". Similarly, Brennan and Dawson JJ. regarded[9] the attempt by the Family Court to meld the welfare of the child with the "clearly inappropriate forum" test as misconceived. The latter determined whether, in certain classes of case, the Court should decline to exercise its jurisdiction, whilst the former governed the manner in which the Family Court *must*[10] exercise the jurisdiction conferred on it by the *Family Law Act.*

The immediate consequence of the decision in ZP is that it will be more difficult for disputes involving children, and which are not covered by the *Hague Convention*, to be litigated outside Australia. ZP, thus, marks a change in policy direction which will be welcomed by some Australians though not others.

On a more local level, some of the other jurisdictional problems which affect Australian Family Law are well illustrated by the decision of Kay J. of the Family Court of Australia in *In the Marriage of Cauchi.*[11] There, consent orders had been made, *inter alia*, that the husband be restrained, by way of injunction, from entering or occupying the former matrimonial home. Shortly afterwards, a police officer laid a complaint and an intervention order was made under State legislation.[12] Further orders were then made, which on this occasion, restrained the husband from approaching or contacting the wife or the children of the marriage – those orders also specified that, attached to them, was a power of arrest pursuant to s 114AA of the *Family Law Act*. In the end, the husband was arrested; however, it was not clear from the material presented to the Family Court as to whether the arrest was consequent on the breach of the intervention order, breach of the injunction or some breach of the criminal law.

---

8   (1994) FLC 92-480 at 80, 999.
9   Ibid at 80, 001.
10 Author's italics.
11 (1994) FLC 92-447.
12 *Crimes (Family Violence Act)* 1987 (Vic).

Kay J. held, first, that[13] a power of arrest automatically attached to injunctions made for the personal protection of persons[14] or injunctions made for the protection of children or their custodians.[15] Otherwise, there is no extant power in the Family Court to attach a power of arrest. It, therefore, followed[16] that the order which specified the power of arrest was made without power and could not stand. The judge considered that, in order to clarify matters for the benefit of the police, it was necessary to prefix any such order with the formula, "These orders are made for the personal protection of the children of the marriage and of the wife". On the continually vexed question of the relationship between Federal and State jurisdiction in the area of domestic violence, Kay J. took the view that, if the prohibition contained in s 114AB of the *Family Law Act* on the taking of proceedings under that Act where State proceedings had already been instituted was aimed at preventing a duplicity of proceedings and providing some protection to the respondent against having to contest the same set of facts in two separate jurisdictions, then that provision did not achieve that end where, as in the instant case, the complaint under State law had been laid by someone other than a party to the *Family Law Act* proceedings. It is a little surprising perhaps that this kind of situation has not occurred more frequently in that it appears[17] that State domestic violence legislation is, for good reason, preferred to its Federal equivalent. At the same time, events which lead up to its use can very well occur in the context of proceedings brought generally under the *Family Law Act*.

II   PARENT AND CHILD LAW

After the decision of the High Court of Australia in *Secretary, Department of Health and Community Services v J W B and S M B*[18] (more generally known as *Re Marion*), which decided that the sterilisation of young women

---

13   (1994) FLC 92-447 at 80, 651.
14   *Family Law Act* 1975 Section 114AA.
15   Ibid Section 70C.
16   (1994) FLC 92-447 at 80, 651.
17   See J H Wade, *Australian De Facto Relationships Law* (1991) para. 73-700.
18   (1992) FLC 92-293. For detailed comment on this case, see P Parkinson, "Children's Rights and Doctors' Immunities: The Implications of the High Court's Decision in *In re Marion*"(1992) 6 *Aust. J. Fam. L.* 101.

with a mental disability could not be authorised by parents but required the authorisation of the Family Court, it would have been surprising had there not been developments in that area.

In *Marion*, the operation was ultimately carried out after authorisation by the Family Court.[19] However, in *L and G M v M M: Director General, Department of Family Services and Aboriginal and Islander Affairs*,[20] Warnick J. of the Family Court declined to grant such an authorisation. The young woman in question (Sarah) was aged 17 and lived in a disabled persons' ward in a country hospital and was dependent on health care providers for her daily needs. She was unable to communicate and could not walk without the assistance of other people. She was unable to operate her wheelchair and her condition would almost inevitably deteriorate. She had begun to menstruate in 1991. As regards her future care, it was admitted that she might be accommodated outside the hospital system. The parents argued that the proposed hysterectomy was necessary in the maintenance of hygiene, to control her epilepsy and to prevent pregnancy. In that regard, the parents relied strongly on their own wishes and the weight which they thought ought to be attached to them.

The basic reason why Warnick J. refused the applications was that he was not, "... satisfied, on the balance of probabilities, but to a firm degree on clear and convincing proof that Sarah's sterilisation [was] in Sarah's best interests."[21] Second, the judge considered that the function of the Court when asked to authorise sterilisation was whether it was, in all the circumstances of the case, in the best interest of the child. That was the view which had been articulated by the majority of the High Court in the *J.W.B.* case.[22] Third, whilst acknowledging that "paramount" did not necessarily mean "sole",[23] he went on to say[24] that, "The best interests of the child is not a 'value' or 'consideration' which sits amongst the pertinent facts and

---

19 In *Re Marion (No 2)* (1994) FLC 92-448. Though not reported until 1994, the decision was made on 1 May 1992.

20 (1994) FLC 92-449.

21 Ibid at 80, 680.

22 (1992) FLC 92-293 at 79, 185 *per* Mason CJ., Dawson, Toohey and Gaudron JJ.

23 See the pre-1976 decision of the High Court of Australia in *Storie v Storie* (1945) 80 CLR 597 at 611 *per* Dixon CJ. It should be said that this writer finds it far from easy to appreciate why this case, given changes in law and policy in Australian family law, should still be continually quoted.

24 (1994) FLC 92-449 at 80, 679.

values in a child welfare case. It is *the perspective* from which all other facts and values must be viewed. It is not part of the evidence and considerations which fall for deliberation, it is the legal principle which provides the focus of the deliberation." There was, his Honour continued,[25] therefore, no room in any final deliberation for the application of some other principle of law which was, inevitably subordinate to that. Hence, in the present case, there was no element of any presumption attaching to the wishes of the parents. "These conclusions," he said, "categorise such matters ... as 'factual material' to which an importance or 'value' will be ascribed, depending on the facts of the case."

On the facts of the case, Sarah's parents were not involved in her daily care and there was no suggestion that their attitudes to, or interaction with, her would change in any way which was dependent on the outcome of the application. On the specific issues which had been raised, the judge concluded[26] that the procedure which was proposed would not increase with any certainty Sarah's capacity to enjoy life or meet a presently unmet need. Expected improvement to hygiene would, the judge thought, be minimal. Likewise, the operation would not improve her health, nor was it necessary to enable her to move into more normal residential accommodation. Finally, Warnick J. considered that, "To make a decision in this case in favour of sterilisation would be virtually equivalent to establishing a policy that all females with profound disabilities resembling those afflicting Sarah should be sterilised ... I cannot think that such an approach is consistent with human dignity, the fundamental nature of the right to personal inviolability and the responsibility of the capable to care for the incapable." It should be said that Warnick J.'s approach is consonant with that of the Family Law Council in an important and recent report which will be discussed later in the commentary.[27]

Given the emotive nature of the topic, there was bound to be further constitutional debate surrounding it. Thus, in *P v P*,[28] the High Court was faced with the relationship between State and Federal jurisdiction.[29] The

---

25   Ibid at 80, 680.

26   Ibid at 80, 681.

27   Below text at note 88.

28   (1994) FLC 92-462.

29   That had not been an issue in the *J.W.B.* case, above at note 18, because the child in question was resident in the Northern Territory.

applicant and the respondent (Mr and Mrs P) had divorced in 1990. Mrs
P. had custody of L, their 16-year-old intellectually disabled daughter, who
was a weekly boarder at a school in New South Wales for children with
intellectual disabilities. At other times, she lived with Mrs P. in that same
State. Mrs. P applied to the Family Court for an order authorising, and
consenting to, an operation on her daughter which would have the effect
of rendering her permanently infertile. It was intended that the operation
would be carried out in the State of New South Wales. However, she had
not applied to the Guardianship Board of the State for its consent. Part 5
of the *Guardianship Act* (N.S.W.) 1987 establishes a legislative scheme
regulating the administration of "medical or dental treatment" to incapable
persons of 16 years or over. More specifically, such treatment is
prohibited[30] unless consent has either been given by the Board or carrying
out of treatment to which consent has not been obtained is authorised by
Part 5. It should be said that especially stringent restrictions are imposed
in relation to sterilisations. Hence, the five questions which were reserved
for the decision of the High Court were based on the view that the circumstances of the case were such that, subject to the effect of the *Family
Law Act* and the jurisdiction of the Family Court, the proposed treatment
would contravene the provisions of the State legislation. In the event, the
High Court answered all of those questions in the affirmative, thus
strengthening Federal jurisdiction as against that of the States. The decision
is, hence, important in the constitutional context of Australian family law
but is also likely to be regarded as representing the adventurous (or foolhar-
dy) qualities of the presently constituted High Court as further represented
by decisions outside the family law area.[31]

Apart from the issue of sterilisation, the matter of medical procedures
and jurisdiction has additionally been canvassed in *Re Michael*[32] and *Re
Michael (No 2)*.[33] The child in question was eleven years old and suffered
from a congenital abnormality whereby the major blood vessels to and from
his heart were transposed. The usual consequence was death. Medical experts
were wholly in favour of the need for surgery, but the parents were opposed

---

30 *Guardianship Act* (NSW) 1987 Section 35(1).
31 See *Mabo v Queensland (No 2)* (1992) 175 CLR 1; *Theophanos v Herald and Weekly
    Times* (1994) 124 ALR 1.
32 (1994) FLC 92-471.
33 (1994) FLC 92-486.

to that course of action. In view of their opposition, the matter was referred to the Public Advocate for the State of Victoria. In this proceeding, the only issue was the standing of the Public Advocate, who relied on the powers granted under State legislation.[34] At first instance, it was held that the legislation[35] permitted the Public Advocate to institute the proceedings and, in addition, that s 63(1) (c) of the *Family Law Act* recognised the Public Advocate as being a person who had an interest in the child within the meaning of the Act.

The major argument advanced on behalf of the parents was that the Public Advocate had neither the power nor a duty to act as a litigant in the Family Court so as to cause a person with a disability to undergo treatment. In consequence, they argued that the litigation function of the Public Advocate was limited to proceedings before the State Guardianship Board or the Federal Administrative Appeals Tribunal. Additionally, they argued that the other prime function of the Public Advocate was to promote the interests of the disabled as a class and, in turn, that that did not entitle the Public Advocate to act as a litigant. In the instant case, the Public Advocate, it was claimed, was not acting for or on behalf of the child as was required by the legislation[36] and should, thus, be regarded having exceeded his statutory powers.

A strong Full Court of the Family Court[37] dismissed the parents' appeal. The first basis for their decision was to be found[38] in s 4(1)(d) of the State legislation which states that one of the objects of the Act is, "... to ensure that persons with a disability ... are informed of and make use of the provisions of this Act." and s 4(2)(b) which requires that "... the best interests of a person with a disability are promoted". Second, the Court took the view that the powers of the Public Advocate extended well beyond a support function to the Guardianship Board, which, they thought,[39] was apparent from the terms in which the State legislation was concerned. Thus, for instance, s 16(1)(e) of the Act permits the Public Advocate to , "... seek assistance in the best interests of any person with a disability from any

---

34   *Guardianship and Administration Act* 1986 (Vic).
35   Ibid Section 16(1)(e), (f).
36   *Guardianship and Administration Act* 1986 Section 16(1)(f)(Vic).
37   Nicholson CJ., Fogarty and Joske JJ.
38   (1994) FLC 92-471 at 80, 892.
39   Ibid at 80, 892.

government department, institution, welfare organisation or service provider..." and the following paragraph enables the Advocate to make representations on behalf of, or act for, a person with a disability. That last power, the Court considered was more than sufficient to provide a basis for the Public Advocate to commence the proceedings. In addition, the Public Advocate was entitled so to act by reason of the *parens patriae* jurisdiction conferred on the Family Court in the *Family Law Act* and recognised by the High Court in the *J.W.B.* decision.[40]

Yet that was not to be the end of the story: prior to the Full Court's decision, a surgeon had indicated that he would be willing to carry out the relevant procedure and, indeed, the Public Advocate's case had, to a degree, been predicated on the surgeon's willingness so to do. However, the surgeon had changed his mind and, at that point, the Public Advocate applied to have the proceedings adjourned *sine die*. On the other hand, the Human Rights Commission argued that the Court ought not to release the child from whatever care and protection the Court could provide for him. The welfare jurisdiction of the Family Court, they submitted, was broadly analogous to that of the *parens patriae* jurisdiction and, as a result, responsibility for the child lay primarily in the Court.

Treyvaud J. regarded[41] the Human Rights Commission's submissions as being attractive, helpful and soundly based in law. Next, he was of the opinion that, once it had become involved in proceedings of this kind, the Court it was shown had primary responsibility for the child, whatever the attitude of the parents might be. Further, it appeared that some incident might arise which, given the circumstances of the case, could require the urgent reconstitution of the Court. Hence, the proceedings should remain on foot. The Court made[42] various orders though these were based on particular undertakings made by the parents to the Court.[43] These undertakings were concerned with the child's receiving appropriate examination and treatment – and, in that context, Treyvaud J. considered that the child's father's approach was, "... one based upon a real understanding and appreciation, not only of the risks which his son runs every day suffering from a cardiac

---

40 Above text at note 22.
41 (1994) FLC 92-486 at 81, 066.
42 Ibid at 81, 068.
43 Ibid at 81, 067.

condition, but of the risks which he would run even if he underwent surgery."

One of the peripheral issues which arose in *Re Michael (No 2)* was a submission made by the Human Rights Commission to the effect that the child's view was important, and best expressed through the office of a separate representative.[44] The role of the separate representative was one of the issues which was considered by the Full Court of the Family Court in the important case of *Re K*.[45] There, the wife had died in late 1992, with her husband being charged with her murder. He was awaiting trial at the time of the initial hearing. That hearing concerned applications by, on the one hand, a maternal aunt and, on the other, the paternal grandparents and aunt, for custody of the child of the marriage who, at the time, was aged three. The husband was also an applicant and was unrepresented in proceedings at first instance. He did not himself make an application for custody, but, rather, indicated that he supported the latter application. The trial judge granted sole custody and guardianship to the maternal aunt and allowed her to remove the child to the United States where she lived. In reaching that decision the trial judge made a finding that, on the balance of probabilities, the husband had killed the wife. The husband, paternal grandparents and aunt appealed, unsuccessfully, against the orders.

On the issue of the husband's appeal, which was based on the grounds that in all the circumstances of the case, the trial judge ought to have made interim, rather than final, orders the Court took the view[46] that any such decision should be made solely on the basis of the welfare of the child. Indeed, the Court considered that the circumstances were such that final orders ought to be made, in that the welfare of the child would not be served by the custody issue remaining in abeyance until the criminal law issue was resolved, which might well take some time.

As regards the paternal grandparents and aunt, the Court noted[47] that the trial judge had examined their proposals in detail, which had included their previous close and loving relationship with the child. However, taking relevant expert evidence into account, he had not regarded that as being

---

44   See *Family Law Act* 1975 section 65.
45   (1994) FLC 92-461.
46   Ibid at 80, 765 *per* Nicholson CJ., Fogarty and Baker JJ.
47   Ibid at 80, 767.

decisive of the issue and could not displace his view that the child's welfare would best be served by being in the custody of the maternal aunt.

In addition though the Commonwealth Attorney-General had intervened,[48] arguing that the case warranted the appointment of a separate representative. There were two bases for this submission: first, because a permanent removal of the child from the jurisdiction was contemplated and this carried with it the consequential likelihood of the cessation of any contact with the remaining parent. Second, because of the relationships and circumstances which existed between the parties and the interveners, the Full Court took the view that a separate representative ought to have been appointed, but the trial judge's failure to do so ought not to lead to the other orders being overturned.

More importantly, the Court set out[49] various guidelines which should govern the appointment of separate representatives. There were 13 such guidelines, set out as follows: cases which involve allegations of child abuse (whether physical, sexual or psychological); cases where there is an apparently intractable conflict between the parents; where the child is apparently alienated from both parents; where sexual preferences of either or both of the parents, or some other person having significant contact with the child, are likely to impinge on the child's welfare; where the conduct of either or both of the parents or some other person having significant contact with the child is alleged to be anti-social to the extent that is seriously impinges on the child's welfare; where there are issues of significant contact with the child; any case in which, on the material filed by the parents, neither seems a suitable custodian; any case in which a child of mature years is expressing strong views and, if those views were given effect, there would be a change in custodial arrangements or a complete denial of access; where one of the parties proposes that the child will permanently be removed from the jurisdiction or permanently removed to a place within the jurisdiction so as to greatly restrict or, for all practical purposes, exclude the other party from the possibility of access to the child; cases where it is proposed to separate siblings; custody cases where none of the parties are represented and, last, applications in the Court's welfare jurisdiction hearing, in particular, cases relating to medical treatment where

---

48 *Family Law Act* 1975 section 91(1)(b).
49 (1994) FLC 92-461 at 81, 773.

the child's interests are not adequately represented by one of the parties. The Court noted[50] that those categories were not intended to be exhaustive and drew attention to the situation where one of the parties was not a natural parent.

That final comment notwithstanding, the situations referred to in *Re K* do seem to be a very useful starting point indeed. However, that was not to be the end of the matter; in *F v MI and NZ*,[51] Kay J. interpreted s 65 of the Act as being limited to children who were directly affected by proceedings and were, in effect, the subject matter of the proceedings. Again, in *In the Marriage of Bennett*,[52] a father sought either to discharge a separate representation order or to remove a particular separate representative who had had a continuing involvement in the litigation. Although Rourke J. conceded[53] that the Court did have the power to remove a separate representative in these circumstances, he refused to do so on the basis that any representative who expressed views inimical to those of the father would be found in the same situation.

One of the issues to which reference was made in *Re K* was the recurrence of child abuse. In 1994, probably the most important decision in that area was that of the Full Court of the Family Court in *K v B*.[54] In that case, the majority[55] applied the earlier decision of the same Court in *In the Marriage of B*[56] to the effect that, in almost all cases where child sexual abuse was alleged, supervised access was not an appropriate safeguard. There was, though, a strong dissent by Kay J. who emphasised[57] that a denial of the opportunity of a relationship between children and their natural parents is a conclusion which the Court should reach with considerable reluctance. At all times, the judge considered, the minimisation of the risk of child sexual abuse had to be weighed against the importance of the continuance of the relationship of parent and child.[58] Without attempting to be determinative of the issue, which both in particular and general terms will be

---

50   Ibid at 80, 776.
51   (1994) FLC 92-493.
52   (1994) FLC 92-463.
53   Ibid at 80, 815.
54   (1994) FLC 92-478.
55   Ellis and Baker JJ.
56   (1993) FLC 92-357.
57   Ibid at 80, 968.
58   Ibid at 80, 969.

ongoing, it should be said that Kay J.'s judgment was notable for a detailed analysis of case law and social science literature.

Another important decision involving child sexual abuse was another decision of the Full Court in *In the Marriage of J.*[59] This case was concerned with a finding at first instance that children had not been sexually abused. The trial judge acknowledged that his decision was contrary to expert evidence and a major factor in reaching that conclusion was that the witnesses concerned had said that they were not conducting an investigation but were intent upon protecting the children. The mother successfully appealed on the grounds that the decision that her husband had not abused the children was not open on the evidence and, especially, it was not open to the judge to reject the expert evidence in the manner in which he had.

On the general issue, the Full Court, whilst noting[60] that it was not every mistake of fact made by a trial judge in a discretionary proceeding which would found a successful appeal, continued by saying that, "... in a case such as this where the question for determination was whether the children had been abused by the husband where a number of experts had concluded that here had been abuse, a mistake by the trial judge as to the nature of the work performed by two of those experts must give rise to serious concerns regarding the trial judge's processes of reasoning." Trial judges, they also commented, did not have to accept the evidence of experts in child abuse cases, but it was essential that there be proper analysis and investigation of the evidence. Accordingly, a new trial would be ordered. After various other recent decisions, *J* does suggest that the utility of expert evidence in child sexual abuse cases has been rehabilitated.

A rather different situation involving family violence was considered by Chisholm J, in *In the Marriage of J. G. and B. G.*[61] which was a contested matter relating to custody and access. Both parties sought custody but were agreeable to the other having access. During the course of the proceedings, various allegations were made relating to physical and verbal violence on the part of the husband. In granting the wife custody, the Judge said that he would identify and set out the legal principles which were relevant to allegations of violence in the context of proceedings relating to

---

59 (1994) FLC 92-476.
60 Ellis, Finn and Chisholm JJ.
61 (1994) FLC 92-476 at 80, 944.

children. The Judge stated[62] that, "In contrast with criminal proceedings or proceedings in tort, it is not the objective of the law in custody and similar proceedings to punish wrongdoers or to provide compensation or redress for victims. But family violence is by no means irrelevant, as it is with divorce: it is to be taken into account if it is relevant to the determination of the child's welfare, which is the paramount consideration. The standard of proof is the civil standard of proof on the balance of probabilities, not the criminal standard of proof beyond reasonable doubt."

Thereafter, he set out[63] various matters which were relevant in that situation: first, the Judge considered that the Court would have regard to the fact that family violence might be directly or indirectly relevant to the welfare of children in a variety of ways and might well be relevant even where it was not witnessed by, or directed at, the children. Further, so far as the evidence allows, the Court will attempt to understand the nature of any family violence which has occurred and its potential effect on the children. Where the evidence permits the Court to make findings in relation to contested allegations of family violence and, where such findings are necessary to determine which orders will best promote the welfare of the children, then the Court will make those findings. On the other hand, it may be open to the Court to refrain from making the findings where they are not needed to decide what orders will best promote the welfare of the children. In such a case, the Court will exercise a discretion as to whether the child's welfare would be promoted by the making of such findings. In the instant case, Chisholm J. did consider that it was necessary to make findings regarding the serious allegations made by the mother in order to arrive at an order which would promote the interests of the children.

III FINANCE AND PROPERTY

Although Australian family law in 1994 has been dominated by policy matters and parent and child law, there have, nonetheless, been some interesting developments in the area of finance and property.

An especially vexed issue in relation to distribution of property has been the relative weight to be given to the various contributions, financial or

---

62   (1994) FLC 92-515.
63   Ibid at 81, 314.

otherwise, made by the parties to the marriage. That matter was considered by the Full Court of the Family Court in *In the Marriage of Money*.[64] The parties had been married for over ten years and the trial judge found that, at the time of the marriage the husband had substantial assets (stage 1) and that the initial financial contribution to the parties assets had been made almost entirely by the husband. As regards contributions during the marriage, the trial judge had found that, before the birth of the elder child (stage 2), the husband's contribution exceeded that of the wife but, after that birth (stage 3), the wife's contribution as homemaker and parent was to be equated with the husband's financial contribution. However, after the separation (stage 4) the trial judge initially apportioned the contributions as being 60% to the husband and 40% to the wife but went on to say that other factors[65] required an adjustment of 10% in favour of the wife. The grounds for the husband's appeal were based around a claim that the trial judge was in error in finding that, where the husband having made effectively all of the initial financial contributions to the parties' assets at the time of the marriage, the appropriate distribution was that which had originally been made, without the latter adjustment. By a majority, the Full Court allowed the appeal.

In the leading judgment in the majority, Lindenmayer J., took the view[66] that, given the magnitude of the husband's contributions during the various stages of the marriage, it was difficult to see how the trial judge could conclude that the husband's contribution was only 10% greater than that of the wife. The trial judge could only have come to that conclusion, he thought,[67] "... if he failed to give any or adequate weight to the vastness and overall significance of the husband's overall contribution. That contribution of capital clearly provided the springboard for the subsequent acquisition by the parties of the property which they had at the time of the hearing."

Second, Lindenmayer J. was of the opinion that the wife's contribution could not be said to have eroded the husband's contribution; the more so as the trial judge had accepted that it was, in stages 2 and 3, no greater than that of the husband. Lindenmayer J. commented that, "The underlying

---

64 Ibid at 81, 318.
65 (1994) FLC 92-485.
66 See *Family Law Act* 1975 section 7592 which sets out the factors to be taken into account in relation to spousal maintenance.
67 (1994) FLC 92-485 at 81, 059.

assumption by [the trial Judge] seems to be that *any* contribution by the wife, whether matched or even exceeded by a like contribution by the husband, would erode his contribution. In my view, that assumption is erroneous, both from the point of view of logic and legal principle. The husband's initial contribution could only be eroded by some *imbalance* of subsequent contributions favourable to the wife."[68] All of that meant[69] that the decision at first instance was manifestly unreasonable and, as such, was subject to the intervention of the Full Court and that an appropriate division was 65% to the husband and 35% to the wife.

Holden J. agreed with Lindenmayer J. but thought[70] that, if Lindenmayer J.'s statement that the husband's initial contribution could only be eroded by some imbalance of subsequent contributions favourable to the wife were correct, then years of equal contribution to the conservation and improvement of an asset introduced by the husband and contribution to the welfare of the family would not be recognised. However, that did not affect the outcome of the appeal.

Fogarty J., though, dissented; he considered[71] that the order of the trial judge which had divided the available property equally did not fall outside the reasonable exercise of discretion under s 79 of the *Family Law Act*. In addition, he stated that the original contribution should not, "... be carried forward as a mathematical proportion; ultimately, when it comes to the trial such a contribution is one of a number of factors to be considered. The longer the marriage the more likely it is that there will be later factors of significance, and in the ultimate the exercise is to weigh the original contribution with all others, both factors and those later factors, whether equal or not, may in the circumstances of the individual case reduce the value of the original contribution."[72] Thus, the *Money* decision emphasises the essentially discretionary nature of s 79.

Another case which related to the matter of contributions was *In the Marriage of Kessey*[73] where the husband had unsuccessfully appealed

---

68   Ibid at 81, 060.
69   See also, *In the Marriage of Lee Steere* (1985) FLC 91-626; *In the Marriage of Crawford* (1979) FLC 90-647.
70   (1994) FLC 92-485 at 81, 061.
71   Ibid at 81, 063.
72   Ibid at 81, 054.
73   (1994) FLC 92-495.

against an order at first instance that the matrimonial home be sold and the proceeds divided 62.5%-37.5% in favour of the wife who had, initially, asked for a 75%-25% division. It was argued on behalf of the husband that the trial judge was in error, first, because it had been found that the improvements to the home, which had been funded by the wife's mother, were a contribution made by, or on behalf of, the wife. Second, the husband appealed against a finding that the contribution from the wife's mother must have had an impact which was most likely to have had a significant impact on the value of the home. Third, the trial judge had relied on evidence regarding the wife's state of health which had initially been excluded.

The Full Court[74] held, first, that a contribution by a parent of a party to the marriage would be regarded as a contribution made by or on behalf of a party to the marriage, "... *unless* there is evidence which establishes it was *not* the intention of the parent to benefit only his or her child."[75] As regards the second ground, the Court considered[76] that , in a case such as the present, it was not necessary to arrive at precise mathematical valuations of the parties' contributions. All that was necessary was to evaluate the weight which should be given to each party's contribution relative to that of the other. Finally, it was open to the trial judge, regardless of the evidence which had been excluded, to conclude that her health was seriously and permanently impaired on the basis of her own affidavit evidence.

To conclude the discussion of matrimonial property issues in Australian family law in 1994, mention must be made of the decision of Coleman J. in *Homsy v Yassa and Yassa; The Public Trustee.*[77] There, the dispute was between the applicant husband and the Public Trustee for New South Wales on behalf of a deceased woman who had been married to the applicant at the time of her death. In the absence of an order from the Family Court, the applicant would retain the major assets of the marriage since they were vested in his name at the time of the deceased's death. The events which had led up to that situation were that the parties had married in 1973 and had separated in 1986. In 1988, the applicant killed the deceased, and, in consequence, had been in prison from 1988 until 1992. Coleman J. of the

---

74 Baker, Finn and McCall JJ.
75 (1994) FLC 92-495 at 81, 150. See also *In the Marriage of Gosper* (1987) FLC 91-818.
76 (1994) FLC 92-495 at 81, 151.
77 (1994) FLC 92-442.

Family Court granted the declaration sought by the Public Trustee[78] that
the applicant was disentitled to any benefit from the estate of the deceased
and was, further, excluded from being a member of the class constituted
by the next of kin of the deceased who, on intestacy, would share in her
estate.[79] The decision, although inevitable, does emphasise strongly that
self aid in the area of family property is not to be encouraged!

As had been traditionally the situation, decisions regarding the Child
Support Scheme were concerned with departure from administrative assessment of the level of support. First, in *In the Marriage of Carey*,[80] the
parties had entered into consent orders relating to the matrimonial property,
but, shortly after the orders had been made, the husband resigned from his
job. He then requested, and received, an amended child support assessment
on the basis of an estimated reduced taxable income. However, as part of
leaving his job, he had received his holiday and long service leave and had
cashed in his superannuation. These payments increased his taxable income
for the taxation year. As a result, the husband received a second assessment
based on his actual taxable income. The husband appealed against the second
assessment, arguing that the income tax base was the wrong base to use
because his assessable income in the year in question included a once only
capital payment (the superannuation payout). He argued that it would be
inappropriate for the Court to demand that he pay child support out of his
superannuation without having regard to the property which the wife had
received as part of the initial agreement.

Kay J. upheld the appeal in part and reinstated the original assessment.
First, the judge considered[81] that it would be unjust and inequitable to
require the husband to pay child support for the year under review based
on his actual taxable income given that it had included the repayment of
capital and that that capital was otherwise adjusted between the parties. On
the other hand, it was inequitable as regards the wife and children to treat
the husband, during that year, as having anything other than an income as
represented by the original assessment. The reason for that, Kay J. stated,

---

78 Ibid at 80, 617.
79 See *Public Trustee v Fraser* (1987) 9 NSWLR 443; *Permanent Trustee Co. Ltd v
    Freedom From Hunger Campaign* (1991) 25 NSWLR 140. For comment, see K Mackie,
    "Manslaughter and Succession" (1988) 62 *A.L.J.* 616.
80 (1994) FLC 92-489.
81 Ibid at 81, 092.

was because the husband could have continued in employment; the only reason why he had chosen not to do so was to avoid his child support obligations. That was clearly not an appropriate reason for a further departure.

A rather different situation was represented by the decision of the same judge in *In the Marriage of Sloan*.[82] In that case, the parties had reached agreement regarding financial matters shortly after their separation. The agreement, which was incorporated into consent orders, provided *inter alia*, for the wife to have custody of the two children of the marriage, that the wife have the matrimonial home transferred to her but, on the other hand, that she would forego any claim for maintenance for herself and the children for a period of ten years after the separation. Almost four years later, the wife applied for child support and the Child Support Agency made an assessment. The Agency was prepared to give the husband credit in respect of child support for a limited period of time based on the transfer of property; however, the husband took the view that he was entitled to ten years of credit from the date of separation. Kay J. agreed with the husband's submission.

Stating that,[83] "You cannot contract out of child support. The Act is clear about that, the authorities are clear about that. The legislation makes it clear that the Court can take into account that the parties have divided their assets in determining the appropriate level of child support.", Kay J. noted that the wife had all of the assets and a rather higher earning capacity. Although the wife had care of the children, the circumstances were such that the administrative assessment resulted in an unjust and inequitable conclusion. It followed that an appropriate way of taking account of the parties' arrangements was to discount the amount of child support payable by the husband from the time of the hearing for the next four years.[84] That order would have the effect of halving the level of child support which the husband paid.

One wonders, given the almost total emphasis on the case law of departures from the administrative formula, whether the formula is itself flawed or, more generally, whether the entire concept itself is not wholly suppor-

---

82 (1994) FLC 92-507.
83 Ibid at 81, 263.
84 Ibid at 81, 264.

table. I have long wondered,[85] whether the entire exercise is not aimed
at reducing the social security budget whilst, at the same time, actually
creating administrative costs in other areas.

IV LAW REFORM

The area of law reform in Australian family law is, presently, rather confused. On a specific issue, to which reference has already been made,[86]
the Family Law Council, in a recent report, *Sterilisation and Other Medical
Procedures on Children*, have urged that there be a new division inserted
into the *Family Law Act* which would seek to regulate the sterilisation of
young people. The thrust of the proposed legislation would emphasise that
it would be unlawful to sterilise a child except under prescribed circumstances.[87] Any such sterilisation would have to be authorised by the Family Court
and, accordingly, the consent of children and/or their parents would not suffice.[88] The Council proposed a three-stage decision making process to
govern the consideration of applications.[89] It is proposed that the legislation
would indicate four situations in which sterilisation would never be
authorised. Those situations are sterilisation for eugenic reasons, for purely
contraceptive purposes, as a means of concealing or avoiding the consequences of sexual abuse and, finally, sterilisations performed on young women
prior to the onset of menstruation, based on predictions of further problems
which might arise in that regard. The legislation should also provide that
no person under the age of 18 should be sterilised unless the procedure is
necessary to save life or to prevent serious damage to the persons' physical
or psychological health. In deciding whether there is serious danger to a
person's physical or psychological health the decision maker would be
obliged to have regard to whether the feasibility of less permanent forms
of contraception, where relevant, had been explored. The Council emphasise
that, once that hurdle is overcome, the decision maker would be required

---

85 See F Bates, "The Context of the Economic Consequences of Divorce in Australia: A
    Brief Comment on Ingleby" (1994) 31 *Houston L.R.* 643.
86 Above text at note 20.
87 Recommendation 1(b).
88 Recommendations 1(c), 4.
89 Recommendation 3.

not to approve the operation unless satisfied that it would be in the child's best interests.

Few, one might think, would object to the substantive proposals contained in the report. Indeed, there was overwhelming support, in the submissions received by the Council, for the view that sterilisation should be confined to exceptional circumstances or as a last resort. However,there was some dispute as to which body or organisation would act as the decision maker. Although, as has been noted, the Report recommended that the Family Court be given the relevant power. At the same time, there was strong support for the appropriate State Guardianship Boards having the power; although the Chief Justice of the Family Court was strongly in support of his own forum, there are quite clear arguments in favour of the more specialist local bodies.[90]

On the broader front, uncertainty prevails. In October 1994, a new Bill (the *Family Law Reform Bill* (1994)) was introduced which attempted to replace the whole of Part VII, which deals with children. Its thrust is very much predicated on the Family Law Council's earlier report, *Patterns of Parenting After Separation*.[91] That Bill, however, has been withdrawn because it is anticipated that, ultimately, it will be amalgamated with the *Family Law Reform Bill (No 2)* (1994) which was introduced into the Senate in December 1994. This Bill deals with matters relating to finance and property and emphases a presumption of equality of division and pre-nuptial agreements.[92] There will be public hearings regarding both Bills and written submissions have been sought. Taken together, these Bills represent the most major changes which have been made to the Act since it came into force in early 1976. What the response to the proposed legislation will be, given the raucous and ignorant response to Australia's ratification of the *United Nations Convention on the Rights of the Child*,[93] remains to be seen. One

---

90 The Medical Powers Committee of the Family Law Council took that view. It should be said that the present writer was a member of that Committee ..!
91 For comment see F Bates, "Australian Family Law in 1992 – The Year of the Loud Report?" (1994) 32 *U. Louisville J. of Family Law* 233.
92 This part of the Bill is derived from the Australian Law Reform Commission's Report, *Matrimonial Property* (ALRC 39, 1987). For critical comment, see F Bates, "Reforming Australian Matrimonial Property Law" (1989) 17 *Anglo-Am. L.R.* 46.
93 See M Otlowski and M Tsamenyi, "Parental Authority and the United Nations Convention on the Rights of the Child" (1992) 6 *Aust. J. Fam. L.* 137 especially at 149 *ff.*

suspects that the emphasis on parental *responsibility*[94] rather than *right*, may precipitate another tonitrual blast from the forces of reaction.

V TENTATIVE CONCLUSIONS

1994 has represented something of a watershed: there are proposed reforms but it is, given the pressures of Parliamentary time, likely to be some way down the line before the changes are effected – if, indeed, they are effected at all. It is now notorious that the Act has, hitherto, been amended 38 times since it came into force. Some of those amendments have been very substantial. One can only anticipate more. The case law has been rather predictable given the legislative uncertainty which Australian family lawyers face.

---

94 For comment, see L Maloney, "Beyond Custody and Access: A Children's Rights Approach to Post Separation Parenting" (1993) 7 *Aust. J. Fam. L* 249.

AUSTRIA

MEIER & MUELLER, MEIER-MUELLER OR MUELLER-MEIER: NEW PRINCIPLES IN THE LAW ON SURNAMES

Erwin Bernat and Helga Jesser**

I   INTRODUCTION

If we assume a case in which a Mr. Meier marries a Ms. Mueller, the question arises as to whether a given legal system should provide binding rules on the surname used after marriage. Furthermore, there also seems to be a need for rules governing the name of the children of this union.

Whereas in Anglo-American law attempts have been made to leave the choice of surnames to the spouses' discretion (Privatautonomie)[1], the legislators in German-speaking countries have put special emphasis on the so-called *regularity principle* (Ordnungsprinzip), which calls for a strict legal regulation of the surname. This principle is based on the idea that the state ought to be able to distinguish between different physical persons[2]. This thinking was already apparent in the original version of the Austrian Civil Code, which dates back to 1811 and provides a stipulation on surnames.

The comprehensive revision of the law on surnames is the latest step in the development of Austrian family law. The novel stipulations form part of the "Act amending the law of the surname" (Namensrechtsänderungsgesetz; hereinafter: NamRÄG)[3] which amends the Austrian Civil Code, the 1938 Marriage Act, the Act on Non-contentious Proceedings as well as the Act on Registry of Births, Deaths and Marriages (Personenstandsgesetz – PStG), among others. To provide the reader with some real insight into the intentions of this act, we shall briefly sketch the historic development of the law on surnames.

---

*   Associate Professor (Dr.iur.), Graz Law School, Department of Civil Law.
** Assistent (Dr.iur.), Graz Law School, Department of Civil Law.

1   Cf. I. Schwenzer, "Namensrecht im Überblick", *FamRZ* (1991) 390 ff; D. Giesen, "Der Familienname aus rechtshistorischer, rechtsvergleichender und rechtspolitischer Sicht", *FuR* (1993) at 65 ff.
2   I. Sagel-Grande, "Die wesentlichen Rechtsgüter im Namensrecht", *Neue Justiz* (1992) 537.
3   NamensrechtsänderungsG, *Fed. Law Gazette* 1995/25.

A. Bainham (ed.), The International Survey of Family Law 1994, 75–85.
© 1996 *The International Society of Family Law. Printed in the Netherlands.*

II   HISTORIC DEVELOPMENT OF THE LAW ON SURNAMES

When the Austrian Civil Code was promulgated in 1811, its marriage and
family law was based on patriarchal principles, which meant that the husband
was seen as the "head of the family", who – in the legislators' conception
– was in charge of "managing household concerns" (section 91 original
version of the Civil Code). The wife – as well as the children – were
automatically named after the husband (sections 92 and 146 original version
of the Civil Code).

It took the Austrian legislature a long time to recognize the principle
of equality between the sexes. It was only in 1975[4] that the original wording
of section 92 came to be abandoned. Although the principle of a common
surname during marriage was upheld, it had at least become possible for
the spouses to opt for the wife's name as a surname: if a Mr. Meier married
a Ms. Mueller, their surname could be Mueller (section 93 para 1 former
wording), if the couple so desired. If there was no express arrangement, the
husband's surname was legally considered to be the surname (section 93
para 1 sent 2 former wording). In this case, the wife was allowed, if she
wished, to suffix her maiden name to her husband's name with a hyphen.
This form of the name could not, however, be used by another person
(section 93 para 2 sent 1 former wording). Nevertheless this provision did
not resolve the question as to whether the husband was allowed to suffix
his name to his wife's, if the wife's name had been chosen as the common
surname. The wording of section 93 para 2 sent 1 former version of the Civil
Code seemed to preclude this possibility. Did this provision then infringe
upon the principle of equality and was it therefore unconstitutional (cf. article
7 of the Austrian Constitutional Act)? An often-cited 1985 Austrian
Constitutional Court judgment adopted this viewpoint. Rightly, the Court
maintained that there is no reasonable ground for denying to those few men
who have opted for their wife's surname as the family name, the possibility
of placing their original surname after the common surname taken from the
wife.[5] Hence, it was again the legislators' turn to remedy section 93's infringement of equality, as the Constitutional Court had demanded. Only one
year thereafter, section 93 Civil Code was amended again[6] within the narrow

---

4   *Fed. Law Gazette* 1975/412.
5   Austrian Constitutional Court, March 5, 1985, JBl 1985, 414 (with a note of H. Pichler).
6   *Fed. Law Gazette* 1986/97.

framework laid out by the Constitutional Court: Solely section 93 para 2 of the former wording of the Civil Code was altered in such a way as to enable each spouse to suffix his/her former surname to the new common surname as legally derived from his/her spouse. The aforementioned principle (which in case of disagreement or a lack of an express arrangement opting for the wife's surname stated that the husband's surname was to become the common surname) remained unchallenged. Furthermore, the legislators upheld the rule that the spouses were to bear the same name during marriage.

This rule stipulating that in case of doubt the husband's surname is to be taken as the family surname, as well as the above-mentioned principle demanding identical names for spouses, has often been criticised during the last ten years both by the general public and by family law scholars.[7] Unlike the German Constitutional Court[8], its Austrian counterpart did not feel compelled to object to the preferential treatment of husbands on the basis of equality in 1993. In this context, the Court held that section 93 para 1 sent 3 of the Civil Code's former wording did not represent a preferential treatment of men, but that it merely took established facts into consideration.[9] Even if only a tiny minority opts for the wife's surname as the common family name[10], this argument given by the *Austrian* Constitutional Court is by no means convincing. As the *German* Constitutional Court has correctly emphasized, force of habit (i.e. of choosing the husband's surname as family name) cannot of itself be seen as constituting sufficient ground for the existence of a rule which gives preference to men in the absence of objective differences. The principle of equality should instead exert a formative influence and not just be a rule that the legislators are obliged to obey. It should also serve as an instrument for overcoming existing discrimination that can still be seen in interaction between the sexes.

Although the Austrian Constitutional Court did not endorse this view, it nevertheless did suggest that the decision of whether to create a new law on family surnames was up to the legislators; the Court did, however, hold

---

7   For a survey see E. Bernat, *ZfRV* (1991) at 390 ff.

8   Decision published, inter alia, in *ZfRV* (1991) at 386 - 390 (note E. Bernat).

9   Austrian Constitutional Court, 18 Dec 1993, *JBl* (1994) at 326 ff.

10 According to statistical surveys conducted because of the amendment of section 93 Civil Code, only 1.23 per cent of all engaged couples opted for the fiancée's as the common family name: see 865 of the appendices to the shorthand records of the National Council (first Chamber of Parliament) (hereinafter: BlgStProt NR), 16th legislative period (hereinafter: GP), 3.

that from the point of view of sexual equality, there was no *constitutional* obligation to do so.

It was not only this 1993 Court ruling which launched the wide-spread discussion on an amendment of the law on surnames. In 1990, the Ministry of Justice had already presented a draft law[11] which, for the first time, questioned the rule of identical names for spouses during marriage. In the course of the following years, the parties of the coalition government[12] did not submit a joint draft law to parliament: obviously, the government parties did not quite manage to reach a compromise on this ideologically controversial issue in family law. Nevertheless, members of parliament started to draw up notices of motion in 1990[13] which – one may rightly say – paved the way for the new common surname stipulations. At the very beginning of the 19th legislative period, the Social Democrats[14] and Christian Conservative Party[15] as well as the Ecology Party[16] submitted motions to the Parliament. On December 16, 1994, Parliament finally passed the Act amending the law on surnames[17]. It went into effect on May 1, 1995.

Most of its provisions are very similar to the Social Democrats' notice of motion (number 4/A).

III BASIC PRINCIPLES OF THE NEW LAW ON SURNAMES

A   Spouses' Surnames

The new provision has again been incorporated into section 93 of the Civil Code. Para 1 of section 93 remains unchanged. Therefore, the *principle* of identical names (sentence 1) has been upheld as well as the rule that in case

---

11   JMZ 4408/21-I 1/90.
12   The Christian Conservatives and the Social Democrats have together constituted the Government in Austria since the 1980s.
13   Namely, in 1990/91: Draft No. 412/A of 6 June 1990, II-11359 BlgStProt NR, 17th GP (Social Democrats); Draft No. 197/A of 8 July 1991, II-2659 BlgStProt NR, 18th GP (Social Democrats); Draft No. 196/A of 8 July 1991, II-2620 BlgStProt NR, 18th GP (Christian Conservative Party); Draft No. 130/A of 18 April 1991, II-1578 BlgStProt NR; 18th GP (Ecology Party).
14   Draft No. 4/A of Nov 7, 1994, 19th GP.
15   Draft No. 21/A of Nov 11, 1994, 19th GP.
16   Draft No. 25/A of Nov 11, 1994, 19th GP.
17   *Fed Law Gazette.* of Jan 5, 1995, No. 25.

of disagreement the husband's surname is to become the common surname (sentence 2).

The novel stipulations are to be found in paras 2 and 3 of section 93. Both are to be welcomed in the light of *equality* as well as that of the *right of personality* of every human being, according to which the name is, above all, an expression of the individuality of its bearer. What has changed?

1   No peremptory provision for identical surnames during marriage

Although section 93 para 1 sent 1 stipulates the principle of identical names, this principle is more or less reversed by para 3: should Ms. Mueller declare before or during the marriage ceremony at the registrar's office – either by means of a public document or by means of a document certified by notary public or a civil court – that she prefers not to assume her fiancé's surname, i.e. Meier, then she is allowed to retain her surname (Mueller) during marriage. According to section 93 para 3 the spouses then keep their original surnames (Meier & Mueller).

2   Hyphenated name instead of only a suffixed name

If the given couple has – according to section 93 para 1 – either agreed upon his (Meier) or her (Mueller) surname, section 93 para 2 grants the "disadvantaged" spouse the possibility of conjoining his/her original surname. Section 93 para 2 differs from the pre-existing model in two ways.

a)   Until now, the "disadvantaged" spouse's possibility of conjoining his/her original surname to the joint surname was a *strictly personal* right. There was no obligation to use a hyphenated name. Hence, German writers did not refer to this sort of family name as a real hyphenated name, but as a merely *suffixed* or *accompanying name (Begleitname)*. Once a Mr. Meier and a Ms. Mueller had agreed on Mueller under the former law, Mr. Meier was under no obligation to call himself Mueller-Meier; on the contrary, this was solely his own right, and he was allowed to exercise it whenever he cared to. Therefore, he was able to sign as Mr. Mueller, or, if he felt so inclined, as Mueller-Meier. Section 93 para 2 as amended represents a new approach. The spouse whose name will not become the family name must decide whether he/she would rather give up his/her present name or suffix it to the new common surname. Should Mr. Meier and his fiancée Ms. Mueller have agreed on the joint surname Mueller (section 93 para 1 sent 2), then he has the right to declare in the registrar's office before or during the marriage ceremony – by means of a public document or a document certified by a notary public or a civil court – that he wishes to join his original surname and the new common family name Mueller. If he makes such a declaration, his new name is henceforth Mueller-Meier. Contrary to the law before this latest amendment, he is now legally compelled to use the name Mueller-Meier (section 93 para 2 sent 2). Should Mr. Meier fail to give the aforementioned declaration in time, then section 93 does not entitle him to appear as Mr. Mueller-Meier.

He too, must consequently use the chosen surname Mueller. This is the main difference between the old and new provisions.

b)   The second main modification facilitates the formation of a hyphenated name. If Mueller is the new common family name as defined by section 93 para 1, then Mr. Meier can opt for either Mueller-Meier or Meier-Mueller. Whereas formerly these provisions used only to allow suffixing one's original surname, section 93 para 2 sent 1 introduces the alternative of placing this name first.

Modifications of the law on hyphenated names closely resemble the German law as completely amended due to the above-mentioned[18] 1993 German Constitutional Court judgment[19].

3   The meaning of the term "common surname"

So far we have concentrated on discussing the main revisions within section 93 Civil Code. We will now focus on the exact meaning of "common surname" as defined in this section. Can a Ms. Mueller whose maiden name was Berger and her fiancé Mr. Meier agree that their family name be Mueller (as stipulated in section 93 para 1 sent 2), if the surname Mueller was from a previous marriage? Whereas this would have been contrary to the former version of section 93 para 3 Civil Code, section 93 as amended includes no such prohibition. Mr. Mueller's divorcée could place the surname Mueller before or after Meier, should the engaged couple come to agree upon Meier as the common surname (section 93 para 2 sent 1 Civil Code).

---

18   Cf. note 8.
19   Act on the amendment of the law of the family name (Gesetz zur Neuordnung des Familiennamensrechts; FamNamRG) of Dec 16, 1993, *Fed. Law Gazette* (1993) I, at. 2054 ff.

Hence, any name borne by one of the parties immediately before marriage can be chosen as the common surname as defined in section 93 Civil Code. It does not necessarily have to be the maiden name, as can be seen in the preceding example.

Let us continue our experiment: a divorced Ms. Mueller wishes to marry a Mr. Meier. Both would prefer her maiden name Berger as the common family name (section 93 para 1 sent 2 Civil Code). Is this legally possible? The amendment to the act has also provided for this contingency. Before her marriage to Mr. Meier, Ms. Mueller must declare in the registrar's office – by means of a public document or a document certified by a notary public or a civil court – that she chooses to resume her maiden name Berger (section 93a sent 1 Civil Code as amended). Then, both Ms. Berger and Mr. Meier have to follow the same procedure to declare that they wish to use Berger as their common surname (section 93 para 1 sent 2 Civil Code).

Mueller & Meier could even take Huber as their common surname, if Ms. Mueller had at any time borne the name Huber in a former marriage with a Mr. Huber. Huber, however, could only be selected as a common surname if there was issue from this previous marriage (section 93a sent 2 Civil Code as amended).

4   Transitional provisions

By way of transitional provisions the act enables those couples who married before May 1, 1995 to take advantage of the new regulations. These transitional stipulations, given in section 72a of the Act on Registry of Births, Deaths and Marriages, permit alterations of the family name within the new legal limits for every spouse who married before May 1, 1995. This option can be exercised until April 30 2007 (section 72e of the said act).

A spouse who has married under the new law (i.e. after May 1, 1995) and has opted for his/her spouse's surname as the common surname (section 93 para 1 Civil Code) cannot place his/her original surname before or after the new family name unless he/she declares such intent at the marriage registrar's office at the latest (section 93 para 2 sent 1). This preferential treatment of "old" marriages vis à vis "new" is indeed astonishing. Yet the legislature has filled this gap elsewhere: the forming of a hyphenated name

– though impossible at the registrar's office – is still feasible through a *change of name* effected before the proper administrative authority[20].

B   The Children's Family Name

The Austrian law of domestic relations still distinguishes between legitimate and illegitimate children. Whereas a 1989 act abolished all differences in succession arising from legitimate and illegitimate descent[21], considerable differences remain in the fields of custody and the law relating to the of-f-spring's surname.

1   Legitimate children

Section 139 Civil Code as amended is in line with the legislative conception that determined the former stipulation; nevertheless it adapts this concept to the new options opened up by section 93 Civil Code as amended.

If the parents bear a common surname in terms of section 93 para 1 Civil Code as amended, then the child is named after them. If one spouse has exercised the option granted by section 93 para 2 Civil Code as amended, the name is still to be seen as a common family name. If Mr. Meier marries Ms. Mueller and both agree on Mueller as their common surname, the children are then named Mueller, even if Mr. Meier places his original name before or after the family name Mueller (according to section 93 para 2 as amended).

The drafters also had to provide for the contingency that Mr. Meier and Ms. Mueller might use different surnames (in the sense of section 93 para 3 Civil code as amended). In this case, section 93 para 3 sent 2 Civil Code stipulates that before marriage, the parties are to agree *unanimously* on the family name of future issue by means of a public document or a document certified by a notary public or a civil court before or at the marriage ceremony at the registrar's office. This means that Mr. Meier and Ms. Mueller have to agree on Meier or Mueller upon marriage at the latest. There is, however, no way to enforce this duty, and certainly not by refusal to

---

20   This option has been granted by sec 2 (1) ((7)) of a public law (*Fed. Law Gazette* 1988/195) which itself has been amended by the NamensrechtsänderungsG.

21   Cf. E. Bernat, "The Final Stages of Three Decades' Family Law Reform", 29 *J.Fam.L.* 285, at 294 ff (1990-91).

perform the marriage[22]. If there is no agreement in terms of section 93 para 3 sent 2 Civil Code, the child is given the father's surname (section 139 para 3 Civil Code as amended). This rule again reflects the patriarchal principle. This may be seen – in the light of the second Constitutional Court ruling on the law of surnames[23] – as not infringing the constitution; but it nevertheless reveals a considerable lack of imagination on the part of the drafters. The German legislators stipulated that in such a case the right of naming the descendants can be transferred to one of the spouses (section 1616 para 3 German Civil Code), although they gave no clue as to which criteria were to be included in the guardianship court's decision. The following alternatives seem plausible: decision by lot; age of father or mother (with precedence for the elder parent, or vice versa); alphabetic order of initial letters (Meier having priority to Mueller or vice versa). In our opinion such a stipulation seems to serve equality far better than the provision in section 139 para 3 Civil Code.

However, section 139 Civil Code also gives rise to jurisprudential doubts. For example, it remains unclear whether Mr. Meier or Ms. Mueller, who bear separate family names during their marriage, can revoke a declaration given before marriage according to which the children are to be named Mueller, and whether they may accordingly designate Meier as the new name for their children.

Since the drafters obviously intended that all the children of parents with different surnames should have the same name[24], one is probably bound to make distinctions: as long as there are no children, the decision can be revoked; otherwise the parents are to adhere to the name that was previously chosen.

2   *Illegitimate children*

In our context, a child is considered as illegitimate if it was born more than 302 days after dissolution of the mother's marriage (section 138 and 155 sent 1 Civil Code). Of course, children are in any case seen as illegitimate if their mother was never married. However, all children born within marriage or within 302 days after the dissolution of the marriage are deemed

---

22   *Thus, report of the judiciary committee (hereinafter: JAB), 49 BlgStProt NR, 19th GP,* 6.

23   *JBl* (1994) 326.

24   JAB, 49 BlgStProt NR, 19th GP, 8.

legitimate (section 138 Civil Code), irrespective of whether they are in fact descendants of the husband. In these cases, children conceived outside of marriage are only considered illegitimate when a paternity case has shown them to be so[25]; they are deemed legitimate until then.

According to the law as it stood before the amendment, the illegitimate child was given the mother's maiden name (section 165 Civil Code former version). If a Ms. Mueller had never been married, her child was also called Mueller under the former law. However, if the said woman had been married to a Mr. Meier and had retained the name Meier after marriage, her child was not named Meier (like herself), but Mueller, if that child was born more than 302 days after the dissolution of the marriage: Mueller was the maiden name of the divorced mother whose married name was Mrs. Meier. Quite obviously, the legislature wanted to avoid a situation which suggested any link between the divorced husband and the child, if only by name. The interest of the divorced man might seem to merit protection, but it has to be – in any case – subordinated to Mrs. Meier (née Mueller)'s child's best interests[26]: it will normally be in the child's best interests that it bear the mother's current surname. Corresponding to this value judgment (which has also been laid down in section 1617 para 1 German Civil Code), section 165 of the Austrian Civil Code has been amended in that the word "maiden name" has been replaced by "surname". Consequently, the illegitimate child is now given the mother's name at the time of birth. If a mother whose maiden name was Mueller is divorced from a Mr. Meier and if she bears the name Mueller-Meier or Meier-Mueller according to section 93 para 2 sent 1 Civil Code, mention has to be made of one exception to the principle described above. The child is simply named Meier (if Meier has been chosen as the couple's common family name), because a different person's family name can only be derived from the common family name (as defined by section 93 para 1 Civil Code as amended), according to section 93 para 2 sent 3 Civil Code as amended.

---

25 According to Art. 4 § 7 of the Familienrechtsangleichungsverordnung, *German Official Reichs-Gazette* 1943 I, at 80 ff.

26 For an analysis of the best interests of the child see E. Bernat, "Das Kindeswohl auf dem Prüfstand des Rechts. Gedanken zur Funktionsbestimmung einer familien-rechtlichen Generalklausel", *ÖstAmtsV* (1994) at 43 ff.

C Miscellaneous

The Act amending the law of the common surname has also amended a large number of further provisions which can only be mentioned briefly: the law of the family name in the context of adoption and legitimation; provisions of the Marriage Act, as well as of the Act on Non-Contentious Proceedings; the Act on the Registry of Births, Deaths and Marriages; and finally several stipulations of an act allowing a person under certain circumstances to change legally his/her first or last name.

IV EPILOGUE

The Act amending the law of the surname, which was passed at the beginning of the 19th legislative period, has abolished one "sacred" principle of Austrian family law: the principle of identical family names during marriage. Thus the Austrian legislature has joined those states which have chosen to give priority to equality and the protection of personality at the expense of an (irrational) maintenance of taboos. There is a tinge of disappointment as the stipulations on common surnames still do not provide complete gender neutrality (again, cf section 139 para 3). Nevertheless, the present amendment can be appreciated as a step – though not a final one – in the direction of a family law that conforms to modern attitudes.

BULGARIA

BASIC ISSUES IN BULGARIAN FAMILY LAW

Anna Staneva[*]

I   INTRODUCTION

Family law in Bulgaria has not undergone any fundamental changes during the last ten years. A Family Code was enacted in 1985 and is still in force. The political and economic changes in the country have had almost no influence on family law regulations. This is one of the reasons why the following is not a study on the latest developments in family law, the other being that Bulgaria has never before been covered in this Survey. So, a general review is more appropriate.

II   MARRIAGE

Marriage is an act through which a man and a woman enter into a certain legal relationship with each other and which creates and imposes mutual rights and duties. A marriage can only be contracted if special formalities are carried out. A number of requirements, relating to the capacity to marry, must also be met in order to have a valid marriage.

Until 1945 marriage in Bulgaria could be contracted only through a church ritual. It was the Orthodox Church that was vested with all the authority relating to marriage and divorce. In 1945 the Marriage Decree was enacted and through it the above matters were transferred to the secular authorities. Since 1945 only civic marriage has legally binding effect. The former religious marriages were however recognized. Nowadays, a marriage ceremony can still be performed according to the rites of the church to which the parties belong but it has no legal effect whatsoever. Marriage is contracted by the mutual consent of a man and a woman given personally before the civic status registrar and in the presence of two witnesses at the local municipality. Marriage is considered valid only after a certificate of marriage is issued and duly signed by the parties and the registrar. The place

---

[*]   Faculty of Law, University of Sofia.

A. Bainham (ed.), *The International Survey of Family Law 1994*, 87–100.
© 1996 *The International Society of Family Law. Printed in the Netherlands.*

where the ceremony takes place has no bearing on the validity of the marriage.

If the above formalities – different sex of parties, personally expressed consent to marry, participation of the civic status registrar, and a signed certificate of marriage – are not adhered to, the marriage is void. It has no legally binding effect ab initio.

In order that a person should have capacity to contract a valid marriage, the following conditions must be satisfied:

a) Both parties must be over the age of 18. Minors above the age of 16 can marry with permission from the head of the regional court if important reasons for an early marriage exist. Parents' consent is not necessary; they only have the right to express an opinion. Through marriage the minor spouse gains full legal capacity.

b Neither party must be already married. No exceptions to monogamy are allowed. A second marriage can be contracted only upon termination of the first one by the death of one spouse, by annulment or divorce.

c) Neither party must suffer from mental disease or imbecility which has lead or can lead to full judicial disablement; neither party must suffer from a disease, representing a serious threat to the life or health of any offspring or the other spouse, unless the ailment is dangerous only for the latter and he or she is aware of the fact.

d) The parties must not be related within the prohibited degrees of consanguinity. Marriage cannot be contracted between any relatives of a direct line of descent, between brothers and sisters, their children and other relatives of a collateral line of descent up to and including the fourth degree. These prohibitions also extend to adoptive relationships. Affinity is not an obstacle to marriage.

Where the above conditions are not satisfied, the marriage is voidable. It is also voidable where one of the parties has been forced to contract the marriage under the threat of a serious and immediate peril. A voidable marriage has to be treated as a valid one in all respects until its annulment is decreed. An action for annulment in the cases of bigamy, consanguinity and disease can be brought before the regional court by each of the spouses or by the attorney general. In the cases of minority and threat an action can be brought only by the minor or the threatened party. Annulment has no retrospective effect and the consequences of divorce are applicable.

III   THE EFFECTS OF MARRIAGE

Spouses have equal rights and obligations in marriage. Their relations are supposed to be built upon mutual respect, faithfulness, common care for the family and children. Spouses are free to choose their respective professions and occupations, and they both have the right to the other's consortium. No enforcement of these rights and obligations is however possible. Breach of any of the above obligations is not in itself a ground for divorce – the only one being, since 1953, the irretrievable breakdown of marriage, together with divorce by mutual consent.

Property relations between spouses are governed by the Family Code. Marital agreements, through which spouses seek to achieve consequences differing from those set forth in the Family code, are still not allowed and are deemed void. According to the law spouses can have two types of property: joint and personal.

Real estate, chattels and bank accounts, acquired during marriage by either of the spouses as a result of common contribution belong jointly to them. The presence of common contribution is presumed by law unless proved otherwise. During marriage spouses have no separate shares in their joint property. That is why they can dispose of it only by mutual consent. The situation with joint bank accounts is somewhat different. When the account is in the name of one of the spouses, he or she is solely entitled to withdraw sums from it; but if, in doing so, this spouse jeopardizes the interests of the family or of the other spouse, the latter may request the court to issue an order for joint handling of the account.

Everything acquired before the marriage was contracted or after its termination belongs to the person (future or former spouse), in whose name the acquisition was made. However, joint property does not cover all acquisitions during marriage. Personal property remains: acquisitions by way of inheritance or donation; chattels serving the ordinary personal needs of each spouse and those necessary in practising his or her profession; all other rights which are not connected with chattels, real estate or bank accounts, such as contractual claims, patents, author's rights, etc. Each spouse is free to dispose of his or her personal property.

IV ESTABLISHING PARENTAGE

Maternity is determined by birth. In most cases, when the fact of birth and the identity of mother and child do not cause doubt, it is the birth certificate through which motherhood is established. This applies whatever the mother's marital status. Bulgaria has a legislative answer to the question of who is the legal mother in cases where the person giving birth is not the child's genetic mother. Our Family Code (art.31, s.1) takes the view that maternity is established by birth even where the child does not biologically belong to the so-called "gestational mother". She is the only mother recognized by law and this is not to be displaced by contract or otherwise. The only possibility for the biological mother to establish a legal relationship with the child is through adoption.

So, motherhood is determined by birth and the latter is in most cases established by a birth certificate. It is however possible that the woman whose name is registered in the birth certificate is not the true mother of the child because she has not given birth to any child at all or has given birth to another child. In such cases an action can be brought before the district court, without any time restrictions, by the woman whose name is on the birth certificate, by her husband (as the presumed father), by the child, by the woman who claims to be the real mother, and by her husband. The aim of such an action is to prove by all possible evidence that the woman registered as mother is not such in fact. The effect of this lawsuit, if successful, is that the child's mother is considered unestablished (unknown) and other ways of establishing parentage can be invoked.

Another possibility for establishing maternity is through a court action. This applies where the mother has not been registered at all in the birth certificate or, in the above cases, where the registration has been proved false. In any case, such an action can be brought before the district court only if the child's mother is legally unknown. The right to bring such an action extends to the woman who claims to be the mother, her husband and the child. No time restrictions are set for bringing the action before the court.

The third way of establishing maternity is through affiliation. This also applies to establishing paternity. This will be discussed later, after analysing the basic legal methods for establishing paternity.

In Bulgaria, as almost everywhere else in the world, the presumption that the mother's husband is the father is legally accepted (art. 32 of the Family Code). In order that it should apply, the following preconditions exist: a) there should be a valid (including voidable) marriage; b) the wife should give birth to a child; c) birth should take place during marriage or within 300 days after its termination. The husband is deemed to be the child's father irrespective of any declarations to the opposite effect made by the spouses and regardless of the time interval between the marriage and the child's birth.

It is possible that the so-called "collision of presumptions" can take place. This is the case when a woman – several months after the dissolution of her first marriage – enters into a second one, and a child is born very soon thereafter. It is in fact born during the second marriage but also within 300 days after the termination of the first one. So, both the former and the present husband of the mother can legally be fathers of the child. This conflict is resolved in art. 32, s. 2 in favour of the present husband of the mother. He is considered to be the more probable father and, in any event, this solution is obviously favourable for the child.

The presumption can be rebutted (art. 33 of the Family Code) if it is established beyond reasonable doubt that the child could not have been fathered by the husband. The action may be brought before the court by the mother not later than a year after birth, and by the presumed father – within a year from the day when the birth became known to him. No other person, even the child, can bring an action to rebut the presumption of fatherhood. If the action is successful, the position of the child is equivalent to that born to an unmarried woman, i.e. the father is unknown. There is only one exception in the above mentioned case of the "collision of presumptions" – if the second husband, for whom the presumption is in force, rebuts it, the former husband will be considered the father of the child. And only after his successful action, will the child be deemed fatherless.

When the child is born to an unmarried woman, there is of course no presumption of paternity. In such cases, together with those where the presumption has been rebutted, the father can be established through a court action, brought by the mother within three years from birth, and by the child up to the age of 21.

Affiliation can be used both by a man or a woman who consider themselves parents of a certain child whose father or mother are not established. Affiliation is a voluntary personal declaration of origin, made before the civic status registrar, and effectively establishing parenthood without the need of any material proof thereof. Any child, regardless of age, may be affiliated but only where parenthood is not established. Even if the child has one known parent, his or her consent is not necessary. The above picture shows that it is quite possible, voluntarily or not, to affiliate a child who is not the child of the declarator. That is why the other parent (if there is one), and the child have the right to contest the affiliation. This right is even given to interested third parties which is rather unusual in the matter of parenthood.

In conclusion I would like to stress the important point that Bulgarian law makes absolutely no distinction between the legal status of "legitimate" and "illegitimate" children. These two terms are not even in use. No matter how the origin of a child has been established (through a birth certificate, affiliation or through a court action), it gives rise to a legal relationship between parent and child, their mutual rights and obligations being the same in all respects – cohabitation, alimony, custody, inheritance, etc.

V   ADOPTION

Since 1968 two types of adoption are known to Bulgarian family law: full adoption (adoptio plena), and partial adoption (adoptio minus plena). Through full (unrestricted) adoption all the parental authority and responsibility is transferred from the parents (if there are any), to the adoptive father or mother, or both. The child is considered legally equal to a biological child of the adoptive parents with all the consequences flowing therefrom. The child is incorporated into the adoptive family and considered to be "related" to all the relatives of the adoptive parents. The legal bonds to the biological parents are severed completely. There are however some remaining effects of the former relationship: e.g. consanguinity remains an obstacle to marriage.

Partial (restricted) adoption, as is revealed by its name, creates a relationship between adoptive parent and child where all the parental rights and responsibilities are vested in the adoptive parent. No legal relationship is created however between the child and the relatives of the adoptive parents. In contrast, the legal relationship with the biological parents is preserved. In fact the child is put in a situation where it can derive benefits from two sources: e.g. alimony should be given by the adoptive parents but if they are not in a position to provide it, the biological parents step in; the child can inherit from both his relatives by blood and the adoptive parents. But if the child should die, only the latter have the right to inherit.

How is the type of adoption determined? In the first place, there are three cases where full adoption is obligatory: where the child's parents are both unknown; where the child has been left in a social institution with a blanket consent for adoption, or it has been left in such an institution for short term rearing but has not been reclaimed for more than one year after the day when it should have been taken back (art. 61 of the Family Code). In all other cases, where the child's parents or at least one of them are known, and they have not left it with a social institution, the type of adoption depends on the coordinated opinions of all the parties whose consent is necessary (as to which, see below).

Adoption is accomplished through a judicial procedure before the regional court. Adoption is granted only if it is in the best interest of the child. In order to make his decision, the Judge can gather and require all sorts of information concerning the applicants and the child. Apart from this information, the Judge must be satisfied that the legal requirements for an adoption to be granted are observed. These are the following:

a) Only a person under the age of 18 may be adopted. Marriage is not an obstacle. Readoption is not possible until the first adoption is terminated. The prohibition does not apply to spouses who may, either simultaneously or consecutively, adopt the same child.

b) The applicant for adoption must be of full age (18) and legal capacity and should not be deprived of parental rights.

c) There should be a minimum of 15 years difference of age between the child and the applicant. Where spouses apply jointly for adoption, it is sufficient if this age differential is satisfied in relation to one of them.

d) Adoption between relatives in a direct line of descent and between brothers and sisters is prohibited. An exception is made for grandparents who may adopt their grandchild if born out of wedlock or whose parents are deceased.

Adoption can be granted only if the necessary agreements are given. The Family Code (art. 54, s. 1) first stipulates the agreement of the "adopter". This goes without saying as this person is usually the applicant who sets the whole procedure in motion. It is obvious that there is going to be no adoption unless he consents.

The most important agreement is that of the parents of the child. Both parents, if legally established and alive, regardless of their marital status, have the right to agree to the adoption or oppose it. If the parents are both unknown or dead, the child's guardian is entitled to express a view but his consent is not required. Finally, if the child is left with a social institution, its director's agreement must be obtained.

The court has power to dispense with parental agreement as a means of securing the child's welfare. But this may only be done on certain specified grounds. These are:

a) When the parent's residence is not known and he or she cannot be found.

b) When the parent is judicially disabled because of mental illness or imbecility. If disablement is only partial, the court has to listen to the parent's opinion but is not bound by it.

c) When the child has been left in a social institution with a blanket consent for adoption or has been left in such an institution for short term rearing but has not been reclaimed for more than one year after the day when it should have been taken back.

d) When the parent permanently disregards the needs of the child, does not take care of it or pay alimony, or brings the child up in a way detrimental to its development.

If the child is over the age of 14, its agreement is absolutely necessary for the adoption. Finally, there is a last group of people whose agreement is needed – the spouses of the "adopter" and of the "adopted". This envisages relatively rare cases, i.e. situations where only one of the spouses adopts a child or where an already married person between the age of 16 and 18 is being adopted.

Only after the court is satisfied that all the above conditions are satisfied and that the adoption will be beneficial to the child, a decree for adoption may be granted.

Adoption, being only a legal relationship and not one "by blood", can be terminated, its termination bearing some similarity to the dissolution of marriage. Partial adoption is terminated through the death of the adoptive parent. In all other cases adoption is terminated by a court decision. The grounds are as follows:

a) Adoption is terminated by the court on the basis of mutual consent of both parties – the adoptive parent and the child, provided that both are of full age and legal capacity.

b) Grounds for termination are serious offences committed by one party against the other or other circumstances leading to a complete breakdown of the relations between them.

c) Voidability of adoption is also a ground for its termination. And it is voidable whenever one of the above requirements for an adoption to be granted are disregarded.

d) Finally, only if it is in the interest of the child, a full adoption can be terminated by the court where the only or both adoptive parents are deceased.

The legal effects of adoption cease with its termination and the rights and responsibilities of the biological parents are restored as they were before the adoption.

VI PARENTAL RIGHTS AND RESPONSIBILITIES

Biological parents, established by one of the ways set out above, and adoptive parents have the same rights and responsibilities towards the child. As it was mentioned before, these do not differ with the sex of the parent or with his or her being married or unmarried. Both parents are equally vested with the rights and burdened with the responsibilities. In normal circumstances each of them can act separately in the name of the child, a mutual consent being presupposed. Only in cases where the parents do not live together due to divorce, lack of marriage or other reasons, can on appeal to the regional court be made in order to decide who is to exercise parental authority.

Only parents can have parental rights. So, no contract transferring such rights to another person will be legally recognized. This, of course, does not mean that the parents cannot use help or services from other people or public institutions. And this does not exclude the necessity of guardianship when the child has no parents or they are deprived of parental rights. However, in all these cases, strictly speaking those "surrogate parents" are not legally entitled to parental rights, but to rights in many respects very similar to them.

In severe cases of child abuse parents can be subject to criminal liability. They are also liable for torts, committed by the child against a third party, under art. 48 of the Contracts and Obligations Act. But parents can also be held responsible under arts. 74-75 of the Family code governing the restriction and deprivation of parental rights. Both measures aim to defend the child from behaviour of the parent or from an objective situation, connected with him or her, which create a potential or real danger to the life, health, education, property, or development of the child. Both measures have a restrictive character but the extent of the restrictions is different. When "restriction of parental rights" is ordered by the court, only part of them is taken away from the parent, e.g. the right to live with the child, representation rights, visitation rights, etc. Deprivation of parental rights has its literal meaning – the parent loses as a result of a court decision all his parental rights. Even some collateral rights are taken away, such as the right to seek alimony from an adult child, the right to become guardian or adoptive parent to another child. Only the obligation to maintain the minor child remains for a parent deprived of parental rights. Whether the court will order restriction or deprivation depends on the severity of the case. When one parent is deprived of parental rights, the other will exercise them; but in cases where this is the only parent or both are deprived of parental rights, a guardian must be appointed for the child.

VII MAINTENANCE

The rules about maintenance are contained in a separate chapter eight of the Family Code (arts. 79-93). They consist of general rules, regulating maintenance between members of a family, and also some specific rules, relating to maintenance of minor children by their parents, children of full age who continue their education, and of former spouses.

Maintenance obligations arise within quite a large family circle – between relatives of a direct line of descent, between brothers and sisters and between spouses and former spouses. Each of these persons can seek alimony from one of the above relatives if he is incapable of work and cannot support himself from his property. No person, except minor children, has the right to alimony irrespective of his property and his own ability to maintain himself. It should be specifically noted that a husband has no obligation to support his wife or his former wife unless she complies with the above general prerequisites. However, where a normal marital relationship exists, both spouses are supposed to enhance the welfare of the family commensurate with their respective property, income and personal capabilities.

The specific cases of maintenance are the following:

a) Minor children under the age of 18 are to be maintained by their parents regardless of whether they are fit for labour or can support themselves from their own property.

b) Children over the age of 18 can also seek alimony from their parents under certain circumstances if they continue their education, but no later than the age of 25.

c) Former spouses are obliged to maintain each other under the general circumstances of inability to work and to support themselves from their own property. There are however some additional conditions that must be observed. Only the party who has not been responsible for the divorce can seek alimony from the other. This alimony is due up to three years after the dissolution of marriage unless a longer term is agreed by the parties or determined by the court. The right to alimony ceases automatically on the remarriage of the recipient.

VIII   DIVORCE

Marriage is dissolved with the death or presumption of death of one of the spouses, through annulment and through divorce.

Until 1945 divorce was under the jurisdiction of the ecclesiastical courts. The grounds for divorce were strictly enumerated (e.g. adultery, desertion, cruelty, insanity, sexual inability), and required in most cases that the respondent had committed a matrimonial offence. With the Marriage Decree of 1945 a major step forward was made. Some of the old grounds for divorce were preserved. But together with them two very important ones were introduced – the irretrievable breakdown of marriage irrespective of the reasons which led to that result, and divorce by mutual consent. Later on (in 1953) the matrimonial offence grounds for divorce were abolished and nowadays the only ground is the irretrievable breakdown of marriage, together with divorce by mutual consent.

The irretrievable breakdown of marriage can be based on any fact connected with matrimonial life – matrimonial offence, disease, character incompatibility, behaviour of third parties, etc. The important thing is that the petitioner should convince the judge that the marriage is only a legal form and not a marriage in substance.

The divorce procedure starts by a petition presented to the regional court (no specialized matrimonial courts exist in Bulgaria), by either of the spouses. The court is then obliged to set a date for a conciliatory hearing which has two main objectives: to define the matters in relation to which the parties are in dispute and, setting out the disadvantages of divorce both for the spouses and children, to encourage the parties to make an effort to preserve the marriage. The court can, in its own discretion or if the parties wish so, set a second conciliatory hearing. If reconciliation is not achieved, a date for the second and essential hearing is set, no sooner than four months after the conciliatory hearing.

At this second hearing several issues must be discussed, the first being, of course, the question of whether the marriage has irretrievably broken down. The second important issue is to establish the fault for the breakdown of marriage. This decision has an impact in two basic directions: for the development of the procedure itself and for the consequences of divorce. The parties can avoid the court's judgement as to fault by submitting a complete agreement, regulating the consequences of divorce regarding the spouses' relationships and their relationships with the children. If such an agreement cannot be achieved, or it is not in the best interests of the child, the court will not accept it, and besides deciding on the party at fault, the court will have to make ex officio decisions as to: the exercise of parental authority by one parent and visitation rights for the other, the use of the family home, the alimony of the children, the family name of the spouse who has changed it by marriage. Property disputes between the parties can also be introduced into the divorce procedure, but they are not necessarily a part of it and are usually examined separately so as not to delay the dissolution of marriage. In the end, being convinced that the marriage has irretrievably broken down and having made a decision on all the collateral issues, the court may grant a decree of divorce. The parties can appeal against it before the district court. Marriage is considered terminated after the decree comes into force.

Divorce by mutual consent is a form of divorce which has caused much controversy. It was introduced in 1945, banned in 1952, and reintroduced in 1968 by the first Family Code. Since then it has always existed as a possibility which can be used only by spouses who have at least three years of marital life. In order to achieve divorce, the parties have to apply jointly to the court, expressing their firm mutual consent for divorce and submitting a complete agreement as to the consequences of the dissolution of the marriage. In this procedure the court has no right to analyse whether the marriage has really broken down or the reasons for it. The court has only to make sure that the spouses' decision is serious and freely taken and that their agreement is in the best interests of the child. If the agreement is not complete or not beneficial to the child, the court will allow a possibility for it to be changed; and if this is not done, the divorce petition will be dismissed. The same will happen if one of the parties does not appear before the court without a reasonable excuse. The absence of one party is considered a sign of hesitation, so it is presumed irrebuttably that there is no longer mutual consent for the divorce.

IX CONSEQUENCES OF DIVORCE

Two aspects of the consequences of divorce can be examined: (a) the relations of the former spouses, and (b) the relations between the former spouses as parents and their children.

a) After the marriage is terminated each former spouse becomes free to contract a new marriage without the necessity of waiting a certain period of time.

Joint marital property is automatically transformed into simple coownership with equal shares for both spouses. They have however the right to apply to the court for a larger share, the main grounds being that the petitioner has been vested with the exercise of parental authority after divorce and this creates great difficulties for him, and that the petitioner's contribution to the acquisition of the joint property has been considerably larger than that of the respondent.

After divorce each of the former spouses may sue for the monetary value of his or her contribution to the acquisition of personal property of significant value by the other.

Former spouses cease to be legal heirs to one another and forfeit all benefits resulting from dispositions in case of death, effected before the divorce. The latter means that if the husband has mentioned his wife in his will and then a divorce takes place, the former wife will be automatically excluded as heiress although the will has not been formally changed. There is no obstacle however for former spouses to make wills in one anothers' benefit after the divorce has taken place.

Divorce is also a ground for revocation of donations of considerable value made in connection with or during marriage by one spouse to the other or by relatives or friends of one spouse to the other.

A remaining important issue after divorce is the assignment of the matrimonial home. It might be joint matrimonial property, property of one of the spouses or of a third party. At issue here is not the ownership but the right to use and to live in the matrimonial home. The question is who is to stay there and who is to leave. If there is no agreement between the parties, the court will have to make the decision according to art. 107 of the Family Code. The solutions can vary, but the dominant criterion is the interest of the child. This means in practice that in almost all cases the parent who has been vested with the exercise of parental authority, will also get the use of the matrimonial home. This applies even if its owners are relatives of the other former spouse. Of course, this is a very undesirable situation and restriction of the owners' rights can last only for a relatively short period of time fixed by the court.

b) Divorce and lack of cohabitation makes it impossible for both parents to take care of the children and supervise their acts. That is why in the divorce procedure one of them is vested with the exercise of parental authority and obligations. It is important to notice that the other parent is not deprived of the rights themselves, he just cannot exercise them. The parent to be chosen depends again on all the circumstances relevant to the interests of the child. No agreement between the parents will be accepted by the court if it is considered detrimental to the child. Even an agreement to separate the children between the two parents will also be deemed as such and rejected, unless certain unusual circumstances make this separation desirable (e.g. one child is heavily ill, or there is too large an age difference between the children, or they have already lived separately for a considerable period of time, etc.).

For the parent, who is going to live separately, visitation rights are fixed. How often, for how long and on what conditions meetings with the child take place, depends entirely on the particular circumstances of the case.

As an exception, where the interests of the child require it, the court may decree that they live with a third party, usually a close relative, or at a social institution. In any event the decree of the court concerning the exercise of the parental rights is not irrevocable. On the contrary, it can be changed without any formal prerequisites if a change in the initial circumstances occurs.

CAMEROON

NULLITY: THE SQUARING OF A QUESTIONABLE DILEMMA

E.N. Ngwafor[*]

I   INTRODUCTION

The bi-jural nature of Cameroon's legal system has been the subject of voluminous legal literature.[1] With 250 tribes spread throughout the national territory, the role of customary law in Cameroon also becomes a pertinent area of study. Small wonder that today customary law stands out as one of the main sources of Family Law in Cameroon.[2] One can therefore say, with equal lack of diffidence, that Cameroon is a multi-jural State.[3] The result has been that on several occasions customary law finds itself on a collision course with the written law.

One would have imagined that, in this confusion, the courts would be plagued with petitions on nullity. But surprisingly this legal problem has hardly ever been canvassed in our courts. Thus, when a petition for divorce came up, it was almost always presumed that the marriage was valid. Counsel on either side never took time to find out if the marriage was void. The last few years have witnessed a dramatic modification in approach. Examples now abound where a spouse would petition for divorce and would be told that his marriage had never ever existed, with the inevitable consequence of changing his prayer from divorce to that of nullity.

---

[*]   Associate Professor of Law, University of Yaounde II.

[1]   C. Anyangwe, "The administration of Justice in a Bi-jural Country - The United Republic of Cameroon": Thesis submitted for the degree of Doctor of Philosophy, (Unpublished, University of London, 1969) at 1-13; C. Anyangwe, *"The Cameroonian Judicial System"*, CEPER, (1987) at 81; E.N. Ngwafor, "Family Law Trends in Cameroon: A Non-Development Process", (1983/84) 8 *Annual Survey of Family Law*, at 16.

[2]   Section 27 (1) of the Southern Cameroons High Court Law, 1955, stipulates:
"The High Court shall observe, and enforce the observance of every native law and custom which is not repugnant to natural justice, equity and good conscience, nor incompatible either directly or by implication with any law for the time being in force, and nothing in this law shall deprive any person of the benefit of any such native law or custom".

[3]   E.N. Ngwafor, "Property Rights for Women: A Bold Step in the Wrong Direction" (1990-91) JFL, 29, at 297; W.J. Kamba, "Comparative Law : A Theoretical Framework, " *(1974) 23 International and Comparative Law Quarterly*, 23, at 485.

A. Bainham (ed.), The International Survey of Family Law 1994, 101–118.

This confusion has been exacerbated by the presence and recognition of two types of marriages in Cameroon. In the first place, the statutory marriage, otherwise known as monogamy; and the customary law marriage, otherwise termed polygamy. The election of one type of marriage instead of the other gives rise to far-reaching consequences. The first one which immediately springs to mind is the choice of a competent court in the event of any matrimonial problem. There is also the problem of the different formalities required for the celebration of either type of marriage. It is with this background information that we shall examine the very recent judgment of Justice Hillman Egbe in the case of ASA'AH v ASA'AH[4], delivered in December 1994.

II   ASA'AH V. ASA'AH: THE FACTS

The parties who now live in London, England got married on December 20, 1988 in Limbe, Cameroon. At a certain stage during their stay in England, their relationship detcrioratcd and according to the wife, the husband became very violent. In fact, by an injunction order dated October 4, 1994 the Court in Kingston-On-Thames stopped the husband from appearing within 200 yards of the matrimonial home. The reasons why the court in England could not hear either party's petition for divorce will be discussed later. It should however be noted that, on October 12, 1994, barely eight days after the injunction order in England, the husband, through an originating summons filed a petition in the High Court in Buea, Cameroon, declaring that their marriage was null and void. As to the type of marriage opted for, it was expressly spelt out in their marriage certificate that the parties were:

> married according to the native laws and customs of the Nweh Mundani people and by Cameroon Civil Status Rules and Regulations.

These contradictions notwithstanding, Justice Hillman Egbe went ahead to hear and try the matter and subsequently pronounced a decree of divorce.[5]

---

4   The unreported judgment of Suit No HCF/66/94 of December 21, 1994.
5   The petitioner's prayer was later changed from nullity to divorce.

A Was the marriage valid?

It would not be a sound judgment if a Court decided to pronounce a decree of divorce on a non-existent marriage. In fact, there must be a valid marriage before a petition is presented. Hence in *NKO v. NKO*,[6] Dervish J., refused to pronounce such a decree, holding that the marriage was invalid.[7] The question now arises whether the Court in *ASA'AH v. ASA'AH* acted properly in trying the matter before it. The ambiguity that surrounds the presence of both statutory and customary law marriages in Cameroon cannot be over-emphasised. One of such difficulties did manifest itself in *ASA'AH v. ASA'AH*.

The parties to a marriage are free to choose between a statutory marriage (monogamy) and a customary law marriage (polygamy). They cannot get married under the native laws and customs of a particular tribe and yet purport to imply a monogamous regime. It has been held that such a marriage certificate must be tendered for rectification.[8] This is precisely what happened in *Kumbongsi v. Kumbongsi*,[9] at the Court of Appeal in Buea. The appellant got married to the respondent in 1960 according to the native laws and customs of the Bali-Nyonga ethnic group. In 1961 and 1970, he took in a second and third wife respectively, with no objection from the first wife. For the purpose of receiving family allowances the appellant and the respondent declared their marriage before the Buea Court of First Instance. They obtained a declaratory judgment dated September 3, 1974; and a marriage certificate was then issued. The appellant did not examine his own copy of the marriage certificate because, as he maintained, he had no reason to do so. Sometime in 1977 he noticed that there was an entry in his marriage certificate which he did not approve of. It read, "monogamy with common property". He then brought the matter to the Court of First Instance for rectification of the marriage certificate by the deletion of the phrase quoted above. He failed. On appeal, Chief Justice Ekema found for

---

6   (1968-1970) UYLR 110.

7   See also *Abili v. Abili*, the unreported judgment of Suit No HCB/3/82 where the purported marriage was by proxy thus infringing section 42 of the Civil Status Law No 68/LF/2 of June 11, 1968. Anyangwe J. found no difficulty in rejecting the petition for divorce and instead held that the marriage was void *ab initio*. cf *Mbiaffie v. Mbiaffie*, the unreported judgment of suit No HCSW/30 mc/85.

8   *Kumbongsi v. Kumbongsi*, the unreported judgment of the Court of Appeal No CASWP/4/84.

9   Ibid.

the appellant and ordered that the document be rectified. Justice Ekema's decision is understandable, for parties cannot opt for a customary law marriage and later decide to change their regime in the course of registering the marriage.

The entries in the marriage certificate in the case of *ASA'AH v. ASA'AH* were most peculiar. For the first time a court was called upon to examine a marriage certificate wherein the Civil Status Registrar had mentioned that the parties were married according to:

> The native laws and customs of Nweh Mundani and by the Cameroon Civil Status Rules and Regulations.

And in this same document it was entered that the parties had chosen "monogamy" as their type of antenuptial settlement. In *Kumbongsi v. Kumbongsi*[10] the interpretation called for was easy to determine because the parties had chosen to be governed by the native laws and customs of the Bali-Nyonga people. The marriage was therefore potentially polygamous. But in *ASA'AH v. ASA'AH* the parties purported to have opted for the two different regimes, namely, the native laws and customs of the Nweh Mundani ethnic group (that is, a potentially polygamous marriage) and at the same time wanted to be ruled by the Civil Status Registration Law[11], (that is a statutory marriage, otherwise known as a monogamous marriage). It is disturbing to note that Justice Hillman Egbe did not address his mind to this contradiction. In fact he did not even cite *Kumbongsi v. Kumbongsi*[12]. The Court of Appeal judgement by Chief Justice Ekema in the latter case would have been of great guidance to Justice Egbe. In ordering for the rectification of the marriage certificate in the *Kumbongsi case*, Chief Justice Ekema, among other things declared:

> "The marriage between the appellant and the respondent although contracted in 1960, was only registered in 1974 by which time the appellant had contracted two other marriages. The appellant and the respondent could not therefore have opted for a monogamous marriage even if it was their intention to do so because *no one man can opt for two different forms of*

---

10   Ibid.
11   Ordinance no. 81-02 of June 29, 1981.
12   Supra.

marriage. A man is either polygamously married or monogamously married but not the two forms simultaneously" (emphasis added).

This is a logical analysis which leads to yet another conclusion, namely that the purported marriage between Mr and Mrs ASA'AH is null and void. If this reasoning is accepted, the Court ought to have heard and tried a case on nullity and not on divorce.

But it is also possible to posit another argument, that ASA'AH v. ASA'AH was a valid customary law marriage. This reasoning results from the interpretation of section 48 of Ordinance no 81-02 of June 29, 1981, which governs Civil Status Registration in Cameroon[13], which stipulates that "marriage shall be celebrated by the civil status registrar". It has been strongly contended that this statement refers mainly to the celebration of statutory law (monogamous) marriages.[14] It does not apply to the celebration of customary law marriages, as Justice Anyangwe implied in one case.[15] There are about 250 tribes in this country and so it would be virtually impossible for the civil status registrar to be conversant with all the requirements of each group. This explains the justification for a declaratory judgment. This happens when, parties who have fulfilled all the requirements for the celebration of a valid customary law marriage now seek documentary proof of their new status of a married couple. The practice is to obtain a declaratory judgment from the Court of First Instance, acknowledging the existence of their marriage. This declaration could be made as long as 10, 15, 20 or 25 years after the said celebration. It is at this point that the parties contact the civil status registrar who merely "registers" the marriage. Note that, he does not "celebrate" but instead "registers" the marriage. And that is why he enters in the marriage certificate that the parties got married according to the native laws and customs of X or Y tribe.

The error has almost always come from the elitist class, who after the phrase, "married according to the native laws and customs of a particular tribe", insist that the word monogamy be included in the declaratory judgment as well as in the marriage certificate. A classic example can be seen in the 1984 declaratory judgment of Magistrate Bill Egbe in the Limbe Court of First Instance wherein he declared:

---

13 Hereinafter referred to as the 1981 Ordinance.
14 E.N. Ngwafor, *Family Law in Anglophone Cameroon*, (1993) at 33-41.
15 *Abili v. Abili*, in the unreported judgment of suit No HCB/3/82.

"Whereas, by virtue of the documents produced and the statements of the witnesses called legally to support his/her prayer, it appears that Desmond Iwu Njuko ... being of the age of 52 years ... contracted marriage on 24/11/60 at Limbe ... with Angelina Anaba ... being of the age of 40 years ... according to the customs of Ibo. Type of marriage ... monogamy."

The presence of the word monogamy is of no significance, for it does not change the fact that the marriage is potentially polygamous. We can also note that although the marriage was contracted in 1960 it was only registered 24 years later, that is in 1984.[16]

As to the distinction between the fact of celebration and that of registration section 81(1) of the 1981 Ordinance is helpful in providing that "customary marriages shall be recorded in the civil status register of the place of birth or residence of the spouses". Such registration (or recording) has nothing to do with the validity of the marriage. It is not the duty of the civil status registrar to start the ceremony all over again. At his level, his job is mainly to record the marriage in the civil status register. In pursuance of his line of action, he could ask the parents and elders of the couple if the necessary customs of the ethnic group in question had been respected. This only goes to prove that the celebration had in fact taken place.

Another argument can be advanced in this same vein namely that when one gets married according to the native laws and customs of a particular tribe, the marriage is simply potentially polygamous and does not necessarily oblige the bridegroom to marry more than one wife. This statement embellishes yet another disturbing contention that it would be proper for such a party to maintain that his customary law marriage is monogamous. This is a very vicious argument because it simply invites another question, namely, what is a customary law marriage? When you get married under customary law, the marriage is polygamous or potentially so. It is irrelevant that the man does not proceed to marry a second, third or fourth wife. One Ghanaian case strongly illustrates this point.[17] Here, the husband went through a customary law marriage with the intention to turn it into a christian marriage. Problems beset the marriage before the husband carried through his intention. The Court of Appeal in England did not hesitate to hold that it did not have

---

16 See the case of *Kumbongsi v. Kumbongsi*, Supra, where registration took place 14 years after celebration.
17 *Sowa v. Sowa* [1961] All E.R. 687, C.A.

jurisdiction. The reasoning of the Court was simple. Since the husband had done nothing to change the initial character of the marriage, it was, in essence, to be regarded as a polygamous marriage. It was irrelevant that the husband had not added to his number of wives.

From these various points of view one can venture the conclusion that once spouses-to-be opt for the native laws and customs of a tribe the marriage is potentially polygamous notwithstanding any other entry in the marriage certificate, to the contrary. Indeed, Justice Nganjie in *Motanga v. Motanga*[18] warned that where the civil status registrar fails to indicate in the spaces provided the type of marriage chosen, the marriage will be presumed to be potentially polygamous. He pointed out that:

> "The spouses must specifically state and must mention in the marriage certificate that the marriage is monogamous, otherwise the presumption is that it is polygamous because a Cameroonian is polygamous by birth."[19]

In the light of these analyses one is quickly tempted to arrive at the conclusion that the marriage in ASA'AH v. ASA'AH was celebrated under customary law.

B   Did the High Court in Buea have jurisdiction?

In analysing this sub-heading issues of validity will again arise in the attempt to find out whether the marriage in the ASA'AH case was celebrated under statutory law or customary law. A marriage could be declared void under statutory law and yet be accepted as valid under customary law. Such a dividing line could give rise to problems of jurisdiction. For example, if the marriage is considered to be a valid customary law marriage, then the customary court, and not the High Court, will have jurisdiction in the event of any matrimonial problem for which one of the spouses seeks redress.

By the provisions of section 7 of the Southern Cameroons High Court Law 1955, original jurisdiction in matrimonial matters is vested in the High

---

18   The unreported judgment of suit No HCB/2/76.
19   Small wonder this same judge in the above case defined marriage in Cameroon as, "the union between a man and one or more women to the exclusion of other men".

Court. Following the harmonisation of our two constitutions in 1972[20], the Judicial Organisation Ordinance no 72/4 of August 26, 1972 was passed. Section 16(1) of this Ordinance provides inter alia that the High Court shall have jurisdiction:

> (b) ... in civil matters to try actions and proceedings relating to status of persons, civil status, marriage, divorce and affiliation, subject to the legal provisions relating to the traditional courts as regards rationae personae jurisdiction.[21]

On the other hand, Section 9 (1)(b) of the Southern Cameroons High Court Law 1955 emphatically provides that problems arising from polygamous marriages must be settled in customary courts. It is therein stated that:

> Subject to the provisions of the Land and Native Rights Ordinance and any other written Law, the High Court shall not exercise original jurisdiction in any suit or matter which is subject to the jurisdiction of a native court relating to marriage, family, status, guardianship of children, inheritance or the dispostion of property on death.

The consequence of this dichotomy is that the High Court will set aside any matter relating to a customary law marriage.[22] But where there is no evidence in the marriage certificate that the parties had opted for a customary law marriage and only the term monogamy is mentioned, then the High Court will have jurisdiction. This was the fact in issue in the interesting case of *Mokwe v. Mokwe*.[23] The petitioner declared in his petition for divorce that he had been married to the respondent around 1982 according to the customary laws of the Bakundu people. But their marriage certificate made no mention of this customary law marriage. In fact, the parties had contracted a monogamous marriage in 1985 according to the provisions of the civil status registration Ordinance, 1981. The High Court dismissed counsel's objection that the court did not have jurisdiction.

---

20   Until 1972, Cameroon was composed of two Federated States: Former West Cameroon made up of Anglophone Cameroon and former East Cameroon, made up of Francophone Cameroon.

21   Now, Section 16(1)(c) of Law No 89/019 of December 29, 1989.

22   See *Kemgue v. Kemgue*, infra; *Ngwa v. Ngwa* infra; and *Tufon v. Tufon*, infra.

23   The unreported judgment of suit No HCB/14mc/89.

Coming back to the ASA'AH *case*, the facts are more complicated. If the petition had been founded on nullity simpliciter, then the High Court would without more have had original jurisdiction. And in that case the court would have arrived at the conclusion that the marriage was void ab initio following the dictum of Chief Justice Ekema in the Court of Appeal case of *Kumbongsi v. Kumbongsi*,[24] that:

> a man is either polygamously married or monogamously married but not the two forms simultaneously.

Another variant of the problem turns on the consequences of marriages by proxy. It is an important requirement that the spouses-to-be must be present during the celebration of the marriage. Where one party is represented by a third party the marriage will be rendered void. Indeed, section 69(1) of the 1981 Ordinance specifically requires the presence of the spouses-to-be. However, an exception has been provided in section 66(1) of the 1981 Ordinance and it arises only where one of the spouses-to-be is in apparent danger of death and cannot appear before the registrar. On this ground alone therefore the marriage in the ASA'AH case could be considered void since the petitioner was represented on the day of the celebration. But this would not be so if the marriage was celebrated under customary law. It is a well-known fact that the celebration of such a marriage is basically by proxy, beginning with the betrothal right to the payment of the bride price.[25] In the early days it was even possible to betroth a girl *en ventre sa mère* in the hope that the mother was carrying a female child.

Although the next point discussed below was not sufficiently articulated in Justice Egbe's judgment in ASA'AH v. ASA'AH, the sworn affidavits show that the parties did not respect sections 53 and 54 of the 1981 Civil Status Registration Ordinance. It is recognised that only a civil status registrar can celebrate a statutory marriage.[26] The Ordinance goes ahead to enact in its section 53 that at least one month before the celebration of the marriage, a declaration mentioning the full names, occupation, residence, age and place of birth of the spouses-to-be and their intention to contract marriage shall

---

24 Supra.
25 See S.N. Chinwuba Obi, *Modern Family Law in Southern Nigeria*, (1966) at 103 et seq.; See generally, E.N. Ngwafor, *Family Law in Anglophone Cameroon*, op. cit. at 43-47.
26 Section 48 of the 1981 Ordinance.

be lodged with the civil status registrar.[27] When this happens, it will be the duty of the civil status registrar with whom the declaration has been lodged, immediately to publish the said declaration by posting it on the notice board of the civil status registration office.[28]

Failure on the part of the spouses-to-be to respect these formalities renders the statutory marriage void *ab initio*. But the validity of a customary law marriage cannot be affected simply because banns have not been published. On the other hand, the tendency is to carry out thorough investigations into the character of the members of both parties by both sides. It is however certain that the marriage in *ASA'AH v. ASA'AH* was by proxy and secondly, that no banns were published as required by sections 53 and 54 of the 1981 Ordinance. Under these circumstances we could aver, without fear of any strong contradiction, that the marriage was contracted under customary law. Hence, the High Court in Buea was not competent to hear and try the matter. In *Ngwa v. Ngwa*,[29] Ndoping J. held that since the parties had been married according to the native laws and customs of the Bafut people, the High Court in Bamenda could not entertain the petitioner's divorce suit. The judge stated that:

> "I find and hold that the petitioner's marriage to the respondent ... continues to be a customary law marriage up to the present. In the upshot, I adjudge that I, presiding at the High Court Mezam, have no jurisdiction to entertain the petition. The petitioner is advised to seek her redress in the Bafut Customary Court which is clearly the tribunal with the jurisdiction in the matter."

Also in *Tufon v. Tufon*,[30] the parties contracted their marriage under the native laws and customs of the Kom people. The wife's petition for divorce based on the husband's adultery was struck out by Asu J. in the Bamenda High Court for want of jurisdiction.[31]

It may be helpful to examine a certain portion of Justice Hillman Egbe's judgment in *ASA'AH v. ASA'AH*. He said among other things that:

---

27   See also Section 38 of the now repealed Law No 68/LF/2 of June 11, 1968.
28   Section 54(1).
29   The unreported judgment of suit No HCB/59mc/83.
30   The unreported judgment of suit No HCB/59MC/183.
31   See also *Kemgue v. Kemgue*, the unreported judgment of suit No HCB/IBMC/83; *Ebako v. Ebako* the unreported judgment of suit No HCSW/42MC/77.

"It is a cultural anathema and an inexcusable wrong for an African woman to evict a husband from their matrimonial home and ban him from access thereto on grounds of assault. Battery is a common feature of African marital life and it may be administered as corrective punishment. Usually, it does not give rise to court action even when it is cruel and reprehensible."

This is again eloquent proof of the confusion that surrounds the difference between statutory and customary law marriages. Justice Egbe must have been referring to the acts of violence perpetrated by the petitioner on the respondent in England which resulted in an injunction order of October 4, 1994, forbidding the petitioner from "assaulting, molesting, harassing or interfering with the applicant or her child". It should be noted that such an application for an injunction order could be made independent of a divorce petition. It is also understandable why the respondent could not petition for divorce in England. English courts do not entertain petitions founded on marriage contracted under customary law.[32]

Justice Hillman Egbe's dictum cited above calls for concern. Placed in the context of a customary law marriage the statement carries a high degree of truth. It is normal practice under customary law for a husband to chastise his wife physically as a means of correction. In fact under this type of marriage a woman is regarded as the husband's property.[33] The judge's statement is not true where the parties opt for a statutory marriage. Cameroonian cases abound which indicate that an action will lie under section 1(2)(b) of the Matrimonial Causes Act, 1973, where one spouse is violent on the other.[34] It should also be noted that even under customary law it becomes abnormal where the beatings are administered frequently. In such a case a decree of divorce will be granted. This was the case in

---

32 *Sowa v. Sowa* (1961) All E.R. 689 C.A.
33 See the unreported judgments of Inglis J. in *Ndumu v. Ndumu* (No 2), suit No HCB/97mc/86 and *Achu v. Achu*, Appeal No BCA/62/86.
34 *Njuaka v. Njuaka* and *Agnes Agbor*, the unreported judgment of suit No HCSW/7MC/82; *Sandjo v. Sandjo*, the unreported judgment of suit No HCSW/74MC/80. The English Matrimonial Causes Act 1973, is applicable in former West Cameroon by virtue of Section 15 of the Southern Cameroons High Court Law 1955 which stipulates that: "The jurisdiction of the High Court in probate, divorce, and matrimonial causes and proceedings may, subject to the provisions of this law and in particular Section 27, and to rules of court, be exercised by the court in conformity with the law and practice for the time being in force in England".

Bwange v. Bwange,[35] where the husband was found to be a man of uncontrollable temper, who would frequently beat up the petitioner and burn
her clothes. In yet another case,[36] the respondent who usually came back
home late, would beat up the petitioner on his return. He continued to do
so even when she was pregnant. The court granted a divorce. A husband
could also succeed in a petition for divorce under customary law on the
ground of the wife's violence. In one case, the Mankon customary court
pronounced a decree of divorce against a wife who had inflicted various
acts of violence on the husband.[37]

From the foregoing we can see that the marriage in the *ASA'AH Case* was
contracted according to the customary laws of the Mweh Mundani tribe and
that only the Mweh Mundani customary court ought to have heard and tried
any divorce petition brought by either party.

C   *The first giant corrective steps*

Cameroon has not witnessed significant legislative activity in Family Law
within the last thirteen years. The courts, on the contrary, have been very
busy. The last decade has seen the passing of landmark decisions in this
area of the law. It has been especially noticeable because the hitherto un-
popular matrimonial relief of nullity suddenly became a cause for concern.
And unlike in Ireland where the interest provoked along these lines turned
on incapacity to consummate a marriage,[38] the controversy in Cameroon
revolved on formalities to marry.

It was noted earlier that only a Civil Status Registrar can celebrate a
monogamous marriage. And that at least one month before this event the
civil status registrar must publish banns, announcing the impending
celebration. In view of the confusion emanating from the presence of both
statutory and customary law marriages in Cameroon there has been the

---

35   The unreported judgment of Customary Law Suit No 68/86-87, CRB 3/86-87, at 67.
36   *Monono v. Monono*, the unreported Customary Law Suit No 81/87-88, CRB 8/87-88
     at 70.
37   *Awah Patrick Chefor v. Siriwah Justine*, the unreported Customary Law Suit No 82/86-
     87, CRB 1/86-87, at 17.
38   William Duncan, "Waning For Divorce" (1985) 9 JFL 155; Paul O'Connor, "Nullity
     and the Judiciary" (1993-94) Vol. 32 JFL, 345.

tendency to ignore the importance of these requirements. And this is all the more so because the formalities mentioned hereabove have no place in the celebration of a customary law marriage. Within the last few years the courts have decided to put an end to this confusion, and as if to set an example, one of the popular cases concerned citizens of the upper class.

In the famous case of *Biaka v Biaka*,[39] Dr Biaka, a gynaecologist contracted a marriage sometime in 1966 with one Josephine Daniloff, at the Kensington County Marriage Registry, in London. After the celebrations the parties cohabited in London up to 1977 when Dr Biaka returned to his native country Cameroon. He immediately joined the medical services of the Cameroon government as a gynaecologist. In 1979, Dr Biaka filed a petition in the Fako High Court to dissolve the marriage contracted in London in 1966. The Court granted a decree nisi in favour of the petitioner in August 1979 and made the decree absolute on November 30 that same year. Barely four days after obtaining the decree absolute, that is on December 3, 1979, the petitioner contracted another monogamous marriage with the respondent based on Law No 68/LF/2 of June 11, 1968 organising Civil Status Registration in Cameroon.[40] The parties cohabited for nine years before their "marriage" became strained. The petitioner then filed a petition for divorce sometime in 1988 for a dissolution of the marriage, contending that the marriage had irretrievably broken down.

It was at the preliminary examination of the case that the issue of the validity of the marriage had to be canvassed. Since the parties celebrated their marriage barely four days after the dissolution of the petitioner's first marriage, it was indisputable that they did not respect the provisions on publication of banns. Surprisingly, however, Justice Nkele at first instance ruled that the marriage was valid and that any debate on nullity was sheer waste of time. On appeal the question was asked if the learned trial judge had not erred in law in raising the presumption of regularity in a marriage certificate established in violation of the mandatory provisions of the law under which it was made. Justice Bawak ably argued that the sections of

---

39 The unreported Court of Appeal Judgment of CASWP/37mc/90 of February 28, 1991.
40 This Law was later repealed and replaced by Ordinance No 82-02 of June 29, 1981 with the same long title. Sections 38 and 39 of the 1968 Law also provided that a marriage should be celebrated by a civil status registrar and that at least one month before the said celebration there should be the publication of banns.

the law prescribing publication of banns were mandatory and went on to
state the few exceptions to the rule:

> "At times it may happen that one of the parties wishing to contract a mar-
> riage was to travel abroad or the bride-to-be is pregnant and the parties wish
> to forestall the chances of the child being born out of wedlock or that some
> serious reasons exist which necessitate the celebration of the marriage before
> the one month period provided for by law, the parties apply to the State
> Counsel having jurisdiction over the area for a 'fiat' dispensing with the
> publication of banns."[41]

It is the overwhelming influence of our customary law that blurs the distinction between statutory law marriages and those contracted under customary law. In Cameroon, as in most African countries, marriage unites two
families and not just two individuals. This explains the vital role of parental
consent, even in cases where the spouses-to-be are adults. The validity of
the marriage rests on the payment and acceptance of the bride price.[42] This
seal is absent where there is no parental consent and this can be deduced
where the girl's parents refuse to accept the bride-price.

Our judges have tended to confuse issues and to a large extent have been
willing to dissolve a statutory marriage contracted between adults on the
sole ground that parental consent was absent. In *Evelyn Fese Njotsa v.
Michael Njotsa*,[43] the petitioner sued for divorce, predicating her case on
the old ground of cruelty. She failed to prove her case but Justice Endeley,
as he then was, however went on to pronounce a decree of divorce. He
stated:

> "I am satisfied that the failure of this marriage has been sealed by the fact
> that it did not when it was being solemnised and does not even now, enjoy

---

41 This procedure is laid down in sections 39-44 of the 1968 Law and Sections 53-54 of
    the 1981 Ordinance. Publication of banns or notice is a very popular and mandatory
    requirement for the celebration of a valid christian marriage even in Nigeria. See S.N.
    Chinwuba Obi, *Modern Family Law in Southern Nigeria*, op. cit. at 188-191; A.B.
    Kasunmu and J.W. Salacuse, *Nigerian Family Law*, 1966, at 52-55.

42 This of course is unmindful of Section 70(1) of the 1981 Ordinance with stipulates that:
    "The total or partial payment or non-payment of dowry, the total or partial execution
    or non-execution of any marriage agreement shall have no effect on the validity of the
    marriage".

43 ((1971-73) UYLR 5.

the blessings of the married couple's respective parents. In these circumstances, it will not be in the interest of the parties to keep it on."

Ordinarily, parental consent ought not to receive recognition in a statutory marriage.[44] But since spouses-to-be under both statutory and customary law marriages feel obliged to fulfil this condition of payment of the bride-price, the difference between these two marriages becomes blurred.

Another aspect of the problem was seen in the case of *Mbiaffie v. Mbiaffie*.[45] The petitioner sued for divorce, alleging adultery and unreasonable behaviour. The parties got married in 1976 under statutory law. The respondent had already been married but had abandoned his first wife in France without any prior matrimonial proceedings. Here again we can see the influence of a very significant aspect of customary law, namely that a man can get married as many times as he so wishes. What is intriguing in this case is the fact that the court would go ahead and pronounce a decree of divorce on a marriage which had never existed.[46] The fact that the respondent had already contracted a first marriage rendered the second marriage to the petitioner void and bigamous.[47]

That same year the Bamenda Court had convicted a husband on a charge of bigamy under the same circumstances, sentencing the accused to six months imprisonment.[48] The judicial error in *Mbiaffie v. Mbiaffie*[49] is very evident. The *Biaka v. Biaka*[50] case is not only salutary but most timely.

---

44   In the Nigerian case of *Ugboma v. Morah* (1940), 15 NLR 78, the validity of a marriage was challenged because the plaintiff, even though of age, had not received the consent of her parents as was required by customary law. This point of view was rejected because, as the court held, the parties were married under the Marriage Act, and as the plaintiff was above twenty-one years parental consent was not necessary.

45   The unreported judgment of suit No HCSW/30mc/85 of October 3, 1985.

46   E.N. Ngwafor, "The *Mbiaffie v. Mbiaffie* Case or the dissolution of a non-existent Marriage" (1989-90) *Revue de Legislation et de Jurisprudence Camerounaise,* 25.

47   See Section 359 of the Cameroon Penal Code and also section 35 of the Marriage Ordinance, Chapter 115- Vol IV of the Revised Laws of the Federation of Nigeria which forms part of our sources of Family Law.

48   *Pierre Ndjiqui v. Cecile Ngo Njock*, the unreported Bamenda High Court Judgment of February 28, 1985. Pierre Ndjiqui was accused and convicted of having abandoned his first wife with whom he had contracted a monogamous marriage in the Bertoua Civil Status Registry, and secretly contracted another marriage with one Samah Grace Fri in Kumbo.

49   Supra.

50   Supra.

A line should always be drawn between the two types of marriages that are recognised in Cameroon and the respective conditions required for their validity should not be confused nor misplaced.

The *Biaka v. Biaka* case is not the first in the line of decisions in which the court had to restate the law as it ought to be. Problems of nullity had also been under fiery debate in another perspective. The earlier cases turned on the interpretation of the provisions of the Law that a statutory marriage shall be celebrated by the Civil Status Registrar.[51] This requirement hardly reflects the simple manner in which customary law marriages are celebrated. In this connection, every stage of the ceremony is oral and there is hardly any documentary proof at the end of the ceremony, although society accepts the parties as husband and wife. And since there is a strong attachment to the importance of the payment of a bride-price even to ceremonies leading to the formation of a statutory marriage, spouses-to-be inadvertently overlook the mandatory nature of the statutory requirement that such a marriage must be celebrated by the civil status registrar.

An early judicial recognition of this requirement came in 1982 in the case of *Abili v. Abili*.[52] In this case, the marriage was celebrated by a Court Clerk without any delegation of powers from the civil status registrar. The purported marriage was declared null and void by Justice Anyangwe. Seven years later a similar question came up in the High Court in Fako, in the case of *Albert Che Niba v. Sussan Embelle*.[53] The parties were married in May 1971. The facts disclosed that the marriage was celebrated by the Senior Divisional Officer in keeping with Section 2 of the Marriage Ordinance.[54] The Senior District Officer was ignorant of the Civil Status Law of 1968 which gave the civil status registrar exclusive rights to celebrate a marriage. Although the parties had lived together as husband and wife for eighteen years and there were several children of the marriage, the judge found no difficulty in holding that the marriage was void. In the words of Justice Moma:

---

51   Section 38 of the 1968 Law and Section 48 of the 1981 Ordinance.
52   The unreported judgment of suit No HCB/3/82 of September 18, 1982.
53   The unreported judgment of Suit No HCF/125mc/89 of April 12, 1991.
54   Before the passing of the 1968 Law and later the 1981 Ordinance, issues on marriage were regulated by the Nigerian Marriage Ordinance, Chapter 115 - Vol.IV, of the Revised Laws of the Federation of Nigeria 1958.

"This marriage is declared null and void. The parties to this suit have never acquired the status of husband and wife according to the existing Law on Civil Status in this country."

III CONCLUSION

The first oddity in the case of ASA'AH V. ASA'AH is the speed with which judgment was delivered. Although the originating summons was filed on October 12, 1994, the divorce petition was first heard on October 17, 1994, barely thirteen days after the injunction order in England against the petitioner. The case suffered four successive adjournments before the petitioner appeared for the first time on November 16, 1994. Within one month the court delivered judgment pronouncing a decree nisi of divorce. In other words the matter was heard and tried within a record time of two months. Although this is not to say that justice hurriedly given may be justice denied, divorce cases in Cameroon have been known to take between two to five years.[55] Even the attempt at reconciliation needs a reasonably long time.

The judgment of Justice Hillman Egbe presents several lacunae. Considering the long list of authorities cited in this work, ASA'AH v. ASA'AH would have turned on nullity proceedings and not divorce. But if the view is taken (and this position will easily receive approval by many scholars) that the marriage was celebrated under customary law, then the High Court in Buea did not have jurisdiction to hear and try the matter. It is regrettable to note that if left unchecked this judgment may set the judicial clock back a decade. The judge failed to cite even one case to support his stance, and did not even distinguish the case with any other earlier judgment.

The Court of Appeal judgments in *Kumbongsi v. Kumbongsi* and *Biaka v. Biaka* still stand out as good law and will continue to guide the courts in drawing a line between statutory and customary law marriages with the concomitant legal consequences. It is with anxiety that one looks forward to reading the decision of the Court of Appeal in ASA'AH v. ASA'AH. If ten years or so ago nullity proceedings constituted a dilemma, then the decisions

---

55 See *Tarh v. Tarh*, the unreported Court of Appeal judgment, No BCA/19/87 which took over five years.

in *Abili v. Abili*,[56] *Albert Che Niba v. Sussan Embelle*[57] and *Biaka v. Biaka*[58] have each shown that it is a questionable dilemma.

---

56   Supra.
57   Supra.
58   Supra.

CANADA

CHILDREN, SAME-SEX COUPLES AND ABORTION

Martha Bailey and *Nicholas Bala***

I   INTRODUCTION

A major focus of recent concern in Canada has been the position of children, especially in the context of divorce. There has been a widely shared view that child support orders have been too low, contributing to the post-divorce poverty of women and children. Several appellate decisions, including one from the Supreme Court of Canada, have indicated that higher child support awards should be made, and the federal government released proposals for guidelines that would facilitate the determination of child support awards.

The Supreme Court of Canada released a judgment in 1994 dealing with international child abduction and the *Hague Convention*, emphasizing the importance of giving jurisdiction to the courts of the family's last common residence. A decision of the Supreme Court in a child protection case emphasized the importance of continuity of care by foster parents, and limited the rights of biological parents to regain custody of children who have been in the custody of a protection agency. But another Supreme Court decision revealed a deeply split bench on whether, in principle, parents involved in child protection proceedings have a constitutionally protected interest in their relationship with their children.

While Canada has a relatively broad legal conception of the "family",[1] there is enormous controversy over same-sex couples. The courts are slowly giving legal protection to these relationships, but recent legislative efforts to consolidate and clarify their position have run into great opposition.

In 1988, Canada's criminal laws governing abortion were ruled unconstitutional. Some provincial governments have been trying to restrict women's access to abortion services under the guise of regulating health care, but recent court decisions have ruled these attempts unconstitutional.

---

*   Assistant Professor, Queen's University, Kingston, Ontario.
**   Associate Dean, Queen's University, Kingston, Ontario.
1   See e.g. Bala, "The Evolving Canadian Definition of the Family" (1994), 8 *Inter. J.L. & Fam.* 293-318.

A. Bainham (ed.), The International Survey of Family Law 1994, 119–143.
© 1996 *The International Society of Family Law. Printed in the Netherlands.*

While access to abortion services remains restricted in many localities, the country is moving in the direction of broader access to abortion services.

II   CHILD SUPPORT

By the early 1990s, if not before, many legal practitioners and academics in Canada recognized that amounts of spousal and child support were, in general, too low.[2] This was viewed as contributing significantly to women and children living in poverty after divorce. In 1992, the Supreme Court of Canada addressed the issue of spousal support in *Moge v. Moge*,[3] a judgment that included discussion of the social and economic context of divorce, and emphasized the need to compensate women for the career sacrifices which they commonly make to assume primary child care roles in marriage. The effect of *Moge* has been a significant increase in the number of women receiving spousal support, as well as in the duration of these orders.[4]

By 1991, governments in Canada[5] began to examine the issue of child support, motivated by a desire to improve the economic position of children and women, as well as a recognition that governments often subsidize inadequate support orders through welfare payments. Measures were taken to improve enforcement of orders, and in most provinces a government agency will now enforce support orders without charge to the recipient.[6]

---

2   See e.g. E D Pask, "Gender Bias and Child Support: Sharing the Poverty" (1993), 10 *Can. F.L.Q.* 33; and M Grassby, "Women in Their Forties: The Extent of Their Right to Alimentary Support" (1991), *30 R.F.L.* (3d) 369.

3   [1992] 3 S.C.R. 813, 43 R.F.L. (3d) 345, 99 D.L.R. (4th) 456.

4   See e.g. Bala, "Canada: Growing Recognition of the Realities of Family Life" (1994), 32 *Univ. Louisville J.F.L.* 269, at 269-273; and Bala, "Spousal Support Law Transformed – Fairer Treatment for Women" (1994), 4 *Can. F.L.Q.* 13-56.

5   Under Canada's *Constitution Act, 1867*, sections 91 and 92 there is concurrent jurisdiction for child and spousal support, with both the federal and provincial governments having authority to enact laws. In the event of conflicting orders, an order made under federal legislation is "paramount".

6   See e.g. F.J. Lynch, "The Family Support Plan Act" (1995), 12 *Can. F.L.Q.* 55-116.

In 1991-92, a series of government discussion papers were released proposing various possible models for child support guidelines,[7] based on similar schemes in the United States, Australia and Sweden, which set a presumptive amount of child support, given different levels of parental income. The reports argued that guidelines would result in more expeditious and less expensive resolution of disputes; as well, most of the models under discussion would have produced significantly higher child support awards than those being made in the early 1990s in Canada. By 1994, the issue of the inadequacy of many child support orders began to reach appellate courts in Canada.

In *Levesque v. Levesque*[8] the Alberta Court of Appeal articulated "guidelines" for child support, reasoning that the legislation offers "little specific guidance" on how judges should apportion child support, but "justice requires a uniformity of approach".[9] The Court of Appeal recognised that the traditional Canadian approach, which required applicants to develop and defend an itemized budget of expenditures for the child, produced cost estimates that were both variable and too low. Inadequate child support orders resulted in a steep decline in the standard of living after divorce, with the custodial parent and children often enjoying a much lower standard of living than the non-custodial parent. Further, the Court believed that the unpredictability of outcomes may encourage litigation, especially for those litigants who have "unreasonable expectations, or who are spoiling for a fight".[10]

The Court of Appeal suggested that trial judges in Alberta should establish detailed guidelines about appropriate amounts, but ruled that until this is done, an approximate "interim litmus test" is for child support to be "20% of the gross income of the parties in the case of one child, and 32% in the case of a two child family."[11] This sum would ordinarily be apportioned between the parents in accordance with their incomes, taking account of the fact that in Canada child support is deductible by the payor, and taxable in the hands of the custodial parents. The approach of *Levesque*

---

7   Federal/Provincial/Territorial Family Law Committee, *Child Support: Public Discussion Paper* (1991, Ottawa); and *The Financial Implications of Child Support Guidelines: Research Reports* (1992, Ottawa).

8   (1994), 116 D.L.R. (4th) 314, 4 R.F.L. (4th) 375 (Alta. C.A.).

9   R.F.L. at 385.

10   R.F.L. at 391.

11   R.F.L. at 394.

results in substantially higher amounts of child support than Canadian courts have generally been awarding, which the Court of Appeal clearly intended. The expectation is that parents, especially non-custodial parents, should reduce their standard of living to support their children.

Soon after the Alberta Court of Appeal decided *Levesque*, the Supreme Court of Canada rendered a judgment in *Willick v. Willick*, another case that emphasized the inadequacy of child support awards. In *Willick*, the father agreed to pay $450 per month for each of his two children in a 1989 separation agreement, as well as $700 per month in spousal support. The agreement was incorporated into a consent divorce decree. By 1991, the father's income had more than doubled since the agreement was made, to about $8,500 per month, plus he received a $4,200 annual housing allowance. On a variation application the trial judge ordered the father's payments to be increased to $850 a month for each child, a decision ultimately affirmed by the Supreme Court of Canada.[12]

Writing for four of the seven members of the Court who heard the appeal, Sopinka J. emphasized the "narrow focus of this case".[13] He ruled that while a separation agreement "operates as strong evidence that at the time ... its terms ... adequately provide[d] for the needs of the children,"[14] it is not binding on a court as parents cannot "barter away" their children's right to support. In a case such as this, where the father's income more than doubled since the agreement was made, the courts have a discretion to overrule the earlier agreement. The children's needs are to be assessed by reference to the means of the parents, and a "significant increase in the means of the payor parent *may* require that the needs of the child include benefits that were not available."[15]

Madam Justice L'Heureux-Dubé, writing for herself and two other justices (including the only other woman on the Supreme Court), provided a broader discussion of child support, and indicated that awards in Canada have in general, been too low. L'Heureux-Dubé J. reviewed social and legal literature on the "context" of divorce, including recognition of the gendered nature of the effects of marital breakdown, and noted in particular "the significant level of poverty amongst children in single parent families and the

---

12   (1994), 6 R.F.L. (4th) 161 (S.C.C.).
13   R.F.L. at 173.
14   R.F.L. at 179.
15   R.F.L. at 182. Emphasis added.

failure of courts to contemplate hidden costs [of child rearing] in their calculation of child support awards."[16] While L'Heureux-Dubé J. was clearly critical of the existing Canadian pattern of child support, she did not endorse the specific target setting approach of *Levesque*. Indeed in *Willick* she appeared at best unenthusiastic about the prospect of legislative child support guidelines,[17] seeming to prefer to rely on the individualized discretion of the judiciary.

At the same time as the judiciary has begun to confront the issue of the inadequacy of the amounts of child support, there have been challenges to the constitutionality of Canada's tax laws governing child support. Under Canada's *Income Tax Act*[18] child and spousal support payments are deductible by the payor, but taxable in the hands of the recipient. When this scheme was established in the 1940s, payors (men) invariably had higher incomes and a higher marginal tax rate than the recipients of support (women), so that the scheme served as a form of "subsidy" to divorced families. At least in theory, this "subsidy" could be used for the benefit of the children and taken into account by judges and lawyers when the amounts of support are set.

However, advocates for women, the vast majority of recipients, have argued that too often in practice deductibility and inclusion are ignored by lawyers and judges at the time that initial support levels are set. Further, with the gradual increase of women's incomes relative to men's, more recipients have had *higher* incomes than payors, resulting in an extra tax burden for divorced families where child support is being paid. Government estimates suggest that there is a net "subsidy" to divorced families of about $330 million as a result of this scheme, with about 67% of the families being "winners" under the scheme (i.e., paying less tax in total than if child support were not deductible by the payor and not included in the income of the

---

16   R.F.L. at 192.
17   R.F.L. at 207. This is consistent with her approach to spousal support in *Moge v. Moge* [1992] 3 S.C.R. 813, and to the "best interests" of children in custody disputes in *Young v. Young*, [1993] 4 S.C.R. 3, 49 R.F.L. (3d) 117 1108 D.L.R. (4th) 193. In both cases L'Heureux-Dubé J. placed significant reliance on the discretion of judges.
18   *Income Tax Act*, S.C. 1970-71-72, c. 63, section 56(1)(b) and 60(b).

recipient), 29% being "losers" (i.e., paying more tax), and 4% finding it neutral.[19]

In 1994, the Federal Court of Appeal ruled in *Thibaudeau v. the Queen* that requiring recipients to pay income tax on child support violated the provisions of the *Charter of Rights* prohibiting discrimination.[20] Interestingly, the Court rejected an argument that the scheme discriminated on the basis of gender, even though the vast majority of recipients of child support are women and a feminist group intervened in support of the challenge. While the Court of Appeal accepted that the taxing of child support adversely impacts women, in that many more women than men are recipients, the Court felt that it could not be said that the law was discriminatory on the basis of gender in that custodial fathers are treated in the same way as custodial mothers.

The majority of the Court of Appeal did rule, however, that the taxation of child support discriminates against custodial parents on the basis of "family status". For example, a *non-separated* custodial parent is not required to include in taxable income payments received from her spouse for the purpose of supporting a child, while a separated *non-parent* having custody, such as a grandmother with custody of a child, is not required to pay tax on support received from a parent. While "family status" is not explicitly named as a prohibited ground of discrimination, the Court accepted it as an "analogous" ground of discrimination and ruled the provision unconstitutional.

The decision in *Thibaudeau* produced a vigorous dissent, and an appeal was argued in the Supreme Court of Canada in January 1995. It is far from certain that the Court of Appeal decision will be upheld by the Supreme Court. While the judgment does not expressly deal with the *deduction* of child support by payors under the *Income Tax Act*, it is certain that the government would respond to a Supreme Court decision upholding *Thibaudeau* by enacting legislation to remove deductibility, thereby reducing the total amount of funds available for child support. Arguably, on *average*,

---

19   *Thibaudeau v. Canada* (1994), 3 R.F.L. (4th) 153, 116 D.L.R. (4th) 261 (Fed. C.A.), at R.F.L. 180 and 186. As noted in the decision, some studies by non-government researchers indicate that the proportion of "winners" may be lower, perhaps just over 50%. See R.F.L. at 178.

20   *Canadian Charter of Rights and Freedoms*, Part I of the Constitution Act, 1982, being Schedule "B" of the Canada Act (U.K.), 1982, C. 11, section 15.

less money will be available for divorced women and their children if *Thibaudeau* is upheld, though a minority of them may be in a better position.

In January 1995, the Federal-Provincial-Territorial Family Law Committee issued its final report on Child Support Guidelines,[21] which recommended a model for payments based on a percentage of only the payor's income, with the percentage adjusted for the number of children and modified slightly at lower income levels. Assuming no changes in the tax law, the percentages work out to about 18% of the payor's gross income for one child, 30% for two children, and 37% for three children. The Committee recommended a strong presumption in favour of these guidelines, narrow grounds for deviation, and provision for periodic variation as the payor's income changes. Many lawyers are arguing that imposition of these proposed guidelines would now tend to result in lowering of average awards (which have been increasing, particularly since *Levesque* and *Willick*), though the existence of guidelines would permit the amounts of support to be determined relatively inexpensively.[22] The formula has also been criticized as being overly simplistic, and in particular for ignoring the income of the custodial parent as a factor is establishing amounts payable.

Since the release of the *Thibaudeau* decision by the Federal Court of Appeal in mid-1994, the federal government has been under increasing political pressure to deal with child support laws, both in their substantive and taxation aspects. While much of the initial impetus for change has come from women's groups, fathers are also organizing and lobbing government. The Minister of Justice has vaguely promised to "overhaul the system", but is awaiting the result of the Supreme Court decision in *Thibaudeau*.[23] Any changes in tax treatment of child support will affect the type of guidelines that might be imposed, while the changes in the child support award patterns are raising questions in some minds about whether it is appropriate to move

---

21 *Federal/Provincial/Territorial Family Law Committee's Report and Recommendations on Child Support* (Ottawa, 1995); available from Communications and Consultation Branch, Department of Justice Canada, Ottawa, Canada, K1A 0H8 (tel. 613 957-4222).

22 See, e.g., "Proposed child support guidelines too low?", *Lawyers Weekly*, Feb. 28, 1995, p. 1 & 24; and "Ont. Crt. hikes support award", *Lawyers Weekly*, March 31, 1995, p. 8. Some critics, however, are arguing that the guidelines are too high; see "N.S.C.A. child support award at odds with fed'l. guidelines", *Lawyers Weekly*, Mar. 23, 1995; and "Support rules unfair, report say", *Globe & Mail*, Feb. 24, 1995.

23 See, e.g., "Child support changes met with scepticism", *Globe & Mail*, Jan. 28, 1995.

to legislative guidelines at this time. A decision in *Thibaudeau* is expected in the summer of 1995, and government action by the autumn.

III INTERNATIONAL CHILD ABDUCTION: THE HAGUE CONVENTION

On October 20, 1994, the Supreme Court of Canada handed down its first decision under the Hague Convention on the Civil Aspects of International Child Abduction[24] ("the Convention"). *Thomson v. Thomson*[25] demonstrated Canada's commitment to the basic principle of the Convention – the protection of children from wrongful removal by ensuring their immediate return to their home jurisdiction. As well, the Supreme Court ruled that interim orders may not be imposed pursuant to domestic legislation to protect the best interests of children who are to be returned, but suggested that it may be possible to make such orders under the Convention itself. The decision also raised questions as to application of the Convention for the purpose of access enforcement.

The Thomsons were married in Scotland in 1991, and a son was born in 1992. The parents separated, and each sought custody of the child. On November 27, 1992, the mother was granted interim custody by a Scottish court, with interim access to the father. The judge ordered that the child remain in Scotland pending a further court order. On December 2, 1992, the mother left Scotland with the child, to stay with her parents in the province of Manitoba in Canada. While visiting her parents, the mother decided to settle in Canada, and she applied for custody in Manitoba on February 3, 1993. The same day, the custody hearing in Scotland was resumed, and the father was granted custody. On February 25, 1993, the father requested the return of the boy under the Convention. In March 1993, the father responded to the mother's Manitoba custody application with an application under Manitoba's *Child Custody Enforcement Act*[26] (CCEA) and under the Convention for the return of the child to Scotland. In April 1993, the mother appealed the Scottish grant of custody to the father, but her appeal was dismissed.

---

24 Can. T.S. 1983 No. 35.
25 (1994), 6 R.F.L. (4th) 290.
26 *The Child Custody Enforcement Act*, R.S.M. 1987, c.C360.

The Manitoba Court of Queen's Bench heard the father's application under both the Convention and the CCEA. The CCEA is the Manitoba legislation that adopts and implements the Convention (in Canada the Convention has been implemented through legislation enacted in each province and territory). The CCEA also provides for custody enforcement in non-Convention cases, and allows a court to make interim custody orders in relation to children who are to be returned to another jurisdiction for a custody determination. The judge determined that the mother's Scottish interim custody order did not include the right to determine the child's place of residence, and that the boy had been wrongfully removed and should be returned to Scotland pursuant to article 12 of the Convention. The judge then made a four-month interim custody order in favour of the mother pursuant to the provisions of the CCEA, on the basis that it would be in the best interests of the child to remain with the mother pending final determination of custody in Scotland.

The Manitoba Court of Appeal dismissed the mother's appeal, and her further appeal to the Supreme Court of Canada was also dismissed. In response to the concern that the father's Scottish custody order (characterized as a "chasing order") gave him the immediate right to custody and precluded return to the status quo as it existed before the wrongful removal, the Supreme Court accepted the father's undertakings not to take physical custody immediately on the boy's return, and to commence proceedings in Scotland to determine the custody issue on the merits. On the question of whether an interim custody order under the CCEA could be made to achieve the same result, LaForest J. for the majority said that a successful application under the Convention preempts a local custody application. If it is determined that the child is to be returned pursuant to the Convention, the court may not make an interim custody order pursuant to domestic legislation.

LaForest J. went on to say that if the father's undertaking had not been forthcoming or had not been acceptable, it might have been possible under the Convention itself to delay the return of the child to allow the mother to obtain interim custody in Scotland. Such a delay would protect the child from being immediately transferred to her father on his return to Scotland, pending final determination of the custody issue. This would be in keeping with the objective of the Convention to restore the status quo, which otherwise would be thwarted by the "chasing order". LaForest J. stated: "Faced with this situation, the court must be assumed to have sufficient control over its process to take the necessary action to meet the purpose and spirit of the Convention".[27]

On the issue of whether the removal or retention was wrongful, the Supreme Court first ruled that there had been a wrongful removal, because the non-removal clause of the mother's interim custody order preserved the jurisdiction in the Scottish court to determine the issue of custody on the merits in a full hearing. Therefore, the Scottish court became an institution with "rights of custody" immediately before the removal of the child, and the mother's breach of those custody rights constituted a wrongful removal within the meaning of the Convention.[28] The mother's removal did not breach the custody rights of the father, who had only an interim access order, but it did breach the custody rights of the court.

The Supreme Court was careful to limit its decision on the wrongful removal issue to cases of interim custody, and made clear that the same reasoning would not necessarily apply where there is a final custody order, even one with a non-removal clause. LaForest J., in his majority judgment, wrote:

> "It will be observed that I have underlined the purely interim nature of the mother's custody in the present case. I would not wish to be understood as saying the approach should be the same in a situation where a court inserts a non-removal clause in a permanent order of custody. Such a clause raises quite different issues. It is usually intended to ensure permanent access to the non-custodial parent. The right of access is, of course, important but, as we have seen, it was not intended to be given the same level of protection by the Convention as custody. The return of a child in the care of a person having permanent custody will ordinarily be far more disruptive to the child since the child may be removed from its habitual place of residence long after the custody order was made. The situation also has serious implications for the mobility rights of the custodian."[29]

---

27 (1984) 6 R.F.L. (4th) 290 at 334. L'Heureux-Dubé J., in a concurring judgment, took a different view on this point, and said that in some cases it would be appropriate to make an interim order under the domestic legislation, even where the child was to be returned pursuant to the Convention.

28 Here the Supreme Court was following the reasoning of Sir Stephen Brown P. in *B. v. B. (abduction: custody rights)*, [1993] 2 All E.R. 144 (C.A.).

29 (1994), 6 R.F.L. (4th) 290 at 323.

These obiter comments indicate that the Supreme Court may be unwilling to apply the Convention to enforce non-removal clauses in final custody orders by ordering the custodial parent to return the child.

On the issue of wrongful retention, the Supreme Court stated that the custody order granted to the father in Scotland after the mother had removed the child did not have the effect of making the retention of the child wrongful. In this case, the father's custody order was assumed to be in the nature of a "chasing order", granted to bolster the father's application for return of the child, rather than a determination on the merits of the custody issue. LaForest J. stated, "There is nothing in the Convention requiring the recognition of an ex post facto custody order of foreign jurisdictions".[30] The "chasing order" standing alone would not have been sufficient to ground a claim under the Convention. LaForest J. noted that in some British and Australian cases "chasing orders" have been granted to establish wrongful retention against a parent with a final custody order at the time of removal, and said that "such an approach taken against a custodial parent (other than one acting on an interim basis, as here) appears at first blush to be directed to protecting interests other than custody rights, to which the remedy of return of the child is confined under the Convention".[31]

In *Thomson*, the Supreme Court emphasized that return of a child would be ordered under the Convention only to protect custody and not access rights. *Thomson* suggests that an access parent will not be considered to have custody rights within the meaning of the Convention simply because the custodial parent does have the right to remove the child without the access parent's consent. In *Chalkley v. Chalkley*, a Canadian Convention case decided after *Thomson*, this issue arose but was not addressed; rather evidence that the mother's removal of the children was wrongful because it violated the father's rights of custody under the law of England was accepted, apparently without challenge by the mother or query by the court as to whether the father's "custody" rights fell within the definition of rights to be protected according to *Thomson*.[32]

In *Chalkley*, the issue that generated attention was whether the very limited exceptions to the rule of immediate return where there has been a

---

30 R.F.L. at 325.
31 R.F.L. at 326.
32 [1994] 10 W.W.R. 114 (Man. Q.B.); [1995] Man. J. No. 21 (Man. C.A.); leave to appeal to S.C.C. dismissed, L'Heureux-Dubé J. dissenting, March 30, 1995.

wrongful removal applied to each of the two children involved. The mother successfully argued that one of her children should not be returned to England, but her second child was ordered to be returned. The first child's serious medical condition and threats of suicide if she were returned to England satisfied the test of one of the exceptions in article 13, because there was "a grave risk" that her return would expose the child "to physical or psychological harm or otherwise place the child in an intolerable situation". Article 13 also allows an exception if the child "objects to being returned and has attained an age and degree of maturity at which it is appropriate to take account of its views". The child was 14 years old at the time of the hearing, and in view of her age and maturity it was found that her strong preference to remain in Canada should be given effect.

The second child was much younger, only two years old at the time of the hearing, and she did not suffer from any medical condition as did her sister. The Manitoba Court of Queen's Bench would have denied the return of the younger child as well, on the grounds that the grievous harm to which the older daughter would be exposed would occur whether both children were ordered to be returned or whether only the younger daughter were ordered to be returned. The Manitoba Court of Appeal upheld the decision that the older girl should not be returned, but allowed the father's appeal as it related to the younger child and ordered her immediate return. There was no evidence establishing that the younger child would suffer any risk from being returned, and it was an error to consider the evidence relating to one child in considering the return of another. The mother's application for leave to appeal to the Supreme Court of Canada was dismissed.

As noted above, the issue that was not addressed in *Chalkley* was the nature of the father's custody rights that were protected by the Convention. In *Chalkley*, as in *Thomson*, the mother was exercising day-to-day care and control of the children at the time she removed them to Canada. The mother had day-to-day care and control of the children after the father moved out of the marital home. The parties did not obtain a court order or make a written agreement as to custody, but for the first month after separation the consensual arrangement was that the children remained in the home with their mother, and their father visited them from time to time. Then the mother removed the children to Manitoba, Canada, in February 1994, without the father's knowledge or consent. The basis for finding that the mother's removal was wrongful was the affidavit of the Official Solicitor of the Supreme Court of England. The affidavit said that in England, pursuant to the *Children Act 1989*,[33] the concept of "custody" has been replaced by "parental responsibility", and that both parents in the Chalkleys' situation would have parental responsibility. It went on to say that

> where no order is in force in relation to the child, the removal of a child
> from the United Kingdom by a parent who is the holder of parental respon-
> sibility without the consent of the other parent who is also the holder of
> parental responsibility is wrongful as defined by Article 3 of the Hague
> Convention because it breaches the remaining parent's "rights of custody"
> as defined by Article 5; that is, the parental responsibility which that parent
> enjoys and enables him or her to care or make arrangements for the care
> of the child and, in particular, to determine the child's place of residence.
> Furthermore, such a removal is in breach of the provisions of the Child
> Abduction Act, 1984 which makes it an offence for a parent to take or send
> his child out of the United Kingdom without "appropriate consent" which
> means the consent of either the child's mother or the child's father if he
> has parental responsibility for him.[34]

The thrust of the domestic law of England, as explained by the Official Solicitor in this affidavit, appears to be that any parent with parental responsibility has "custody rights" within the meaning of the Convention, and that removal of a child by the other parent without consent will be wrongful and entitle the first parent to an order of return.[35] Since according to the law of England a parent who does not live with the children, does not have day-to-day care and control of the children, and who simply visits the children may still have "parental responsibility", the question is whether the Convention should be applied to protect the rights of such a parent, who in Canada would be considered to have "access" and not "custody" rights. The point

---

33 *Children Act 1989*, c.41.
34 [1994] 10 W.W.R. 114 at 118-19.
35 It would seem that even if the mother had obtained a "residence order" in England pur-
    suant to the *Children Act*, providing that the children would live with her, the position
    would have been the same. The *Children Act*, s.13(1)(b) specifically provides that a
    parent with a residence order may not remove the child from the United Kingdom
    without the consent of every person with parental responsibility or leave of the court
    [except for trips of less than a month pursuant to s.13(2)]. It should be noted that a
    "residence order" would not be made as a matter of course, because of the "no order"
    principle in the *Children Act*, s.1(5), which provides that a court shall not make an order
    "unless it considers that doing so would be better for the child than making no order
    at all."

was not raised or addressed in *Chalkley*, but in the light of LaForest J.'s obiter comments on this issue in *Thomson*, the question is bound to resurface.

IV RIGHTS OF PARENTS IN CHILD PROTECTION PROCEEDINGS

The Supreme Court of Canada has long held that where biological parents voluntarily surrender care of their children to individuals who become psychological parents, the "best interests" of the child will favour preserving continuity of care. Long-term psychological parents are invariably permitted to retain custody or proceed with an adoption despite challenges from biological parents.[36] In a 1994 decision the Supreme Court of Canada unanimously ruled that the same emphasis on continuity of care by psychological parents should apply where a child is taken into the custody of a state child protection agency and placed with foster parents who then want to adopt the child.

In *Catholic Children's Aid Society of Metropolitan Toronto v. C.M.*[37] a single mother had parenting difficulties and voluntarily sought the assistance of the child protection authorities. When the girl was two, the mother was hospitalized for psychiatric problems and the child came into agency care. The mother consented to an initial wardship order, and continued to visit with the child. About four months after the child came into care, the agency sought to have the mother's parental rights terminated and to have the child adopted. The initial hearing did not conclude for almost two years, but the original trial judge ultimately ordered the child to be returned to her mother's care. The agency appealed the decision through various court levels, with the child remaining in the care of a foster family selected by the agency pending resolution of the case. By the time the case reached the Supreme Court of Canada the child was 7 years of age. The mother had remarried and there was evidence that she was emotionally capable of caring for her

---

36 *King v. Low*, [1985] 1 S.C.R. 87, 44 R.F.L. (2d) 113; *Racine v. Woods* [1983] 2 S.C.R. 173, 36 R.F.L. (2d); and *Sawan v. Tearoe* (1993), 48 R.F.L. (3d) 392 (B.C.C.A.), leave to appeal to S.C.C. refused (1994), 3 R.F.L. (4th) 196.

37 [1994] 2 S.C.R. 165, 113 D.L.R. (4th) 321, 2 R.F.L. (4th) 313; some of the comments here about *C.M.* are an edited version of portions of Bala, "The Supreme Court and Best Interests of the Child" (1995), 6 *Supreme Court L.Rev.* (forthcoming) (Butterworths, Toronto).

child, but the child had a "strong negative reaction" to visits with the mother. The foster parents had "bonded" with the child and were eager to adopt her.

In *C.M.* the Supreme Court was called upon to apply Ontario's *Child and Family Services Act*,[38] which requires decisions about the return of a child to parental care to be based on the "best interests of the child." The Act contains a lengthy statutory definition of "best interests", and L'Heureux-Dubé J. acknowledged that a legislative scheme regulating intervention in family life by a state agency is not identical to the statutory provisions that govern private disputes between divorced or separated parents, even though the same basic phrase – "best interests of the child" – is used in both types of legislation.[39]

> "Equal competition between parents and the Children's Aid Society is not supported by the construction of the Ontario legislation. Essentially ... the Act has as one of its objectives the preservation of the autonomy and integrity of the family unit and that the child protection services should operate in the least restrictive and disruptive manner, while at the same time recognizing the paramount objective of protecting the best interests of children ..."

While recognizing the onus on the state agency to justify initial intervention in the family, and to establish that the child continues to be in need of protection by the state, L'Heureux-Dubé J. ultimately took a "flexible approach" when characterizing this type of hearing. In particular, once the child has been in the care of foster parents, the court must consider not only whether the biological parent is fit to resume care of her child, but also must consider the emotional harm that might result from removal of a child from her "psychological parents" (i.e. the foster parents).

The ultimate decision in *C.M.* may well be justifiable in terms of the particular case before the Court, where the child had spent some five years with the foster parents. However, a consideration of the "context" and implications of this type of decision is lacking in *C.M.* There is no discussion of the fact that child protection cases typically involve biological parents of limited educational, social and economic background litigating against state agencies with staff and foster parents who have a higher social and

---

38   R.S.O. 1990, c.C.11, s.37(3).
39   R.F.L. at 342.

economic position. Often in Canada the biological parent is a member of a visible minority group or aboriginal, while staff and foster parents are generally white. Although child protection agencies face budget constraints, to the parents they appear to be massive institutions with seemingly limitless resources, while parents are usually represented by lawyers on legal aid certificates.

In developing her analysis, L'Heureux-Dubé J. cited various Canadian precedents, but most of these were cases involving "private disputes" between biological parents and psychological parents who had gained custody as a result of direct, voluntary placement with them by a biological parent.[40] What is disappointing is not the conclusion on the facts in *C.M.*, but the Court's failure even to address the underlying social and legal issues that arise in this type of litigation.

The "psychological parent" and "bonding" analysis developed in *C.M.* is based on a theory originally propounded by the American mental health professionals Goldstein, Freud and Solnit in 1973 in their book *Beyond the Best Interests of the Child.*[41] While L'Heureux-Dubé J. does not explicitly cite their theories in *C.M.*, they clearly lie at the root of her analysis.[42] Regrettably, she failed to acknowledge that the significance of concepts like "psychological parent" is quite controversial among mental health professionals. There is a large literature challenging the significance of these concepts for determining whether to terminate the rights of biological parents of children in foster care.[43] American courts,[44] after thorough discussion of conflicting theories, have not placed nearly as much weight on the work of Goldstein, Freud and Solnit as the Supreme Court of Canada did in *C.M.* The debate over concepts like "psychological parent" will not be easy to resolve, but it is disappointing that in *C.M.* the controversy was not even addressed.

---

40 See e.g. *King v. Low* [1985] 1 S.C.R. 87, 44 R.F.L. (2d) 113; 16 D.L.R. (4th) 576.

41 (1973), New York, The Free Press.

42 Interestingly L'Heureux-Dubé J. cites their work in her decision in *Young* (1993), 49 R.F.L. (3d) 117 at 180 as supporting limitations on the rights of access parents, but makes no *explicit* reference to their work in *C.M.*

43 See, e.g., P.C. Davis, "Use and Abuse of the Power to Sever Family Bonds" (1983-84), 12 *Rev. L. & Soc. Change* 557; D. Fanshel, "Urging Restraint in Terminating the Rights of Parents of Children in Foster Care" (1983-84), 12 *Rev. L. & Soc. Change* 501; and T.L. Mosikalsana, "Case Comment: Sawan v. Tearoe" (1993), 11 *Can. F.L.Q.* 89.

44 See e.g. *Matter of Guardianship of J.C.*, 608 A 2d 1312 (N.J. 1992).

By way of contrast to the unanimous Supreme Court decision in *C.M.*, the January 1995 case of *R.B. v. Children's Aid Society of Metropolitan Toronto*[45] revealed a Supreme Court that was deeply split over whether, *in principle*, parents should enjoy constitutional rights in litigation with a child protection agency.

R.B. arose out of a case where Jehovah's Witness parents were refusing, on religious grounds, a blood transfusion for a new born child suffering infantile glaucoma. Doctors felt that surgery, which would require a blood transfusion, was necessary to save the child's life. A court order was sought by the child protection agency to have the child made a temporary ward of the agency. The trial judge made the order, and the agency consented to the operation and transfusion. Although the operation was concluded and the child returned to parental custody, the parents appealed the original decision on the ground that it had violated their constitutional rights to a relationship with their child. After a lengthy appeal process, the Supreme Court of Canada upheld the original order and the constitutional validity of the child protection legislation in question. However, the Supreme Court divided sharply over the broader question of whether there were any circumstances in which the Constitution might apply to this type of case.

Justice La Forest, writing for four of the nine justices, adopted a constitutional analysis which was originally developed in the United States[46] and recognized that parents have a constitutionally-protected interest in their relationship with their children. In particular, the concepts of "liberty and security of the person", protected in section 7 of Canada's *Charter of Rights and Freedoms*, include a significant element of parental rights. Accordingly, state action to restrict parental autonomy must accord with the "principles of fundamental justice". Justice La Forest wrote:[47]

"our society is far from having repudiated the privileged role parents exercise in the upbringing of their children. This role translates into a protected sphere of parental decision-making which is rooted in the presumption that

---

45 [1994] S.C.J. No. 24, released Jan. 27, 1995.

46 See e.g. *Meyer v. Nebraska*, 262 U.S. 390 (1923); *Stanley v. Illinois* 405 U.S. 645 (1972). This analysis was long advocated by Canadian legal scholars; see e.g. Bala & Redfearn, "Family Law and the 'Liberty Interest': Section 7 of the Canadian Charter of Rights" (1983), 15 *Ottawa L. Rev.* 274, quoted by La Forest J. in *R.B.*

47 At para. 85.

parents should make important decisions affecting their children both because parents are more likely to appreciate the best interests of their children and because the state is ill-equipped to make such decisions itself. Moreover, individuals have a deep personal interest as parents in fostering the growth of their own children. This is not to say that the state cannot intervene when it considers it necessary to safeguard the child's autonomy or health. But ... parental decision-making must receive the protection of the Charter in order for state interference to be properly monitored by the courts, and be permitted only when it conforms to the values underlying the Charter."

While the legislation and state action in this case did satisfy the requirements of "fundamental justice", and hence was constitutionally valid, if the approach of La Forest J. is followed, there may well be situations in which parents can invoke the constitution to protect their rights.[48]

While La Forest J., with three other judges concurring, took a broad view of parental rights, four other judges of the Supreme Court took a narrow view of any *constitutional* rights that parents might have. Justices Iacobucci and Major expressed a concern that "the family is often a very dangerous place for children",[49] and felt that any concern about parental "liberty" must be balanced against the child's constitutionally protected rights to "security of the person". The difficulty with this analysis in a case like *R.B.* is that the child lacked the capacity to articulate any views, and the effect of this type of argument is that a state agency can purport to use the *child's* constitutional rights to limit parental rights.

The ninth judge, Sopinka J., refused to issue an opinion on whether section 7 of the *Charter of Rights and Freedoms*, with its protection of "liberty and security of the person", included parental rights, but did conclude that the parents in this particular case were entitled to some constitutional protection for their religious freedom, an interest protected by section 2 of the *Charter*. The four judges who took a broad view of section 7, as including parental rights, agreed that parental religious freedom was infringed in a child protection proceeding if religious beliefs are the basis for resistance to state interference with the child.

---

48   See e.g. Zylberberg, "Minimum Constitutional Guarantees in Child Protection Cases" (1992), 10 *Can. J. Fam. L.* 257-281.

49   Para 219.

The judicial division of opinion in *R.B.* about whether parents involved in child protection proceedings have constitutionally recognized procedural rights to due process probably reflects a deeper division of views about the role of the state in family life. While the disagreement did not affect the outcome in the specific situation before the Court, it is likely that future cases will require the Court to address directly the issue and provide some judicial resolution to this controversy.

V SAME-SEX COUPLES

In 1994, there were legislative reform initiatives at both the federal and the provincial level aimed at diminishing discrimination against homosexuals and expanding the rights of same-sex couples. Although these initiatives did not actually result in legislative change, the federal government has indicated that it will proceed with its efforts at legislative reform in 1995, and it is expected that Canada will continue to broaden the equality rights of gay and lesbian individuals and couples. In addition to the efforts at legislative reform, there were court challenges in which it was argued that legislative definitions of "spouse" that did not include same-sex partners discriminated on the basis of sexual orientation, thereby violating the equality rights guaranteed by the *Charter of Rights and Freedoms*. As well, some employers voluntarily extended "spousal" benefits to the same-sex partners of their employees,[50] while others who attempted to exclude same-sex partners from "spousal" benefits were successfully challenged in grievances under the anti-discrimination clauses of collective agreements.[51]

With regard to law reform efforts, the federal government introduced Bill C-41,[52] which would allow for stronger penalties for hate crimes, including crimes motivated by hatred for homosexuals. The problem of crime

---

50 Dennis Slocum, "TD Gives Gay Couples Benefits", *Globe & Mail*, Dec. 30, 1994. Some employers, however, have resisted voluntary extension of benefits to same-sex partners, despite vigorous requests from employees, on the grounds that current Canadian legislation does not require it: Dennis Slocum, "Imperial Oil Rejects Same-sex Benefits", *Globe & Mail*, Apr. 20, 1995.

51 *Canadian Telephone Employees' Association v. Bell Canada* (1994), 43 L.A.C. (4th) 172.

52 Bill C-41, *Act to amend the Criminal Code (sentencing) and other Acts thereof*, 1st Sess., 35th Parl. Canada, 1994.

motivated by homophobic intolerance received considerable attention in 1994, in part because of public hearings held by the Quebec Human Rights Commission, at which evidence was presented that 14 homosexual men were murdered in Montreal over the previous four years, and that an average of one serious physical assault is reported to Quebec's gay community hotline each day. Bill-41 became stalled at the committee stage, and faced vocal opposition by renegade members of the majority Liberal government, who vowed to vote against it on the grounds that it violated the country's moral values and gave special status to homosexuals. It is expected that Bill C-41 will be brought to a vote in 1995.

The federal government has promised to introduce further legislative changes after Bill C-41 has been dealt with, in particular, amendments to the *Canadian Human Rights Act* to add sexual orientation to the list of prohibited grounds of discrimination with regard to areas of federal responsibility.[53] The amendment will bring the *Canadian Human Rights Act* into conformity with current court rulings, which have held that sexual orientation must be "read into" the prohibited grounds of discrimination in the Act, because otherwise the Act itself would violate the *Charter of Rights and Freedoms* protection against discrimination.[54]

A related matter under consideration by the federal government is the issue of "spousal" benefits for the same-sex partners of federal employees. Currently the federal government is faced with many individual claims for spousal benefits for same-sex couples, and legislative reform would eliminate the current problems of dealing with the issue on a case-by-case basis. The government has expressed support for extending benefits to those who are in a relationship of interdependency similar to that of common-law or married couples,[55] and has withdrawn its appeal of a labour arbitration ruling that awarded a gay federal employee the same family-leave benefits enjoyed by heterosexual employees.[56] The government's support for same-sex benefits will probably take the form of legislative amendments in 1995.

---

53 The provinces of British Columbia, Manitoba, New Brunswick, Nova Scotia, Ontario, Quebec, and Saskatchewan, and the Yukon Territory already prohibit discrimination on the basis of sexual orientation for matters within their jurisdiction, such as public services, housing, employment, and professional and trade association memberships.

54 *R. v. Haig and Birch* (1992), 9 O.R. (3d) 495 (C.A.).

55 Geoffrey York, "Benefits Proposal Praised", *Globe & Mail*, May 28, 1994.

56 Margaret Philp, "Ottawa Acquiesces on Gay Spousal Leave", *Globe & Mail*, 15 April 1995.

The Supreme Court heard an appeal in *Egan v. Canada*,[57] an important case on the rights of same-sex couples in November 1994, and reserved its decision. In *Egan*, the Federal Court of Appeal ruled that the definition of "spouse" in the *Old Age Security Act*, which was limited to married and cohabiting heterosexual partners, was not discriminatory, because it was based on spousal status rather than sexual orientation.[58] Other persons, e.g., two sisters living together, were not included in the definition of "spouse", and there was no reason to extend benefits to one group – same-sex couples – that did not meet the definition and not to others. The result of the decision was that Egan's homosexual partner of 47 years was not entitled to claim spousal benefits from Egan's pension, although an unmarried heterosexual partner could have obtained such benefits. The *Egan* case will provide the Supreme Court of Canada with an opportunity to make a ruling on the role of the *Charter* in defining same-sex rights.

In particular, the Supreme Court of Canada will be able to make a ruling on whether or not sexual orientation is a prohibited ground of discrimination covered by the *Charter*. The *Charter* enumerates prohibited grounds of discrimination, but "analogous grounds" are covered as well, and the test to be applied is whether the group is a "discrete and insular minority" that historically has suffered discrimination by virtue of a personal characteristic.[59] Many judgments have accepted that sexual orientation is an analogous ground of discrimination covered by the *Charter* (including the Federal Court of Appeal in *Egan*, which accepted this as settled law,[60] although it ruled against Egan and Nesbit on another basis), and it is widely expected that the Supreme Court of Canada will confirm this. The implications of a ruling in favour of Egan and Nesbit that the exclusion of same-sex couples from the provisions of the *Old Age Security Act* violates their *Charter* rights would

---

57 *Egan and Nesbit v. Her Majesty the Queen in Right of Canada* (1992), 87 D.L.R. (4th) 320 (Fed.Ct. T.D.); (1993), 103 D.L.R. (4th) 336 (Fed. C.A.); leave to appeal to the Supreme Court of Canada granted.

58 *The Old Age Security Act*, R.S.C. 1985, c. 0-9, defines "spouse" as including, in relation to any person, a person of the opposite sex who is living with that person, having lived with that person for at least one year, if the two persons have publicly represented themselves as husband and wife.

59 *Andrews v. The Law Society of British Columbia*, [1989] 1 S.C.R. 143 at 182.

60 *Egan and Nesbit v. Her Majesty the Queen in Right of Canada* (1993), 103 D.L.R. (4th) 336 (F.C.A.) at 381.

be far-reaching, and would necessitate a review of all federal statutes to ensure that gay and lesbian couples are treated equally.

At the provincial level, the Ontario government introduced ambitious legislation that would have extended to same-sex couples the same rights enjoyed by heterosexual common law couples, including the right to claim spousal support from a same-sex partner, the right to spousal benefits, and the right to adopt children.[61] Ontario had already enacted legislation giving a homosexual partner the same right as a heterosexual partner or spouse to consent to medical treatment in cases where the other partner lacked capacity to give consent,[62] but Bill-167, the 1994 legislative proposal, went much further. The social democratic government allowed its members to have a free vote on the legislation. When it became clear that Bill-167 was not going to pass, the government offered to amend the Bill to make it more palatable to a majority, in particular by removing the provision that would have allowed same-sex couples to adopt children.[63] Despite removal of the adoption clause that many had objected to, Bill 167 was narrowly defeated in a free vote, on June 9, 1994. Supporters were frustrated by the defeat, and some activists responded by planning to launch a vigorous programme of court challenges to the approximately 75 provincial statutes and more than 200 federal statutes that arguably discriminate against same-sex couples, thereby continuing the pressure to enact legislative reforms.[64]

One important court challenge to Ontario legislation is *M. v. H.*, in which the plaintiff is arguing that the exclusion of same-sex partners from the right to claim spousal support on the breakdown of a relationship violates the guarantee of equality in the *Charter*.[65] Ontario's *Family Law Act* provides that heterosexual couples who have lived together for at least three years or who have had a child together in a relationship of some permanence may claim spousal support from one another.[66] The plaintiff in *M. v. H.* is asking the court to include same-sex couples in the current statutory regime, so that parties like herself who have cohabited in a same-sex relationship for

---

61   Bill 167, *An Act to Amend Ontario Statutes to Provide for the Equal Treatment of Persons in Spousal Relationships*, 3rd Sess., 35th Leg. Ont., 1994.

62   *Consent to Treatment Act*, 1992, S.O. 1992, C.31, proclaimed in force April 3, 1995.

63   "Boyd Backs Off on Gay Spouses", *Globe & Mail*, June 9, 1994.

64   John Beaufoy, "Lawyers Plan to Challenge Laws After Defeat of Bill 167", *The Law Times*, June 20-26, 1994, p.1.

65   (1994), 1 R.F.L. (4th) 413 (Ont. Gen. Div.).

66   *Family Law Act*, R.S.O. 1990, c.F.3, s.29.

at least three years could claim spousal support. This case is on hold pending the Supreme Court of Canada decision in the *Egan* case.[67]

Alberta, Prince Edward Island, Newfoundland, and the Northwest Territories are the only Canadian jurisdictions that have no prohibited discrimination on the grounds of sexual orientation in their human rights legislation. In Alberta, the constitutional validity of the province's *Individual Rights Protection Act*[68] was successfully challenged in *Vriend v. Alberta*, on the basis that the failure to include sexual orientation as a prohibited ground of discrimination violated the *Charter* guarantee of equality.[69] The remedy granted by the Alberta Court of Queen's Bench was to "read into" the legislation the missing ground of discrimination, thus clearing the way for Mr Vriend to challenge his dismissal for homosexuality from employment as a teacher.

Reducing discrimination against individuals on the basis of their sexual orientation and expanding the spousal benefits available to same-sex couples will continue to receive a great deal of attention in Canada, as legislatures and Parliament continue to be pressured to catch up with the rulings of courts and administrative bodies that declare existing laws unconstitutional. Politicians seem willing, at present, to have judges take the lead in dealing with this controversial issue.

VI ABORTION: CONTROVERSY OVER ACCESSIBILITY

In 1988 the Supreme Court of Canada ruled unconstitutional the provisions of the *Criminal Code* that controlled access to abortion services,[70] and the year following the Court decided that the putative father of an unborn child has no standing to restrict a woman's right to an abortion.[71] In 1991 an attempt in Parliament to reimpose a criminal law regulating abortion was narrowly defeated.[72] Since then there has been no serious effort at the

---

67 Martha A. McCarthy, "Recognition of Same-sex Spouses is an Issue of Rights *and* Responsibilities", *The Lawyers Weekly*, Feb. 24, 1995, p.10.
68 *Individual's Rights Protection Act*, S.A. 1980, c.1-2.
69 *Vriend v. Alberta*, [1994] A.J. No. 272 (Alta. Q.B.).
70 *R. v. Morgentaler*, [1988] 1 S.C.R. 30, 37 C.C.C. (3d)449.
71 *Daigle v. Tremblay*, [1989] 2 S.C.R. 530, 62 D.L.R. (4th) 634.
72 See Bailey & Bala, "Canada: Abortion, Divorce and Poverty" (1992), 30 *Univ. Louisville J.F.L.* 279, 279-281.

national level to legislate with respect to abortion, though some individual candidates were elected in the 1993 federal election with a strongly "pro-life" stance.

The major focus of efforts of "pro-life" activists in Canada has been in demonstrating at abortion clinics, and in lobbying provincial governments to use their jurisdiction over health care to restrict access to abortions. Demonstrations by "pro-life" activists have been directed at women entering abortion clinics, as well as at the homes and offices of doctors who perform abortions. There have also been incidents of violence, including the 1992 bombing of a Toronto abortion clinic, and in 1994 the near fatal shooting of a doctor in Vancouver who performed abortions.[73] As a consequence of pressure, lobbying and demonstrating, many doctors and hospitals have been unwilling to perform abortions, and women in many places in Canada have had to travel to the few major cities where there are free standing abortion clinics.

In 1994, the government of Ontario, which is strongly "pro-choice", was able to obtain a court injunction to restrict the activities of protesters.[74] While recognizing that the injunction constituted a restriction on the protesters' constitutionally protected freedom of expression, the court gave precedence to protection of the privacy interests of women in ordering protesters to remain at least 60 feet away from the abortion clinics. Further the court ruled that picketing of doctors' residences had an intimidating effect, and ordered protesters to remain at least 500 feet from their homes.

A Prince Edward Island court ruled that an attempt by the provincial government sympathetic to a "pro-life" position to restrict public funding for abortions was *ultra vires*.[75] The government promulgated regulations restricting payment by the public medical care plan for abortion services only when performed in hospitals and determined to be "medically required" by the Health and Community Services Agency. The court held that the regulation was based on "social and moral perceptions of undesirable con-

---

73 See e.g. "Shooting unbelievable: B.C. doctor recalls", *Globe & Mail*, Dec. 15, 1994; and "Abortion: The Last Gasp Death Threats, Physical Attacks, Covert Harassment", *Globe & Mail*, January 28, 1995.

74 *Attorney General of Ontario v. Dieleman* (1994), 20 O.R. (3d) 229 (Ont. Gen. Div.). The British Columbia government is also considering enacting legislation to protect abortion clinics; see e.g. "How to protect clinics? B.C. ponders law to deter anti-abortion violence", *Globe & Mail*, January 5, 1995.

75 *Morgentaler v. Prince Edward Island*, [1995] P.E.I.J. 20 (S.C.).

duct", and ruled the regulation was inconsistent with provincial health care funding states. While there remains pressure on some provincial governments to end all funding for abortions,[76] such a step would likely violate Canada's national public health insurance legislation.[77]

VII CONCLUSION

Judicial decisions and legislative initiatives in 1994 demonstrated a continuing concern with the interests of children, but relatively little consideration of the rights of children. The rights of parents, on the other hand, received considerable attention. Discussion of the extent to which Canada will provide constitutional protection for parental rights will continue, as will consideration of the application of the Hague Convention to protect parental access rights. With regard to same-sex couples, legislative defeats have been discouraging to gay and lesbian rights advocates, but given the court rulings under the *Charter of Rights and Freedoms*, legislative action at some point will become inevitable. Abortion rights have been maintained in Canada, but these legal rights may be undermined by threats posed to the availability of services by guerilla tactics from "pro-life" activists and continuing financial pressures on the Canadian health system.

---

76 "On public funding of abortions", *Globe & Mail*, April 7, 1995.
77 See "Morgentaler seeking full funding for N.S. clinics", *Globe & Mail*, February 4, 1995.

CHILE

A NEW PATRIMONIAL REGIME IN MARRIAGE

*Inés Pardo de Carvallo**

I   INTRODUCTION

On September 23, 1994, Law no. 19.335 was published in the Official Journal of the Republic of Chile establishing modifications to legislation in the areas of patrimonial regimes in marriage, adoption, alimony, the decriminalisation of adultery and other topics of lesser importance.

The reform constituted an advance in the field of equality of rights between spouses in the administration and disposition of the property of the marriage, in as far as both agree to adopt the new system, but this still has not produced the absolute equality between the parties that would be desirable.

In this article we will analyse the most relevant aspects of the modifications, but will limit ourselves to commenting only on those that have a direct relation to the marital regime.

II   THE REGIME OF PARTICIPATION IN PROFITS OF THE MARRIAGE

A   *Characteristics*

1   The regime established by Law no. 19.335 is contractual and consequently optional or elective. It is contractual in that for it to govern the relationship between spouses it must first have been adopted by the parties.

However, while the source of creation is contractual, its development and application is meticulously regulated by the law, which in certain cases prohibits any agreement or contract on specific matters, such as terminating the operation of the regime.

The regime may be assumed before contracting marriage in the civil marriage contract, in the act of marriage itself or during its subsequent existence. In this last example, the spouses will substitute the regime of

---

*   Professor of Law, Catholic University of Valparaíso. Translated by Andrew Burge LLB (Bris.).

A. Bainham (ed.), The International Survey of Family Law 1994, 145–154.

conjugal society for that of participation or of total or partial separation of goods under the new system.

The law changes in part the principle of immutability of the total separation of property which, up to the enactment of the new law, was absolute in our legislation.

Spouses that are now governed by a system of total legal or contractual separation of property may agree to participate in the increases in the value of each patrimony that occurred during the marriage (to be subsequently referred to as the profits of the marriage).

2   It is a mixed regime. There is patrimonial separation, in that at no time does there exist unity of property or debts during the existence or the dissolution of the marriage. There is no common mass. This separatist characteristic guarantees the reciprocal economic independence of the spouses.

Each one administers his or her property, uses it, enjoys it, collects any income and disposes of it independently, save in a few exceptions that will be indicated.

Only at the end of the system is there participation in the excess profits of the marriage after adjustments, which is referred to as a credit. This is the only time that the new system reflects the community property system.

3   It is a form of participation that is purely lump sum and calculable, and applies only to the profits of the marriage, if there are any.

In the Chilean system, the division is by halves. The law will not accept a participation by any other proportion, as occurs for example in Spanish legislation, where under Article 1429 of the Civil Code a different distribution is permitted in some situations.

There is no participation in the losses which must be borne by the spouse that suffered them.

4   The pact of participation does not admit any condition, time period or mode of operation.

5   It is a solemn agreement and subject to the observance of formalities. There are three different formulas:
a) Where it is made between the parties before the marriage by Deed and a subinscription is made in the margin of the inscription of marriage at the moment of celebration or within the following 30 days.

b) If it is agreed in the act of marriage, the spouses will declare this accordingly before the official of the civil registry, who will include it in the inscription.

c) If the spouses decide to adopt the regime during the marriage, they will have to do so by Deed and subinscribe in the margin of the inscription of marriage within 30 days thereafter.

B   Analysis of the System

1   Dominion of the property
Each spouse is the exclusive owner of the property that is in their name, regardless of whether at the time of coming under their patrimony the property was acquired for value or gratuitously.

Thus, the spouse is the owner of the property from when it is acquired and maintains the real rights over it while it is not alienated. The dominion of the things that are in a spouse's name does not change because of the matrimonial regime. There are not cases, as occurs in conjugal partnerships, of conversion of a real right into a personal right. Consequently there are two patrimonies. Those of the husband and those of the wife.

However, in order to determine what the law defines as profits of the marriage, it is necessary to consider the patrimonial collection of property and in the first place analyse the initial patrimony, a concept that only has importance at the end of the regime rather than during its existence. This essentially means that which each spouse had at the beginning of the marriage.

The law establishes that the spouses or those contemplating marriage must make an inventory of property at the moment of electing to participate in the new system.

In the absence of an inventory, the patrimony may be proved by means of other instruments, such as registers, receipts or credit titles.

To this original patrimony must be added any property acquired for value during the existence of the system, whose origin or title of acquisition precedes participation in the system.

Gratuitous acquisitions must be considered as property of the original patrimony with a previous deduction of charges. If both parties receive gratuitous title, then their respective patrimonies will be increased by the proportions of their interest in the gratuitous title, or in equal parts if such proportions can not be established.

Conversely, the following will not be considered as part of the original patrimony: profits generated by the property of the spouses, including those provided by the initial collection of property, interests in mines owned by one of them, remuneratory donations, property subsequently acquired for value or income of any type.

2　Administration

All the movable or immovable goods acquired by one spouse, whether for value or gratuitously and regardless of the moment of incorporation, are administered exclusively by them.

While the law does not expressly make the distinction, we must be clear that we are dealing with spouses of full capacity. If they were not of full capacity, as for example with minors or someone whose capacity has been diminished in some way, then the rules of guardianship would be applied.

The separation of administration is practically all embracing. The only exceptions are:

a)　The situation where the spouses, both being owners of property, form between them a community which is governed by the rules of this quasi-contract. This will apply to property acquired for value or gratuitously.

b)　Sureties personally given to guarantee the obligations of third parties. To be valid, this type of attached obligation requires the consent of the other spouse. An absence of authority nullifies the guarantee. The law characterizes this as relative nullity and establishes a time period of four years for the commencement of an action, commencing the day that the spouse that challenges the act first had knowledge of it. However no action may be brought more than ten years after the completion of the act or the contract.

The legislation does not give any guidelines on the level of proof required to establish knowledge, and this absence will give rise to numerous arguments between the parties.

c)　The alienation or encumbering, the promise of alienation or encumbering or the concession of personal rights of use and enjoyment to a third party of family property in which the volition of both spouses is required, under penalty of nullification.

3 Termination of the Regime

The law specifies the causes for which the regime terminates. These are:

a) The death of one of the spouses. The demise of the husband or wife puts an end to the regime of property. Unlike the B.G.B. code in Germany, there is not envisaged a separate form of liquidation in this event.

b) By presumption of death of one of the spouses. The provisional decree of possession of the property of the missing spouse puts an end to the regime.

c) By declaration of nullity of the marriage. The law does not consider the different forms that this can take, which are: simple nullification of marriage or a putative marriage.

If the marriage was simply nullified, it is said that there was never good faith nor just cause of error on behalf of either of the participants and neither the marriage nor the regime of property will ever have existed, so as such the system is terminated. The reality is that there was never a patrimonial state, and each one being the owner of the goods that appear in his or her name will continue in this manner without the possibility of demanding credit for profits of the marriage.

A different situation is produced if the marriage was putative, as the regime will have been created and will have produced its own effects while there lasted good faith and just cause of error on the part of at least one of the parties.

d) By Sentence of Perpetual Divorce. When a divorce is granted for one of the reasons indicated by the Law of Civil Marriage, and bearing in mind that in Chilean legislation a divorce does not dissolve the marriage bond, the regime of participation will end and the spouses will be considered as completely separated in terms of property.

e) By a Judgement that Declares the Separation of Property. Where the regime of participation in profits of the marriage exists, the husband or the wife may request the judicial separation of the property for reasons indicated by the Civil Code, the Law of Civil Marriage or the Law concerning Abandonment of the Family and Alimony.

C Effects of the Dissolution of the Regime

Once the cause for dissolution exists or in some areas has been proven, the process for the determination of any possible participation of one party in the share of the profits of the marriage of the other begins.

1 Determination of Final Patrimony

The first stage of the process is the double valuation. Within three months following the end of the regime, the law obliges the spouse (though it should say the spouse, beneficiary or transferee according to the manner in which the regime terminated) to prepare and deliver a signed and valued inventory detailing the property that comprises his or her final patrimony (the first valuation). From this list is excluded property of personal use and furniture acquired during the regime. This last category is presumed to be communal unless there is contrary proof. Such proof must be contained in written antecedents.

There is, therefore, a presumption of communal dominion in relation to moveable property, of which half of the value will correspond to the patrimony of each party.

The inventory will also refer to the obligations that comprise the final patrimony at the same date.

The time period of three months may be extended by the judge for one further period of three months. This is a period of judicial grace that may or may not be granted in each case.

The inventory will serve as proof in favour of the other spouse in determination of the final patrimony, and may be challenged by him or her on the grounds that it is not reliable, and in this event all the probative means permitted by law are available. Without prejudice to the above, any of the spouses may request the solemn, notarized verification of the inventory.

The property is valued in the state in which it exists at the time of the dissolution of the system, a determination that may be effected by the spouses, by a third party or by the judge in a subsidiary role.

2 Liabilities will be determined in the same way

Is the valuation unilateral or must it be made jointly? The law is not clear. In my opinion it must be made by both parties, and if they are not in agreement it will be referred to the judge for decision.

In a complementary rule in relation to the determination of the final patrimony, the law makes further provision against what is referred to as the concealment or exclusion of property from the inventory or the creation of false obligations by one of the spouses, with the intention of reducing the value of their final patrimony. These provisions carry the consequence of a penalty of double the value of the property or of the debts excluded or concealed.

The final patrimony of a spouse, determined in accordance with the above mentioned rules, may be increased by certain aggregations which the law defines as "imaginary additions".

There will be accredited sums by which the assets have been reduced as a consequence of acts done during the existence of the system and corresponding to:

a   Irrevocable donations

b   Fraudulent acts or squandering

c   Certain specific payments or expenses made or incurred by a spouse.

a   Irrevocable Donations

If one of the spouses has made donations which do not correspond to the proportionate fulfillment of moral debts or social uses, then these total amounts donated must be included in his or her inventory.

It is worth asking what is meant by "moral debts". They would be to our understanding, gratuitous distributions that do not constitute an obligation as such and are motivated by a conscientious imperative, for example maintenance paid to a distant relative, indirect relation or contributions to charitable institutions etc. It would not appear that these amounts are cumulative to the assets. Neither will donations given on marriage, birthdays etc. be collated.

b   Fraudulent acts or Squandering

If the assets of a spouse have been disminished as a consequence of the perpetration of fraudulent acts or by the squandering by one spouse to the prejudice of the other, the corresponding amount will be included.

With regard to the acts of squandering, it is necessary to take into account that the only sums that will be accredited are those that represent the value of property which has left the patrimony of the squanderer, if the intention of the act or contract was to prejudice the other party. If there was no such intention (a matter which must be proved) then they are not accumulated.

c   Certain specific payments or expenses of the spouse
Finally, the law orders the accumulation of payments of the price of annuities
and pension schemes and other expenses that ensure a future income to the
spouse ... with the exception of those made through the social security systems.

If property was alienated to effect the donation, fraudulent act or the
purchase of a future income, it must be considered in the state in which it
existed at the time of its alienation. The above mentioned accumulations
will not be made if the acts were made with the consent of the other spouse.

It is not surprising that the authorization of the other spouse, a type of
veiled renunciation of the right to collation, is considered by the legislator
as releasing in the case of donations or of payments for future income, but
faced with the supposed "fraudulent acts or squandering", how can
authorization impede collation?

It is difficult to imagine a case in which an injured spouse, knowing that
an act of fraud is intended, will give prior consent. If the spouse did not
know that the act was fraudulent and was deceived or surprised by the other
spouse and gave his or her authorization, the law does not give the right
to effect the collation, a situation that appears unjust to us. We believe that
the injured party should be able to request the invalidation of the act in
accordance with the general law, as long as the action is not out of time.

Once the final patrimony has been determined, this figure must be
compared to that of the original patrimony, which must be calculated according to the state of the property at the time of entering the system or the
aquisition of the property (the second valuation).

From the fixed value must be deducted the value of obligations that were
in existence on the same date.

If the liabilities were greater than the assets then the original patrimony
will be taken as having been without value, or an initial patrimony of zero.

The value (the law says price) of the original patrimony is thus determined, and will be prudently increased to reflect inflation up to the date
of the termination of the system. It may be difficult to determine the value
that the property had at the time of entry into the system, especially if the
regime has lasted for a long period of time.

If the final patrimony of a spouse results in a smaller sum than that
initially owned, only that spouse will bear the loss or deficit.

Conversely, if the comparison between the initial and the final patrimony
results in a positive difference, the increase represents profits of the regime.

"What is meant by profits is the difference in net values between the original patrimony and the final one of each spouse."

We then have to proceed to compare the situation of one spouse to that of the other. If both have suffered losses then there will be nothing to participate in.

If only one has obtained profits, the other will participate in half of its value.

If, on the other hand, both spouses have positive gains then there is a cancelling out up to a point of concurrence of the figure of the lowest value, and then the spouse with the lesser gain has the right to receive payment of half of the excess figure from the other. They have a participation credit, which is pure and simple and will be paid in cash. In all of this, if the operation of the above causes serious injury to the debtor spouse or to his or her children in common and this can be duly proven, then the judge will be able to set a one year period for the payment of this debt, which in such an event will be fixed at re-adjusted values. The law also permits the spouses to agree on payment of goods other than cash. If payment is made with something of value in place of money, and this is subsequently awarded to a third party in proceedings (evicted), then the debt is re-created in the terms previously indicated. It is interesting that the legislator has given to the institution of eviction the effect of re-creating the debt, not being the applicable consequence in other areas which it exhaustively regulates, for example in contracts of purchase and sale.

III FAMILY PROPERTY

The aforementioned law no. 19.335 introduces to the Chilean legislation system what it terms "family property", a type of protected patrimony, which applies regardless of the system that governs the marriage: conjugal society, separation of goods or participation in profits.

This family property consists of the immovable property of both spouses or of one of them, as well as the movable property that furnishes them, as long as the immovable property serves as the principal residence of the family and that the judge in brief and summary proceedings declares them as such on the petition of one of the spouses. The rights and shares that the spouses have in property associations of the principal residence also possess the characteristics of family property.

The property declared family property may not be alienated, voluntarily encumbered, or be the object of a contract to alienate or encumber or grant rights of use or enjoyment, without the consent of both spouses. The absence of this proprietary consent of the spouse will occasion the possible petition of nullification of the transaction concerned. The designation as family property is not perpetual, given that the law is empowered to establish mechanisms for ending the designation. The spouses may make a common agreement or the owner may petition the judge to end it, based on the grounds that the property is no longer serving the purpose for which the designation as family property was originally given.

The law upon which we have commented took effect on December 23, 1994, and as such it is impossible to evaluate the effect that it will have on Chilean society or the way it will be received by those who are actually married or those who will contract marriage in the future.

CHINA

WOMEN TO THE FORE: DEVELOPMENTS IN THE FAMILY LAW OF THE PEOPLE'S REPUBLIC OF CHINA, 1992-4

*Michael Palmer**

I INTRODUCTION

In the years 1992-4 the People's Republic of China (hereinafter, the PRC) continued to develop a system of family law designed not only to reflect socialist values, but also to encourage rapid economic development, and to promote political stability. In the post-Mao years the family has re-emerged as the basic unit in China's development policy, and the authorities have sought both to use and to control the family. The family has been made central to the system of economic production in the countryside, the provision of care, and is the key institution through which population growth is to be contained.[1] An earlier Survey noted the recent introduction of special legislation designed to protect young people[2] and the most significant legal change occurring during the period considered in this essay was the introduction of similar legislation designed to bolster the legal and social position of women: the Law for the Protection of Women's Rights and Interests (in force 1 October 1992).[3] In addition, as part of the official policy of protecting the rights and interests of socially disadvantaged categories of person, provincial legislation provided more detailed rules safeguarding the position of returned overseas Chinese and their family members.[4]

---

* Senior Lecturer, Department of Law, School of Oriental and African Studies, University of London.

1 For a more general discussion of the post-Mao law and policy on the family see Michael Palmer, "The Re-Emergence of Family Law in Post-Mao China: Marriage, Divorce and Reproduction", no. 141 *The China Quarterly* 110-134 (1995).

2 See Michael Palmer, "Minors to the Fore: Developments in the Family Law of the People's Republic of China", 15 *Annual Survey of Family Law* [1991] 299-308 at 301-05 (1992-93).

3 *Zhonghua Renmin Gongheguo Funü Quanyi Baozhang Fa* (Law of the People's Republic of China for the Protection of Women's Rights and Interests) 1992, *Zhongguo Falü Nianjian* 1993 (Law Yearbook of China 1993) 220-22 (1993).

4 See, for example, *Heilongjiang Sheng Shishi "Zhonghua Renmin Gongheguo Guiqiao Qiaojuan Baohu Fa" Banfa* (Procedures of Heilongjiang Province for Implementing the Law of the People's Republic of China on the Protection of the Rights and Interests of Returned Overseas Chinese and the Family Members of Returned Overseas Chinese),

A. Bainham (ed.), *The International Survey of Family Law 1994*, 155–179.
© 1996 *The International Society of Family Law. Printed in the Netherlands.*

In 1994, as a result of continuing difficulties with the system of marriage registration, further reforms were introduced in new Regulations for the Administration of Marriage Registration.[5] In the previous year the Supreme People's Court introduced further changes to the law governing custody, child support arrangements, and division of property at divorce.[6]

The efforts of the PRC authorities to control the number and quality of births continued throughout this period, with more rigorous enforcement of restrictions on family size, and the introduction of new and important provincial legislation. The most significant development was the Regulations of Guangdong Province on Family Planning, in force 24 December 1992.[7] In addition, however, there was an unsuccessful attempt at the end of 1993 to introduce a national law on eugenics. The draft was subsequently revised and reintroduced as the Law Protecting the Rights and Interests of Mother and Child. This was promulgated on 27 October 1994, came into force on 1 June 1995, and for reasons of space will be discussed in next year's Survey. Suffice it to say here that the law in its revised form remains very concerned with questions of eugenics and is clearly intended to form a central element in China's population programme.[8]

---

28 February 1992, *Zhongguo Falü Nianjian* 1993 (Law Yearbook of China 1993) at 592-94 (1994).

5　For accounts of earlier changes to the system of marriage registration see Michael Palmer, "The People's Republic of China: New Marriage Regulations", 10 *Annual Survey of Family Law* [1986] 39-57 (1987-88); Michael Palmer, "The People's Republic of China: More Rules but Less Law", 13 *Annual Survey of Family Law* [1989] 325-342 at 328-333. The new rules are: *Hunyin Dengji Guanli Banfa* (Regulations for the Administration of Marriage Registration), *Fazhi Ribao* (Legal System Daily), February 25, 1994 at 2.

6　*Zuigao Renmin Fayuan Guanyu Renmin Fayuan Shenli Lihun Anjian Chuli Zinü Fuyang Wenti de Ruogan Juti Yijian* (Several Concrete Opinions of the Supreme People's Court Regarding the Problems of Bringing Up the Children in Divorce Cases Handled by the People's Courts), November 3, 1993, *Zhongguo Falü Nianjian* 1994 (Law Yearbook of China 1994) 812-13 (1994); *Zuigao Renmin Fayuan Guanyu Renmin Fayuan Shenli Lihun Anjian Chuli Caichan Fenge Wenti de Ruogan Juti Yijian* (Several Concrete Opinions of the Supreme People's Court Regarding the Problems of Dividing Property in Divorce Cases Handled by the People's Courts), November 3, 1993, *Zhongguo Falü Nianjian* 1994 (Law Yearbook of China 1994) 813-14 (1994).

7　*Guangdong Sheng Jihua Shengyu Tiaoli* (Regulations of Guangdong Province on Birth Planning) *Nanfang Ribao* (Southern Daily) December 24, 1992, at 2.

8　Another important legal development at the national level dealing with the question of birth planning is concerned with the system of punishment to be applied in case of violation of birth control norms: see *Zuigao Renmin Fayuan, Zuigao Renmin*

The legal framework for safeguarding the rights and interests of children was further expanded, following the PRC's ratification at the very end of 1991 of the Convention on the Rights of the Child, by the coming into force of the Adoption Law on 1 April 1992,[9] and the promulgation and introduction on 14 March 1992 of Rules for Implementing the Law on Compulsory Education.[10] The latter attempt to strengthen the system of compulsory education in the People's Republic, and stipulate that parents will, if necessary, be forced to send their children to school (Article 13), that parents who fail to ensure that their children attend school will be subject to criticism and fines (Article 40) and that employment of school-age children will be punished (Article 41).

In addition, there continued to be significant changes in the regulation of "lifestyle" problems, with new rules introduced on prostitution and the

---

Jianchayuan, Guanyu Yifa Yancheng Pohuai Jihua Shengyu Fanzui Huodong de Tongzhi (Notice of the Supreme People's Court and the Supreme People's Procuracy Regarding the Punishment by Law of Criminal Activity which does much Damage to Birth Planning), *Zhongguo Falü Nianjian* 1994 (Law Yearbook of China 1994) 795-96 (1994).

9   See Michael Palmer, "Minors to the Fore: Developments in the Family Law of the People's Republic of China", 15 *Annual Survey of Family Law* [1991] 299-308 at 305-08 (1992-93). Further support for the implementation of the 1992 Adoption Law and related rules was given by the introduction of: first, a Supreme People's Court Notice on publicity for the new code, secondly, a Notice issued by the Supreme People's Procuracy on rigorous enforcement of the Adoption Law, thirdly, implementing measures for the adoption of Chinese children by foreign persons, and fourthly, a Notice from the Ministry of Justice on problems of notarising customary adoptions. See *Zuigao Renmin Fayuan Guanyu Xuexi, Xuanchuan Zhixing "Zhonghua Renmin Gongheguo Shouyang Fa"* (Notice of the Supreme People's Court on the Study, Publicising and Implementation of the Adoption Law of the People's Republic of China), *Zuigao Renmin Fayuan Gongheguo Gongbao* (Gazette of the Supreme People's Court), no. 2 for 1992, at 47; *Zuigao Renmin Jianchayuan Guanyu Yange Zhixing "Zhonghua Renmin Gongheguo Shouyang Fa" de Tongzhi* (Notice of the Supreme People's Procuracy on the Strict Implementation of the Adoption Law of the People's Republic of China), *Zuigao Renmin Jianchayuan Gongheguo Gongbao* (Gazette of the Supreme People's Procuracy), no. 2 for 1992, at 27; *Sifa Bu, Minzheng Bu Waiguoren Zai Zhonghua Renmin Gongheguo Shouyang Zinü Shishi Banfa* (Implementing Measures of the Ministry of Justice and the Ministry of Civil Affairs for the Adoption of Children in the People's Republic of China by Foreign Persons) *Fazhi Ribao* (Legal System Daily) November 13, 1993 at 2.

10   *Zhonghua Renmin Gongheguo Yiwu Jiaoyu Fa Shishi Xize* (Detailed Regulations for Implementing the Compulsory Education Law), *Quanguo Renmin Daibiao Dahui Changwu Weiyuanhui Gongbao* (Gazette of the Standing Committee of the National People's Congress), no. 6 for 1992, at 172-79.

patronage of prostitutes,[11] as well as the system for dealing with juvenile offenders. In addition, clarifications were made by the Supreme People's Court and the Supreme People's Procuracy of several questions relating to the 1991 legislation on the severe punishment of people dealing in women and children.[12]

Finally, in 1992 the Supreme People's Court introduced a significant interpretation of the 1991 Civil Procedure Law and this, *inter alia*, offered some clarification of the place of mediation in the process of judicial divorce and the conflicts rules by which foreign divorces will be recognised by the PRC authorities.[13]

The present essay examines and attempts to assess the importance of the new law protecting Chinese women's rights, (see below, Section V) and also considers some of the other important developments in PRC family law occuring during the period 1992-94 – in particular, it looks at the key areas

---

11   *Maiyin Piaochang Renyuan Shourong Jiaoyu Banfa* (Measures for the Detention and Education of Prostitutes and those who Patronise Prostitutes) *Fazhi Ribao* (Legal System Daily), September 11, 1993, at 2; *Zuigao Renmin Fayuan, Zuigao Renmin Jianchayuan, Guanyu Zhixing "Quanguo Renmin Daibiao Dahui Changwu Weiyuanhui Guanyu Yanjin Maiyin Piaochang de Jueding" de Ruogan Wenti de Jieda* (Explanation of the Supreme People's Court and the Supreme People's Procuracy on Several Questions Regarding the Decision of the Standing Committee of the National People's Congress on the Strict Prohibition of Prostitution and the Patronage of Prostitutes), *Zuigao Renmin Jjianchayuan Gongbao* (Gazette of the Supreme People's Procuracy) no.1 for 1993, at 20-21; *Gongan Bu Guanyu Xiugai Maiyin Piaochang Renyuan Bufu Shourong Jiaoyu de Shensu Chengxu Guiding de Tongzhi* (Notice of the Ministry of Public Security on Revising the Provisions on Appeal Procedures for Persons Engaged in Prostitution or Whoring), August 14, 1992, *Zhongguo Falü Nianjian* 1993 (Law Yearbook of China 1993) 754 (1993).

12   *Zuigao Renmin Fayuan, Zuigao Renmin Jiancha Yuan, Guanyu Zhixing "Quanguo Renmin Daibiao Dahui Changwu Weiyuanhui Guanyu Yancheng Gauimai, Bangjia Funü de Jueding" de Ruogan Wenti de Jieda* (Explanation of the Supreme People's Court and the Supreme People's Procuracy on Several Questions Regarding Implementation of the Decision of the Standing Committee of the National People's Congress on the Severe Punishment of Criminals Who Abduct or Sell, or who Kidnap, Women and Children), *Zhongguo Renmin Jianchayuan Gongbao* (Gazette of the Supreme People's Procuracy), no.1 for 1993, at 18-19.

13   *Zuigao Renmin Fayuan Guanyu Shiyong "Zhonghua Renmin Gongheguo Minshi Susong Fa" Ruogan Wenti de Yijian* (Opinions of the Supreme People's Court Concerning Certain Problems in the Application of the "Civil Procedure Law of the People's Republic of China"), *Zuigao Renmin Fayuan Gongbao* (Gazette of the Supreme People's Court), no. 3 for 1992 at 70-94.

of marriage (Section II), divorce (Section III), and family planning (Section IV).

II MARRIAGE REGISTRATION

During the period surveyed there was a further important development in the state control of marriage and related matters – the promulgation on 1 February 1994 (in force on the same day) of another revised set of marriage registration regulations. The new rules are the third to be introduced in some fifteen years, and the relatively rapid pace of legislative change in this area of marriage and family reflects the very considerable difficulties that the authorities have experienced in marriage registration work. Much of the concern relates to the family planning programme. As births are permitted only within marriage,[14] the control of marriage becomes particularly important for a regime concerned to limit the quantity and to improve the quality of the offspring born to its people. This concern has become particularly acute in the post-Mao era, but marriage registration has always be a difficult matter in socialist China because the requirement of registration is not welcomed by a peasantry that prefers to conclude its marriages by means of customary celebration.[15] The judicial solution has been to develop the notion of *shishi hunyin* or *de facto* marriage in order to assume jurisdiction in matrimonial cases.

The new rules represent a further legislative restriction on the notion of *de facto* marriage.[16] Indeed, Article 24 appears to leave little or no room for the courts to find that a *de facto* marriage has been created – relations between parties who live together as "husband and wife but have not applied for marriage registration are invalid and not protected by law." The article confirms that a registered union is the only acceptable form of marriage

---

14 See Michael Palmer, "The Re-Emergence of Family Law in Post-Mao China: Marriage, Divorce and Reproduction", no. 141 *The China Quarterly,* 110-134, at 113-114 (1995).

15 On peasant preference for customary formalities see Michael Palmer, "The Re-Emergence of Family Law in Post-Mao China: Marriage, Divorce and Reproduction", no. 141 *The China Quarterly* 110-134, at 118-19 (1995).

16 On *de facto* marriage see Michael Palmer, "The Re-Emergence of Family Law in Post-Mao China: Marriage, Divorce and Reproduction", no. 141 *The China Quarterly* 110-134, at 119-122 (1995).

regardless of the age of the parties.[17] The entrenched problem of underage marriage is further addressed in Article 32 which empowers the provincial authorities to introduce special measures in order to ensure that couples do not marry under the minimum legal ages (twenty for women, twenty-two for men). However, the extent to which this rigorous approach to unregistered unions can be maintained in the face of the continued peasant preference for customary unions is uncertain. Moreover, the 1989 Supreme People's Court rules on judicial dissolution of unregistered unions are less generous to women in matters of custody and property, and the more restrictive policy and law will therefore work to their disadvantage.

The benefit to the parties of properly registered marriage is stressed in the part entitled General Principles at Article 3: "the lawful rights and interests of the parties registering their marriage in accordance with the law are protected by law." The chapter that follows repeats the provisions contained in the 1986 Regulations which laid out the functions of, and training for, marriage registration personnel, but specifies more clearly the various functions of marriage registration offices: marriage registration (including divorce by mutual consent and restoration of marriage)[18] and the issuance of marriage certificates, responding to attempts to breach the requirements of marriage, and its registration, and to promote public awareness of the laws governing marriage.[19] In the chapter dealing with the actual process

---

17 For earlier attempts to restrict the scope of *de facto* marriage see Michael Palmer, "The People's Republic of China: New Marriage Regulations", 10 *Annual Survey of Family Law* [1986] 39-57 (1987-88); and Michael Palmer, "The People's Republic of China: More Rules but Less Law", 13 *Annual Survey of Family Law* [1989] 325-342 at 328-333 (1990-91).

18 Divorce by mutual consent is handled by administrative procedures under Article 24 of the 1980 Marriage Law: "divorce shall be granted if husband and wife both desire it. Both parties shall apply to the marriage registration office for divorce. The marriage registration office, after clearly establishing that divorce is desired by both parties and that appropriate arrangements have been made for the care of any children and the disposition of property, shall issue a divorce certificate without delay." Restored marriage refers to the process by which parties formerly married to each other restore their marital ties - an institution found in PRC law because Chinese society still prefers unhappy couples not to divorce.

19 This responsibility to promote public awareness appears to be especially onerous in relation to the policy of eliminating customary unions for marriage registration personnel are enjoined not only to "publicise laws governing marriage" but also to "promote civilised marriage customs".

of marriage registration the new regulations are more detailed and complex than the 1986 rules. They also promote the use of physical examinations before marriage (Articles 9 and 10), a policy clearly connected with the PRC's growing concern with eugenics. This chapter also introduces stricter, and significantly more detailed, requirements in cases of divorce by mutual consent and restoration of marital ties (*huifu fuqi guanxi*). Chapter IV deals with the administration of marriage registration records, and introduces clearer rules on the process by which a marriage certificate may be reissued.

The next section (Chapter V), not only specifies the requirement of registration noted above (Article 24) but also deals with the failure of parties to meet marriage registration requirements. Thus, Article 25 stipulates not only that fraudulently based attempts to secure marriage, restored marriage, or divorce registration will result in a revocation of the registration and a fine of not more than 200 *yuan*. Marriage registry personnel are also obliged by Article 26 to report to the procuracy attempts to register a bigamous union. Article 27 requires the marriage registry staff to report and to encourage the use of administrative punishments (*xingzheng chufen*) in cases in which the work unit of one of the spouses has provided false documentation. Finally in this section, parties are advised that they may lodge appeals against marriage registry decisions either by the process of administrative review (*xingzheng fuyi*) or administrative litigation – that is, judicial review (*xingzheng susong*).

III DIVORCE

In 1994 the Supreme People's Court issued an important Opinion on custody and child support issues in divorce cases. For several years there have been acute difficulties in this area of PRC family law, and to a significant extent these stem from the very limited guidance offered to the courts by Articles 29 and 30 of the 1980 Marriage Law.[20]

The new Opinion attempts to deal with some of the difficulties through the provision of detailed guidelines. To a significant extent these guidelines

---

20 Articles 29 and 30 deal with custody and support issues respectively in only the most cursory manner.

concern the tensions which often arise in Chinese families at the time of divorce between traditionally based views that children, especially male children, should remain in the custody of their father and his family after the marriage has come to an end,[21] and a policy axiom that a young child is better cared for by its mother. To a significant extent, however, the tension is reflected in rather than resolved by the Opinion.

Thus, Article 1 provides that, "a child who is not yet two years of age in general shall live with its mother." However, in any one of several circumstances the father shall be made the custodial parent: in particular, if the mother is seriously ill and it is not appropriate for the child to live with her, or the conditions in which the mother is trying to bring up the child are adequate but the mother is unable to fulfil her duties and the father has applied for custody. In addition, the father may be made the custodial parent of a child below two years of age if there is an agreement between the parties and the proposed arrangement is "clearly not harmful to the healthy development of the child." If the child is two years of age or above, but still a minor, there is no presumption in the Opinion that the mother is the more appropriate custodial parent; instead, where both wife and husband apply for custody of such a child preferential treatment is to be given to one of the parties if one of the following conditions apply: that party can no longer reproduce because, for example, she or he has been sterilised; secondly, the child has already been living with that parent for a longer period of time than it has with the other parent; thirdly, that party has no other children whereas the other party does have one or more additional offspring; or, fourthly, the other party is suffering from serious illness or is in some other circumstance which is not conducive to the physical and mental health of the child. In addition if there has been significant grandparent involvement in the raising of the child, and the grandparents are willing to continue to assist, this is a factor to be taken into account in deciding the issue of parental custody.

Somewhat surprisingly, the Opinion does not deal with the question of access for non-custodial parents, although it does at least provide for a form of joint custody: "permission may be given for the parties to make an

---

21   In traditional times, of course, divorce rates were low and the termination of marriage primarily occurred through the death of one of the spouses. Even where it was the husband who died, and the widow sought remarriage, the children were expected to continue to reside with their father's family.

agreement in which custody of the child is rotated between them" (Article 6). In addition, both parties are permitted to alter a custody arrangement by agreement (Article 17). If, during the divorce proceedings, neither parent is willing to support the child, the court may make a ruling temporarily imposing custody on one party (Article 20). It is open to the non-custodial parent to alter the arrangements in a number of circumstances including failure of the custodial parent to fulfil her or his obligations, maltreatment of the child by the custodial parent, or other circumstances in which the co-residence with the child "has a detrimental influence on the physical and mental development of the child" (Article 16). If there is failure by one or both the parties to comply with a judgement, ruling or mediation agreement on custody and support arrangements, a people's court may impose a compulsory measure (that is, summons to court by warrant, a fine, or detention) in accordance with the provisions of Article 102 of the 1991 Civil Procedure Law, Article 21).

Child support given by the parents is dealt with in Article 7 and is determined on the basis of, first, "the actual needs of the child", secondly, "the actual circumstances of the father and mother", and thirdly, "the actual living costs of the area." As with custody, the parties may agree between themselves that one party should bear the entire burden of providing support. However, if such an arrangement does not, in practice, work effectively and adversely affects the child's development, this one-sided arrangement will not be approved. In most cases it is expected that responsibility for providing support will be shared between the divorcing spouses. In the Opinion an average rate of payment for those with a fixed source of income is suggested: 20 to 30 per cent of total monthly income. This payment level is expected to be higher where there are several children who require support, but in general the level of payment should not "exceed 50 per cent of the total monthly income." If a parent has no income, or disappears without trace, her or his property "may be sold off to pay for the child's support."

In general, support is to be maintained until the child is eighteen years of age, but this assistance may not be withdrawn in certain circumstances – for example, if the adult child is unable to support itself, or is unable to work, or is in continuing education and so on. Any child dissatisfied with the level of provision may seek an increase on the ground that existing payments are below the actual standard of living in the locality, that additional support is required because the child is in bad health or still receiving education, and so on.

Special provision is made for two areas of Chinese family life in which tensions often arise namely, step-parenthood and adoption. According to the Opinion, in a divorce between a natural parent and a step-parent there is no obligation on the latter to continue to contribute to the maintenance of the child. If the step-parent is unwilling to continue to provide support then the former husband or wife, as an original parent, should provide the necessary assistance (Article 13). More importantly, a divorced father or mother may not refuse to make child support payments on the ground that the child has changed its surname. This is consistent with the policy of encouraging step-parent adoptions, and is primarily intended to deal with non-custodial fathers who become upset at attempts by their former spouse to integrate the child into the reconstituted family by step-parent adoption. If the adopted child is the father's only son the change in surname will be a major threat to the natural father's social identity.

In cases in which the child has been adopted, the rules that apply to ordinary families also apply,[22] but a specific rule is introduced by the Opinion in order to deal with customary adoptions in which one parent did not genuinely consent to the adoption. If the non-custodial parent did not really consent to the adoption, she or he is not required to continue to provide support.

On the same day that it published its Opinion on custody issues, the Supreme People's Court issued another Opinion which dealt with division of matrimonial property.[23] In China, as elsewhere, this is also a highly contentious issue which is frequently a source of conflict between the divorcing spouses. The Opinion on property division is a detailed document which makes a serious effort at handling the often complex issues of ownership, use, and compensation that need to be settled. For reasons of space it is not possible here to look at the rules which the Opinion introduces in detail. Suffice it to say that, in my view, the policy requirement laid out in the introductory paragraph that the division of the matrimonial estate should

---

22   Marriage Law 1980 Article 20: "The state protects lawful adoption. The relevant provisions ... governing the relationship between parents and children shall apply to the rights and duties in the relationship between adoptive parents and adopted children."

23   *Zuigao Renmin Fayuan Guanyu Renmin Fayuan Shenli Lihun Anjian Chuli Caichan Fenge Wenti de Ruogan Juti Yijian* (Several Concrete Opinions of the Supreme People's Court Regarding the Problems of Dividing Property in Divorce Cases Handled by the People's Courts), November 3, 1993, *Zhongguo Falü Nianjian* 1994 (Law Yearbook of China 1994) 813-14 (1994).

benefit production and not disrupt too much existing living arrangements will, in the social context of the Chinese countryside, tend to work against the interests of women, as will the provisions on division of property between persons whose customary marriage has been characterised as illegal cohabitation (Article 22).

IV BIRTH PLANNING REGULATIONS

The post-Mao Chinese leadership's concern to develop birth control regulations at the provincial rather than the national level has been noted elsewhere.[24] Article 12 of the Marriage Law 1980 and Article 49 of the 1982 Constitution made family planning mandatory for married couples, and linked to these legal provisions have been a number of important policy statements on the need for a drastic limitation of fertility. Throughout the 1980s and early 1990s there has been a basic policy of restricting to one child nearly all families in which the wife is at a child-bearing age. In exceptional circumstances, the birth of two children is permitted.

One province in which the regulations that implement these national policies have been particularly subject to change is Guangdong, an area in which traditional kinship values and the ideal of a large family have persisted, especially among the rural population. However, Guangdong is also the economically most rapidly growing area of China, and now has an immigrant population of some 10 million,[25] swelling its total population to more than 65 million. The transient workers or "floaters" (*liudong renkou*) are especially unreceptive to family planning controls, and the rapid growth of the migrant or "floating" population is one important consideration prompting a further major revision of the provincial family planning regulations.[26] The new rules also extend control over reproduction by persons registered

---

24 *See* Michael Palmer, "The Re-Emergence of Family Law in Post-Mao China: Marriage, Divorce and Reproduction", no. 141 *The China Quarterly* 110-134, at 126 (1995).

25 Interview with Guangdong Provincial Procuracy, June 1993.

26 Note: *Guangdong Sheng Jihua Shengyu Tiaoli* (Regulations of Guangdong Province on Birth Planning) *Nanfang Ribao* (Southern Daily) December 24, 1992, at 2, replacing the Guangdong Sheng Jihua Shengyu Tiaoli (Regulations of Guangdong Province for Birth Planning), promulgated and in force, 1 June 1986.

as Guangdong residents but who, in fact, currently reside elsewhere or who are married to Chinese persons resident in Hong Kong, Taiwan and so on.[27]

The revised rules, introduced at the very end of 1992, are divided into seven sections. The first, entitled General Provisions, places a significant degree of responsibility for attaining population planning targets on the various levels of people's government in the province. The local birth control committees, which had principal accountability for family planning under the 1986 Regulations (Article 4), retain a significant degree of responsibility for family planning and the enforcement of the provincial regulations. However, they are now defined as "functional bodies" (*zhineng bumen*) and are clearly expected to share their duties with a wide range of institutions. Thus, organizations "such as Villagers' Committees, Neighbourhood Committees, Trade Unions, the Communist Youth League, the Women's Federation, and Family Planning Associations," are expected to "organize and educate the public with a view to accomplishing jointly the work of family planning" (Article 6). What is more important, ultimate accountability for the effectiveness of the birth control programme lies with the "principal leaders of the people's governments at various levels." The relative importance of this concern with the birth control programme in their work is reflected in the provision in Article 4 of the new regulations that "an important criterion for assessing the achievements of people's governments at various levels and their leaders is whether or not population planning has been accomplished and family planning work carried out satisfactory." This emphasis on the duty of local government leaders to make a success of the birth control programme is paralleled by a concern to ensure co-operation between the various bodies with responsibilities in this area: "departments and units at various levels must work out feasible measures on the basis of the duties they assume, and jointly accomplish the work of family planning" (Article 4).

The new regulations, as did the rules that they replace, oblige married couples to practise family planning. Unlike the earlier Guangdong codes, however, they now also stress that birth control is a legal duty for married couples: "it is against the law [*weifa xingwei*] to fail to practice family

---

27 *See* Article 12 in the new rules.

planning" (Article 2). Moreover, in Chapter Two, entitled "Birth Control", it is laid down that "child bearing outside the plan is strictly prohibited" (Article 14). The preferred remedy for failure to adhere to this rule is stated in Article 17: "women who are pregnant outside the plan should adopt timely remedial measures" – that is, they should undergo an abortion at the earliest opportunity. A provision in Chapter VI ("Restrictions and Penalties") enables local governments or ward offices (*jiedao banshichu*) to fine, among other types of offender, "those who have children before reaching their legally marriageable age and those who have children born out of wedlock." Such persons are now liable to "a levy for having children outside the birth plan for a period of two to five years." The same article specifies that those who have children born out of a bigamous union or cohabitation "shall be dealt with in the same manner as for bearing excessive children outside the plan." Failure to pay such financial penalties is initially sanctioned, according to Article 36, by one or more of a variety of bureaucratic responses. The Public Security Bureau, industrial and commercial authorities, and the labour authorities are empowered to impose a wide range of administrative sanctions including the temporary revocation of business licences, vehicular driving licences, temporary residence cards, and works permits. In addition, if the offenders are immigrants "the units and proprietors concerned should cancel any contracts (*chengbao*) or leases" to which they are a party, and "dismiss these persons and recover possession of their houses" (Article 36). Indeed, the Regulations recommend that an individual should agree to family planning commitment when entering into a "contract, lease or labour agreement of more than one year" with an organ, enterprise or "institution" (*shiye danwei*).

Provision is made, at Article 40, for administrative or judicial review of decisions taken to impose penalties on those parents – transients or otherwise – who bear children in excess of the limits imposed by the family planning rules. These possibilities were absent from the 1980 and 1986 codes, and are consistent with the development since at least the late 1980s of mechanisms in administrative law and practice by means of which the aggrieved citizen may attempt to secure redress against the state. At the same time, however, local authorities may now make applications to the courts for enforcement of their administrative decisions which are being resisted (Article 41). In this respect, at least, the new regulations may be considered to represent a small but significant step forward in that they encourage greater judicial involvement in the regulation of administrative acts in this area of social life.

The new rules do not relax the existing restrictions on the exceptional circumstances in which an urban couple may attempt to bear a second child;[28] for the rural population the provision in the 1986 Regulations that an application for permission to bear a second child may be made (and, perhaps, granted) if a couple's first child is female is not repeated in the 1992 Regulations.[29] Instead, each application is to be considered on its merits and we must assume that in practice the rules have been tightened because the official commentary on the new rules complains that in rural areas of Guangdong the problem of excessive births is "rather serious" (*bijiao yanzhong*).[30] In this connection we should also note that the 1992 Regulations contain a new restriction on misuse of amniocentesis and other tests which are able to reveal the sex of an unborn child: "units and in-dividuals are strictly prohibited from identifying the gender of the foetus without authorisation" (Article 16). There is also a greater concern in the new rules with eugenics – to the ban contained in the 1986 Regulations on childbearing from those suffering serious hereditary disease is now added a requirement that if such a pregnancy does occur "it must be terminated" (*bixu zhongzhi renshen*) (Article 16).

As indicated above, a major development in the new regulations is the introduction of detailed provisions on the management of family planning among the migrant or transient population. Article 22 requires the various departments of the local government of the place of temporary residence

---

28 According to the 1992 Regulations, the circumstances in which an urban couple may attempt for a second child are: the first child is disabled; or the wife and husband have produced children by other marriages but not retained custody; or the wife has been certified as having been correctly sterilised for five years, then adopted a child, but subsequently finds herself to be pregnant; or the wife and husband are themselves single children; or one or both of the spouses is engaged in a dangerous occupation.

29 For an account of the debate on the question of the circumstances in which a second child should be allowed see Michael Palmer, "People's Republic of China: Reacting to Rapid Social Change", 12 *Annual Survey of Family Law* [1988] 438-460, at 447-49 (1989-90).

30 *Jihua Shengyu bixu shixing yifa guanli* (The administration of birth planning must be carried out according to the law) *Nanfang Ribao* (Southern Daily), December 24, 1992 at 1.

to work together effectively in the task of limiting migrants' births. Article 23 calls for co-operation between the government of the place of temporary residence and the government of the place of permanent residence,[31] and places on both special administrative duties including, in particular, the issuing and checking of family planning certificates and the maintenance of birth control registers for the migrants. Article 24 requires immigrants of child-bearing age to be issued with family planning certificates before leaving their home area, and to hold a birth permit issued in the place where their household is registered in order to give birth in their place of temporary residence. Infringements of these rules are punished by the local authorities in the place of temporary residence (Article 25).

V   LEGAL PROMOTION OF GENDER EQUALITY

The status of women in contemporary Chinese society has for many years been a matter of considerable controversy, both within China and in the comparative study of gender equality. At the onset of the PRC's post-Mao reforms programme, the authorities reaffirmed in the Marriage Law 1980 the principle of gender equality first enshrined in China's socialist law in the 1954 Constitution.[32] However, the reforms of recent years have in practice tended to undermine the ability of the state and the Communist Party to enforce the law and policy of gender equality. Efforts to bolster gender equality have often been impaired directly or indirectly by the reform programme itself through the relaxation of state control over the economy, the stress placed on the family as a unit of care, the birth limitation policy and so on.

In traditional Chinese society, males were seen as inherently superior to women, so that in China's basic binary characterisation of the natural and social worlds they are central to the *yang* or positive principle, whereas women are viewed as a key expression of the *yin* or the negative principle. Accordingly, it was men who occupied positions of power and authority

---

31   That is, the place at which the household registration or *hukou* is maintained.
32   Constitution of the People's Republic of China 1954, at Article 96; it should be noted, however, that the Common Programme 1949 (or provisional constitution) also proclaimed gender equality: "women shall enjoy equal rights with men in political, economic, cultural, educational, and social life (Article 6).

and when a family could afford to educate its children it was the sons who were educated, usually so that they might gain status and wealth for their natal family through service in the imperial bureaucracy. Within the family, a woman occupied a position subordinate to the father, husband, and sons in their life. Female infanticide, child betrothal and arranged marriage, concubinage, unequal rights of divorce, and female seclusion were among the more important manifestations of the social and legal subordination of women.

This subordination, however, was by no means complete: within the family a mother often wielded considerable power, the daughter of a wealthy family might be given an elaborate dowry indicating to the bridegroom's family not only its high social status but also an unwillingness to condone any abuse of its married-out women.[33] In addition, the emphasis in imperial Chinese law on hierarchy – which meant that an offence committed by a married woman against her husband was punished more severely than the same offence committed outside the family context – was counterbalanced by a Confucian humanitarianism in which the law extended certain privileges to weaker members of society: women, the aged, the young and the infirm.[34]

Moreover, even before the arrival of socialist rule, significant attempts were made to enhance the status of women. Thus, for example, women's sectarian movements sought explicitly to furnish members with an identity and an existence quite different from those provided by ordinary marital arrangements.[35] The Taiping Rebellion (1851-64) proposed and implemented

---

33 See, for example, M. Freedman, *Chinese Lineage and Society: Fukien and Kwangtung* 58-59 (1966).

34 For a general discussion of this feature of imperial Chinese law, unfortunately not written with particular reference to the position of women, see Derk Bodde, *Age, Youth and Infirmity in the Law of Ch'ing China*, *Essays on China's Legal Tradition*, 1980 (Jerome A. Cohen, R. Randle Edwards and Fu-mei Chang Chen, eds.).

35 Marjorie Topley, "Marriage Resistance in Rural Kwangtung", *Women in Chinese Society*, 1975 (Marjery Wolf and Roxanne Witke, eds.); Janice E. Stockard, *Daughters of the Canton delta: Marriage patterns and economic strategies in South China*, 1860-1930 (1989).

briefly radical reforms in family life, and an enhancement in the status of women.[36]

Missionaries, especially Protestants, were committed to improving the status of women and were especially important in crusading against footbinding. The resulting pressure led to the abolition of footbinding in 1902. Protestant missionaries also played a very significant role in promoting educational opportunities for women. The May Fourth Movement[37] extended criticisms of Chinese family life that had been first put forward in the last decades of imperial rule, and its efforts to promote egalitarian principles in family life resulted, *inter alia*, in the various reforms introduced by the Nationalist Government in Books Four and Five of the Civil Code 1930.[38] These reforms included the introduction of a requirement of consent on the part of intending spouses (Articles 972 and 997), the right of women to sue for divorce (Article 1052), and the right of women to inherit (Article 1138).

In areas of China controlled by the Communist Party, radical reforms were from the very beginning also introduced in family and related law.[39] Thus, in the late 1920s the Jiangxi Soviet's earliest land law proclaimed that all men and women, old and young, were to be entitled to equal distribution, although subsequent legislation adopted a somewhat less radical stance. The Provisional Constitution 1931 also emphasised that the new Soviet Government would guarantee the fundamental liberation of women, and the Marriage Regulations of the same year declared that the feudal marriage system was to be overturned and explicitly banned various manifestations of gender inequality including arranged marriage, minor marriage, contracts for the sale of women, concubinage, and inequality of divorce rights. In addition, women were granted significant rights of custody and property. Subsequent legislation revised some of the more radical rules, with divorce rights for Army wives being restricted, and women's rights of custody and

---

36 Vincent Y.C. Shih, *The taiping ideology: its sources, interpretations, and influences*, 60-79 (1967).

37 The May Fourth Movement was a popular attempt in the aftermath of the First World war at effecting cultural and socio-political change in Chinese society.

38 Promulgated 26 December 1930, in force 5 May 1931.

39 In particular, until the past decade or so, family and land reform were always seen as closely interrelated. It is some measure of the significance of the changing policies of the post-Mao era that land reforms have proceeded without any real reference to the impact of these reforms on the family.

maintenance significantly reduced. In later years, the Party continued to move further away from radical policies enhancing the status of women, preferring instead to seek political support in the patriarchal world of the Chinese peasantry and to make the family a fundamental component of socialist development.

The 1950 Marriage Law of the PRC was based on the experiences of family reform gained in the pre-Liberation territories under Communist Party control. Among the reforms which it promoted in order to enhance the status of women were prohibitions on child betrothal and the payment of bride wealth, and the requirement that there was to be free choice of marriage partner, monogamy, rights for widows to remarry, and equal rights of divorce and in the children of the marriage. In making the family a key institution in the new society, the Marriage Law 1950 called for reciprocity in parent-child ties and in relations between spouses.

Thus, husband and wife were placed under a duty to "love, respect, assist and look after each other, to live in harmony, to engage in productive work, to care for the children, and to strive jointly for the welfare of the family and for the building of the new society" (Article 8). The new law insisted that the reformed, socialist, family system was based, *inter alia*, on "equal rights for both sexes"[40] but immediately added that it was also founded on the "the protection of the lawful interests of women and children," suggesting that the policy of gender equality might well encounter social resistance.

One area of the Marriage Law that met with particular opposition was freedom of divorce,[41] so that the new law soon became popularly known as the "divorce law" and the "women's law" – reflecting the fact that most petitioners for divorce were women. Reconciliation through mediation replaced the initial policy goal of severing "feudal" marriages, and the Party became critical of attempts to characterize the Marriage Law as being primarily concerned with the promotion of women's rights and interests.

---

40   Note: This principle was buttressed by a number of specific provisions requiring, for example, consent as a [precondition] for marriage (Article 3), equal status in the home (Article 7), equality in choice of occupation (Article 9), equal rights in family property (Article 10), use of surname (Article 11), and inheritance of the property of a spouse (Article 12).

41   Article 17 of 1950 Marriage Law.

Economic and political priorities encouraged the Party to stress the virtues of harmonious family life. Peasant resistance meant that in many respects the legal reforms in marriage and family life were not effectively implemented in the countryside.[42]

Even in urban areas, where the law was much more successfully imposed, the progress towards more equal relations between sexes was by no means certain, so that even by the early 1980s Whyte and Parish had to conclude that "the current situation still falls considerably short of full sexual equality."[43]

In the post-Mao era, as noted above, the relaxation of state control over production, the enhanced reliance on the family for the provision of social care, the single-child family policy and so on have tended to work against women's interests, and the authorities have sought to remedy the problem through legal change. As pointed out in earlier Surveys [44]freedom of divorce was introduced by the Marriage Law 1980, and the law governing divorce was further reformed in 1989.[45] In addition, various legislative efforts have been made to improve the position of women in education and at work. In 1980, the PRC became a party to the Convention on the Elimination of All Forms of Discrimination Against Women (in force, 26 November 1982), and on 3 April 1992 the National People's Congress of the PRC approved the Law of the PRC for the Protection of Women's Rights and Interests (in force, 1 October 1992). The new law is an ambitious effort to promote a higher status for women. It provides a domestic legislative statement that encourages gender equality in several of the areas of socialisation which tend to promote the development of inequality in gender roles, namely, education and family life. It also attempts to enhance the position of women in areas of social life in which women are systematically denied equal access: power, property and status.

---

42 At the end of 1953 "the marriage reform campaign dropped into the phase China watchers call 'low ebb'; not abandoned but with little energy being expended on it" (Marjery Wolf, "Chinese Women: Old Skills in a New Context", *Women, Culture and Society*, 1973 (Michelle Zimbalist Rosaldo and Loiuse Lamphere, eds.).

43 Martin King Whyte & William L. Parish, *Urban life in contemporary China*, 227 (1984).

44 *See* Michael Palmer, "Some General Observations on Family Law in the People's Republic of China", 9 *Annual Survey of Family Law* [1985] 41-68, at 63 (1986-87).

45 *See*, Michael Palmer, "The People's Republic of China: More Rules but Less Law", 13 *Annual Survey of Family Law* [1990] 325-342, at 333-36 (1990-91).

The General Principles Chapter of the law lays out important dimensions of the PRC's policy on women. The basic postulate of gender equality is emphasized in Article 1: "this law is enacted to safeguard women's lawful rights and interests (and) to promote equality between man and women." Articles 4, 5, and 7 in this section encourage governmental bodies and relevant mass organizations such as the Women's Federation and trade unions to protect women's rights and interests. In order to enhance the prospects for effective implementation of women's rights, the new law has a special section on "Legal Responsibility" which provides apparently new opportunities for women to obtain relief against discriminatory conduct. Thus, Article 48 gives women the right to demand that the relevant government department remedy the deficiency or to bring suit in a people's court. Moreover, Article 50 specifies that administrative discipline (*xingzheng chufen*) may be taken against state officials who are responsible for discriminatory conduct against women in the following specific areas: first, in dealing with complaints that women's rights are being infringed; secondly, in employment matters; thirdly, in allocations of land and housing in rural areas; and finally, in educational matters. In addition, the same article also stipulates that not only is there the prospect that administrative discipline will be imposed on state functionaries who take retaliatory action against those who lodge complaints against them but also that "if the reprisal is criminal, [the functionary] shall be dealt with in accordance with the criminal law."

However, elsewhere in the General Principles section there are indications that the commitment to equality of status is not entirely whole-hearted. Thus, Article 1 also states that gender equality in the PRC is valued not only for its own sake but also because it will assist women to contribute more effectively to "socialist modernisation" (*shehui zhuyi xiandaihua*). The addition of this functional justification of an enhancement of the role of women in China's socialist development may well serve to perpetuate inequality. It encourages the view that in circumstances in which the protection of women's rights and the promotion of gender equality do not obviously contribute to economic advances there is less need to take action against discrimination. This qualified view of the importance of gender equality is reinforced by the provisions of Article 6. These suggest that women are to some extent responsible for the discrimination that they suffer, for women are now urged to "have self-respect, self confidence, to stand on their own feet, to improve themselves [*ziqiang*], and to use the law [*falü*]to defend their own lawful rights and interests."

Moreover, in a manner consistent with the PRC's important jurisprudential principle that there should be a balance of rights and duties women are advised by the second paragraph of the same article to "observe the laws of the state, respect social ethics and fulfil the obligations prescribed by law." Elsewhere in the Law the concern with duties is manifested in matters of family planning. This concern with social ethics is particularly important, however, because it not only again indicates that women's rights are contingent rather than absolute, but suggests that women have a particular responsibility to bear for the decline in moral standards that the Chinese leadership feels has taken place in the post-Mao era.

Article 2 prohibits not only discrimination (*qishi*) against women but also abuse (*lüedai*) and injury (*canhai*). This concern with physical abuse of women is not, however, extended into more detailed areas of the women's law, and it is not clear in what ways, if any, these provisions afford greater protection than those already available in the Criminal Law 1979. Moreover, the emphasis in the Legal Responsibility section is on administrative rather than judicial redress of discriminatory conduct, and in practice this will mean that many disputes are handled through mediation and compromise, methods which are themselves often disadvantageous for women.

Much of the protection offered in Chapter Seven, which deals with marriage and family rights (*hunyin jiating quanyi*), replicates safeguards found elsewhere in the law.

The provision in the new law at Article 41 protecting a woman's right to marry a partner of her choice is already legally guaranteed in the Constitution 1982 (Article 49), the Marriage Law 1980 (Articles 2 and 3), and the General Principles of the Civil Law 1986 (Article 103). Article 47 deals with problems of reproduction, and does attempt to improve significantly the position of married women by declaring not only that women have the right to bear children[46] but also that they may choose not to have children. The former provision is designed, *inter alia*, to assist women who give birth to daughters; the latter is a new right for which it will be difficult to secure popular acceptance in a social world in which the traditional female gender role stressing the woman's reproductive and nurturing functions remains important. The same article, in its second paragraph, "balances" this uncertain right by reminding spouses that they have a duty to "practice family planning in accordance with the relevant provisions of the state" and that the pertinent government departments have a duty not only to provide proper contraception facilities but also to "protect the health and safety of women having birth control surgery."

Article 43 reaffirms the equality of rights of women in the matrimonial estate, but Article 44 attempts to address the problem of housing at the time of divorce. If the matrimonial home is either jointly rented or jointly owned the presumption is that favourable consideration will be given to the rights and interests of the wife and children. However, especially in urban areas, the normal practice is for a married woman to live in the accommodation provided by her husband's work unit and this often places an unhappy wife in a difficult position. The possibility of expulsion from the family home puts pressure on her to tolerate conduct from her husband that she otherwise would not accept and to refrain from bringing a divorce suit. In such cases the new law does attempt to afford some relief in that the husband is urged in Article 44 "to do all he can to help the wife solve her housing problem." Such exhortation may well prove to be inadequate as a protective mechanism.

There are no provisions in the Marriage and Family section dealing with the problem of domestic violence. This issue is addressed to some extent in Chapter VI "Rights of the Person." Article 33 declares that "the state protects the rights of the person, which women enjoy equally with men,"

---

46   The actual text reads, "women have the right to bear children in accordance with the relevant principles of the state." That is to say, they do not have the right either to bear children outside marriage or to give birth in violation of the provincial regulations which implement the single child policy. See Palmer, "The Re-Emergence of Family Law in Post-Mao China: Marriage, Divorce and Reproduction", no. 141 *The China Quarterly* 110-134 (1995).

and Article 35 insists that "women's rights to life and health brook no infringement." Some detail is also added by Article 35 which reaffirms the prohibitions on maltreatment of baby girls (including female infanticide), and forbids maltreatment of a woman in a number of specific circumstances: if she seeks to exercise her right not to bear children, if she gives birth to a female child, if she is elderly, or if there is use of "superstitious" or "violent" methods to injure her. The latter provision has to be read in the social context of rural China as a ban on the often tolerated physical abuse of women, rather than as a licence allowing a bullying husband to abuse routinely his wife. Nevertheless, it does suggest that many incidents of domestic violence will continue to be dealt with by people's mediation rather than by the courts.

In other Chapters too, efforts are made to respond to the disadvantaged position of women in post-Mao society. The most significant of these endeavours to promote change are to be found in the sections of the Law dealing with property and employment. The former reaffirms women's rights of inheritance, and rights to farm land under the rural responsibility system. The succession rights of widows are given special protection but little more than that already provided in the Inheritance Law 1985. Additional protection is, however, afforded in one particular type of circumstance – thus, the succession rights of the widow who has been a particularly dutiful daughter-in-law are expressed in terms significantly stronger than those used in the Inheritance Law itself. Article 32 of the women's law insists that there shall be no infringement of the inheritance rights of a married woman who has taken principal responsibility for providing care for her mother-in-law or father-in-law. She is a first order heir and takes equally with the children of the deceased. Given the continued importance in the Chinese countryside of traditional attitudes on widow's rights, it is likely that the widow who intends to remarry will continue to be barred in social practice from retaining possession of the property that she has inherited. For this reason Article 31 of the new law emphasises the widow's right to dispose freely of the share of the estate which she has inherited and "no one is permitted to interfere with the disposal." Articles 31 and 32 do, however, appear to reflect not so much the state's concern with women's rights as its policy that the household should function effectively as a unit of care. That is to say, women's rights are here given special protection because they contribute to China's economic development policies.

Gender discrimination in employment matters is another major concern for the new law. Building on legislation introduced in the late 1980s the new law attempts to address the problem of unequal treatment of women at work, and stipulates that there is to be equality in the right to work and in matters of hiring, pay, housing and other material benefits, and promotion (Articles 21 to 24). The welfare needs of physically disadvantaged women are given special attention in Article 27: "the state should develop social insurance, social relief and medicare systems to provide material assistance for old, sick or disabled women." Discrimination against women in relation to bearing children is also addressed – along with the prohibition in Article 26 on dismissal of a woman worker on grounds of marriage, pregnancy and childbirth, specific safeguards are offered in Article 25 for women during pregnancy and for a period after childbirth. However, paragraph 1 of Article 25 may well serve to reinforce traditional gender stereotypes in the world of work. It speaks of "women's special needs" (*funü tedian*) as a basis for limiting access to certain kinds of work – a unit "should not assign women any work or labour that is unsuitable for them." Moreover, the specific safeguards afforded women in relation to pregnancy and associated matters may also have unintended consequences inimical to the employment position of women as the law appears to assume that the current system – in which it is the wife's unit that will bear the cost of such protection – will continue.

The chapter on political rights contains little more than some encouragement to women and relevant governmental and legislative bodies to improve the position of women in public life and, in Article 13, for the authorities to ensure that complaints about the infringement of women's rights and interests are dealt with properly. The following chapter deals with educational matters, and *inter alia*, reminds parents and guardians of their duty to ensure that their daughters receive compulsory education (Article 17). It also encourages the state to continue the good fight against female illiteracy. Chapter VI is concerned with rights of the person and reaffirms provisions in the Criminal Law 1979, recent amendments to the Criminal Law, and the General Principles of the Civil Law 1985 that protect women's rights to life, portrait, and reputation.

The women's protection law attempts to address the continuing problems of gender stratification in socialist China. It identifies many of the more intractable difficulties which Chinese women face, but is much stronger on exhortatory language than it is on concrete, effective measures to enhance the status of women and to protect the rights and interests of women. To this, and the other limitations noted above in our discussions of the General Principles Chapter, we should note that the very introduction of such a law may have unintended consequences that work against the intention of the law. In particular, PRC law now provides for the special treatment of women, the disabled, the young and the elderly in a curious parallel to the law of imperial China. By identifying women as a socially disadvantaged category in need of special protection there is the danger that the law will strengthen social definitions of women as being less than the equal of men and thereby perpetuate inequality between the sexes. Moreover, as we have seen in earlier parts of this paper, recent developments in other areas of the law have tended to work against, rather than to promote, the status of women. Indeed, the Women's Law itself tends to deal with the position of women in a social world in which the economy is still dominated by the government and public ownership. As a result, it is even less equipped to deal with issues raised by the emerging private sector. In my view, the Law tends also to deal with the symptoms rather than the causes of gender discrimination – little attention is given in the law to the role of family, education, the media, the single child policy and so on in the creation of gender stratification.

CZECH REPUBLIC

NEW PROBLEMS AND OLD WORRIES

*Jiri F. Haderka**

I   NEW FRONTIER IN EUROPE

On New Year's Eve 1992, the Czechoslovak Federation lived its last hours. At midnight, a new frontier in Central Europe was born, running from the Pass of Jablunkov at the Polish border through the chain of the Beskydy mountains to Breclav at the right bank of the Morava river near Lower Austria's lowlands. The old historical Czech Lands (i.e. Bohemia, Moravia and a part of Silesia) remained on the west of this line. Slovakia, created after the First World War by the Trianon Treaty as an integral part of the unitary Czechoslovak Republic, appeared on the east.

The cheer below the Bratislava Castle, fomented by sausages and wine freely distributed by the Government, did not reflect the general mood there. Prague retained a relatively quiet face with several more wrinkles on it.

The dismemberment of the Federation was peaceful.[1] No shot was fired, nobody was hurt or even killed.

The extinction of the Federation was prepared by the last Federal Constitutional Act no. 1992-524 C.L. (Collection of Laws) and was executed in accordance with it.

The new Czech Constitution, enacted two weeks before the dismemberment, entered into vigour on January 1, 1993 and was published under no. 1993-1 C.L. It conserved the former Czechoslovak Charter of Fundamental Rights and Freedoms as a part of the constitutional system. The old flag was not the only reminder kept from the preceding period. Another Constitutional Act no. 1993-4 C.L. accepted the former law and order and confirmed that the new succession state took over the international

---

*   Judge, and Professor of the Faculty of Law at the Palacky University in Olomouc.
1   This article follows up the previous contribution by the same author: "Czechoslovakia: Decline and Fall of the Federation and Its Family Law", in: (1992) University of Louisville Journal of Family Law, Annual Survey of Family Law, 16, 281-291.

A. Bainham (ed.), The International Survey of Family Law 1994, 181–197.
© 1996 *The International Society of Family Law. Printed in the Netherlands.*

obligations as well as the rights resulting from international treaties concluded by its predecessor.[2]

In its art. 10 the Czech Constitution also proclaimed its will to give primacy to obligations resulting from ratified and published international treaties on human rights and fundamental freedoms as immediately binding before national Parliamentary Acts.

The unwanted creation of the new state as a necessity evoked by the Slovak decision to separate has brought many complications from the point of view of international public law. One of them was the need to apply for new admission to the Council of Europe, realized on June 30, 1993.[3]

The Slovak Republic achieved the same result simultaneously, having provided guarantees concerning rights of the Hungarian minority.

Complications also afflicted home law and order because it was necessary to create new authorities and institutions to implement the Constitution and to rebuild the economic structure on the diminished territory, as only 2/3 of inhabitants and 3/5 of the former territory remained in the frame of the Czech Republic. All that menaced the pace of transition to market economy and restructuralization of law and order.[4]

---

2   Cf. D. Jilek: Mezinarodnepravni pohled na ustanoveni cl. 10 Ustavy Ceske republiky (Art. 10 of the Constitution of the Czech Republic from an International Law Point of View), Casopis pro pravni teorii a praxi, (1), (1993), 1: 111-120, in comparison with the former Federal Constitution as analyzed by J. Malenovsky: Mezinarodni smlouvy o lidskych pravech a cs. ustavni pravo (International Treaties on Human Rights and Czechoslovak Constitutional Law), in: Pravnik, (131), (1992), 11: 931-949.

3   Cf. J. Malenovsky: K pravnim aspektum prijeti Ceske republiky do Rady Evropy (On Legal Aspects of Admission of the Czech Republic to the Council of Europe), Pravnik, (132), (1993), 10-11: 886-902, J. Capek: Evropska Umluva o ochrane lidskych prav a clenstvi Ceske republiky v Rade Evropy (European Convention on Human Rights Protection and Membership of the Czech Republic in the Council of Europe), Pravni praxe, (42), (1994), 2: 69-72, J. de Morzellec: Nastupnictvi statu – priklad rozdeleni CSFR (Succession of States – Example of Dismemberment of the C.S.F.R.), Pravnik, (132), (1993), 9: 777-784.

4   J. Hrebejk: Ustavni poradek CR (Constitutional Order of the Czech Republic), Pravnik, (132), (1993), 5: 441-442, J. Barta: Nektere pravni souvislosti samostatnosti CR a tzv. recepcni zakon (Several Legal Circumstances of Independence of the Czech Republic and the so-called 'Conservation Act', ibidem, pp.365-373, V. Sevcik: Vyhledy ustavnosti v novem state – Pokus o analyzujici sondu (Constitutionality Prospects in the New State – An Analysis Attempt), Pravnik, (133), (1994), 12: 1011-1027, V. Mikule: Zruseni cs. federace z hlediska ustavniho prava (Abolition of the Czechoslovak Federation from the Point of View of Constitutional Law), Pravnik, (132), (1993), 9: 785-794.

In the days in which I am writing these lines, i.e. at the beginning of 1995, the majority of the economic and legal difficulties have been overcome, but what remains to the present are consequences of the dismemberment for the human factor: the impact of the new frontier on families.

II FAMILY RELATIONS IN THE LIGHT OF CZECH-SLOVAK INTERNATIONAL PRIVATE LAW

A A small lesson in demography

In the twenties, Czech-Slovak marriages became a very common phenomenon. The Slovaks lacked their own developed stratum of intelligentsia. Czech judges, teachers, officers and clerks streamed to Slovak towns and villages in a considerable number. There has never been a significant understanding barrier between Czech and Slovak – as it does not exist between English and Scottish from the Lowlands or langue d'oc and langue d'oie in France – though Slovak evolved to a different literary language in the middle of the 19th century. The Czechs and the Slovaks were considered as two branches of the same Czechoslovak nation. Czech husbands and Slovak wives often had children born in the Slovak environment, with siblings born in the Czech environment, often speaking both languages.

After Munich and the following Nazi occupation of the Czech Lands, a reverse movement began: expulsion of the majority of the Czechs by the government of the semi-fascist rest of Slovakia, diminished by the Viennese Arbitration in 1938, to its mountainous regions for the benefit of Hungarian demands. Most of the expatriated families remained in the Czech Lands even after the end of the Second World War, not challenging a new beginning in the eastern part of the liberated country.

After 1945, transfer of the majority of the German population from the Czech border areas back to Germany, resulting from the Potsdam Treaty, gave occasion to Slovak peasants and craftsmen to move to the western part of the Republic. Later, in the fifties, Slovak steel workers and miners flowed to the industrial basin around Ostrava in North-Eastern Moravia. A considerable part of them founded families, marrying Czech women.

Middle and Eastern Slovakia was the home of the Gypsy population. They had their adverse experience, won between 1938-1945, and penury

of their daily life in dreary clay villages influenced their slow and in-
conspicuous move to Bohemian and Moravian towns.

At present, it is estimated that approximately 300,000 persons of Slovak
origin live in the Czech Lands and that 300,000 Gypsies are settled here,
though only 33,000 of them adhere to Gypsy nationality.

In the last years, a new phenomenon acceded to all that: that of social
orphans in tender age, placed in Czech children's homes and abandoned
by their mothers who had come mostly from Slovakia. Inaccurately, they
are called "children from the E-55 road" as those unfortunate women had
made themselves frequently known as prostitutes seeking customers on E-55
travelling here from or to eastern Germany. At present one estimates the
number of those E-55 children at 1,200. They were born on the Czech
territory, with unclear Philistine and doubtful citizenship. They mostly remain
blocked in collective care because of helplessness of social care inspectors
and hesitations of lawyers.[5]

B   *Problems of citizenship*

Now we must proceed to questions of citizenship, before we approach the
problems of Czech-Slovak international private law and procedure.

Citizenship, is of key importance as the so-called "connecting factor"
not only for solution of the dilemma of Czech or Slovak courts' jurisdiction
in family matters but also for solution of the collision rules dilemma. Luck-
ily, the conflicts of laws are rather latent, as until present the Czech family
law and the Slovak family law, inherited from the times of the former
Federation, have the same wording.

Between 1918 and 1968, in a unitary state, citizenship in Czechoslovakia
was also unitary and the same for everybody. After federalization in 1968
two-fold citizenship emerged: national Czech or Slovak on one hand, and
Federal on the other hand. Originally, national citizenship had been
introduced as primary, and Federal citizenship was deduced from it. Later
Federal citizenship was accorded precedence to avoid cases of persons having
only national citizenship and not Federal citizenship at the same time. In

---

5   A very good report on the problem is given by I. Jirku: Deti na odsun (Children for
    Transfer), Mlada fronta dnes October 27, 1994. For further evaluation cf. articles in
    the Lidove noviny newspaper from January 12-14, 21, 26, 1995.

normal cases, everybody should have had Federal citizenship accompanied by a national one: extraordinarily, cases of only Czechoslovak citizenship could occur.

The end of the Czechoslovak Federation brought a new problem. It was clear that Federal citizenship would disappear – but how would it be possible to legislate now on Czech citizenship and Slovak citizenship? It was undoubted that the legislative solutions should be coordinated at least to a certain degree. The Slovak legislative team showed more inclination to admission of the possibility of a two-fold, i.e. cumulative Czech and Slovak, citizenship. The Czech team was against it and strived to create exclusive Czech or Slovak citizenship.

The result of Czech legislative effort ended in this manner and is enacted in the Czech Citizenship Act 1993-40 C.L., as amended by the Act 1993-272 C.L. Several articles of this Act were attacked by an aggrieved group of mostly left-wing deputies and submitted to the Czech Constitutional Court. Its decision no. 1994-207 rejected the grievance as unfounded. The Act remained without further changes, though in its singular sections it had been criticized by home and foreign observers, including two U.S. senators. But litigious points will not be the object of our inquiry.

For our purpose it seems necessary to report the following content of the above-mentioned Act:
Czech citizenship can be acquired
·   by birth, if at least one of the child's parents is a Czech citizen or if they are persons without any citizenship and at least one of them has his/her permanent residence in the Czech Republic and the child was born on the Czech territory (art. 3);
·   by adoption of the child, if at least one of the adopters is a citizen of the Czech Republic, with consequences since the day of the final adoption judgement (art. 3A);
·   by determination of paternity in case of a child born out of wedlock, if his/her mother is a foreign citizen or has no citizenship and his/her father is a Czech citizen, as from the day of the concurrent declaration of the parents about paternity or since the day of the final judgement determining the paternity (art. 4);
·   in case of a foundling who has not attained 15 years of age, if he/she was found on the Czech territory and if it is not proven that he/she has acquired citizenship of another state (art. 5);

·   by declaration of the person concerned, if he/she did not have either Czech or Slovak citizenship on December 31, 1992, but was a citizen of the Federation (art. 6);

·   by bestowing it upon the person concerned on his/her request under five conditions determined in art. 7, with four of them pardonable. In the case of a minor under 15 years of age, the parents are entitled to include him/her in their request. The request of the legal guardian of a minor of the above-mentioned age can also be handed over separately. We should add that in case of disagreement between the parents, it is the court which is entitled to resolve their discord according to art. 49 of FC (Family Code). If the legal guardian functioning in the place of parents is a tutor or curator, he/she needs the court's approval to the request.

Loss of Czech citizenship is possible by

·   dismissal from the state bond on request (art. 14);

·   declaration by the citizen (art. 16);

·   acquisition of foreign citizenship under conditions of art. 13 and 17.

Special alleviative means for acquisition of Czech citizenship in the transitional period till the end of 1993 were enacted in coincidence with extinction of the Czechoslovak Federation for citizens of the Slovak Republic. They had special regard for children and the elderly (art. 18-19).[6]

C   Main rules of international private law concerning Czech-Slovak family law relations

Both the succession states inherited the old Federal Act 1963-97 C.L. concerning Private International Law and Rules of Procedure Relating Thereto as amended by the Acts 1969-158 C.L., 1992-234 C.L. and 1992-264 C.L.

Art. 2 of the Act states that its provisions shall be applied only if an international treaty does not provide otherwise.

---

6   Foreign criticism of the Czech Citizenship Act, 1993 concentrated on pre-requisites of bestowal of Czech citizenship according to art. 7. E.g. U.S. Congressmen S.H. Hoyer and D. De Concini criticized it from the point of view of human rights and evoked President Havel's reaction that the law seemed to be in order, only its application was sometimes inadequate. Cf. Lidove noviny November 14, 21; December 7, 1994; January 12, 1995. Afterwards, the matter was mentioned in the U.S. Report on Human Rights in the World. Czech explanations are expected.

A treaty of this kind was concluded between the Czech Government and the Slovak Government on October 29, 1992. The circumstances of conclusion of the treaty "On Legal Aid Provided by Judicial Authorities and on Regulation of Selected Legal Relations in Civil and Criminal Matters" were very anomalous.

At the time of its signing, the Czech Republic and the Slovak Republic were parts of the Czechoslovak Federation and could not be considered as fully entitled subjects of international public law. On the other hand, it was clear that the Federation would not survive and that it was necessary to achieve regulation of its parts' relations for the time when they would emerge as fully entitled public international law subjects.

The treaty was ratified thereafter and published in 1993. For the Czech Republic it entered into force on April 5, 1993. It is accompanied by a Final Protocol as its integral part.

In my opinion, the treaty has not led to good results. The former Federation had bilateral treaties with its neighbours which went far further in encouraging legal collaboration than this one. The negotiators should have been aware that in future the Czech Republic and the Slovak Republic would have very intensive need of contacts in the private law area, first of all in family law matters. It was as if they had been afraid to respect the peculiar situation of the new countries, for three generations parts of a common state, and to transgress the line of cool pragmatism. Instead of negotiating special bilateral rules, the treaty repeatedly invokes the Hague Conventions and in many regards does not follow the model of other bilateral treaties, as concluded e.g. with Poland, Hungary, East Germany etc.

Nevertheless, the general spirit of political correctness breaks through in several points. E.g. courts are entitled to collaborate directly without interference of the Ministries of Justice (art. 9 and 10 of the treaty).

We must admit that at the time of conclusion of the treaty it was superfluous that it contained rules on conflicts of laws (the so-called collision rules). The reason was the lasting uniformity of substantive law in civil and criminal law areas. But what is lacking, is the fact that the treaty itself does not contain rules on problems of international Czech and Slovak jurisdiction. This deficiency is only partly remedied by the Final Protocol. If we leave aside its art. III and IV, which had only temporary importance, we should concentrate on art. I and II – the only ones concerning civil law matters.

Art I. states:

> "In procedures concerning legal relations between parents and children, the jurisdiction will belong to the court of that contracting party on whose territory the child had his/her permanent residence at the time of initiation of the procedure. Yet in case of divorce of marriage the jurisdiction belongs to the court which is competent to the divorce proceedings."

This article has evoked many uncertainties and hesitations. Its terminology is not quite clear and is rather ambiguous. The leading case 13 CO 654/94 of the Regional Court in Ostrava issued on December 29, 1994, gave the following explication of it:

Under the term "legal relations between parents and children" all the relations of substantive law contained in the second part of FC should be understood. These parts have the same wording for both the contracting parties till now and they did not differ at the time of conclusion of the Final Protocol. This term encompasses all topics forming the content of art. 30-84 of FC, i.e. not only relations between children and parents in a narrower sense, but also matters of adoption, tutorship and curatorship. The term "permanent residence" of the child should be explained as indicated in art. 88 of the Code of Civil Procedure (CCP), then also identical for both the contracting parties. That means that the child has his/her permanent residence as agreed by his/her parents, or determined by the court's decision or by other crucial circumstances, such as lasting placement of the child in institutional care if no other possibility remained.

Art. II of the Final Protocol deals with custodianship jurisdiction and has in mind cases of incapacitated persons and care for their personal and property matters.

Other questions of jurisdiction are not settled by the bilateral treaty and its complementary Final Protocol. Therefore it is necessary to use the rules of Act no. 1963-97 C.L. as mentioned above.

Here citizenship of persons involved in family law relations plays a considerable role both in relation to jurisdiction and collision rules.

III RECENT CHANGES IN FAMILY LAW LEGISLATION

There is not too much to report on changes to the Czech family law. In 1993-1994 the Czech FC remained untouched by legislators.

As to the Foster Care Act (FCA), we reported its partial modifications in our preceding contribution.[7]

Since that time it was only slightly modified by the Act no. 1993-307 C.L. in its art. 5, section 5, where a sentence was added, enlarging the rights of the entrusted child to allowance for coverage of his/her needs till 18 years of age if he/she cannot be employed.

Other partial changes are contained in governmental ordinances 1993-154, 1993-336 and 1994-245 C.L. They deal only with the amount of allocations paid in connection with foster care, successively raised to compensate for the level of inflation.

Further partial changes were introduced by the ministerial regulation 1993-136 C.L. which displaced the former regulation 1973-52 C.L., complementing the FCA.

In general, the last two years were a period of relative stagnation of family law reform preparations.

The sentiment that something should happen and that a start to continuation of the reform must be given was growing particularly among social care inspectors and Faculties of Law. Perhaps the turning point was the conference on family law codification organized by the Faculty of Law of the Charles University in Prague in May, 1994.[8]

The fact that 1994 had been declared as the "International Year of the Family" by the UNO and was accompanied by such world congresses as those in Cardiff, Brussels[9] and The Hague worked as an incentive.

The Ministry of Labour and Social Affairs and the Ministry of Justice entered into an exchange of opinions, the Office for Legislation and Administration was involved, the deputies of the Parliament interested. After local elections, the moment for the decisive action seemed to appear. In the

---

7   Cf. Note 1.
8   The results of the conference were successively published in the monthly Pravni praxe, (42), (1994), 8: 501-502.
9   Czech reports on the congresses by myself cf. in Pravni praxe, (42), (1994), 9: 560-565, and ibidem: 10: 626-633.

first days of January 1995 the Government adopted its ruling on the matter (no. 1995-1, from January 4, 1995).

Preparatory materials for the Government suggested that family law reform should be divided into two successive steps.

The first step should include the amendment of the FC with the aim of its depuration from ideological admixtures originating from the totalitarian period and bring it to harmony with the Constitution and the exigencies of international treaties and other instruments of international law. This step should be realized before the end of 1995.

The second step should be incorporation of family law into a quite new General Civil Code, which would be prepared approximately 2-3 years later; this reform should be accompanied by adoption of a special Act on legal and social protection of the family. Thus legal relations belonging to the frame of private law should be separated from those belonging to the area of public law.

The above-named Office and Ministries should be entrusted with the responsibility for the legislative work.[10]

The final version as adopted by the Government conserves nearly all important features of this concept inspired by the conference of Law Faculties in May 1994, with one exception.

It leaves out the two-step method and imposes the realization of the reform all at once, in the frame of the completed Civil Code. The principles of the reform should be ready for submission to the Government by September 30, 1995 and the complete text of the draft by autumn 1996.

IV RECENT EVOLUTION OF JUDICATURE

A *Recognition of foreign decisions in matrimonial matters*

The Act no. 1963-97 C.L. concerning Private International Law and Rules of Procedure Relating Thereto, as amended, governs recognition of foreign decisions in matrimonial matters and determination of paternity in a specific manner. This occurs by way of the so-called "delibation procedure" before the Czech Supreme Court.

---

10   Cf. short reports in the Czech press, e.g. Lidove noviny, January 5, 1995.

Recently, decision D 1994-46 has given an example of this kind in a case including a German international element. It is the Czech Supreme Court's judgement no. Ncu 182/93 dating from March 30, 1994.

To make the topic better understandable, we begin with quotation from several articles of the above-mentioned Act.

Art. 67

"1) Final foreign decisions in matrimonial matters[11] and in matters involving determination (ascertainment or denial) of paternity, in which at least one of the parties is a Czech citizen, shall be recognized in the Czech Republic only on the basis of a special decision, unless barred by provisions of the articles 63 and 64, letters b, c, and d.[12]

2) Only the Supreme Court of the Czech Republic may pronounce the recognition of the decisions listed in sec. 1 after hearing the opinion of the Attorney General of the Czech Republic. Besides the parties, the motion

---

11   According to art. 38, section 1 proceedings concerning divorce, invalidation of marriage and determination of existence of marriage.

12   Art. 63 states: "Decisions of judicial authorities of a foreign state in the matters listed in art. 1, as well as foreign judicial settlements and foreign notarial papers in these matters (further referred to only as 'foreign decisions') shall have legal effect in the Czech Republic if they have become final according to an affidavit of the respective foreign authority and if they have been recognized by the Czech authority."
The cited art. 1 indicates the purpose of the Act and in this connection states that it governs civil law, family law, labour law and other similar relations including an international element.
Art. 64 has the following wording:
"A foreign decision may not be recognized or executed if:
a) its recognition is hindered by the exclusive jurisdiction of the Czech authorities or if the proceedings could not be carried out by any authority of the foreign state, should the provisions concerning the competence of the Czech courts be applied to the consideration of the jurisdiction of the foreign authority;
b) a Czech authority has issued a final decision on the same legal relation or if the final decision issued by an authority of a third state was recognized in the Czech Republic;
c) the foreign authority deprived through its procedure the party against whom the decision is to be recognized, of the possibility to take proper part in the proceedings, in particular if the latter had not been personally served with the summons or the motion to initiate the proceedings, or if the defendant had not been personally served with the motion to initiate the proceedings;
d) the recognition is contrary to the Czech public order;
e) reciprocity is not guaranteed; reciprocity shall not be required if the foreign decision is not directed against a Czech citizen or juristic person."

may be filed by any person who proves his/her legal interest and, in the public interest, also by the Attorney General of the Czech Republic. The Supreme Court of the Czech Republic shall decide by judgement; it need not order a hearing.

3) The decisions listed in sec. 1 may be recognized only if the facts of the case have been ascertained in a manner which basically conforms to the respective provisions of Czech law."

Art. 68:

"1) If at the decisive time all parties were citizens of the state whose decision is involved, the decisions listed in art. 67, sec. 1 shall have, without further proceedings, the same legal effect in the Czech Republic as final Czech decisions, unless they are contrary to public order.

2) The same shall apply to decisions issued by the authorities of other foreign states, if such decisions are recognized in the home states of all the parties."

The sentence of the decision D 1994-46 states:

"The motion requiring recognition of a foreign decision pronouncing in-validity of marriage of spouses from whom at least one has been a citizen of the Czech Republic cannot be satisfied if the marriage concerned was concluded on the Czech territory after the preceding marriages of both the spouses had been finished by divorce pronounced by a final decision of a Czech court. It all relates to such a case where the ground for deter-mination of nullity of the marriage, stated by a foreign court, was the fact that the decision of the Czech court on the divorce, foregoing the conclusion of the above-said marriage, had not been in relation to one of the spouses, who had had also a foreign citizenship, yet recognized by the authority competent for the territory of the state whose citizenship one of the spouses had acquired."

The underlying facts can be briefly summarized as follows:

The marriage of J.K. and his wife E.K., formerly E.R., was concluded on Czech territory on April 29, 1967 before the competent Czech authority. It was terminated by divorce by a Czech court on February 16, 1981 and the decision of this competent authority became final on April 6, 1981.

The marriage of R.H., born R.H., and her husband V.H. concluded on Czech territory, was terminated by a Czech court on June 17, 1980 and this decision became final on June 20, 1980.

At that time all the persons concerned were Czech citizens, living on Czech territory.

The man J.K. and the woman R.H., now R.K., concluded thereafter a new marriage in the civil form on Czech territory on June 13, 1981. According to the Czech law and order, i.e. art. 1 and 11 section 1 of the Czech Family Code (then Czechoslovak FC) there was no legal impediment to the validity of marriage of J.K. and his new wife R.K., formerly R.H.

In contrast to the woman R.K., who had always been exclusively a Czech citizen, the man J.K. had acquired in addition to his Czech citizenship, which has preeminence according to art. 33 of the Act, a second citizenship – that of the Federal Republic of Germany before he divorced in the Czech Republic in 1981. On the day of conclusion of his second marriage with R.H. on Czech territory in 1981, the divorce of his preceding marriage had not been yet recognized by the competent German authority. On this basis the German court in the town of D. declared the marriage of J.K. and R.K. void from the point of view of German law and order. Thereafter, the first J.K.'s wife initiated delibation proceedings, aiming at recognition of the final decision of the German court in the Czech Republic.

The Czech Supreme Court declined the motion, in accordance with the opinion of the Attorney General. It pressed the point that such recognition would be contrary to the postulates of art. 64 of the Act 1963-97 as amended by the Acts 1969-158, 1992-234 and 1992-264 C.L.

Evaluation of preconditions of the valid conclusion of J.K.'s and R.K.'s marriage was in the exclusive competence of the Czech authorities according to art. 64 a) of the Act. Recognition of the German court's decision on nullity of this marriage is barred in the first place by the clause of art. 64 d) of the same Act. An opposite view would signify that the matter could not be evaluated according to Czech law but according to foreign law – without legal grounds for its use.

B   Affiliation matters

Here we are obliged to report two decisions.

1   The first of them, D 1993-43, concerns a special case of paternity determination in which the man susptected of having had sexual intercourse with
the child's mother in the critical period before the birth of the child died
before the initiation of the proceedings before the court. In this rather exceptional group of cases, the motion is filed against a special guardian in the
place of the dead putative father, instituted by the court before the initiation
of the proceedings, as stated in art. 55 of FC. According to the principles
of art. 54 section 2 of FC, the plaintiff (the child or the mother) must prove
the existence of the sexual intercourse and the guardian as the defendant
should prove that the deceased could not be the biological father of the child,
even if the intercourse in due time had been proven.

The aim of the decision D 1993-43 is to emphasize that the procedure
should not be considered as a mere formality but that it should follow all
the rules governing other procedures relating to the third paternity
presumption.

The decision states that all important evidence must be brought during
the proceedings, i.e. not only evidence by witnesses and documentary
evidence, but that also expert evidence, such as haematological examination,
comes into consideration. I would add that the DNA-analysis should be also
taken into account – if there is a possibility of its reasonable use.

2   The second decision, D 1994-42, has in mind the case of a special motion
of the Attorney General according to art. 62. of FC aimed at denial of paternity if the interest of society requires so.

The decision states that the Attorney is not entitled to file an appeal if
the decision has satisfied his motion: formerly, before the change of art.
35 of the Civil Procedure Code in 1991, it was deemed that he had this
possibility because of his extraordinary position which differed from that
of other participants.

C   Maintenance

1   The decision D 1993-18 deals with a general problem which is important
on a large scale for all categories of maintenance cases. Its subject is the
legal character of the so-called "compensation money" paid to employees

at the end of their labour relation: it does not represent an equivalent of the wage. This special character must also be taken into consideration when evaluating the economic situation of the obliged person in deciding on alimony.

2   D 1994-17 deals with the situation of an entrepreneur in the position of an obliged person vis-à-vis the maintenance right of his/her child. Here the court is bound to investigate his/her income in the past calendar year as indicated in his/her income tax return declaration and confirmed by a tax administration authority. This sort of evidence does not absolve the court from the duty to use other available kinds of evidence important for this purpose.

3   D 194-22 clarifies decision-making on alimony after placement of a child in foster care. Parents or other relatives obliged to pay maintenance for the child pay to the district authorities who pay the allocations on the child's maintenance in advance to the foster parents.

4   The situation of a child who has finished his/her compulsory school education but continues preparing for his/her future career by attending supplementary special school extensions is treated in D 1993-11: such a child retains in principle his/her right to maintenance from the parents.

5   In D 1994-37 the principle is deduced that a divorced woman has no alimony right from the property of her former husband's parents.

D   Community property of spouses

In the field of matrimonial property relations we have only three decisions to mention.

The first one relates to a rather procedural problem. D 1994-10 states that bringing a partial judgement in matters of this kind does not come into consideration.

The second decision, D 1993-44, deals with the question under what preconditions a yet unfinished building belongs to the community property of the spouses and which stage of construction is decisive for the evaluation.

The last decision, D 1994-66, confirms that a hired TV set does not belong to the community property of the spouses.

E   Joint tenancy of a flat by husband and wife

The following group of published decisions deals with matters related to the joint tenancy of a flat by a husband and wife.

In D 1993-28 it is stated that the court's decision on evacuation to a substitutional flat has, in the light of the new regulation under the amendment to the Civil Code by the Act no. 1991-509 C.L., the character of a decision in merito and not only of that about the maturity of the principal claim. Thus the legal position of the evacuated becomes stronger.

D 1993-29 affirms that the claim on abolition of the right of a joint tenancy by spouses, the determination of the future exclusive tenant and the duty to evacuate the flat in dependence on acquisition of a substitutional flat are indivisible. If the appeal aims only against one of them, all are subjected to the revision.

Finally, D 1993-26 states that in case of judicial abolition of the common tenancy right to a cooperative flat by former spouses, the spouse who is obliged to evacuate the flat is entitled to move to a substitutional flat and not only to a lower category accommodation.

V   CONCLUSIONS

The hope that the period 1993-1994 would bring transformation of family law in the Czech Republic evaporated: the stimulus brought by the International Year of the Family was too feeble against the internal forces resisting the legislative approach.[13] The Ministries quarrelled over to whom the duty to initiate the legislative efforts belonged, the Parliament was overwhelmed by other tasks which it considered more important, and the Government adopted its directive on family law reform only after the end of the year. Its contents seem not to have awakened too much enthusiasm in the circles which will be entrusted with the realization of the governmental ruling no. 1995-1 from January 4, 1995. No wonder: the words are ambiguous in several places, the supposed time spans too short and danger of pressures from various interested groups very vividly aroused.

---

13   Evaluation in a rather biting critical tone cf. J. Ondrackova: A tak uplynul Rok rodiny.... (And So the Year of the Family Passed...), Lidove noviny January 24, 1995.

Perhaps in our next contribution we will be able to report more on the long awaited deeds.

ENGLAND

ENGLAND IN THE INTERNATIONAL YEAR OF THE FAMILY

*Michael Freeman**

I   IMAGES OF THE FAMILY IN 1994

1994 was the "International Year of the Family". In England (more accurately for these purposes Britain) little more was heard of the "back to basics" campaign of the previous year[1]: its final demise, like his, came when a Tory M.P. was found hanging with an orange in his mouth and clad only in stockings and suspenders. The Government hesitated on divorce reform, wisely perhaps in the light of sustained criticism of its proposals from professional pressure groups and leading family law scholars.[2] The number of divorces rose to their highest ever.[3] The number of marriages hit a 150-year low.[4] At 31 per cent the incidence of illegitimacy was the highest ever recorded.[5] The number of children on child protection registers also increased sharply.[6] So did the number of children living in poverty (now it is a staggering one in three).[7] We all retain our images of the year: to me the abiding ones are of police dragging away protesters in wheelchairs angry at a government blocking a bill on disabled persons' rights[8] and of the Christmas scene in Rhyl where a baby of 18 months died of thirst whilst

---

*   Professor of English Law, University College London.
1   See M.D.A. Freeman, "Back To Basics" (1995) 33 *University of Louisville Journal of Family Law* 329.
2   For criticisms see G. Davis (1994) 24 Fam Law 103, C. Barton (1994) 24 Fam Law 104; (1994) 24 Fam Law 349: more positively see S. Roberts (1994) 24 Fam Law 204.
3   There were 160,385 decrees in 1992. This is the highest rate so far recorded of 13.7 persons divorcing per thousand married population. See Office of Population Censuses and Surveys, *1992 Marriage and Divorce Statistics: England and Wales* (London: HMSO).
4   *Ibid.* And see *The Times*, February 24, 1995.
5   Office of Population Censuses and Surveys, *Population Trends*, 771 (1994). See, further, David Utting, *Family and Parenthood* (York: Joseph Rowntree Foundation, 1995).
6   There were 24,500 additions to the register in 1992 (see Department of Health, *Child Protection: Messages from Research*) (London: HMSO, 1995, p. 28).
7   House of Commons Social Security Committee, *Low Income Statistics. Low Income Families* 1979-1989 (London: HMSO 1993) (one in four living at official poverty line: a third living within 140 per cent margin of basic benefit level.)
8   And see Ian Parker, "Spitting on Charity", *The Independent On Sunday* April 9, 1995.

A. Bainham (ed.), The International Survey of Family Law 1994, 199–225.
© 1996 The International Society of Family Law. Printed in the Netherlands.

his parents overdosed and the family lay dead for up to five weeks before their bodies were found.[9]

Of the many reports on the family in 1994, two, published shortly after the end of the year, stand out. Of the Rowntree inquiry little need be said: it charts rising inequality and its impact upon the family and is a powerful indictment of the 1980s and beyond.[10] The report of the United Nations' committee on the rights of the child may be of greater interest to family lawyers.[11] Given that Mrs Thatcher gave a "solemn undertaking" at the World Summit on children in 1990 to give a high priority to the rights of children, this report demonstrates a huge chasm between pious words and real actions. The British Government is castigated for failing children in nearly every aspect of their lives. Serious concern is voiced about the number of children living in poverty[12], as well as about social welfare cuts. The committee is alarmed at the number of children begging and sleeping on the streets – and, though it does not say so, this number is likely to increase rather than decrease.[13] Although the report welcomes the Children Act of 1989 and initiatives on bullying in schools, cot deaths and sexual abuse of children, it expresses concern on sixteen different issues ranging from treatment of children as young as 10 under Northern Ireland's emergency powers legislation to the extent of child poverty and the plight of child refugees.

In particular, the United Nations calls for legislation to ban corporal punishment in private schools and to outlaw "chastisement" at home (this would bring the law into line with that in Sweden, Norway, Finland, Austria and Cyprus).[14] The committee reported that it was deeply concerned about

---

9   *The Guardian*, January 28, 1995. A leader "Walking By On The Other Side" in the same
     issue linked this to the UN Committee Report on the Rights of children in Britain.
10   *Income and Wealth* (York: Joseph Rowntree Foundation, 1995).
11   See *The Guardian*, January 28, 1995 (also *The Independent* January 28, 1995). Gerison
     Landsdown, "Minor Offences", *The Guardian*, January 18, 1995 anticipates the criticism.
     The Government's Report is published as *The UK's First Report to the UN Committee
     on the Rights of the Child* (London: HMSO, 1994).
12   See also Carey Oppenheim, *Poverty: The Facts* (London: Child Poverty Action Group,
     1993).
13   Few who examine the rights of street children think it necessary to look at countries
     such as Britain. See Judith Ennew, "Outside Childhood: Street Children's Rights" in
     B. Franklin (ed), *The Handbook of Children's Rights* (London: Routledge, 1995), p.
     201.
14   Cyprus was the latest to pass such legislation in 1995 (see EPOCH newsletter).

legislation which allows moderate and reasonable chastisement of children by parents[15] and, in the light of recent developments, sanctions it also by childminders.[16] Although a Department of Health civil servant, representing the Government, told the committee this meant only "a light smack",[17] a member of the UN committee referred in response to a recent court case in which a mother was acquitted of assault after she beat her daughter with a leather strap until she bled.[18]

The committee also castigated the plans to set up detention centres for offenders aged 12 to 14, holding this to be incompatible with the UN Convention on the Rights of the Child,[19] and called for the raising of the age of criminal responsibility. This is currently 10, though as the law now stands it is necessary to prove that a child between the ages of 10 and 14 knows that his/her act is seriously wrong as opposed to just naughty.[20] Legislation is, however, expected to overturn this *doli incapax* presumption which has stood since at least the fourteenth century.[21] By contrast the age of criminal responsibility is higher in all comparable Western European democracies save Switzerland (where, incredibly, it is 7).[22]

The committee also called for the establishment of a children's ombudsman, such as exists in Norway,[23] Sweden,[24] New Zealand and Costa Rica. This has been advocated in Britain for some years, including by myself.[25] Greater rights for children in the education system – the report talks of children being consulted over the running of their school – is also

---

15   See Children and Young Persons Act 1933 section 1 (7).

16   See *London Borough of Sutton v Davis* [1994] 1 FLR 737 (and *post*, p. 218).

17   As quoted in *The Guardian*, January 28, 1995.

18   Quoted *idem*.

19   And see *Community Care* February 2-8, 1995, p. 4.

20   *C v D.P.P.* [1995] 2 All ER 43.

21   See W. Holdsworth, *A History of English Law* (London: Methuen, vol IX, 1926) p. 140.

22   On France, where the age of criminal responsibility is 13, see J. Bourquin, *Social Work in Europe*, 1 (1), 42 (1994).

23   On which see Malfrid Flekkøy, *A Voice for Children* (London: Jessica Kingsley, 1991). See also her "Child Advocacy in Norway", *Children and Society* 2 (4), 1989.

24   See M. Koren (1995) 3 *International Journal of Children's Rights* 101.

25   See Martin Rosenbaum and Peter Newell, *Taking Children's Rights Seriously* (London: Calouste Gulbenkian, 1991).

welcome advice.[26] So is the insistence, also in the report, that children should be taught about their rights.

The Government's response to this criticism – "Britain can hold its head up high on child welfare, and every parent knows that"[27] – is hardly likely to convince. Nor I fear is the Minister responsible for the family's assessment of the state of the family in Britain at the end of the International Year of the Family.[28] As the positive achievement of the "Year", she singled out the Prime Minister's commitment to offer all four-year-olds a nursery place (it seems via a voucher scheme which has been concocted in a peculiarly ham-fisted way),[29] additional support for low-income working families to help with childcare costs,[30] and the fall in the number of children in local authority care[31] (which she attributes to the Children Act providing a clearer focus on "helping families to help themselves").[32] The Minister's statement oozes complacency (the article is entitled "Safe in our Hands" and, though she will not, necessarily,have chosen this, it accurately depicts the sentiments she expresses). She does, it is true, pick up a key theme from the International Year, namely the need for better education, information and advice on parenting issues. But it is to the voluntary sector that she looks to fulfil this need. Her article ends, as my *Survey* article began last year, with a reference to the James Bulger tragedy.[33] The reaction to this case, she notes, "expressed a nation's fear of a deep malaise within our society". But she does not share this pessimism. "The more we strengthen families and the more we strengthen the communities around them, the easier we shall feel about the way we live now", she concludes. The gulf between the Rowntree report and the UN committee's report and this assessment is unbridgeable, and, sadly, a reflection of how out of touch the Government is with the health of the family in Britain today.

---

26   And see Michael Freeman in Ron Davie, *Listening to Children in Education* (London: Fulton, 1996).

27   See John Bowis, the health minister responsible for children, quoted in *The Guardian*, January 28, 1995.

28   "Safe in our Hands", *The Guardian*, December 28, 1994. And see the criticism in a leading article "Facts of Family Life" on the same day.

29   Offering parents £1000 (which will not pay for a place) and relying on the "market" to supply the shortfall in places.

30   And see *Community Care* October 6-12 1994, p. 28.

31   See *Child Protection: Messages from Research* (London: HMSO 1995).

32   *Op cit*, note 28.

33   *Op cit*, note 1, at 329-330.

II THE LEGISLATION OF AUTONOMY

There was no major family law legislation in 1994. 1995 and 1996 are likely to be much busier as family homes and domestic legislation is promised[34] and both divorce reform[35] and adoption reform[36] is expected. The opportunity was, however, taken in 1994 finally to lay to rest the marital rape immunity.[37] The legislation confirms the decision in *R* v *R*[38] and affirms the right of a wife to say "no" to sexual intercourse with her husband. English law is thus brought into line with that in most civilised countries. The final demise of this incident of the "sexual contract",[39] astonishingly only on the agenda for the last twenty years,[40] enables us to take domestic violence more seriously. Seemingly it escaped attention during the International Year of the Woman: we must be grateful for this positive response to the International Year of the Family.

Autonomy was also enhanced by the passage of the Marriage Act of 1994, the result of a Private Member's Bill.[41] The Act extends the premises at which marriages may be solemnised beyond those conventionally listed (churches and register offices). Civil marriages may now be solemnised on premises approved by local authorities. Most of these authorities have interpreted their new power conservatively and those who wish to marry underwater or in motorway service stations will still have their desires thwarted. But it is now possible for marriages to be celebrated in a variety of "tasteful" surroundings and the new facility is being used.

---

34 The Family Homes and Domestic Violence Bill 1995, published in February 1995 and now forming part of the Family Law Bill 1995, will implement most of the Law Commission report, *Domestic Violence and Occupation of The Family Home* (Law Com. 207, 1992).

35 See Lord Chancellor's Department, *Looking to the Future – Mediation and the Ground for Divorce*, Cm. 2799 (April 1995): a Bill is anticipated in the Autumn of 1995.

36 See Department of Health, *Adoption: the Future*, Cm 2288 (November 1993).

37 Criminal Justice and Public Order Act 1994 section 142.

38 [1992] 1 AC 599.

39 See Carole Pateman, *The Sexual Contract* (Oxford: Polity Press, 1988). See also Richard Collier, *Masculinity, Law and the Family* (London: Routledge, 1995).

40 See Diana E.H. Russell, *Rape in Marriage* (New York: Macmillan 1982) and David Finkelhor and Kersti Yllo, *License to Rape* (New York: Free Press, 1985).

41 The initiative of a Tory M.P. [formerly] a comedian, Gyles Brandreth.

III MONEY AFTER DIVORCE

The Law Reports were dominated in 1994 by cases on children. The Children Act 1989 was probably the most interpreted Act of the year. This *Survey* will look at some of these developments in due course but concentrates initially on some other case law developments in 1994.

There were more reported cases on financial provision issues in 1994 than for some time. Discussion of two of the more important cases, *Brooks v Brooks*[42] and *Crozier v Crozier*[43] was squeezed into last year's *Survey*.[44] The problems raised in each of these cases will be taken up by legislation in 1995[45] so that the issues (pensions and the impact of a child support assessment upon a clean break order) will be reserved for a future *Survey* article.

The cases that were reported are indicative of the problems now occurring. Many relate to so-called changes of circumstances, unemployment, redundancy, negative equity, dependence of children beyond majority and the impact of these on previous orders. The principles in which a court will allow applications for leave to appeal out of time in financial provision cases were set out by Lord Brandon in *Barder v Caluori* in 1987:

"A court may properly exercise its discretion to grant leave to appeal out of time from an order for financial provision or property transfer made after a divorce on the ground of new events, provided that certain conditions are satisfied. The first condition is that new events have occurred since the making of the order which invalidate the basis, or fundamental assumption, upon which the order was made, so that, if leave to appeal out of time were to be given, the appeal would be likely, or very likely to succeed. The second condition is that the new events should have occurred within a relatively short time of the order having been made. While the length of time cannot be laid down precisely, I should regard it as extremely unlikely that it could be as much as a year, and that in most cases it will be no more than a few months. The third condition is that the application for leave to

---

42 [1994] 2 FLR 10 (upheld by the House of Lords in June 1995: see [1995] 3 All E.R. 257).

43 [1994] Fam 114.

44 *Op cit*, note 1, at 333, 348.

45 In the Pensions Act 1995 and Child Support Act 1995 respectively. At the time of writing (April 1995) both of these measures are at Bill stage.

appeal out of time should be made reasonably promptly in the circumstances of the case".[46]

A fourth condition, involving prejudice to third parties, was not in issue in any of the reported cases in 1994.

One of the more extraordinary sets of facts testing the *Barder* principles occurred in *S* v *S.*[47] Six years of cohabitation followed by eight of marriage and then, after a divorce with a consent order, fifteen more years of cohabitation provided the back-drop to this litigation. The ex-wife wanted to appeal out of time a consent order made fifteen years previously in order to obtain a lump sum to reflect her share of a jointly owned house and to assist with additional housing costs, furniture and car replacement, and to provide an annual income on a clean break basis. The court had no difficulty in finding a change of circumstances within the *Barder* test, and it was satisfied that the new events occurred within a relatively short time of the order. But never before had as long a period of time elapsed as in this case. This did not disturb the judge. The third condition, he held, had to be judged "according to the circumstances of the case".[48] These included "the fact that [the ex-wife] remained under the same roof with her [ex-] husband, cooking, cleaning, sharing meals, and looking after him and the daughter ... while at the same time her solicitors were clearing their minds as to how to proceed".[49] The judge was persuaded that she had acted with reasonable promptness. The case is also of interest for the way it treats cohabitation. The judge found himself constrained by precedents from 1976[50] and 1981[51] to hold that, for the purposes of standard of living enjoyed before breakdown of the marriage and duration of the marriage,[52] regard could only be had to the period between the date of the marriage and its break-down, though he conceded that public opinion on living together outside marriage had changed in the interim.[53]

In *Worlock* v *Worlock*,[54] *Penrose* v *Penrose*[55] and *Cornick* v *Cor-*

---

46   [1988] AC 20, 43.
47   [1994] 2 FLR 228.
48   *Ibid*, at 234.
49   *Ibid*, at 236.
50   *Campbell* v *Campbell* [1976] Fam 347.
51   *Foley* v *Foley* [1981] Fam 160.
52   Section 25 (2) (c) and (d) of the Matrimonial Causes Act 1973 (as amended) respectively.
53   See *op cit*, note 47, at 246.
54   [1994] 2 FLR 689 (but decided in 1991).

nick,[56] courts refused to allow subsequent events to undermine orders. In *Worlock*, the supervening event was the transfer of shares from the ex-husband's mother to the ex-husband but this had taken place two years after the clean break order. On *Barder* principles it was far too late for the consent order[57] to be set aside on grounds of fundamental change. In *Penrose*, tax liability greatly in excess of previous estimates was held to be capable of being a "new event" in the *Barder* sense, but the court refused to upset the original order[58] where the new circumstances could have been established beforehand. The ex-husband had been less than truthful with the Inland Revenue. Both Balcombe L.J. and Nourse L.J. invoked the policy consideration of the need for there to be "an end to litigation",[59] and refused his application for leave to appeal out of time. In *Cornick*, Hale J. held that the increase in value in the husband's assets was not a "new event" in the *Barder* sense, even though the alteration was unforeseeable. She noted that the "case-law, taken as a whole, does not suggest that the natural processes of price fluctuation, whether in houses, shares or any other property, and however dramatic, fall within [the *Barder*] principle".[60] The ex-wife was potentially saved from a large loss in *Cornick* because it was not a clean break case: she was thus free to apply for a variation of her periodical payments.[61]

The cases of *Richardson* v *Richardson*[62] and *Smith* v *McInerney*,[63] raise another issue of policy, and test the limits of autonomy. In *Smith* v *McInerney* what the parties agreed in a separation agreement was, with the hindsight of the husband's redundancy, much more favourable to the wife than to the husband. But Thorpe J. was clear that: "As a matter of general policy ... it is very important that what the parties themselves agree at the

---

55   [1994] 2 FLR 621.
56   [1994] 2 FLR 530.
57   The order had not been recorded as a consent order but it was not disputed that the order was made with the consent of both parties.
58   A lump sum order.
59   *Per* Balcombe L.J., *op cit*, note 55, at 632; *per* Nourse L.J., *ibid*, at 636. See also Hale J. in *Cornick*, *op cit*, note 56, at 536.
60   *Op cit*, note 56, at 536.
61   And presumably obtain a lump sum since it was open to the parties to compromise her application for an increase in her periodical payments in this way.
62   [1994] 1 FLR 286 and (No 2) [1994] 2 FLR 1051.
63   [1994] 2 FLR 1077.

time of separation – would be upheld by the courts unless there are overwhelmingly strong considerations for interference".[64] The courts sought, however, to aid the husband by extracting from the wife an indemnity in respect of the substantial periodical payments which it was envisaged the Child Support Agency would require of him.[65]

The limits of autonomy are also acknowledged in *Richardson* v *Richardson*.[66] The parties had agreed that the husband would pay periodical payments to the wife for three years. A consent order was made to this effect and it was further ordered that at the end of the three year period claims by either party for financial provision would be dismissed. The order did not contain a direction[67] precluding the wife from making an application seeking to extend the period. When the wife made such an application, it was held that the court had jurisdiction to entertain it. The suggestion that the court use its inherent jurisdiction[68] to amend the order to include the direction was rejected. When the case returned to court the duration of the periodical payments order was extended to five years, and this time there was a direction preventing her from making applications for a further extension. The court justified the extension and the departure from the principle in *Edgar* v *Edgar*[69] by pointing to the continuing responsibility the wife had for the children of the family. The court recognized that, although they were no longer minors, their dependence would probably far exceed their majority, independence being likely to come only after completion of their education.

Although the end of conduct has been heralded by Government promises on divorce,[70] it will not entirely disappear, remaining as a factor in matters relating to financial provision where it would be inequitable to disregard it.[71] Two striking examples of this were reported in 1994. Thus, in *Whiston*

---

64 *Ibid*, at 1081.
65 The CSA would ignore the fact that, pursuant to an agreement, he had transferred to his wife his half-share in the matrimonial home and collateral endowment policies in consideration of, inter alia, release from any obligation to maintain his children. And see *Crozier* v *Crozier*, *op cit*, note 43.
66 *Op cit*, note 62, at 295.
67 See Matrimonial Causes Act 1973 section 28 (1A).
68 *Cf Thynne* v *Thynne* [1955] P. 272, 313 *per* Morris L.J.
69 [1980] 3 All ER 887.
70 See *op cit*, note 35.
71 Matrimonial Causes Act 1973 section 25 (2) (g), as amended in 1984.

v *Whiston*,[72] the wife's entitlement was reduced by 10 per cent because the marriage she had entered into was bigamous. The husband's argument that public policy demanded she should have no claim at all was rejected. The judge expressed the view that "bigamy towards the close of the twentieth century does not carry the gravity that it did when the statutory offence was created in 1861".[73]

H v *H*[74] resembles the leading case of *Jones* v *Jones*,[75] though this is not discussed in Thorpe J.'s judgment. After the breakdown of the marriage,[76] the husband carried out a "brutal and perverted"[77] assault on the wife. She was hospitalised: he was sentenced to 3½ years' imprisonment. The court took this conduct into account in ordering transfer of the husband's half-share in the matrimonial home to the wife. It is difficult to quarrel with this conclusion[78] but, if conduct is to be removed from the frame, it could have been reached without recourse to the conduct provision. The court could equally have focused on such matters as earning capacity, resources, needs and mental disabilities. The husband's conduct had caused the wife's loss of earning capacity and had increased her needs. It had also psychologically scarred her. But would public opinion – said to be the gravitational force behind the conduct provision[79] – tolerate its departure from money and property questions as well?

IV DIVORCE – SOME CONFLICTS' ISSUES

In three reported cases in 1994 attempts were made, in each case unsuccessfully, to cast doubt on family law procedures in other countries. In each of the cases parties (or a party) had voluntarily participated in a foreign divorce or marriage and had then sought to impugn the proceedings (in the marriage case the ceremony) in an English court. That all the attempts failed

---

72 [1994] 2 FLR 906.
73 *Ibid*, at 908. The statutory offence was created long before 1861 (in fact in 1603).
74 [1994] 2 FLR 801.
75 [1976] Fam 8.
76 Attributable (in part no doubt) to the wife's lesbian relationship with another woman.
77 *Op cit*, note 74, at 802.
78 Though Evelyn Ellis did with *Jones* v *Jones* (see [1976] 39 MLR 97) on the ground that the husband was being punished twice.
79 See, for example, *W* v *W* [1976] Fam 107 (see Sir George Baker P. at 114).

shows both comity and a reluctance to allow parties to renege on obligations undertaken abroad. In a fourth case (*D* v *D*),[80] though, the attack was successful.

In *McCabe* v *McCabe*[81] what was in dispute was a marriage ceremony in Ghana. English conflict of laws refers matters of formalities to the *lex loci celebrationis*:[82] no question of essential validity arose in the case.[83] The husband came from Southern Ireland, the wife from Ghana: they met, it seems, in London, where she twice became pregnant by him. A marriage was then arranged by the wife's great-uncle. The husband "was told that he needed to provide £100 and a bottle of Schnapps".[84] In fact he substituted gin. The ceremony was then performed near Accra in Ghana by Uncle Nelson (the great-uncle being ill and unable to attend) in the wife's father's house before members of her family. Neither husband nor wife was present. Part of the £100 was distributed within the family and some of the gin drunk as a blessing. The couple lived together and had two children. when she petitioned for divorce in England, he argued that they were not married, since no valid marriage had taken place. The Court of Appeal did not agree: on the evidence, the essential components of a valid marriage under Akan customary law had been complied with. The wife was granted her divorce. The decision displays an open-mindedness beyond what might have been expected in the past and contrasts sharply with the attitude English legislation[85] and courts[86] take to divorces of similar informality.

In *Eroglu* v *Eroglu*[87] the couple (a Turkish husband and a British wife)[88] divorced in Turkey in order to enable the husband to evade national service (a privilege he forfeited by being married to a foreign wife). It was a "sham" divorce. The wife now sought a divorce in England. This could

---

80 [1994] 1 FLR 38. The case is less interesting than the other three. Recognition of a Ghanaian customary divorce was refused because it was not "effective" under Ghanaian law and no reasonable steps had been taken to notify the wife of the proceedings (see Family Law Act 1986 section 51 (3) (a) (i)).

81 [1994] 1 FLR 410.

82 See *Berthiaume* v *Dastous* [1930] AC 79.

83 Which is fortunate because we are not told of the domiciles of either of the parties.

84 *Op cit*, note 80, at 411. The Schnapps re-appears in *D* v *D*, *op cit*, note 79a, at 44 (given in this case, to the wife's mother on divorce).

85 Family Law Act 1986.

86 See *Chaudhary* v *Chaudhary* [1985] Fam. 19; *Zaal* v *Zaal* [1982] 4 FLR 284.

87 [1994] 2 FLR 287.

88 Again we are not told the domicile of either party.

only be granted if the Turkish divorce could be refused recognition as being "manifestly contrary to public policy".[89] Thorpe J. refused so to hold. The discretion to refuse recognition was one to be exercised sparingly and the motive for the divorce was irrelevant. Fraud was not a ground for refusal of recognition. The court conceded that where one party had deceived both the other and the foreign court, such deception might be relevant to the exercise of the statutory discretion: here, however, both parties had been aware that the Turkish court was being deceived. Said Thorpe J: "Those who play games with divorce decrees expose themselves to a variety of risks and, having enjoyed the desired benefits during cohabitation, cannot reorder their status now that they have fallen out".[90] With the Turkish divorce recognised, the "wife" was able to seek financial relief from the English courts.[91] But what of the children? Were they legitimate?[92] Was the cohabitation after the "sham" divorce a "putative marriage"?[93] Should we look at "sham" divorces as we do "sham" marriages?[94] Perhaps the decision provokes more questions than it answers.

In the third case, *M* v *M*,[95] the question centred upon the appropriate forum for a divorce and its ancillary matters of an English couple ("The quality of their Englishness is perhaps reflected in the fact that the marriage was celebrated in the church at Stoke Poges")[96] who had spent most of their married life in France. Divorce proceedings in France not having achieved all she wanted, she sought a "second bite at the cherry"[97] by invoking Part III of the Matrimonial and Family Proceedings Act 1984. It would appear that the wife had come out of the French proceedings with a package considerably weaker than that which she might have expected from an English court. Her counsel referred to her "appalling hardship ... to find herself with two children after 15 years of marriage with no home

---

89 See Family Law Act 1986 section 51 (3) (c) and *Kendall* v *Kendall* [1977] Fam 208.
90 *Op cit*, note 86, at 290.
91 Under part III of the Matrimonial and Family Proceedings Act 1984. The question remains as to whether the court's attitude to the Turkish divorce would have been different if this jurisdiction had not existed.
92 *Cf Shaw* v *Gould* (1868) L.R. 3 H.L. 55 with *Re Bischoffsheim* [1948] Ch. 79.
93 See Legitimacy Act 1976 section 1 (1), amended by section 28 (1) of the Family Law Reform Act 1987.
94 See *Vervaeke* v *Smith* [1983] 1 AC 145.
95 [1994] 1 FLR 399.
96 *Ibid*, at 400. The church is the site of Gray's "Elegy".
97 *Ibid*, at 405-406.

and no prospects of a home" and argued that "if that is the product of French justice it cannot be relied upon to prevent her seeking fair relief from the family justice system in the country of marriage, in the domicile that she has never left and in the society which provides home and income, not only to herself and children, but also to their father".[98] But, held the court, the case could not be "decided on the basis of compassion for a seemingly disadvantaged mother"[99] "Wisely or unwisely the wife has either chosen or accepted that the breakdown of the marriage should be referred to the court at Versailles. Wisely or unwisely she has pursued her financial rights in that court to a very full extent. The court at Versailles is a court of competent jurisdiction in one of our nearest neighbouring friendly states and the principles of comity require that I should recognise and respect its order".[100] Both "common sense" and "comity" were offended by the possibility of allowing a litigant to start again from "scratch" having taken financial claims to a realistic conclusion within the French system.[101] The case points to the need for good advice from family lawyers with understanding of private international law. Whether the courts will decide similarly where the foreign court is not a neighbouring (or perhaps Commonwealth) jurisdiction remains to be seen, but I would hazard a guess that the chauvinism which Thorpe J. was anxious to avoid in *M* v *M* might erupt more readily if the foreign divorce proceedings were more "foreign".

V   DOMESTIC VIOLENCE

As ever, the law reports were replete with domestic violence cases. With major reform anticipated in 1995,[102] a discussion of only one of the more significant decisions is warranted.

---

98   *Ibid*, at 407. A contrast with *R* v *R* [1994] 2 FLR 1036 is apposite: there the court refused to stay English divorce proceedings, the case in favour of them resting on the ability of the English court to make more extensive orders than the alternative Swedish court.

99   *Idem. Cf Radwan* v *Radwan (No. 2)* [1973] Fam 35.

100   *Idem*, at 407-408.

101   *Idem*, at 408.

102   There is to be legislation forming part of a wider Family Law Bill which will also incorporate divorce reform.

Perhaps the most interesting case is *Pearson* v *Franklin*.[103] This brings
out both the complexity of the law and the interface between domestic
violence legislation and children's legislation. As in many domestic violence
cases, there was no violence.[104] The relationship of twins' parents (they
were not married) had broken down permanently: there had been serious
arguments, but no violence to the mother or the children. Though headlined
a domestic violence case, in reality it was a dispute over who should occupy
the rented house.[105] The mother having moved out with the twins, she
now lived with her parents in quite unsuitable accommodation. An ouster
order was not available under the Matrimonial Homes Act 1983 because
they were not married. Nor could an eviction order be sought under the
Domestic Violence and Matrimonial Proceedings Act 1976 because they
were not living together as husband and wife, she having moved out some
six months before she sought to have him ousted.[106] Denied these avenues,
the mother sought two alternative paths. She invoked the Children Act 1989
and applied for a specific issue order.[107] It was contended on her behalf
that such an order should be granted because of the paramountcy of the
children's welfare,[108] and because the mother had sole parental responsibility for them.[109] The Court of Appeal held that, although the question
of where a child should live would usually be suitable for determination
on an application for a specific issue order, that could not be so where a
right of occupation would be interfered with. Said Nourse L.J.: "However
you were to dress it up, for whatever reason it was made, it would in
substance be an ouster order. Such orders having become very familiar to
Parliament by 1989, it cannot have been intended that they should be capable
of being made under the guise of specific issue orders".[110] Alternatively,
it was argued that the mother was entitled to an injunction under the inherent

---

103 [1994] 1 FLR 246.
104 *Vaughan* v *Vaughan* [1973] 1 WLR 1159; *Smith* v *Smith* [1988] 1 FLR 179; *Spindlow*
     v *Spindlow* [1979] Fam. 52.
105 It was a housing association joint tenancy.
106 See *O'Neill* v *Williams* [1984] FLR 1.
107 See section 8.
108 See section 1 (1).
109 Unmarried fathers do not have parental responsibility automatically, though they may
     acquire it (see section 4 of the Children Act 1989).
110 *Op cit*, note 102, at 249.

jurisdiction of the court. This argument had failed in *Ainsbury v Mil-lington*[111] and the Court of Appeal is bound by its own decisions.[112] The court admitted that, had the parties been married, it would have been possible to invoke the inherent jurisdiction if this was necessary to protect children.[113] The incoherence of the law was addressed by both judges: thus Thorpe J. thought it "questionable that children of parents who have been divorced should be any better protected than children of parents who have ceased to cohabit",[114] and, under reforms urged by the Law Commission, to be embodied in the new family homes legislation, this will no longer be so. In the interim a way was found round the thickets of the law: the mother was allowed to apply under the Children Act for an order requiring the father to transfer to her, for the benefit of the children, his interest in the joint tenancy of the home.[115] But, it may be commented, Parliament no more intended this provision to be used in this context than it intended the specific issue order to be so utilised. The court, perhaps not surprisingly gave no consideration to the criteria which would govern such an application: if a child's welfare is not paramount in an ouster application,[116] could it possibly be so here? It would be a strange irony if this were so.

IV SOME PROPERTY ISSUES

Barclays Bank v O'Brien[117] was considered in last year's *Survey* article. The banks' concern that this was not a one-off but a problem likely to recur can be seen in reported cases in 1994. It was followed in *Midland Bank v Greene*[118] and *Midland Bank v Massey*.[119] In *Greene* it was held that the wife's reliance on her husband's financial advice was such as to give

---

111 [1986] 1 FLR 331.
112 *Young v Bristol Aeroplane Co* [1944] K.B. 718.
113 See *Quinn v Quinn* [1983] 4 FLR 394.
114 *Op cit*, note 102, at 251-252.
115 See section 15 and Schedule 1, para. 1 (2) (e) (i). Such an order would give her, as against the father, an exclusive right to occupy the home.
116 *Richards v Richards* [1984] 1 AC 184 stating that the criteria are those in the Matrimonial Homes Act 1983 section 1 (3) and *Lee v Lee* [1984] FLR 243 holding that the same criteria apply to those who are not married.
117 [1993] 4 All E.R. 417 (also now [1994] 1 AC 180 and [1994] 1 FLR 1).
118 [1994] 2 FLR 827.
119 [1994] 2 FLR 342.

rise to a presumption of undue influence on his part in procuring the mortgage on their home. Since a mortgage charging the property as security for the husband's present and future debts was a transaction manifestly disadvantageous to the wife, it followed, the bank having taken no steps to advise the wife of her position, that the bank was fixed with constructive notice of the surety's right to set aside the transaction, and the court was entitled in the exercise of its equitable jurisdiction to set the transaction aside. But all was not lost for the bank because the court also held that, in exercising that jurisdiction where *restitutio in integrum* was impossible, the court should do what was practically just in all the circumstances. It was inequitable for the wife to be able to avoid the mortgage without discharging the debts she had incurred to procure her interest in the property. She was ordered to pay a sum of money in order that the mortgage security be set aside. Otherwise, there would be an order enabling the bank to take possession.

In *Midland Bank* v *Massey* the surety was not a wife. Nor was she a cohabitant. But she had had a stable sexual and emotional relationship with the man who had induced her to grant a legal charge over her house in favour of the bank to finance a business venture of his. Steyn L.J. recognised that this was "an extension of the approach enunciated by Lord Browne-Wilkinson" [in *Barclays Bank* v *O'Brien*], but he had "no doubt that in terms of impairment of Miss Massey's judgmental capacity this case should be approached as if she was a wife or cohabitee of Mr Potts".[120] But, also following Lord Browne-Wilkinson in *O'Brien*,[121] the judge held that the bank had complied with the requirement of ensuring that Miss Massey received independent advice. In fact her lover accompanied her to the solicitor and she was not seen alone. Although conceded not to be "good practice",[122] it did not, so the court held, undermine the independence of the advice received. The result was that the bank was not affected by constructive notice and Miss Massey lost her home. All she was left with is the rather speculative action against her lover (or former lover) for fraudulent misrepresentation. Those who were crying tears for the banks a year ago may wish to reflect on the results of these two cases.

---

120 *Ibid*, at 345.
121 [1994] 1 AC 180, 196-197.
122 *Op cit*, note 118, at 347. See also now *Banco Exterior International* v *Mann* [1995] 1 FLR 602.

A duped mother came out rather better than Mrs Greene or Miss Massey in *Abbey National* v *Moss*.[123] A daughter had persuaded her mother[124] to transfer her house into their joint names to simplify the transfer of the property on her death on condition that it would not be sold in her lifetime. The daughter then borrowed a large sum of money from a building society on the security of the property. To do this she forged the mother's signature. Two years later the daughter stopped paying and left the country. At first instance, it was held *inter alia* that the property be sold.[125] The Court of Appeal did not agree. Accepting that it was elementary law that the assignee of a donee could not acquire a better right than the donee had but took his interest subject to all the equities affecting the interest of the donee, and that the court would not allow trustees for sale to ignore the requirement of consent, it held that the trust for sale would not be enforced so long as there was a collateral purpose[126] still subsisting requiring the retention of the property. The court refused to allow the trust for sale to defeat the purpose of providing a home for the mother, even where there had been an assignment to another who was being kept out of the enjoyment both of the property and the proceeds of sale. As a matter of family law this may be a satisfactory conclusion, but it is one difficult to reconcile with a series of bankruptcy decisions,[127] which hold that where a husband and wife are still living together in the matrimonial home and one of them becomes bankrupt, the collateral purpose comes to an end. Peter Gibson L.J. was aware of this and expressed a concern that the House of Lords might have to revise the bankruptcy authorities or *Jones* v *Challenger*,[128] but the Court of Appeal was clearly bound by the attempt to reconcile them by Nourse L.J. in *Re Citro*.[129]

Bankruptcy was in issue in *F* v *F*.[130] A husband had himself declared bankrupt to evade an application by his divorcing wife for ancillary relief. She successfully had his bankruptcy order set aside. The court then ordered him to pay a lump sum of £150,000 to the wife. The court expressed the

---

123 [1994] 1 FLR 602.
124 Who had been recently widowed.
125 Under the Law of Property Act 1925 section 30.
126 Following *Jones* v *Challenger* [1961] 1 QB 176.
127 The latest of which is *Re Citro* [1991] Ch. 142.
128 *Op cit*, note 122, at 314.
129 *Op cit*, note 126, at 158-159.
130 [1994] 1 FLR 359.

opinion that in the circumstances where a husband had deliberately presented a false picture of his financial circumstances, it was better that the court should make an order which was unfair to him than one that was unfair to his wife.

VII FAMILY PROVISION

Two cases on the Inheritance (Provision for Family and Dependants) Act 1975 are worthy of note. In *Stock* v *Brown*[131] a widow of nearly 90 was allowed to apply out of time for additional provision made to her out of her deceased husband's estate. There had been no independent advice, there was no suggestion of prejudice to or objection from other beneficiaries, and no application would have been necessary but for a decline in interest rates which halved her income from investments. Given that many such applicants will be elderly, it may be that the limitation period for such applications should be relaxed, but there is no information as to what injustice, if any, the present rule is causing.

A more intriguing case is *Re Jennings*.[132] The applicant, a man of 50 living in comfortable circumstances, sought provision out of the estate of a deceased father who had had no contact of any kind with him since the age of four. Ten shillings in a birthday card on his second birthday seems to have been the only financial provision ever made. At first instance Wall J. awarded the adult son £40,000, out of an estate worth about £300,000. He interpreted "any obligations and responsibilities which the deceased had towards [the] applicant"[133] to include those "arising in infancy which were not discharged".[134] The Court of Appeal did not agree. It was "irrelevant that this father behaved as he did – however much this behaviour may be deplored. It is not the purpose of the 1975 Act to punish or redress past bad or unfeeling parental behaviour where that behaviour does not still impinge on the applicant's present financial situation".[135] "Some undischarged responsibilities from the past may still be current – for instance a child of

---

131 [1994] 1 FLR 840.
132 [1994] 1 FLR 536.
133 See Section 3 (1) (d) of the 1975 Act.
134 *Op cit*, note 131, at 542.
135 *Ibid*, at 548 *per* Henry L.J.

the deceased might have given up a university place to nurse the deceased through his long last illness and now wish to take up that place. The moral obligation there would be both current and clear. But where the undischarged responsibility does not amount to an obligation present at the date of death, the statute does not require it to be taken into account".[136] As a general rule, it was held, the reference in the statute to obligations was to those the deceased had immediately before his death. "An Act intended to facilitate the making of reasonable financial provision cannot have been intended to revive defunct obligations and responsibilities as a basis for making it".[137] This decision could have implications elsewhere, though not, it must be assumed, in the context of the Child Support Agency.

VIII   INTERPRETING THE CHILDREN ACT

There were numerous decisions on the Children Act 1989 in 1994. Two cases reached the House of Lords. In *Birmingham City Council* v *H (No. 3)*[138] the House determined that where both the parent and the child were children, it was only the child about whom a question as to upbringing arose whose welfare was paramount.[139] In *Re M*[140] the Lords interpreted "is suffering significant harm", the threshold condition for a care order,[141] to mean was so suffering at the time when protective proceedings were initiated. Lord Templeman saw the appeal as "an illustration of the tyranny of language and the importance of ascertaining and giving effect to the intentions of Parliament by construing a statute in accordance with the spirit rather than the letter of the Act".[142] In effect the House of Lords came to the same conclusion as it had done with previous child protection legislation.[143]

---

136 *Ibid*, at 547 *per* Henry L.J.
137 *Ibid*, at 543 *per* Nourse L.J.
138 [1994] 1 FLR 224.
139 Under section 1 (1) of the Children Act.
140 [1994] 2 FLR 577.
141 See section 31 (2) of the Children Act 1989.
142 *Op cit*, note 139, at 588.
143 *D* v *Berkshire County Council* [1987] 1 All E.R. 20, discussed in an earlier *Survey* article (see 1988) 27 *Journal of Family Law* 101, 105-109.

One of the most controversial decisions of the year vindicated the childminder refused registration by a local authority for not agreeing to the authority's "no smacking" policy. There was, said Wilson J., nothing in the Children Act or in the *Guidance and Regulations* to oblige the authority to adopt an inflexible policy in relation to corporal punishment.[144] Guidance was later given by the Department of Health and this sanctioned smacking,[145] to the consternation of many local authorities which apparently persist in refusing to take childminders who believe in hitting their charges.[146]

This case attracted most publicity though cases of children purporting to "divorce" their parents ran it close.[147] The metaphor of divorce had come from the Gregory Kingsley case in the United States[148] and it came as a made-to-measure package complete with (misleading) associations. There had been cases in 1993[149] and concern was such that a ruling by the President of the Family Division had ensured that cases were heard in the Family Division.[150] The Children Act, by allowing children to apply with leave for a residence order,[151] had made this possible, though it has to be said the uses to which it was put were not in contemplation. In *Re SC*[152] it was made clear that, whilst a residence order could not be made in favour of the child herself, she could seek leave to apply for a residence order in favour of someone else (in this case the family of a long-standing friend). The child must have "sufficient understanding"[153] to make the application: the courts have pitched the level of this quite high.[154] But even if sufficient understanding is established, the court still has a discretion whether to grant leave.[155] 1994 saw a conflict of first instance decisions on the relevance of the paramountcy principle to the application for leave. In *Re SC* Booth

---

144 *London Borough of Sutton* v *Davis* [1994] 1 FLR 737.
145 D.H. Circular 96/94.
146 See *Community Care*, March 16-22, 1995, at 5.
147 See Michael Freeman "Can Children Divorce Their Parents?" in (ed) Michael Freeman, *Divorce – Where Next?* (Aldershot: Dartmouth, 1995).
148 623 So 2d 780 (Fla dist. C.A. 1993).
149 These are discussed in detail in *op cit*, note 146.
150 [1993] 1 FLR 668.
151 Section 10 (8).
152 [1994] 1 FLR 96.
153 See Section 10 (8).
154 See *e.g. Re S* [1993] 2 FLR 437.
155 So held by Booth J. in *Re SC, op cit*, note 151 at 98.

J. held that, since the initial application for leave did not raise any question about the child's upbringing, the child's welfare was not the paramount consideration.[156] But in *Re C*[157] Johnson J. extended the application of the welfare principle to the whole question of leave on an application by a child. In *Re C* a 15-year-old girl sought leave to apply for a residence order to live with a boy-friend's parents and a specific issue order to go on holiday with them to Bulgaria. Johnson J. could see no identifiable advantage in making a residence order at the present time – he accordingly adjourned the application for leave. As far as the holiday was concerned, he took the view that this was not the kind of issue which Parliament contemplated being litigated when it allowed children to make applications for leave – this leave application was therefore refused. These cases, and there were others,[158] stirred a fair amount of excitement and some concern, but in reality were merely tentative testing of the scope of a new statutory provision.

The importance of the paramountcy principle is strikingly illustrated by the decision of the Court of Appeal in *Oxfordshire County Council v M*.[159] It had earlier been decided that local authorities do not have the benefit of legal professional privilege in respect of experts' reports in care proceedings.[160] Thus, they were obliged to disclose to all parties all relevant documents and experts' reports which are in their possession. The *Oxfordshire* case extended this principle to the other parties to care proceedings. The Court of Appeal ruled that legal professional privilege had to yield to the overriding principle that in both the Children Act and in the wardship jurisdiction the interests of the child are paramount.

In the past English courts have set their face against joint parenting orders.[161] But the Children Act does allow for a residence order to be made in favour of more than one person[162] thus it gives its blessing to joint parenting. The problems of shared residence were illustrated in *Re J*,[163] where residence was divided between the parents, as a result of an arrangement between them. But the 3-year-old child played one parent off against

---

156 *Ibid*, at 99, following *Re A* [1992] 3 All E.R. 872.
157 [1994] 1 FLR 26.
158 On these see *op cit*, note 146.
159 [1994] 1 FLR 175. See now also *Cleveland C.C. v F* [1995] 1 FLR 797.
160 *R v Hampshire County Council ex parte K* [1990] 2 QB 71.
161 *Riley v Riley* [1986] 2 FLR 429.
162 Section 11 (4).
163 [1994] 1 FLR 369.

the other and developed such a degree of anxiety and stress as to lead the court welfare officer to recommend that she spend rather more of her time with one parent than the other. In two cases reported in 1994 different views were expressed in the Court of Appeal as to when shared residence orders were appropriate. In *Re H*[164] Purchas L.J. took the view that the establishment of two competing homes only leads to confusion and stress and is, therefore, contrary to the paramount interests of the child. His view accordingly is that such an order "would rarely be made and would depend upon exceptional circumstances".[165] In *A v A*,[166] Butler-Sloss L.J. disagreed with Purchas L.J's remarks to the effect that exceptional circumstances only could justify a shared residence order.[167] She preferred to describe the shared residence order as "an unusual order which should only be made in unusual circumstances".[168]

The problems attendant upon the proof of abuse continued to exercise the courts' minds. The propriety of using covert video surveillance – in the case under consideration it was used to observe a mother who suffered from Munchausen's Syndrome by proxy – was examined by Wall J. in *Re DH*.[169] He held that there is no objection to the admissibility of evidence produced by means of CVS. As the judge acknowledged: "Counsel were agreed that even if the evidence were unlawfully or improperly obtained, it would still be admissible in civil proceedings and a fortiori in proceedings relating to a child where the welfare of the child plainly requires that the truth of the manner in which he was abused should be ascertained".[170] The judge also ruled that the consent of the non-abusing parent is not required prior to such procedures.[171] He did, however, express "unease at

---

164 [1994] 1 FLR 717 (decided in December 1992).
165 *Ibid*, at 728. Cazalet J. thought shared residence might be a way of reducing differences between the parties but added that, where there were differences, the child should normally have his settled home with one parent (at 726).
166 [1994] 1 FLR 669.
167 *Ibid*, at 678.
168 *Idem*.
169 [1994] 1 FLR 679, 709-715.
170 *Ibid*, at 709. There is no equivalent in civil proceedings to the provision in the Police and Criminal Evidence Act 1984 (section 78) which permits a court to refuse to admit evidence where the court believes it would have an "adverse effect on the fairness of the proceedings".
171 *Ibid*, at 714.

the abrupt manner in which a procedure designed to establish a medical diagnosis turned into a criminal investigation".[172]

The courts have long had to find the appropriate balance between the need to disclose evidence in fairness to parties and the imperative to preserve confidences to protect children.[173] In *Re B*[174] the Court of Appeal acknowledged that a court has power in a children case[175] to act upon evidence adduced by one party, or given by a welfare officer, which is not disclosed to the other party. But it held that this power should only be exercised in most exceptional circumstances, and only where the court is satisfied that the disclosure of evidence would be so detrimental to the welfare of the child as to outweigh the normal requirements for a fair trial. In *Re G*[176] the welfare officer had received information from an informant relating to the mother's parenting ability and had given a promise of confidentiality. She wished to place before the court what the informant had said, but did not wish that information to be disclosed to the parties. The Court of Appeal ruled that the assurance should not have been given. Only where there was a serious threat to the welfare of children would the fundamental rule which provided that a party should be informed of all the evidence against him be relaxed. Further questions were raised in two cases in 1994. In *Re M*[177] the views and anxieties of children (aged 13 and 9) were contained in the welfare report. Understandably, the children did not wish their mother to see this. The Court of Appeal held that, in determining whether or not disclosure of a confidential welfare report should be withheld, the test was whether "real harm"[178] would ensue from the disclosure, not the less stringent test of whether there was a significant risk of harm. The Court of Appeal did not believe this report should remain confidential. This decision frustrates the expectations of the children and arguably tilts the balance too far in favour of natural justice and too much against the interests of children. The second case of note is *Re K*.[179] A father sought leave to disclose at his trial for rape evidence adduced in proceedings brought under the Children

---

172 *Ibid*, at 715.
173 An early example of the dilemma is *D v NSPCC* [1977] 1 All E.R. 589.
174 [1993] 1 FLR 191.
175 *Official Solicitor v K* [1965] AC 210 had held this to be the case in wardship cases.
176 [1993] 2 FLR 293.
177 [1994] 1 FLR 760.
178 *Ibid*, at 764.
179 [1994] 1 FLR 377.

Act. He wished to challenge the credibility of the mother by reference to the previous inconsistent statements made by her in the Children Act proceedings. The court permitted disclosure. Whilst it had to have regard to the interests of the children concerned,[180] it had to balance the importance of confidentiality and the frankness that engendered in the Children Act proceedings against the public interest in seeing that the interests of justice are properly served. In this case, there could be no detriment to the children concerned for it was in their interests that their father got a fair trial.[181]

The standard of proof where abuse is alleged also exercised the courts' minds in 1994. In *Re W*,[182] a case of alleged sexual abuse, where the issue was whether there should be contact between the father, the supposed perpetrator, and the children, the court, whilst accepting the civil standard of proof (the balance of probabilities), ruled that the more serious the allegation, the more convincing was the evidence that was needed to tip the balance in respect of it. Although, said the court, it was settled that in civil proceedings charges of sexual abuse did not require proof beyond reasonable doubt (the criminal standard), the standard of proof to be required was nevertheless commensurate with the serious nature of the issues raised. A similar approach was adopted in *Re M (No. 2)*,[183] a case of neglect and physical abuse where a small child's cries for help were silenced by a court which seemed to prioritise the interests of her mother and step-father. As a five-year-old she was admitted to hospital with numerous bruises, seriously underweight and suffering from duodenal haematoma. She said, when interviewed by a psychologist, that she had been punched in the stomach by her mother and kicked there by her father (that is her step-father) and that her father had put a pillow over her head and hit her with a belt on her bottom. She made it clear that she did not want to return to her mother and step-father and dearly wished to go to her maternal grandparents. How any court could interpret this as a child "with ambivalent feelings in the short

---

180 And see *Re D* [1994] 1 FLR 346.

181 Another example of this is *Re F* [1994] 2 FLR 958 (leave given for the disclosure to the special adjudicator in immigration proceedings of documents used, and a transcript of the evidence given, in proceedings which had been brought under the Children Act).

182 [1994] 1 FLR 419.

183 [1994] 1 FLR 59.

term about a return home"[184] beggars belief. Nor is it easy to repose much confidence in a court which put the child's views down to "immaturity" preventing her from viewing her real hopes and wishes "objectively in the light of her own best long-term interests".[185] The Court of Appeal held that the trial judge was right to conclude that he should not find the incident with the belt had taken place or that the duodenal haematoma had been caused by either or both parents, unless the evidence was of a weight appropriate to the seriousness of those allegations. The trial judge had said that "given the seriousness of the nature of the allegation and the personalities and relationships involved, it is a proportionately higher standard of probability than otherwise for less serious allegations".[186] The implication of this, as Spencer rightly observed, is that "the worse the danger the child is in, the less likely the courts are to remove her from it".[187] This child almost lost her life, and there can be no doubt why. If social workers rather than a court had taken the decision to return her to her mother and step-father, they would have been pilloried.

Other decisions about children may be noted more briefly. A result of *Nottinghamshire C.C. v P*,[188] discussed in last year's *Survey* article, was that Devon County Council sought to protect children from a sex offender by invoking the inherent jurisdiction of the High Court.[189] The culprit was not a member of the family (in the *Notts* case he was the father) so that neither a care order nor a supervision order was appropriate. Inherent jurisdiction could be exercised, held Thorpe J., to protect the children. A distinction was drawn between a local authority seeking to have protective powers conferred upon it through resort to inherent jurisdiction (prohibited by s. 100 (2) (d)), and a local authority inviting the court to exercise its inherent powers to make an order which does not give any powers to the authority itself. Inherent jurisdiction was also successfully invoked by a local authority to oust a father in *Re S*.[190] Since no other alternative order had been suggested, the case, it was held, came within s. 100 (4) (a), and, since

---

184 *Ibid*, at 66.
185 *Ibid*, at 67.
186 Quoted *ibid*, at 67.
187 [1994] 6 *Journal of Child Law* 160.
188 [1993] 2 FLR 134 (and see [1995] 33 *University of Louisville Journal of Family Law* 329, 342-344).
189 *Devon County Council v S* [1994] 1 FLR 355.
190 [1994] 1 FLR 623.

on the facts the court had reasonable cause to believe that if its inherent jurisdiction was not exercised, the children were likely to suffer significant harm within s. 10 (4) (b), it granted the orders sought by the local authority. These two cases illustrate a reluctance by the judges to be held to a restrictive interpretation of s. 100. Such a reluctance was anticipated.

It was also to be expected that the "in need" provisions[191] of the Act would run into difficulties and that the courts would be reluctant to second-guess the ways local authorities allocated their resources. Cases in 1994 demonstrated these difficulties. Barnet's closure of day care nursery centres, Brent's failure to provide the caretakers of an autistic boy with suitable accommodation, Kingston's refusal to fund accommodation and support for a Vietnamese child in a Vietnamese Children and Young People's Project were all challenged by judicial review and all three were unsuccessful.[192] The courts made it clear that they would not undertake the exercise of investigating the choice between priorities that had to be considered by the local authority. They also pointed to the other routes of appeal, in particular the complaints procedure,[193] and showed a clear preference for this over judicial review.[194]

Another context in which the relationship between courts and local authorities and their respective decision-making powers arose was in relation to so-called care plans. As observed in a previous *Survey* article,[195] the courts can no longer monitor the administration of a child's upbringing by a local authority once a care order is made.[196] The dilemma of a court which believes a care order is appropriate but disagrees with or is unhappy about the authority's plans for the child was deliberated upon in *Re J*.[197] There was, said Wall J., a need for a proper balance to be struck between the need to satisfy the court about the appropriateness of the care plan and the avoidance of over-zealous investigation into matters within the ad-

---

191 Children Act section 17.

192 *R v London Borough of Barnet ex parte B* [1994] 1 FLR 592; *R v London Borough of Brent ex parte S* [1994] 1 FLR 203; *R v Royal Borough of Kingston-upon-Thames ex parte T* [1994] 1 FLR 798.

193 Under section 26 (3) of the Children Act.

194 See, in particular, Ward J's judgment in the *Kingston* case at 812-815.9

195 *Op cit*, note 1, at 347-348.

196 *Re B* [1993] 1 FLR 543. Nor may the court direct that the guardian continue her involvement in the case (*Kent C.C. v C* [1993] 1 FLR 308).

197 [1994] 1 FLR 253.

ministrative discretion of the local authority. Courts cannot make care orders unless the threshold criteria[198] are met and making the order would be better for the child than making no order at all.[199] The absence of a coherent care plan makes it difficult to be satisfied of the latter. In *Re J* the plan was inchoate, but, perhaps surprisingly, did not prove a stumbling block to the making of a care order.

It has been shown several times that courts are reluctant to interfere with the ways local authorities carry out their duties. It was to be expected that sooner or later there would be an attempt to claim damages for personal injury resulting from negligence or breach of statutory duty by a local authority. It happened in 1994 in the case of *X and others* v *Bedfordshire County Council*[200] which held that the legislation does not support the view that Parliament had intended to confer a cause of action in damages on a child or other person in respect of breach of the statutory duties imposed on local authorities under the Children Act or otherwise. Nor, it held, would any action lie in negligence in respect of a local authority's alleged failure to exercise its statutory duties. In late June 1995 the House of Lords dismissed appeals against this decision.[201] They cannot have found it easy: judgment was reserved for nine months.

---

198 See section 31 (2) of the Children Act.
199 See section 1 (5) of the Children Act.
200 [1994] 1 FLR 431.
201 *The Times*, June 30, 1995.

FINLAND

A LONG, LONG WAY TO THE HAGUE - THE RATIFICATION AND IMPLEMENTATION OF THE HAGUE CONVENTION ON THE CIVIL ASPECTS OF INTERNATIONAL CHILD ABDUCTION

*Matti Savolainen**

I   INTRODUCTION

The Hague Convention on the Civil Aspects of International Child Abduction was adopted and opened for signature at the Fourteenth Session of The Hague Conference on private international law on October 25, 1980. The Convention entered into force on December 1, 1983 following the ratifications by Canada, France and Portugal. Although Finland took an active part in the preparatory work of the Convention, it took almost 14 years since the adoption of the Convention in 1980 for Finland finally to become the 39th State Party to the Convention on August 1, 1994.

One of the main reasons for the delayed ratification was that the relevant Finnish legislation on children and parents in 1980 was outdated and in many respects diametrically opposed to the underlying principles of the Convention.

The defects of the Finnish law on child custody would not have been an absolute impediment to ratification of The Hague Convention immediately after its adoption. Certainly, having regard to child abductions from Finland, it would have been difficult in several cases even to determine whether the removal or the retention of the child was unlawful in terms of Article 3 of the Convention. It is also obvious that often, especially where custody was based upon foreign law or a foreign custody order, the answer produced by Finnish law would have been felt to have been arbitrary and wrong. Nevertheless the Convention could have been applied although it would not have worked properly or at least not in the best possible way.

A far greater problem might have been cases where the child had been unlawfully removed to Finland or unlawfully retained there. As indicated above, a typical feature of Finnish law, as reflected in judicial practice, was its hostility towards the application of foreign custody laws and towards

---

*   Senior Legal Adviser, Ministry of Justice, Helsinki.

A. Bainham (ed.), The International Survey of Family Law 1994, 227–240.
© 1996 *The International Society of Family Law. Printed in the Netherlands.*

the recognition of foreign custody orders in addition to the considerably extensive jurisdiction exercised by Finnish courts.

These "nationalistic" attitudes were demonstrated in particular in cases where in mixed marriages a Finnish parent, in most cases the mother, had abducted the child to Finland. In those cases Finnish courts did not hesitate to assume jurisdiction, even immediately after the child had been brought to Finland, and as a rule sole custody was granted to the abducting parent of Finnish nationality. Within this judicial atmosphere there might have been a considerable risk that Finnish courts would not have been able to comply properly with the primary obligation imposed by the Convention: to order a child unlawfully removed to or retained in Finland to be returned. One could envisage cases where a Finnish court might have refused to return the child on the grounds that a five year old child "objects to being returned", that sending the child from Finland to a foreign country would in itself "expose the child to psychological harm" or, in cases where the child was a Finnish national, that the return of the child would not be permitted by the fundamental principles of the Finnish Constitution concerning the fundamental freedoms of a Finnish national.

Under these considerations the Ministry of Justice decided that the ratification of the Hague Convention should be postponed until the ongoing revision of child custody legislation was completed and that a full revision of private international law relating to child custody should be undertaken at the same time as the legislation on the ratification and implementation of The Hague Convention was presented to the Parliament. It was also understood that simply "incorporating" the provisions of The Hague Convention into Finnish law by a Parliamentary Act was not sufficient but that it was necessary to use the so-called "transformation" techniques by issuance of sufficiently detailed, unambiguous and strictly binding provisions in an internal implementation statute.

The new Child Custody Act (1983) entered into force on January 1, 1984. The Act on the revision of the Child Custody Act (1993) of March 4, 1994 (186/94), which contained the new provisions relating to private international law on child custody and on the implementation of The Hague Convention, entered into force almost ten years later, on August 1, 1994 when also The Hague Convention entered into force in respect of Finland.

II THE IMPLEMENTATION OF THE HAGUE CONVENTION

The provisions on the implementation of The Hague Convention adopted in 1994 were inserted into the 1983 Child Custody Act as a new chapter 5, immediately after the generally applicable private international law rules which appear in chapter 4 of the Act. In addition, new chapters 6 and 7 also contain several provisions applicable to the procedures on the return of abducted children under The Hague Convention. These rules reflect the principle expressed in several provisions of The Hague Convention that the Convention shall not prevent any Contracting State to go further towards facilitating the return of abducted children than what is necessarily required by the Convention. (alav. Article 18, Article 29 and Article 36). In general they attempt to create as effective and rapid a national procedure for the return of children as possible. The most important adaptations of The Hague provisions are the following:

A *Making The Hague Convention universally applicable*

The Hague Convention only applies in cases where the abducted child was habitually resident in a Contracting State immediately before any breach of custody or access rights (Article 4). This provision has also been adopted as a main rule under the Finnish implementation provisions. Where a child abducted to Finland was not habitually resident in a Contracting State, the rules on the "prompt return" do not apply. On the other hand, in these cases the child as well as the holders of custody rights will be protected by the generally applicable new rules which give Finnish courts and other competent authorities wide powers to recognise and to enforce a custodial relationship lawfully established abroad whether by operation of law, by a court order or otherwise. In addition, the new provisions give the Government the power to make The Hague rules on the return of the child applicable by a Government Decree mutatis mutandis even in cases where the child, before the breach of custody rights, was habitually resident in a State other than a Contracting State. However, until now the Government has not yet made use of these powers.

B   *Retroactive application*

Possibly having regard to its late admittance to The Hague Child Abduction Club, the Hague rules of the Finnish Child Custody Act have been made applicable also to cases where the child has been taken to Finland, lawfully or unlawfully, before the entry into force of the Act on August 1, 1994 and the child is at that date being unlawfully retained in Finland in terms of The Hague Convention.

C   *The children protected*

The Finnish provisions have not adopted as such the rigid rule of Article 4, second sentence, according to which the application of the Convention as a whole shall cease when the child attains the age of 16 years. Instead of excluding these children from the scope of application of The Hague rules adopted in the Finnish Child Custody Act, it is only provided that the child shall not be ordered to be returned nor a return order enforced after the child has attained the age of 16 years.(alav Section 34, para. 2, Section 46, para. 3). This solution means that all the other the Hague mechanisms, such as the services of the Central Authority in locating the child, taking of appropriate provisional protective measures, provision of legal aid and advice, securing in appropriate cases the voluntary return of the child and organising contacts between the child and the parents are available even after the child has attained the age of 16 years, provided that the child under the law applicable to the custody of the child, at the time such measures are to be taken, can still be deemed to be under legal custody.

D   *The Central Authority and its powers*

The Finnish Central Authority responsible for the duties under The Hague Convention is the Ministry of Justice, which also has full statutory powers to represent the applicant in return proceedings, either directly or through a delegated advocate in private practice. Both social authorities and police authorities must upon request provide all necessary assistance for the Ministry in discovering the whereabouts of the child and in the making of the appropriate enquiries as well as to secure the enforcement of the return order and to prevent the removal of the child outside the country.

E   One single competent court

According to the centralized model chosen in the Finnish Child Custody Act, only one court, the Court of Appeals of Helsinki, has jurisdiction in return proceedings. The court may hold its sessions anywhere within the country. This court also acts as the executor authority in "ordinary" proceedings relating to the recognition and enforcement of foreign custody orders.

F   Simplified urgent procedure

The application for the return is determined in special summary proceedings where the person alleged to have removed or retained the child must be given the opportunity to be heard if his or her whereabouts are known and this would not cause delay in proceedings. Where necessary, the Court of Appeals may also make any provisional (ex parte) orders relating to the child's residence, custody or access. Where the decision has not been made within six weeks from the application the Court of Appeals shall, upon the request by the Central Authority or by the applicant, explain the reasons for delay.

G   "Fundamental principles" not a ground for refusal

Article 20 of The Hague Convention contains an ingenious provision under which the return of the child may be refused, not only on the grounds mentioned in Article 13, but also if this would not be permitted by the fundamental principles of the requested State relating to the protection of human rights and fundamental freedoms. This provision seems to be far from clear. In particular one might speculate on what might be the cases where the return could not be refused on the grounds mentioned in article 13, but where the refusal would be possible under Article 20. How for instance could there be a case where the return of the child would not "place the child in an intolerable situation", but the return "would not be permitted under the fundamental principles relating to human rights of the requested State"? Could it be possible that a grave violation of the fundamental principles of the requested State could be deemed to be "tolerable" by that State? In order to eliminate these problems of interpretation, the Child Custody Act has not adopted any provision comparable to Article 20 which therefore cannot be invoked in Finland as a ground for refusal to return the child.

H   Immediately enforceable return orders, direct physical surrender

A return order made by the Court of Appeals is always immediately enforceable. The enforcement procedure is "automatic" i.e. the order is sent directly by the Court to the competent enforcement authority which is requested to enforce the order urgently. In all cases enforcement is carried out by direct enforcement measures, by physically surrendering the child. "Soft" enforcement measures, such as conciliation with a view to obtaining voluntary surrender of the child or pecuniary sanctions are not applicable.

I   Appeal and stay of enforcement

An appeal against an order whereby the child has been ordered to be returned may be made to the Supreme Court within 14 days from the order. On request the Supreme court may also order that further enforcement of the order should be postponed.

J   Free proceedings

Finland has made the reservation on free court proceedings allowed in Article 26 paragraph 3 of the Convention. Although Finland is thus not under the international obligation to provide free proceedings except to the extent that the costs will be covered by the ordinary Finnish system of free legal aid, such free proceedings are provided for by the internal provisions of the Child Custody Act. Accordingly any applicant will be provided full legal aid and advice without regard to the applicant's financial situation.

III THE FIRST THREE CASES

As expected, all the first cases were cases where the removal of the child to or retention in Finland had occurred before The Hague Convention entered into force in respect of Finland on August 1, 1994 (see above II, 2). The first case is particularly interesting:

A Case 1 (Kostiainen)

The parents of child X (a son, born March 3, 1985), father A, a Finnish national and mother B, a naturalized Finnish national had in July 1991 moved to California with the intention of establishing their permanent residence there. In January 1992 A moved back to Finland and on June 26, 1992 the Superior Court of Kern granted legal separation to the spouses and physical custody of child X was given to mother B. On January 13, 1993 father A removed child X from California to Finland and on February 8, 1993 the Court of First Instance of Helsinki granted divorce to the spouses and gave custody of child X to father A. The mother, who had moved to Finland in July 1993 and lived there permanently, made an appeal to the Court of Appeals of Helsinki but by a decision issued on May 25, 1994 the appeal was rejected. The mother made a further appeal to the Supreme Court.

While the case was still pending in the Supreme Court the mother made an application on August 12, 1994 to the Court of Appeals of Helsinki, after the period of one year from the removal on January 13, 1993 had elapsed, and requested that child X be promptly returned to her. When the application was to be served on father A it was discovered that the father had moved abroad with child X on August 27, 1994. In consequence, father A did not appear in proceedings.

The Court of Appeals of Helsinki stated in its procedural rulings that child X had been taken from Finland to another State and referred to Section 37 paragraph 2 of the Child Custody Act, according to which proceedings relating to the return of the child may be stayed or dismissed when there are reasons to believe that the child has been removed to another State. However, the Court decided to continue the proceedings because father A and child X, having regard to their dwelling, nationality and the child's school, had close contacts with Finland to the extent that their stay abroad could not be assumed to be permanent. The court also ruled that proceedings might be continued according to Section 38 although the application was not served on the father A since his whereabouts were unknown.

In its decision, issued within five weeks of the date of application on September 16, 1994 (No 4253), the Court of Appeals ordered the child X to be "returned to live with his mother". When stating its reasons the Court established that the removal of child X from California (13.3.1993) by father A was an unlawful removal in terms of The Hague Convention and Section 32 of the Child Custody Act which, according to its transitional provisions, applies even where the child has been taken to Finland before the entry into force of the relevant provisions of the Act.

The court further decided that in accordance with the objectives of the Act (on the implementation of The Hague Convention), which are aimed at providing effective protection in international cases to the relationship between the custodial parent and the child and to prevent arbitrary removals of the child, it should apply its provisions, although the mother B had during the custody dispute moved to Finland (July 1993), because her main motive had been that she could act more effectively to obtain custody of the child while residing in Finland.

The Court also noted that, according to Article 17 of The Hague Convention, the sole fact that a decision relating to custody had been given in the requested State should not be a ground for refusing to return a child under the Convention. It concluded that the decision given by the Court of Appeals itself on May 25, 1994 and which had not become final was therefore not a ground to refuse the return of the child under the Convention.

Finally, the Court stated that father A had prevented mother B from visiting the child X and that it was evident that he would continue to do so in the future. Cutting off the relationship between the child and the mother was, according to the opinions of the medical experts, detrimental to the development of the child and the Court therefore considered that "it [was] in the interests of child X that he [should] be ordered to be returned to live with his mother".

The case is remarkable. Practically every step in the Court's reasoning was wrong and as wrong as it could be. The case is an example of what a court should not do in an alleged international child abduction case. It provides a "Never Again"-checklist.

First, regarding the removal of the child X on January 13, 1993, this was no longer international and thus outside the scope of application of The Hague Convention on International Child Abduction. The mother B had since

July 1993 for more than one year been resident in Finland with the obvious intention of remaining in Finland. This was also the State of habitual residence of child X and father A. All of them were Finnish nationals. In addition, proceedings relating to the custody of child X were pending in Finland, upon the appeal lodged by mother B in the Supreme Court.

In her application mother B did not even request that the child be returned to California or to any other foreign jurisdiction nor were there any indications in the application that the applicant herself intended in the future to leave Finland with the child.

The removal of child X from Finland by the father on August 27, 1994, which was not the subject of the proceedings concerned, was an international removal, but fully lawful since the father had obtained sole custody of the child by the Court of Appeals decision of May 25, 1994.

The decision by the Court of Appeals, even according to its explicit wording, was in fact not at all a return order in terms of The Hague Convention, but in fact a residence order. The child was ordered "to be returned to live with his mother" who clearly intended to stay in Finland with him. The result of the Court's decision was that the mother obtained the "physical custody" of the child while the father, by virtue of the previous Court of Appeals Decision of May 25, 1994, still held sole "legal custody" of the child. In other words, under the disguise of a Hague return order, but obviously in good faith, the Court simply modified its previous custody order by transforming it into a "split custody order": physical care of a child (who in any event was not in Finland, but abroad with the father) to the mother with legal custody to the father. Moreover, the making of such split custody orders is contrary to Finnish custody law which requires that a person having physical custody should also in principle have the necessary legal custodial powers to represent the child. Finally, custody proceedings may not in the first instance be initiated in the Court of Appeals but in the court of first instance and not even in that court while proceedings relating to the custody of the same child are still pending in the Supreme Court.

The application was made after the period of one year from the unlawful removal (13.1.1993) had already elapsed. Under Article 12, paragraph 2 of The Hague Convention the child should also in that case be ordered to be returned, unless it is demonstrated that the child is now settled in its new environment (e.g. a crack smoking community in Zürich).

In order to facilitate the return of the child in these cases, and to avoid certain difficulties in its interpretation, this "environmental" clause has in

Finnish implementation provisions been reproduced in a provision under which the return of the child may be refused if the return would be contrary to the best interests of the child. This test, however, was not applied by the Court of Appeal. Instead, the Court applied the ordinary, "positive" best interests test applicable in custody disputes by stating explicitly that it "[considered] that it [was] in the best interests of child x that he [should] be ordered to be returned to live with his mother".

Finally, it is interesting to note that the Court of Appeals, in its procedural rulings, did not make use of the possibility offered to the Court by Section 37, paragraph 2 of the Child Custody Act either to dismiss the case or to stay proceedings where there are reasons to believe that the child no longer is in Finland, i.e. in the State which is being requested to return the child, but has been taken to another State. In the case before the Court there were not only "reasons to believe" that the child was no longer in Finland, but in fact it was even established that the child had been taken out of the country on August 27, 1994. Irrespective of whether or not the child was taken to a State Party to The Hague Convention it is difficult to understand why the Court still wanted to issue a return order under The Hague rules while knowing that the child was no longer in Finland. Such a Finnish order would be unenforceable and would have no effect in the State where the child was present. The reasons given by the Court as a ground for the making of a Finnish return order that the child, no longer present in Finland, was otherwise closely connected with Finland, are simply beyond understanding.

B   Case 2 (Demetri)

Mother A and father B had been living in Sweden together with their daughter x, born on December 17, 1986. The parents were unmarried and custody of the child x belonged to the mother under Chapter 6, section 3, paragraph 1 of the Swedish Code of Parents. The parents separated and the father had been permanently resident in Finland at least since 1991. Child x, who had been living with the mother in Sweden, was taken to Finland in September 1991 to live with father B.

In January 1992 mother A, who still had sole custody, made an application in summary administrative enforcement procedures under the revised Child Custody Enforcement Act (1983) and asked for the surrender of the Child. The application was rejected by the decision of the County Administrative Court on February 15, 1993 (i.e. more than one year after the application) on the grounds that, having regard to the best interest of the child, the matter had to be decided in ordinary court proceedings and instructed the parties to initiate custody proceedings in the competent Finnish court. Proceedings were never initiated. Instead, in March 1993 father B voluntarily returned child X to mother A in Sweden.

Child X lived with mother A in Sweden till the end of September 1993. After that the child was sent voluntarily on October 1, 1993 to visit the father. No formal rights of access were established for the father by court order nor had the parents made any clear stipulations on the exercise of the access rights by the father in October 1993, in particular as to the duration of the visit. Child X stayed with father B in Finland from October 1993 and the father refused to return the child to the mother in Sweden, despite several requests, including those made in writing by the mother's lawyers on January 17 and June 29, 1994.

On September 13, before a period of one year had elapsed, mother A applied to the Court of Appeals of Helsinki for the return of child X. After the application was served on the father, he opposed the return on the grounds that:

·   he had in practice been the primary caretaker of child X almost throughout her whole life and she had lived for more than 5 years with him and his new family;

·   mother A lived in Sweden whereas child X did not speak Swedish;

·   mother A was leading an "asocial life" and had often changed her residence and the development of child X had regressed every time the child had stayed with the mother;

·   child X was 8 years old and, having regard to her age, had attained such a maturity that her opinion should be taken into account;

Accordingly, the defendant claimed that the return should be refused by virtue of Section 34 of the Child Custody Act since there was a grave risk that child X, who could not speak Swedish, if returned, would be exposed to serious mental injuries (i.e. Article 13, para.1, subpara. (b) "psychological harm" exception) and that the child objected to the return (i.e. Article 13, para 2 exception).

In its decision (No 4951), issued within four weeks of the application, on October 14, 1994, the court ordered the child to be returned, referring to Section 34 of the Child Custody Act (Article 13 of The Hague Convention). It stated that no such evidence, upon which it would be deemed to be probable that the return of the child to her custodian in Sweden would expose the child to physical or mental injuries or otherwise place the child in intolerable conditions, was produced in the case. In addition, the court stated that, having regard to the fact that the child was less than eight years old, it was obvious that the child was not capable of making independently autonomous decisions of the parents and her environment and that therefore it would not be appropriate to interview the child in order to discover her views.

C Case 3 (Comet-Codina)

The parents, father A and mother B, were married to each other and living in Switzerland (Geneva) with children X and Y. A was a British national domiciled and habitually resident in Switzerland since 1959 (born 1955), while B was a Finnish national habitually resident in Switzerland since 1976. The mother B left Switzerland for Finland with children X and Y who were in joint custody of A and B on November 3, 1993.

The father A lodged an application with the Court of Appeals of Helsinki on November 27, 1994. In his application A explained that mother B came to Finland with the children on November 5, 1993 and it was not until Easter 1994 that he A discovered that B had no intention of returning to Switzerland or to allow children X and Y to return to their home. Since that time he had made several attempts to have the children returned or to visit them, but with modest results. He had only been able to meet the children in Christmas 1993 (one week), Easter (three days) and 7 hours on August 1, 1994. In an application made to the court of first instance on June 10 mother A had applied for a maintenance order as well as a custody order.

During his last visit to Finland in October 1994 father A was compelled to sign an agreement before the competent social authorities. According to this he and B agreed that X and Y should live with mother B and that he should have specified access rights in October 1994 with the undertaking that he should not attempt to remove X or Y outside Finland. The agreement was to serve as a basis for an interim order to be applied for from the court where the application made by B was pending. The court issued an interim order on residence and rights of access in accordance with the agreement on October 12, 1994.

In his application A claimed that the agreement signed on October 10, 1994, as well as the following interim order by the court of first instance of October 16, 1994, should be disregarded and requested that the children be returned to Switzerland. He claimed that he was compelled to sign the agreement under threat that otherwise he would not be allowed to have access to the children. Furthermore, he was given misleading information about his legal rights by the authorities as well as by his lawyers. It was not until October 19, 1994 that he, for the first time, had heard about the new law relating to child abductions which applied to his case. Therefore he considered that he had signed the agreement under coercion and, having been innocently mistaken of his rights, he had not given his genuine consent that the children might stay in Finland.

The agreement of October 10, 1994 was signed in the presence of the lawyers of both A and B and this was not contested by A.

In its decision, issued within six weeks of the application on December 7, 1994 (No 6376) the Court of Appeals rejected the application on the grounds that no evidence was produced to indicate that A had signed the agreement under coercion and that A by that agreement should be deemed to have given his approval to the non-return of the children within the meaning of Section 32, paragraph 2 of the Custody of Children Act (i.e. the "acquiescence" exception in Article 13, para. 1, subpara (a) of The Hague Convention. In consequence, the return of the children should not be deemed to be unlawful.

IV CONCLUSION

From the point of view of the practical operation of The Hague Convention a critical and pessimistic reader might conclude that in Finnish judicial practice one third of cases will be complete blunders (Case No 1), the child will be returned in one third of cases (Case No 2) and that the return will be refused in one third of cases (Case No 3). This, however, would certainly amount to drawing big conclusions from small samples. A closer look at the files in cases 2 and 3 (and the claims and counterclaims made by the parties and how they were treated by the Court) might suggest a far more positive conclusion.

As usual, the defendants made all possible efforts to use the "grave risk or intolerable situation" exception (Article 13. para. 1 subpara (b) of The

Hague Convention, Section 32, para. 1, subpara. 2 of the Finnish Child Custody Act) as well as the "objection by a mature child" exception (Article 13, para. 2 of The Hague Convention, Section 32, para. 1, subpara. 3 of the Finnish Child Custody Act) in order to avert the return, to block the proceedings and delay the prompt return and to convert the summary return proceedings into an ordinary custody dispute under the best interests test.

The arguments presented by the lawyers included inter alia that a parent was unfit, asocial, alcoholic, lesbian, that a child who does not speak Swedish (the second official language of Finland) would suffer grave mental injuries if returned to Sweden (the State of the child's habitual residence before the unlawful retention), that a 5 year old child had reached "an age and maturity at which it is appropriate to take account of its views" and that the return of the child should be refused because of the polluted air of Geneva. In case 2, where the child was ordered to be returned, these kinds of objections were rejected forthwith by a simple statement that there was nothing in the case to support the use of the "grave risk or intolerable situation" exceptions. It is also interesting to note that the Court rejected the typical dilatory request to interview a child, who was almost 8 years old, simply by making reference to his age without entering into inquiries whether or not the child might nevertheless have attained, in this individual case, such a maturity that his opinion should be taken into account.

As a whole the Court made it fairly clear (in Case 2) that return proceedings are urgent summary proceedings on the physical return of the child to another State, not ordinary custody proceedings. The only task of the Court is, in principle, to decide whether this is an unlawful removal or not and, if so, to order the return. The exceptions to the return must be given a very narrow and strict interpretation and they can only be applied in extremely rare cases. It was also made clear that not only does the burden of proof as to the exceptions lie on the defendant, but also that the defendant must be prepared to present immediately conclusive evidence to support them. Otherwise the objection will be disregarded. In addition, no delaying tactics such as social reports and interviewing the child will be tolerated. It is only to be hoped that these principles adopted in Case 2 will be followed in future cases and that the unfortunate Case 1 will soon be forgotten.

FRANCE

REFORMS AND CONTROVERSIES

J. Rubellin-Devichi *

Recent times in France have been marked by intense legal activity, both legislative and judicial, on sensitive questions about which opinions among judges and legislators alike are divided.

I   ABORTION

The most striking development concerns termination of pregnancy (abortion). This has become a matter of live current interest through a conjunction of three factors: First, the United Nations declared 1995 the Year of Women; stress had already been laid, at the Cairo World Population Conference, on the need for a means of birth control other than infanticide for women of the third world. This was pressed, in particular, by Mme Veil, then Minister for social affairs, health and the urban community. Controlling of procreation and women's rights over their own bodies must be two of the most important problems to be raised, particularly by French delegates, at the Fourth World Congress on Women, in Beijing, in September. Secondly, 1995 saw the twentieth anniversary of the law of January 17, 1975, enacted on the initiative of Mme Veil, decriminalising abortions performed under defined conditions of timing (abortion during the first ten weeks of pregnancy is permitted) and of procedure (obligatory counselling, consent of a parent for young minors...), and the passions of supporters and opponents of legalising abortion were stirred by militant anti-abortion societies (Laissez-les-vivre, SOS-Tout-Petits): a hundred or so "anti-abortion commandos", have been identified since 1990 – these intervene with varying degrees of violence, chaining themselves to beds and medical equipment, or chanting psalms and prayers to induce distress and guilt among the staff. A law of January 16, 1993, passed on the initiative of Mme Neiertz, then Secretary of State for women's matters, made obstruction of an abortion a punishable offence

---

*   Professor at Jean Moulin University, Lyon 3, Director of the Centre du droit de la famille.
    Translated by Peter Schofield.

A. Bainham (ed.), The International Survey of Family Law 1994, 241–257.

and courts have frequently handed down suspended sentences of imprisonment, no doubt the most appropriate penalty, given that it is always the same
people who form these commandos. Thirdly, the opposing positions were
to manifest themselves anew in connection with the amnesty law. There is
a tradition in France that a new President of the Republic, on taking office,
puts forward a Bill to declare amnesty – a relic of the royal prerogative of
mercy – with the objective of obliterating certain offences, whether brought
to trial or not. President Chirac's Bill included, inter alia, minor breaches
of road traffic law (illegal parking), terms of imprisonment of three months
or less, suspended terms of imprisonment of up to nine months. In the course
of debates, the National Assembly wanted the anti-abortion commandos to
be excluded from the amnesty, but the Senate, against the advice of the
Minister of Justice, by a narrow majority (5 votes) voted to give the benefit
of the amnesty to non-violent actions, failing to take sufficient account of
the fact that psychological pressure is itself a kind of violence. Finally a
compromise was reached, anti-abortion commandos got no amnesty, but
nor did those sentenced for "provocation, propaganda or publicity". In fact,
even if this bargain was a small price for the refusal of absolution to the
anti- abortion commandos (since 1984 only four cases were reported by the
Ministry of Justice), it does possibly provide ammunition for those wishing
to make difficulties for family planning centres, particularly when they
criticise the brevity of the time limits, which force women who have gone
beyond the tenth week to go abroad for treatment, or when they point out
how inhuman and dangerous it is to require the consent of a parent of a
pregnant minor. Despite all these vicissitudes, it would be unimaginable that
there could be a return to the previous state of the law on abortion, which
would bring back widespread recourse to illegal abortions with all their
dreadful results. According to figures issued by the United Nations office
for population in its 1995 report, more than half the forty million abortions
carried out each year are performed illegally, and the estimated cost is 67,000
deaths.[1] Whatever a very small minority of fanatics may do, there is no
real prospect of Parliament withdrawing the freedom granted to women by
the "loi Veil".

---

1   *Libération,* July 12, 1995.

II THE UNITED NATIONS CONVENTION ON THE RIGHTS OF THE CHILD

The recent period is also remarkable for the strange way in which the Cour de cassation has decided to give effect to the United Nations Convention on the Rights of the Child, and by the resistance shown by some doctrinal writers and lower courts.

It is generally known that France was among the first signatories to the United Nations Convention on the Rights of the Child, on January 20, 1990, and was also among the first to ratify it on August 6, 1990, enabling it to be given speedy implementation. It would have been expected that our country, cradle of the Rights of Man, would have set its heart on advancing children's rights, the more so since France, like Belgium, Luxembourg, the Netherlands and Portugal (to mention only European countries) and unlike the United Kingdom, Ireland, Iceland and Sweden, among others, incorporates treaties directly into internal law, by virtue of Article 55 of the Constitution. The Cour de cassation could have been expected to apply the New York Convention wherever French law made no provision and even where its provisions were at variance with the Convention.

Not a bit of it. On March 10, 1993[2], in a case where a father, relying on Article 12 of the Convention, complained that the judges at first instance had failed to give the child a hearing, and despite the fact that the appeal could have been easily rejected on the ground that the child had been heard through a court social worker and an expert witness, the Cour de cassation held that "the provisions of the Convention relating to the rights of the child [...] cannot be relied on before the courts, the said Convention, which only creates obligations falling on the participating States, not being directly applicable in internal law." On June 2, 1993[3], in a case where a natural father complained that the Cour d'appel had made him go to Mexico, where the child lived with the mother, in order to exercise his visitation rights, in breach of Article 8-1 of the Convention, the Cour de cassation rejected the appeal in the same terms. On July 15, 1993[4] the court (civil chamber) stuck to that position; in one case a Pakistani complained that the Cour d'appel had upheld the decision of the juge des enfants extending the placement of his six year old son in the care of the welfare authority (Aide

---

2   Cass. civ. March 10, 1993, Bull. civ. I n° 103.
3   Cass. civ. June 2, 1993, Bull. civ. I n° 195.
4   Cass. civ. July 15, 1993 (2 arrêts), Bull. civ. I n° 259.

sociale), in breach of Article 30 (among others) of the Convention which provides for the child's right to keep his cultural roots; in a second, a divorcing father contended that, in deciding that the children, subject to joint parental authority, should continue to live with their mother, the judges had taken into account the interests of the children only as a simple factor, not as a paramount one as required by the Convention. This inflexible position[5] taken up by the Chambre civile reappears, along with the same reasoning, in a decision of the Chambre sociale of July 13, 1994[6] reversing a decision of the Cour de Paris. The latter, following a closely reasoned opinion of its advocate general, had held that a sixteen year old woman who did not work and was not a student should, by virtue of Article 26 of the Convention, be regarded as the third party beneficiary under the life assurance policy of her father.[7] In another decision of January 4, 1995[8] the civil chamber [of the Cour de Cassation], rejecting an appeal against the court of Montpellier, once again decided not to join a young man born in 1977 as a party to the case. His parents had divorced in 1982, and his father had applied for a residence order, by which the boy would live with him, in 1990. The application was refused at first instance and the father appealed. The minor, after being heard by the judge, having a premonition that the application was about to be refused, applied to be joined as a party, but this was considered improper and lacking in decency (inconvenant) by the first instance court. Many writers expect a change in this trend of the line of decisions. Two senior judges, in a note to the Consultative Commission on Human Rights consider, on the basis of the decisions of June 2 and July 15, 1993 that the Cour de cassation "would no longer lay stress on the fact that the Convention is not applicable in internal law, relying rather on the point that some of its provisions could not be relied on in national courts".[9] They even

---

5   All the more inflexible considering that in all four cases the appeals could have been rejected on numerous other grounds.

6   Cass. soc. July 13, 1994, Bull. civ. V n° 236.

7   Paris, November 27, 1992, Gaz. Pal. April 15, 1993, concl. Domingo.

8   Civ. January 4, 1995, unreported. See H. Bosse-Platière and O. Matocq, "La parole de l'enfant dans le divorce de ses parents" (The child's right to be heard in his parents' divorce), *Petites Affiches*, special issue for the congress of notaries, April 1995, *The child and the law*, p. 83.

9   R. de Goutte, "A propos des arrêts récents de la 1ère chambre civile de la Cour de cassation sur la Convention des Nations Unies relative aux droits de l'enfant", *Rev. dr. de l'enfant et de la famille* 1994/3 n° 40, p. 120.

list a number of articles they think should be recognised as "self-executing", but they are probably wrong in fact; the latest decision of the chambre civile does not signal any change in the monolithic position taken so far. Monsieur le Conseiller Massip, who presided in the 1st chamber when the decision of March 10, 1993 was announced, recently also recalled that the refusal of the Cour de cassation to allow that some provisions of the Convention were directly applicable probably derived from a view that "such a distinction [would be] calculated to give rise to casuistry and to difficulties of application which it had been hoped to prevent".[10] Judges in lower courts show resistance. Among their decisions[11], we pick out that of March 16, 1993 of the cour de Rennes[12], relying on Article 12 of the Convention to allow joinder, through an avocat, of a ward (pupille) of the State, under twelve years old, who wanted and obtained an adoption order in favour of the foster family, despite the refusal of consent of the aide sociale à l'enfance (social services). Most interesting was the case before the cour de Rennes on June 13, 1994[13]; in refusing to impose an order for deportation, following a conviction for unlawfully failing to leave on a young woman from the Côte D'Ivoire who did not want to go leaving her five month old baby behind, the court stressed that direct application of the Convention, or at least of provisions in it that were sufficiently complete and precise, followed from the general principle of integrating treaties into the internal legal order.[14]

The Conseil d'Etat, the highest administrative court (on the level of the Cour de cassation on the civil side), agreed, in two decisions of February

---

10 J. Massip, "L'application par la Cour de cassation de conventions internationales récentes relatives à l'enfance", *Petites Affiches*, loc. cit. p. 41.

11 See the writer's observations in *Chronique du droit de la famille*, JCP, 1995.I.3813 and the decisions there cited.

12 D.1995, p. 113, note G. Geoffroy and D. Desgue.

13 Rev. trim. dr. civ. 1994, p. 81, obs J. Hauser; Rev. dr. san. soc., 1994, p. 503, obs. F. Moneger.

14 There has been a yet more striking case; police, giving effect to a judgment of the tribunal de Douai of February 2, 1995, imposing a sentence of three months imprisonment (suspended) and three years exclusion from France for being illegally in the country, on a Senegalese woman, mother of children aged 3 and 5 years, had placed the children in a home run by the aide sociale à l'enfance, and forced the woman into the dilemma of either parting with her children (expulsion of minors is forbidden) or leaving the country without them voluntarily. The case went to the cour d'appel (*Libération*, July 21, 1995), but the method seems to have government approval.

17, 1993 and June 30, 1993, to consider grounds of appeal based on breach of the Convention, and held them not to be made out on the facts.[15] On July 29, 1994[16], the Conseil d'Etat declared that Article 9 of the Convention (not the Convention as a whole) only creates obligations between states and does not grant rights to individual parties, thus showing that it was receptive to the opinion of Mme the Commissaire du Gouvernement that "it will be appropriate, in due time, to examine each of the provisions of the Convention".

The Committee on the Rights of the Child has considered the precise place of the Convention in internal law, in relation to the decisions of the French Cour de cassation.[17] Members of the Parliament and judicial administrators of the Council of Europe, aware of the problems the French attitude creates, have set up a "Project for a Convention on the exercise of children's rights"[18] which will include, inter alia, in Article 8, the possibility of the judge taking up a case proprio motu (se saisir d'office) in proceedings affecting a child, an ingenious means of ensuring the child's access to justice. Whatever may be said, the need for the proliferation of international texts is regrettable, but we are forced to it. Another approach, to combat the attitude of the French Cour de cassation – which threatens to infect both neighbouring countries and former French dependencies, as was pointed out by the First Secretary of the Hague Conference in his General Report to the European conference on the monitoring of children's rights[19] – is being sought in the idea that the Committee on children's rights should draw up a list of provisions of the Convention it considers to be self-executing,

---

15 CE February 17, 1993 (party cannot rely on the provisions of Articles 8, 9 and 10 of the International Convention on the Rights of the Child to object to refusal of a residence permit), Journal du droit des jeunes, juin 1994, n° 136; June 30 and July 28, 1993 (grounds of appeal relied on by a man from Mali to call for annulment of a deportation order, based on Articles 9 and 12 of the Convention not made out on the facts), Journal du droit des jeunes, November 1993, p. 33 and Rec. Lebon, tables, p. 778.

16 CE July 29, 1994, AJDA November 20, 1994, concl. Mme Denis-Lindon; Gaz. Pal. July 8, 1995, p. 24, note Y. Benhamou; it concerned a Tunisian couple, parents of eight children, seeking annulment of a deportation order, which had been granted at first instance.

17 *Journal du droit des jeunes*, June 1994, n° 136.

18 Announced by the Council of Europe on 25 April, 1995, see L. Pettiti, "Le projet de convention européenne sur l'exercice des droits des enfants", P.A. n° cited above, p. 31.

19 European Conference on Monitoring Children's Rights, Ghent, December 11-14, 1994, General Report of Hans van Loon.

and seek to persuade States which automatically integrate treaties into the internal legal order to apply those articles directly. This will be difficult to achieve in France, where it could represent a threat to national sovereignty and the separation of powers. The French Cour de cassation takes orders from no one.[20] This is further evidence of the current malaise in the French courts.

Unable to have the New York Convention applied in the French Courts, the child can obtain this before the European Court of Human Rights, applying as an individual without conditions of capacity. France holds the record for individual applications (some 400 annually since 1991), and has repeatedly been condemned. One of the first decisions of the Cour de cassation about transsexualism, on May 31, 1987[21], was taken to the European Court which, on March 25, 1992[22], condemned France, for breach of Article 8 of the Convention, to pay compensation to the complainant. Eight months later, on December 11, 1992[23], the Cour de cassation in assemblée plénière fell into line with the European Court: "when a person...no longer has all the characteristics of his original sex, and has taken on a physical appearance approximating to that of the other sex to which his social conduct corresponds, the principle of respect for privacy justifies the indication on his registration of civil status of his apparent sex".[24] We must logically expect that the Assemblée plénière will similarly intervene in relation to the New

---

20 Demonstrated at the ceremonial re-opening when, after the Minister of Justice had set aside the reform proposed by the Premier président of the court, aimed at cutting down the number and the length of cases, the Procureur Général rose to say he was refusing to give the traditional address as a sign of protest.
21 Cass. civ. May 31, 1987, RTDciv. 1989, 725, obs. J. Rubellin-Devichi, and references there cited. The rejection of the change of sex had been subsequently confirmed by four decisions of May 21, 1990 (Bull. civ. n° 117; RTDciv. 1991, 289, obs. J. Hauser; *Revue Droit de l'enfance et de la famille*, 1990/3, p. 27, note P. Murat).
22 ECHR March 25, 1992. RUDH 1992, p. 316; *Revue Droit de l'enfance et de la famille* 1992/2, p. 27 note P. Murat; RTDciv. 1992, p. 540, note J. Hauser; F. Sudre, Droit de la Convention européenne des droits de l'homme, chronique de l'actualité, JCP 1993.I.3654, n° 19.
23 Cass. ass. plén. December 11, 1992, JCP 1993.II.21991, concl. Jépl, note G. Memeteau.
24 See the reference to this question in J. Rubellin-Devichi, "L'état de la personne et les Conventions internationales", in *Le droit français et la Convention Européenne des droits de l'homme, 1974-1992*, directed by F. Sudre ed. Engels, 1994, p. 165.

York Convention, without waiting for the condemnation of the European Court, which cannot be long delayed.[25]

III   LAW OF JANUARY 8, 1993

Only one of the two legislative projects on family law, presented by the Government on December 23, 1991 and which we mentioned as imminent in the 1992 Annual Survey[26], has passed into law – the law of January 8, 1993 "relating to civil status, the family and the establishment of the juge aux affaires familiales".

This law, whose provisions are to be welcomed, falls within the general development of family law. It takes account of recent advances in biology (particularly positive proof of paternity), and gives greater scope to the wishes of the individual as well as simplifying procedures as a result.

Λ   Civil status

Regarding civil status, the main reforms concern first names, changes of surname, neonatal deaths.

1.   Henceforth, parental choice of first names is free: reference to calendars and known personages of ancient history is gone. Hitherto, the registrar had to reject first names considered not to be capable of being registered, and to refer the case immediately to the Procureur de la République, who could put the case before the tribunal de grande instance, citing the parents, to have the child named. Now, the registrar has to register the names chosen by the parents, and if these seem to be contrary to the child's interests, or to the rights of third parties to protect their family name, he must forthwith inform the juge aux affaires familiales (the JAF, established by the same law,

---

25   As the decisions of the European Court do not bind national courts, the transsexual denied an amendment to his civil status registration could not have the case retried; what is more, the Cour de cassation is free to disregard decisions of the European Courts, as was recently restated (Crim. February 3, 1993, D. 1993, p. 515, note J.-F. Renucci; May 4, 1994, D. 1995 p. 80, note J.-F. Renucci), though this could result in yet another judgment against France.

26   French version, Regards sur le droit de la famille dans le monde, P.U.L. Lyon, 1993, p. 177, (yet to appear in English Annual Survey).

and who took office on February 1, 1994). This new procedure was applied in the cases of two little girls, one born in January and the other in May of 1993. The parents of one wanted to call her Babar (a children's story animal with a trunk and enormous ears, which would, the judges considered, be detrimental to her). The other's parents chose Jani, Vercise, Onasis (counterfeiting the name of a commercial clothing park and the patronymic of a Greek family, which caused the parents' choice to be rejected). Change of the given names, allowed where there is a legitimate interest, is on the application of the person concerned or his representative and to the JAF, not, as previously, to the tribunal de grande instance.

2. The administrative procedure for change of surname, authorised in case of legitimate interest (usually because the party has a ridiculous or odious surname, but sometimes because of the desire to protect a surname from extinction – for instance that of the maternal family), is somewhat simpler. The change only applies to the party's children under 13; for older children and adults, their individual consent is needed.

In general, even when the change of surname flows from a change of filiation, by its establishment or alteration, it does not apply to children who have attained majority without their consent (Article 61-3 of the Civil Code). This rule is welcome, for it was a shock for an adult, frequently already father of a family to lose the surname (for instance his mother's) he had hitherto held and transmitted to his own children, when a (true or false) father recognised him and married his mother after long delay. But it does strike a blow at the link between transmission of surname and filiation.

3. The Civil Code (Article 79-1) contains a new measure to relieve the pain of parents of a child born alive and viable, but who dies before being registered (which must be within three days of delivery). On production of a medical certificate, registration of birth and of death takes place, not, as previously, of a stillborn child (enfant sans vie).

B   Filiation

Concerning filiation, the law contains long awaited and highly innovative provisions to bring French law into line with the International Convention on the Rights of the Child.

1. The out-of-wedlock child takes the surname of the parent who is first to recognise him. To give him his father's surname more easily (on the

model of the legitimate family) the parents can make a joint declaration while he is still a minor. This is not before the JAF, nor, as formerly, the juge des tutelles, but before the chief registrar of the tribunal de grande instance and, if over 13, the child must also consent (Article 334-2).

2. Reform of adoption as a whole is currently under examination (the Mattei Report, commissioned by the Prime Minister was submitted on February 4, 1995[27], and France signed the Hague Convention on International Adoption in April 1995). Meanwhile certain specific provisions have been enacted. In particular when a child already has an established filiation in relation to one birth parent, it will no longer be possible for a subsequent spouse of the other birth parent to obtain an order for full adoption of that child; also it is required that judgment must be given on an adoption application within six months. The latter reform was anyway otiose as most courts were disposing of cases much more speedily.

3. The terms "legitimate" and "natural" filiation are retained, but the methods of establishment are brought closer together. The terms in no way connote a value judgment on the diverse forms of family, concubinage being totally socially acceptable. This is why the percentage of out-of-wedlock births is so high (over 33% of births – the highest ratio among European and Western States).

But, while some States, such as Belgium, have abolished the distinction in terminology, but retained a significant discrimination between the methods of its establishment[28], French law has taken equality in this field to its logical conclusion – if one allows for the fact that there is no equivalent available for the presumption pater est quem nuptiae demonstrant.

In relation to out-of-wedlock paternity suits, the law of 1993 abolishes the notorious conditions for allowing a claim to be made (rape or abduction at the time of conception, fraudulent seduction, letters or writings from the father admitting his paternity, open concubinage between mother and putative father, contributing as a father to the maintenance or establishment of the

27 J. Rubellin-Devichi and B. Trillat, "L'adoption: Réflexions sur le rapport Mattei", *Petites Affiches*, n° cited above, p. 136.

28 By the law of March 31, 1987, the minor child of parents not married to each other can only be recognised by the father if the mother consents. The Belgian Cour d'arbitrage held, on December 21, 1990 and October 8, 1992, that this provision was contrary to the constitution (See *Annual Survey of Family Law*, 1992, Belgium, by M.-T. Meulders Klein).

child) along with the grounds for not allowing one (notorious misconduct of the mother, relations with another man). Proof of paternity is henceforth possible, by any means, if there is a strong presumption or indication, and only proof of non-paternity can cause the action to fail. Further, the new certainty of proof of paternity afforded by the blood test and genetic fingerprinting has meant the abolition of the former defence to the child's action for maintenance against a man who had sexual relations, at the time of conception, with the mother, based on the latter's dissolute lifestyle. This is an important action lasting throughout the child's minority, not barred by two years' delay like the paternity action.

As to out-of-wedlock maternal filiation, the novelty, at least apparent, for it existed already in the Code de la famille et de l'aide sociale (Article 47), was the introduction in the Civil Code of the right of a woman to give birth anonymously.[29] Ending one of the most fundamentally divisive controversies in the Parliament, the law provides a ground for the rejection of an action to determine maternity (Article 341, para. 1). No matter what one may think of this possibility[30], it must be stressed on the one hand that it applies to the married and the unmarried woman alike, for the presumption of paternity rests on maternity (conception or birth in wedlock); insofar as establishing maternity is impossible, there can be no legitimate filiation. On the other hand, it is wrong to allege that this text is contrary to Article 7 of the United Nations Convention on the rights of the Child.[31] In fact, the mother's right to remain anonymous makes it specifically impossible for the child to know his parents.

---

29 B. Trillat "L'accouchement anonyme, de l'opprobre à la consécration", *Liber amicorum* Danièle Huet-Weiler, LITEC/PUS, 1994, p. 527.

30 Some justifiably consider this freedom is of benefit to both mother and child, for it avoids abortion, infanticide and abuse (on this see J. Rubellin-Devichi, "Droits de la mère et droits de l'enfant. Réflexions sur les formes de l'abandon", RTDciv. 1991, p. 695). Others invoke the need for the individual, at the time he is developing his personality, to know his genetic parents, without recognising that the individual in question will have largely passed the age of development when he starts his search for his origins.

31 The child has the right to know his parents and to be brought up by them "so far as possible".

C   Parental authority

On the matter of parental authority the law makes two innovations: first Article 387 of the Civil Code sets out in the case of divorce the principle of continued joint exercise, the judge intervening to fix the child's residence only in default of agreement or if the agreement seems to him to be contrary to the child's interests. In fact, on this point, all the law of 1993 does is to legislate judicial practice: only in rare cases and for well defined reasons were judges granting exclusive exercise to one parent.[32] Further, Article 372 restates the basic rule for the child of married (or by implication former-ly married) parents or of parents living (or formerly living) in concubinage: parents of a legitimate child exercise parental authority in common; so do those of a natural child, but on two conditions. First the recognition must come before the child is a year old (which seems logical, fathers who mean to take charge of them normally recognise their children before birth, and recognition which does not take place during the first year is often not willingly given). Secondly they must be living together at the time of the second recognition, which can – and according to the prevailing inter-pretation of the national education department must – be proved by act of the JAF. This second condition, the result of a compromise between the two legislative chambers, is unanimously criticised by doctrinal writers, for it is impossible to apply and in fact destroys the automatic nature of the at-tribution of joint exercise to natural parents. Fortunately, exclusive attribution to the mother (Article 374, para. 2) can be avoided, and joint exercise chosen, by a joint declaration before the chief registrar of the tribunal d'instance (Article 374, para. 3 réd. loi du 8 février 1995).

D   The Juge Aux Affaires Familiales

Concerning the creation of the JAF, the law brings to fruition a reform set in motion more than ten years ago, to end what was denounced as the scattering of jurisdiction in contentious family matters, whereby these were conducted before a dozen different courts. Henceforth the JAF is the sole

---

32   H. Fulchiron, "Enquête réalisée à la demande du ministère de la Justice sur l'exercice de l'autorité parentale depuis 1988", accepted for publication in Revue Droit de l'enfance et de la famille.

judge of divorce and its consequences. He can refer the case to a collegial bench and must do so if either party requests it. He rules on disputes over given names, grandparents rights of access, difficulties over the exercise of parental authority, on urgent matters provided for under Article 220-1 in case of a crisis in the working of the matrimonial regime, and he has inherited from the first instance judge jurisdiction over maintenance obligations. This is a welcome reform, but it brings with it an overload of powers which ought to be matched by an increase in the number of judges so that decisions can be reached with the speed required in family matters. The Legislature has preferred to favour recourse to mediation (law of February 8, 1995), which we are beginning to see can be the worst, as well as the best, solution.

E Children's right to be heard

Regarding the hearing of children in court and the defence of their interests, the law is inspired by Article 12 of the United Nations Convention on the Rights of the Child: Article 388-1 of the Civil Code now generally allows a minor if, and only if, "capable of understanding (discernement)", to be heard by the judge or by a person nominated by the judge "in any proceedings which concern him". The child's request, which may be to be heard with an avocat or person of his or her choice, can only be set aside "by a decision for which specific reasons are given". But there is no appeal against this decision, which opens the door to arbitrariness as appears from a number of recent cases. Article 388-2 also establishes as a general principle that, in case of conflict between the interests of a child and those of his legal representatives, an administrator ad hoc must be nominated. This is an enormous advance for French law which regards the child only as someone under incapacity, whose protection and representation fall to his parents. But the child remains incapable of bringing his own action in place of, or even against, uncaring parents.[33] Contrary to some colleagues[34], we remain

---

[33] Except in relation to a supervision order (assistance éducative) where Article 375 of the Civil Code ("If the health, safety or morality of an unemancipated minor are in danger, or if the conditions of his education are gravely compromised...") allows direct application to the juge des enfants.

of the opinion that the right of access to justice, accorded to every individual by the European Convention, must be given to the child – which does not mean the judge will accede to his or her demands – and that the reform made by the law of January 8, 1993 is clearly inadequate.

IV EQUALITY OF CHILDREN

The other legislative project laid before the Parliament on December 23, 1991 completed equality between children. It contained two sets of important provisions, one improving the succession rights of a surviving spouse, which are surprisingly small in France[35]; the other removing all discrimination against children conceived in adultery. Probably it was to obtain the equality of children that the two sorts of reforms were lumped together. However, while the vote on the measure was delayed by other urgent matters, the Minister of Justice in the Balladur Government presented it anew on February 8, 1995 "with the exception of the rights of adulterine children, which it is proposed to leave as they are", since the existing law was "a balanced compromise between the two main interests, respect for marriage as an institution and the desire not to penalise descendants."[36] Fortunately the project – which drew hostility from most lawyers, avocats and notaries – is unlikely to be presented in this state in Parliament. Recent news reports have shown two children born of adultery, one the daughter of a famous singer, rejected by her father and reduced to bringing a paternity suit; the other, daughter of the highest person in the State, taken up and educated by him. These two examples provide a perfect illustration of the fact that

---

34 See particularly the brilliant article of Jean Hauser, "L'enfant et la famille: de l'hexagon à l'ensemble vide? Eloge de compromis." Petites Affiches, 1995, n° 94, p. 17.

35 At present, if there are children, the surviving spouse receives only the usufruct in one quarter of the assets of the deceased (Article 767 C. civ.), always provided the latter has not disinherited the survivor, which is always a possibility, for the survivor has no reserved rights. The project grants, if there are children, the choice between the usufruct of the whole of the assets and receiving a quarter outright. If disinherited wholly or in part, the survivor has a claim to what is already being called a minimum guaranteed inheritance to ensure the maintenance of her/his standard of living (periodical financial provision and occupancy of the accommodation that was the main home at the date of the death).

36 Reply to a question to the Minister (Question n° 7768, November 15, 1993, JOAN May 16, 1994, p. 2502).

present law on divorce, surname and parental authority give the father the power to choose the fate of his adulterine child, thus creating an even more shocking inequality and injustice than that which resulted only from the law.[37] We consider it unthinkable that Parliament could vote for such a counter-reform, which the European Court has several times condemned in other States – States which have, moreover, reformed their law since".[38]

V BIOETHICAL LAWS

So-called bioethical laws have at last been passed. Three projects were laid before Parliament on March 25, 1992, required by an alleged need to "fill an important gap in our law", and to affirm, after civil and social rights, "biological rights" and complete the "trilogy of fundamental rights".[39] Following a number of fine reports and significant parliamentary effort, from these projects three laws have emerged.[40] They could hardly be described as highly polished, and it is hard to believe they have been so long in the making. The project was ambitious, the field vast, which explains many of the ill-advised provisions; moreover the Legislature has chosen to lay down the law in a most rigid manner, on questions which were not really within its competence.

The law of July 1, 1994 gives a legal framework for the management of files held for Health research. The two laws of July 29 are closely linked and insert provisions into the Civil Code, Penal Code and Public Health Code. They lay down on the one hand the rules – hitherto deduced from general principles – underlying the status of the human body and governing

---

37 As was perfectly demonstrated by A. Tisserand (L'enfant adultérin, thèse, Strasbourg, 1990).

38 See examples cited in our article in *Le droit français et la Convention européenne des droits de l'homme*, 1974-1992, directed by F. Sudre, ed. Engels, 1994, p. 165.

39 Address of the Minister of Justice, Journées nationales de l'éthique, December 23, 1991.

40 Law of July 1, 1994 relating to personal data held for the purposes of health research, amending the law of January 6, 1978 relating to electronic database, files and liberties. Unlike the two that follow, this law was not submitted to the Conseil constitutionnel – hence its date. Law of July 29, 1994 relating to respect for the human body. Law of July 29, 1994 relating to the giving and use of parts and products of the human body, in aid of medical assistance of procreation and prenatal diagnosis. The last two have been declared consistent with the Constitution, respecting the safeguard and the liberty of the human person, which it was alleged they threatened.

the giving and use of its parts and products, and on the other hand the particular rules of such gifts and their utilisation. They also regulate medically assisted procreation and medical practice to that end.

We find it strange that Parliament, representing society in general, should have considered itself to have sufficient scientific authority to say that insemination must be carried out using frozen semen, that mixing of semen is forbidden, that the embryo obtained by in vitro fertilization must be placed in a woman within eight days of conception, that frozen embryos must be destroyed at the end of a period of five years, that doctors can have recourse to procreation with third party donated gametes only after attempts to fecundate with the sperm of the husband or concubine have failed, that any one donor's sperm may only be used five times (the practice of centres was to use it for up to five families), etc.

Fearing that individuals would choose the sex of their child by diagnosis before implantation, this had been forbidden from the first vote: it took the efforts of Professor Mattei, author of the final report on genetics and also a deputé, to convince members, at the time of the second vote in the Assemblée Nationale, that such a prohibition would be inhumane, leaving those families carrying a genetic defect only the choice of abortion or of abstention from having children.

The law has in many ways lacked moderation: it declares void all contracts with the object of procreation or gestation for another person, so making illegal the loan of a womb to a couple where the wife has ovules and the husband viable sperm, so that they are capable of creating an embryo, whereas it permits and regulates the gift of gametes of either sort, or even that of an embryo. Where a couple has recourse to in vitro fertilization, and surplus embryos are created and frozen for later attempts, the death of one of the couple ends the possibility of reimplantation, the embryos must be destroyed, there is only the possibility for the survivor to give away the embryo – his or her child – to strangers, whereas if the woman is the survivor, her wish would be to carry the child herself, as she had done for the others, so as to give birth to a child, genetically and biologically, fraternally related to the older siblings.

It seems to us perfectly proper that the law, following the ethical rules set out by the CECOS[41], should restrict to couples, married or concubines of two years standing, the facility of having recourse to medically assisted procreation. But we consider most ill-advised the provisions which forbid all challenge to filiation once the couple has consented. First, this child on whom a forced – and rather repugnant – paternity is imposed, for everyone knows it not to be biological paternity, is bound to suffer damage; he cannot be the subject of full adoption. Then, as the law has had to make exception for the case where "it has been held that the child is not conceived by assisted procreation", the husband who wants to deny paternity can only do so by proving positively that the child is that of his wife's lover; the woman who wants to attribute paternity to her lover will have little difficulty in snatching her child from her husband, who, having consented to artificial insemination, thought his paternity was unassailable.[42]

If we add that determining paternity or maternity by genetic fingerprinting can only take place in the course of judicial proceedings, obliging people to go to foreign laboratories or to start a trumped-up action, and that it is a rather bizarre logic that leads to building this form of proof into such a rigid system, it can readily be understood why the hope expressed in a large part of doctrinal writing is that the Legislature will have an opportunity to reexamine its work and tidy it up.

---

41 CECOS – Centres d'Etude et de Conservation du Sperme Humain. They number more than twenty, formed into a federation.

42 There have already been many such cases. In one current case, the woman wants her husband to consent to divorce; she has gone to Belgium to obtain DNA fingerprinting of herself, the child and her lover, and explains to the husband that he must leave the child with his "real" parents.

GERMANY

TWO LIVELY DISCUSSED REFORM ACTS

Rainer Frank*

I   INTRODUCTION

This report focusses on two law reforms which have already been passed and come into effect: the Act for the Reform of Family Name Law ("Familiennamensrechtsgesetz") and the Act for Social Insurance against the Risk of Nursing Care ("Pflegeversicherungsgesetz"). This report is also concerned with a bill by the German government on the equal rights of illegitimate children to succeed to a deceased's estate ("Erbrechtsgleichstellungsgesetz"). The last part of the report deals with a decision by the Federal Court of Justice on the issue of whether in the case of artificial insemination a sperm donor is entitled to damages for pain and suffering where his frozen sperm are destroyed by the fault of another.

II   FAMILY NAME REFORM ACT

A   Reason for the reform

The Family Name Reform Act[1] which became effective on April 1, 1994 is based on a decision handed down by the German Constitutional Court on March 5, 1991.[2] In this decision, the Constitutional Court held parts of the previous law on family names to be unconstitutional and, at the same time, deviated from a traditional principle of German law. According to the old law, spouses were required to bear the same family name. It was only possible to choose the husband's or the wife's family name as the married name. If, prior to their marriage, the couple was unable to agree on a married name, the man's family name automatically became the married name in accordance with § 1355 par. 2 s. 2 BGB which was then held unconstitutional

*   Professor of Law, Freiburg I. Br. University.
1   Gesetz zur Neuordnung des Familiennamensrechts from 16.12.1993. BGBl. 1993, I. 2054; cf. Wagenitz, FamRZ 1994, 409-416 and Diederichsen, NJW 1994, 1089-1097.
2   BVerfGE 84, 9=NJW 1991, 1602 = FamRZ 1991, 535; cf Frank, J.Fam.L. 31 (1992/93), 347-354.

A. Bainham (ed.), The International Survey of Family Law 1994, 259-269.
© 1996 The International Society of Family Law. Printed in the Netherlands.

in the decision rendered on March 5, 1991. The court found that this provision violated the constitutional principle of equality of the sexes and, therefore, declared this rule of law to be null and void. The new Family Name Reform Act serves to bridge this gap in the law.

B   The new law: the principle of the common family name

The legislature did not fully renounce the principle that spouses are to bear the same family name. The new § 1355 par. 1 s. 1 BGB states that spouses should bear the same family name. However, they are not required to by law. They have the option of keeping the family names they had previously.

The legislature did not provide much leeway with regard to the name that can be selected as the common family name. Only the family name that either spouse received at birth may become the married, i.e. family, name. This means the following: a family name which was acquired as a result of a previous marriage may not be chosen as the common married name in a subsequent second or third marriage. Ms. A who was married to Mr. B in her first marriage and since then is called Ms. B only has the choice between her maiden name A and the family name of her second husband; the family name B which she received by her first marriage may not be used in the second marriage. The combination of different family names is also not allowed: when Ms. A and Mr. B. marry, they may not call themselves Mr. and Mrs. A-B or B-A. The legislature was afraid that the formation of double names could create an undesired multiple linkage of family names in the next generation.

C   The addition to the family name

A spouse who waives the use of his own family name can either place his previous family name before or after his new married name (§ 1355 par. 4). Such an addition, however, may not be passed onto children born from the marriage; the children may only bear the common family name.

D Selection of a common family name at a later point in time

Should the spouses not decide on a common family name at the time of their marriage, each spouse will continue to bear his or her previous family name (§ 1355 par. 1 s. 3 BGB). A common married name, though, may be selected at a later point in time. Spouses may decide on a common family name within a period not exceeding 5 years after the consummation of their marriage. The reason for this rule is that the desire to have a common family name sometimes arises only after the birth of a couple's first child.

E The effect of divorce or a spouse's death on the family name

In the event that a marriage is terminated by divorce or the death of a spouse, the married name may still be used. However, a spouse may go back to using his or her previous married name or family name received at birth or may attach such a name to the present married name (§ 1355 par. 5 BGB).

F The child's family name

As under the old law, the new law provides that legitimate children are to bear the married name of their parents (§ 1616 par. 1 BGB). The new law also has not changed the rule that a child born out of wedlock automatically receives the family name that the mother has when the child is born (§ 1617 par. 1 BGB).

Should the parents of a legitimate child not have the same family name, the parents may elect a family name for the child pursuant to § 1616 par. 2 BGB. They may choose whether the child is to receive the family name of the mother or father. Double names are not allowed. The family name they decide upon becomes the family name of all subsequently born children so that siblings have the same family name.

Difficulties arise when parents who do not have the same family name cannot agree on the family name for their children. This issue was ardently discussed during the draft stages of the reform law. The legislature finally agreed to leave this issue for the guardianship court. Should the parents be unable to reach an agreement, the guardianship court may appoint one of the parents as the one to decide on the family name pursuant to § 1616 par. 3 BGB.

G *Later changes in the family name*

Problems often arise when a woman remarries after the divorce of her first marriage and assumes the name of her second husband. The woman's change of name does not automatically affect the name of her children from the first marriage. Especially in the case of younger children, however, it is often desirable for them to bear the same name as their mother and step father. As under the old law, the only way for a mother and her children to have the same family name under these circumstances is by way of a special name changing procedure in accordance with the law on name changes. Pursuant to this law, a change in name requires substantiation of an "important reason". Whereas the courts used to allow name changes only in rare cases, today they are much more flexible and act in the child's best interests.[3]

II   THE INTRODUCTION OF MANDATORY NURSING CARE INSURANCE

On January 1, 1995 a new mandatory nursing care insurance law went into effect in Germany[4] which affects the entire population. This insurance is premised on the basic notion of shifting an individual's financial risk of becoming in need of nursing care to a community of insured individuals.

A   *The underpinnings of the act in aspects of family law*

The introduction of mandatory insurance within the ambit of social insurance (in addition to the already existing health, accident, pension and unemployment insurance) has its underpinnings in § 1601 BGB with regard to matters of family law. This provision places immediate family members

---

3   Cf. BVerfG from 7.1.1994, FamRZ 1994, 439-441.
4   Gesetz zur sozialen Absicherung des Risikos der Pflegebedurftiükeit (Pflegeversicherungsgesetz) from 26.5.1994. BGBl I, 1014; cf. Schellhorn, Familie und Recht (=FuR) 1994, 317-327.

under a duty to support each other. This obligation to provide support also extends from children to their parents. Should parents in later years become in need of financial support because they cannot afford to pay for household nursing care or live in a nursing home, then their children were required by the old law to support their parents commensurate with their income and financial circumstances. It was only when the children or other immediate relatives were unable to render support that the government was required to provide financial assistance within the framework of social welfare (i.e. governmental aid for the poor). Therefore, the children of elderly persons were primarily responsible for paying the costs of nursing care before mandatory nursing care insurance was introduced. In the past, this situation caused great hardships especially for those between the ages of 50 and 60 because these people often had to bear the costs of their own children's education and their parents' nursing care at the same time.

B   The financing of nursing care insurance

Starting on January 1, 1995, workers and employees earning below a certain income level and who pay into mandatory health insurance will have to insure themselves against the risk of needing nursing care. Children without an income and the spouse of the beneficiary are also covered by the insurance. Governmental employees, freelancers and highly-paid employees are required to take out such an insurance policy with a private insurance company. The new law creates an obligation to take out insurance. In the future, insurance coverage will only be available together with nursing care insurance. Whoever is already pensioned must also obtain insurance; however, special conditions do apply here.

   In the beginning, the insured's contributions to the nursing care insurance will amount to 1,0 % of his gross income, later this percentage will rise to 1,7 %. The insured and his employer will each bear one half of the total amount of contributions (in the case of pensioned persons: the social security insurance authority).

C *Nursing care insurance coverage*

Nursing care insurance is supposed to cover the additional expenses of those people who, due to illness, physical incapacity or old age, rely considerably on outside assistance with regard to ordinary or day-to-day chores. Depending on their need for support, the beneficiaries are placed in different categories which determine what kind of coverage they are entitled to.

People who are highly in need of nursing care receive, for example, benefits enabling them to pay for nursing care providing assistance in daily grooming, meals and physical activities. This is intended to alleviate wives and mothers, in particular, who in three out of four cases are the ones responsible for taking care of the family. The objective is thus to make it possible for such persons to hire outside help at least once a year so that they can take a rest. Whoever needs nursing care more than three times a day is classified as a severe case and is entitled to larger benefits from the insurer. Those who are in such severe need of nursing care that they must be cared for around the clock receive full benefits which enable them to pay for care in a hospital.

D *Evaluation*

The introduction of mandatory nursing care insurance has been criticized on the grounds that the social security carriers are having to shoulder a greater portion of the national product and Germany is becoming less and less attractive as a site of investment as a result of the employers' increasing financial burden. The bill was close to failing due to the lobby of the employers. Finally, though, a compromise was reached according to which the employers' financial burden caused by the costs of nursing care insurance is supposed to be offset by other types of financial relief such as limitations on continued pay in case of illness or the deletion of a holiday.

On the other hand, mandatory nursing insurance is a considerable relief for all those who either take care of a family member themselves or support him financially. By earmarking the necessary funds for financing nursing care, the new law is designed to counteract the tendency of putting elderly persons in impersonal nursing homes. Moreover, the new law is supposed to enable people to grow old in their familiar surroundings at home.

IV REFORM OF THE LAW OF SUCCESSION WITH REGARD TO ILLEGITIMATE
CHILDREN

Although the purpose of the 1969 law on illegitimacy was to do away with
the unequal treatment of legitimate and illegitimate children, the German
law of succession continues to differentiate between legitimate and illegitimate children. The bill presented by the German government on March
18, 1994[5] is supposed finally to change this.

A Current law: the claim of an illegitimate child to receive the equivalent
of his statutory share in the estate and the premature settlement of the
illegitimate child's future rights of succession

In the case of the statutory right of succession of an illegitimate child,
German law distinguishes whether the illegitimate child succeeds to the estate
of the mother or father. In the first scenario there are no special rules: an
illegitimate child succeeds to the estate just as a legitimate child. This,
however, is different in relation to the father: if an illegitimate child is to
succeed to the father's estate next to legitimate children or the surviving
spouse, he only has a claim to receive the equivalent of his statutory share
in the estate pursuant to § 1934 a BGB. This means: an illegitimate child
does not have joint ownership of an estate with the other co-heirs; he has
no right to be heard with regard to the administration of the estate or its
assets. He merely has an (in personam) monetary claim against the co-heirs.
This claim, however, is for an amount equal to the value of the share of
a legitimate child in the estate. Therefore, an illegitimate child does not end
up suffering a financial disadvantage.

If the father of an illegitimate child dies without leaving behind any
legitimate children or a spouse, the illegitimate child automatically becomes
an unconditional statutory heir.

Current law is premised on the following notion: if an illegitimate child
becomes a joint owner of his deceased father's estate along with the

---

5 Gesetzentwurf zur erbrechtlichen Gleichstellung nichtehelicher Kinder (Erbrechtsgleichstellungsgesetz), Bundesratsdrücksache 219/94; cf Stintzing, FuR 1994, 73-82;
   Barth/Wagenitz, Zeitschrift fur Jugendrecht (=ZfJ) 1994, 61-67; Bosch, ZfJ 1994, 224-
   232; Bosch, Der Amtsvormund (=DA Vorm) 1994, 538-554.

deceased's wife and (or) legitimate offspring, tension and conflict can be anticipated in the distribution of the estate because the interests of the illegitimate child necessarily come into conflict with those of the spouse and legitimate children. This holds especially true in the case of the continued running of an industrial or commerical business which can then cause considerable problems.

German law also contains a special rule which is unfamiliar to other legal systems: an illegitimate child between the ages of 21 and 27 can seek from his father a premature settlement of his future rights of succession pursuant to § 1934d BGB. This premature settlement, though, is not equal in value to the expected estate, but is a lump sum payment which normally is three times the amount of annual child support paid by the father. This sum can easily reach or even exceed 20,000 DM. Should the child settle his share prematurely, all statutory claims against the deceased's estate as well as claims to a compulsory portion of the estate become extinguished.

The reason for this (odd) provision is that legitimate children often receive financial assistance from their fathers when they first begin to work. Illegitimate children, by contrast, do not have this kind of support. The premature inheritance settlement is intended to provide them with similar financial means at the beginning of their working careers. It is true that an illegitimate child who asserts a claim for a premature inheritance settlement forfeits his rights against the deceased's estate as well as to a compulsory portion of that estate. However, the financial foundation of a young person is often more valuable for the life of an illegitimate child than a later inheritance which is usually affected to the child's disadvantage by inter vivos dispositions made by the father.

B Plans for reform

The current government draft completely does away with the special provisions in the law of succession which up until now have governed the rights of illegitimate children. It totally repeals the provisions on an illegitmate child's claims for the equivalent of his statutory share in an estate as well as premature inheritance settlements. In the future, illegitimate children will become joint owners of a deceased's estate in intestate succession just as legitimate children.

Three reasons have been given for changing the status of illegitimate children in their right to succeed to a deceased's estate:

1) first, a change in society: children born out of wedlock no longer constitute an occurence of peripheral importance. Illegitimate children often live with their parents in a stable environment which only then ceases to exist when one of the parents dies. The argument that illegitimate children create strife among the legitimate offspring and surviving spouse as co-heirs of the estate is no longer acceptable considering modern social demographic developments. In the light of the fact that nearly one out of every three marriages ends up in a divorce, the possibility that in the case of a remarriage legitimate children from a previous marriage will stir up conflict within the group of co-heirs is numerically much greater than the potential for conflict provoked by illegitimate children.

2) From a constitutional point of view, current law is questionable. The fact that illegitimate children are worse off than legitimate offspring, since they are only entitled to a claim for the equivalent of their statutory share in the estate, is hardly disputed nowadays. A mere monetary claim that is based on the value of the estate at the time of death of the deceased is not commensurate with the property rights of the co-heirs in the estate along with their possibility of administering the estate and being entitled to a share in any increased value of the estate after the death of the deceased. An illegitimate child remains burdened by the difficulties of assessing the estate's assets and enforcing his claim. He is also not sufficiently protected against a removal of assets from the estate. Premature inheritance settlements do not offset these disadvantages.

3) Reunification has also necessitated a reform of the law of illegitimacy in a particular sense. Under to the law of the former GDR, illegitimate and legitimate children had equal rights in the estate. The rights which illegitimate children were allotted under the laws of the former GDR should be preserved post-reunification. For this reason, the unification treaty (Art. 235 § 1 par. 2 EGBGB) provides that the provisions concerning a legitimate child's right to succeed shall be applicable to illegitimate children born prior to reunification instead of the provisions regulating claims for the equivalent of the statutory share in the estate and premature inheritance settlements. This special rule has created a legal discrepancy between the German states

in the east and west. The new law intends to rectify the uncertainties resulting from the current situation.

V   DAMAGES FOR PAIN AND SUFFERING DUE TO THE DESTRUCTION OF SPERM
     BY FAULT

The Federal Court of Justice, the highest court in Germany in civil matters, was confronted with the following case in its decision from November 9, 1994[6]: The plaintiff was to undergo surgery for cancer, aware of the fact that it would result in sterility. Therefore, prior to the operation, he had his sperm frozen and deposited in the hospital so that he would still be able to father children. Later, the plaintiff married and wanted to fulfill his wish to have children by artificial insemination of his sperm. However, it turned out that the sperm deposited in the defendant hospital had been destroyed by an oversight. The plaintiff sued the hospital for damages for pain and suffering in the amount of 25,000.- DM.

A   Applicable law

German law does not allow for monetary compensation of immaterial damage in cases of breach of contract (§ 253 BGB). Therefore, despite the breach of the custody agreement between the plaintiff and the hospital, the plaintiff could not assert a contractual claim for damages against the hospital.

However, quite apart from contract law, German tort law sometimes allows for the compensation of immaterial damages under special circumstances. § 847 par. 1 BGB, for example, provides for damages for pain and suffering in cases of bodily injuries and other injuries to one's health. Case law has treated bodily injuries and other injuries to one's health as an invasion of the general right of personality. The issue presented was, therefore, whether the destruction of the frozen sperm qualified as such an invasion.

---

6   BGH 124, 52-57 = NJW 1994, 127-128 = FamRZ 1994, 154-156; cf. Laufs/Reiling, NJW 1994, 775-776; Rohe, JZ 1994, 465-468.

B The decision

Frozen sperm is in and of itself no longer a part of the human body so that from a legal point of view its destruction is more like damage to property than bodily injury. However, in the opinion of the Federal Court of Justice, the concept of the human body and bodily injury have to be construed broadly. It reasoned that the protection that tort law extends to the human body can ultimately be traced back to the worthiness of protection of the general right of personality. Therefore, a bodily injury is to be assumed where parts of a living organism are removed for therapeutic reasons in order to be implanted at a later time. Such a functional unity exists, for example, where skin or bone is removed for the purpose of reimplantation in the same person as well as in the case of blood donations for oneself. The court then concluded that the same must also apply to the egg cell removed from a woman which is to be reimplanted at a later time as well as to removed sperm which are to be inseminated at a later time, as in the case at bar. The court held that a donor who has his sperm preserved in order to be able to produce offspring in the event of his sterility has a claim for damages for pain and suffering based on bodily injury where his sperm are destroyed by the fault of a third party.

C Criticism

The reactions to this decision are controversial. The court's construction of the concept of bodily injury aroused opposition. In the opinion of those critical of the decision, the judges exceeded the letter of the law with their interpretation. They argued that in terms of its common usage alone, the destruction of sperm does not entail a bodily injury. From a dogmatic point of view, critics also raised objections based on the argument that German tort law does not provide for comprehensive protection of the right to family planning. From a political standpoint, critics pointed to the danger of well-defined tort law becoming futher eroded by this decision.

REPUBLIC OF IRELAND

CONSTITUTION AND THE FAMILY

Paul O'Connor

Paul O'Connor[*]

I INTRODUCTION

A remarkable feature of Irish Family Law is the extraordinary position which the family occupies in the scheme of constitutional protection.[1] In Article 41 of the Constitution the family is recognised by the State "as the natural primary and fundamental unit group of Society, and as a moral institution possessing inalienable and imprescriptible rights antecedent and superior to all positive law"[2] This Article provides, further, a guarantee on the part of the State to protect the family in its constitution and authority[3] and "to guard with special care the institution of Marriage, on which the Family is founded, and to protect it against attack".[4] The best known and perhaps the most controversial of the provisions contained in Article 41 pertains to divorce where it is provided that no law shall be enacted providing for the grant of a dissolution of marriage.[5] Finally, reference should be made to Article 42 where it is acknowledged by the State "that the primary and natural educator of the child is the Family" and, accordingly, it "guarantees to respect the inalienable right and duty of parents to provide, according

---

[*] Dean of the Faculty of Law, University College Dublin.
[1] For a general discussion on the constitutional protection of the family see Casey, *Constitutional Law in Ireland* (Sweet and Maxwell, 2nd ed., 1992); and J. M. Kelly, *The Irish Constitution* (Butterworths, 3rd ed., 1994, ed. by Hogan and Whyte).
[2] Article 41.1.1.
[3] Article 41.1.2. See discussion in *In re J.H. (an infant)* [1985] I.R. 375 on the rights enjoyed by the family founded on marriage.
[4] Article 41.3.1. It should be noted that the Constitution does not provide any definition of the word "family" which appears in the section. In the *State (Nicolau) v. An Bord Uchtála* [1966] I.R. 567 the Supreme Court observed that the family referred to in Article 41 is clearly the family founded on the institution of marriage. For further illustrations of the State's obligation to protect the family see *Murray v. Ireland* [1991] ILRM 465 and *Fajujonu v. Minister for Justice* [1990] 2 I.R. 151.
[5] Article 41.3.2. It is, however, possible to have a marriage annulled in Irish Law. See O'Connor, *Key Issues in Irish Family Law* (Round Hall Press, 1988) and by the same author, Ireland : Nullity and the Judiciary (32) *University of Louisville J. of Fam. Law* (1993-94) at 345-58.

A. Bainham (ed.), The International Survey of Family Law 1994, 271–298.
© 1996 *The International Society of Family Law. Printed in the Netherlands.*

to their means, for the religious and moral, intellectual, physical and social education of their children".[6]

Given the nature, breadth, and constitutionally entrenched status of these rights it is not surprising that virtually every major legislative initiative in the family law area has raised constitutional issues and, in some cases, has been the subject of constitutional challenge.[7] While the following treatment does not purport to embrace all of the constitutional issues currently affecting the family[8] it does include consideration of the more important cases decided in the years 1993 and 1994.

II   JUDICIAL SEPARATION

The Judicial Separation and Family Law Reform Act 1989 represents a major and extensive piece of reforming legislation which, in effect, provides the legal infrastructure for a modern system of divorce save for the right to re-marry. Divorce with freedom to re-marry will only become legally possible if, and when, the prohibition on divorce is removed by constitutional referendum.[9]

In *F v. F.,Ireland and the Attorney General*[10] an interesting, but so far unsuccessful challenge, was raised with respect to a number of provisions in the 1989 Act. In *F* the applicant's wife had successfully petitioned for

---

6   Article 42.1.
7   See, for example, *Re Article 26 and the Adoption (No. 2) Bill 1987* [1989] I.R. 656 where, what was to become the Adoption Act 1988, was declared constitutional. On the other hand, in *Re Article 26 and the Matrimonial Bill* 1993 [1994] 1 I.R. 305 the Bill in question was pronounced to be repugnant to the provisions of Article 41 of the Constitution. See also constitutional challenge to Judicial Separation and Family Law Reform Act 1989 in *F v. F* [1994] 2 ILRM 401 and challenge to Child Abduction and Enforcement of Custody Orders Act 1991 in *J v. R* unreported, Supreme Court, February 17, 1993.
8   e.g. issues pertaining to the right to receive information on abortion, abortion facilities available in foreign jurisdictions, and the right to travel to such jurisdictions for the purpose of obtaining an abortion. See Eighth and Thirteenth amendments to Constitution, and decision of Supreme Court in *Attorney General v. X* [1992] 1 I.R. 1.
9   The present Government is committed to introducing a constitutional referendum on divorce in 1995. An earlier referendum, intended to delete the provision on divorce was defeated in 1986. Article 46 of the Constitution provides for the amendment of the Constitution by referendum submitted to the decision of the people.
10 [1994] 2 ILRM 401.

a decree of judicial separation on the basis of Section 2 (f) 1 of the Act. This section provides that a decree may be made on the ground "that the marriage has broken down to the extent that the court is satisfied in all the circumstances that a normal marital relationship has not existed between the spouses for a period of at least one year immediately preceding the date of the application". The applicant contended that the section was un-constitutional having regard to Article 41 of the Constitution. The essence of his argument was that the 1989 Act allowed for a much too easy basis for judicial separation or, as the court characterised the applicant's case, the section set "too modest a standard or too low a threshold for the granting of an order which would have the effect of impairing his constitutional rights in relation to his marriage and the institution of marriage generally."[11] If this was the case, so the argument went, the State would be failing in its constitutional obligation to guard the institution of marriage and protect it against attack. In addition the applicant, it would appear, relied on Article 40 of the Constitution, whose relevant provisions provide:

"40.3.1. The State guarantees in its laws to respect, and, as far as prac-ticable, by its laws to defend and vindicate the personal rights of the citizen.

40.3.2. The State shall, in particular, by its laws protect as best it may from unjust attack and, in the case of injustice done, vindicate the life, person, good name, and property rights of every citizen."

In terms of the personal rights of the citizen these include, in the context of marriage, the right to marry,[12] the right to procreate,[13] and "all of the basic rights deriving from the relationship of marriage, such as, the right of the married couple to cohabit, the right of each spouse to give and receive from the other moral as well as financial support and the right of spouses to make and adhere to decisions made in relation to family property".[14]

The applicant sought to advance a specifically Christian view of marriage whose rights derived from natural law, and argued that it was in this context

---

11 *Ibid* at 413.
12 See *Ryan v. Attorney General* [1965] I.R. 294.
13 See *Murray v. Ireland* [1985] I.R. 532.
14 *F v. F, supra*, note 10, at 410. See also right to marital privacy which was established in *McGee v. Attorney General* [1974] I.R. 284.

that his rights as a party to the marriage should be determined.[15] This provided the court with the opportunity to pronounce on how the provisions of the Constitution, relevant to the applicants's case, should be interpreted and applied. Would the court accept the invitation to explore the content of the rights to which marriage gives rise by reference to natural law? The court firmly rejected this invitation and, in so doing, declined to hear the evidence of theologians on the rights which natural law protects and, additionally, on what constitutes the essential features of Christian marriage. Murphy J., giving judgment, wrote:

> "It may well be that 'marriage' as referred to in our Constitution derives from the Christian concept of marriage. However, whatever its origin, the obligations of the State and the rights of parties in relation to marriage are now contained in the Constitution and our laws and ... it falls to me as a judge of the High Court to interpret those provisions and it is not permissible for me to abdicate that function to any expert, however distinguished".[16]

What was of particular concern to the applicant was the power given to a court under Section 2 f(1) permitting it to grant a decree of judicial separation in the absence of any requirement to establish fault by a petitioner, or need to obtain consent from a respondent, coupled with the relatively brief time requirement that the marriage breakdown be for only twelve months.

This concern inevitably raised the troublesome issue of when it could be reasonably and fairly said that a marriage has broken-down. It can be argued that one of the implications arising from the applicant's argument was that his marriage had not broken down in the sense that he firmly believed that, through counselling, the marriage relationship could be restored. Murphy J. conceded that the concept of the break-down of marriage was difficult to define. He, nonetheless, observed:

---

15 See observations of Kennedy C.J. on natural law in *The State (Ryan and Others) v. Lennon* [1935] I.R. 170, at 204-5. See also judgment of Kenny J. in *Ryan v. Attorney General, supra*, on personal rights of the citizen which stem from the Christian and democratic nature of the State.

16 *Ibid*, at 409.

"It seems to me that breakdown of marriage, though difficult to define, presupposes the previous existence of a functioning marriage and thus the loss or even the conscious and deliberate withdrawal by one of the spouses of an essential ingredient or component of the marriage which brings about the breakdown. It is not necessary to identify how or when or for what reason the marriage broke down to satisfy the requirements of the Act but it must be proved to the satisfaction of the court, on the balance of probabilities, that it did so".[17]

Referring to the non-consenting party the judge had this to say:

"But in my view it must be recognised that such an essential ingredient includes the consent of either party because the implacable opposition of one or other of the spouses to the continuation of the marriage – however unjust or unreasonable – must destroy the fundamental relationship".[18]

In conclusion Murphy J., while accepting that the granting of a decree on the ground contained in s.2 f(1) might hinder attempts at reconciliation, was strongly of the view that the section constituted little more than official recognition of an existing and usually tragic state of affairs. Accordingly, therefore, the applicant's challenge failed.

The decision in *F* is of significance in that the court made it abundantly clear that when it comes to deciding what constitutional rights attach to marriage the approach which will be adopted is one which must take into account social and cultural change brought about by the passage of time. As far as the breakdown of marriage is concerned the court recognised this as a reality and that if one of the parties to such a marriage wishes to separate then that party should be able to do so. In recognising the reality of marital breakdown, and responding to it in the instant case, the court was not prepared to be encumbered with theological and natural law considerations. One can, in the result, identify a strongly secularist component in the judgment of Murphy J. in the sense that it represents a particularly strong endorsement of the view that in a pluralist society the courts will

---

17 *Ibid*, at 415-6.
18 *Ibid*, at 416.

not choose between the views of different religious denominations on the nature and extent of natural rights.

III MATRIMONIAL PROPERTY

It is hardly surprising that the great bulk of property disputes between married couples arise out of failed marriages. Typically, disputes involve a claim by one spouse to an interest in property the title to which is very often vested in the other. Given that the family home is usually the most substantial asset litigation has, naturally, centered on questions of ownership of the house and entitlement to interests in it by the respective spouses.

It is the common law system of separate property which largely governs property transactions in Ireland. Under this system the parties to a marriage stand in the same relationship to property rights as if they were unmarried.[19] It is still the case that, despite the power of the courts to make various ancillary orders upon the granting of a decree of judicial separation,[20] the property rights which the parties to a marriage enjoy are done so largely on the basis of title.[21]

Criticisms of the separate property system have been made on the now familiar grounds that it does not adequately take into account the contributions of a spouse, normally the wife, in looking after the household and any children of the marriage.[22]

---

19 See Kahn Freund, "Inconsistencies and Injustices in the Law of Husband and Wife" 15 *Mod. L. Rev.* 133, 135 (1952).

20 See Part 2 of the Judicial Separation and Family Law Reform Act 1989 which specifies the ancillary orders which can be made with respect to maintenance, property, custody, and the family home.

21 For a discussion on family property see Lyall, *Land Law in Ireland* (Oak Tree Press, 1994) Ch. 17 and ensuing discussion on the extent to which direct and indirect contributions give rise in Ireland to a beneficial interest in the matrimonial home. See, in particular, judgments of Supreme Court in *McC v. McC* [1986] ILRM 1 and *BL v. ML* [1992] 2 I.R. 77.

22 It should be noted that Article 41.2.1 and 2 provide respectively, that
"In particular, the State recognises that by her life within the home, woman gives to the State a support without which the common good cannot be achieved.
The State shall, therefore, endeavour to ensure that mothers shall not be obliged by economic necessity to engage in labour to the neglect of their duties in the home."
Barr J. in *BL v. ML, supra*, note 21, remarked that those provisions were "in harmony with the philosophy to regard marriage as an equal partnership in which a woman who

With the publication of the Matrimonial Home Bill in 1993 the legislature attempted to alter the law by introducing an important reforming measure which purported to vest in each spouse equal rights of ownership in the matrimonial home. The constitutionality of this Bill was considered by the Supreme Court pursuant to an Article 26 reference by the President.[23] Section 1 of the Bill provided that, in the situation where the matrimonial home was one in which either or both spouses had an interest, but was not owned by them as joint tenants or tenants in common in equal shares, the interest in the home would vest in both spouses as joint tenants. This measure purported to create, in effect, a regime of matrimonial property with respect to the family home. As such it represented a quite definite restriction on property rights which the State, in the interest of the common good, obviously felt was justified. The case, however, was (a little surprisingly) decided not on the basis of Article 43 of the Constitution which guarantees the right to private property[24] but, rather, on the basis of Article 41, which it will be recalled, embodies the State's guarantee to protect the family in its constitution and authority.

The Attorney General, who argued in favour of the constitutionality of the Bill, identified the chief merits of the measure in the following terms: it strengthened the family; enhanced the economic position of the dependent spouse and dependent children in relation to the family home; recognised the connection between family life and the home in which it was conducted; and supported the institution of marriage as an equal partnership. In short the Bill would provide, overall, greater security for the dependent wife and any children residing in the family home.

As the provisions of the Bill were applicable to every matrimonial home occupied by a married couple as their sole or principal residence on or after June 25th, 1993, the issue was whether it represented an overly broad measure or in the words of the Supreme Court "a reasonably proportionate

---

elects to adopt the full-time role of wife and mother in the home may be obliged to make a sacrifice, both economic and emotional, in so doing. In return for that voluntary sacrifice... she should receive some reasonable economic security within the marriage" (at 98).

23 *Re Article 26 of the Constitution and the Matrimonial Home Bill 1993* [1994] 1 I.R. 305. In the situation where the President doubts the constitutionality of a Bill that Bill may be referred to the Supreme Court for a ruling pursuant to Article 26.

24 Article 43.1.1 and 2.

intervention by the State" having regard to the inalienable and imprescriptable rights possessed by the family under Article 41.[25]

The Supreme Court accepted that it was in the common good to encourage, by appropriate means, joint ownership of the family home. This, according to the court, was "conducive to the dignity, reassurance and independence of each of the spouses and to the partnership concept of marriage which is fundamental to it."[26] What was, however, of chief concern to the court was the invasion of the fully and freely made joint decisions of spouses concerning ownership of the family home and the fact that these would now be set aside through the imposition, in effect, of joint ownership. In examining the provisions of Article 41 the court wrote:

> "It is the opinion of the Court that the right of a married couple to make a joint decision as to the ownership of a matrimonial home is one of the rights possessed by the family which is recognised by the State in Article 41, s.1, sub-s.1 of the Constitution as antecedent and superior to all positive law and its exercise is part, and an important part, of the authority of the family which in Article 41, s.1 sub-s.2 the State guarantees to protect."[27]

In ruling that the Bill was unconstitutional Finlay C.J. wrote:

> "Having regard to the extreme importance of the authority of the family as acknowledged in Article 41 of the Constitution and to the acceptance in that Article of the fact that the rights which attach to the family including its right to make decisions within its authority are inalienable and imprescriptible and antecedent and superior to all positive law, the Court is satisfied that such provisions do not constitute reasonably proportionate intervention by the State with the rights of the family and constitute a failure by the State to protect the authority of the family".[28]

The decision of the Supreme Court, even if viewed as a robust vindication of the rights of the family and a sharp setback to liberal and reforming government policies, amply confirms the existence of a quite marked, if somewhat ill defined, constitutional boundary between the State and the

---

25 [1994] 1 I.R. 305,326.
26 *Ibid* at 326.
27 *Ibid* at 325.
28 *Ibid* at 326.

family. The Supreme Court was firm and decisive in its decision to uphold and proclaim the constitutional importance of preventing excessive and unwarranted encroachment by the State on the essentially private decisions of spouses which fall within the ambit and competence of the family. Even the strongly laudable objective of protecting economically vulnerable "homemaker" spouses was made to yield to the freely entered agreement of spouses to decide what is best for them on matters pertaining to the ownership of the family home.

In *F v. F*[29], considered above, the applicant claimed, in addition, that an order made under s.16(a) of the Judicial Separation and Family Law Reform Act 1989, giving his wife the right to occupy the family home to the exclusion of himself, was unconstitutional in that it constituted an unjust attack on his property rights and in consequence, was contrary to Article 40.3.2.[30] Murphy J., in rejecting the applicant's contention, expressed the view that a right of residence does not amount to an adjustment of property rights. The judge, in so ruling, took the opportunity to identify the functions served by the family home. He remarked:

> "First, it provides the ordinary residence for the family, and secondly, it represents or may represent an asset of significant value. In addition to the immediate and practical value of the right to reside or to continue to reside in a family home – particularly for a non-income earning spouse – and the possible asset value of the family home, the courts have long since identified the psychological value of the family home in providing a point of unity around which the children of a broken marriage may preserve or rebuild some of the physical and personal relationships on which the development of the family would depend (see *B v. B* [1975] I.R. 54 at p. 59)."[31]

Murphy J. refused to consider the issue of the right of residence in isolation from the various other ancillary orders which a court has jurisdiction to make under the 1989 Act. In this regard the judge pointed out that an exclusive right of residence given to a non-owning spouse could be balanced by a reduction in the amount of maintenance payable to that spouse on the part

---

29 [1994] 2 ILRM 40 1.

30 This provision reads: "The State accordingly guarantees to pass no law attempting to abolish the right of private ownership or the general right to transfer, bequeath, and inherit property."

31 [1994] 2 ILRM 401, at 417-8.

of the other. In holding that there was no unjust attack on the property rights of either party Murphy J. said that the power to grant a right of residence to one spouse to the exclusion of the other was

> "... merely one feature in the difficult and unhappy task of attempting to ensure that provision is made as far as practicable in the best interest of both spouses and their dependent children in the unhappy circumstances which have arisen and which will ordinarily create severe financial as well as emotional problems for them."[32]

IV   RECOGNITION OF FOREIGN DIVORCES

The recognition of foreign divorces has, over the years, proved to be an awkward and contentious issue in Irish law. From the time when such divorces were first deemed to be legally capable of recognition within the jurisdiction the courts' attention has been almost wholly directed to determining whether the parties to the dissolved marriage were domiciled within the jurisdiction where the divorce was obtained.[33] As domicile is the only basis upon which Irish courts will accord recognition to a foreign divorce the following questions, which specifically concern wives, have arisen: Is the wife's domicile dependent on that of her husband? Is the wife capable of acquiring a domicile of her own? Is it sufficient, for the purposes of recognition, that either spouse have been domiciled in the jurisdiction at the time when the divorce was obtained?

The enactment of the Domicile and Recognition of Foreign Divorces Act 1986 helped to clarify matters and reformed the law by providing new rules for recognising foreign divorces. The Act abolished the wife's domicile of dependency[34] and substituted the rule that a divorce would be recognised if granted in the country where either spouse is domiciled.[35] The difficulty with the legislation, however, was that these provisions were to be applied

---

32   *Ibid* at 419.
33   See, for example, *Mayo-Perrott v. Mayo-Perrott* [1958] I.R. 336; *Bank of Ireland v. Caffin* [1971] I.R. 123; *Gaffney v. Gaffney* [1975] I.R. 133; *K.D. v. M.C.* [1985] I.R. 697; *C.M. v. T. M.* [1991] ILRM 268.
34   See section 1.
35   See section 5.

prospectively i.e. after the coming into force of the legislation.[36] S.2 of the Act makes it clear that the domicile that a person had at any time before its commencement "shall be determined as if this Act had not been passed". This implied that as far as pre-1986 marriages were concerned the wife's domicile of dependency was preserved and that, if a divorce was to be recognised, both spouses would have to be domiciled in the country where the divorce was granted.

It is somewhat surprising that the legislature drew this distinction between domicile pre and post 1986 because some doubt had, earlier on, been cast on the constitutionality of the dependent domicile rule for married women.[37] Matters, however, were not allowed to settle and the courts were soon presented with the opportunity to pronounce on the constitutionality of the acquisition by a wife, upon marriage, of her husband's domicile. In *C.M. v. T.M.*[38] it was stated by Barr J.:

> "I would have no hesitation whatever in holding that the old rule was the relic of matrimonial female bondage which was swept away by principles of equality before the law and equal rights in marriage as between men and women which are enshrined in the Constitution – see in particular Article 40.1 and 3 and Article 41. It appears that the only possible argument against such a conclusion is that it might create some uncertainty for spouses and others who may have been affected by the rule in times past. It does not seem to me that that argument could possibly save an alleged rule of law which is patently unconstitutional and can be unjust and unreal in its application...."[39]

The implication which undoubtedly arises from these remarks is that the wife's domicile of dependency did not become part of Irish law following the enactment of the Constitution in 1937.[40] This issue, along with the rule of recognition which is applicable to foreign divorces obtained prior to 1986,

---

36 Section 3 reads: "The domicile that a person has at any time after the commencement of this Act shall be determined as if this Act had always been in force".

37 See judgments of Walsh J. in *Gaffney v. Gaffney* [1975] I.R. 133 and McCarthy J. in *K.D. v. M.C.* [1985] I.R. 697.

38 [1988] ILRM 456.

39 *Ibid* at 470.

40 See Article 50 which provides that laws which were in force prior to the coming into operation of the Constitution shall continue to be of full force and effect provided that they are not inconsistent with the Constitution.

was authoritatively considered in the recent Supreme Court case of *W v W*.[41]

The facts of *W* were, briefly, as follows: the plaintiff married the defendant in Ireland in 1973 having previously married one J.E. in England in 1966. She divorced J.E. in England in 1972 shortly before she married the defendant. It was the defendant's contention that at the time when the English divorce was obtained the plaintiff was not domiciled in England as she had, by then, resumed her Irish domicile of origin. As such there was no basis in Irish law for recognising the divorce and the 1966 marriage was, as far as Irish law was concerned, still valid.

The Supreme Court agreed, first of all, with the observations of Barr J. in *C.M.* that the wife's domicile of dependency was inconsistent with the equality guarantee embodied in Article 40.1 of the Constitution.[42] Blayney J. expressed the views of the court in these trenchant terms:

> "... I have no doubt that if the rule were still in force a married woman would not be held equal before the law. She would be in a position of inequality firstly by comparison with her husband, and secondly by comparison with women who are not married. As between the married woman and her husband, he would retain the independent domicile which he enjoyed before his marriage while his wife would lose the independent domicile which she had previously enjoyed. Furthermore, her independent domicile previously enjoyed would become converted by law into a domicile dependent on that of her husband. So the law would clearly be giving unequal prominence or importance to the husband by providing that it was his domicile which would be the common domicile of the couple throughout their marriage".[43]

The judge also pointed out that the rule would have the effect of treating, unequally, married women in comparison to unmarried women as the former's domicile was dependent on marriage whereas the latter's was independent.[44]

While these constitutional objections to the dependent domicile rule were entirely convincing the position was still decidedly unclear as to what rule

---

41   [1993] ILRM 294.
42   The Article reads: "All citizens shall, as human persons, be held equal before the law."
43   See note 41, at 308.
44   *Ibid* at 308.

of recognition should be applied to a divorce obtained prior to 1986. There were two main possibilities : either the court would insist that both parties to the marriage would have to be domiciled in the jurisdiction where the divorce was obtained, or, that it would be sufficient if either of the spouses was domiciled in the jurisdiction granting the decree. If the latter possibility was accepted it would imply the judicial creation of a new rule of recognition.

The Supreme Court displayed a readiness for innovation and decided that it would recognise the plaintiff's divorce on the ground that her then husband was domiciled in England. In making this decision the court stressed that what was involved were common law, judge-made rules which were not immutable and, further, that the issue of recognition should be answered by the court in light of present day policy.[45] What, however, was the scope of this newly fashioned rule of recognition? Blayney J. refused to confine the rule to situations where only the husband was domiciled in the divorce jurisdiction. To do so would be constitutionally unacceptable as it would, again, create inequality in the position of the spouses by enabling, for the purposes of recognition, a domiciled husband to divorce but not a domiciled wife. Accordingly it was accepted that Irish courts would "recognise a divorce granted in a country in which either of the parties to the marriage was domiciled at the time of the proceedings".[46]

The Supreme Court based its decision explicitly on public policy. This policy included, in part, the desirability of avoiding limping marriages which would, inevitably, have been the situation in the instant case had the court refused to recognise the plaintiff's English divorce (she was validly divorced according to English law).[47] Public policy was, however, given a much broader application by the court. In ruling that it was essential to consider the issue of recognition in the light of the changes effected by the 1986 Act Blayney J. was content to say that the court, "as a matter of public policy, should independently modify the judge-made rule in order to do justice to the plaintiff".[48]

---

45 *Ibid* at 314.
46 *Ibid* at 314.
47 In this regard the court placed reliance on the decisions in the two English cases *Travers v. Holly* [1953] 3 WLR 507 and *Indyka v. Indyka* [1969] 1 AC 33.
48 [1993] ILRM 294, at 314.

It is hard to resist the conclusion that what the Supreme Court did was to supply the legislative gap in the 1986 Act by, in effect, applying retrospectively the changes contained in Section 5(1) of the 1986 Act.[49] As this Act was specifically designed to amend the law relating to domicile and the recognition of foreign divorces it is arguable that effect should have been given to Sections 2 and 3 which implicitly acknowledged that the rules of recognition are not the same as regards divorces obtained before and after the commencement of the 1986 legislation. This distinction which the legislature sought to preserve was rejected by the Supreme court when it created the same rule of recognition as that created by the legislature. In the result the legislative and judicial processes were combined to establish a uniform rule of recognition. A seamless legal reality governing the recognition of foreign divorces was created; one which is applicable to the period commencing with the enactment and coming into force of the Irish Constitution up to the enactment of the 1986 legislation.

V   CHILD ABDUCTION

The Child Abduction and Enforcement of Custody Orders Act 1991 gave effect in Ireland to the Convention on the Civil Aspects of International Child Abduction (the Hague Convention) and the European Convention on Recognition and Enforcement of Decisions concerning Custody of Children and on Restoration of Custody of Children (the Luxembourg Convention). Prior to the adoption of these Conventions Ireland had not been a party to any international agreement concerning child abduction nor were there any arrangements in place whereby custody orders made by the Irish courts would be recognised and enforced in other jurisdictions. The two Conventions, dealing as they do with the civil aspects of international child abduction, address the issue of the wrongful removal of a child from one country to another. Referring to the Hague Convention Denham J. observed that its spirit "is to protect children from the harmful effects of wrongful removal or retention, and to return them promptly to, the country of their habitual residence".[50]

---

49   This is the section which contains the new rule of recognition.
50   *P v. B* unreported, Supreme Court, December 19, 1994.

The issue which was raised in *Wadda v. Ireland*[51] was whether the provisions of the 1991 Act were consistent with the Constitution. The plaintiff, an Irish citizen, who was habitually resident with her husband, a Moroccan citizen, in England, removed the only child of the marriage to Ireland and, soon afterwards, applied to the Irish High Court to be made sole guardian and custodian of the child. The husband, in response, instituted proceedings under the 1991 Act seeking the return of the child to England. The High Court ruled that the husband was entitled to the relief which he sought but imposed a stay on the order to return the child pending a determination of the plaintiff's constitutional challenge.

The declaration which she sought was based on the grounds that the provisions of the 1991 Act failed to protect and vindicate the personal rights of the child; that they failed to ensure access for the plaintiff and her child to the Irish courts; and that they failed to protect the family as the primary and natural unit group of society.

Keane J., who gave judgment, referred to the Hague Convention in the following terms:

> "The convention was entered into by the signatory states in the interests of children and in order to protect them from the harmful effects of their wrongful removal from the states of their habitual residence. Article 13 expressly empowers the relevant authority (in Ireland the High Court) to refrain from ordering the return of the child where there is a grave risk of exposing the child to physical or psychological harm or otherwise placing the child in an intolerable situation. By so providing, the framers of the convention were allowing a significant margin of discretion to the authorities of the requested state, which enables those authorities to refuse to order the return of the child where it might not be in the child's interests to do so".[52]

Turning to Article 20 of the Convention, which provides that the return of a child may be refused if this would not be permitted by the fundamental principles of the requested state, the judge ruled that these must, in the context of Ireland, refer to the provisions of the Constitution. He wrote:

---

51 [1994] ILRM 126.
52 *Ibid* at 132.

"Articles 40 to 44 inclusive of the Constitution appear under the heading 'Fundamental Rights' and define, either expressly or by implication, rights of the citizen which cannot be modified or abridged by any of the organs of government except to the extent permitted by the Constitution itself. These provisions reflect an acknowledgement by the Constitution that there are rights regarded as of such importance in a democratic society such as Ireland as to warrant recognition in this manner by the fundamental law of society, in our case the Constitution".[53]

The expression "human rights and fundamental freedoms" referred to in Article 20 of the Convention include those rights set out in Articles 40 to 44 of the Constitution.[54] The order to return the child to the United Kingdom did not, therefore, violate any of these rights. Keane J. concluded that the State guarantee in Article 40.3.1 to respect and vindicate the personal rights of the citizen are fully protected by the provisions of the Convention. The judge went further and held that the Convention actually provided additional machinery for the protection and vindication of constitutional rights in the situation where children, who are Irish citizens, are wrongfully removed from the jurisdiction.[55]

Given that the Convention requires the return of a child, who has been wrongfully removed, to the jurisdiction in which it is habitually resident the issue arises as to whether the consequent ousting of the jurisdiction of the Irish courts to determine such issues as guardianship and custody is constitutionally permissible. Keane J. took the view that giving the force of law to conventions such as the Hague Convention was in accordance with Ireland's acceptance of generally recognised principles of international law and was thereby consonant with constitutional objectives.[56] Additionally, given that the purpose of the Convention was to protect the interests of children, the Irish Parliament was entitled to give legal effect in this jurisdiction to those provisions which conferred jurisdiction on foreign courts in cases having an international dimension.[57] In this regard it was necessary

---

53 *Ibid* at 132.
54 *Ibid* at 133.
55 *Ibid* at 135.
56 *Ibid* at 136.
57 *Ibid* at 136.

that the jurisdiction of one country should be ousted in favour of the jurisdiction of another.[58]

Finally, because the courts in Ireland are empowered to refuse to order the return of children when, to do so, would violate their constitutional rights Keane J. held that the Convention in no way infringed the constitutional guarantee of fair procedures[59] or the plaintiff's right as a parent to invoke the protection of the Irish courts with respect to the welfare of her child.[60]

Earlier, in *C.K. v. C.K.*,[61] Denham J. held that the Child Abduction and Enforcement of Custody Orders Act 1991 must be presumed constitutional and read so as to encompass existing constitutional rights. In that case, where the children were wrongfully removed from Australia, the High Court rejected the contention that there was a constitutional obligation to hold an inquiry into the welfare of the children before ordering their return to Australia. In this regard the children did not have a constitutional right to such an inquiry nor a constitutional right to have the concept of their welfare as the first and paramount consideration determined. In the event that the return of the children entailed a potential breach of constitutional rights then Articles 13 and 20 of the Convention could be relied upon.[62]

VI ADOPTION

One of the most significant features of the Adoption Act 1988 is that it enabled, for the first time, the adoption of children born within marriage in circumstances where one or both parents are still alive. Whether the extension of the categories of adoptable children to those born within marriage implied that all children were now potentially adoptable was considered by the Supreme Court in *T.M. and A.M. v. An Bord Uchtála*.[63] The child,

---

58 It was recognised in *In re Haughey* [1971] I.R. 217 that Article 40.3 of the Constitution provides a guarantee to the citizen of basic fairness of procedures. See, also, *The State (Healy) v. Donoghue* [1976] I.R. 325. In *Garvey v. Ireland* [1980] I.R. 75 it was stated that "by Article 40, s. 3, there is guaranteed to every citizen whose rights may be affected by decisions taken by others the right to fair and just procedures." (at 97).

59 [1994] ILRM 126, at 136.

60 Unreported, High Court, November 27, 1993.

61 See pp. 25-271.

62 [1993] ILRM 577.

63 *Re Article 26 and the Adoption (No. 2) Bill* 1987 [1989] I.R. 656.

who was the subject of adoption proceedings, was born in India and was brought to Ireland by the applicants both of whom were domiciled in Ireland. The authorities in India did not know the identity of the child's parents nor their marital status. It was plain, however, that the child had been abandoned and placed in an orphanage in Delhi. As far as the adoption proceedings in Ireland were concerned the issue was raised in the High Court as to whether the 1988 Act had any application to children born of alien parents. The court ruled that it had no application to this category of child. Its decision was based on constitutional considerations, specifically, that when the constitutionality of the 1988 Act was considered (pursuant to an Article 26 reference)[64] the legal issues were analysed in the context of the rights and duties which parents have by virtue of the Constitution. Alien parents, according to the High Court, who are not based in the jurisdiction, have no constitutional duties under the Constitution. The essence of the judgment may be summarised in the following terms: since the 1988 Act did not contemplate any limitation on the rights of alien parents it, therefore, followed that their children were excluded from the provisions of the Act.

The Supreme Court, allowing the applicants' appeal, held that nowhere in the Irish adoption code was the word "child" defined or qualified by reference to its particular nationality or citizenship nor was the word "parent" qualified as to citizenship, nationality, or domicile. Chief Justice Finlay said of the 1988 Act that it

> "... is a very significant step forward in the capacity of our society to care and provide for children in need of care and protection. Unless compelled by its terms to do so the courts should not, in my view, construe it as unavailable to any child within their jurisdiction who would otherwise qualify for adoption and, in particular, such exclusion based on nationality, citizenship or place of birth would not appear to be supportable".[65]

It is important to point out that the changes effected by the 1988 Act with respect to the categories of children who may be adopted and the circumstances in which they may be adopted are entirely consistent with the provisions in the Constitution. Article 42.5, for example, permits the State to supply the place of married parents where, for physical or moral reasons, they fail

---

64   [1993] ILRM 577, at 586.
65   Note 63, at 663.

in their duty towards their children. When the Supreme Court came to consider the constitutionality of the Act it found that the constitutional guarantees afforded to the family did not mean that where there was a failure on the part of parents, of the kind envisaged by Article 42.5, that a child so affected by such failure could not be incorporated into an alternative family.[66]

In the instant case the Supreme Court held that the reference to the words "parents" and "children" in that Article was not confined to Irish citizens. It would, according to the court, be remarkable if Article 42.5 "could not be invoked to protect any child in the State who is left, in effect, parentless".[67] Accordingly, the court rejected the High Court's interpretation of the Adoption Act 1988 and authorised the relevant bodies to proceed with the adoption.

Had the appeal been unsuccessful it would have meant that the child could not be adopted by the applicants. The resulting legal relationship between the child and the applicants would have been limited and would have fallen short of the constitutionally protected relationship which is established through adoption. An adoption order made in favour of the applicants would, from a constitutional law perspective, have the effect that the child would belong to a unit group (the family) possessing inalienable and imprescribable rights; it would have the right to protection by the State of the family to which it belongs; and the right to be educated by the family and to be provided by its parents with religious, moral, intellectual, physical and social education.

The area of consent and its revocation in adoption proceedings continues to prove troublesome as far as the Constitution is concerned where the most frequently encountered problem relates to the natural mother's initial agreement to place her child for adoption and whether, in so doing, she abrogates her constitutional right to custody.

The legal relationship which exists between the natural mother and her child was extensively explored in the leading case *G. v. An Bord Uchtála*[68] where it was decided that the mother has an alienable, constitutionally protected natural right, to the custody and to the control of the upbringing

---

66   [1993] ILRM 577, at 589.
67   In re *J.H.* [1985] I.R. 575.
68   *G. v. An Bord Uchtála* [1980] I.R. 32.

of her child. As far as the child itself is concerned it has a constitutional right to bodily integrity and an unenumerated right to an opportunity to be reared with due regard to its religious, moral, intellectual, physical and social welfare.[69] The source of these rights, it has been said recently, stem from the natural relationship which exists between a mother and her child and arise from the child's total dependency and helplessness and the mother's natural determination to protect and sustain her child.[70] Given the rights which are involved it is a fundamental requirement that the mother give her consent to the placing of her child for adoption. In this regard the consent must "amount to a fully informed, free and willing surrender or an abandonment" of the mother's rights.

In *M. O'C v. Sacred Heart Adoption Society*[71] the natural mother, having given her written consent to the placement of her child for adoption, refused to give her consent to the making of the adoption order and issued proceedings seeking the return of her child. The mother argued that the consent which she gave was defective in that it was not an informed consent as she had never been expressly told that she was surrendering her constitutional right to the custody of her child. The court, in finding that the mother's consent was valid, in the sense that it was voluntarily given and fully informed, made these important observations

"... what is required for the consent to be a fully informed consent is that the mother should be aware that the right that she has, and the right that she is choosing to surrender, is an absolute right to the child which cannot be taken away from her against her will. She must be aware that the right is one fully protected by law. I do not accept that the use of any such phrase as 'a constitutional right' is necessary for the consent to be a fully informed consent. I do not believe that the use of such words would be of advantage in bringing home to a mother the strength of her rights. Providing that the person about to surrender his or her rights is fully aware that the right she possesses is an absolute right and one that will be protected and enforced to the full by the law then, in my view, the surrender of that right is given

---

69   *Ibid* at 44.
70   In *G.*, *supra*, note 68, O'Higgins C.J. stated that the mother's right to custody "arises from the infant's total dependency and helplessness and from the mother's natural determination to protect and sustain the child." (at 55). The same point was made by Budd J. in *M.N v. V.W.*, unreported, High Court, November 10, 1993 at 63.
71   [1995] 1 ILRM 229.

by someone who is fully informed. Put another way, in my view an empty formula of words does not and never could replace the full knowledge and realisation of the fact that rights of the nature described above exist."[72]

The decision in *M.O'C* provides support for the view that the legal standards applicable to the waiver of constitutional rights, while exacting, will not be set at such an excessively high standard as to make it well nigh impossible to say whether a consent given was truly free and fully informed.[73] What is important is that the mother has a full appreciation of what in substance is involved, and what the resulting legal implications are, when she agrees to put forward her child for adoption.

The importance in determining whether the mother has surrendered her constitutional rights with respect to her child is that, in the event that she has not, the adoption process will be rendered much more difficult. When the mother refuses, fails, or withdraws her consent it is frequently the case that the prospective adoptive parents will seek an order dispensing with her consent. The High Court is empowered under Section 3 of the Adoption Act 1974 to make an order authorising the Adoption Board to dispense with the requisite consent when it is satisfied that it is in the best interests of the child to do so. In *M.N. v. V.W. and J.W.*[74] Budd J. expressed the view that Section 3 could not be applied in the situation where the mother retains her constitutional rights. The section, according to the judge, is only operative when there is a consensual abandonment on the part of the mother of her constitutional rights.[75] What this implies is that the mother has agreed and acted in such a manner as to abrogate her constitutionally recognised right to the custody of her child and that she has full knowledge of the consequences which follow as a result of the agreement to place her child for adoption.[76]

---

72 *Ibid* at 235.
73 On this point see observation of McWilliam J. in *McF v. G and G and The Sacred Heart Adoption Society* [1983] ILRM 228 at 232-3.
74 Unreported, High Court, November 10, 1993 at 71.
75 *Ibid* at 71.
76 *Ibid* at 67.

VII GUARDIANSHIP AND CUSTODY

The most important decision handed down in this branch of family law in 1994 was that of the European Court of Human Rights in *Keegan v. Ireland*.[77] While *Keegan* did not, as such, raise any constitutional law issues for the court's determination it does, nonetheless, have consitutional implications for the legal relationship between a natural father and his child. This case had its origins in the unsuccessful attempt by a natural father to be appointed guardian of a child which he had by his unmarried girlfriend. In Irish law it is the natural mother who is the guardian of a child born outside of marriage and it is she, and not the father, who enjoys constitutional rights with respect to the child. This, legally very weak, position of the father was improved somewhat as a result of an amendment to the Guardianship of Infants Act 1964 which provides as follows:[78]

> "Where the father and mother of an infant have not married each other the Court may, on the application of the father, by order appoint him to be a guardian of the infant".

The natural father in *Keegan* applied to be made a guardian of his daughter. At the time when the child was born the father's relationship with the mother had ceased and she, shortly after the birth, placed the child for adoption. The father opposed the adoption and sought custody of the child. He was, initially, successful in his application to be made a guardian which implied that his consent to the impending adoption would now have to be obtained. The prospective adoptive parents appealed to the High Court but were unsuccessful in that the court found that the father was a fit person to be appointed guardian. Certain questions, however, were stated for consideration by the Supreme Court which concerned the vital matter of what test should be applied in determining whether the natural father should be appointed guardian. The test applied in the High Court was to the effect that the father has a right to guardianship subject to it being established that he is a fit person to be appointed guardian and that there are no circumstances based

---

77 Eur. Court H.R., 1994, Series A, No. 291; (1994) E.H.R.R. 342.
78 S. 6A of the Guardianship of Infants Act 1964. This section was inserted into the Act by section 12 of the Status of Children Act 1987.

on the welfare of the child which suggest that he should not be appointed in such capacity.

The Supreme Court rejected this test on the basis that it assumed that the 1964 Act, as amended, created a right to guardianship as opposed merely to a right to apply for guardianship.[79] It was conceded that the natural father may have rights of interest or concern arising from the blood link between father and child but he had no constitutional right to guardianship. The High Court, in the light of the Supreme Court's ruling, and having regard to the requirement that it consider the welfare of the child as the first and paramount consideration, ordered that the child remain with the applicant parents who, subsequently, were successful in their efforts to have the child adopted.[80]

The European Court considered whether the natural father's right to respect for family life had been violated in that his child had been adopted without his consent. It was claimed, further, that the State had violated this right by denying the father a defeasible right to be appointed guardian. Article 8 of the European Convention on Human Rights provides:

"1. Everyone has the right to respect for his private and family life, his home and his correspondence.
2. There shall be no interference by a public authority with the exercise of this right except such as is in accordance with the law and is necessary in a democratic society in the interests of national security, public safety or the economic well-being of the country, for the prevention of disorder or crime, for the protection of health or morals, or for the protection of the rights and freedoms of others."

The court observed that the State must act in a manner which is calculated to enable family ties with a child to be developed and that legal safeguards must be created which render possible the child's integration into its family.[81] It was recognised that the mutual enjoyment by parent and child of each other's company constitutes a fundamental element of family life

---

79   *J.K. v. W.* [1990] 2 I.R. 437 at 446-7.
80   See *K v. W* (No. 2) [1990] ILRM 791.
81   (1994) E.H.R.R. 342, at 362.

even in the situation where the relationship between the parents has broken down.[82]

The court went on to rule that Irish law, in permitting the secret placement of the child for adoption, without the father's knowledge or consent, leading in turn to the bonding of the child with the prospective adoptive parents, and its adoption by them, amounted to an interference in the father's right to respect for family life. Such interference, according to the court, could not be justified and as such constituted a violation of Article 8.

As the case was decided on this basis there was no consideration of the father's claim that he had a defeasible right to be appointed guardian. It is, thus, possible that Irish law, in failing to provide such a defeasible right, may be in breach of Article 8. What should be borne in mind, however, is the Supreme Court's unambiguous statement that the natural father has no constitutional right to the custody of his child.[83] On the other hand the child does have constitutional rights, which constitutional reality is in part reflected in the requirement that the welfare of the child in guardianship and custody proceedings be regarded as the first and paramount consideration. In the event that the father was to be given a defeasible right to custody such right would, of necessity, be statutory in nature compared to that of the mother which derives from the Constitution.

It can be argued that Irish law, as it currently stands, is strongly biased in favour of the child in that it places the onus on the natural father to show why he should be appointed guardian. In placing the welfare of the child at the centre of its analysis a court is, in the result, able to review the quality and significance of the father's relationship and involvement with his child. It can ask, for example, whether the relationship is non-existent, or so casual and minimal, as to make it indefensible to appoint the father as legal guardian or whether the situation is one where the child was born as the result of a stable and established relationship.

It is submitted that, on balance, it is doubtful, given the natural father's constitutional position, that the failure to accord him a defeasible right to guardianship, or even to create a presumption of guardianship in his favour, amounts to a violation of his rights in respect of his private and family life.

---

82   *Ibid* at 362.
83   *State (Nicolau) v. An Bord Uchtála* [1966] I.R. 567; *G. v. An Bord Uchtála* [1980] I.R. 32.

It would seem to be a most difficult proposition to sustain that the State, in attaching primacy to the position of the child, and in obliging the father to satisfy the court that he should be appointed guardian, has erred too much on the side of protecting the child's legal and constitutional interests.

VIII   TAX AND SOCIAL WELFARE ALLOWANCES

The point has been established in Irish law that when the constitutionality of a tax law is impugned the courts will not embark on an analysis of taxation policy nor evaluate the government choices which are embodied in such policy.[84] All such matters, it has been said, relating to the object and range of taxation "are matters of national policy which cannot, as such, be considered by the courts".[85] What the courts will be concerned with, however, is whether what has been done by the State adversely affects consitutitional rights, obligations or guarantees.[86]

In *Mhic Mhathúna v. Ireland* [87] the plaintiffs contended that alterations to income tax legislation which resulted in the abolition of a tax free allowance for the dependent children of married parents, and inadequate increases in the social welfare allowances for such children, constituted a violation of the constitutional guarantee to equality and the constitutional rights which the family, based on marriage, enjoy by virtue of Article 41. The argument founded on equality was to the effect that the State, in terms of its support, had discriminated invidiously between the marital and non-marital family or, to put it somewhat differently, between married parents and single parents. What, in short, had happened was that over a period of time the allowances for unmarried parents had substantially increased while those for married parents had substantially decreased.

The Supreme Court, on appeal, considered this issue of discrimination and agreed with the finding in the High Court that the plaintiffs had failed to establish that the discrimination in question was unconstitutional in the sense that it was in any way invidious. Article 40.1 permits discrimination

---

84 *Somjee v. Minister for Justice* [1981] ILRM 324, at 327.
85 *Madigan v. Attorney General* [1986] ILRM 136, at 159.
86 *Ibid* at 159.
87 [1995] 1 ILRM 69.

so long as it is not unjust, invidious or arbitrary.[88] The Article permits the State to have due regard in its enactments to differences of capacity and social function. In this regard the Supreme Court agreed with the views expressed in the High Court that the functions performed by married and unmarried parents are different.

These different functions stem in part from the Irish Constitution's preference for the marital family which, as already noted, is recognised to be the primary and fundamental unit group of society and, unlike the extra-marital family, possesses inalienable and imprescriptible rights. In the *State (M) v. Attorney General*,[89] for example, it was pointed out that the legitimate child is part of a family unit which is specifically provided for by the Constitution and, typically, enjoys the protection of joint decisions by its parents. The child born out of wedlock, however, does not belong to such a unit. Interestingly, the court adverted to the realities which frequently obtain in the family which exists outside marriage. Finlay P. (as he then was) observed:

"... in my view there is much weight in the submissions on this point made on behalf of the respondents to the effect that in the generality of cases the mother of an illegitimate child may be subjected to strains, stresses and pressures arising from economic and social conditions which fully justify the legislature in making special provisions with regard to the welfare of that child, which provisions are not considered necessary for the welfare of a legitimate child".[90]

Subsequently, in *Murphy v. Attorney General*,[91] the Supreme Court held that the less favourable treatment of cohabiting married couples under the income tax code when compared to that of unmarried cohabiting couples did not violate the equality guarantee because it had to be set against the many favourable discriminations made by the law in favour of married couples.[92] At the centre of the court's analysis in *Mhic Mhathúna* was the

---

88   See *de Bùrca and Anderson v. Attorney General* [1976] I.R. 38; *Dillane v. Attorney General* [1980] ILRM 167; *O'B v. S* [1984] I.R. 316; *Hyland v. Minister for Social Welfare* [1990] ILRM 213; *Murphy v. Attorney General* [1982] I.R. 241.

89   [1979] I.R. 73.

90   *Ibid* at 79.

91   [1982] I.R. 241.

92   *Ibid* at 284.

different roles which married and unmarried parents occupy under the Constitution. Given these roles the Supreme Court ruled that "(o)nce such justification for disparity arises the court is satisfied it cannot interfere by seeking to assess what the extent of the disparity should be."[93] It was no function of the court, irrespective of whether a piece of legislation was successfully impugned on constitutional grounds, to direct the legislature to enact new and different provisions.

Turning to Article 41 the court conceded that there were circumstances, such as removing entirely the financial support from the family, which would imply a violation of the constitutional obligations imposed on the State by that Article. In the instant case, however, there was no absence of support or removal of support by the State. The issue raised by the plaintiffs was, instead, one of the sufficiency of State financial support. What the measure of support should be was in the court's view a matter peculiarly "within the field of national policy to be decided by a combination of the executive and the legislature that cannot be adjudicated upon by the courts."[94]

Some attempt should be made at this point to distinguish the cases of *Murphy* and *Mhic Mhathúna*. In the former the Supreme Court decided that the unequal treatment, for income tax purposes, of married couples compared to unmarried couples did not violate the constitutional guarantee of equality. The court, however, found that the higher tax liability of married couples constituted a breach of the constitutional pledge by the State to guard with special care the institution of marriage and to protect it against attack.[95] This conclusion was reached even though the court accepted that the State had conferred various social, revenue and other privileges and advantages on married couples and their children. These, however, were not sufficient to outweigh the increased tax burden on married couples.[96]

---

93 [1995] 1 ILRM 69, at 79.

94 *Ibid* at 80.

95 [1982] I.R. 241, at 287.

96 The decision in *Murphy* was subsequently relied upon in the cases *Hyland v. Minister for Social Welfare* [1987] I.R. 624 and *Greene v. Minister for Agriculture* [1990] 2 I.R. 27. In the latter Murphy J. observed that the decision in *Murphy* required him to conclude "that the imposition of a scheme by the State or any of its agents on married couples living together which is substantially different from one placed on unmarried couples living together is in breach of the pledge by the State to guard with special care the institution of marriage and to protect it against attack." (at 26).

It is submitted that it is difficult to reconcile the two decisions. Interestingly, *Mhic Mhathúna* makes no reference to *Murphy* and this may be because the approach taken in the former, reflecting as it does a large measure of deference to State policies in the areas of tax and social welfare, is at odds with the approach taken in *Murphy*. In the latter the court, in effect, did the following: it evaluated the sum total of the advantages and privileges enjoyed by the marital family; it concluded that there was a breach of Article 41; and that this breach was not compensated for or justified by such advantages and privileges. To the extent that the decision in *Murphy* can be read as a prohibition on the State penalising marriage[97] it is perfectly defensible. The difficulty, however, with this approach lies in determining when a particular measure may be said to penalise the marriage state. In seeking to answer this question a court runs the risk that its inquiry may unjustifiably intrude upon government policies in the tax area; policies which, given limited resources, often involve finely balanced and delicate judgments as to what will best promote the common good. It is submitted that the restrained and non-interventionist approach taken in *Mhic Mhathúna* is to be preferred.

Once it was accepted that social policy can be legitimately invoked to differentiate between single parents and married parents the plaintiff's task in mounting a successful constitutional challenge became insuperable. Nothing short of a total failure of financial support would justify the court's scrutiny of the relevant tax and social welfare provisions. It is submitted, however, that the court's cautious approach and its refusal to interfere with what, in effect, would be the government's financial management and implementation of social policy was entirely proper. The court is simply not competent to second guess the legislature's actions or choices in these matters.

---

97   See *Muckley v. Ireland* [1985] I.R. 472, at 485.

ITALY

REFORM OF THE LAW OF CITIZENSHIP

Anna Galizia Danovi[*]

I   INTRODUCTION

After repeated attempts at a general reform of the law of citizenship, in 1992 the Italian Parliament approved an Act the purpose of which was to reorganise this subject and to replace the previous Act of June 13, 1912, which generally governed citizenship, together with the partial reforms brought about by the Acts of May 19, 1975 n. 151, April 21, 1983 n. 123 and May 15, 1986 n. 180.

II   ACQUISITION OF CITIZENSHIP

Act 91/1992 leaves unchanged the traditional principle regarding the acquisition of citizenship, "iure sanguinis" (by nature of blood). This is however revised taking into account the constitutional principle of equality of the sexes and equality between spouses (article 3, first paragraph, and article 29, second paragraph of the Constitution). Act 555/1912 provided for filiation as a fundamental criterion for the acquisition of citizenship. This notion reflected the continuing influence of the figure of "pater familias" in that Italian citizenship through their father was transmitted to the children while the mother's citizenship was only secondarily relevant.

Under the 1992 legislation different rules for the acquisition of citizenship are contained in various provisions. Article 1 of the Act of 91/1992 keeps as the principal criterion that of filiation of an Italian father or mother. This was previously introduced by Act 123/1983 following the constitutional court's decision of February 9, 1983 n. 30. The obligation imposed on children with double citizenship of choosing one on attaining majority has been definitively abolished. This abolition suggests a neutral (if not actually favourable) attitude towards cases of double citizenship. Such cases, which are going to increase in the future, will nevertheless have to take into account the international conventions in force, among which we might recall in

---

[*]   Lawyer in Milan. Translated by Prof. Avv Rafaella Lanzillo.

A. Bainham (ed.), The International Survey of Family Law 1994, 299–302.
© 1996 The International Society of Family Law. Printed in the Netherlands.

particular the European Convention on the reduction of cases of multiple citizenship and that on military service obligations in the case of multiple citizenships concluded at Strasbourg on May 6, 1963 and ratified by Italy in the Act of October 4, 1966 n. 876.

The acquisition of citizenship by filiation can arise either at the moment of birth or during the minority of the child and it can be the result of subsequent recognition, judicial declaration of parenthood or an order for maintenance of the child (article 279 Civil Code). Where these acts occur during the majority of the child, the acquisition of citizenship is dependent on an express declaration of will of the child. This can cause the loss of the "status civitatis" (citizenship) of origin where this is stipulated by the laws of the state in question or by any international conventions in force at the time. Following the rule contained in Act 123/1983, article 3 of the new text provides for automatic acquisition of Italian citizenship by foreign minors adopted by couples, at least one of whom is Italian. In contrast, for adults adopted by Italian citizens the different procedure of naturalization is envisaged. In accordance with one of the fundamental principles of the Act of 1912, the purpose of which was the elimination of cases of stateless persons, article 1 of Act 91/1992 provides in a residual way two further criteria for the acquisition of citizenship in accordance with the principle of "ius soli" (by virtue of birth in the territory): Italian citizenship is conferred on anyone who was born in the territory of the Republic, if both parents are unknown or stateless, or if the child does not follow the parents' citizenship according to the laws of their country of provenance. The new Act moreover envisages, as did the Act 555/1912, the acquisition of citizenship by operation of law. This requires a declaration of will by the person concerned, but obviates the need for any measure of the Public Administration.

The following conditions are prescribed in relation to the acquisition of citizenship by foreigners or stateless persons. The foreigner or stateless person must have Italian origins (father, mother or ancestors to the second degree who are Italian citizens by birth) or, alternatively, must have been born in Italy and have had legal residence there until the age of majority. In the case of reliance on Italian origins one of the following further conditions is required:

1. Military service for the Italian state together with a declaration of will regarding the acquisition of Italian citizenship;

2. Public employment, including employment abroad, in the service of the Italian state together with a declaration of will regarding the acquisition of Italian citizenship;

3. Legal residence in Italy for at least two years before attaining the age of majority and a declaration of will regarding the acquisition of Italian citizenship. In the case of those born in Italy and resident there until majority a declaration of will is required within a year of reaching the age of majority. Article 5 of Act 91/1992 provides for the acquisition of citizenship by "iuris communicato" (communication of law), reproducing the rule already introduced by law 123/1983 and reinforcing the irrelevance of marriage regarding the automatic loss and automatic acquisition of Italian citizenship by the wife. This is in accordance with the consistent trend of decisions of the Constitutional Court on the matter.

With this proviso, the law establishes that the foreigner or stateless person who marries an Italian citizen acquires, in turn, citizenship if he or she has been resident in Italy for at least six months before the marriage, or if the marriage continues without dissolution, annulment, interruption of civil effects or legal separation for at least three years.

III NATURALIZATION

Finally, article 10 of Act 91/1992 provides for the attribution of Italian citizenship by means of naturalization. For this purpose, not only the will of the interested person is required, but also a decree of the President of the Republic, issued after hearing the opinion (necessary, but not binding) of the State Council, on the proposal of the Minister for Home Affairs.

In order to obtain naturalization specific conditions must be satisfied, among which are legal residence in Italy for a minimum time period (at least four years for citizens of a member state of the EC, five years for stateless persons, ten years for foreigners) and the foreigner's having been employed by the Italian state whether in Italy or abroad for at least five years. In any event, even where these conditions are not satisfied, Italian citizenship can be conferred on any foreigner who has rendered high services to Italy or where an exceptional interest of the state is involved.

IV LOSS OF CITIZENSHIP

The rules concerning the reasons for loss of citizenship have also been reformed by Act 91/1992 in the following way.

First, the legislator has favoured the principle of act of will in the loss of Italian citizenship, applying it also to the case of voluntary acquisition of a foreign citizenship. As a consequence, Italian citizens, who also have a foreign citizenship and are resident abroad, can waive Italian citizenship.

Automatic loss of citizenship occurs in exceptional cases, and in particular:

1. In the case of failure to observe an order emanating from an Italian authority to leave an employment or a public service in a state or a foreign public organisation or an international organisation or military service done for a foreign state;

2. In the case of failure to leave, positions analogous to those indicated above in times of war between Italy and the other state concerned. Another instance of the loss of citizenship arises in relation to the minor children of someone who acquires or re-acquires Italian citizenship in any of the ways indicated above. The children of such individuals are permitted to waive Italian citizenship on attaining the age of majority if they have another citizenship. Finally, the loss of Italian citizenship is envisaged in the case of minors adopted by Italian citizens whose adoption is later revoked [for reasons imputable to the minor] with the proviso that the minor in question must have another citizenship, or be in a position to acquire it again, in order to avoid a case of statelessness.

JAPAN

FAMILY LAW REFORM AND IN-COURT MEDIATION IN THE JAPANESE FAMILY COURT

Fujiko Isono and *Satoshi Minamikata*[**]

I   INTRODUCTION

Since the 1960s, families in Japan have shown drastic changes in their structure and role within society. Subsequently, it has been observed that the number of married women working in the labour market has been steadily increasing, along with the upward surge of divorce and it has been noted that disputes among family members have become more complicated.

Under such circumstances, the voice for reforming Family Law (the fourth and fifth part of the Japanese Civil Code, enacted in 1947) has become stronger in society, particularly among women, since some Family Law provisions are far behind providing appropriate protection to the parties involved in family disputes. It has been emphasised that the Family Court should be re-examined if Family Law is to be reformed in the future. The Family Court, which was set up in 1949 as a nation-wide special court, provides various services, for example in-court mediation and adjudgment, to the parties involved in family problems; disputes over divorce, custody, adoption and succession, etc. In Japan, the majority of families with problems still tend to resolve their conflicts in out-of-court settings, a lesser number may settle their disputes at family courts. The ordinary court is regarded merely as a last resort. In this respect, the Family Court works as an important institution in solving family problems and it should be studied along with Family Law reforms.

This paper will first sketch an outline of the social background to the recent family law reform proposals. Secondly it will discuss such proposals and, finally, delve into the issues concerning the Family Court, particularly focusing on in-court mediation.

---

[*]   Part-time lecturer at Japan University of Social Welfare (1957-1962); now an independent research worker.

[**]   Professor of law, the Faculty of Law, Niigata University.

A. Bainham (ed.), *The International Survey of Family Law 1994*, 303–319.

II FAMILY LAW REFORM AND ITS SOCIAL BACKGROUND

Significant changes within Japanese society since 1960 have affected various aspects of family life.

First, the number of working women has upsurged in accordance with the rising number of women continuing on to higher education. The ratio of women students attending universities and colleges is 40.8%, in contrast with 37% men in 1992 (Economic Planning Agency:110). Meanwhile, approximately 40% of all employed people are women and about 70% of married women work (Forum:30, 31). However, in terms of working conditions, such as wages, women are in many cases still discriminated against notwithstanding the enactment of the Equal Opportunity for Employment Act 1985. The average annual wage of a woman is estimated at about 60% of that of a man's wage (Forum:51). In spite of such a situation, women are gradually gaining the opportunity to become more independent financially, in and out of their homes.

Secondly, it is observed that the average age of marrying couples has risen. In 1951, the average age of marrying men was 25.9 and that of women 23.1 and in 1991, 28.2 and 25.9 respectively (Economic Planning Agency:22). It is understood that an increasing number of the young studying at higher education and furthermore the changing attitudes of young women towards marriage have caused the rise in the marriage age. However, the view that married women should be mainly in charge of domestic chores still prevails amongst men. Consequently, marriage sometimes translates as an institution in which women face new obstacles against their working and social activities, rather than the traditional expectation of financial security. For even some young men, marriage is not regarded as a necessity, since they are able to obtain from the service industry (such as house keepers) various domestic services which used to be expected within a marriage. In addition, it is observed that a certain number of men are inclined not to become involved in complicated human relationships, thus they are likely to avoid considering marriage.

All these views and attitudes of young people towards marriage and human relationships seem to lead to developing vulnerability within a marriage.

Thirdly, the increase of divorce reflects social attitudes towards marriage. The number of divorce cases has risen for 30 years and in 1993 it totalled approximately 190,000. That the number of young people preferring "love marriage" to "arranged marriage" has increased since the 1960s, indicates that "affection" or "love" is regarded as a crucial factor for maintaining marriage. Accordingly, people are likely to support the view that marriage can be dissolved if they feel that the "affection" or "love" between them has been lost (Tokyoto:56).

Fourthly, the principle of equality between the sexes has come to prevail widely among people, particularly women. The view that husband and wife should be treated equally in their home affects the attitudes of married women towards marital property and financial matters in marriage. For instance, according to a survey even in 1968, 87% of wives thought that they were entitled to claim half of the husband's income and their matrimonial property (Seronochosa:8).

Under such circumstances, the need for changing the present Family Law in order to promote a more equal protection within the family has become more distinct in society.

III PROPOSALS FOR FAMILY LAW REFORM

In 1991, the Family Law Reform Committee (Hosei Shingikai Mimpobukai Mibunho Shoiinnkai) recognised that some provisions of the present Family Law should be modified for the purpose of providing appropriate protection to the parties in a changing society.

Family Law is based on individualism and the principle of equality of the sexes, which are spelled out in the Constitution (Articles 14 and 24) and its ideal family is that of "a conjugal family". In this respect, the Family Law was hailed as a "democratic" statute to emancipate people, especially women, who were discriminated against under the old Family Law system.

However, some provisions of the new Family Law have been criticised for going against the philosophy of the Constitution, since they failed to achieve sufficient protection for family members, such as married women or illegitimate children. Accordingly, the Family Law was revised on various occasions: in 1962 the provisions concerning "a missing person", "dissolution of adoption" and "financial provision to a person particularly related with a deceased". In 1976 the provision on changing the surname of a divorced person. In 1980 the provisions relating to a spouse's shares in succession and to a family member's special contribution to a deceased person's assets were changed. In 1987 the special adoption scheme (one of court order rather than contract), which is equivalent to the Western adoption system, was introduced.

After the International Year of the Woman 1975 and the International Year of the Child 1979, the already existing wish for advancing the equality principles in Family Law and promoting further protection to family members became stronger in many sections of society.

Under such circumstances, in 1991 the Family Law Reform Committee commenced on the task of revising some provisions of the present Family Law and published the report with several proposals for the reformation of such law in 1994.

The fundamental aims of the current law reform are: first, to promote further "individualistic views" in the law and secondly, to improve equality between family members.

A   Reforms on surnames in marriage

The individualistic views in Family Law can be strongly seen in the proposals: a system by which parties to marriage should opt for choosing their surname and maintain it after marriage and the "non-fault divorce" principle with more limited restrictions.

Concerning parties' surnames, section 750 of the Civil Code stipulates that "Husband and wife assume the surname of the husband or wife in accordance with the agreement made at the time of the marriage". One party to marriage shall be required to take the other's surname and in fact more than 97% of wives do take their husbands' surnames at the time of marriage. It is claimed that this gives rise to various issues of principle and practical issues, such as the following.

It was understood under the old Family Law system that a wife was to be taken into the husband's family group by marriage. In this way, the fact that the wife took her husband's surname constituted a symbolic aspect of a marriage. However, under Article 24 of the Constitution, it spells out that a marriage shall be valid based on the free will of both parties on an equal basis. A wife does not need to think that she should move to her husband's family group through marriage, but instead she could create a separate family group with her husband. Consequently, it is possible that a wife can maintain her own surname after marriage.

Under such circumstances, it is claimed in some quarters that to maintain one's own name should be a human right by emphasising that a name is regarded as representing one's own individuality. Now, section 750, which usually requires a wife to abandon her family name, is criticised because it infringes upon her right of equality.

In addition, from the practical viewpoint, the present law causes inconvenience to the party changing his or her surname. Presently, many women who are engaged in employment and social activities under their maiden names, change to their husbands' on marriage. When they are required to change their surnames, they face a lot of cumbersome tasks. For instance, it is necessary to alter their surnames to their husbands' in every official document, such as a driving licence or a national health service card. Some people cannot understand why the process should be such a nuisance.

The changing attitude is illustrated in a recent case (Tokyo District Court November 19, 1994: Hanrei Taimuzu No.835, at 58). A woman professor, working at a state college, brought an action against the Japanese Government for damages. She claimed that the fact that she was forced to change her maiden name and to use her husband's surname, at her office, after marriage under the current law, infringed upon her Constitutional freedom as a fundamental human right.

Recognising such social trends, three options for reviewing the present Family Law were proposed in the report (Report:2-8). Though the three options differ in detail, they share the basic principle: new provisions should provide for a spouse either to maintain his or her surname after marriage, whilst respecting an individual's right to his or her own name.

B Modification of divorce provision

Family Law provides three ways of obtaining divorce: divorce by consent, divorce through in-court mediation or adjudgment (we do not refer to adjudgment here since it is rarely used) in the Family Court and divorce by decree in the Ordinary Court (District Court, High Court and Supreme Court).

If the parties agree over the divorce and related issues, including the distribution of property and arrangements for custody, they are required merely to file for a notification form with the family registry section of the relevant local authority. In this respect, divorce by consent is not a judicial, but an administrative process. Approximately 90% of all divorce cases are divorce by consent. In a contested case, the parties should go to in-court mediation at the Family Court under the "system of compulsory in-court mediation prior to litigation". If an agreement is reached, it is incorporated in an "in-court mediation document on divorce"; its binding force is e-quivalent to a court decree. These cases occupy about 9% of the total number of divorces. If not, the parties file for a divorce petition to the District Court. The court will issue a divorce decree following the grounds of Section 770 (Civil Code).

On some occasions, however, the court faces difficulties in applying this section to a divorce petition. Section 770 is based on the principle of "i-rretrievable breakdown" stating that "Husband or wife can bring an action for divorce only in the following cases: 1) If the other spouse has committed an act of unchastity; 2) If he or she has been deserted maliciously by the other spouse; 3) If it is unknown for three years or more whether the other spouse is alive or dead; 4) If the other party is attached with severe mental disease and recovery therefrom is hopeless; 5) If there exists any other grave reason for which it is difficult for him or her to continue the marriage".

If the last sub-section is construed literally as a "no-fault divorce clause", even a party who is to be blamed for the marital breakdown is entitled to file for divorce, claiming that the marital relationship has broken down ir-retrievably. Indeed, many cases have demonstrated that a husband may allege the breakdown of the marriage, after he has committed marital misconduct, wanting to leave his wife, who is vulnerable socially and financially.

Until 1987, the Supreme Court had rejected the petition for divorce by such a "guilty party" by interpreting the "no-fault divorce clause" strictly for the purpose of protecting the "innocent party". For instance, the Supreme Court declared that such a petition was against public policy (Supreme Court February 19, 1952: Minshu 6-2-110).

However, such interpretation of "no-fault divorce" gave rise to much controversy. It is pointed out that, the fact that one party should continue the marriage despite he or she having already lost affection or love toward the other, is against the fundamental view that marriage should be based on the parties' free will and love. In other words, a "tolerant" view towards divorce is accepted in society. Moreover, it is asserted that it is quite difficult to discover which party should be blamed as the "guilty party" under the present divorce proceedings. Therefore, it seems that the court is likely to rely upon an "objective" test, such as the period of separation, rather than "subjective" factors, when granting divorce, especially when accepting the petition filed by the "guilty party".

Eventually in 1987 the Supreme Court granted divorce to a "guilty party" under the following conditions: an "innocent party" is provided with sufficient financial security by the "guilty party", the couple has no dependent children and they have lived apart for a certain period of time (Supreme Court September 2, 1987: Minshu 41-6-1423).

Concerning the period of separation, the Committee cites in the report that the figures of the average number of years between the beginning of a separation and the time of the divorce granted, is approximately three years (Report:88). The survey of 1993 shows that in 88.8% of all divorce cases the parties get divorced within five years of the commencement of a separation (Nihonbengoshirengokai: 158). In a 1987 case, the period of separation was approximately forty years and in a 1989 case (Supreme Court November 8, 1989: Kagetsu 40-7-171), it was eight years. The courts, thus, shortened the period of separation for granting divorce. Considering such circumstances, the Committee puts forward, as a reasonable proposal, that a divorce can be granted on the ground of five years separation without agreement.

Some, however, criticise this proposal by pointing out that an "innocent party" (vulnerable wives in many cases) may face various difficulties after divorce, whilst a "guilty party" can enjoy the freedom of desertion. Responding to such criticism, the report makes clear that the new divorce provision will contain a "hardship clause". It states that a divorce must not be granted if one of the parties and/or children will face grave financial and social difficulties in the granting of such a divorce (Report:11).

C Equality between husband and wife

As stated earlier, though Family Law is based on the equality principle, the reality is in some respects far from the idealistic purpose of the provisions. The report examines some provisions on matrimonial property in order to encourage equality in the financial position of spouses (Report:8-10).

Section 762 (Civil Code) adopts the separate property regime stipulating that "(1) Property belonging to either a husband or wife from a time prior to the marriage and property acquired during the subsistence of the marriage in his or her own name constitutes his or her separate property. (2) Any property, in regard to which it is uncertain whether it belongs to the husband or the wife, is presumed to be the property in their co-ownership." However, this separate property doctrine causes, in many cases, injustice to wives. It is difficult for a house wife, for instance, to acquire property under her own name, while her husband can obtain property such as the matrimonial home under his name, at the expenditure of his wife's labour at home. In the case of many working wives, it is not easy for them to gain their own property because of comparatively low wages under present working conditions. In addition, they feel injustice at home, since they have to do most of the domestic chores, whilst their husbands spend little time aiding them (Forum:13, 44). Under such circumstances, the courts have made efforts in protecting and promoting the financial situation of married women, by adopting flexible interpretations of the provisions on matrimonial property.

For instance, the courts now accept the doctrine that a wife is entitled to claim her share to the property acquired under her husband's name, if she has made sufficient financial contribution to their marital life. This doctrine, however, can be applied only to the disputes between husband and wife. If a third party is involved (for example, if a third party purchases the matrimonial home from the husband, registered under his name, whilst his wife has made certain financial contributions for obtaining or maintaining the home), he or she must be given a priority of protection as a bona fide purchaser under the ordinal rules of the Civil Code. Similar to the situations in other countries, a divorcing wife often faces the difficulty of finding accommodation, if she has to leave the matrimonial home when her husband sells it to a third party at the time of divorce. Many lawyers claim that a special provision should be included in the reformed Family Law for the purpose of protecting the right of one party to live in the matrimonial home after divorce. Although the report does not propose any reform in relation to the matrimonial home, it declares that this issue is important and should be discussed in the future (Report:61-64, 97).

The reformed provisions will be implemented within a few years. Although many disputes are still settled in informal settings, such as arrangements between the parties, the total number of the cases dealt with at the Family Court has increased. Therefore, whether the basic principles of Family Law reform can be realised, will depend upon how the Family Court operates. In this respect, the role of the Family Court has become more important for protecting the parties involved. The next chapter will discuss the issues concerning the Family Court by focusing on in-court mediation.

IV THE JAPANESE FAMILY COURT AND IN COURT MEDIATION

While in some Western countries, discussions are going on over whether it is advisable to set up a special Family Court, in Japan the idea of a Family Court dates back to 1919, when the Cabinet set up a Provisional Council to revise the existing law. The reason for this move was stated as follows: "It has been recognised that the Civil Code now in force (enforced in 1898, and now called the Meiji Civil Code) includes provisions which are not compatible with the excellent ethics and laudable tradition of our country. What should be the main points to be changed?"

In the course of deliberation, the conservative members, who had been greatly dissatisfied with the existing articles concerning the family (here including relatives; extended family), demanded drastic law reform to make it compatible with their ideal of the traditional family *Ie* system (an extended patriarchal family headed by the eldest son of the former Head of the Family), while the more progressive members made efforts to remove the *Ie* elements and make the law more suitable for the actual state of family life which had changed a great deal since the modernisation which started in the latter half of the 19th century. Heated discussion raged between these two factions (See Isono, 1988).

Nevertheless, the first point the two parties agreed on was to create some kind of system in which family disputes would be settled without recourse to a court trial based on rights and obligations of the two parties. The conservatives welcomed creation of a special system to settle domestic disputes amicably on the principle of a traditional ethical code and magnanimity through mediation by persons of high social status who were widely respected. They considered such a device the best way to guarantee the laudable system of *Ie*, and that its creation should be given priority to any law reform.

The progressive members also had no objection to the idea of settling family disputes through mediators. Having been chosen from among prestigious gentlemen, they were not primarily for equal human rights; but they were more sympathetic to under-privileged people and advocated that the privileged should treat them with magnanimity. Their attitude may be best described as "paternalistic". They also thought that it was an excellent idea for the State to solve conflicts for the family of the people.

The most authoritative interpretation, then, of Family Law, stated by one of the relatively liberal professors, was that the law concerning the family was not meant to regulate any rights of individual members of the family but to protect the unity of the family as a whole. His theory of the "guardian role of the State" seems to imply that Family Law was a set of rules which the State should refer to in dealing with family matters. Even after the war, his theory continued to be a standard interpretation of family law (Nakagawa 1942: 6-17, 1959: 3-19).

It is true that in Japan there was, and still is to some extent, a very strong negative attitude towards taking a case to a court of law. For the ruling class this would prevent the awareness of individual rights to develop among the ruled; and ordinary people used to regard law as something connected with punishment. After the First World War, however, there grew up popular aspirations after liberalism. This relatively liberal period is called the period of "Taisho Democracy". Taisho is the reign title of the Emperor who was on the throne from 1912 to 1926. Under strong public pressure the Bill of Universal (male) Suffrage was finally adopted in 1924, but almost at the same time the notorious Law for Maintenance of the Public Peace (which was to make Japan an actual police state) was enforced.

Whilst discussions in the Council were dragging on, in 1924 the Tenant Mediation Act and in 1926 the Labour Mediation Act were passed, instead of a regular tenancy law and labour law, which were on the agenda of the Council. These Acts were an appeasement to prevent peasant unrest and labour movements, mediation being used as a convenient method to put psychological pressure on the weaker to acquiesce in the decision favourable to the stronger.

In the meantime, Japan started a wholesale invasion of Northeast China (Manchuria), and the Council's proposals about family and relatives (1925) and inheritance (1927) which had been presented to the government were shelved. Therefore the only positive outcome of the Council was the idea of family conflict mediation and this materialised in 1939 as an Act for Mediation of Human Affairs (family matters). The government supported it as "the most recommendable approach to safeguard our laudable system concerning the family and relatives" (Isono 1958: 52). In the Diet the Minister of Justice made a speech saying, "Concerning conflicts on the family, individual rights should not be given too much attention, and the family mediation should be based on our laudable family ethics" (Isono 1958: 51-52)

Hozumi Shigeto, one of the leading "liberal" members of the Council, was appointed the first male member of the Mediation Committee together with a well-known woman leader and a judge. According to verbal evidence, he proudly described the system as "modernisation of the go-between mediation". Traditionally, marriage was arranged between two families through a go-between couple, who knew both families and usually had a social status higher than the two parties. If some trouble arose, the go-between couple was asked to mediate, and the decision of the go-between couple, backed by their prestige, had to be accepted by both parties. Hozumi's argument was: "In a modern society, the married couple does not necessarily live in their native region, and this makes their go-betweens not easily available. So, the State provides an alternative to the go-between mediation" (Hozumi).

In fact, at that time the authorities felt an urgent need to introduce such a system. There was a growing number of quarrels arising in families of men killed in the war, (officially "the men who died gloriously for the Emperor"), concerning inheritance and the question of who were entitled to receive pensions. The parents, for example, claimed the pension which was given to the widow. The government had to take some measures to avoid legal confrontations among relatives of such deceased patriots.

During the war years (1931-1945), with the growing fanatic nationalism, the ideology of a "Family State" was inculcated in the mind of the Japanese people, especially through the education system which was entirely subject to the Ministry of Education. The Emperor was the head of the family of the Japanese people, and according to traditional ethics, the people who were the children owed an absolute obedience to the Emperor, the Father (in reality, whatever order the government issued in His name). "Theirs was not to reason why, theirs was but to do and die", was literally enforced. Labour movements were mercilessly crushed, and instead of the labour union, the slogan of "Enterprise is a Family" was made the order of the day.

For public education, three months before the start of the regular war against China in July 1939, the Thought Control Bureau of the Education Ministry published a booklet entitled *The Fundamental Principle of the Japanese Polity*; and a few months before Pearl Harbour, the Education Bureau of the same Ministry issued *The way of the Imperial Subjects*, which was followed by the *Manual for Guidance about Family Life* (1942). All of them were intended to mobilise public sentiment to support the ideology of the Family State.

When Japan finally surrendered in August 1945, the centre of the official concern was to "defend the Japanese Polity", namely the "Family State" headed by the Emperor. Immediately after the surrender a new cabinet was formed with the brother-in-law of the Emperor as Prime Minister, and its Minister of Education proclaimed: "The promotion of democracy in education should aim at the ideal Japanese form of democracy based on the principle of *One lord (Emperor) and The thousand Imperial Subjects* with the lord-vassal relationship as the norm of conduct and the father-son relationship for their emotional attachment" (Isono 1958: 58)

Their illusion, however, was dashed when in October Japan was placed under the Allied (in fact U.S.) occupation, and directives issued by the General Headquarters under General MacArthur guaranteed the freedom of criticising the Emperor System, which had been the strictest taboo, together with formation of labour unions, liberation of women and so on. Education was democratised and most of the restrictions which had been forced upon people under the former regime were removed.

Naturally, the revised Constitution, with special articles on the definition of the family was to be based on the free agreement of a man and a woman, and for equality of both sexes. This amounted to the collapse of the *Ie* system. Scandalised conservatives, who constituted a majority of the then existing Diet, (the Lower Chamber elected during the war and the House of Peers), made frantic efforts to preserve the system of *Ie*. Most of the people also thought that the abolition of *Ie* meant denial of family life itself. The idea of a nuclear family was misunderstood as legal authorisation to neglect parents. This popular misapprehension was enhanced by the utter disruption of effective communication between parents who had been brainwashed through the former education and children who were now being taught the new democratic behaviour at school, such as expressing their opinions differently from those of the parents.

Nevertheless, women hailed the emancipation, and in spite of some confusion of individualism with egoism, the younger generation welcomed their newly obtained freedom from the *Ie* restrictions; and in the course of time, the movement for restitution of the *Ie* died down. On the other hand, the confusion caused by the sudden change increased conflicts within the family. In 1946 the long-standing idea of family mediation was incorporated in the Domestic Section of the District Court, and in 1947 an independent Family Court was inaugurated, combining the Domestic Section and the Juvenile Tribunal, which had been set up in 1923. The Family Court is directly attached to the Supreme Court. Each prefecture has its own Family Court and some branch offices.

The Domestic Section is divided into mediation and adjudgment parts. The latter mainly deals with cases such as the appointment of a guardian for a minor or applications for changing names after divorce and so on, and also deals with cases with precise regulations by law, like inheritance etc., on which the parties cannot agree. The main point of this paper being mediation, we do not go into the adjudgment part of the Domestic Section, neither the Juvenile Division, which mainly deals with delinquency, and thus, limit the discussion to the Mediation Panel.

The Mediation Panel consists of a man and a woman and a judge, who in many cases appears only on finalisation of the agreement, and the agreement reached at the Family Court is legally binding. The mediators are chosen from among persons with higher education and respectable social status; many of the male members used to be retired public servants or businessmen, but now there are increasing numbers of those who have the experience of studying family problems. Women members were mainly recruited formerly from among graduates of the pre-war women's university (they were a small minority group of female intellectuals), or even the wives of local big names; but in recent years there are more women mediators specialising in relevant subjects.

There is no professional screening about the suitability of their personality as mediators. Formerly, they were considered to represent public opinion and sentiment, but now are officially appointed as a part of the legal apparatus, and receive a small amount of remuneration. While there used to be no retirement age, it is now set at 70, except for special cases.

It should be pointed out here that, with the tradition of "not to pay too much attention to the law", much of the Family Law is relegated to the Family Court and a lot is left to the discretion of the Mediation Panel.

The Mediation Panel is often assisted by "investigation officers". This is usually translated as "probation officers", but this translation is misleading because their roles and competence are not the same. The investigating officers' main task is to provide the Mediation Panel with information about the applicant parties. They are recruited, through regular examination, mainly from among university graduates who studied law, sociology, psychology, education or similar subjects, but they are not statutorily authorised to engage in counselling on their own, though sometimes they do counselling only at the order of the Mediation Panel. In Tokyo and Osaka, and in some other places, there are investigation officers specially appointed for counselling. Nevertheless, the question about confidentiality does not seem to have been raised, as they are required to present a written or verbal report to the Mediation Panel. Unfortunately, the use of investigation officers as counsellors is said to be on the decline, due to financial reasons and the problem of work load for the officers.

The parties concerned are required to appear at the mediation session together. If the mediation fails, or the parties or one of them cannot be satisfied with the decision, the case may theoretically be taken to an ordinary court of law; but the expense and delay are a formidable deterrent. In any case, there is a firmly established system of compulsory in-court mediation prior to litigation, the conflicting parties cannot go straight to an ordinary court, but have to go first through compulsory mediation by the Family Court (See Numabe 1994).

It is not surprising that after the enforcement of the new Civil Code (1947), the number of divorces increased considerably. Considering that there is no system of legal separation, the percentage is not very high (1.45 in 1992). The reasons for this relatively low rate, such as the Japanese woman's lower level of expectation in married life, especially about her personal relationship with her husband etc., cannot be discussed here.

Mediation is primarily aimed at the reconciliation of the married couple, but in recent years most of the "successful" mediations have resulted in divorce by mutual consent with arrangements for children and property being agreed upon. It seems that the marriages taken to the Family Court are already past remedy. In Japan divorce by consent has never been contested. This may seem very progressive, but in the Meiji Civil Code this was used as a device to "remove" from the *Ie* the *yome* who was considered unsuitable. The *yome* is not exactly "daughter-in-law" but a term to denote the status of the son's wife in the *Ie*. In the West the breaking up of a family means divorce, but under the system of *Ie*, an undesirable *yome* had to be removed as a disruptive element for the unity of the *Ie*. As it was not possible to put such a practice in the written law, mutual consent was used because it was extremely difficult for the *yome* to refuse to consent.

The process of divorce has been made so simple that, if marriage partners agree, divorce can be made legally valid by just presenting at the family registry section of the relevant local authority, or even post by mail, a printed notification form bearing the names and seals (signatures do not count and the names can be written by others) of the two parties with those of two witnesses. As the seal does not have to be the personal seal specially registered, one of the two parties can very easily file in the form of divorce even without the other party knowing. In order to protect a possible victim from such a treacherous action, you can find at the office a printed form stating that "If a person under such a name should file in a divorce notice, please do not accept it". Because of the facility to legalise divorce, the number of divorce cases brought to the Family Court is only a fraction of the divorces actually effected. It is generally estimated that more than 90% of the divorced do not go through any administrative or legal check. Arrangements about children and property are entirely left to the parties, unless quarrels arise on some special points and then they are taken to the Family Court. Even though divorce represents the majority of the cases handled by the Family Court, the Court also deals with inheritance, property, custody and other conflicts relating to the family. The applicant can be represented by a lawyer, and a certain amount of legal aid is available, if necessary.

The Japanese approach to treat family conflicts, as much as possible, out of the legal sphere looks very similar to the end results of the long process of marriage law reform in England and Wales. The difference is that while English law reform came out of the recognition of the complexity of human psychology and the futility of trying to bind quarrelling married couples together by force of law, the Japanese system grew out of the strong objections of the traditionalists to the recognition of individual rights for members of the family. The former involves the importance of counselling efforts to encourage the parties to make their own decision, and the latter, originating in the idea of the State, as the guardian, to solve the problem for the parties, still retains some paternalistic overtones.

It is not easy to get frank comments from those who have the experience of having applied for in-court mediation at the Family Court; but there is a report of an investigation made in 1964 revealing that one half of the women who had received mediation at the Family Court felt that at the mediation session they had been "pressurised to endure the present situation"(Numabe:17). As the Mediation Panel is supposed to represent the "good sense" of society, and as mediators are mostly elderly persons, their good sense tends to be conservative, and not being familiar with the social science approach to the problem, they are apt to give moralising lectures as experienced persons with the aim of making the applicants reform their ways. This data is now 20 years old, and it is hoped that the attitude of mediators has since been improved.

In Japan, the Family Court is taken so much for granted that there have not been enough analytical or probing studies about the structure and working of the Family Court. In view of the difficulty inherent in mediation, it cannot be expected that all or even a majority of the cases filed at the Family Court will be successfully mediated. The estimation is that about 30% of the cases reach some kind of agreement, and others are listed as agreements not reached or as withdrawn.

In Japan divorce is no longer a stigma, while cohabitation has not yet been regarded as so respectable as in the West. On the other hand, legal registration and the marriage ceremony are not linked; marriage has to be registered separately. Therefore, a marriage that has passed through a formal ceremony, but not been officially registered, is socially quite acceptable, though legally invalid. There have been various legal devices to protect a woman left in a very disadvantageous position as the result of such a union.

It is a pity that the Family Court, whatever its origin was, cannot be more effectively used for the mediation of family problems. The applicants can have their case heard for a nominal fee and minimal expenses such as for postage (unless they prefer to be represented by a legal adviser). If the investigating officers were used as real trained social workers with the competence to conduct counselling with a guarantee of confidentiality, and the Mediation Panel was asked to deal with material arrangements such as custody and property, people might find the Family Court more attractive. The difference between the Family Court and an ordinary law court is now widely understood, and the question of in-court or out-of-court counselling will not bother people too much. The greatest obstacle to any reform seems to be the general complacency of the people concerned (not applicants) about the Family Court.

It must be added, however, that the question still remains whether all conflicts can be or should be settled by "mediation". As far as psychological or emotional conflicts are concerned, many cases may be at least alleviated by expert counselling; but when it comes to disputes about practical arrangements, if one is too eager to settle them by mediation, the end result is apt to be that the more obstinate party gets what they want and the weaker gives up in desperation. In domestic disputes should the idea of justice based on legal rights be entirely discarded?

Sections I, II and III were written by Satoshi Minamikata. Section IV was written by Fujiko Isono. The authors are very grateful for the advice and the assistance of Miss Michelle Gooden of Cardiff Law School.

References

Economic Planning Agency (1993), *The Arrival of the Society with a Small Number of Children – Annual Report on the National Life for Fiscal 1992*, Printing Bureau, Ministry of Finance Tokyo.

Forum Josei no Seikatsu to Tenbo (ed.)(1994), *Zuhyodemiru Onna no Genzai (Statistics on Current Situation of Women)*, Mineruvashobo Kyoto.

Homusho Minjikyoku Sanjikanshitsu (1994), *Koninseidoto ni Kansuru Mimpokaiseiyoko (Report on the Family Law Reform)*, Homusho Minjikyoku Sanjikanshitsu Tokyo (cited as Report).

Hozumi, S. (1939), what Hozumi Shigeto told F. Isono, his niece, in 1939, after the first session of mediation.

Isono S. & F. (1958), *Kazoku Seido (The System of Ie)*, Iwanamishoten Tokyo.

Isono, F. (1988), "The Evolution of Modern Family Law in Japan" *Journal of Law and the Family* Vol.2.

Katayama, T. (1939), Jinji Chotei Ho Gaisetsu (An Introduction to Act for Mediation of Human Affairs) Ganshodo Tokyo.

Nakagawa, Z. (1942), *Nihon Shinzoku Ho (Japanese Law on Family and Relatives)*, Nihonhyoronsha Tokyo.

(1959), *Shintei Shinzoku Ho (Law on Family and Relatives, revised)*, Seirinshoinshinsha Tokyo.

Nihonbengoshirengokai (ed.) (1994), *Korekaranokekkonn to Rikon (Marriage and Divorce in the Future)*, Akashishoten Tokyo.

Tokyoto (1994), *Tokyo Josei Hakusho 93 (White Paper on Women 1993)* Tokyoto Tokyo.

Numabe, A., Noda, A. and Hitomi, Y. (eds.)(1994) *Shin Kaji Chotei Dokuhon (Revised)(New Textbook on Mediation)*, Ichiryusha Tokyo – gives a comprehensive description of mediation in the Family Court.

Sorifukohoshitsu, *Danjobyodo (The Equality of the Sexes)* Seronchosa (Opinion Poll) November 1975.

Wagatsuma, S. (ed.)(1956), *Sengo ni okeru Mimpo Kaisei no Keika (The Process of the Postwar Reform of Civil Code in Japan)*, Nihonhyoronshinsha Tokyo.

MALAWI

THE NEW CONSTITUTION AND THE FAMILY

Garton Kamchedzera[*]

I INTRODUCTION: A NEW CONSTITUTION

Landmark constitutional developments took place in Malawi in 1993 and 1994. Concerted internal and external pressure forced Dr H. K. Banda and his Malawi Congress Party (MCP) to accept a referendum on whether the country should adopt a multiparty system of government. Malawians overwhelmingly voted, on 17 June 1993, for multipartyism. Ended were the MCP's thirty year autocracy and Dr Banda's legalised life presidency.[1] On 17 May 1994, a new party and a new president were elected to govern.[2] On the same day, a new constitution[3] came into force and repealed the 1966 constitution.[4]

The new constitution is mainly a result of the new parties' idea-trading. Constitutional conferences, under the auspices of the National Consultative Council,[5] were followed by the operation of a constitution drafting committee. No attempts were made to have politically neutral constitutional framers.[6] Instead, partisan lawyers were entrusted to draft the constitution. Consultation was insufficient as the main goal was to replace the 1966 constitution before the newly elected government took office. Hence, the constitution will provisionally apply for one year.[7] It is hoped that during the first year idea-trading will be facilitated to improve the constitution.[8] The present parliament's power to amend the constitution is limited.[9]

---

[*] Senior Lecturer in Law, University of Malawi; currently research scholar, Clare Hall, University of Cambridge.
[1] Provided by Sections 4 and 9 of the 1966 Constitution.
[2] Under the Parliamentary and Presidential Elections Act 1993, Act No 31 of 1993.
[3] Under the Republic of Malawi (Constitution) Act 1994, Act No 20 of 1994.
[4] Section 2 of the Republic of Malawi Constitution Act 1994 and sections 212 and 214 of the 1994 Constitution.
[5] Established under section 3 of the National Consultative Council Act 1993, Act No 20 of 1993.
[6] As suggested by John Rawls, for example: John Rawls, *A Theory of Justice* (Oxford, Oxford University Press, 1972), at 17-22.
[7] Section 212(1) of the 1994 Constitution, *supra*, note 3.
[8] Section 212(4).
[9] Under section 196.

A. Bainham (ed.), The International Survey of Family Law 1994, 321–327.

Provisions on the following matters can only be amended with the approval of a referendum:[10] Establishment and description of the republic, application and interpretation of the constitution, fundamental constitutional and national policy principles, human rights, citizenship, the franchise, and the independence and jurisdiction of the judiciary. Such provisions nevertheless may be amended by Parliament with two thirds majority if the amendment does not affect the substance of the constitution.[11] The remaining provisions may be amended by parliament provided that two thirds of the total national assembly members support such amendment.[12]

The Constitution drafting committee was free to use international standards. Indeed the new constitution's interpretation will partly be guided by current international law norms and comparable foreign case law.[13] Any international agreement ratified by an Act of parliament is part of the Republic's law if such an Act so provides.[14] International agreements binding on Malawi before the new constitution came into force are also part of Malawi's law subject to parliament's subsequent contrary provision.[15] Also part of Malawi's law is customary international law that is consistent with the constitution or a Malawian Act.[16] Not only does the 1994 constitution contain civil and political rights.[17] The constitution further incorporates economic, social, cultural, and solidarity rights.[18] It is worthwhile briefly to note how the new constitution's provisions on family law relate with the international standards that Malawi has ratified.

---

10 Section 196(1)(a).
11 Section 196(3).
12 Section 197.
13 Section 11(1)(c).
14 Section 211(1).
15 Section 211(2).
16 Section 211(3).
17 Eg. political rights (section 40); freedom of association (section 32); freedom of conscience (section 33); freedom of opinion (section 34); freedom of expression (section 35); freedom of information (section 36); access to information (section 37); freedom of assembly (section 38); freedom of movement and residence (section 39); freedom to participate in political activities (section 40); and access to justice and legal remedies (section 41).
18 Eg., the right to marry and found a family (section 22); the right to education (section 25); the right to choose language and culture (section 26); the right to property (section 28); the right to economic activity (section 29); the right to fair and safe labour relations (section 31); the right to development (section 30), and the right not to be held in servitude.

II GENDER EQUALITY

The 1966 constitution had no specific provision on gender equality. Gender equality is one of the principles of national policy in the 1994 constitution.[19] Accordingly, the Bill of rights enshrines the woman's right to full and equal protection by the law and not to be discriminated against because of gender or marital status.[20] Laws that discriminate against a woman are invalid.[21] Similarly, customs and practices that infringe the gender-and-status equality principle should be abolished by legislation.[22] The constitution gives examples of the rights that women in Malawi should have. Women have rights to enter into contracts,[23] to acquire and maintain rights in property,[24] and to have parental responsibility.[25] A woman can acquire and retain citizenship and nationality on her own.[26] The woman is further entitled to fair maintenance and to a fair distribution of family property held jointly after marriage dissolution[27]. The 1994 constitution specifies sexual abuse, harassment, violence, discrimination at work, business or public affairs, and deprivation of property, "including property obtained by inheritance", as examples of practices that should be eliminated.[28] Surprisingly, the constitution assumes that access to property through inheritance is fair.

There were attempts in the 1994 constitution to emulate the Convention on the Elimination of All Forms of Discrimination Against Women 1967.[29] The 1994 constitution regrettably fails to match the coherence and commitment of the convention especially in the area of affirmative action. For example the Convention obliges states to adopt temporary special measures accelerating *de facto* equality between men and women as a way of eliminating discrimination against women without delay.[30] The 1994 constitution embeds patriarchy. For example, the constitution assumes that

---

19 Section 13(a).
20 Section 24(1).
21 Section 24(2).
22 Ibid.
23 Section 24(1)(a)(i).
24 Section 24(1)(a)(ii).
25 Section 24(1)(a)(iii).
26 Section 24(1)(a)(iv).
27 Section 24(1)(b)(i and ii).).
28 Section 24((2).
29 Proclaimed by the General Assembly Resolution 2263(XXII) of 7 November 1967.
30 Article 4 of the Convention, *supra*, note 29.

access to property through inheritance is equitable.[31] Further, by granting
the woman fair distribution of joint property only, the new constitution in-
dividualises the family unit and thereby condones male-domination by not
recognising housework and emotional and other contributions that male-
domination does not recognise as economically valuable. To individualise
the family is to contradict the very idea of marriage that the parties normally
share on the formation of the family.

III THE FAMILY

The new constitution endorses the international standard recognition of the
family as "the natural and fundamental group unit of society".[32] The state
and society have a duty to protect the family.[33] Proper construction suggests
that the state's and society's obligation to protect the family entails
facilitating civil, political, economic, social, cultural, and solidarity rights
to the family as a unit and not just to individuals.

Like in many African countries,[34] there is no definition of "family" in
the constitution.

All men and women have a right freely[35] to "marry and found a
family."[36] It is not unreasonable to conclude that the constitution assumes
that marriage is a condition for a family. It is right to conclude that the new

---

31 Section 24(2)(c) of the 1994 Constitution, *supra*, note 3.

32 Section 22(1), repeating Article 6 (3) of the Universal Declaration of Human Rights
1948, adopted and proclaimed by General Assembly Resolution No 217 A (III) of 10
December 1948. Section 13(i) of the 1994 constitution, *supra*, note 3, recognises the
family as "a fundamental and vital social unit."

33 Section 22(1) of the 1994 constitution, *supra*, note 3, complying with Article 16 of the
Universal Declaration of Human Rights, supra, note 32.

34 Alice Armstrong, Chaloka Beyani, Chuma Himonga, Janet Kabeberi-Macharia, Athaliah
Molokomme, Welshman Ncube, Thandabantu Nhlapo, Bart Rwezaura, and Julie Stewart,
"Uncovering Reality: Excavating Women's Rights in African Law", (1993) 7 *Inter-
national Journal of Law and the Family*, 314. at 318-320.

35 Complying with the Convention on Consent to Marriage, Minimum Age for Marriage
and Registration of Marriages 1962, ratified by the General assembly by Resolution
1763 A (XVII) of 7 November 1962 (hereinafter referred to as Marriage Convention).
Note the subsequent Recommendation on Marriage, Minimum Age for Marriage and
Registration of Marriages 1965, adopted by General Assembly Resolution No 2018(XX)
of 1 November 1965, (hereinafter referred to as Marriage Recommendation).

36 Section 22(3) of the 1994 constitution, *supra,* note 3.

constitution recognises marriage by law, marriage by custom, marriage by repute, and permanent cohabitation as the ways of founding a family. Section 22(5) provides that the right freely to marry and found a family applies in all marriages at law, custom, and marriages by repute or by permanent cohabitation. The design was clearly to cover all socially recognised marriages.

There are attempts to prevent child marriages whilst promoting freedom to marry. A person over the age of eighteen cannot legally be barred from entering into marriage.[37] A person between fifteen and eighteen years old may legally marry subject to parental or guardian consent.[38] The state has a duty to "actually discourage" (not prohibit) a marriage where one or both of the parties are under the age of fifteen.[39] A child is a person under sixteen years of age.[40] Hence, persons between sixteen and eighteen years of age, technically "children" under the 1994 constitution though not in international law, need parental or guardian consent. The constitution's provisions also entail that child marriages for persons between fifteen and sixteen years of age are lawful if there is parental or guardian consent.

Once a family is founded, family members are entitled to some rights. Each member of the family has to enjoy full and equal respect.[41] The law should protect all family members against all forms of neglect, cruelty and exploitation.[42] However, there is no definition of "a family." To equate the family with a social union is to neglect single people with no children, single parents, and other social units that are socially recognised as families. Although the new constitution attempts to cover all marriages, it does not cover all families.

The new constitution has been accused of eroding social cohesion in Malawi in so far as it recognises cohabitation as equal to marriage. It is often stated that marriage in Malawi and many African countries is not just a union

---

37 Section 22(6).
38 Section 22(7).
39 Section 22(8).
40 Complying with Article 1 of the Convention on the Rights of the Child 1989, Adopted and opened for ratification and signature by General Assembly 44/25 of 20 November 1989, UN Doc. A/44/736 (1989), hereinafter referred to as Rights of Child Convention).
41 Section 22(2) of the 1994 Constitution, *supra*, note 3.
42 Ibid.

of two parties. Marriage is a further union of two extended families.[43]
Traditional formalities of African marriages are designed to unite the two
parties to the conjugal marriage as well as uniting their respective extended
families. As such, social cohesion is facilitated and human relations are built.
To recognise cohabitation is to encourage individualism, and hence, to erode
social cohesion.

IV THE CHILD

Malawi ratified the United Nations Convention on the Rights of the Child
1989[44] in 1992. The convention's aim is to facilitate the survival, development, participation and protection of the child.[45] The underlying principle
is that the best interests of the child should be paramount in matters relating
to the child.[46] The underlying assumption is that the child has intrinsic
worth as a vulnerable person. The convention is further transcended by the
principle of "first call for children"[47] which states that

> the lives and normal development of children should have a first call on
> society's concerns and capacities and that children should be able to depend
> upon the commitment in good times and in bad, in normal times and in
> times of emergency, in times of peace and in times of war, in times of
> prosperity and in times of recession.[48]

The new constitution's provisions on the rights of the child are a missed
opportunity. The constitutional provisions are parochial and restrictive of
the UN convention's potential. The statement of national policies urges the
state to "promote conditions for the full development of healthy, productive

---

43 T. O. Elias, *The Nature of African Customary Law* (Manchester University Press, 1956),
     at 145-146.
44 Rights of the Child Convention, *supra*, note 40.
45 United Nations Centre for Human Rights and UNICEF, Overview: Convention on the
     Rights of the Child, Information Kit (New York, United Nations Centre for Human
     Rights and UNIEF, 1990), at 2-3.
46 Article 3 of the Rights of the Child Convention, supra note 40.
47 UNICEF, *The State of the World's Children 1990* (Oxford; Oxford University Press,
     1990), (hereinafter referred to as *UNICEF: State 1990*), at 7.
48 *UNICEF: State 1990*, *supra*, note 47, at 8.

responsible members of society".[49] Such a principle arguably facilitates the survival, development, and protection of the child. It is however doubtful whether the participation of the child is facilitated. The child's inherent worth and dignity are not recognised. Absent from the constitution is the principle that the best interests of the child should be paramount in all matters affecting the child. The principle of "first call for children" is also missing. Indeed, it is not recognised that some children are specially vulnerable due to poverty. Instead, the constitution prescribes that all children, regardless of birth (and not religion, opinion, property, among other factors) are entitled to equal treatment before the law.[50] All children have a right to a name and a nationality.[51] Children have a right to know and be raised by their parents.[52] Their health, education, physical, mental, spiritual and social development should be protected.[53] To such ends, children should be "protected from economic exploitation or any treatment, work or punishment that is, or is likely to" be prejudicial or hazardous.[54]

V CONCLUSION

Problems to be addressed by family law remain in Malawi. For the first time, a constitution has attempted to address some family law issues and to provide the direction of legislative and judicial development. Regrettably, the root of gender problems has not been tackled, many families remain legally unrecognised, social cohesion has been threatened, and the rights of the child have been shrouded in parochiality. It is hoped that Malawians will improve many of the provisions relating to family law during the constitution's one year provisional operation.

---

49   Section 13(h) of the 1994 constitution, *supra*, note 3.
50   Section 23(1).
51   Section 23(2).
52   Section 23(3).
53   Section 23(4).
54   Ibid.

MALTA

THE IMPACT OF CEDAW AND THE AFTERMATH

*Ruth Farrugia**

I   INTRODUCTION

December 1, 1993 was an important day for Family Law in Malta. After centuries of the patriarchal system, the House of Representatives legislated to honour its commitments under the Convention on the Elimination of All Forms of Discrimination Against Women (commonly referred to as CEDAW) and amendments to the Civil Code were enacted whereby discrimination between men and women was intended to be reduced to a dead letter.

Family lawyers will not be surprised to learn that this step has hardly just begun to remedy past injustices. Although the law is now clear in the granting of equal status, society has some catching up to do. This past year has been encouraging in the response it has generated from both sexes, from all walks of life, but the procedural framework for the functioning of the amendments has not yet received due attention and neither has the issue relating to the rights of children.

II   THE CIVIL CODE: SOME BACKGROUND

Civil law in Malta finds its roots in the ius commune of Roman Law and although in 1784 the Code de Rohan sought to supplement the ius commune in making a collection of Maltese legislation, statutes, bye-laws and regulations, it was not until eighty years later that the Civil Code took the form known today. Sir Adrian Dingli was appointed Crown Advocate in 1853 and set about producing a Civil Code by tackling twenty-one ordinances over a period of fourteen years, two of which deal with the law of persons and contain some 2,200 sections.[1]

As its model, Sir Adrian Dingli used the French Civil Code, the Code Napoleon of 1804. He also widely consulted the Code of the Two Sicillies, the codes of various Italian states, the Code of Louisiana, the Austrian and

---

*   Lecturer in Family Law, University of Malta.
1   R. Cremona, *Notes on Civil Law*, University of Malta (1980).

A. Bainham (ed.), The International Survey of Family Law 1994, 329–343.
© 1996 *The International Society of Family Law. Printed in the Netherlands.*

Dutch Codes and the first Italian Code enacted in 1865. It still remained thoroughly based on the ius commune which continued to regulate civil law practically throughout the whole of Europe.[2]

The Ordinances dealing with the Law of Persons were consolidated into one ordinance – Ordinance I of 1873 until this was incorporated into a Civil Code known as Chapter 23 of the Revised Edition of the Laws of Malta 1942. Following the enactment of the Statute Law Revision Act in 1980, the Law Commission set up under that Act set about revising the Laws of Malta again and on January 1, 1984 the finalised version came into effect with the Civil Code now becoming Chapter 16 of the Laws of Malta.

In March 1989 the Ministry for Social Policy established the Commission for the Advancement of Women and entrusted its members with the task of drafting recommendations for a new Code of Family Law aimed at eliminating the existing gender-based discrimination in the Civil Code. On December 1 1993 amendments to the law came into effect.

Today, the law pertaining to the family is still to be found within the Code of Civil Law under the Roman heading: Book First "Of Persons". Other legislation relating to the family has been enacted outside the Civil Code and the question is often raised whether it would be more logical to incorporate all legislation regarding the family into one Family Code. Given that this was the original mammoth task which continues to be entrusted to the Commission for the Advancement of Women, it may well be pertinent to suggest that such an undertaking is taken up by an independent Commission whose priority is not elimination of discrimination but rather the amalgamation of and review of family legislation in the interests of the family as a whole, although the Commission maintain that this is their guiding spirit.[3]

---

2   Ibid.
3   Department of Information, *Equal Partners in Marriage: Updating of the Family Law*, (1991).

III THE MUTUAL RIGHTS AND DUTIES OF SPOUSES

Prior to the 1993 amendments, spouses were deemed to "owe each other fidelity, support and assistance".[4] The husband was the "head of the household" and he was "bound to protect his wife, to receive her in the matrimonial home, and to maintain her according to his means and position".[5] The wife was expected to "take the surname of her husband", "to live with him and to follow him wherever he [deemed] fit to establish the matrimonial home" and was "bound to contribute to the maintenance of her husband if he [did] not possess sufficient means".[6] Should the wife leave the matrimonial home "the liability of the husband to maintain his wife [should] cease" where she "[should] refuse, without reasonable cause, to return".[7]

The first premise is now that "(t)he Law promotes the unity and stability of the family". The husband is no longer head of the household and instead, both spouses "shall have equal rights and shall assume equal responsibilities during marriage. They owe each other fidelity and moral and material support".[8] It is interesting to note that the recommendation of the Commission was to include the traditional "assistance" to the obligations of fidelity and support but this was left out of the final draft. Similarly, the original "the spouses shall co-operate with one another in the interest of the family, and are bound to live together in the matrimonial home"[9] was also discarded when the proposals reached the House of Representatives.

The choice of matrimonial home is now to be established where the spouses "by their common accord" may determine, provided that the choice is "in accordance with the need of both spouses and the overriding interest of the family itself". This last proviso was added by the legislator as it does not appear in the White Paper presented by the Commission. Similarly, with regard to maintenance the legislator ended up amplifying this section of the law so as to ensure that the concept of family interests was included:

---

4   *Laws of Malta*, Chapter 16, Article 2 (pre 1993).
5   Ibid., Article 3 (pre 1993).
6   Ibid., Article 4(3) (pre 1993).
7   Ibid., Article 6 (pre 1993).
8   Ibid., Article 2.
9   Department of Information, ibid., Article 2 (as proposed).

"Both spouses are bound, each in proportion to his or her means and of his or her ability to work, whether in the home or outside the home as the interest of the family requires, to maintain each other and to contribute towards the needs of the family."[10]

This section was meant to accord to the wife who remained at home to care for the children some recognition of her contribution to the needs of the family. Whether such contribution can ever be expressed in monetary terms is often hotly disputed and its importance cannot be underestimated, particularly in a society where most women with young children do not work outside the home. Furthermore, the concept of loss of maintenance following separation as a result of breakdown imputable to one spouse is crucial to the importance of maintenance within this scenario. The issue will be discussed under separation.

An interesting addition to the law appears now at section 3A whereby the matrimonial home belonging wholly or in part to one spouse may only be alienated by title inter vivos with the consent of the other spouse. Should such consent be "unreasonably withheld", recourse to the Court of Voluntary Jurisdiction is then possible. This brings me to pose the obvious question whether it should be a Court, albeit one of so-called voluntary jurisdiction, that should attempt a reconciliation between parties in disagreement over the matrimonial home.

The issue of surnames raised controversy and debate far out of proportion to the weight of the argument. The law still declares that the spouses are to take the surname of the husband but the wife may add her maiden name after it. The wife may also decide to retain her maiden surname and add her husband's to it, in which case she must make a declaration before the Registrar at the Public Registry, in accordance with the Marriage Act, prior to the reading of the banns. In no place does the husband have the option of adding his wife's surname to his own and children must take the surname of their father, after which they may add the maiden surname of their mother.[11] The suggestion that the children should take the surname of the mother was a serious attempt to eliminate the stigma attached to illegitimacy but was thrown out before it even reached the legislators for discussion.

---

10   *Laws of Malta*, Chapter 16, Article 3.
11   Ibid., Article 4.

Should there be any disagreement between the spouses then either party may apply to the court of voluntary jurisdiction for its assistance and the judge "after hearing the spouses *and if deemed opportune any of the children above the age of fourteen years residing with the spouses*" must then seek to bring about an amicable settlement of the disagreement. (The italicised words are my own.) The commission suggested that "any of the children of the marriage" which the court deemed "proper" should be heard by the court with the guiding principle being "the unity of the family and of family life". This latter idea has been retained by the legislator in establishing the basis for the solution given by the judge.

In the case of the spouses failing to reach an amicable settlement, and where "the disagreement relates to the establishment or change of the matrimonial home or to other matters of fundamental importance"[12] the spouses may together expressly request the presiding judge to determine the matter himself" by providing the solution which he deems most suitable in the interest of the family and family life".[13] Where this choice has been made, no appeal is possible from the judge's decision.[14]

IV PERSONAL SEPARATION

Malta is one of the few remaining countries in the world where it is not possible to terminate marriage by divorce obtained through its own Courts. It is acceptable for a foreign divorce decree from a competent court to be recognised by the Maltese Courts and in this way it is possible for Maltese nationals to establish their domicile in a country which recognises divorce, sue for divorce in that country and then return to Malta and have the judgment registered there. The lobby in favour of introducing divorce in Malta is ever present, but traditional views regarding the unity of the family at all costs and the predominant Catholic tradition of the Island make its introduction a highly controversial step.

Marriage is therefore – as in other countries – assumed to be a lifelong contract which is terminated by death. It is possible to request personal separation before the competent civil court whereby "the obligation of

---

12   Ibid., Article 6A(2).
13   Ibid., Article 6A.
14   Ibid., Article 6A(3).

cohabitation of the spouses shall cease for all civil effects".[15] Other obligations are therefore assumed to be still operative so that the duty to provide support and to maintain fidelity does not cease once separation is pronounced. The fact that the latter obligation, in particular, is often blatantly flouted has not been reflected in the 1993 amendments, presumably in the continued effort to ensure "the unity and stability of the family".[16]

Separation is possible as the result of litigation or, increasingly these days, "subject to the authority of the court, ... effected by mutual consent of the spouses, by means of a public deed". In both instances, the spouse and/or spouses must first request leave from the Court of Voluntary Jurisdiction to proceed with the separation and it is only when the court feels that all hope of a reconciliation is gone that such permission is granted. In practical – and legal – terms, however, the courts never withhold their permission to proceed to separation although the Judge in the Court of Voluntary Jurisdiction has the weighty responsibility of trying to effect a reconciliation of sorts.[17]

It is a moot point whether such responsibility should be laid at the door of a court at all. Many practitioners in this field today feel that the advent of a family court in the true sense of the word, where it is possible to have relevant back-up services for spouses with marital problems, is long overdue. With all the good will in the world, it is unreasonable to expect a judge, with purely legal training and dealing with a lengthy list of petitioners, to be able to effect a reconciliation in a matter of minutes between parties who have been wrangling over their matrimonial dispute for weeks or months and, sometimes, years.

Furthermore, to continue to call it a Court of Voluntary Jurisdiction is decidedly a misnomer since the 1983 amendments to the Code of Organisation and Civil Procedure rendered this court responsible for the determining of a provisional maintenance allowance pendente lite subject to the opposition of the other spouse whom it should hear before reaching a prima facie decision.

The Commission for the Advancement of Women is entrusted with the drawing up of amendments to set up a family court and the issue regarding the validity of the double hurdle through Civil Court, Second Hall (the Court

---

15   Ibid., Article 35(1).
16   Ibid., Article 2(1).
17   Ibid., Article 37.

of Voluntary Jurisdiction) and Civil Court, First Hall (Family) must certainly have come up for discussion. Similarly, the role of the judge in matters relating to the family and issues central to the treatment of children, which will be discussed further on, must also have provided much food for thought – at least, one hopes so. Separation may be requested on the grounds of:

1   Adultery;[18]
2   Excesses, cruelty, threats or grievous injury on the part of the other against the plaintiff, or against any of his or her children;[19]
3   Desertion for two years or more;[20]
4   Irretrievable breakdown of marriage.

Since 1981, a fresh ground was added whereby spouses may plead that they "cannot reasonably be expected to live together as the marriage has irretrievably broken down".[21] This ground may only be raised, however, where the spouses have been married at least four years. Prior to the introduction of this ground, separation was only possible where fault could be attributed to one or both of the parties. The importance of this lay in the apportioning of the community of acquests subsequent to the separation, to the allocation of maintenance and even to the care and custody of children.

The situation prior to 1993 was that where the spouse at fault was the husband and he was the sole breadwinner he forfeited, amongst other things, the right "to compel, under any circumstance, the other spouse to supply maintenance to him by virtue of the obligations arising from marriage"[22] and "any right which he [might] have to one moiety of the acquests which [might] have been made during the marriage by the industry chiefly of the other spouse".[23]

In those cases where the husband was the sole breadwinner, he was clearly, therefore, in a no-lose situation. The law even went so far as to state that "where it [was] the wife who gave cause to the separation ... she [should] also forfeit her right of dower ... and ... it [should] be lawful for the husband to retain, during the wife's lifetime, the usufruct of the

---

18   Ibid., Article 38.
19   Ibid., Article 40.
20   Ibid., Article 41.
21   Ibid., Article 40.
22   Ibid., Article 48(1)(d) (pre 1993).
23   Ibid., Article 48(1)(c) (pre 1993).

dowry".[24] Where the husband was at fault, the wife was entitled to the return of her dowry.

In an effort to balance this inequity, the amendments have set a date following which a new penalty will begin to run as follows: "any right which he or she may have to one moiety of the acquests which may have been made by the industry chiefly of the other spouse after a date to be established by the court as corresponding to the date when the spouse is to be considered as having given sufficient cause to the separation". But more important, (my italics): "*in order to determine whether an acquest has been made by the industry chiefly of one party, regard shall be had to the contributions in any form of both spouses....*".[25]

It remains to be seen how the courts interpret this section and what monetary value is placed on the contribution of the housewife and mother in reaching an acceptable conclusion in a case where it is brought into issue. As yet, there is no case law to clarify the point.

V   MAINTENANCE

Important variations have been made to deal fairly with the sexes with respect to practical issues arising pendente lite. It is now an obligation on both spouses to supply maintenance during the pendency of the action of separation since now either spouse, whether plaintiff or defendant, may demand a maintenance allowance "in proportion to his or her needs and the means of the other spouse and taking into account also all other circumstances of the spouses".[26] Prior to 1993 it was the responsibility of the husband to provide maintenance to his wife although she was bound to live in the place appointed by the husband in order to receive such allowance and the wife was expected to maintain her family only where the husband was unable to do so.

Once the separation is pronounced, maintenance may now be awarded as a lump sum "which the court deems sufficient in order to make the spouse independent or less dependent of the other spouse, as the case may be". The court shall even "among the circumstances, consider the possibility of the

---

24   Ibid., Article 49(1).
25   Ibid., Article 48(1)(c).
26   Ibid., Article 54(2).

person to whom maintenance is due, of receiving training or retraining in a profession, art, trade or other activity or to commence or continue an activity, which generates an income, and order the lump sum for that purpose".[27] These are innovative ideas reflected in the growing demand for women to assume their economic independence. It is refreshing to note that the legislator has taken the plunge in opening the door to such an equalising process.

The modalities of payment may be determined by the court so that a lump sum may be payable in instalments or the assignment of property may be made whether in full ownership in usufruct, use or habitation. The aim is clearly to ensure that both spouses are given every opportunity to achieve as great a degree of independence on separation as is possible. Although this bodes well for the recognition of equity between men and women, it surely begs the question whether it augurs the introduction of a more definitive means of termination of marriage.

VI MATRIMONIAL HOME

The brightest innovation relates to the allocation of the matrimonial home. Previously, the wife and children more often than not left the matrimonial home in search of shelter where the husband was violent towards them. Or the wife might introduce her adulterous partner into the matrimonial home and refuse to permit her husband to enter. There are legal remedies enforceable through the execution of warrants to provide a just solution to these problems, but the 1993 amendments now give a truly expeditious means of resolving this issue. Section 46:

"During the pendency of the action for separation, either spouse, whether plaintiff or defendant, may leave the matrimonial home and may, whether or not he or she has left the matrimonial home, demand that the court shall determine who of the spouses if any shall reside in the matrimonial home during the pendency of such action."

On pronouncement of the judgement of separation, the court, if asked to do so by either of the spouses, shall decide according to the circumstances

---

27   Ibid., Article 54(4).

whether any one of the parties shall be entitled to reside in the matrimonial home.

VII CHILDREN

The amendments to the civil code necessarily also brought about changes in the legal responsibility attributed to parents committed to the upbringing of children. A new section states:

> "Marriage imposes on both spouses the obligation to look after, maintain, instruct and educate the children of the marriage taking into account the abilities, natural inclinations and aspirations of the children."[28]

Until the 1993 amendments, the institute governing the care of children fell under the title "Of Paternal Authority". It is tempting to add: need one say more? A child was "subject to the authority of his parents" but this authority was exercised by the father.[29] The father was the representative of his children, born or to be born, in all civil matters and his was the role of administrator.

"A child shall obey his father in all that is permitted by law"[30] has now been substituted with "A child shall be subject to the authority of his parents in all that is permitted by law" and wherever the word "father" was indicated this has been substituted by "parents" in order to respect the concept of equality between the sexes in the realm of parenting as well as in other areas. However whilst this is certainly a step in the right direction, little or no attention has been paid to the rights of the child within this context.

Suffice it to say that in the case of "disagreement between the parents on matters of particular importance, either parent may apply to the court of voluntary jurisdiction indicating those directions which he or she considers appropriate in the circumstances".[31] Hopefully the forthcoming Children Act will ensure that these rights are introduced where necessary, then ade-

---

28   Ibid., Article 3B.
29   Ibid., Article 131 (pre 1993).
30   Ibid., Article 131.
31   Ibid., Article 131(3).

quately safeguarded and respected from the viewpoint of the child through child-centred legislation.

Where the child has reached the age of fourteen years, the Court shall also hear the child before making "those suggestions which it deems in the interests of the child and the unity of the family".[32] The overriding concept throughout the Civil Code is, however, embodied within Section 149 whereby:

> "Notwithstanding any other provision of this Code, the court may, upon good cause being shown, give such directions as regards the person or the property of a minor as it may deem appropriate in the best interests of the child."

Other legislation relating to the care of children is provided under the Children and Young Persons (Care Orders) Act and there are the obvious references within the Education Act, the Juvenile Court Act and other laws which directly or indirectly affect the welfare of the child. In the forthcoming Children Act it is hoped to group all legislation referring to children in one code and to ensure that institutions such as fostering which are not yet provided for under Maltese Law receive due attention.

The days are now gone when a mother would take her child to the public library and be unable to place her signature to guarantee the care of the books taken out on loan. Following the 1993 amendments both parents are now equally responsible for their children's actions and the situations which reflected a bygone era handed down from Roman times are happily resolved within the context of the twentieth century.

VII DOWER AND DOWRY

Gone also are the institutions of dower and dowry, the latter forming a salient part of our country's culture and tradition. The Commission for the Advancement of Women felt that the institution discriminated in favour of women in that it was only the female who had the right to dowry and that men should also have this right if there was to be parity, failing which the institution should be scrapped altogether. Section 26 used to read:

---

32 Ibid., Article 131(4).

"1. A son has no claim against his parents to compel them to make to him any provision in contemplation of marriage or for any other cause.

2.   A daughter, however, if not possessed of sufficient property of her own, has, on the occasion of her marriage, a claim for the settlement of a dowry, against her father, or in subsidium against her mother, or her paternal grandfather, or, lastly, her maternal grandfather."

It is very true that there are practically no young women left today in Malta who do not take up gainful employment on leaving school, whether at 16 when compulsory school age ends, or later after receiving further education at college or university. The idea behind the giving of dowry was to ensure that women received some form of monetary asset when they entered into marriage and this was particularly relevant in the case of those women who had no financial assets of their own because the idea of their going out to work was considered unacceptable. This was the case in many families, particularly until the Second World War, after which women started making their way into the market place more frequently, at least until they married, thereby earning money of their own.

The practice, however, continued to prevail that girls be given a dowry over and above this amount although its value varied according to the means of the family and the social background from which they came. Although the institution has recently been abolished, so far it would seem that the practice is still with us and is now taking the form of donation. It will be interesting to see what social impact this kind of legal amendment could have on our people.

IX CUSTODY ISSUES

In fact the changes ensuing from the connection between law and society can already be observed to some extent in the context of the amendments to the civil code regarding care and custody of children both pendente lite and following judgement in a separation case.

Whereas prior to 1993 the court was required to place the children "in the custody of the spouse on the demand of whom the separation shall have been pronounced", unless alternative placement was shown to be in the "better welfare of the children"[33] the court is now expected "to direct to which of the spouses custody of the children shall be entrusted".[34] At the end of the day, the effect was identical. However the working of the law now reflects the situation whereby fault attributable within the separation proceedings, referred to above, does not extend also to the care and custody of children.

Two fresh subsections have been added. One whereby the court may also consider it in the best interests of the child to direct that he or she be placed in the custody of third parties or in alternative forms of care and the other in empowering the court to determine that "one or both of the parents shall be deprived wholly or in part of the rights of parental authority".[35]

In the context of a country which, as yet, does not permit legal representation of children by an independent party and where the child is considered under the authority of his parents, this is indeed a serious step forward in the acknowledgement of rights for children, although the giver of these rights is restricted to the person of the judge within this particular setting.

Where the separation is concluded amicably through a personal separation by mutual consent concluded through a public deed or where any agreement has been reached between the spouses with respect to the custody of the children, either spouse or "any relative of either of the spouses" may seek its annulment where "the interests of the children so require".[36] At no stage of the amendments was any step taken towards providing children with a voice in the assessment of such a situation let alone in giving them the right to be heard in the variance of an arrangement directed primarily to their interests. Probably, as the matter was not a gender issue, it was simply not addressed.

The lobby for men's rights and for acknowledgement of the rights of fathers in the care and custody of their children has been the subject of considerable polemic in Malta. Whereas the law formerly gave the rights and responsibilities over children to their father, in practice, the courts tended to give the day to day care to the mother. Many men caught up in separation cases contesting custody therefore felt that they were being discriminated against on the grounds of sex and have vociferously campaigned to eliminate

---

33 Ibid., Article 56(1) (pre 1993).
34 Ibid., Article 56(1).
35 Ibid., Article 56(2) and (5).
36 Ibid., Article 61(1).

the tendency to award the custody, particularly of young children, automatically to the mother.

In the white paper produced by the Commission for the Advancement of Women, the suggestion was made that joint custody be introduced.[37] However this proposal never made it into the final legislation and the child is still sent off to one parent or the other with access being awarded to the other party. In a country as small as Malta, where the greater number of parents do try their utmost to resolve their differences in the best interests of their children, it is surprising that this suggestion was not acted upon. True, the situation is far clearer in the context of a sole parent having custody but it is surely questionable whether this is always in the best interests of the child.

X   QUO VADIS?

The 1993 amendments have resolved many problems between the sexes which were gender based ab initio. The greater part of them reflect the reality of Maltese society today. There are, however, a number which are providing for the future and legislating for an eventuality is not an easy talk. It can be met with opposition and discontent and can induce disrespect for the law. It is true that equality between the sexes is a truth which needs to be acknowledged and protected by the law. It is also true that such equality has a social dimension as well as a legal one and it is sincerely hoped that the two will catch up with each other in all aspects so that their amalgamation will produce receptive ground for the introduction of legislation directed to the benefit of the child from a child-centred basis.

As I write, a fresh piece of legislation has just been enacted although it has not yet come into force. It provides for the annulment of religious marriages through an ecclesiastical tribunal rather than through the civil courts. Any marriage celebrated in the Catholic church (and Malta is predominantly Roman Catholic) will now be subject to the Metropolitan Tribunal if one of the spouses should choose to institute proceedings there. The judgement passed by the tribunal would then be entered into the civil courts and considered also to produce civil effects.

---

37   *Department of Information*, ibid., page 27 in Article 56(1).

As one can imagine, this has brought about a violent reaction from many groups who either consider that the church should not have any vires in this matter, or who feel that the inquisitorial method used before the tribunal might prejudice the right of audi alteram partem et cetera. A case has been brought before the Constitutional Court in a popular action permitted under the Constitution of Malta to abrogate this legislation. Only time will tell the outcome.

In the meanwhile CEDAW is being observed, the unity of the family respected and life goes on.

THE NETHERLANDS

AN IDENTITY CRISIS – THE OUTER LIMITS OF EUTHANASIA, THE ABOLITION OF CHIVALRY AND OTHER ADVENTUROUS PROVISIONS

Caroline Forder[*]

I LEGISLATION

A New family law procedure

A new procedure for family law cases has been introduced,[1] which links to the new divorce procedure in force since January 1, 1993,[2] in order to assimilate family law procedure to the procedure applicable in general civil law cases: the written application procedure (*verzoekschriftprocedure*). The Act also departs from the previous rule that for differing family law actions different procedures had to be followed. A special feature of the Act is the new right of the parent involved in proceedings for the suspension or termination of parental rights to request the court to hear expert evidence. The court must honour the request whenever the expert evidence pertains to the decision and the appointment of an expert witness is not contrary to the child's interests.

B Maintenance subject to a cut-off date

Maintenance for an ex-spouse need only be paid for twelve years from the date of divorce, in the case of divorces decreed after July 1, 1994. The period can be extended by the court, on the application of the recipient of maintenance, where termination of maintenance would be manifestly unreasonable. Persons divorced before July 1, 1994 are subject to transitional provisions; maintenance is payable for fifteen years from the date of divorce. This means that where maintenance has already been paid for fifteen years,

---

*   Faculteit der Rechtsgeleerdheid, Rijksuniversiteit Limburg, Maastricht.
1   Wet van 7 July 1994, Staatsblad 1994, 570; (implementation instrument 14 October 1994, Staatsblad 1994, 774); in force on 1 April 1995 (Implementation instrument 14 October 1994, Staatsblad 1994, 774).
2   Wet van 11 June 1992, Staatsblad 1992, 286.

A. Bainham (ed.), The International Survey of Family Law 1994, 345–363.

the liable spouse can apply forthwith to the court to terminate maintenance. The court will do so unless this would be very unfair to the recipient spouse. Relevant factors in the court's decision are: age of the recipient, whether there are children, the length of the marriage and any entitlement of the recipient of maintenance to the pension rights of the liable spouse.[3] The law on the settlement of pension rights was regulated in the Settlement of Pension Rights on Divorce Act 1994.[4]

See item II.D below for case law developments.

C Legal position of older people

The court may appoint, on the application of the persons specified, a mentor to act for an older person who, by reason of mental or physical condition, is temporarily or permanently hindered from taking care of his or her non-property interests. When choosing the mentor, the court must follow the expressed wishes of the person whose interests are to be protected, unless there are persuasive reasons to the contrary. The mentor acts for the older person in questions of care, nursing, treatment and supervision. The mentor is obliged to involve the older person in the decision-making as far as possible and to stimulate his or her independence. In other matters the mentor must watch over the older person's interests and give advice.[5]

The possibility of appointing a mentor is a less interventionist alternative to the existing power to order "*curatele*", which has been perceived to be overprotective, at least in certain cases. In the latter type of order the curator has a sort of guardianship in respect of the older person, who loses all contractual and dispository capacity and even voting rights.

---

3   Wetten van 28 April 1994, (Staatsblad 1994, 324, 325) came into force on 1 July 1994 (implementation instrument 19 May 1994, Staatsblad 1994, 365).
4   Wet verevening pensioenrechten bij scheiding, 28 April 1994 (Staatsblad 1994, 342) in force 1 May 1995 (Implementation instrument 9 August 1994, Staatsblad 1994, 615).
5   Wet van 29 September 1994, Staatsblad 1994, 757; came into force on 1 January 1995 (implementation instrument 28 October 1994, Staatsblad 1994, 779).

D Compulsory reception into psychiatric care

The Reception into Psychiatric Hospitals Act 1994[6] replaces the Insane Persons Act 1884, significantly improving the position of psychiatric patients. The Act provides for compulsory admission where the person is a danger to himself or to others, which danger can only be averted by compulsory admission. The rights of the compulsorily admitted patient, once inside the hospital, are laid down in the Act. Each patient has the right to a treatment plan (which the responsible physician must discuss with the patient), the right to correspond by post or telephone (which may only be restricted in prescribed circumstances), and an unlimited right to inspect his or her own medical files.

It is now possible to request transfer to another institution; there is unrestricted access to advisors and the Mental Health Inspector. The hospital must appoint an officer who is specifically concerned with the interests of patients, and there is a new complaints procedure. (The complaints procedure will also apply to patients voluntarily admitted, pending enactment of other provisions.) The hospital has a duty to take account of the views of a child aged twelve to eighteen years who is subject to involuntary admission; such minors exceptionally acquire certain procedural rights. For the voluntary admission of a patient under twelve years of age, the consent of the parent(s) alone is required. For the admission of a child aged twelve to sixteen the consents of the parent(s) and the child are required. The admission in respect of a child sixteen or over requires only the child's consent.[7] In the category aged twelve to sixteen difficult questions will arise where the parents and child do not agree. The government has said that the crucial question for the resolution of such conflicts is whether the child is capable of appreciating the situation and forming his own judgment. Thus the test comes close to that used by the English House of Lords in *Gillick v West Norfolk and Wisbech Area Health Authority*[8] and is a welcome improvement on the decision of the European Court for the Protection of Human Rights in

6   Wet bijzondere opneming in psychiatrische ziekenhuizen (BOPZ) came into force 17 January 1994, (implementation instrument 21 December 1993, Staatsblad 1993, 755).

7   Van der Linden, "Bijzondere opneming van minderjargien in psychiatrische ziekenhuizen" *Tijdschrift voor familie- en jeugdrecht* 16 januari 1994 at 9-15.

8   [1985] 3 All E.R. 402.

Nielsen v Denmark.[9] However, one can feel concern for the child under the age of twelve who is capable of appreciating the matters relevant to the decision, but who need not even be asked.

The Inspectorate for Mental Health acquires a new set of tasks under the Act; namely, "to safeguard the health interests of all patients whose mental faculties are disturbed in questions of: supervision of compulsory admission, the deployment of any kind of restraint and placement in isolation".

For handicapped and psycho-geriatric patients capable of understanding the admissions procedure the Act brings safeguards as to admission and confers rights whilst in the institution. There is the possibility to object to compulsory admission. Those incapable of giving a valid consent to admission will have their cases decided by an admissions committee. Within nursing homes and houses for the mentally handicapped all treatment must be registered and is subject to supervision by the Inspectorate for Mental Health.

E   Sham marriages

The Sham Marriages Act[10] is an attempt to combat sham marriages. A foreigner intending to marry a Dutch Citizen is required to have a right of residence in the Netherlands or evidence that s/he has applied for entry to the Netherlands or is not intending to reside in the Netherlands. Upon the application of the Minister a marriage can be declared null and void as a sham transaction and incompatible with Dutch *ordre publique* if the intention of the spouses, or one of them, "was not directed to fulfillment of the obligations flowing from marriage, but rather with the acquisition of entry to the Netherlands".

---

9   Judgment 28 November 1988, Series A no. 144.
10 Wet van 2 June 1994, Staatsblad 1994, 405, (date of coming into force to be determined by statutory instrument).

F   Euthanasia

In 1993 Professor Rood-de Boer reported that the Disposal of the Dead Act
had come into force, but that there had been no new legislation on euthanasia
because of disagreement between political parties. She reported that a practice had developed by which physicians reported voluntarily to the public
prosecutor when they had performed an act of euthanasia.[11] On June 1,
1994 this voluntary reporting procedure became mandatory. The form of
reporting is prescribed in the statutory instrument, passed under the authority
of Article 10(1) of the Disposal of the Dead Act, which introduces this
change.[12] Euthanasia and other acts of assistance to terminate life performed
by a physician must be reported to the public prosecutor, who has to consider
whether to instigate criminal proceedings. The physician's actions remain
criminally punishable, but the public prosecutor has to decide whether the
physician's reliance upon an "emergency situation" (in which he has to
choose between the lesser of two evils in his care for the patient) provide
sufficient reason to abstain from prosecution. If the prosecutor does not
accept the argument there must be a prosecution. There will always be a
prosecution when the patient did not explicitly ask for his or her life to be
terminated.

The central issue is the patient's freely formed wish, which must be
explicitly and repeatedly expressed, to be given euthanasia. The physician must
establish that the patient has no prospect of improvement, has an untreatable
complaint, and is suffering to an unacceptable degree. The treating physician
should consult another independent physician in regard to the request. The
form which the physician has to fill in contains five sections: the history
of the illness; the request to end life (a distinction is made between patients
with a physiological illness and those suffering from mental illness); termination without express request; consultation with another doctor; and the
manner of termination.

The reform follows the recommendations of the Remmelink Committee
in 1991. The number of reports made by physicians is on the increase. In
1991, 591 cases of euthanasia were reported (1 prosecution ensued). In 1992

---

11   See Professor Rood-de Boer's report in the survey 1992-1993, at 393-394.
12   Disposal of the Dead (Amendment) Act 1993 (2 December 1993, Staatsblad 643);
     Statutory Instrument 17 December 1993, Staatsblad 1993, 688 (Implementation instrument
     29 April 1994, Staatsblad 1994, 321).

there were 1323 cases reported, (4 prosecutions ensued), in 1993, 1318 reports and 14 prosecutions. In 1994, 452 cases were reported before May 1, 1994, with 3 prosecutions ensuing, representing a slight increase on the same period in the previous year.

In the *Chabot* case, decided on June 21, 1994, the Dutch Supreme Court held that, under certain conditions, and subject to more safeguards than in cases of physical illness, euthanasia could also be performed on patients whose suffering and wish to die was due to mental illness.[13]

II DEVELOPMENTS IN CASE LAW

A   *Dutch family law is condemned by the European Court for the Protection of Human Rights*

On October 27, 1994 the European Court, following broadly the decision and reasoning of the European Commission,[14] held by seven votes to two that Dutch law infringed Article 8 ECHR by failing to give a married mother any possibility to deny that her husband was the father of a child born during marriage.[15] The Court held that a legal system must make it possible for the presumption that the husband was the father of the child to be rebutted and a legal relationship to be established between the child and the biological father. In Dutch law this takes place through the mechanism of recognition. The *Kroon* case is most notable for the extensive interpretation given to "family life" which the state is obliged to respect and goes further than the earlier European Court case law on the definition of family life.[16] An unmar-

---

13 Nederlandse Jurisprudentie 1994, 656.
14 Appl. 18535/91, report 30 March 1993. I analysed this decision and its implications in my paper "The non-marital child's relationship to the father under Dutch law and the European Convention for the Protection of Human Rights" given at the eighth conference of the International Society of Family Law, Cardiff, 1994.
15 *Kroon, Zerrouk and M'Hallem Driss v The Netherlands* Eur. Court H.R. judgment 27 October 1994, Series A no. 297-C.
16 I.e. *Marckx v Belgium*, Eur. Court H.R. judgment 13 June 1979, Series A no. 31; *Johnston v Ireland* Eur. Court H. R. judgment 28 December 1986, Series A no. 112; *Abdulaziz, Balkandali and Cabales v United Kingdom*, Eur. Court H.R. judgment 28 May 1985, Series A no. 94; *Berrehab v The Netherlands* Eur. Court H. R. judgment 21 June 1988, Series A no. 138; *Keegan v Ireland* Eur. Court H. R. judgment 26 May 1994, Series A no. 291.

ried couple, who do not and never have lived together, and who deliberately choose not to marry nevertheless have a relationship qualifying as "family life" entitling them to the protection of Article 8 ECHR. It was enough for the Court that Kroon and Zerrouk's relationship was long-standing and that they had four children together.

Just to show that direct applicability of the European Convention does not, unfortunately, always safeguard human rights as well as it might, the Dutch Supreme Court has driven a coach-and-four through the European Court's ruling in *Kroon*. On November 4, 1994, only *one week* after the European Court's ruling in *Kroon*, Budike and Watson, a couple in a situation indistinguishable from that of Kroon and Zerrouk, presented themselves to the Dutch Supreme Court, seeking the possibility to challenge the presumption of paternity in favour of the husband, who had disappeared, and for the child's relationship to the biological father to be established by recognition. Astonishingly, the Dutch Supreme Court held that it could give the parties no remedy, since to do so would usurp the function of the legislature (which is now entering the fourteenth year of preparation of legislation on the subject). The Supreme Court *refused to determine* whether Article 8 ECHR was infringed by these facts. Even if there were an infringement, said the Supreme Court non-committantly, the grant of a remedy in this case would cause it to exceed its judicial function and usurp the legislative function. In particular, were the mother to be given a right to challenge the presumption of legitimacy, this right would have to be circumscribed by restrictions to protect the rights of the child, as the government's most recent bill purported to do.[17] As Jan de Boer remarks in his note under the decision,[18] the Supreme Court's refusal to grant a remedy to Budike and Watson, who had rights protected by the ECHR which must be recognised by every conceivable system which the legislator might introduce, is unconvincing. The Dutch legislator is as much bound by the European Court's decision in *Kroon* as is the Dutch Supreme Court. It seems inevitable that there will be another application to the European Court...

---

17 Rechtspraak van de Week 1994, 226.
18 Nederlandse Jurisprudentie 1995, forthcoming.

B   *Some other problems with recognition*

The recognition system causes very many problems in Dutch family law, frequently providing a hurdle to the legal establishment of de facto relationships. Polman, whilst he was married to Anneliesje Baams, fathered a child, Nadia, by Gerritje Langelaar. Polman attempted to recognise Nadia, but the Registrar, applying Article 224(1) Book 1 Dutch Civil Code which prohibits recognition by married men, refused the recognition. Polman commenced proceedings but died before there was any outcome. The refusal to allow recognition was alleged to violate Article 8 ECHR (failure to respect the family life of Polman and Nadia). The President of the Rechtbank Utrecht held, on June 23 1994, that recognition must be allowed.[19] He took account of the fact that Polman was Nadia's guardian, that he visited her three times a week, that Nadia had a good contact with Polman's two marital children, and that Polman's lawful wife was in agreement with the recognition, as was Nadia's mother.

Under Article 224(1) Book 1 Dutch Civil Code it is not possible for a man to recognise a child without the mother's consent. Without recognition the father cannot apply for custody of the child. On April 8, 1988 the Dutch Supreme Court held that Article 8 ECHR required that the mother's consent could be substituted with that of the court if her refusal to consent was motivated by "an interest not deserving of any respect whatsoever". In that case the mother was not living with the child.[20] In subsequent case law the Supreme Court has emphasised that in the usual case, when the mother and child are living together, the mother's consent will not be substituted.[21] But in a case decided by the Dutch Supreme Court on October 28, 1994 the mother's consent was substituted.[22] The parties had been married and had two children during the marriage. There were two children born during a period of cohabitation after the marriage was dissolved. The father had recognised one of these children, but the mother withheld her consent to recognition in respect of the other child, S. S was thus the only one of four siblings not to have a legal filiation link with the father. The children, although under the custody of the mother, had been placed with foster

---

19   Kort Geding 1994, 298.
20   Dutch Supreme Court 8 April 1988, Nederlandse Jurisprudentie 1989, 170.
21   Dutch Supreme Court 18 May 1990, Nederlandse Jurisprudentie 1991, 374-375.
22   Nederlandse Jurisprudentie 1995, 221.

parents under a supervision order. The father visited them regularly and wished to obtain custody in respect of the children. However, his inability to recognise S was an absolute barrier to obtaining custody of S. On the mother's own admission, the mother's only reason for refusing to consent to recognition was to prevent the father establishing a legal relationship with the children. I have no doubt that the decision on the facts is the right one. But the Supreme Court's reasoning is in my view unsatisfactory. The right result – that the father was able to recognise the child – could have been achieved by applying the ruling of April 8, 1988: the mother's refusal to consent to recognition was motivated by an interest not deserving of any respect whatsoever. But the Supreme Court applied another test. It said that the test just mentioned only applied to the "usual" situation in which the mother was living with the children and bringing them up.

In the "unusual situation" where, as in the case before the Supreme Court, the children are subject to a supervision order and are living with foster parents, another test, which gives less weight to the mother's interests, should apply. Namely, the court should ask whether "the mother, taking into account the disproportionality between the father's interests in recognition and the mother's conflicting interest – always having regard to the child's interests – could not reasonably have refused consent to recognition".[23]

This development is unsatisfactory for a number of reasons. First, the rule concerning substitution of the mother's consent, which was reasonably clear, has become unnecessarily complicated. This extra rule was certainly not necessary to dispose of the case in hand. Second, the courts now have to distinguish between "usual" and "unusual" situations. Borderline cases are inevitable. What, for example, is the position when the child is subject to a supervision order but still living with the mother? Third, and much more seriously, the court's attention is now diverted from the essential issue. The essence is not whether the situation is usual or unusual, but should be whether the mother, in taking her decision, has the interests of the child at heart or not. This diversion, if followed, leads to judicial time-wasting, forced reasoning and possibly an incorrect balance in the Article 8 ECHR rights concerned in future cases.

---

23   The Supreme Court relied upon an earlier decision, Dutch Supreme Court 20 December 1991, Nederlandse Jurisprudentie 1992, 598.

C An application of the Marckx case

On April 15, 1994 the Dutch Supreme Court applied the European Court
of Human Rights' decision in *Marckx*[24] to facts involving elements of
private international law. The mother, Vera, gave birth to the child Gaiety
Parinah Braga, in Brazil on March 11, 1991. The mother's aunt, Joana Braga
dos Santos, registered the birth on April 16, 1991, falsely declaring herself
to be the child's mother. In 1990 the aunt had informed the Dutch foster
parents, Mr and Mrs Mooijman, about the child which her neice was then
carrying and for which the neice would not be in a position to provide. Joana
agreed to bring the child to the Mooijmans in the Netherlands. The precise
content of the agreement concerning the character and duration of the child's
residence with the foster parents was disputed. The aunt – Joana – arrived
in the Netherlands on May 23, 1991 with the child, who in the Netherlands
rejoiced in the name Amber, and handed her to Mr and Mrs Mooijmans.
Amber has lived with them until the date of the present action. And so things
might have remained, but for the arrival of the mother, Vera, in the Netherlands in July 1992, and the commencement of proceedings by her with a
view to obtaining custody of Amber. Vera underwent scientific tests which
established with a high degree of probability that she was Amber's mother.
In October 1992 the court granted Vera visiting rights in respect of Amber.
International Social Services investigated Vera's social circumstances in
Brazil to establish whether she was fit to have custody of Amber. In inter-
locutory proceedings Vera requested the court to order the foster parents
to hand Amber to her, pending resolution of the custody proceedings.

At first instance the president of the *Rechtbank* ordered the foster parents
to return Amber to her mother. This decision was reversed by the
Gerechtshof, on the grounds that Vera was unable to prove that she had
parental rights in respect of Amber according to Brazilian law or that she
would obtain such rights within the forseeable future. Brazilian law, being
the law of the mother's nationality, was the *lex causae* according to normal
rules of Dutch private international law. The correction of the false
registration in the Brazilian birth register would involve proceedings of
uncertain duration and outcome. The Supreme Court disagreed. The mother
and child were both resident in the Netherlands and therefore were both

---

24 *Marckx v Belgium* Judgment of 13 June 1979, Series A no. 31.

entitled, according to Article 1 ECHR, to the full protection of the Convention rights and freedoms. The mere fact of birth and the biological link implied "family life" between Vera and Amber, within the meaning of Article 8 ECHR. The Supreme Court said: "An essential element of this 'family life' is the right of mother and child that the child be cared for and brought up by the mother and the right to mutual enjoyment of one another's company. The obstruction of such enjoyment was an interference within the meaning of paragraph 2 of Article 8 ECHR." Moreover, the interference could not be justified by the mere fact that Brazilian law did not recognise Vera to be Amber's biological mother. The Supreme Court ordered interim custody of Amber to Vera and directed the case to be reconsidered by another *Gerechtshof* to examine whether Amber's interests required her to be brought up by Vera or by the foster parents.

D Some maintenance problems

Case law on maintenance abounds, but still I would like to mention several interesting decisions by the Dutch Supreme Court. Under Article 160 Book 1 Dutch Civil Code the obligation to pay maintenance to an ex-spouse terminates when the person entitled to maintenance remarries or cohabits with someone "as if they were married". This provision is controversial, not least because the dependent ex-spouse will acquire no new maintenance rights against the new partner with whom he or she cohabits. Moreover, there are formidable difficulties in establishing whether and when a cohabiting relationship is sufficiently like a marriage to be covered by Article 160.

Accordingly the provision is interpreted restrictively. It does not apply when the person entitled to maintenance commences a homosexual relationship.[25] It is uncertain whether the provision could be applied when the new partner is still married. The question is whether a relationship can be held to be like a marriage when an actual marriage between the parties is forbidden by law. On November 25, 1994[26] the Supreme Court held that, if a cohabitation relationship is to be covered by Article 160 it must be es-

---

25 Dutch Supreme Court 29 April 1994, Nederlandse Jurisprudentie 1994, 625.
26 Rechtspraak van de Week 1994, 253C.

tablished that: (a) the parties live together, and (b) they run a joint household, and (c) they care for each other, whether financially or in kind. There is the possibility that the provision may be scrapped insofar as it applies when the recipient of maintenance does not re-marry but merely cohabits. There is much to be said for scrapping.

Even though the spouse paying maintenance may be unable to request the court to terminate definitively the maintenance obligation under the provision just explained, he or she may be able to request, under Article 401 Book 1 Dutch Civil Code, a reduction in maintenance in the light of any decrease in the dependent spouses's needs caused by the cohabitation.[27] In this way it is possible to take account of improvements in the dependent spouse's financial circumstances; if these circumstances later take a turn for the worse, due for example to the disappearance of the new partner from the scene, there is always the possiblity of raising the level of maintenance.

In a case concerning the claim to maintenance of a famous Dutch trumpetter against his much younger wife, the *Gerechtshof* (second instance court) had held that the wife's maintenance obligations ceased on the husband's 65th birthday. The husband, who had in his time commanded a substantial income, had had full opportunity to make provision for an occupational pension for his old age. The wife argued, and the *Gerechtshof* agreed, that the fact that he had not done so could not now be laid at the wife's door. The Supreme Court disagreed. The decision had in effect the character of a final termination of the wife's maintenance obligations; the Supreme Court held that the lower court's decision did not reach the high standards which were required of decisions which have such a drastic effect. In particular too little weight had been attached to the fact that the husband was unable to turn the clock back. Although the failure to provide for his old age was a relevent consideration the *Gerechtshof* had failed to consider: (a) whether it was usual in the profession of free-lance musicians to provide for an occupational pension, and (b) whether the wife had played any part in the decision not to make such provision.

In two further cases[28] the Supreme Court considered how to resolve the problem of two concurrent maintenance claims when the liable person had insufficient resources to meet both obligations in full. The facts con-

---

27 Dutch Supreme Court 7 October 1994, Nederlandse Jurisprudentie 1995, 61.
28 Dutch Supreme Court 25 November 1994, Rechtspraak van de Week 1994, 254; 2 December 1994, Rechtspraak van de Week 1994, 260.

cerned a man who was obliged to support a child born to a former partner and who subsequently began living with a woman who had no income of her own. The Supreme Court, reversing the *Gerechtshof* on this point, held that there is no rule that maintenance responsibilities to a child have priority over maintenance responsibilities to a new partner, whether married or not. The Supreme Court said that the needs of the individuals dependent upon maintenance must be balanced against one another. The fact that the father of a child begins a new family is not of itself any reason to decrease the maintenance obligations owed to the child; however, a proof of factual circumstances may indicate that a reduction is justified. The Supreme Court mentioned that the arrival of children in the father's new family (whether or not they were his own or the partner's children) might justify a reduction, but that it would also be necessary to consider whether the father and his new partner were taking all reasonable measures to maximise resources i.e. a partner might reasonably be expected to go out to work.

E   The emergence of the right to know one's parentage: the second Valkenhorst case

This year the Dutch Supreme Court made a very important ruling on the right to know one's parentage. In 1921 the institution "*Moederheil* (literally: salvation of women)" was founded and run by a Catholic order with the object of achieving the "moral and social elevation of fallen women". The functions of *Moederheil* have since been taken over by the respondent institution, Valkenhorst. The applicants in the Valkenhorst litigation were the children of mothers who had turned to *Moederheil* for help in the 1920s and 1930s. Valkenhorst held a collection of files compiled when the mothers were admitted to the institution. The files contained details of the persons the mothers had stated were the fathers of their children. The information had been given at the request of the institution, to enable Moederheil to pursue the father with a view to recouping the costs of helping the mother and child. The applicants sought to have access to these files, as they had no other way of discovering the identity of their fathers. In the first case brought against Valkenhorst, *Roovers v Valkenhorst*, the Gerechtshof 's-

Hertogenbosch[29] held that the applicant, Maria Roovers, whose mother had died in 1944, had a right to know the identity of her father which weighed more heavily than the mother's right of privacy.[30] After this decision Valkenhorst revised its policy on disclosure of the files. Valkenhorst was prepared to disclose the identity of the mothers in all circumstances. The father's identity would be disclosed if the mother was dead and had made no objection or, if alive, she had consented. If the mother, who was living, refused to consent to disclosure, Valkenhorst would "keep mum". This new policy was the subject of the second Valkenhorst case, *Monteyne/de Ruyter/Derks v Valkenhorst*.[31] The first two instances had upheld Valkenhorst's policy as applied to the facts. The applicants appealed to the Dutch Supreme Court. The Dutch Supreme Court reversed the lower court's rulings and quashed the decisions.

First, the Supreme Court held that there was a right to know one's parentage in Dutch law. The court ruled that basic rights such as respect for private life (Article 8 ECHR), freedom of thought and conscience and religion and freedom of expression are all aspects of a more general underlying freedom of personality.[32] This implicit freedom of personality includes, according to the Supreme Court, the right to know the identity of one's parents. The court acknowledged that the right is recognised in Article 7 of the United Nations Convention on the Rights of the Child.[33]

---

29 The Gerechtshof 's-Hertogenbosch is a court of second instance; appeal lies to the Supreme Court.

30 Gerechtshof 's-Hertogenbosch, 18 September 1991, Nederlandse Jurisprudentie 1991, 796 (noted L.F.M. Verhey NJCM-Bulletin (1992) 17-2, at 156-161 and Van Vliet, Nemesis, 1992-3, at 9); appeal from the Arrondissements Rechtbank te Breda, 20 June 1989, Nederlandse Jurisprudentie 1989, 726, noted Tijdschrift voor Familie- en Jeugdrecht 1989, 7, at 168, P. Vlaardingerbroek. This case is discussed in my article: "Constitutional principle and the Establishment of the Legal relationship between the Child and the Non-Marital Father: A Study of Germany, the Netherlands and England" (1993) International Journal of Law and the Family, at 71-73.

31 Gerechtshof 's-Hertogenbosch, 25 November 1992, Nederlandse Jurisprudentie 1993, 211.

32 Dutch Supreme Court 15 April 1994, Nederlandse Jurisprudentie 1994, 608, o.w. 3.2. noot Hammerstein-Schoonderwoord.

33 The child shall be registered immediately after birth and shall have the right from birth to a name, the right to acquire a nationality and, as far as possible, the right to know and be cared for by his or her parents. The Convention was ratified by the Netherlands on December 21, 1994 (see Part III below).

According to Heringa[34] the Supreme Court allowed itself to be guided by the reference to the case law of the German Federal Constitutional Court[35] by Advocaat-General Koopmans in his advice to the Supreme Court. The likeness between the phrasing of the Dutch Supreme Court and the Federal Constitutional Court is indeed striking. It is not the first time that the Dutch Supreme Court has "borrowed" from the Federal Constitutional Court's doctrine.

Second, the Supreme Court held that the right of personality of the child was not absolute; the right had to be weighed against other countervailing rights. In the Supreme Court's view the lower court had made two mistakes in weighing up the three countervailing interests. The three interests are: the "child's" interest in knowing his or her origins, the mother's right of privacy, and a "social function" interest arising from the need for Valken-horst to be able to ensure confidentiality to future clients.

The Supreme Court held, contrary to the lower court, that the "social function" interest was, in the circumstances, not applicable.[36] The lower court had said:

> "Insofar as the applicant's [De Ruyter's] contentions make a balancing of the individual interests possible, the appellant's mother's interest in privacy must, in combination with the above-mentioned social interest, and in the absence of statutory regulation, weigh heavier than the appellant's interest. The social interest includes the consideration that *to fail to respect in advance the wishes of the mother* will in general create the possibility that, in fear of such *absolute claims to information concerning parentage which are not suspectible to balance against other interests*, damage might be done to a (born or not-yet-born) child or that care might be withheld with possibly

---

34 NJCM-Bulletin 19-6 (1994), at 650 (nr. 5).
35 The cases are Federal Constitutional Court, 18 January 1988 (right of a non-marital adult child to learn from her mother the identity of her father); Federal Constitutional Court 31 January 1989, Entscheidungen des Bundesverfassungsgerichts 79, 256 (conditions under which a marital child may challenge the presumption of legitimacy even when the mother is still married to the man whom the child doubts is the real father); Federal Constitutional Court, 26 April 1994, Zeitschrift für das gesamte Familienrecht 1994, 881 (the rule (§ 1598 second phrase German Civil Code) which restricts the right of the marital child to challenge the presumption of paternity later than two years after the child attains majority regardless of the applicant's knowledge of circumstances casting doubt on the identity of her real father, is unconstitutional).
36 HR 15 april 1994, NJ 1994, 608, o.w. 3.4.2.

much more damaging consequences than the lack of information about parentage."[37]

The Supreme Court did not agree. I think the Supreme Court was right. Secrecy is frequently defended with arguments about supposed consequences which have no foundation in reality. Valkenhorst should have been put to proof on the supposed consequences of making information available *sometimes* even when the mother had stated her opposition to such disclosure. It is far-fetched to assume, without evidence, that, in present-day – happily – rather tolerant social and moral conditions, women would be deterred from seeking help from an institution like Valkenhorst – let alone abandon or ill-treat the children – just because details of the father might, at some time in the future be disclosed. On different facts, for example the case of parenting by artificial donor insemination, it is in my view, possible that the "social function" interest might play a role, but the existence of this interest must, in my submission be empirically proven.

There is a mass of evidence which demonstrates that the child's interest in knowing his or her parentage is weighty and urgent.[38] But, as Koopmans says, "an interest, however great, cannot yet be regarded by definition, as a right."[39] The international law provisions, Article 8 ECHR and Article 7(1) of the UN Convention on the Rights of the Child do not provide that the right must be enforceable in all cases. In Koopmans' view the mother's right to privacy still has quite a considerable weight. The Supreme Court's approach is different. The Court held that the interest of the applicant must prevail. It gave two reasons: first, the vital character of the "child's" interest, and second, the fact that the mother is responsible (jointly with the father) for the child's existence.[40] I must confess to entertaining some doubts about the logic of the Supreme Court's reasoning; but after this case there can be no doubt about the right to know one's biological parentage will be given far more weight than the right of privacy of the parent, at least when that information is held by a third party.

---

37   Gerechtshof 's-Hertogenbosch 25 November 1992, NJ 1993, 211, o.w. 4.14.
38   See, for example, J. Masson/C. Harrison, "Mapping the Frontiers", paper given at the conference of the International Society of Family Law at Cardiff, 1994.
39   Dutch Supreme Court 15 April 1994, Nederlandse Jurisprudentie 1994, 608, A-G conclusie, nr. 6.
40   Dutch Supreme Court 15 April 1994, Nederlandse Jurisprudentie 1994, 608, o.w. 3.4.3.

III TREATIES

On December 21, 1994 the Netherlands passed an Act ratifying the United
Nations Convention on the Rights of the Child, November 20, 1989, New
York.[41]

IV LEGISLATIVE PLANS

A Registration of cohabitation

In the Annual Survey of 1992-1993 Professor Rood-De Boer mentioned
that some municipal councils had developed a practice of registering
cohabitation between persons who could not marry but who wished for some
official "seal" upon their relationship.[42] On June 8, 1994 a Bill was
presented to parliament which, if enacted, will introduce a legislative
registration procedure. Registration will be possible for persons who, by
reason of legal incapacity (being of the same sex or within the prohibited
degrees), are unable to marry. This goes against the recommendations of
the Kortmann Committee, who did not wish to confine the possibility to
those who are unable to marry each other. Under the proposal partners are
to declare to the Civil Status Registrar that they wish their relationship to
be registered. The registrar must investigate whether all requirements are
satisfied; i.e. that neither partner is married to, or has a registered relationship
with, another living person; and that both partners have reached the age of
majority.

The procedure is open to Dutch nationals and European Union nationals
lawfully resident in the Netherlands. When these conditions are not satisfied
the applicants must have been lawfully resident in the Netherlands for at
least one year immediately preceding the application. These provisions
purport to prevent sham registrations and "registration tourism".

Registration is to have the same effects as marriage vis-a-vis the public
sector (taxation and social security), unless international or Community Law
requires another result. In the private sphere registration is to have broadly
the same effects as marriage . But registration is to have no effect upon the

---

41 Wet van 24 November 1994, Staatsblad 1994, 862 (K. 22 855).
42 Loc. cit n. 11, at 394-395.

parties' relationship to any children living with one of the partners (but see the proposal in section IV. B. below).

Proposed consequent amendments to taxation and nationality law are scheduled for discussion in spring 1995.

B   *Custodianship for non-biological parents*

According to a new legislative proposal[43] it will become possible for a person, not being the biological parent, who is living with, and sharing the care for, a child, to apply for a custodianship order. The proposed Bill contemplates an applicant who has a "close personal relationship" with the child and who lives with a person who is the child's biological parent. The Bill will make it possible for these two adults to apply to the court for an order which will enable them to share custody jointly. The rights enjoyed are not to be equated with "joint custody" of divorced parents or unmarried parents; particularly when the rights of the biological parent terminate, the rights of the custodian are subordinate to and dependent upon the biological parent's rights. The Bill aims at strengthening the legal position regarding the child, of, for example, step-parents, or the lesbian or homosexual partner of the parent with custody, whilst making a clear distinction between the custody rights enjoyed by biological parents and other persons.

A custodianship order will not be able to be made if the biological parents have joint custody. Where there is a biological parent without custody, the request will only be granted if the custody order has been in force for at least three years. The biological parent without custody must be heard by the court before the court reaches a decision. If the custodianship order is made, the biological parent without custody retains rights of access and to receive information. In the event of the custodial parent's death, the custodian becomes sole custodian by operation of law. However, the non-custodial (biological) parent may apply for a variation of custody order on the grounds of a change in circumstances. Custodianship may be terminated on the application of the custodial biological parent or the custodian. Furthermore custodianship ends whenever the biological parent's right of custody

---

43   TK '1994' 1995 wetsvoorstel 23 714 (medevoogdij en gezamenlijke voogdij).

ends, whether because of a variation in custody, or because of suspension or termination of parental rights.

The same legislative proposal provides for a form of joint custody which can be ordered in respect of child being brought up by a married or unmarried couple, neither of whom is a biological parent of the child. Unlike the situation described in the paragraph above, these custodians will have an equal position in relation to the child.

This proposal is linked to a separate proposal to place joint custody held by the biological parents, whether married, divorced or unmarried, on a legislative footing.[44] The Dutch Civil Code at present excludes joint custody, but the Dutch Supreme Court has held that Article 8 ECHR requires that divorced and unmarried parents are able to share custody when they both wish to do so and the child's interests do not indicate to the contrary.[45] The custodianship proposal has been subject to some criticism. In particular Carla van Wamelen, whilst approving the general objective of affording some legal basis to the child's de facto relationships, points to a number of problems. She asks why it is considered necessary for the couple seeking custodianship to apply to court, rather than simply imposing a registration requirement. In the legislative proposal the custodianship provisions are thus equated to the position of divorced parents applying for joint custody rather than to an unmarried couple seeking joint custody. She compares the position of an unmarried heterosexual couple with a lesbian couple. In the former case a man who is not the child's biological father can nevertheless recognise the child and then acquire joint custody by a simple registration procedure. The mother's lesbian partner, by contrast, is obliged to use court proceedings. These differences are not justified by the protection of the child's interests. Van Wamelen further criticises the three year waiting period when there is another biological parent without custody; she suggests the period, if any period is really necessary, should be one year.[46]

---

44 Wetsvoorstel 23 014.
45 Dutch Supreme Court 4 May 1984, Nederlandse Jurisprudentie 1985, 510; Dutch Supreme Court (Harbinger of Spring decisions) 21 March 1986, Nederlandse Jurisprudentie 1986, 585-589.
46 *Tijdschrift voor Familie- en Jeugdrecht* 1995 afl. 1, pp. 8-11.

NEW ZEALAND

NEW ZEALAND FAMILY LAW 1994 –
MORE PROMISE THAN ACHIEVEMENT

*Bill Atkin**

I   INTRODUCTION

Two broad reflections emerge from a review of family law in New Zealand
in 1994. First, the year has been one of promise rather than achievement.
The celebration of the International Year of the Family occurred with the
expected round of conferences and public statements. While much was said
in connection with the Year, little positive action was actually taken. Some
changes to family law were however foreshadowed. Certain to be enacted
in 1995 is new legislation on domestic violence. Further on the horizon is
a revamp of the law on matrimonial property, inheritance and de facto
relationships. The ratification of the Hague Convention on inter-country
adoption is now government policy but a fuller reform of the Adoption Act
1955 still looks a long way off. Reports on the child support scheme and
on assisted human reproduction are awaiting Government reaction.

The second reflection is that family law is becoming increasingly international in its ambit. New Zealand is a sea-bound nation and travel to other
jurisdictions involves more planning and expense than in other parts of the
world. However there is a steady pattern of immigration from the Pacific
Islands, and in some instances illegal overstaying in New Zealand by people
from the Islands and elsewhere. This can raise acute problems where the
overstayer has family members including children in New Zealand. To solve
this kind of problem, the New Zealand courts have resorted to the United
Nations Convention on the Rights of the Child, which New Zealand ratified
in 1993.[1] There is also an increasing number of international child abduction
cases, most of which involve the application of the Hague Convention which
was incorporated in legislation by the Guardianship Amendment Act 1991.

---

*   Reader in Law, Victoria University of Wellington.
1   See especially the Court of Appeal decision, *Tavita v Minister of Immigration* [1994]
     2 NZLR 257.

A. Bainham (ed.), The International Survey of Family Law 1994, 365–385.

II DOMESTIC VIOLENCE

The principal legislation on domestic violence in New Zealand is the Domestic Protection Act 1982. While this Act has worked reasonably well and has led to only a small number of appeals against Family Court decisions, its scope has been regarded as too limited and its orders too inflexible. Towards the end of 1994, the Minister of Justice introduced a new Domestic Violence Bill into Parliament and it is expected that this will be passed during 1995. Two reports fed into the process of law reform. In 1993 the Department of Justice released for public consultation a report on the existing law and options for reform.[2] Secondly, a former Chief Justice, Sir Ronald Davison, was asked to investigate a tragic case where a man killed himself and his three children in circumstances where he had legitimate care of the children, the Bristol inquiry.[3] The Family Court had granted a consent order for shared custody three months earlier. In making the consent order, the court relied on the independent legal advice given to each of the parties, the support of court-appointed counsel and the report of a commissioned psychologist. The backdrop to these events were allegations that the father had been abusive towards the mother. The Davison report exonerated the Family Court of any blame:[4]

"In my opinion there was nothing whatever in the material placed before the court from which a Judge could have been alerted to the probability or even the possibility that to give the children into the custody of their father might create a situation of danger for them."

But the report was critical of the law which allowed this kind of situation to occur. Sir Ronald Davison thought that once a person had used violence against a spouse or child "then such person should be presumed (unless exceptional circumstances are shown to exist for deciding the contrary) to be unsuitable either to have custody or unsupervised access to the child until such time as such person can establish that it is safe for the child to be given

---

2   *The Domestic Protection Act 1982 A Discussion Paper* (Department of Justice, Wellington, 1993).

3   *Report of Inquiry into Family Court Proceedings Involving Christine Madeline Marion Bristol and Alan Robert Bristol* (Report to the Minister of Justice, no official publisher, undated).

4   Ibid at 34.

into his/her custody for him/her to have unsupervised access to that child".[5]
Among several recommendations made in the report to try and overcome
the Bristol type of tragedy were the following:

· If allegations of violence are made in a custody or access case, the court
  should satisfy itself whether or not the allegations are true.

· The principle of the welfare of the child should be modified to include
  a presumption that a violent parent is not a fit and proper person to have
  custody or unsupervised access.

· The court's power to make consent orders should be exercised only if
  the court is satisfied that the consent was freely given.

Whether these proposals would have saved the lives of the Bristol children
and their father is moot.[6] How practical they would be if taken literally is
also open to debate. The implication is that the Family Court judge is to
be proactive in checking to see whether there has been violence in a relationship, especially where the judge is presented with a proposal for a consent
order. But in a recent decision under the Domestic Protection Act, the Family
Court was chided by a High Court judge for doing this very kind of thing.[7]
Greig J referred to:

"...the fundamental premise that a Judge is to determine the questions and
issues on the evidence and the material before him. It is not for a Judge
to investigate the facts. He must leave the matter to counsel. Counsel and
the parties take the risk that if they fail to produce the appropriate evidence
or material the decision may go against them."

---

5   Ibid at 42.
6   Stewart analyses the recommendations and concludes that they would have made no
    difference: "Domestic Violence: the Bristol case and the Davison Report" (1994) 1
    Butterworths Family Law Journal 116. See follow-up comments at 149 and 150. See
    also Busch and Robertson, "I didn't know just how far you could fight: Contextualising
    the Bristol inquiry" (1994) 2 *Waikato LR 41* and Robertson and Busch, "Not in front
    of the children – the literature on spousal violence and its effects on children" (1994)
    1 *Butterworths Family Law Journal* 107.
7   *Wells v The Family Court* [1995] NZFLR 145, 149. The case concerned an application
    for an occupation order with respect to the apartment which a couple had lived in. The
    apartment was in fact owned by a family trust and had been tenanted since the parties'
    separation. The Family Court judge took an initiative in requiring the man to show how
    the apartment could be tenanted. This was criticised by Greig J.

This traditional notion of the role of the judge runs counter to the Davison ideas. Likewise it may be asked what resources the investigating judge would be able to call upon. At a time when government funds for legal aid and for expert reports to the Family Court are being restricted, it is hard to see another pot of gold emerging to pay for a new style of judging. One Family Court judge, speaking at an International Year of the Family conference, has suggested that the Family Court should continue to do what courts do best:[8]

> "The roles and responsibilities of parents and others working with families should not be fudged or blurred by an implied extension of the functions of the Court into areas for which it has neither the expertise nor the resources. However, there is a real danger that legislative reaction to such recommendations and the publicity surrounding them will create an expectation that the Family Court, as presently structured, serviced and resourced can never meet."

This concern about the burdens which might be placed on judges is less apparent in the legislation introduced late in 1994 into Parliament. The Domestic Violence Bill will amend provisions in the Guardianship Act 1968 relating to custody and access. First, where there is an allegation that a party has used violence against a child or the other party, the court is required to determine whether the allegation is true "on the basis of evidence presented to it by or on behalf of the parties to the proceedings".[9] This means that the court does not have an investigative role. The onus of proof is presumably on the person making the allegation and the standard of proof will be the balance of probabilities.[10] A mere allegation without some back-up evidence should therefore lead to the conclusion that the allegation is

---

8   Judge Ellis, "The Family Court as decision-making forum for families and children" in *Rights and Responsibilities* (International Year of the Family Committee, Wellington, 1995), 149-150.

9   Clause 105, which will insert a new section 16B into the Guardianship Act.

10 The decision of Smellie J in *T v T* [1994] NZFLR 586 may be noted. A finding of sexual abuse by the mother was overturned on appeal because it was not proven on the balance of probabilities, but by the same token Smellie J was not able to reach a positive conclusion that the mother had not been present during abuse. Sexual abuse claims are easy to make, hard to prove and hard to disprove. See also the Court of Appeal decisions in *M v Y* [1994] 1 NZLR 527 and *S v S* [1994] 1 NZLR 540, decided at the end of 1993.

not proved. What constitutes violence is obviously crucial. The Bill states that "violence":[11]

"(a) Means physical abuse or sexual abuse; but
(b) Does not include force lawfully used in self-defence, or by way of correction towards a child."

This definition excludes by implication emotional or psychological abuse. "Abuse" may suggest a pattern of violent behaviour rather than an isolated incident and it bears the connotation of taking improper advantage of a situation, so that something more than the mere application of force, as in the minimum criterion for battery, is necessary. On the other hand, a one-off incident may be so serious that it should surely fall within the notion of physical abuse.

A complication is that there may be cross-allegations of violence and, in some situations, mutual abuse may be apparent. Such a finding may be awkward in relation to the second major amendment to the Guardianship Act. Where violence has been proved, the court must not grant custody or unsupervised access to the violent party "unless the Court is satisfied that the child will be safe while the violent party has custody of, or, as the case may be, access to the child". The safety test will essentially be a factual question. It is not clear whether the judge is expected to embark on an independent enquiry but the judge may take nine factors into account in assessing safety: the nature and seriousness of the violence, whether the violence occurred recently, the frequency of the violence, the likelihood of further violence, the harm to the child, whether the other party considers the child will be safe and consents to the order, the child's wishes, steps taken by the violent party to prevent further violence occurring, and any other matters the court considers relevant. Where both parties have been violent, it may be possible to show that one party was provoked and reacted out of powerlessness. The safety of the child may not therefore be in issue in relation to that parent. However situations can also be envisaged where the court can grant custody to neither parent. The child may be left in a legal limbo until separate care and protection proceedings can be instituted.

---

11   In a new section 16A.

Normally in custody and access cases, the welfare of the child is the paramount consideration and the child's wishes must be taken into account. However the child's safety now appears to be an overriding requirement qualifying the wider notion of the child's welfare and wishes. The point has been graphically made by a Family Court Judge:[12]

> "...where older children have clearly expressed wishes to continue contact with a person who has had a history of violence, are we in danger of diluting the 'best interests of th child' concept by imposing society's expectation of an appropriate role model? Overriding all other considerations save violence may mean that we end up with a group of angry young people who feel abandoned by their parent because, against their wishes, there has not been any contact."

Some instances of violence will be obvious and the courts should have little difficulty in implementing the new law in these cases. Indeed they are able to do what the new law proposes already, as illustrated in *V v T*[13] where a judge cancelled an access order largely on the basis of the father's violence towards the mother. In assessing the welfare of the children, Judge Green took into account their safety, the father as a role model, the mother's fragility and the threat to the children's settled existence if access were enforced.

The Domestic Violence Bill, in addition to making changes to custody and access laws, will replace the Domestic Protection Act 1982. The court can make three main orders under the existing law, non-violence, non-molestation and occupation orders. The rules relating to occupation orders remain largely unchanged in the Bill, but the other two orders will be replaced by a new order called a protection order. The following points are noteworthy in relation to protection orders:

·   A protection order can be made only if (i) the respondent has committed an act of domestic violence or has engaged in behaviour which viewed as a whole amounts to domestic violence, and (ii) an order is "necessary for the protection of the applicant or a child of the applicant's family, or

---

12   Judge Green, "A note on privacy and access in relation to the Family Court" in *Rights and Responsibilities* (International Year of the Family Committee, Wellington, 1995), 152.

13   [1994] NZFLR 454.

both".[14] "Violence" is defined more broadly than in the amendment to the Guardianship Act. It includes not only physical and sexual abuse but also psychological abuse which is expanded to include intimidation, harassment, damage to property threats of abuse and a child's witnessing of abuse of an adult family member.[15] In assessing the "necessity for protection" test, the court is required to consider whether minor or trivial acts form a pattern of behaviour from which the parties need protection and, where the basis of the application is a threat, whether the threat is likely to be carried out. A novel provision is found in clause 13(5):

"Without limiting the matters that the Court may consider when determining whether to make a protection order, the Court must have regard to-
(a) The perception of the applicant or a child of the applicant's family, or both, of the nature and seriousness of the act or behaviour in respect of which the application is made; and
(b) The effect of that act or behaviour on the applicant or a child of the applicant's family, or both."

Thus, the court must look at the situation from the victim's point of view and this has been included largely in response to evidence that victims often feel they are not believed or listened to. However, just how the courts will give effect to the victim's point of view is unclear. The threshold tests for an order must still be met, ie proof of violence and need for protection. A court is not justified in granting an order simply because the applicant says there has been violence and says that he or she needs protection. The standard of proof is the balance of probabilities[16] and some applicants may fail to meet this standard.

· One of the criticisms levelled at the current law is that it is not available against a range of people such as an abusive son or non-cohabiting boyfriend. In future, protection orders can be sought not only against spouses but also against others with whom the applicant has a "domestic relationship". This phrase is defined to include partners (including same-sex partners), family members, people who ordinarily share the same household (although this does not include landlord/tenant and employer/employee

---

14   Clause 13.
15   Clause 3.
16   Clause 68.

relationships, which presumably ought to be dealt with under other branches of the law), and people who share "a close personal relationship".[17] The latter may cover the boyfriend/girlfriend situation but is not limited to sexual relationships.

· An application can be made by a child.[18] This is a very rare feature in New Zealand family law, which has usually limited the ability to institute family law proceedings to adults even where the interests of children are central.

· The Bill envisages the possibility that both parties may allege violence and claim the need for an order. But the court will be able to make "mutual" orders only if both parties have applied in the proper manner and each application has been determined by the court.[19]

· A protection order will normally be aimed at preventing the respondent from abusing or threatening to abuse the applicant, damaging property and intimidating and harassing. Other conditions may be incorporated into the order.[20] Contravening a protection order constitutes an offence which on the first occasion may attract up to six months' imprisonment or a fine of $5000, substantial increases on the existing maximum penalties for breaching a non-molestation order of 3 months and $500.[21]

· On making a protection order, the court must direct the respondent to attend counselling or a programme such as anger management "unless there is good reason not to do so".[22] The applicant may also ask to be directed to counselling (in which case the State will usually bear the cost)[23] but the applicant and respondent cannot be required to attend joint counselling.[24]

---

17   Clause 4.
18   Clause 8.
19   Clause 16.
20   Clauses 17 and 18.
21   Clause 32.
22   Clause 21.
23   Clause 19.
24   Clause 20.

III MATRIMONIAL PROPERTY, DE FACTO RELATIONSHIPS AND INHERITANCE

New Zealand has a mixed bag of laws dealing with property issues. Inter vivos claims involving married persons are dealt with under the Matrimonial Property Act 1976. Succession matters for widowed spouses are dealt with under the Matrimonial Property Act 1963, the Family Protection Act 1955 and the Administration Act 1969. The discrepancy between the way in which inter vivos and succession claims of spouses are handled has been recognised ever since the 1976 Act was introduced into Parliament. De facto partners have to rely by and large on the law of contract (if they have a cohabitation contract) or the law of trusts and restitution. Although the Court of Appeal has settled on a liberal standard for determining de facto cases, the law is still seriously deficient. Solicitors find it hard to give clear advice to their clients, litigation has to begin in the High Court rather than the Family Court, and it can be protracted and expensive. The wide variance in result between the married spouse and the de facto partner is seen as unfair and unjust.

The Government's position on reform has until recently been muted. A Justice Department Working Group prepared a report on reform options in 1988 but that has lain dormant ever since.[25] However, at a conference in November 1994, the Minister of Justice indicated that he was now prepared to reform the law on de facto and de iure partners and had instructed his department to work on these issues.[26] It is not certain that any new legislation will equate de iure and de facto spouses, especially given the shades of definition which can be given to the notion of "de facto relationship".[27] But some movement towards a principle of equal division which already operates in the matrimonial context is likely to apply to stable de facto relationships of long standing.

---

25 *Report of the Working Group on Matrimonial Property and Family Protection* (Department of Justice, Wellington, 1988).

26 Hon DAM Graham MP, "The Minister of Justice's opening speech" (1995) 25 *VUWLR* 3.

27 For a discussion of some of the options, see Atkin and Cull, "De facto Property – Law Equity and the Unmarried Couple" in NZLS Family Law Conference *The Family Court Ten Years On* (1991) and Atkin, "Family property law reform" (1995) 25 VUWLR 77.

The Law Commission has been undertaking a major project on succession issues.[28] The focus here has been on the rules, currently found in the Family Protection Act 1955, which enable some family members (but not including de facto survivors[29]) to apply for a share of the deceased's estate. The question here is, assuming that the spouse obtains a half share under revised matrimonial property rules, upon what basis should that spouse and other family members be entitled to provision from the estate, contrary to the testator's will? Should the sole basis for such provision be proven need or do the principles of family solidarity justify a very liberal system for spreading a person's estate around family members who feel they gained insufficient recognition in the will?

In the meantime, as we wait for concrete reform proposals on these matters from the Government, the courts continue to process a sizeable amount of litigation. The following Court of Appeal decisions are noteworthy. *Lankow v Rose*[30] involved a de facto relationship of 10 years standing. At the beginning of the relationship the man's indebtedness cancelled out his considerable assets but, with the help of the woman, by the end of the relationship his finances had prospered so that his assets totalled about $625,000 while the woman's totalled $30,000. The woman had contributed $22,000 to the cost of the house which the parties had lived in and a similar sum for the purchase of vehicles for the man. The High Court judge held that the woman was entitled to a half share in the house (the house being worth $260,000) and this was upheld on appeal. The Court of Appeal rejected the notion that there should, by analogy with matrimonial cases, be a presumption of equal sharing in *de facto* cases. This, the court thought, "ignores the fundamental difference between a legal marriage and a de facto marriage... In the case of a de facto union the claimant does not start from a presumptive half share but rather from nothing. A de facto claimant must demonstrate first a case for an interest and then what that interest should be".[31] Obviously in some cases, an equal share will be justified but it must

---

28 See Sutton, "Law Commission succession project: Communal family property?" (1995) 25 *VUWLR* 53.

29 Some de facto survivors have been able to claim against their deceased partner's estate under the Law Reform (Testamentary Promises) Act 1949 but the ground rules for such a claim are quite different from the family protection claim: see Atkin, *Living Together Without Marriage The Law in New Zealand* (Butterworths, Wellington, 1991) ch 8.

30 [1995] NZFLR 1.

31 Ibid at 20.

be made out on the basis of the extent to which the respondent has been unjustly enriched and this in turn depends on the amount of the claimant's sacrifice. Tipping J set out the following four factors which a claimant must show:[32]

1 Contributions, direct or indirect, to the property in question.
2 The expectation of an interest therein.
3 That such expectation is a reasonable one.
4 That the defendant should reasonably expect to yield the claimant an interest.

If the claimant can demonstrate each of these four points equity will regard as unconscionable the defendant's denial of the claimant's interest and will impose a constructive trust accordingly.

An important aspect of the contributions element is that "contributions in the home may qualify as contributions to the home"[33] and this was vital in an earlier Court of Appeal decision, *Nash v Nash*,[34] where the woman's claim "rested almost entirely on the provision of spousal services of housekeeping and child rearing."[35] The Court of Appeal allowed the woman a quarter share not only in the house but also in six hectares of surrounding land which formed a "lifestyle block" used by the whole family.

Lankow v Rose is to be appealed to the Privy Council, which may take a less generous view than the New Zealand Court of Appeal of the basis upon which these claims can be made. With one main exception, however, the facts may be sufficient to uphold the claim even on a more conservative test. The exception relates to an answer the woman gave during cross-examination. She was asked about her efforts on behalf of Mr Lankow and his company, which she said were done with the idea of saving the company and Mr Lankow money: "then they were not done with the idea of gaining for yourself an interest in the property?" to which the answer was "Not at all".[36] Counsel for Mr Lankow argued that this showed that Ms Rose had no expectation of receiving a share in the property. The Court of Appeal

---

32 Ibid at 19. These factors are all discernible in previous Court of Appeal decisions, especially *Gillies v Keogh* [1989] 2 NZLR 327 and *Phillips v Phillips* [1993] 3 NZLR 159.
33 Ibid at 20.
34 [1994] NZFLR 921.
35 Ibid at 925.
36 Ibid at 21.

rejected this argument, saying that it confused the concept of expectation with that of motivation and that there was other evidence to indicate that the woman expected to gain a share in the property.

The international aspects of family property law arose in *Samarawick-rema*.[37] The parties were married in Sri Lanka in 1966 and came to New Zealand in 1987, separating two years later. They had assets in New Zealand worth approximately $85,000, the main item of which was the matrimonial home. In addition, the husband owned a property in Sri Lanka which, although bought before the marriage, had been largely developed during the course of the marriage. Under New Zealand law, matrimonial property is normally divided equally. However, by section 7 the Matrimonial Property Act 1976 Act does not apply to immovable property situated overseas. No doubt moved by the potential injustice of totally ignoring the Sri Lankan property, the Family Court judge, supported on appeal in the High Court,[38] granted the wife $77,800 worth of the property in New Zealand and directed her to sign a document abandoning any claims to the Sri Lankan property to the extent of the value of the assets vested in her. The Court of Appeal held that this approach was wrong as it in effect treated the Sri Lankan property as matrimonial property which could be reflected in the division of the New Zealand property. This breached section 7 of the Act. Furthermore the renunciation of any claim to the Sri Lankan property assumed that the wife would have an equal interest in the property under Sri Lankan law:[39]

> "The claims in respect of the foreign property are to be decided by the local law, and should not be the subject of compensating adjustments in respect of the New Zealand assets to ensure that the final division of the total assets reflects a New Zealand approach."

This of course echoes conventional conflict of laws rules. But it means that a woman in the position of Mrs Samarawickrema must go to the expense and trouble of establishing her claim in the foreign jurisdiction. This will be beyond the resources of many people.

---

37   [1994] NZFLR 913.
38   [1994] NZFLR 321.
39   Ibid at 919-920.

The case of *Grace v Grace*[40] touches on matters which are of increasing importance in the development of law and policy in New Zealand. A couple separated after 37 years of marriage and seven children. The case would have automatically attracted the equal division rules of the Matrimonial Property Act 1976 but for the fact that the matrimonial home was in the husband's name and was on Maori land. By virtue of section 6, Maori land is outside the scope of the Act and is dealt with under separation legislation, Te Ture Whenua Maori Act 1993. Instead, the wife sought an order that the husband held the property on trust for both himself and the wife in equal shares, invoking principles similar to those which have been used by parties to de facto relationships. The wife was careful to seek monetary compensation rather than a vesting order in the Maori land, the latter being impossible under the 1993 Act. The husband argued that jurisdiction rested solely with the Maori Land Court under the 1993 Act, but the Court of Appeal rejected this argument. The Court saw nothing in the 1993 Act to exclude the jurisdiction of the High Court in such situations and allowed the case to proceed. Despite the cultural sensitivities at stake in this decision, any other result would have been grossly unfair to the wife, as she would almost certainly have received no share of the house or its equivalent in monetary terms.

IV ADOPTION

In May 1994, the Government introduced legislation on inter-country adoption. There were two main aspects to the proposals. The first was to empower the Director-General of Social Welfare to enter into inter-country adoption agreements with other countries. The second was to permit the Director-General to delegate the implementation of any such agreement to suitable organisations which applied for the purpose.

Several groups within the community were concerned that this legislation was to be enacted without being fully thought through and in isolation of wider reforms of adoption laws. In addition, it was argued that the Government should heed the Hague Convention on inter-country adoption and that the legislation was not entirely consistent with the Convention. In

---

40 [1994] NZFLR 961.

the light of these concerns, the Government withdrew the legislation from Parliament and decided to work towards ratification of the Hague Convention. Although the full review of adoption laws may still be some way off, revised inter-country rules may return to Parliament in the foreseeable future.

V   CHILD SUPPORT

Since it came into force in 1992, the Child Support Act 1991 has had a bad press. Unlike the Australian legislation on which the New Zealand Act was based, it applied across the board to all cases of financial support for children, even those which had been settled amicably many years previously. There are many instances of satisfactory agreements, negotiated on the basis of very different laws, being upset, to the disadvantage of one party or the other. In some instances, liable parents suddenly found themselves paying much more, while in others, custodians saw vast reductions in what they were entitled to receive. It is commonly accepted that it was a policy blunder to apply the Act retrospectively in this way.[41] There have been many other criticisms of the scheme. For instance, because it is based on taxable income, it is easy for the self-employed to pay far less than their real financial resources would allow and so, "there is a developing child support avoidance industry".[42] On the other hand, liable parents and their new families complain that the system can generate real hardship for second families, which can be a bitter pill to swallow where the custodian is well placed financially.

In 1993, a review of the Act by the Child Support Agency led to one significant change and a suggestion that another independent review of the Act was necessary. The change, brought about by legislation in 1994, was to empower the Agency itself to grant departures from the amount of child support a liable parent is obliged to pay under the statutory formula. Prior to this, departure orders could be obtained only from the Family Court, even where the application was entirely straightforward. It is now possible to avoid the expense of litigation by using the administrative departure

---

41   *Child Support Review 1994 Report of the Working Party* (1994) (commonly known as the "Trapski Report" after its Chairperson) paras 3.2, 4.4 and 7.1.

42   Ibid at 29.

procedure and appealing to the court only where that procedure produces an unsatisfactory result.

The independent review of the Act, the Trapski Report,[43] consulted widely and heard many submissions from people around the country. The Report was produced in November 1994 and awaits implementation. While the Trapski Report makes numerous recommendations, many of them are cosmetic and it is hard to see how they will assuage critics of the scheme. As time goes on and the transitional cases have fully worked themselves out, the level of discontent and the extent of litigation will doubtless lessen. There is already some evidence of this, with fewer cases reaching the courts. But this does not remove some fundamental question marks surrounding the general approach – among them, how does the scheme really advance the welfare of children, how can it avoid Maori understandings of family relationships which are based on the wider family network rather than the parent/child relationship, how can the scheme operate fairly in isolation from the other issues which arise in marriage breakdown situations, and what will be the long term effects of a scheme which has built in disincentives to settling by agreement?

The Trapski Report's main recommendations are:

· The objects of the Act should include a recognition of the welfare of the child. While this move is fine in principle, there is little in the Report's general recommendations to give it practical effect.

· The formula for calculating child support should be changed. At present the child support liability is a percentage of the amount of money left after deducting a "living allowance" for the liable parent from the liable parent's taxable income. Trapski recommends doing away with the living allowance and simply dividing a "set percentage" of the liable parent's income between all birth and adopted children, plus those stepchildren whom the liable parent proves are dependent (taking into account "the extent of that dependency"). Although the Report states that the Working Party "experimented with models in these terms and have satisfied ourselves that such a formula can work",[44] no examples of this are given and the crucial "set percentage" is left undisclosed. No consideration appears to be given to a dependent partner or new spouse (as in the living allowance at present). Extra weighting

---

43   See note 41.
44   Ibid at 25.

will be given "to recognise the additional costs of a first child" but it is not clear whether this relates to the first child in the household of the custodian or the liable parent or both. The rules on stepchildren may be complicated. How is dependency to be proven so that administrative simplicity is preserved? How will the "extent of that dependency" be taken into account without introducing complexity and scope for dispute into the scheme? Sadly, the Report is very light on detail in relation to this important recommendation.

·   At present taxable income acts as the starting point of the formula. Trapski would widen this by enabling the Child Support Agency to take into account such matters as depreciation, tax losses, developmental farming expenditure, livestock adjustments, income spreading, fringe benefits, and income received from a trust or company which is tax free in the hands of the liable parent. An "anti-avoidance" rule would be included in the Act to enable certain transactions to be void for child support purposes. These recommendations, while not likely to endear themselves to the rural sector of New Zealand, are inevitable if a fair scheme is to operate. Using taxable income penalises the ordinary wage and salary earner and lets many wealthy liable parents go with minimal obligation. But the proposals will add more complexity to the scheme and scope for dispute. The ideal of a simple formula looks more and more distant.

·   Trapski recommends that the rules on departure orders be redrafted to avoid what is described as the present "analytical maze".[45] But the few changes offered will do little to reduce the complexity of what is the main vehicle for balancing the inflexibility of the formula approach. Trapski fails to address whether the current rules are adequate to ensure that the courts, and now Child Support Agency review officers, can do justice as between the parties.

The Trapski Report considered a number of other potentially significant changes but instead opted for the status quo. Among them are the following:

·   The Report thought that there should be no "pass-on" to the custodian of a proportion of child support payments where the custodian is on a social security benefit. At present, payments are simply retained by the State.

---

45   Ibid at 48. The phrase had earlier been used by Tipping J in *Ewing v Ewing* [1993] NZFLR 849, 861.

·   Te Puni Kokiri, the Ministry of Maori Development, asked that adoptions by Maori custom be recognised in the scheme but this was rejected.

·   The Report rejected the inclusion of the custodian's income in the formula. The Working Party members recognised the perception of "inequity for liable parents in the current policy" but, ironically, thought that a change "would introduce unnecessary complexities and difficulties".[46]

·   Voluntary agreements can be easily undermined by either party's applying for a formula assessment. The Trapski Report made no recommendation to make agreements more durable and binding.

Apart from the Trapski Report, two matters about the current scheme are worthy of note. First, the rate at which child support is being collected, always a problem under previous systems, is proving encouragingly high. The current year's collection rate is 77% and the rate over all years since the scheme has been operating is 82%. As arrears are paid off, the rate for earlier years will continue to increase. Possible reasons for these results are the efficiency of the Child Support Agency, as part of the tax department, in tracking people, and the fear factor which comes from heavy penalties for failure to pay. These penalties reflect those for non-payment of income tax and can be punitive.

Secondly, the Court of Appeal has clarified some issues relating to departure orders in the case of *Lyon v Wilcox*.[47] In this case, the liable parent saw his obligations rise from $10 per week under a maintenance agreement to $156 under the formula. The child in question was born during a brief relationship, when according to the father the mother had failed to use contraception after having agreed to do so. An adoption had been agreed upon but the mother had not proceeded with this. The mother and son lived in Scotland with the mother's husband who had effectively acted as the boy's father for eight years. The liable parent had nothing to do with the boy. He had also bought a house subject to a substantial mortgage, not expecting to have to pay out large sums on child support. The mother's financial situation was better than the father's and this, coupled with his outgoings, was essentially the basis for the departure application. However, the mother's position was significantly better only when taking into account her husband's income. Under section 105 of the Child Support Act, a new spouse's income

---

46   Ibid at 43.
47   [1994] 3 NZLR 422; [1994] NZFLR 634.

is relevant only if there are "special circumstances". The Court of Appeal, in what may be seen as a rather narrow reading of the provision, held that the only circumstance which was relevant was the fact that the mother's husband had acted as the boy's father for at least eight years and that this was not "special" because step-parenting is very common. The broader context in which the husband acted as father was irrelevant. The Court of Appeal then considered the specific ground which the liable parent relied on, namely that "the income, earning capacity, property, and financial resources of either parent" rendered the level of child support unjust and inequitable.[48] On the facts, having excluded the husband's income from the calculation, the Court thought that the disparity in financial position between the parties was too small to fall within the terms of the ground. But in any event, "special circumstances" must again be shown before any of the grounds are satisfied. On another rather narrow construction of the Act, the Court held that, in relation to the ground relied upon by the liable parent, "the focus is on economic considerations and it follows that only matters of this kind are relevant to deciding what is just and equitable and what constitute special circumstances".[49] No departure order was therefore allowed.

VI ASSISTED HUMAN REPRODUCTION

New Zealand has six clinics which perform in vitro fertilisation and a small number of additional locations where donor insemination is carried out. These services are provided by a mixture of state and private clinics but all have accreditation with the Australian Reproductive Technologies Accreditation Committee. New treatments such as intracytoplasmic sperm injection (ICSI) are submitted to a national ethics committee on assisted reproductive technologies. That committee has approved ICSI in 1994 but has twice rejected applications for IVF surrogacy, ie where a woman (usually a relative or friend) will be implanted with an embryo produced by the gametes of another couple who are unable to carry a pregnancy but intend to bring up their biological child. The ethics committee's decisions are not

---

48   S 105(2)(c)(i).
49   [1994] 3 NZLR 422, 432; [1994] NZFLR 634, 645.

binding according to statute but gain their authority from the professional demand to act ethically.

New Zealand has no licensing system for operators in this area, and the only specific legislation is the Status of Children Amendment Act 1987, the general thrust of which is to treat the birth mother and her partner as the legal parents of a child born following the use of an assisted reproductive technique. In the absence of other State regulation, the Minister of Justice appointed a two person committee to investigate the position in New Zealand and prepare a report outlining options for the future. That report was handed to the Minister in July 1994.[50]

The Ministerial Committee thought it unnecessary to establish a special State licensing system for providers of assisted reproductive technologies. Given the professional controls which exist already through accreditation and given the small pool of expertise available to staff a licensing system, it was thought more important to tighten some loopholes and establish a different kind of agency to safeguard the public interest. One loophole was the possibility that a health professional could operate without being accredited. There is some evidence that this has happened with respect to donor insemination, where there are risks to a child if the donor suffers from a condition such as HIV. Accredited clinics are careful to test semen over a period of six months before using it. A long awaited revised Medical Practitioners Bill has now been introduced into Parliament and, when passed, should give the professional authorities powers to lay down conditions on the practice of special areas of medicine.

Another significant recommendation of the Committee was for the Government to establish a new Council on Assisted Human Reproduction. The Council would have a co-ordinating and watchdog role, as well as advising the Government and other agencies on issues associated with assisted reproduction. An important task would be to work with providers, consumers and interested members of the public to produce codes of practice on such matters as obtaining consent, the storage and use of embryos and gametes, and such matters as the number of embryos which should be

---

50 *Assisted Human Reproduction Navigating Our Future* (Report of the Ministerial Committee on Assisted Reproductive Technologies, Wellington, 1994). The writer was one of the two members of the committee, the other being Dr Paparangi Reid, a Maori woman doctor.

implanted at any one time. The Council would also have an educational function and would foster research, including psycho-social research.

Two specific issues required careful consideration by the Ministerial Committee. The first related to the accessibility of services. There were two aspects to this. One was whether reproductive services should be part of the public health system or whether they should be left to the private sector. On this, the Committee saw value in a mix of public and private provision. While it is hard to defend devoting vast public resources to expensive technologies, some sectors of the community can afford these technologies only if they are largely free. One problem with private provision is the unwillingness of health insurers to provide cover. The Committee recommended that insurers should reassess their position on this, particularly in the light of human rights legislation which outlaws discrimination on the grounds of disability. The other aspect of access to services proved predictably to be highly controversial. Can clinics discriminate on the grounds of sexual orientation and refuse to offer their services, for example, to a lesbian couple who wish to have donor insemination? Similar questions can be asked about single women, elderly women, and people suffering from physical or intellectual handicap. As the Human Rights Act 1993 bans discrimination in the provision of services on the grounds of sexual orientation, it was hard for the Committee to reach a conclusion which would permit such discrimination. While in specific instances there may be genuine medical reasons for turning particular people down (this might be especially true of post-menopausal women), a blanket rule excluding a whole category of people would be difficult to justify.

The Committee also addressed the question of access to identifying information about donors in a donor insemination programme. In years gone by, donors donated semen anonymously and records were often not kept. More recently, clinics have adopted assiduous practices of keeping records and in some cases require donors to agree to identification at a later stage in the life of any child who may be born. Because of the Status of Children Amendment Act, no legal consequences, such as the obligation to pay child support, will flow for the donor. The consequences will be emotional and psychological for the parties. Whether a DI child can gain access to identifying information without the consent of the donor is moot. The information is personal information about both the child and the donor and prima facie under the Privacy Act 1993 the child has a right of access. This is however qualified where access would infringe the privacy rights of another individual. If a donor refuses to consent to the release of the information, the prima facie right may be abrogated. In the light of this and other uncertainties, the Committee recommended that the Privacy Commissioner prepare a special code, including a provision that future donations must be on the basis of the possibility of identification.

The Ministerial Committee's report has not been acted upon by the Government. The area is not one perceived by the Government as requiring urgent action and so, legislation is unlikely in the near future.

VII INTERNATIONAL CHILD ABDUCTION

New Zealand gave statutory effect to the Hague Convention on the Civil Aspects of International Child Abduction when the Guardianship Amendment Act 1991 was passed. A considerable number of cases is now brought invoking the Convention.[51] One difficulty with the 1991 Act was that, while the Convention was contained in a Schedule, the body of the legislation departed in places from the terms of the Convention. One example was the definition of the phrase "rights of custody". By an amendment passed late in 1994, Parliament altered the definition to conform to that found in the Convention. In the meantime, the Court of Appeal had decided in *Gross v Boda*[52] that access rights, in this instance every other weekend and alternating vacations, fell within the phrase "rights of custody". The fact that there was a separate definition of "rights of access" was not thought significant because the definitions of custody and access were overlapping. The new formulation of "rights of custody" refers to "rights relating to the care of the person of the child and, in particular, the right to determine the child's place of residence". It is submitted that the rule in *Gross v Boda* will continue to apply, as a parent with access rights will still during the period of access have rights relating to the care of the child, including where the child is to live.

---

51 For a sample of the 1994 cases see *B v B* [1994] NZFLR 497, *F v T* [1994] NZFLR 565, *S v S* [1994] NZFLR 657, *M v H* [1994] NZFLR 825, *Pickersgill v Grantham* [1994] NZFLR 854, *McDonnell v Collins* [1994] NZFLR 885, *McKendrick v Denholm* [1994] NZFLR 986 and *Boy v Boy* (1994) 12 FRNZ 89.
52 [1995] NZFLR 49.

NORWAY

REGISTERED PARTNERSHIP IN NORWAY

*Peter Lødrup**

I   INTRODUCTION – THE REGISTERED PARTNERSHIP ACT

The Norwegian Act on *Registered Partnership for Homosexual Couples of April 30 1993 no. 40* reads as follows:

"Section 1
Two persons of the same sex may register their partnership, with the legal consequences which follow from this Act.

Section 2
Chapter 1 of the Marriage Act, concerning the conditions for contracting a marriage, shall have corresponding application to the registration of partnerships. No person may contract a partnership if a previously registered partnership or marriage exists.

Chapter 2 of the Marriage Act, on verification of compliance with conditions for marriage, and Chapter 3 of the Marriage Act, on contraction of a marriage and solemnization of a marriage, do not apply to the registration of a partnership.

A partnership may only be registered if one or both of the parties is domiciled in the realm and at least one of them has Norwegian nationality.

Verification of compliance with the conditions and the procedure for the registration of partnerships shall take place according to rules laid down by the Ministry.

Section 3
Registration of partnerships has the same legal consequences as entering into marriage, with the exceptions mentioned in Section 4.

The provisions in Norwegian legislation dealing with marriage and spouses shall be applied correspondingly to registered partnerships and registered partners.

---

*   Professor of Law, University of Oslo.

A. Bainham (ed.), The International Survey of Family Law 1994, 387–394.
© 1996 *The International Society of Family Law. Printed in the Netherlands.*

The provisions of the Adoption Act concerning spouses shall not apply to registered partnerships.

Section 5
Irrespective of the provision in Section 419a of the Civil Procedure Act, actions concerning the dissolution of registered partnerships that have been entered into in this country may always be brought before a Norwegian court."

In the Bill presented to the *Storting*[1] (The Norwegian Parliament) the Ministry discusses the principal issues and the practical aspects of registered partnership at length. In the following, I will present the reasoning of the Ministry of Children and Family Affairs as it is laid out in the Bill. The Bill has – in a shortened version – been translated into English, and I will base this presentation largely on this version.

The main purpose of the Act is to give homosexual couples the possibility, by registration of their partnership, to be treated as married as regards all legal consequences of marriage (Section 3). The only exception relates to the right to adopt children (Section 4).

The Act came into force on August 1, 1993.

II THE NEED FOR LEGISLATION FOR HOMOSEXUAL COUPLES

1   The Ministry takes as a starting point the need to regulate the mutual financial and legal rights and obligations between the partners themselves and towards society. It is emphasized that, regardless of attitudes on the origin of marriage and its central importance, a marriage is *also* a legal contract that regulates the financial situation of two people who live in a close union and become dependant on each other. Others than married couples may live in such close fellowship that they need to regulate their joint economic affairs. The economic conditions under which homosexual couples live are of the same nature as those for married couples, apart from those concerning responsibility for children. Gay and lesbian couples have the same emotional and practical reasons for desiring reciprocal rights and obligations, and there is the same need to protect the weaker party.

---

1   Ot. prp. no. 32 (1992-93).

Furthermore, discussing the main principles on which the Bill is based, the Ministry states that homosexual couples have the same opportunities as cohabiting heterosexual partners to enter into private legal contracts on *inter alia* inheritance and joint ownership of their residence and household goods. To some extent they can thus achieve what married couples are automatically entitled to under the law. However, such agreements are often not sufficient. There are legal limits to how far private contracts may go. Experience also shows that like cohabiting heterosexual couples, very few homosexual partners make use of the opportunity to enter into such agreements, partly because they do not foresee the need for them in case of crisis, such as the death of one of the couple or dissolution of the relationship in other ways.

There is little doubt as to the necessity for legislation in such areas. It is difficult to dispute that a couple who has lived with a joint economy for many years should be able, for example, to inherit from one another without having to make a will and that the survivor should be able to retain the joint residence and property.

It is added, that most of the legislation that applies to marriage is based on the practical need to regulate the economic and legal relations between spouses on the one hand, and between the married couple and society on the other hand. The pragmatic, practical basis of this legislation is illustrated by the fact that although marriage is a central institution in most cultures, legislation governing marriage varies considerably. Homosexual couples have the same need for these rules. In this respect they resemble married couples more than they resemble other people who live together, such as friends or relatives. Their emotional closeness leads to the same close economic and practical relationship as for married couples.

2   In addition to these more economic considerations, the Ministry have important comments on the moral values that an opportunity to register partnerships between homosexual couples necessarily touches upon.

It is a fact that legislation governing homosexuality has changed dramatically over the last twenty years. In Norway, homosexual relations between men were considered a criminal offence until 1972. Prohibition of discrimination against homosexuals followed only nine years later. A more tolerant attitude has developed along with increased knowledge of the nature of homosexuality and the social situation of gays and lesbians.

The Ministry believes that it is a strong argument – which is put forward by homosexuals themselves – that legal regulation will promote stability and reciprocal obligations. There is little information available as to whether homosexual relationships are more transitory than heterosexual ones. It would not be surprising if this were the case. All relationships go through periods of crisis. When married couples have problems, many factors are mobilized to prevent an immediate break-up of the relationship. Support from family and friends, the responsibility for children, and a long tradition that break-up is a last resort are significant factors. For homosexual couples the situation is usually different. Most of these relationships are stigmatized and the couples keep them secret. There is generally no open relationship with family and friends that makes it natural to turn to them for help. It is difficult to mobilize support from a family that does not approve of the situation. A partnership act will not solve all these problems, but will have a stabilizing effect.

A formal, registered partnership will be a signal from a gay or lesbian couple to their families, friends and society that they wish to enter into a committed relationship. This will be emphasized by their formal, legal status. Many homosexual couples find it a great injustice that even after many years' cohabitation, they are still regarded – legally, economically and socially – merely as two people who share a residence.

Furthermore, a formally established partnership will in itself represent a commitment. It is a sign to others that the couple wishes to form a lasting relationship. This commitment may mean that greater efforts are made to avoid a break-up if the relationship undergoes a crisis. A registered partnership will imply openness, and a departure from the traditional invisibility of gay and lesbian relationships will provide many homosexuals with positive role models. Stable relationships provide security and a sense of belonging. Most homosexuals live alone and are liable to be lonely and socially isolated. But most of them wish to live as couples. Homosexuals have the same need for security and growth within a lifelong relationship as do heterosexuals, and should therefore be given the same support in establishing permanent, committed relationships.

Finally, an Act which opens for registration homosexual partnerships, will mean a public acceptance of such partnerships. Such an Act will consequently encourage more gays and lesbians to come out, and thus reduce the problems created by their need to hide their own nature and live in isolation. 3   The discussion of an acceptance of homosexual partnerships necessarily brings up the consequences for marriage as an institution and the view that it will increase family dissolution. The Ministry is very firm in rejecting the objection that acceptance of homosexuals will weaken marriage and have a negative impact on family stability.

Marriage is the fundamental social institution and the natural environment for upbringing of children. Marriage is a relationship between a man and a woman. Lifelong monogamy is the ideal that most people hope to achieve. Many married couples fail to live up to this ideal, and divorce, often followed by remarriage, is increasing, affecting a large number of children. Divorce and the prevalence of unmarried cohabitation have reduced the importance of marriage as the dominant family institution. But this applies to relations between men and women. It is not homosexual relationships that have weakened the status of matrimony and contributed to the dissolution of families.

Marriage has a twofold purpose. It has traditionally been a social and religious institution whose prime function is to care for children and for the mother while the children are dependent on her. More recently another purpose has become increasingly important: marriage is a stable and preferably lifelong relationship between two adults – a relationship that involves strong feelings, closeness and vulnerability, and which has its own value whether or not the couple have children. Most people consider that a close and stable relationship with another person, with mutual respect, care and support, is one of the most desirable aims in life. Many couples wish to give this an institutional framework in order to demonstrate to society their mutual commitment, and that they intend it to last for life. Couples who form such an attachment, wish their relationship to be binding. This encourages the kinds of attitudes and a mutual sense of support which make it more difficult to separate when crises arise.

Couples who know that they will not be able to have children, for example because of sickness or old age, nevertheless often choose to marry. Their reason is based on this second aspect of marriage – creating a stable and lifelong setting for a life together.

Homosexual couples have the same desire to form such a framework around their relationship. The proposed legislation is intended to enable them to achieve this. That gays and lesbians wish to give greater commitment to their relationships is a confirmation of the ideals of marriage – a desire for a permanent relationship based on mutual caring. A homosexual relationship can however never be the same as a marriage, neither socially nor from a religious point of view. It does not replace or compete with heterosexual marriage. The only other option available to a homosexual couple is for their relationship to remain unregulated. The opportunity for homosexuals to register their partnerships will not lead to more people opting for homosexual relationships rather than marriage.

III COMMENTS ON THE BILL FROM VARIOUS GROUPS AND ORGANISATIONS – THE DEBATE IN THE *STORTING*

1   Before the Bill was presented to the *Storting*, it was commented upon by various groups and organisations. The majority favoured the Bill, or were neutral in their comments. Of special interest may be the comments from the majority of the bishops. They stated the fundamental difference between the ethical responsibility of the individual on one hand, and the responsibility of the legislator on the other. The Bill went, in their opinion, too far in giving homosexual partners the same status as married couples. They also underlined that marriage is the fundamental form of cohabitation, and that the Bill will weaken the position of marriage in society. These opinions were shared in the comments from the great majority of clerical organisations. The Faculty of Theology at the University of Oslo, however, had a positive attitude towards the Bill.

2   In the *Storting* the great majority was in favour of the Bill. Only one party, the Christian Peoples Party, was unanimously against it. The arguments of the opponents followed closely the objections from the majority of the bishops. It was argued that an adoption of the Bill would devalue and undermine the positive monopoly of marriage between man and woman.

IV SOME REMARKS ON THE ACT[2]

1   The purpose of the Act is to open for registration homosexual couples who wish that their relationship should have the same legal consequences as marriage. It cannot be disputed that the Act thus recognises such partnerships as equal to marriage from a legislative point of view. Personally, I welcome the Act, and cannot see that it devalues marriage as an institution,

---

2   The Act is commented upon in Holmoy og Lodrup: Ekteskapsloven og enkelte andre lover med kommentarer, Oslo 1994 at 572-578 and Strandbakken in Jussens Venner, Oslo 1993 at 300-352.

because registration is only open to persons that cannot enter into marriage since they are of the same sex. Consequently, Norwegian law now offers the same choice to both heterosexual couples and homosexual couples: They may cohabit within or outside the legal framework which is attached to marriage. It may be added that the legal effects of marriage are regulated in about 120 different acts, and that the common denominator for these rules is that they regulate the position of two adults that live in a close economic and emotional relationship.

2   In Section 1 it is stated that only persons of the same sex can register a partnership. Consequently, cohabiting heterosexuals who can, but do not want to, get married, cannot through this act be subject to the same legal rules as married couples. It should also be noted that the term "register" is somewhat misleading – also a marriage is subject to registration. As regards homosexual partners, a ceremony very similar to the marriage ceremony has been made obligatory. This has been instituted by Section 2 (4).

To be registered, one of the partners must have domicile in Norway, and one of them must have Norwegian citizenship. Thus close connection to Norway – which is stronger than for those who want to contract a marriage in Norway – is motivated by the assumption that a registered partnership may not be recognized in many countries. On the other hand, if a person having registered a partnership in Norway according to the Act gets married in another country, it is assumed that it should be recognized as a valid marriage in Norway. Consequently, there will be a situation of bigamy with its legal implications.

If a person is living in a partnership registered in Sweden or Denmark, he or she may not be registered in Norway. On the other hand, Norwegian law will recognize such registrations in the said countries, and similar systems which may be enacted in other countries.

3   In Section 3 (1) the very important rule of the effects of a registration is given. As mentioned above, a registration has the same legal effects as a marriage. This is repeated in Section 3 (2). The only exception is given in Section 4. It is still only married couples that may adopt a child. In this respect, registered partners are treated like cohabiting heterosexual couples.

V   ANNUAL REGISTRATIONS

When the Bill was prepared, the Ministry assumed that between 300 and 400 couples would register annually. From August 1993 until the end of that year, 154 couples had registered their partnerships.

RUSSIA

BEFORE RADICAL REFORM OF FAMILY LAW

*Olga Khazova**

*Olga Khazova**

I   INTRODUCTION

Strictly speaking, the reform of Russian Family law has already begun and, after several quiet years, family law was put at last into motion in 1994. First, the new Russian Civil Code (Part One) was adopted in 1994 being, no doubt, one of the most important legal events of recent years. Though family relations do not fall within the sphere of civil law and are dealt with by separate family legislation, the Civil Code also contains provisions of extreme importance for family law. In particular, it concerns property relations between the spouses, legal capacity of under-aged persons and custody and guardianship. Second, there were two family law acts enacted in Russia recently. Finally, there is a project relating to the new Family Code which is currently being debated in the Russian Parliament.

II   PROPERTY RELATIONS BETWEEN SPOUSES

Regarding family matters, one of the most important innovations of the new Civil Code[1] is the introduction of the institution of marriage contract into Russian law – an institution absolutely forbidden in this country for the last 77 years. Though only a few words in the Civil Code are devoted to the marriage contract, the significance of the changes they make in the law is difficult to overestimate. According to Article 256, "Property acquired by spouses during the marriage is their joint property, if another regime of their property is not established by an agreement between them".

Under the traditional soviet family law, the spouses were not allowed to deviate from the matrimonial property regime stipulated by law. Family law provided imperative rules on this matter and it was only the regime of common joint property (similar to the continental regime of matrimonial community) that was recognized as a legal one.

---

*   Institute of State and Law, Russian Academy of Sciences, Moscow.
1   Sobranije Zakonodatel'stva Rossiiskoi Federatsii. 32 (1994) Para. 3301.

A. Bainham (ed.), The International Survey of Family Law 1994, 395–401.

The new Civil Code contains no detailed provisions concerning the conclusion of marriage contracts, obviously leaving this matter to family legislation. But since there are still no special regulations in family law on this matter, there continues to be some confusion about the form in which a marriage contract should be concluded and other conditions that should be observed.

As to the legal regime of matrimonial community, operating in the absence of a marriage contract, the Civil Code has introduced no changes and has just repeated the corresponding provisions of the Code on Marriage and the Family. As it was previously, the regime of common joint property means that all the property acquired by the spouses (jointly or separately) during the marriage automatically becomes their joint property. Personal property of each of the spouses constitutes that acquired before the marriage and that given to each of them as a gift or inherited by each of them during the years of marriage. Things intended for the individual or professional use of one of the spouses belong to that spouse personally. Personal property of a spouse may be considered by the court as belonging to both of them jointly, if it is established that the other spouse contributed to the property greatly, and as a result thereof the value of the property significantly increased.

Where family property is divided the shares of the spouses are considered to be equal. The court is entitled to depart from this general rule only in a few cases established in the law.

These are the main features of the matrimonial regime of common joint property, which is stipulated by Russian law. It operates now, if the spouses do not prefer to have their own arrangements and do not conclude a marriage contract.

III LEGAL CAPACITY OF MINOR CHILDREN

Under Russian Civil law a person acquires full legal capacity when he/she attains 18 years – the age of majority. Until that time children remain under their legal representatives' custody or guardianship. Children under 14 years are considered in law as not having any legal capacity at all (i.e., active capacity to acquire by their acts civil rights and to create for themselves civil duties) and remain under their parents' custody. (The new Civil Code lowered this age from 15 to 14). For minors under 14 years transactions are concluded by their parents or guardians, as their legal agents. Persons whose duty is to care for minors are responsible for damage inflicted by them. However, the Civil Code recognizes the right of minors between 6 and 14 years to conclude for themselves small everyday and some other transactions (section 28).

Minors between 14 and 18 years have partial legal capacity and remain under guardianship of their parents (section 26). Without their parents' consent they are entitled to dispose of their earnings, grants and other incomes; to execute their author's rights; to place money on deposit and to dispose of it; to conclude small everyday transactions. Other transactions may be concluded by them only with the consent of their legal agents. The new Civil Code[2] strengthens protection of minors rights and interests; in particular, it provides that a child can be deprived of his right to dispose himself of his earnings and other incomes (or his right can be restricted) only in court proceedings. Previously such questions were decided by custody and guardianship bodies alone.

The most important innovation in this connection was made in section 27 of the Civil Code, which introduced the institution of emancipation of minor children. For years there had been only one ground for granting full legal capacity to an under-aged person: where a minor, having attained 16, was allowed to marry before marriageable age (18 years) by a competent authority, from the day of marriage he/she became fully capable. The new Civil Code provides that an under-aged child, having attained 16, may be declared as having full legal capacity, if he works on a contract or with his parents', adopters' or guardians' consent is involved in business activity. Emancipation of an under-aged child is effected by custody and guardianship bodies with the consent of the child's legal representatives, or, if they do not give their consent, – by court decision. After being emancipated "a child" himself bears full responsibility for all his obligations, including damage caused by his actions.

---

2   Kommentarii k Grazdanskomu Kodeksu Rossiiskoi Federatsii. Moscow. 1995. P. 52.

IV NEW RUSSIAN FAMILY LAW ACTS

There were two questions that could not wait for the radical reform of family law to take place in the country and needed to be solved immediately. These related to maintenance of children and intercountry adoptions.

A *Code on Marriage and the Family (Changes and Amendments) Law 1994*

1 *Maintenance provisions*

Russian courts began to experience difficulties when dealing with maintenance claims for the support of children long ago. Our transition to a market economy has made the problem especially urgent. Under the previous law, maintenance of a child usually took the form of periodic payments, the amount of which was strictly determined as a proportion of the parent's earnings. The form of periodic payments determined as a fixed sum could be used rarely and only in cases stipulated by law. The amount of maintenance was also established by law and was for one child – 1/4, for two children 1/3 and for three or more children – 1/2 of the parent's earnings. It is not difficult to imagine that such rigid rules needed to be seriously improved and that family legislation needed to be brought into line with real life circumstances, when families' incomes differ to a much greater extent. It was necessary to give judges more discretion and the right to depart from these strict rules. It was necessary also to give parents more freedom in the settlement of maintenance conflicts by their own agreement.

First of all, the Law of 1994[3] gave the court much more freedom in defining the amount of maintenance. Preserving the old criteria (1/4, 1/3 and 1/2 of earnings) as a general rule, it is possible now for a court to reduce or, conversely, to increase the amount of maintenance paid monthly, taking into account the financial position of the parties or other circumstances.

The Law also significantly increased the possibility of using the form of maintenance determined as a fixed sum. Now there are in fact no restrictions, and it may be used as an alternative to the form determined as a proportion of earnings. Under the new version of section 71, in cases where a parent obliged to pay maintenance has irregular or changing earnings (income), or he is paid in foreign currency, or he has no earnings (income)

---

3   Sobranije Zakonodatel'stva Rossiiskoi Federatsii. 35 (1994) Para. 3653.

at all, or when it is difficult or impossible to determine the amount of maintenance as a proportion of his earnings or if it is contrary to the interests of one of he parties, the court is entitled to determine the amount of monthly paid maintenance in a fixed sum or simultaneously – as a proportion of earnings and as a fixed sum. It means that the law has given to a court the right to make the decision it thinks is the best in the circumstances.

Further, if the earnings of a parent obliged to maintain a child are not sufficient, it is possible now, in accordance with the new Law, to collect maintenance payments from his bank accounts or from sums invested in enterprises. Moreover, if this appears to be insufficient, then recourse may be had to the payer's property as well (section 91-1).

The Law of 1994 enlarged also the rights of parents in deciding their maintenance disputes themselves. In particular, it is now possible for parents to settle questions on children's maintenance during the marriage or after divorce by their own agreement (concluded in a written form). They can choose any form of maintenance they like, but the monthly paid sum cannot be lower than that established in section 68 of the Code (i.e. 1/4, 1/3 and 1/2 of earnings) (section 67).

B   The Law on Adoption

The Law on Changes and Amendments to the Code on Marriage and the Family, Criminal Code, Criminal Procedure Code and Administrative Offences Code of March 7, 1995[4] introduced new provisions, as is clear from the Law's title itself, to different branches of Russian law. They all concern the same point – adoption. The Law aims to exclude sale of children and to prevent offences in the field of adoption, principally intercountry adoption.

The problem was that Russia appeared to be absolutely unprepared to resolve all the problems connected with foreign adoptions, and it was necessary to take urgent measures to give greater protection to children without families. In the absence of proper legal rules in Russia there has been a moratorium on intercountry adoptions for nearly three years which aimed to stop abuses in this field.

---

4   Sobranije Zakonodatel'stva Rossiiskoi Federatsii. 11 (1995) Para. 939.

In accordance with the new version of section 98 of the Code on Marriage and the Family, in the Law of 1995, intercountry adoptions of Russian children are permitted only if it appears to be impossible to place the child in a family in Russia or to pass him to his relatives irrespective of their place of residence or citizenship. The Law requires the Russian Government to establish a special Centralized body for registration of all children that need to be settled. A child can be made available for intercountry adoption after the expiration of a 6 month period after he has been registered in such a centralized body (for children under 3 years the Law provides for a 3 month period) (section 122 of the Code).

The period of 6 months is considered to be too long, and the Law has been justly criticized in this connection; the search for a proper family for a child on Russian territory or among his relatives should be performed much more quickly, taking into account that during this period a child has to live in a special children institution, and that this can do him a lot of harm.[5]

Another obvious shortcoming of the new Law[6] is that it forbids performance of intercountry adoptions by means of adoption agents even if they have a special licence, while simultaneously permitting those made by private persons under a power of attorney notarially certified (section 98 of the Code). Such a situation could hardly make intercountry adoptions for foreigners easier, but will definitely not prevent adoption from being used for mercenary purposes.

The Law of 1995 establishes criminal responsibility for the sale of minor children and for illegal adoption (sections 125-2 and 162-9). Corresponding amendments are introduced into the Criminal Procedure Code and Administrative Offences Code. The latter, in particular, is amended by the new section establishing administrative responsibility for the heads of children institutions and local authority officials for breaches of adoption procedure or terms under which they must present information about children without families, or presentation of false information about such children, or for other actions aiming to withhold children from adoption or transfer to families (section 193-1).

---

5   O.A. Dyuzheva, "Problems of Legislation on Intercountry Adoption". – Gosudarstvo
     i pravo.6 (1995) P. 46.
6   Ibid.

V   THE NEW FAMILY CODE PROJECT

The Code on Marriage and the Family that is still in force in the territory of the Russian Federation was adopted in 1969. It goes without saying that the majority of its provisions are outdated and do not correspond to present day demands and recent legislation. The main task of the project of the new Family Code that is under discussion in the Russian Parliament now is to bring our law into line with modern trends.

In the draft-Code an attempt is made to extend family rights and to give them more protection, to give members of the family more freedom in deciding their family matters and to strengthen their responsibility for non-fulfilment of their family duties (principally concerning their parental obligations); to limit courts' interference to cases where it is necessary for protection of the rights and interests of members of the family and when parties cannot reach an agreement, and, on the other hand, to give judges much more discretion in deciding matrimonial disputes than they have ever had before. With these aims in view the project removes all the formal restrictions for paternity proceedings, protects the rights of minor parents, defines the rights of those involved in "artificial procreation" procedures, contains provisions on marriage contracts and agreements between spouses, provides an easier procedure for divorce by mutual consent, putting, however, all the questions concerning children's maintenance under the court's control if there is no agreement between the parents or their agreement does not correspond to the child's best interests. It is one of the main ideas of the project to make the "child's best interests" the main criterion in settling matrimonial disputes and to give minor children many more rights. Particularly, the project stipulates the child's right "to have a say" when matters that concern his life are discussed, and the right to apply himself to local authorities and, from 14 years, to a court to protect his rights and interests. The draft-Code tries to give more protection to children without families, it introduces a court procedure for adoption and extends the possibilities of placing children without parental care in families of different types.

So, these are the main features of the new Russian project. Whether it becomes law and how it will work in practice only the future can show.

SINGAPORE

WOMEN, FAMILY, PROPERTY AND THE LAW

Peter de Cruz[*]

I   INTRODUCTION

Family Law in Singapore is a rich cocktail of English common law, local case-law and statutes and elements of customary law. The most important non-Muslim statute is the Women's Charter.[1] English law in Singapore derives from the Second Charter of Justice[2] which was granted by the British Crown on November 27 1826. This was subsequently interpreted by judges in Singapore as having imported into the Colony of the Straits Settlements[3] the law of England as it stood on that date subject to such modifications as were necessary to prevent injustice or oppression to the local inhabitants.[4] The Singapore courts therefore had to determine the extent of application of English law relating to marriage, succession, legitimacy and other related matters and whether the custom, religion, practices and usages of the Chinese, Muslim and Hindu communities should be recognised. The early law was developed by the judges, who were British expatriates and legislative intervention was fragmentary and infrequent.

The Women's Charter (the Charter) was first enacted in 1961 and has had its greatest impact upon the status of non-Muslim Singaporean women, particularly in relation to marriage and divorce although it covers other areas of family law. It has undergone several revisions and is the main statute for most of non-Muslim Family Law in Singapore, supplemented by judicial

---

[*]   Professor of Law, Staffordshire University, England. The author wishes to acknowledge the assistance of Jane Carter, a graduate of Keele University, who worked as his research assistant in the Summer of 1995 and provided him with many of the cases and materials referred to in this article.

[1]   This was first enacted in 1961; see now Cap. 353. Singapore Statutes, Rev. Ed. 1985.

[2]   This was issued by the British Crown under the authority of King George IV: see 6 Geo. IV c.85, and was therefore an Imperial Act passed in 1825.

[3]   Singapore belonged to this until 1946.

[4]   See Braddell *The Law of the Straits Settlements. A Commentary* (2nd edition) Vol.I, at 1-61; see further Wee "English Law and Chinese Family Custom in Singapore: The Problem of Fairness in Adjudication" (1974) *16 Mal. L.R.* 52, 53-62; see more generally Leong Wai Kum *Family Law in Singapore. Cases and Commentary on the Women's Charter and Family Law* (1990).

A. Bainham (ed.), The International Survey of Family Law 1994, 403–418.

decisions. The enactment of the Charter has led to an enhancement of the status of women in Singapore although this is not immediately obvious even from a close reading of the law reports. Indeed, a leading writer on Family Law in Singapore[5] has commented that since Singaporeans are made up of Chinese, Indians, Jews and a number of smaller racial groups, apart from Malays (to whom the Charter does not apply), the acceptance and endurance of the Charter demonstrates how Singaporeans have forsaken their culture. Having lived in Singapore for over twenty years, and having practised Family Law at the Bar, the present writer would respectfully suggest that the Charter has achieved widespread acceptance (which is not synonymous with popularity), because it enshrines some of the values and norms which are acquiring, or have acquired, universal acceptance and it introduced provisions which enhanced the position of women and children in many respects.[6] It also provides a structure which is stable, familiar, and flexible, and enjoys the benefit of State enforcement and an effective administrative machinery which was lacking under the previous customary law regimes.

This Article focuses on the interpretation of the Charter provisions in relation to non-Muslim cases dealing with (i) the division of matrimonial assets upon divorce; and (ii) the special significance of contributions made to the Central Provident Fund in post-divorce distribution of marital assets. It also notes the courts' approach to the division of property between unmarried couples which is still governed by English law and is outside the Charter.

---

5   See Leong Wai Kum, *supra*, at 1.

6   The Charter allows scope for consideration of *both* parties' contributions to the matrimonial assets which English, Australian and New Zealand legislation also allows. In practice, this tends to be an allowance for the non-financial contribution of the *wife*, which reflects the underlying philosophy of the various legislatures. The Charter also abolished polygamy for non-Muslim men and the concept of the wife's dependent domicile which meant that a deserted wife could henceforth divorce her foreign husband in Singapore without having to travel to her husband's country to commence divorce proceedings. Provisions were also introduced under the Charter which enhanced the enforcement of maintenance for the wife. Further, nearly all "developed" jurisdictions have adopted the concept that the child's welfare (or "best interests") is a primary consideration: see section 119 of the Charter which makes the welfare of the child the first and paramount consideration in any custody proceedings; under section 117 of the Charter the High Court cannot make absolute any decree of divorce or nullity of marriage or grant a decree of judicial separation unless it is satisfied that "the best possible arrangements have been made for the welfare of the child".

II DIVISION OF MARITAL PROPERTY

A Background

Partly as a result of its British colonial heritage, the Singapore legislature has sometimes seen fit to borrow legal concepts from statutes enacted by the British Parliament,[7] the Australian and New Zealand legislatures. However, this has not always resulted in immediate legislation. For example, the original Singapore Women's Charter of 1961 actually reproduced a great deal of the law found in English law as at 1937. On the other hand, the Singapore legislature sometimes introduced legal reforms before the British Parliament had done so.[8]

As far as property division upon dissolution of marriage is concerned, Singapore *prima facie* follows the English common law so that the notion of "separate property" prevails. Consequently, a man and his wife will be beneficially entitled to any property which they have acquired before and during the course of the marriage, unless, of course, there is evidence of a variation in ownership rights with regard to any particular property.[9] Indeed, in Singapore, the right of a woman to retain her own property was created by what is now section 49 of the Women's Charter, allowing her to hold property which belonged to her as a married woman, which she acquired or which devolved upon her, as a femme sole, which she has the right to dispose of accordingly.[10] As in England, the shortcomings of the separate property regime have frequently been exposed in Singapore cases, particularly when a marriage has broken down, since it has often failed to

---

7 See eg The Divorce Ordinance XXV of 1910 which conferred jurisdiction in divorce and matrimonial causes on the Supreme Court, which used as its model the English Matrimonial Causes Act 1857. The Singapore Parliament also enacted various changes to divorce law that had already been brought into effect in England and Wales in 1923 and 1937 by the Matrimonial Causes Acts of those years.

8 For instance, in 1967, Singapore introduced separation as a ground for divorce before the British did, by following the initiative of Australia and New Zealand.

9 As with English courts, the Singapore courts have a judicial discretion conferred by statute to make allowances and variations taking account of the particular marital relationship, evidence of written agreements and financial arrangements. For the English approach see sections 21-25, especially section 25 of the English Matrimonial Causes Act 1973 (as amended). The Singapore position is discussed in the text of the present Article.

10 This followed section 2 of the English Married Women's Property Act 1882.

reflect the true respective contributions of the parties to the marriage in financial *and* non-financial terms. The prevailing trend in Singapore, in keeping with the more traditional roles of spouses, has been for the husband to be the sole breadwinner and to accumulate considerably more wealth than the wife often because the wife has looked after the needs of the home and the children and has chosen not to pursue a full-time career or to delay embarking on such a career indefinitely. In other words, at the time of the termination of the marriage, there was a need to recognise the contribution of the wife as a homemaker since English common law only recognises such a contribution under very restrictive circumstances.[11] One such circumstance would be if the courts were able to find evidence of a common intention for the spouses to share the proceeds of the matrimonial property.

Parliament therefore enacted section 106[12] of the Women's Charter, giving the courts a discretion to adjust property rights upon dissolution of a marriage. However, unlike its divorce provisions, which were generally taken from the English Family Law Reform Act 1969, section 106 of the Singapore Women's Charter has not been simply copied from the present English equivalent under the Matrimonial Causes Act 1973.

Section 106 reads as follows:

106. *Power of court to order division of matrimonial assets*
1) The court shall have power, when granting a decree of divorce, judicial separation or nullity of marriage, to order the division between the parties of any assets acquired by them during the marriage by their joint efforts or the sale of any such assets and the division between the parties of the proceeds of the sale.
2) In exercising the power conferred by subsection 1) the court shall have regard to
a) the extent of the contributions made by each party in money, property or work toward the acquiring of the assets;
b) any debts owing by either party which were contracted for their joint benefit; and

---

11   E.g. if there has been a direct financial contribution to the purchase price of the matrimonial home, or towards a deposit, or by paying the mortgage: see the House of Lords' cases of *Pettitt v Pettitt* [1970] AC 777; *Gissing v Gissing* [1971] AC 886; and *Lloyds Bank v Rosset* [1990] 1 All ER 1111.

12   This was formerly numbered section 100 prior to the 1985 Revised Edition of the Charter.

c) the needs of the minor children (if any) of the marriage, and, subject to those considerations, the court shall incline towards equality of division.

3) The court shall have power, when granting a decree of divorce, judicial separation or nullity of marriage, to order the division between the parties of any assets acquired during the marriage by the sole effort of one party to the marriage or the sale of any such assets and the division between the parties of the proceeds of the sale.

Subsection 4) then continues:

4) In exercising the power conferred by subsection (3) the court shall have regard to

a) the extent of the contribution made by the other party who did not acquire the assets to the welfare of the family by looking after the home or by caring for the family; and

b) the needs of the minor children, if any, of the marriage, and, subject to those considerations, the court may divide the assets or the proceeds of sale in such proportions as the court thinks reasonable; but in any case the party by whose effort the assets were acquired shall receive a greater proportion.

5) For the purposes of this section, references to assets acquired during a marriage include assets owned before the marriage by one party which have been substantially improved during the marriage by the other party or by their joint efforts.

It is clear that, in keeping with its well-established practice of legal transplantation,[13] Singapore's approach to the division of matrimonial assets[14] is statute-based but it derives from a Kenyan Report first submitted in 1968.[15]

---

13 See Alan Watson, *Legal Transplants* (1974) wherein he explores the notion of legal concepts "transplanted" from their original provenance to another foreign jurisdiction where they often appear to co-exist happily with more indigenous concepts.

14 The wording of section 106 also suggests that "matrimonial assets" in the present context refers to "assets acquired during the marriage"; the terms "matrimonial assets" and "family assets" are not used in the legislation and the courts have pointed out that the use of such terms cannot be taken as having the same meaning as in English law: see *Neo Heok Kay v Seah Suan Chock* [1993] 1 SLR 230; see also Tan Cheng Han *Matrimonial Law in Singapore and Malaysia* (1994) esp. at 184-192 for a discussion of the scope of "matrimonial assets" and section 106 in general.

15 See *Commission on the Law of Marriage and Divorce*; cited in the Malaysian Royal Commission Report on the Law of Non-Muslim Marriage and Divorce laws; see also Crown, "Property Division on Dissolution of Marriage" (1988) 30 *Mal. LR* at 41.

This was the source of identical Malaysian legislation which was itself the immediate source of the Singapore provision![16] However, it appears that although the Kenyan Commission did not state any source for its report, the relevant clause dealing with division of property is redolent of ideas which were to be found in English cases in the 1950s and 1960s. So once again the influence of English law continues to cast its long shadow even in the post-colonial, postmodernist era. As far as the section itself is concerned, it is certainly much shorter than the detailed "checklist" contained in section 25(2) of the English Matrimonial Causes Act 1973.[17]

With these considerations as a backdrop to the Charter, we turn to consider some recent examples of the judicial interpretation of the section.

B   Recent interpretation of section 106

Within the last three years, the courts have not been unduly burdened with cases requiring an interpretation of section 106 except with regard to the relevance of the Central Provident Fund (CPF) and its relationship to section 106. The CPF is a fund to which all Singapore employees and workers must compulsorily contribute a percentage every month, in a separate account with the CPF board, from which they will eventually derive their pension, which will then benefit themselves and/or their families. In addition, the employer must also contribute an amount based on a percentage of its employee's salary to that employee's CPF account. CPF monies are therefore part of wages or salaries. The question which has recently arisen for the courts is whether money in a married person's CPF account should be taken into account in calculating the total assets for the purpose of division under

---

16   This appears to be the antecedents of section 106 of the Charter: see Crown, "Property Division on Dissolution of Marriage" (1988) 30 *Mal. LR* 34 at 36-43.

17   Section 25(2)(f) of the 1973 Act mentions as one of the matters to be taken into account by the court, in exercising its discretion on property allocation, "the contributions which each of the parties has made or is likely in the foreseeable future to make to the welfare of the family, including any contribution by looking after the home or caring for the family". s. 25(3) of the 1973 Act mentions the "financial needs of the child". In any event, an overriding guideline under the English legislation is that in deciding whether to exercise its wide powers under the statute in relation to division of marital property, the court must give "first consideration" to the welfare of a minor child of the family (ie under 18 years of age): section 25(1).

section 106. Clearly, if the CPF fund is taken into account, this will increase the total value of matrimonial property available for division.

Within the last two years, the first instance courts have gone either way on this question. In *Ong Chin Ngoh v Lam Chin Kian*[18] Chan J did not see why the courts could not take into account the value of the CPF fund of each of the parties to the marriage, for the purposes of determining the corpus of the matrimonial assets in divorce proceedings. However, in a subsequent case, *Neo Heok Kay v Seah Suan Chock*[19] Coomaraswamy J disagreed with this approach arguing that even if CPF monies are assets acquired during marriage, they must also by law be "available" for division between the parties under the express words of section 106. However, in the light of restrictions stipulated in the CPF Act[20] on the use of CPF monies, such monies cannot be the subject of an order under section 106. Thus, he sees the availability of the monies as an *additional* requirement although the word "available" does not actually appear in section 106. In any event, the matter appears to have been resolved by the Singapore Court of Appeal in *Lam Chih Kian v Ong Chin Ngoh*[21] wherein it endorsed the first approach. Goh Joon Seng J expressed the view that the restrictions imposed by the CPF Act did not make money held in a CPF account any less of an asset, provided the fund has been accumulated during the marriage. In those circumstances, the CPF monies constituted an asset acquired during the marriage and were therefore within the scope of section 106.

In the High Court case of *Lau Eng Mui v Ee Chin Kee*[22] the initial question arose as to whether, once the CPF member's account had been treated as part of the matrimonial assets consequent upon the dissolution of marriage, and the share of the member's spouse in the matrimonial assets had to be satisfied from an eventual payment from the CPF monies, it was open to the court to place a charge on such monies in favour of the spouse of the CPF member. Two further questions followed: (i) whether such a charge takes effect immediately on the member becoming eligible to withdraw, or only upon the member actually withdrawing the money standing

---

18   [1992] 2 SLR 414.
19   [1993] 1 SLR 230.
20   Central Provident Fund Act (Cap. 36, 1991 Ed).
21   [1993] 2 SLR 253.
22   [1995] 1 SLR 110.

to the credit of his account; and (ii) whether the CPF Board was obliged to make payment direct to the person in whose favour the order is made.

The facts of the case were that the respondent had been ordered to pay a lump sum of 20,000 Singapore dollars in lieu of maintenance for the children of the marriage, the sum to be paid out and charged against the respondent's CPF monies when he was entitled to withdraw and did withdraw them from the fund. There were three children of the marriage and the respondent had no regular job, so there was doubt as to whether he would be able to pay periodical maintenance.

Khoo, J enunciated the following principles:

(i) In a case where the whole or a predominant part of the matrimonial assets to be divided consequent upon a dissolution of marriage consists of CPF monies, and where a spouse's entitlement on a division can only be satisfied from an eventual payment from the CPF monies, the judgment of the court ordering that the spouse's share of the matrimonial assets be satisfied from a portion of the CPF monies in the member's account gives rise to a proprietary interest in the CPF monies as opposed to a mere personal claim against the CPF member.

(ii) This interest is a real and substantial interest, even though the monies to which it is attached cannot be withdrawn from the fund until the circumstances prescribed for withdrawal have arisen in accordance with the CPF Act.

(iii) A charge on the funds standing to the credit of the member's CPF account is no more than a device to protect this interest and the position of the spouse in whose favour the judicial process has brought this interest into being is different from that of an ordinary claimant or judgment creditor.

(iv) On considerations of principle and expediency, it followed that the charge should be imposed on the monies standing to the credit of the member's account.

(v) Once an order imposing a charge has been made in these circumstances and served on the CPF Board, the Board should ensure that no withdrawal from the relevant account is made without leaving in the account a sufficient sum to meet the charge.

(vi) Once the right to withdraw monies from the fund in accordance with the provisions of the Act has arisen, the spouse in whose favour the order is made is entitled to apply to the Board for payment direct to him or her and the Board should act accordingly.

In *Rayney v Spencer*[23] the question before the High Court was whether ordering the postponement of repayment of sums withdrawn from a member's account with the CPF, or ordering non-repayment in favour of the wife and children on the wife's application for a division of assets, are proper exercises of the court's discretion under section 106 of the Women's Charter. Additional factors were that there was a charge on the property and the provisions of the CPF Act and its procedural rules had to be considered.

The facts of the case were that the parties married on June 29, 1974. There were three children from the marriage. The husband was a safety consultant and the wife was unemployed. The marriage began to fail and the parties executed a deed of separation on October 20, 1990. The wife petitioned for divorce on the ground that the marriage had irretrievably broken down because the husband had behaved in such a way that she could not reasonably be expected to live with him. The petition was granted and one of the orders made was a transfer to the wife of the husband's interest in the property (the flat) upon the wife reimbursing the husband's CPF account, without interest, pursuant to a clause in the deed of separation.

At the hearing for ancillary relief, the wife, who had custody of the three children, said that it would be extremely difficult for her to refund her husband's CPF contributions with interest accrued. The judge ordered the husband to transfer his share in the flat to the wife and the wife not to reimburse the husband's CPF account with contributions made by the husband. The wife was required to serve a draft order of the court on the Housing and Development Board (HDB) and the CPF Board. The HDB and CPF Board were at liberty to file an affidavit in reply stating objections, if any, to the transfer of the flat by May 30, 1994.

The initial question which arose was whether the ancillary relief order was made in the proper exercise of the court's discretion under section 106 of the Charter, in particular whether the powers of the court to order division between the parties of any assets acquired by them during marriage by their joint efforts ceased to have any effect where the property was under a charge arising from the provisions of the CPF Act. However, on October 21, 1994, counsel for the wife informed the court that the wife was able to raise a loan and reimburse the husband's CPF account. The court proceeded to give its views on the other issues raised.

---

23   [1995] 2 SLR 153.

Rajah, JC, held, *inter alia*, varying the initial order:

(i) Where undue hardship would be caused to the wife and dependent children, the husband could, in a proper case, be ordered to transfer the property to the wife without her having to reimburse his CPF account sums contributed by him. However, since the wife's financial difficulties had ceased to be an issue, the earlier order was annulled and she was ordered to pay the husband's CPF contributions without interest.

(ii) The words "otherwise disposed of" in reg 7 of the CPF HDB-HUDC Regulations could not include disposal pursuant to an order of the court and a measure of the court's powers under section 106 of the Charter could be gathered from the provisions of section 131 of the Charter which empowered the court to set aside dispositions of "any property".

(iii) The power of the court under section 106 of the Charter was not limited to dividing the assets and ordering the sale and division of the proceeds of sale and that further orders to enforce the orders cannot be made. The Charter empowered the court to divide or order the sale of assets and such powers must be understood to be also conferred as were reasonably necessary to enable the court to divide or order the sale, and to enforce its orders.

(iv) A member was not a borrower of money from his CPF account. He could withdraw his money before he was entitled to do so for a purpose approved by law. The charge on the property ensured repayment.

(v) The underlying policy of the Charter was not to allow the husband to deprive the wife and children by diminishing his assets. The charge on "residential property" and the requirement for full repayment of sums withdrawn where they operated to diminish assets, when the needs of the wife and children may be greater and compelling, were factors that must be considered in the division of assets. The position taken by the CPF and the conflicting interests of husband/wife and children must be balanced to ensure that justice is done on the facts of the case.

III   THE EFFECT OF MAINTENANCE AGREEMENTS BETWEEN SPOUSES

Another area of family law that has exercised the Singapore courts is the question of whether the courts will give effect to maintenance agreements concluded between husband and wife, and if so, on what basis? To begin with, section 110 of the Women's Charter provides:

"An agreement for the payment, in money or other property, of a capital sum in settlement of all future claims to maintenance, shall not be effective until it has been approved, or approved, subject to conditions, by the court, but when so approved, shall be a good defence to any claim for maintenance."

Section 113 of the Charter further provides that subject to section 110, the court has the power, at any time, to vary the terms of any agreement as to maintenance made between husband and wife where it is satisfied that there has been any material change in the circumstances and notwithstanding any provision to the contrary in any such agreement. The position therefore seems to be that the parties are free to enter into maintenance agreements but that such agreements will remain subject to court approval.

In *Tan Kai Mee v Lim Soei Jin*[24] Sinnathuray J opined that it was not open to married parties to contract out of the Women's Charter. However, the clause in that case was unusually restrictive,[25] and it is thus conceivable that the courts might approve one that is less restrictive, particularly if the parties appeared to be quite happy with its terms, provided it does not seek to oust the jurisdiction of the court.

In the High Court case of *Chia Hock Hua v Chong Choo Je*[26] detailed judicial guidance was given on how the courts would assess the validity of a maintenance agreement. The issues were (i) whether the agreement to pay the wife 30,000 Singapore dollars and its payment to her in May 1991 was a valid and reasonable agreement; and (ii) whether the agreement should be sanctioned by the court under section 110 of the Women's Charter; and (iii) if it were not to be sanctioned, whether the wife was entitled to maintenance.

The facts of the case were that the petitioner (husband) and the respondent (wife) married in Perth, Western Australia in 1987 but separated in December of that year. They returned separately to Singapore but the wife returned to Australia in March 1993. The husband filed a divorce petition with a certificate of consent on the grounds that the marriage had irretrievably broken down as the parties had lived separate and apart for three

---

24 [1981] 1 MLJ 271.
25 It stipulated that the wife "shall not at any time apply to the courts to vary the maintenance order".
26 [1995] 1 SLR 380.

years immediately preceding the presentation of the petition and that the wife consented to the decree being granted. In the petition, the husband stated that he had paid the wife 30,000 Singapore dollars, an agreed lump sum in full and final settlement of her claims to ancillary relief. In her answer, the wife admitted receiving the lump sum but denied the basis of the payment. She alleged that the money had been given to her by the husband to buy a car and she had been tricked into going to her husband's lawyer's office to sign the divorce documents. The decree nisi was granted to the petitioner on December 16, 1992 and the wife brought proceedings for ancillary relief for maintenance.

Amarjeet, JC, dismissed the application and held:

(i) Section 110 of the Women's Charter confirmed the position in common law that the wife cannot enter into a binding agreement and thereby waive her rights to claim maintenance unless that agreement met with the approval of the court, the rationale being that a wife should not be maintained out of the public purse.

(ii) The words in section 110 "An agreement ... shall not be effective until it has been approved or approved subject to conditions ..." did not mean that the law denies the existence of an agreement-only that when approved it becomes effective and provides a good defence to any claim for maintenance. The effectiveness and approval of the agreement would also depend on the same common law principles determining the validity of the agreement under section 7 of the Divorce Reform Act 1969 (UK).

(iii) The principles which the courts would consider before a mutually agreed arrangement was endorsed are as follows: the court must be satisfied that the parties were *ad idem*; and whether the question of the benefit of legal advice was necessary if the case was a complicated one; whether there was extreme pressure applied by the husband resulting in the wife accepting an unsatisfactory financial agreement; whether unforeseen circumstances had arisen which made it impossible for the wife to work or otherwise maintain herself; whether the agreement had been reached at arm's length and the parties had been separately advised, which facts if found would constitute prima facie evidence of the reasonableness of its terms; whether poverty and ignorance produced an unfair and unacceptable arrangement for one side; whether on the construction of the agreement there was a good and effective consent; whether there was mistake, duress or undue influence such as the husband being in a superior bargaining position and taking an unfair advantage by exploiting his position and the agreement being entered into without the wife having full knowledge of all the relevant facts and/or legal advice; and the weight to be given to the conduct of the parties and circumstances of the case.

The court then observed, somewhat laconically, that "It may well be that there may be other considerations which affect the justice of the particular case".

(iv) The court found that the wife in this case was a highly educated person who could look after herself (she was a highly trained computer scientist who had become a marketing executive) and her allegations that she had been forced to collect the cheque could not be believed. The receipt which the wife signed stated in clear language that it was a full and final payment in settlement of her claim for maintenance or in lieu thereof and/or periodical payments and whatsoever claim, if any she might have.

(v) The argument that because the document was termed a "receipt" and so did not amount to an agreement was unacceptable. The terms of the "receipt" clearly spelt out an agreement which the wife acknowledged by signing the same.

(vi) The certificate of consent was signed before an independent lawyer and not the husband's lawyer. The wife must therefore have consulted him and had independent legal advice.

(vii) There was nothing unreasonable in the capital sum settlement of 30,000 Singapore dollars reached by the spouses having regard to their financial standing in 1991. There was nothing exceptional or adverse in the financial fortunes of the wife which the court was required to consider.

The courts have certainly approached this area of law with great circumspection and thoroughness but the diverse range of arrangements within each relationship makes it necessary for each case to be scrutinised on its own merits and the Charter provisions are merely the starting point in the court's deliberations.

IV COHABITATION OUTSIDE MARRIAGE: A NEW LEGAL BATTLEFIELD?

Finally, we look briefly at an illustrative case dealing with the division of property between unmarried couples. It would appear that the social phenomenon of cohabitation outside marriage, although by no means new, is now reaching the Singaporean courts in greater numbers. Apparently this has also been happening in West Malaysia[27] particularly within the last few years. Cohabitation of this nature has a long history and first reached public prominence in England, Western Europe and the United States in the 1960s and 1970s. However, even in jurisdictions such as England and the United States, the law has taken a long time to develop, ostensibly because of the immorality of the practice, its perceived threat to the State-endorsed institution of marriage and intrinsic uncertainty in recognition of status. English law is currently an *ad hoc* cocktail of judicially decided cases, domestic violence statutes, and a hotchpotch of property law and contract law principles. The position in Singapore appears to be that cohabitation is not officially recognised by law or State, although everyone accepts that it exists, but the courts are quite prepared to rely on English law to divide property between cohabitants in dispute where their relationship has terminated. In the High Court case of *Chia Kum Fatt Rolfston v Lim Lay Choo*[28] a dispute arose between an unmarried couple concerning the ownership of a flat. The couple became acquainted in February 1988 and by April 1988 they were living together in the plaintiff's studio apartment. This apartment was, however, too small for them and there was also some discussion about marriage. They started looking for another home. Two years later, the plaintiff obtained an option to purchase property for which he paid the option fee of 5,000 Singapore dollars and a further sum of 35,000 Singapore dollars when he exercised the option. The plaintiff also obtained credit facilities of 370,000 Singapore dollars made up of an overdraft and a 20-year housing loan. The purchase of the property was completed in the joint names of both the plaintiff and the defendant. A few months later, the defendant made several payments into the overdraft account the plaintiff held with the bank, amounting to 30,338.93 Singapore dollars. The parties moved into the house and lived there until their relationship broke down in the middle of 1991. The plaintiff wished to sell the property but the defendant refused. On May 19, 1992, the plaintiff took out an originating summons for an order for sale of the property and division of the proceeds. At the hearing, counsel for the plaintiff submitted that the parties' shares in the equity of the property should be in proportion to their respective financial contributions while counsel for the defendant contended that the parties should have equal shares.

---

27   See Pillai "Cohabitation: The New Social Phenomenon" [1994] 2 MLJ li.
28   [1993] 3 SLR 833.

Khoo J considered English authorities on the matter[29] and allowed the plaintiff's application, ruling that:

(i) Where there is no express declaration of trust and no express agreement or understanding about the matter, the respective shares of the parties are to be ascertained according to the circumstances and the parties' respective contributions, direct and indirect, in terms of money or in kind or in services. There is no presumption that the maxim "equality is equity" is applicable.

(ii) In this case, the non-monetary contributions made by both parties to the acquisition of the house, and holding it as a home, were difficult to quantify. In the circumstances, the parties' shares in the net equity of the property should, in principle, be in proportion to the respective financial contributions made by them without taking into account their non-monetary contributions.

The parties were therefore left to agree a figure, and failing agreement on this, would have to return to the court for a determination.

It would seem that a new battlefield involving unmarried couples is developing alongside the well-established battleground occupied by divorcing couples fighting over property. As a country becomes ever more sophisticated, at least in Western terms, it is surely inevitable that greater equality between the sexes will be recognised by the courts, and this is a consequence of women's greater economic and social freedom and independence in Singapore. Cohabitation is not only growing in popularity but is also gaining more widespread social acceptance.

V CONCLUSION

This brief survey of Family Law in Singapore reveals a society that is developing as speedily as ever, and one that is absorbing even more Western norms and attitudes with regard to divorce, property disputes and the family. However, with growing sophistication, Singapore is also attempting to come to terms with modernity while trying to preserve its more traditional religious, cultural and ethnic heritage. The majority of the population is, of course, young, and the young have less memories of colonial history to shake off than their elders. Nevertheless, Family Law in Singapore, is a

---

29   Such as *Goodman v Gallant* [1986] 1 All ER 311 (distinguished) and *Bernard v Josephs* [1982] 3 All ER 162 which he followed.

heady cocktail which is strikingly like English law in its philosophy and style but which is striving to develop a *zeitgeist* of its own. This will assuredly come, but its present approach to family, law and society is still very much in a state of flux and this process continues. Although the Women's Charter is its guiding light, a great deal of family law cases now coming before the courts will be navigating uncharted waters since Singapore still relies heavily on English case-law which is often unpredictable and *ad hoc*. Nevertheless, its Family Law so far is a success story in reconciling a multi-cultural population's needs within a foreign framework. The way it shapes up in the next millenium will be an important indication of how far Singapore's socio-legal development can continue to thrive in the quest for a truly Singaporean identity.

SOUTH AFRICA

SOUTH AFRICAN FAMILY LAW AT THE CROSSROADS: FROM PARLIAMENTARY SUPREMACY TO CONSTITUTIONALISM

*Ronald Thandabantu Nhlapo**

I   INTRODUCTION

The single most important legal development in South Africa in 1994 was the coming into force of the interim constitution.[1] This document has set in train some far-reaching changes, not only in the field of law, but also in social and political relationships within the country. It is a constitution born out of a deep desire by South Africans to rectify the mistakes of the past and to ensure that such abuses do not happen ever again. And since those mistakes were largely about discrimination, repression and inequality, the interim constitution is strong on non-discrimination, freedom and e-quality. These aspirations have been embodied in the Bill of Rights,[2] a part of the constitution seen by many South Africans as the guarantee for a future that will finally erase the memories of the country's apartheid past. The constitution as a whole must be viewed in this light: it represents a settlement negotiated between former adversaries, in which the past (and how to avoid its recurrence) loomed large.

The quest for a "non-racist, non-sexist and democratic South Africa" based on respect for human rights found expression in the Preamble to the constitution which reads:

> "*Whereas* there is a need to create a new order in which all South Africans will be entitled to a common South African citizenship in a sovereign and democratic constitutional state in which there is equality between men and

---

*   Professor of Law, University of Cape Town.
1   Passed in 1993 as the *Constitution of the Republic of South Africa Act No. 200 of 1993* the interim constitution came into effect on April 27, 1994. It stipulates that a final constitution must be adopted by May 1996. The task is being undertaken by the 490 members of the House of Assembly and the Senate, sitting as the Constitutional Assembly.
2   Chapter 3 of the interim constitution, headed "Fundamental Rights".

A. Bainham (ed.), The International Survey of Family Law 1994, 419–434.

women and people of all races so that all citizens shall be able to enjoy
and exercise their fundamental rights and freedoms..."

It has been convincingly argued that, reading the constitution as a whole
in the context of the interests represented in its formulation, the two main
pillars of the new South African state are equality and non-discrimination.[3]
Although the main motivation for these strong assertions of freedom and
equality in the constitution was political, areas of private law are beginning
to feel the effects as well.

II   FAMILY LAW IN THE CONSTITUTION

Before the constitution was finalized in late 1993 there were various attempts
to include broad protections for "the family" in the Bill of Rights. Thus,
Article 2(29) of the draft Bill of Rights published by the African National
Congress in February 1993 provided for the rights to marry and to establish
a family; such marriage to be based on the free consent of both spouses.
Earlier the South African Law Commission[4] had produced a draft Bill of
Rights which protected the family's integrity and the right to choose a spouse
freely. It is interesting to note that the basis for these protections was
monogamy.[5] Between them, the Democratic Party[6] and the Nationalist
Government[7] both published drafts in which the protection of the integrity
of the family was prominent.

     Somewhere along the way, the idea of introducing general protections
for "marriage" and "the family" was dropped and the interim constitution
contains no language to that effect. But it does contain a general non-
discrimination provision which seems destined to have a profound effect
on family law. Section 8, headed "Equality" reads as follows:

---

3   F. Kaganas and C. Murray, "The Contest Between Culture and Gender Equality Under
    South Africa's Interim Constitution" 21 *Journal of Law and Society* No. 4 (1994) 416-
    418.
4   Project 58: Group and Human Rights Interim Report (1991).
5   Article 19.
6   Article 10.
7   *Charter of Fundamental Rights* (1993), article 12.

"8.(1) Every person shall have the right to equality before the law and to equal protection of the law.

(2) No person shall be unfairly discriminated against, directly or indirectly and, without derogating from the generality of this provision, on one or more of the following grounds in particular: race, gender, sex, ethnic or social origin, colour, sexual orientation, age, disability, religion, conscience, belief, culture or language."

There is widespread acknowledgement that these rights are granted to all South African citizens and that their ousting by "closed shop" units of civil society such as families and cultural groups is unacceptable.[8] Doubts exist, however, on how these rights can be extended to the private sphere in the face of the apparently clear language of section 7(1) of the constitution,[9] which reads:

"This Chapter shall bind all legislative and executive organs of state at all levels of government".[10]

This opens up the classic debate about whether or not the Bill of Rights may have "horizontal" or "vertical" application. On the face of it section 7(1) renders only legislation and administrative action challengeable on the basis of being in conflict with the Bill of Rights, leaving out rules of common law and of African customary law which have not found their way into legislation. The position is further complicated by section 7(2) which specifies that the Bill of Rights shall apply to "all law in force...and all administrative decisions taken..." during the period of operation of the Constitution.

---

8 Kaganas and Murray op cit note 3; A. Sachs, *Protecting Human Rights in a New South Africa* (1990).

9 The language which found its way into the provision apparently represents a compromise between the African National Congress and the Nationalist Government. The former had wanted the Bill of Rights to cover fully private relationships while the latter insisted on restricting the operation of Chapter 3 to organs of government.

10 Compare with section 4(2) which provides that "this *Constitution* shall bind all legislative, executive *and judicial* organs of state..." and is thus wider than section 7(1) in its ambit. (Emphasis added.)

Commenting on these provisions, Professor June Sinclair[11] suggests
that the language in section 7(2) should be given its literal meaning, to give
a wide interpretation to "all law in force". This would obviate the need to
distinguish between law that "resides sufficiently in legislation to be vulnerable to attack"[12] and other rules. She concludes by pointing out that
the matter remains unresolved.[13]

III STATUTORY REFORMS

Despite such doubts, there continues to be a general belief that the Bill of
Rights will, in one way or another, achieve "horizontal" reach, and that
family law will inevitably feel the brunt of the non-discrimination provision.
Obviously in anticipation of this (and in an effort to steal the high moral
ground as champions of human rights months before the election) the
previous government enacted the *General Law Fourth Amendment Act 132
of 1993*, which came into force on December 1. The Act abolishes the
marital power from those marriages within which it had continued to exist
after the reforms of 1984 and 1988.[14]

Further enactments that were obviously prompted by the anticipated
advent of a justiciable Bill of Rights included the *Family Violence Act 133*

---

11 J. Sinclair, "Family Rights" in Van Wyk *et al* (eds) *Rights and Constitutionalism: The
    New South African Legal Order* (1994) Juta and Co 522. I am indebted to this, the most
    comprehensive analysis yet of the state of family law in South Africa, for most of the
    facts and figures in this report.

12 Ibid at 523.

13 These are issues that must necessarily await clarification by the courts once constitutional
    litigation gets truly underway.

14 Section 11 of the *Matrimonial Property Act 88 of 1984* had removed the marital power
    from all marriages contracted after November 1, 1984 by white, "Coloured" or "Asian"
    couples: black spouses were expressly excluded. The position was remedied four years
    later when the *Marriage and Matrimonial Property Law Amendment Act 3 of 1988*
    abolished the marital power in the marriages of black people, again prospectively.
    Thousands of South African marriages contracted *before* November 1, 1984 (for whites,
    Coloureds and Asians) and December 2, 1988 (for blacks), respectively, thus continued
    to be subject to the marital power in the face of criticisms by the bench, the practising
    profession and legal academics.

of 1993;[15] the *Domicile Act 3 of 1992;*[16] and the *Guardianship Act 192 of 1993.*[17]

IV THE CASE OF AFRICAN CUSTOMARY LAW[18]

The interim constitution is clearly a compromise document, reflecting a political accommodation between many parties and groupings which, in some respects, is more a peace treaty than a fundamental law. This means that there are many provisions in the constitution which are incompatible with one another or whose consequences appear to be in conflict. Nowhere is this more obvious than in the treatment of African customary law in the document. During the negotiations the traditionalist lobby found itself in a relatively powerful position and it was able to win a number of significant concessions, the most important of which was the inclusion of Constitutional Principle XIII[19] which guaranteed the continued existence of the institution of traditional leadership and of customary law.

At the same time the feminist lobby, fighting a rearguard battle, organized successfully to prevent an outright victory by the traditionalists.

---

15 Which removed the "marital rape exception".
16 Among other innovations, this Act abolished the sexist "domicile of dependence" for married women, thus freeing every adult to acquire a domicile of choice.
17 This introduced the concept of joint guardianship by both parents over legitimate children.
18 Sometimes termed indigenous law, African customary law is the system of norms which governs the lives of millions of black people, particularly (but not exclusively) in the rural areas. It is a custom-based system and its legitimacy lies largely in its claims to a direct link with the past and with tradition. Nowadays it is accepted that customary law has undergone profound changes through various kinds of interaction with the colonial state and with European culture. This has led to the growth of "official" customary law which consists of rigid rules, embedded in judicial decisions and statutes, which have lost the characteristics of dynamism and adaptability for which African custom was famous. In their daily lives, however, people tend to ignore "official" customary law, preferring instead to order their lives according to what we may term "living" customary or folk law.
19 The Constitutional Principles, contained in Schedule 4 of the constitution, represent the political agreements concluded during the negotiations. In terms of these agreements the Constitutional Assembly in drawing up the final constitution cannot depart from the thirty-four Principles set out in the Schedule. They are the negotiated guidelines prescribing the form of the final constitution, covering issues ranging from the shape of the civil service to the system of elections.

(In particular, they managed to keep out of the constitution any language insulating customary law, or "culture" in general, from the reach of the Bill of Rights – which is what the traditional leaders had proposed). The result is that the interim constitution contains language favourable to both tendencies, without clearly indicating which tendency is to prevail in the event of a clash. Thus customary law is recognized – in my opinion, quite strongly – in the constitution, yet it is made subject to Chapter 3 and to legislation. There are also guarantees to the enjoyment of "cultural life" and to the promotion of cultural diversity, yet the Bill of Rights prohibits discrimination on the ground of culture, among others.

References to customary law in the Constitution include the following:

a) Section 33(2) and (3) – which set out the relationship between the fundamental rights enshrined in Chapter 3 and "any law" including customary law. Thus customary law may not limit a fundamental right: on the other hand the existence of a fundamental right does not imply the denial of any other rights or freedoms conferred by customary law "to the extent that they are not inconsistent" with Chapter 3.

b) Section 35(3) – in interpreting customary law courts should have regard to the spirit of the bill of rights.

c) Section 126(1) – provincial legislatures shall have concurrent competence with Parliament to make law with regard to "indigenous law and customary law". (This was achieved by an amendment – the *Constitution of the Republic of South Africa Amendment Act No. 2 of 1994* – which inserted customary law into the list of matters within provincial competence which is set out in Schedule 6).

d) Section 191(1) and (2) – recognising traditional authorities which observe "a system of indigenous law" and making that law subject to "regulation by law".

e) Section 182 – entitlement of traditional leaders of communities "observing a system of indigenous law" to ex officio status in local government.

f) Constitutional Principle XIII (in Schedule 4) read with section 71(1)(a) – the final constitution must recognize indigenous law (subject to fundamental rights and legislation) and the institution of traditional leadership based on such law.

In addition, there is language in the interim constitution which protects the right of South Africans to participate in the language and culture of their choice. Thus, section 31 acknowledges the right of everybody to their "cultural life"; constitutional Principle XI (read with section 71(1)(a) requires the final constitution to promote and protect the diversity of language and culture; and the new Constitutional Principle XXXIV (inserted by *Act 2 of 1994*) acknowledges "the notion of the right to self-determination by any community sharing a common cultural and language heritage" (subject only to the right of "South African people as a whole" to self-determination).

[One may observe, as an aside, that these latter provisions – Principle XXXIV and the amendment to section 126 – are perfect examples of the point made earlier about the interim constitution being a peace treaty. Both amendments were passed early in 1994 and were aimed solely at persuading the Inkatha Freedom Party to participate in the elections of April 27, 1994. The result is that we are left with horrendously difficult questions such as how to interpret the notion of "overlapping rights to self-determination": the self-determination of a group bound by a common language and culture, and the self-determination of the people of South Africa as a whole.]

The cumulative effect of these references seems to be clear: of the three options theoretically open to the constitution-makers to

i   specially entrench customary law,

ii   recognize it, or

iii   abolish it,

the path that was followed was to recognize customary law in fairly strong terms. My own feeling is that, in view of Constitutional Principle XIII and the additions to section 126, such recognition is as close to entrenchment as one can get without requiring special majorities for any contemplated alterations to the status quo.

The indigenous package thus has a very strong presence in the interim constitution: what is more, it has a guaranteed life in the final constitution. This is so, despite language in the constitution subjecting customary law and culture to "fundamental rights", to "regulation by law" and to the "values underlying an open and democratic society based on freedom and equality".

Indeed that is where the problem lies. The constitution does not provide any guidelines for the resolution of conflicts should this clearly recognized system clash with the countervailing modern values found in the constitution, especially in the bill of rights[20].

---

20   See generally R.T. Nhlapo, "The African Family and Women's Rights: Friends or Foes?" (1991) *Acta Juridica* 135-146 for the ways in which customary law poses a problem for human rights.

V   PROBLEM AREAS IN CUSTOMARY LAW

For the first time, then, areas of customary law will be subject to a written constitution which guarantees all the classical liberal entitlements in a justiciable Bill of Rights.[21] Most of the problems which will need to be addressed centre around marriage:[22] the formation of marriage, rights within marriage, and divorce. But underlying all of these is the sensitive and emotive issue of polygamy or, more properly, polygyny.[23]

A   Polygyny

From very early on[24] South African Law made it clear that it could not recognize customary marriages (and Muslim marriages) because of their potentially polygamous nature. For decades, the official view has maintained a strict distinction between a "union" and a "marriage": the former referred to a relationship contracted in accordance with African customary rites while the latter meant a civil, or a proper, marriage.[25] With the negotiations for a final constitution currently underway, the issue has once again become topical: does polygyny offend against the Bill of Rights? In what ways? And what should the Constitution do about it?

---

21   This is going to necessitate consideration of issues that have been "ducked" over the years by successive South African parliaments. T.W. Bennett, *A Sourcebook of African Customary Law for Southern Africa*, Juta and Co. (1991) Cape Town explains: "It would be generous to attribute the want of attention to an unconscious neglect; it is more probably the result of a deliberate policy to exclude Africans from full participation in the South African legal system". He concludes that the marginalization of customary law has led to it being "ignored in the legislative processes that, in the past two decades, have preceded reform of the common law of divorce, intestate succession and matrimonial property" (Preface v).

22   African society, even more than others, constructs its foundations in the notions of family and kinship. Rules relating to the formation and dissolution of families are thus taken very seriously: marriage must surely rate as the single most important ceremony in traditional life.

23   Amongst the indigenous peoples of South Africa polygyny – when one man may marry more than one wife – is the culturally prevalent practice. Polyandry – when one woman may marry several husbands – is unknown.

24   See the case of *Seedat's Executors v. The Master (Natal)* 1917 AD 302.

25   Section 35 *Black Administration Act 38 of 1927.*

The argument most often advanced is that in a country that is governed by a Constitution whose primary social and political goal is equality, a form of marriage in which one man can marry a multiplicity of wives (but not vice versa) cannot survive: it is discriminatory and it fosters inequality.[26] Echoing the same view, but careful to lay the blame where it belongs, Kaganas and Murray[27] argue that patriarchy rather than polygyny is the culprit but that the latter plays an important supporting role to the former. Maintaining polygyny makes it that much more difficult to eradicate patriarchy.[28]

On the other hand Dlamini[29] mounts a vigorous defence of polygyny, arguing that it caters for women who would otherwise not find husbands and that it reduces levels of divorce. (He is unhappy about the high divorce rate in Western marriages, referring to it as "serial polygamy"). Kaganas and Murray themselves concede that there might be some benefits for women in polygamous households: providing companionship, sharing of the workload (and of the sexual demands of the husband), facilitating the spacing of children etc.[30] June Sinclair correctly summarizes this debate in the words: "These diverse views reveal that moral condemnation of one form of marriage in favour of another is unhelpful."[31]

The demands of the constitution for equality and non-discrimination may necessitate some readjustment to the "package" that comes with the customary marriage, but the process should be handled with care. It is naïve to think that social practice can be changed simply by enacting legislation.[32] Even more importantly, outlawing a system in which thousands of women are actively involved would deny them the protection of the law which they currently enjoy[33] without putting anything else in its place. Moreover, it is arguable that failure to recognize customary marriage violates section 8(2)

---

26 A. Sachs, "The Constitutional Position of the Family in a Democratic South Africa" in Sachs op cit note 8.

27 1991 *Acta Juridica* 116 at 130.

28 Ibid; see also Sinclair op cit note 11 at 563.

29 "The Role of Customary Law in Meeting Social Needs" (1991) *Acta Juridica* 71-85.

30 Op cit note 3 at 130.

31 Op cit note 11 at 563.

32 See C.R.M. Dlamini who decries the creation of "paper law" which he describes as "law at variance with the practices of the people, and therefore lacking in legitimacy, as well as effectiveness", in "The Future of African Customary Law" in A.J.G.M. Sanders (ed.) *The Internal Conflict of Laws in South Africa* (1990) Butterworths 3.

33 Sinclair op cit note 11 at 563.

which prohibits discrimination on grounds of culture; the corollary being that recognition may have to be in spite of polygyny, rather than contingent upon monogamy.[34]

Fortunately, in the South African debate there is a growing body of serious analyses of the interplay between culture and human rights.[35]

B   Lobolo or bridewealth[36]

Perhaps second only to polygyny in notoriety is the question of lobolo in customary marriage. Long misunderstood as wife-purchase, the institution is well described by Fannin (writing of the Swazi) who says:

> "Lobolo means cattle (or their equivalent in money) which the bridegroom, his father or his guardian agrees to deliver to the father or guardian of the bride for the purpose of ratifying the matrimonial contract between the group of the bridegroom and the group of the bride and of ensuring that the children of the marriage adhere to the family of the bridegroom."[37]

It is not necessary here to go into the various explanations for the lobolo practice. It now appears fairly settled that an important rationale in the minds of those who practice the custom is that the cattle transferred to the woman's

---

34   Many have argued for the latter position, eg Sachs op cit note 8. To my mind not enough thought has been given to whether there really exists any factor that distinguishes *morally* between polygyny and monogamy, especially "serial polygamy". The debate has not received the serious attention it deserves, mainly because of an automatic assumption that any "civilised" person would opt for monogamy. See Kaganas and Murray op cit note 27 at 127 who find assumptions of the inherent superiority of monogamy (from an equality standpoint) "dubious".

35   Kaganas and Murray op cit note 3; T.W. Bennett, "Human Rights and the African Cultural Tradition" in W. Schmale (ed) *Human Rights and Cultural Diversity* (1994) Keip Publishing, Goldbach 269-280; T.W. Bennett, "The Equality Clause and Customary Law" (1994) *South African Journal of Human Rights* 122-130; R.T. Nhlapo, "Cultural Diversity, Human Rights and the Family in Contemporary Africa: Lessons from the South African Constitutional Debate" *International Journal of Law and the Family* 9 (1995) 208-225. These will provide much-needed material on the state of the debate should the Constitutional Court ever be seized with these questions.

36   Known also as *bohali*, *bogadi*, *rovoro*, *ikhazi* and *munywalo* in the languages of Southern Africa, the practice is an abiding feature of marriage by customary rites.

37   *Preliminary Notes on Principles of Swazi Customary Law* 1967 Lozitha: (unpublished) p.13, an influential research report frequently cited in court.

family compensate them for the loss of their daughter and her reproductive capacities. These cattle are then used to "marry" a bride for one of her brothers, thus bringing in another "reproductive unit" and keeping the groups in a state of equilibrium.[38] There are also suggestions that the practice serves as a guarantee of the good conduct of the spouses;[39] as security for the woman in the case of marriage breakdown;[40] as an indication of the groom's seriousness and sense of responsibility; but there is no doubt that the function of legitimating the children of the marriage is paramount.

The lobolo custom is now protected by statute in South African law. Section 1(1) of the Law of Evidence Amendment Act 45 of 1988 provides for the recognition of customary law in all courts subject to the condition that such customary law should not be opposed to the principles of public policy or natural justice. In a second proviso the statute states quite clearly: "...it shall not be lawful for any court to declare that the custom of lobola or bogadi or other similar custom is repugnant to such principles".[41]

Under the interim constitution, challenges to the custom of lobolo will mostly emanate from the feminist lobbies who frequently attack the custom for treating women as property. There are also attacks against the monetisation of the practice[42] and the subsequent distortions that have seen

---

38   J.F. Holleman *Shona Customary Law: with reference to kinship, marriage, the family and the estate* 2nd ed. (1975) Manchester University Press, Manchester; A. Chigwedere *Lobolo: The Pros and Cons* (1982) Books for Africa, Harare; M. Chinyenze "A Critique of Chigwedere's Book *Lobolo: The Pros and Cons* in relation to the Emancipation of Women in Zimbabwe" *Zimbabwe Law Review* Vol. 1 and 2, 1983-84; J.M. Hlophe "The KwaZulu Act on the Code of Zulu Law – a guide to intending spouses and some comments on the custom of lobolo" 1984 XVII *CILSA* 163; C.R.M. Dlamini "Should lobolo be abolished? A reply to Hlophe" (1985) XVIII *CILSA* 361.

39   B.A. Marwick *The Swazi* (1940) Frank Cass & Co., London, 133.

40   S. Burman "Capitalizing on African Strengths: Women, Welfare and the Law" (1991) 7 *South African Journal of Human Rights* 215.

41   The history of the second proviso makes interesting reading. A *Law 4 of 1885* had granted courts in the Transvaal jurisdiction to apply customary law subject to restrictions similar to the 1988 Act. Having decided that the customs of polygyny and *lobolo* were "repugnant to the principles of humanity observed in the civilized world" the judges in the Transvaal refused to recognize the customary marriage. The effect of course was to render all relationships stemming from matrimony "illegitimate", which in turn amounted to a virtually total withholding of recognition from some of the most fundamental institutions and principles of customary law. The second proviso to section 1(1) of the 1988 Act aims to ensure that the repugnancy clause is never again used to tear the heart out of customary law in this way.

42   Bennett, op cit note 21 at 201.

the custom become a "get rich quick" device for the fathers of prospective brides.[43] Whether it survives these attacks will depend on whether it can be shown that the custom contributes to the subordination of women.[44] A likely outcome is that lobolo will continue to be seen by African spouses as an important aspect in their marriages[45] but will increasingly become optional and symbolic.[46] Lobolo is an essential element in the contracting of a customary marriage, except in KwaZulu and Natal, where the Codes – section 38 of *Law 16 of 1985* and s38 of *Proc R151 of 1987*, respectively – make it optional. Its total disappearance from African marriages, both civil and customary, is highly unlikely.

C   Inequality of rights within marriage and at its dissolution

A constitutional confrontation between the terms of section 8 and the dominant position of the man within an African customary marriage is inevitable. The whole of African family law is permeated by the principle of patriarchy which accords a pre-eminent position to males in society, especially male elders. Within the family this is expressed in the form of a wide ranging marital power of the husband over his wife. The notion is closer to guardianship in its ordinary sense: the husband has the final say in matters concerning both the person and property of his wife. (Needless to say, in customary law this power cannot be excluded by ante-nuptial contract.) In some systems this power includes the right to administer corporal punishment on the wife "for purposes of correction".[47] Instead of easing the plight of African women in this regard, South African law has formalised this minority status in legislation. Section 11(3)(b) of the *Black*

---

43   Sachs op cit note 26.

44   Sinclair op cit note 11 at 566.

45   At present, it is routinely paid even in consideration of a civil/Christian marriage.

46   Judicial decisions from Zimbabwe suggest that this may be the inevitable consequence of removing the stigma of perpetual minority from African women. An Age of Majority Act which confers full adult status on women, and which is made fully applicable in the traditional setting, would seem to be incompatible with a father's right to demand *lobolo*, sometimes to the extent of making his consent to the marriage conditional upon its payment. See *Katekwe v Muchabaiwa* S.C. 87/1984.

47   See generally R.T. Nhlapo "International Protection of Human Rights and the Family: African Variations on a Common Theme" (1989) 3 *International Journal of Law and the Family 1.*

Administration Act 38 of 1927 deems wives married by African customary rites and living with their husbands to be minors under the guardianship of their husbands, except for those living in Natal.

The breakup of the marriage, too, is characterised by inequality. The grounds for divorce are not identical;[48] the woman's freedom to activate the divorce process is restricted;[49] and her rights to maintenance and to the custody of her own children[50] are circumscribed.

A measure of amelioration of some of these rules has already occurred in KwaZulu/Natal where section 11(3)(b) of the Black Administration Act is inapplicable.[51] The Natal and KwaZulu Codes represent the only codified customary law in South Africa and, though it has been possible to enact some progressive provisions into these compilations, assessing their meaning and their reach is "inordinately complex"[52] because of the re-incorporation of the former "homelands and self-governing territories" into South Africa.[53]

VI POSSIBLE CONSTITUTIONAL APPROACHES

The devices available in the interim constitution for the resolution of the problems set out above are largely inconclusive. While the directives contained in section 8 are clear, language such as "unfair discrimination" will still generate problems of interpretation and some debate. There will possibly be some discrimination (ie difference in treatment) that is deemed to be fair.

---

48 In customary law adultery is committed when a married woman has sexual intercourse with a man other than her husband. The implications of this rule are that a man, married or single, commits adultery only if he has sexual intercourse with a married woman. Adultery as a ground for divorce is thus available only to the husband, not the wife.

49 Because she did not negotiate the marriage, she is dependent on her guardian to negotiate the dissolution on her behalf – a position that has been confirmed several times by the courts: *Sweleni v Moni* 1944 NAC (C&O) 31; *Nhlabati v Lushaba* 1958 NAC 18 (NE).

50 Traditionally maintenance is a duty placed upon her father or guardian as the holder of the *lobolo* cattle; similarly the *lobolo* indicates where the children go on divorce. If *lobolo* has been fully paid (or the instalments are deemed to be satisfactory) custody of the children will vest in their father's lineage.

51 By the *KwaZulu Act on the Code of Zulu Law 6 of 1981*, but see Sinclair op cit note 11 at 566-567 on doubts whether this reform is rendered nugatory by the retention of the marital power of the husband in the Code, contrary to the statutory position in South Africa as a whole.

52 Sinclair op cit note 11 at 567.

53 See below.

In addition, section 33(1) – the limitation clause – will allow, in appropriate circumstances, a right entrenched in Chapter 3 to be limited by a "law of general application". Those circumstances will be when the limitation is found to be reasonable and justifiable in a democratic society based on freedom and equality, and when such limitation does not "negate the essential content of the right in question". Moreover, some rules will find protection in the terms of section 229, which provides for "all laws" to continue in force until they are repealed or amended.

Where the rule challenged cannot be protected in these ways then it must "take its chances" under the Bill of Rights. Even here the answers are largely speculative. Will the Bill of Rights apply "horizontally" despite the wording of section 7(1)? When there is a head-on clash between rights equally entrenched in the constitution, which one should prevail and why? In the final analysis, section 98(5) will bear the brunt of the task. That section provides:

> "In the event of the Constitutional Court finding that any law or any provision thereof is inconsistent with this Constitution, it shall declare such law or provision invalid to the extent of its inconsistency: Provided that the Constitutional Court may...require Parliament or any other competent authority, within a period specified by the Court, to correct the defect in the law or provision..."

At the end of the day, many problematic areas of customary law will be subjected to this kind of adjustment, if they have not already been modified by statute.

VII CONCLUSION

Since the elections of April 27, 1994 South Africa has moved from the notion of parliamentary supremacy (where the courts had limited scope to question the laws issuing from the legislature) to constitutionalism, where both the common law and legislation have to comply with a Bill of Fundamental Rights protected by the Constitutional Court. This is having a profound effect on all branches of the law, including family law.

For the first time the legal system of the indigenous population will have to be reckoned with more seriously than has been the case in the past. That system is largely about family relations, and the task of adapting it to constitutional norms will call for a great deal of effort from lawyers, social scientists, anthropologists and politicians alike.

That task will have to be performed against the background of a uniquely South African phenomenon: the past policy of "separate development". As a result of apartheid's attempts to divide the country into a "white South Africa" surrounded by nominally independent satellite "tribal" states, there came into existence the TBVC[54] states. Together with the so-called "self-governing territories" these entities had power to make their own laws in a range of fields which included family law.

On April 27 all these areas again became part of the "national territory" of the Republic of South Africa.[55] By this time many had used their legislative powers to enact laws regulating family matters. Thus the "self-governing territory" of KwaZulu entrenched the marital power of the husband over his wife,[56] following a similar move by the "independent" homeland of Transkei[57] where such marital power cannot be excluded by antenuptial contract. The same Transkei enactment makes it lawful for a man to marry more than one wife.[58]

At the same time wideranging legislative reforms of marriage and family law were taking place in the Republic of South Africa.[59] These were naturally not applicable to KwaZulu and Transkei. Immediately prior to the election the position was thus that "in the Republic proper":

i   the African customary marriage was not recognized; and
ii the marital power had been abolished in all civil marriages.

In KwaZulu and Transkei the marital power was alive and well; and in Transkei a statutorily recognized polygamous marriage had existed for over

---

54   The abbreviation stands for: Transkei, Bophuthatswana, Venda and Ciskei, the four "homelands" which had formally accepted the version of independence offered by the apartheid regime. Their "sovereign" status was recognized only by South Africa. Self-governing status denoted the level of autonomy immediately preceding "independence": at the time of the 1994 election some six territories enjoyed this status.

55   By section 1 of the Constitution, read with schedule 1.

56   Section 27(3) of the KwaZulu Code Act 16 of 1985.

57   Section 39 of the Transkei Marriage Act 21 of 1978.

58   Section 3(1) and (2).

59   See note 14 above.

a decade.[60] The Constitution preserves the laws of the TBVC and "self-governing territories" by section 229 which provides that such enactments will continue in force until repealed or amended. There is no language stipulating what the position of "national" legislation is *vis á vis* these territories. The stage is thus set not only for conflicts between the "preserved" laws and the Bill of Rights[61] but also between these preserved laws and national South African law.

The last word on this must surely go to Professor Sinclair, who concludes:

> "What emerges from all of this is that for the ordinary citizen, and even the experts, the law is inordinately complex. To make the fundamental right of equality for women a reality may require protracted litigation followed by a period of waiting for appropriate legislation...A code of family law drawing together the disparate common-law and statutory rules and making uniform their application is overdue."[62]

In addition to the statutory and common law rules, there will clearly be a need to weave in the rules of indigenous law as well.

---

60 In both Transkei and KwaZulu, of course, the customary marriage, with all its implications, had existed for centuries outside of statutory arrangements. See C.B. Mndaweni, "Limping Marriages in the New South Africa?" XXIV *Comparative and International Law Journal of Southern Africa* (1991) 215-225.

61 Which apparently would be resolved in favour of the Bill of Rights.

62 Op cit note 11 at 543.

SPAIN

MARRIAGE BEFORE THE MAYOR AND OTHER MATTERS

*Gabriel Garcia Cantero**

I   INTRODUCTION

It would seem that the period of major reforms in Family Law, following on the Constitution of 1978, has ended in Spain.[1] Nonetheless there have been reforms of detail in the field of the celebration of civil marriage; certain legal problems arising from the marriage of persons afflicted by mental illness; and administrative decisions made by the authorities responsible for the Register of Civil Status have highlighted the nature of the right to marry (jus connubium) as a fundamental human right recognised under Article 32 of the Constitution.

II   INTERNATIONAL TREATIES

On March 2, 1994, Spain signed an agreement with the United Kingdom, under the Hague Convention of 1980, on the abduction of children across frontiers. It provides that documents sent by Spain to the United Kingdom central authorities will be drawn up in Spanish, while those sent by the United Kingdom to the Spanish central authorities will be in English. This will simplify proceedings.

On May 31, 1994, Spain formally signified acceptance of the Convention of September 4, 1958, on the international exchange of information about civil status.

III   NATIONAL LEGISLATION

The Statute of December 23, 1994 authorises celebration of civil marriage by Mayors. The Statute amends articles 49, 51, 52, 53, 55, 57, 62 and 73 of the Civil Code, so as to allow mayors to perform the marriage ceremony

---

*   Professor of Civil Law, University of Zaragoza. Translated by Peter Schofield.
1   See the writer's article, "Family Law in the Eighties", J.F.L. 1988-1989, at 281 ff.

A. Bainham (ed.), The International Survey of Family Law 1994, 435–439.

for citizens who have chosen to marry in civil form. It should be noted that mayors already had authority to do this, but their role was subordinate to that of the Judge responsible for the Civil Status Register. The amendment gives them an authority concurrent with that of the Judge. It could be that the Legislature was seeking to resolve an "historical conflict" since, traditionally,[2] Judges alone have been competent for the celebration of marriage. Their monopoly ended in 1981. The new Law places the Judge and the Mayor on an equal level, and it is for the contracting parties to make their choice.

During 1994, the Government introduced a draft law on unmarried couples, and another to simplify the system of divorce and separation, but, because of political instability, it is not possible to predict whether they will be enacted.

IV   ADMINISTRATIVE DECISIONS REGARDING THE RECORDING OF MARRIAGE IN THE REGISTER OF CIVIL STATUS

Under the law currently in force, all acts in relation to a person's civil status must be registered in the books of the appropriate Register. Although classed as an administrative act, control of this Register falls within the competence of the Judge of First Instance (in large towns this means a specialised Judge, devoted full time to this activity). The process of registration is subject to appeal ultimately to be determined administratively by the Ministry of Justice (Directorate General of Registers and Notaries); and against the decisions of this administrative body appeal lies to the Civil Courts. The regime of the Civil Register is governed by the Act of 1957, and Regulations of 1958, much modified following the reform of Family Law.

To assess the effect of administrative decisions in 1994, in relation to marriage, the principles governing the jus connubium must be borne in mind. Under the Constitution, Article 32 para. 1: "The man and the woman have the right to contract marriage in full legal equality." The right to marry is covered by articles 42 to 107 of the Civil Code, as reformed by the Law of July 7, 1981. In accordance with article 44 of the Civil Code "the man and the woman have the right to contract marriage as provided in this Code."

---

2   Scil. from 1870, in which year civil marriage was introduced in Spain.

Doctrinal writers note that this text is somewhat restrictively drafted in relation to the Constitution. But in fact the law recognises, alongside the civil form, marriage according to the rites of the Roman catholic and protestant churches, jewish and islamic religious marriage, and also marriage celebrated abroad under the lex loci; and to complete this legal framework, one must add that, under Article 61, para. 1, "marriage takes legal effect from the moment of its celebration."

Apart from brief periods (1870-1875, 1932-1938) canon law marriage had legal effect in Spain. The Concordat of 1970 now in force between the Holy See and the Spanish State requires the recording of church marriages in the Civil Status Register in order to affect the rights of third parties. The repealed law required this to be done within five days, but this rule disappeared in the 1981 Law. A Resolution of May 24, 1994 requires the Judge to register, even if application is made after the expiry of the five day limit, without the need for special administrative procedure for registration out of time.

Certain conditions are imposed for foreign divorce to be recognised in Spain. Under the Resolution of June 2, 1994, registration of the second marriage, celebrated abroad by a Spanish citizen, was refused registration on the ground that the divorce decree had not received an exequatur in Spain. Since the first marriage was between two Spaniards, its dissolution would have had to be registered in the Civil Register in order that the second could be registered.

Marriage of people with mental troubles raises delicate problems. Under present law, while soundness of mind is no longer a condition precedent for contracting marriage, there is uniformity of doctrine supporting nullity where a person was not in full enjoyment of intellect and liberty at the time of the ceremony. What the new regime does is to address a special rule to the administrative officer, authorising him:"where a party suffers from psychiatric defect or abnormality...to call for a medical report as to that party's capacity to consent." Against the decision of the Judge or Mayor, there is an appeal to the Directorate General of Registers and Notaries; and in this matter 1994 has seen interesting decisions.

A   Resolution of March 12, 1994

This concerned a female suffering from chronic oligophrenia with a mental age of 14 years; medical opinion was that marriage would be beneficial, to develop the personality of the young woman, and the Judge was in favour of the marriage, but the Ministère Public intervened to oppose it. The Directorate General rejected this opposition, because the jus nubendi is recognised in the Constitution as a fundamental human right and the freedom to marry enjoys the benefit of the doubt.

B   Resolution of March 18, 1994

In this case, a mother opposed the marriage of her adult daughter, judicially declared incapable. Medical opinion and the Judge favoured the marriage. It was held that persons judicially declared incapable can, in certain cases, perform such civil acts such as making a will or marrying; here the legally required conditions were fulfilled for the validity of a civil marriage, and the mother's opposition could not prevent the exercise of a constitutionally guaranteed right; consequently the Resolution confirmed the Judge's decision to permit the celebration of the patient's marriage.

C   Resolution of March 24, 1994

A contrary solution was reached in the case of the Resolution of March 24, 1994; here medical opinion, that of the Ministère Public and the decision of the Judge came down against the celebration of the marriage; unlike the preceding case, there had not been a judicial declaration of incapacity, but the Resolution considered that Article 56, para. 2, of the Civil Code applied, and refused authorization on the ground that the person lacked capacity to give consent to a marriage.

V BIBLIOGRAPHY

Over the past decade, much has been published on Spanish Family Law, as a result of the major legislative reforms that have taken place. In the period covered by this article, two important works must be noted:

Comentarios a las reformas del Código civil, (Commentary on the reforms of the Civil Code), edited by R. Bercovitz, Tecnos, (Madrid 1993).

Castan Tobeñas, Derecho de Familia. Relaciones conyugales, (Family law. Conjugal relations), tome V, vol.1 of Derecho civil español, común y foral (Spanish civil law, national and regional), 12th edition, revised by Gabriel Garcia Cantero and José Ma. Castan Vazquez, Reus, (Madrid 1994), 1220 pages.

Over 900 pages of the first book are given over to commentary and exegesis of the recent enactments relating to family law: Law of November 11, 1987, on adoption, Law of December 15, 1990 against discrimination on grounds of sex, and Law of December 17, 1990 on nationality; explanatory comments are by specialists, mainly university professors.

José Castan Tobeñas (1889-1969), former president of the Court of Cassation, and University Professor, is one of Spain's most renowned civil lawyers. He wrote a treatise on civil law which was carried on after his death by other authors; perhaps this is the most accessible source for foreigners, as it takes account of European doctrinal writing, of common law, of Latin American countries and of those of the former socialist block. In this volume, there is a detailed study of the family and of general questions of family law, of marriage and its formalities and of conjugal relations, both personal and proprietary. An important place is given to presentation of the economic regimes affecting marriage, at national level and at that of the regions, which have their own civil law; in the main these are regimes based on community, although the Balearic Islands and Catalonia have established a regime of separate property.

SWEDEN

THE RIGHTS OF CHILDREN TO SPEAK FOR THEMSELVES AND OBTAIN ACCESS TO INFORMATION CONCERNING THEIR BIOLOGICAL ORIGINS ETC.

Åke Saldeen *

I INTRODUCTION

This report first describes some details concerning the Registered Partnership (Family Law) Act which was passed by the Riksdag (Swedish Parliament) in 1994 and entered into force on January 1, 1995. Further, a brief review is made concerning the amendments to the Secrecy Act whereby adults were afforded the right to obtain access to information held by the social welfare committee in order to learn of their biological origins. A short commentary is also made on the amendments to the Code on Parents, Children and Guardians concerning, inter alia, the adminstration by parents of their infant children's property. Finally, some observations are made concerning the legislative proposals aimed at improving the opportunities for children to speak for themselves in judicial and related issues.

However, by way of introduction, I would also mention that the legislation concerning an extension of the liability of parents and other custodians for the injurious actions of children, which I described in my report for 1993, entered into force on January 1, 1994.[1]

II REGISTERED PARTNERSHIP

I also mentioned in my report for 1993 that during that year a proposal was put forward by the so-called Partnership Commission. The proposal related to the introduction of two new acts, namely an act concerning partnership (i.e. domestic partnership of persons of the same sex) and also an act concerning cohabitees of the same sex. The conservative government then in power was divided on the very controversial issue of whether any legislation should be passed or not in this field and consequently that Government did not

---

* Professor of Private Law, Faculty of Law, Uppsala.
1 See Saldeen in 33 U. Louisville *J. Fam. Law* at 513-521 (1994-95).

A. Bainham (ed.), The International Survey of Family Law 1994, 441–448.

present any government bill proposing such legislation. The Riksdag itself then took up the matter of legislation and passed the Registered Partnership (Family Law) Act.[2] By this Act, two persons of the same sex may permit their partnership to be registered.[3] Such registration means that most of the rules applicable to marriage also apply to a registered partnership. However, it is not possible for registered partners to have the joint custody of a child nor to adopt a child, jointly or individually. Nor do they have access to artificial insemination or fertilization outside the body, which is regulated in Sweden.

The registration is effected by a procedure reminiscent of a marriage ceremony and performed by a judge of the district court or by a person appointed by the county administrative board. It may also be mentioned that even though the legislation is primarily provided for homosexual couples, there is no requirement laid down concerning any particular sexual inclination or that the parties should have a joint life. At least one of the parties must be a Swedish national and domiciled in Sweden. The reason for this is that one has assumed that no other countries, except Sweden itself (and also Denmark and Norway which have previously introduced similar legislation), will recognize registered partnerships. Nor is it the intention that foreign couples should be able to come to Sweden and obtain registration of their partnership here as this will not have any legal effects in their home country.

The Registered Partnership (Family Law) Act entered into force on January 1, 1995. During the first two months, i.e. January and February 1995, 85 couples registered partnerships. In the majority (4/5) of cases it was male couples who were registered.

---

2   It is very unusual for legislation to be passed by such a procedure in Sweden. Usually acts are passed by the Riksdag following government bills.
3   Parliamentary Standing Committee on Civil-Law Legislation Official Report 1993/94:28.

III THE RIGHT OF A CHILD TO OBTAIN INFORMATION WHICH IS OTHERWISE SUBJECT TO SECRECY CONCERNING ITS BIOLOGICAL ORIGINS

In Swedish law, according to the Code on Parents, Children and Guardians (Chapter 2), when an unmarried woman gives birth to a child the municipal social welfare committee is under a duty to investigate the issue of paternity. The investigation usually terminates in the acknowledgment of paternity by the man indicated by the woman. (However, besides the mother, the social welfare committee must approve such an acknowledgement and such an acknowledgement may only be provided if the man may be assumed to be the father of the child.) If the man whom the committee assumes may be the father refuses to acknowledge paternity the committee may, on behalf of the child, institute judicial proceedings concerning the determination of paternity. There are four specially given cases in the Code where the committee are permitted to discontinue the paternity investigation. One example of this is when it proves impossible to obtain sufficient information to determine the issue of paternity. (It should be added that a decision for the discontinuance of a paternity investigation is not definitive. If, for example, new facts come to light the investigation may be resumed. A decision concerning the discontinuance of a paternity investigation may not be appealed against.) In certain cases a child may have a great interest, particularly where a paternity investigation has been discontinued, in obtaining access to the information contained in the social welfare committee files concerning the paternity investigation in order that the child, with the help of this information, may seek to obtain knowledge concerning its biological origin. Such an interest may of course also exist where paternity has been established but the child perhaps doubts that the true paternity has really been established.

However, by reason of secrecy, the child has not always previously had the right to obtain access to such information. Under the rules of the Secrecy Act (SFS 1980:100) concerning disclosure to parties, the child has only had the right of access to information held by the social welfare committee when the child has been considered to be a party in the paternity case. Such information may concern for example which men the mother had sexual intercourse with during the period within which the child may have been conceived. In those cases where the paternity investigation is discontinued the paternity case is considered to be concluded by the social welfare committee on the day the child attains the age of majority. There is thereby no longer any case where the child is a party. Consequently the adult child has not been considered to have any right of access to the information subject to secrecy contained in the social welfare committee's files. The problem was raised, inter alia, by a number of private members bills in the Riksdag in association with Sweden's adoption of the 1989 UN Convention on the Rights of the Child. This secrecy question was, with other secrecy issues, dealt with by the Ministry of Justice by a memorandum including certain proposals to amend the Secrecy Act.[4] On this basis in 1994 the Government submitted a government bill to the Riksdag with proposals for, inter alia, amendments to the Secrecy Act permitting adult children to obtain access to information concerning facts of importance for determining who are their biological parents (Secrecy Act, Chapter 7, Section 4).[5] The government bill was passed by the Riksdag.

The government bill emphasized that a child's interest in obtaining knowledge concerning its biological origins is very great and the protection of the integrity of the mother and any men must be secondary to the child's interest. However, it was also stated that the secrecy should only be broken when the information to which the child wishes to obtain access is really of importance in order for the child to obtain knowledge concerning who the biological parents are. It is not intended that a child should obtain such access to information by reason of simple curiosity. It should also be mentioned that the new rule does not distinguish between adopted and other children. Thus an adopted child may also obtain information of importance in acquiring knowledge its biological parents.

IV RELAXATION OF STATE CONTROL OF THE ADMINISTRATION BY PARENTS
    OF THEIR CHILDREN'S PROPERTY

In 1994 the Riksdag passed a government bill proposing certain amendments to the provisions of the Code on Parents, Children and Guardians concerning

---

4   Några frågor om sekretess [Some Issues concerning Secrecy] (Ministry Publication: Ds
    1993:55).
5   Government Bill 1993/94:165.

guardianship.[6] The new rules enter into force on July 2, 1995 and, above all else, result in the rules concerning the administration by parents of their children's property being considerably relaxed except where such property is of considerable value.

The administration of infants' property by parents and other guardians was placed under strict public control by the legal rules relating to guardianship which were introduced into Swedish law as early as 1924 by the Guardianship Act.[7] These rules were later included in the Code on Parents, Children and Guardians which was passed in 1949 and entered into force in 1950. Amongst other things, the administration is placed under the supervision of the chief guardian (or the chief guardian committee which is a public authority within each municipality). The chief guardian is in turn subject to judicial control by the district court. Supervision by the chief guardian means, inter alia, that the guardian must submit annual accounts of the administration to the chief guardian. It can also be mentioned, for example, that money which is not required to maintain the infant must be deposited in a restricted bank account whereby the funds may not be removed by the guardian without the consent of the chief guardian.

As regards the administration by parents of their children's property, which property is not infrequently donated by the parents, the above rules have for many years been considered to be antiquated and unrepresentative of modern realities. It was probably the case that parents often neglected to observe the applicable rules of administration. The amendments now passed result in the rules being modernized and more suitably adapted to real needs.

The basic rule is now that the chief guardian will only supervise administration by guardians who are the parents in cases where the child's assets exceed a value of eight times the base sum under the National Insurance Act (SFS 1962:381). In 1995 this sum is SEK 285,600 as the base sum is fixed at SEK 35,700. Irrespective of the value of the property the chief guardian's consent is also required in the future in relation to various measures such as, for example, the sale of real property belonging to the

---

6   Government Bill 1993/94:251.
7   See further for example Saldeen, *Family Law* (in H. Tiberg, F. Sterzel & P. Cronhult, Editors. *Swedish Law – A Survey* (1994) at 359ff.)

child and where the child is to incur debts or run a business. In principle, the previously applicable rules continue to apply in relation to adminstration by parents where the child's property exceeds the above mentioned amount and this also applies to guardianship administration exercised by specially appointed guardians. The rules concerning the placement of the infant's assets have, however, been adapted to the requirements resulting from Sweden's participation in the EEA. (As is known, Sweden is now a member of the EU.) It should be mentioned that, even though the value of a child's property does not exceed eight base sums under the National Insurance Act, the more stringent rules concerning supervision by the chief guardian may apply to administration by parents. If special reasons exist the chief guardian may decide that the rules shall, completely or partially, apply to the administration. Further, where a condition of a will, gift or other endowment so provides, a special chief guardian supervision applies to property acquired by an infant by gift, inheritance, will or other beneficial insurance endowment.

V   THE RIGHTS OF CHILDREN TO SPEAK FOR THEMSELVES ON ISSUES CONCERNING THEIR INTERESTS

Under Article 12 of the UN Convention on the Rights of the Child, a child has the right to express its views on all issues concerning it. Even if Swedish law has not been considered to conflict with the Convention a need to make certain improvements of the rules has been considered necessary. It may be mentioned that there have been discussions for many years in Sweden about whether children should be afforded a right of audience in cases concerning custody and access. Thus it was proposed in 1979 by an Official State Report (SOU), presented by the commission appointed in 1977 to investigate the rights of the child, that children be afforded such rights of audience.[8] In a later report the commission presented such a proposal.[9]

---

8   Om föräldraansvar m.m [The Liability of Parents etc.] (Official State Report – SOU 1979:63).

9   Barnets rätt 3. Om barn i vårdnadstvister – talerätt för barn m.m. [Children's Rights 3. Children in Custody Disputes – Rights of Audience for Children etc.] (Official State Report – SOU 1987:7).

However, now such rights of audience for children in such cases has been introduced.

A memorandum prepared by the Ministry of Justice which reviewed cases and matters in the courts concerning children was presented in 1994.[10] This report also made proposals for certain improvements regarding the opportunity of children to speak for themselves in such cases and matters. However, this report did not contain any proposal to introduce rights of audience for children in cases and matters concerning custody and access. But it did discuss in detail the advantages and disadvantages of such rights of audience, and concluded that the disadvantages predominated. Amongst other things, it was stated that a right of audience for children might result in parents, to a greater extent than hitherto, endeavouring to influence the child in certain respects. It was also considered that such a right of audience would further complicate the process of dealing with such cases and matters with the result that there would be a risk that today's lengthy procedures would be even more protracted.

The memorandum proposed instead that an express reminder was introduced into the Code on Parents, Children and Guardians concerning the court's duty to afford particular attention to the wishes of the child having regard to the child's age and maturity. It is now possible to hear a child in court in a custody or access case if there are special reasons justifying it and it is clear that the child will not be harmed by being heard (Code on Parents, Children and Guardians Chapter 6, Section 19). This rule which was introduced to the Code by legislation in 1983 is, according to the travaux préparatoires, intended to be applied restrictively and this has in fact been reflected in judicial practice. It should be mentioned that, according to the memorandum, there is no reason to support developments towards children being heard more often in court. Instead information concerning the views of children may be obtained by the court by means of the custody investigation undertaken by an officer of the municipal social welfare committee. Such investigations have sometimes been criticised as inadequate as regards the description of the child and its needs. For example, there have been

---

10 Barns rätt att komma till tals. Regler för familjerättsliga och sociala mål och ärenden [Children's Rights to be Heard. Rules for Family Law and Social Cases and Matters] (Ministry Publication – Ds 1994:85).

instances where the investigator has only met the child once or not met the child at all. The Ministry memorandum suggests eliminating any such unsatisfactory state. It is therefore proposed that a new express legal rule be introduced whereby those responsible for conducting custody and access investigations shall be bound to endeavour, unless it is inappropriate, to establish the child's views and report them. This means that the investigator must seek to discover the views of a child in a dispute. This is often, according to the memorandum, inappropriate. But the investigator must try to acquire such contact with the child that the investigator can personally form an opinion about whether the child has a view which should be afforded weight when determining the issue of custody and/or access.

Finally, it should be mentioned that the Ministry memorandum, which has not yet led to any legislation, also contains proposals for the introduction of rules emphasizing the importance of children being afforded the opportunity to speak for themselves on issues such as, for example, adoption and change of name.

TURKEY

DIVERSE ISSUES, CONTINUING DEBATES

Esin Örücü [*]

I INTRODUCTION

Changes in Turkish Family law in the last four years are few.[1] However, there are a number of areas worthy of attention. These are areas where certain traditional social values have been reinforced and others where they have been changed or where change is on its way.

One significant event was the ratification of the Convention on the Rights of the Child by Turkey, but with one important reservation. This was in January 1995.

It is interesting to read the reasoning of the Constitutional Court (Anayasa Mahkemesi), which in July 1992 finally published its decision reached in November 1990, finding the right of the husband to give to or withhold from his wife permission to work outside the home to be unconstitutional.[2]

There were also three important decisions of the High Court (Yargitay). The first was on the relationship of a natural father to his natural and illegitimate children, the second on the severe maltreatment of members of the family which may be understood to include rape in marriage, and the third regarding a wife's killing her husband who had anally raped her as a case of justification or defence. These are all significant, the first for responding to traditional values in society, the second for furthering the discussion on rape in marriage and the third in keeping with similar developments in other legal systems.

A new Amnesty Act[3] was passed in 1991 to allow the legalisation of

---

[*] Professor of Comparative Law, School of Law, University of Glasgow and Professor of Comparative Law, Erasmus Universiteit Rotterdam.

[1] For the picture up to 1990 see Örücü, "Turkey: Reconciling Traditional Society and Secular Demands", 26 *J.FAM.L.* 221 (1987-88) and Örücü, "Turkish Family Law: A New Phase", 30 *J.FAM.L.* 431 (1991-92). Also see generally on law of persons, family law and succession, Ansay & Wallace (eds.), *Introduction to Turkish Law*, 3rd ed, Kluwer (1987) Chps. 4-7, 1.

[2] See Örücü, "Turkish Family Law: A new Phase", 30 *J.FAM.L.* 436-437 (1991-1992).

[3] Amnesty Acts or Legitimacy Acts are passed from time to time allowing the registration of consensual marriages for those without a civil marriage contract who are living together as husband and wife and who have a child born into this relationship, where no marriage impediment exists. These Amnesty Acts make the legitimation of thousands

A. Bainham (ed.), The International Survey of Family Law 1994, 449–463.
© 1996 *The International Society of Family Law. Printed in the Netherlands.*

illicit relationships and to give legitimacy to children born into cohabitation not condoned by the formal legal system.[4]

There were also a number of decisions given by the High Court on various topics that are of interest, such as the social value of virginity, the conditions under which gifts are to be returned after an engagement (nisan) is broken, the liability of the head of the household for the torts of minors, whether a still born baby is a person, and a number of cases on divorce and compensation, and the discretion of the judge in granting divorce by mutual consent or upon irretrievable breakdown of marriage.

The above issues will be examined in this survey. Some aspects of Turkish family law regarded as in need of reform, under discussion at present in Turkey in legal circles and women's interest groups, will also be brought to light.

II SURVEY

A   The Convention on the Rights of the Child

The Convention on the Rights of the Child signed by Turkey in 1990 was at last ratified on January 27, 1995. This ratification is noteworthy in view of a rather general attitude to children in Turkey. Two sayings illustrate the traditional attitude to the value of the child especially in rural areas. One is, "God gives, God takes". This is used when a young child dies and expresses the view that sees death as an act of God alone rather than as a possible result of poor conditions of feeding, hygiene and health care. This is also an indication that life is often held to be cheap. The other saying is, "His flesh is yours, his bones are mine". This is what parents say to a teacher when a child begins school, indicating that the teacher should feel free to use physical punishment. It remains to be seen what changes will be

---

of children possible and validate their status. The first was passed in 1933, then in 1945, 1950, 1956, 1965, 1975 and 1981. The last one was introduced in 1991.

4   For an analysis of the problem see Örücü, "Turkey: Reconciling Traditional Society and Secular Demands" 26 *J.FAM.L.* 226-227 (1987-88) and for a general assessment of cohabitation and its consequences Örücü, "Turquie" in Jacqueline Rubellin-Devichi (ed) *Des concubinages dans le monde*, Paris (1990) 237-251.

introduced, and more important, implemented in the field of the rights of the child in Turkey.

As known, this Convention grants children a number of rights among which there are some related to their having access to information and material from a diversity of national and international sources for their benefit in accordance with Article 29 (Article 17). Article 29 states that the parties to the Convention agree, among other things, that the education of the child shall be directed to the development of his personality and talents to their full potential, of his respect for human rights, his parents, his own cultural identity, language and values, the national values of the country in which he is living, the country from which he originates and for civilisations different from his own. Article 30 addresses the States in which ethnic, religious and linguistic minorities exist; stating that a child belonging to such a minority shall not be denied the right, in community with other members of his group, to enjoy his own culture, to profess and practice his own religion or to use his own language. It is here however that Turkey reserved the right to interpret and apply the provisions of these three articles in conformity with the words and the spirit of its own Constitution and the Treaty of Lausanne of 1923. This reservation must be understood within the framework of the separatist claims in the East of Turkey.

B   Can a wife work outside the home?

In 1990 the Turkish Constitutional Court annulled as unconstitutional section 159 of the Civil Code which stated that a wife needs her husband's explicit or implicit permission to work outside the home.[5] This decision was finally published in the Official Gazette, and hence came into effect in July 1992. Two observations are worth making here. The first is that this section 159, and others in the Civil Code, which remain as yet unchallenged, all giving the husband superiority in certain matters such as choosing the abode, having the last word in the bringing up of the children, giving his surname to his wife and being the head of the household, have never been challenged during the period since 1961 when the possibility of challenging their

---

5   90/31; 29/11/1990. This case was reported in Örücü, "Turkish Family Law: A New Phase" 30 *J.FAM.L.* 431 (1991-92).

constitutionality arose with the introduction into the Constitution of the concept of equality of the sexes. The reason could be that in the traditional family, still the predominant pattern in Turkey, the wife does indeed see herself as a second class citizen subject to her husband's will. The reason may also be, of course, that husbands do not use these rights in practice, so that there is no problem. It could also be that this area is regarded as a marginal issue on the Turkish political agenda; an agenda full of serious economic and political considerations of national importance. The second observation is that the Constitutional Court, while finding this section un-constitutional and drawing Parliament's attention to other such articles in the Civil Code in need of removal, went to great pains to point out that their decision should not be taken to mean that they condone a new lifestyle where the working wife neglects her mission in life, that is her family duties as home-maker for her husband and her children. The last paragraphs of an otherwise excellent reasoning read as an apology to appease the traditionalists. It is also interesting that the Court took about two years to publish its reasoned decision and that it felt under an obligation to end a very progressive and learned discussion upon this apologetic note.

C   Who inherits?

A child whose natural father has been established by a court is considered an illegitimate child (section 443 of the Civil Code) and has the same rights as a legitimate child in succession. The High Court decided in 1993[6] that the existence of blood ties alone is not sufficient in itself to create rights of succession and that the existence of such ties must be established by law. The law determines the relationship of a child to the father either through birth within marriage (section 241 of the Civil Code), the marriage of the parents after the birth of the child (section 247), the correction of legitimacy by the judge (section 249) or through the Amnesty Acts where the legitimacy of children born into cohabitation not tied to a secular marriage contract foreseen by law are administratively corrected. No other means exist to establish this relationship. This is so even when the tie between the father and the child is well known to everyone or the father admits to this through

---

6   93/603,4179; 26/4/1993.

other means than those foreseen by law. Thus all children born out of wedlock are natural as to their father. In 1987 the Constitutional Court annulled[7] section 443/1 of the Civil Code which stated that the succession rights of illegitimate children were only one half of those of legitimate children. The gap that was thus created in the Civil Code was filled by the legislature in 1990.[8] It now reads, "illegitimate relatives have the same rights of inheritance as legitimate relatives". There is nothing in the new wording of section 443 to indicate that natural children can inherit from their fathers, since it does not deal with the distinction between a natural child and an illegitimate child. However, in a recent case a lower court insisted on the reverse interpretation claiming that natural children are to be classified automatically as illegitimate children and thus benefit from the arrangements of the new section 443/1. The High Court, this time in a plenary session, decided[9] on the issue of the rights of succession of the natural child from the natural father. According to the Constitutional Court children, legitimate or illegitimate, whose paternity has been resolved, will secure inheritance on an equal footing. The High Court said, "when the natural father of a natural child has been legally determined, then that child becomes an illegitimate child and therefore should inherit on equal terms with the legitimate children. The lower court is right in its insistence on this view". In saying this, the High Court reversed its stance on this matter. This supports my opinion expressed earlier elsewhere,[10] that concessions were being made to societal practices and values. In a single year between 1993 and 1994 the High Court totally changed its position moving towards the views of the traditionalist section of society through re-interpretation. Moreover, this later position is a firmer one being a General Council decision.

This decision had however attached to it two dissenting opinions signed by five judges who were very disturbed by the turn of events.[11] The dissenting opinions expressed a preference for a literal interpretation. They also expressed concern that the Constitutional Court, instead of only annulling a repugnant provision, laid down rules as the legislature would do and indicated its preference by saying "natural children should also have rights

---

7   1/18; 11/9/1987.
8   Reported in Örücü, "Turkish Family Law: A New Phase" 30 *J.FAM.L.* 431 (1991-1992).
9   94/2-244,463; 29/6/1994.
10 See, Örücü, "Turkish Family Law: A New Phase" 30 *J.FAM.L.* 431 (1991-1992).
11 94/2-244,463; 29/6/1994 at 1599.

of succession from their father". The dissenting judges claimed that, had
it been the case that natural children could inherit from their father, an
Amnesty Act would not have been passed in 1991. When the doctrine is
reviewed however, though the dominant view is in agreement with the
dissenting judges, some authors are seen to pander to the traditionalist view
by simply relying on the reasoning of the Constitutional Court.

D   The Amnesty Act 1991

At this point it is appropriate to mention that Turkey passed its most recent
Amnesty Act on May 8, 1991, the previous one being in 1981. This created
another possibility of legitimising the status of children born out of wedlock.
This legislative enactment reiterates the fact that the status of natural
children, whose paternity cases have not been resolved, remains unchanged
in the Civil Code. Thus it could be said that there is no gap in the law here
and that the law does not attribute the status of heirs to this group of
children. The importance of Amnesty Acts, or as they are sometimes called
"Legitimacy Acts", which are passed from time to time with the express
purpose of administratively correcting the status of thousands of children,
otherwise doomed to remain either natural or illegitimate, cannot be overes-
timated in Turkey even today.

E   Can there be rape in marriage?

There is no reference to rape in marriage in Turkish law. However, it has
always been the case that a wife whose husband forces sexual intercourse
on her, especially if it entails the use of force, can use this as a ground for
divorce under the clause "severe maltreatment" according to section 130
of the Civil Code. She can also claim that the act constitutes behaviour
leading to irretrievable breakdown of marriage (section 134) and again use
this as a ground for divorce. It is possible that a wife can use section 161
saying that her husband's behaviour endangers her life, that it subjects her
to degradation and moral and physical damage and ask the judge to interfere;
she might claim the right to live separately from her husband (section 162)
and then ask that section 416 of the Criminal Code be applied and, if there
is bodily harm, can make a complaint under section 456 of the Criminal

Code. Nowhere however is the term "rape" used in connection with the family. It is also very unusual for a wife to initiate any action in Criminal Law against her husband. However case No. 94/6217 (7/7/1994) is such a case where the High Court stated that the husband, who had anal intercourse with his wife without her consent, was guilty of the offence of "severe maltreatment of the members of the family". This offence is regulated by section 478/1 of the Criminal Code. The husband in this case was given a prison sentence of six months and this decision was approved by the High Court. Time will show whether this is the first step towards regarding intercourse by force without consent as falling under this section. What is more noteworthy is the very extensive dissenting opinion of the Chief Judge of the Fourth Criminal Chamber where the case was reviewed. He says that the law should be now talking of rape in marriage.[12] He opines that if there is no material or moral pressure and the intercourse is anal and without consent then section 478 should apply; but, if there is violence and material/and or moral pressure, then whether anal, vaginal or oral, the offence is rape, and the more general section 188/2 should apply; yet, as in the instant case, if a husband uses only threats, which is moral violence, then the offence falls under section 416.[13] After a wide ranging survey of several legal systems, the Chief Judge states that any intercourse without consent violates sexual freedom and is against public policy. He points out that there is no norm in law which allows the use of violence and threats within the family and that this applies equally to sexual intercourse in marriage.

Actually in the definition of rape given in the Turkish Criminal Code all that is specified is sexual penetration of a person without his/her consent. There is no differentiation of man or woman, or that the penetration should be vaginal, anal or oral; therefore, there would be no legal difficulty in introducing the offence of rape in marriage into the system. However, Turkish society is male dominated and the prevailing view on the expected roles of the spouses in marriage is that it is the role of the woman to give

---

12 94/6217; 7/7/1994 at 1848-1852.

13 Section 416/1 states: "A person who rapes someone who has completed his/her fifteenth year of age by using force or threats or rapes someone who is incapable of resisting the act because of a mental or physical illness, for another reason unrelated to the act of rape, or as a result of the perpetrator's using deceitful means, will be given a sentence of 'heavy imprisonment' for not less than seven years".

and of the husband to take. Therefore there would be additional difficulties in securing general acceptance of the view that rape can take place in marriage. The Turkish word for rape is "irza gecme" which literally means "to violate, ravish or dishonour", "irz" itself meaning "chastity, purity and honour". The concept of rape therefore has connotations of penetrating the moral wholeness of a person. An outsider is capable of doing this, but the husband who is responsible for the moral wholeness of the wife could not, by definition, be culpable of such an offence. Although, as pointed out above, there is no difficulty in interpreting the existing provisions to allow such an understanding that there could be rape in marriage, in view of an old High Court decision following the linguistic argument on the meaning of the word "irz" and therefore not accepting the possibility of rape in marriage, there is a need for the High Court to reverse its opinion. It may be also that, given the time and the inclination, Parliament will change the word "rape" to "sexual offences" as was done in Canada for example. Until that is done however, the change of approach in the High Court is very welcome, especially if its Chief Judge has persuasive powers upon the Fourth Criminal Chamber.

F   A wife kills her husband

In 1991 the High Court decided[14] that a woman who killed her husband who had tried to have anal intercourse with her without her consent, using threats and violence, should benefit from the defence provided by section 49 of the Criminal Code. Section 49 regulating instances of "justification", states that no punishment shall be imposed if the perpetrator has acted in the immediate necessity to repel an unjust assault against his/her own or another's person or chastity. This is the second such decision of the High Court and marks a very significant development. Without going into a conceptual analysis of the "battered wife syndrome", the Court is building a new area of law, re-interpreting the "justifications" provision in Criminal Law. Although, in the light of what has been said above, one could be forgiven for thinking that a husband can use any means "to take his wife", obviously there are limits to what the courts expect the woman to suffer.

---

14   91/4, 39; 18/2/1991.

G Some other issues dealt with by the High Court

Decisions of the High Court are always worth looking into for the purpose of discovering how the Court addresses and assesses traditional values and tries to integrate them into a western secular formal legislative framework.

1 The value of virginity

This traditional value was considered by the High Court in a decision relating to the attempted rape of a virgin. The Court held[15] that the hymen and virginity were social values and since in the instant case the hymen had not been torn, there was no offence of rape, and that the loss of virginity is essential for punishment or in considering a sexual assault as rape. The offender in this case had attempted intercourse with the victim under a promise to marry her.

2 An engagement is broken

It was decided by the High Court that when an engagement is broken, damages cannot be claimed for expenses incurred towards food and clothing in the expectation of a wedding. However, the return of gifts beyond the ordinary can be asked or their cost be claimed and that here fault is not relevant. Moreover, if the non-faulty party has suffered excessive psychological damage because of the breaking of the engagement, then moral damages can be granted.[16] The amount of the compensation depends on the duration of the engagement and the reaction of the social environment to the event. Engagement is an unenforceable contract regarded as a serious promise of marriage. It maintains its importance in Turkey, being in many cases the acceptable means for young members of opposite sexes to come together socially, and of giving young women the opportunity to go out at all and young men to go out with "respectable" girls. As a result of this special status of engagement however, its breach without good cause is a serious matter especially in rural areas, with certain legal consequences (sections 84-85); hence there are always many cases for moral compensation before the courts.

---

15   93/1610, 1984; 6/5/1993.
16   94/6159, 7437; 9/5/1994.

3   Who is liable for the acts of a minor?

In 1993 the High Court decided[17] that if at the date of the tort attributed to a minor the parents are divorced, then the courts have to determine which parent has parental authority over the minor and decide on liability accordingly, the general principle being that one of the parents, as head of the household, is liable for the acts of the minor (section 320 of the Civil Code). The facts of the case were the kidnapping and violation of the virginity of a minor with her consent by another minor. The demand was for material and moral compensation from the offender and his parents. The lower court did not find the parents liable, but the decision was reversed by the High Court.

4   When does "one" become a "person"?

In a case where a pregnant woman went to hospital as an emergency case, after the time of expected birth had passed, the doctors did not immediately act or take appropriate measures and the baby died. The lower court decided that the doctors' negligence amounted to manslaughter (section 455/1 of the Criminal Code). The High Court was of the opinion that the status of "person" could only be gained at the actual time of birth;

> "To be considered a person a baby must be safely and completely delivered. Since this overdue baby died in the womb after the process of birth had started, it cannot be regarded as a person and section 455/1 of the Criminal Code does not apply, but section 230 should be considered which simply covers negligence in the performance of one's duties".[18]

5   Divorce: custody and foreign law

In a case where the central issue was divorce and custody, the High Court decided that when a divorce case has a foreign element, the judge is not bound by the declaration of the parties but can ask for their cooperation in the determination of the applicable law. The Court stated that

> "demand for a divorce is a personal right of the married couple, they alone can bring a divorce case to court, and therefore it is necessary to see the document proving marriage. Since the birth registry entry of the plaintiff

---

17   93/2301, 14550; 13/12/1993.
18   94/738, 2971; 8/4/1994.

does not show the plaintiff as married, the fact of marriage has to be proved in another way. This case has a foreign element in that, though at the time the defendant was a Turkish national, the plaintiff is a citizen of Iceland and the marriage took place in Iceland. There the requirement of the law of Iceland will determine the fact of marriage. However, such documents have to be ratified by Turkish officials and there is nothing in the file to indicate that there has been such a marriage. Though there is a Convention on eliminating the requirement of ratification for foreign documents which was ratified by Turkey in 1984, there must be a search into whether Iceland is a party to this Convention. Neither is it obvious whether the plaintiff has gained Turkish nationality by marriage, and if not, what is the law of their place of residence. In view of all this, Turkish law cannot automatically apply to this divorce and therefore the decision of the lower court based on the fact that there is no dispute between the parties, is reversed."[19]

The High Court, this time, now through its General Council, reiterated that

"in order to decide on divorce and custody, the parties must be married in accordance with the law; foreign documents cannot be regarded as legally binding unless ratified, as pointed out by this Court earlier; the existing document therefore, cannot be used. It is also necessary to determine the citizenship of the parties in this case; the plaintiff claims that the mutual applicable law is the law of Iceland, however, it is not obvious whether the defendant has lost her Turkish nationality, this must be established. How the custody of a child is to be determined is differently settled for a child born into or outside wedlock. For this reason also it is very important to confirm the nationality of the parties. The custody of the child is suspended until his legitimacy is determined as to his father whereupon the child would acquire the father's surname and nationality. The court has to appoint an administrator for the estate of the child to protect his interests. The result is that these issues cannot be resolved until the nationality of the parties and whether they are married or not is determined; the insistence of the lower court in its view is wrong."[20]

6   Divorce for desertion

Among the several grounds of divorce provided in the Civil Code, an interesting one is "desertion". When one spouse deserts the other in order not to

---

19   93/2-949, 94/189; 30/3/1994 at 871.
20   Ibid.

perform marital duties or does not come to the marital home for at least three months without good cause, the other spouse can sue for divorce (section 132). In the instant case a husband moved to a new address but the wife did not follow. The husband filed for divorce on the ground of desertion. The High Court stated that an official warning from the court to the wife is a condition of cognizance of a divorce case relying on this ground. This would be sent upon the request of the husband and to be effective must include the following: the full address of the new home; the money for the costs involved in getting there for the wife; an invitation to the wife to come to the new matrimonial home within a month from the date of the warning; and the fact that in case of non-compliance with the warning a divorce suit would ensue.[21] As this is an absolute ground for divorce, at the end of the month divorce will be granted.

7   Divorce and the loss of legitimate expectations

Still on divorce, this time relating to compensation, the High Court consistently decides[22] that a wife who is not at fault in the events leading to divorce, and who has lost the support of her husband and her legitimate expectations as a result of the divorce, must be given appropriate compensation according to both section 143/1, which stipulates that the spouse without fault can claim compensation for his/her present and future legitimate expectations, and also the general section 4 of the Civil Code laying down the principles of fairness and justice. However, in order to decide on appropriate compensation, there are pre-conditions: there must be such a demand, a present or future legitimate expectation must be lost as a result of the divorce and the party demanding this compensation must not be at fault. This pecuniary compensation is an accessory of divorce and can be demanded orally or in writing at any time during the divorce suit. According to the Court, the interests to be considered must be determined by looking at the general structure of the society, the conditions of the country and the realities of life, and must be those that one spouse can expect the other to provide in a reasonable, serious and continuous manner.[23] In the calculations, the court must also assess educational level and age, so as to determine the chances of re-marriage of the spouse demanding compensation,

---

21   93/2312, 3130; 1/4/1994.
22   93/8938, 9751; 22/10/1993; 93/11319, 12087; 10/12/1993; 94/1130, 1582; 15/2/1994.
23   93/8938, 9751; 22/10/199 at 1058.

and whether the demands can be met in any other way. The Court also takes the traditional view of the role of the wife in the wording of such decisions:

> "within the marriage union it is both spouses' duty to provide happiness for the marriage union (section 151), and the future of the wife is guaranteed by the support of the husband, who as the head of the union, has to support the family (section 152). The wife devotes her labour and total capacity to the union without concern for her future, since the husband will take care of her future. Upon divorce, the wife without fault loses this support, the loss of which justifies the demand of the wife for fair compensation".[24]

8 *Divorce and discretion of the judge*

As to the discretion of the judge in divorce cases, the general attitude of the High Court is that divorce suits are of interest to public policy and therefore the judge has a wide discretion and the parties do not have great freedom to act as they like. The judge must, as far as possible, preserve the marriage union which has been formed by a contract in law. The Court considers that the public interest in the preservation of the family, the smallest unit of society, must be paramount; therefore, only when the union is detrimental to social order, is creating problems for society or has collapsed both morally and socially, or if there is no benefit in its preservation either for the spouses or the children, is the best solution deemed to be to bring such a marriage to an end. The judge must gather evidence as to the above points and must find out from the witnesses whether the union has indeed irretrievably broken down.[25] That the parties agree as to the facts does not bind the judge (section 150/3); the facts must be provided and proved and the judge must be "deeply convinced" of them.

This direction taken by the High Court further undermines the possibility of allowing easier divorce and reducing the pre-eminence of fault introduced into the Turkish Civil Code in 1988 by the new section 134.[26] Accepting divorce by mutual consent represented an attempt to make divorce easier and to limit the discretion of the judge in divorce cases. The High Court does not appear prepared to give up its intervention in divorce cases. The rather narrow view taken in the first years of the amendment now seems

---

24 93/11319, 12087; 10/12/1993 at 1059-1060.
25 94/476, 1005; 1/2/1994 at 1060-1062.
26 See Örücü, "Turkish Family Law: A New Phase" 30 *J.FAM.L.* 431 (1991-92).

to be permanently established. It could very well be said that the Court is trying to protect the rights of the wife and the children in divorce cases in the knowledge that they are very vulnerable given the specific character of the marriage union in Turkey. There is a general belief that divorce apparently by mutual consent will adversely affect women.

III NEED FOR REFORM

Various areas of family law are regarded in legal circles as in need of reform.

First, there are still provisions of the Civil Code such as that the husband is the head of the family (section 152/1) in which capacity he chooses the place of abode (section 152), he represents the family (section 154), the wife must carry his surname (section 153), she may acquire his nationality but he cannot acquire hers, the children carry his surname and nationality (section 259) and, although parental authority is shared, his decision prevails in cases of dispute. All these are at odds with the principle of equality of the sexes. The Constitutional Court alluded to these while discussing section 159, as seen above. These sections are in need of removal or amendment by the legislature.

Second is the problem of establishing the acceptability of claims of rape in marriage in a male dominated society in the light of the views discussed above. As stated, there is no legal impediment to this change and it may be coming.

Third; the area of matrimonial property works to the detriment of the average Turkish woman, who is generally not financially independent or secure, has no profession and is a full-time housewife. The legal regime is one of separation of property (section 170, 186-190) which at a cursory glance is attractive for those who aspire to equality. However, it is well established that where marriage has no impact on the status of the property of the spouses, other arrangements must be made to achieve some level of equality at the termination of marriage. This unsatisfactory regime is under discussion at present in Turkey and there are draft bills in preparation to introduce a kind of "deferred community" after the German model. This is important in that very few couples would opt for the other forms of matrimonial regimes provided by the Code by ante-nuptial contract.

Fourth; although section 134 introduced irretrievable breakdown as an objective ground for divorce and was specifically meant to solve the problem of limping marriages created by divorces obtained abroad by Turks living abroad, this did not happen.[27] In order to have effect, foreign judgments must be recognised by Turkish courts. In cases where the divorce ground is "mutual consent" or "irretrievable breakdown", the Turkish courts are keen to establish that the foreign court has found that the marriage has lasted for at least one year, that the parties express their consent freely in court, and that a contract is submitted to the court as to the arrangements of financial matters and children's welfare. The court investigates the evidence provided rather than simply accepting the evidence presented by the spouses.[28] Unless counsel alert the foreign court to the necessity of including such a statement in the reasoning of the decision, the chances are that the Turkish courts will not recognise the foreign judgment.

IV CONCLUSION

This author said in 1990 that, "major controversies exist in Turkey that are not merely academic; they reflect the present social, political, religious and legal realities. No doubt further substantial developments are to be expected".[29] Having here looked at a handful of diverse issues and continuing debates, the author can say the same today.

---

27 Ibid. Also see Örücü, "A review of Turkish divorce law", in *Recht van de Islam* 8, RIMO (1991) 47-62.
28 See for example, 89/10796, 2176; 22/2/1990.
29 Örücü, "Turkish Family Law: A New Phase" 30 *J.FAM.L.* (1991-92) 437-438.

UKRAINE

THE MARRIAGE RELATIONSHIP IN UKRAINE

*Irina V. Zhilinkova**

I   INTRODUCTION

Ukraine sprung up on the world map as an independent state on August 24, 1991; after a proclamation by the National Parliament, the Deed of Sovereignty, she left the USSR. This event became a cause of important socio-economic changes in the country. Today, Ukraine is carrying out a search of its own internal and external policy and looking for new ways of development. Such a complicated transitional period, unfortunately, has provoked a lot of negative consequences – a catastrophic collapse of production, uncontrollable inflation, and social instability.

All of this has exerted an influence on the conduct of the people of Ukraine in all spheres of life, including the family. The population has sharply reacted to the abrupt drop in the standard of living during the past few years. The number of registered marriages has constantly decreased, and the numbers of divorces and family conflicts have increased.

According to the majority of specialists, Ukraine is now facing a heavy demographical crisis. Ukraine has the lowest birth rate among the former republics of the USSR. One-child families are typical. People generally postpone the birth of second and third children for better times. Families with three or more children make up only 6% of all families. As a result of the fall of the birth rate in Ukraine, the republic's population decreased by about 730,000 each year, which has given her a negative population growth rate since the year 1991.[1] The state intends to support young families and families with children.[2] However, against a background of total economic crisis, such help becomes less and less prominent each year.

---

*   Professor of the Civil Law Department at the Ukrainian Law Academy, Kharkiv.
1   N. Lakiza-Satchyk. I demografichne vyzhyvannya. Polituika i chas. No 4. S.18. (1994).
2   Special Law of Ukraine "On the State Help to Families with Children" was adopted by the Supreme Soviet of Ukraine on November 21, 1992.

A. Bainham (ed.), The International Survey of Family Law 1994, 465–481.
© 1996 *The International Society of Family Law. Printed in the Netherlands.*

Another negative result that is evident is an increase in the number of cohabitations, which were not characteristic of the country in previous years. In Ukraine, this has led to a situation in which a lot of young people are reluctant to marry and now live more easily with many different personal contacts.

The dissolution of the USSR and the proclamation of independence also had an influence on family legislation in Ukraine. When the USSR existed as a united state, family law had two different levels. The first was represented by all-union laws on marriage and the family which operated in the country's entire territory. This was "The Fundamentals of Legislation of the USSR and Union Republics on Marriage and Family". The second level consisted of Ukrainian legislation – The Marriage and Family Code of the Ukrainian Soviet Socialist Republic adopted in 1970 – and other laws. The laws of the USSR were the highest legal authority in the territory of the country and were obligatory for all of the republics. In turn, the laws of the Ukraine were subordinate, and were required to correspond completely with all-union legislation. After the break-up of the USSR, all-union laws about marriage and the family became invalid in the territory of the Ukraine. As a result, the Family Code of the Ukrainian Soviet Socialist Republic remained the basic law concerning marriage and the family. Since June 23, 1992, its name has been The Marriage and Family Code of Ukraine (hereafter referred to as "MFC of Ukraine").[3] This Code is still operative at the present time.

Currently in Ukraine, a tremendous amount of work is going on in order to update and revise our family legislation and to create a new Ukrainian Family Code. At present the first draft of the Family Code is ready. It is expected that the new Code will be adopted in the near future. It has preserved the main content and basic principles of the previous code. First of all, changes and amendments have been introduced to the spouses' relationship, especially their property rights and obligations. This Code will take into account the changes which have taken place in Ukraine in recent times.

---

3   The Law of Ukraine, "On Changes and Amendments to the Code on Marriage and Family of the Ukrainian SSR" of June 23, 1992. Vidomosti Verhovnoi Rady Ukrainy. No36. St. 528. (1992).

The second part of the Family Code of Ukraine, "Marriage", includes legal rules adjusting the relations between spouses, their personal and property rights, and their obligations. Principles connected with divorce and the invalidity of marriage are also included here.

The Family legislation of Ukraine begins with the main principles applying to conjugal relationships. The first of them states that: spouses have equal rights and duties in the family unit. The operative provisions of the family law of Ukraine, in general, correspond to the Resolution of CE (78) 37 "On Equality of Spouses in Civil Law." The family legislation does not restrict directly nor indirectly conjugal rights depending on the sex, race, nationality, religion, domicile, education or financial position of the spouses (Article 4 MFC of Ukraine). Neither spouse has a more advantageous position than the other. The wife and the husband jointly make decisions regarding family life and their children's education (Article 20 of the MFC of Ukraine). Spouses are free to choose their family name, common residences, trade, professions or education (Article 19, 21 of the MFC of Ukraine). Both spouses have equal rights and duties concerning their common children. These rights continue to exist even after divorce.

The draft of the new Family Code of Ukraine is based on these principles.

II   THE SUBSTANTIVE REQUIREMENTS

Conjugal rights and duties only arise in the case of registering a marriage. Family legislation envisages a series of substantive requirements which are obligatory to obtain the legal status of a marriage. If one of them is violated, the marriage may be recognized as invalid by the court and annulled (Article 45 of the MFC of Ukraine).

The free and mutual consent of spouses intending to marry is the first obligatory requirement of the marriage's validity (Article 15 of the MFC of Ukraine). It signifies the absence of threat, duress, fraud and any other illegal coercion or domination of the will of one or both of the intending spouses. Family legislation provides that consent to marry must be expressed by each of spouses personally in front of the registration authority. Representation in this situation is prohibited. If one of the intending spouses cannot appear before the registration authority for good reasons (as a rule because of illness), the marriage registration is carried out at the spouse's home or in the hospital. According to the legislation, the presence of witnesses at the marriage registration is not required. At the same time, they generally are present at the ceremony. This tradition is so strong that most people are convinced that without witnesses, a marriage can not be registered. Receipt of the parents' or other persons' consent to a marriage is not required by law, even in the marriage of minors. However, if minors intending to be spouses want to conclude a marriage contract, the consent of their parent or guardian is necessary.

The legal age for marriage in the Ukrainian family legislation depends on the sex of the party concerned. The minimum age for marriage is 18 for men and is 17 for women (Article 16 of the MFC of Ukraine). Exceptionally, for good reason (as a rule, pregnancy of a young woman), the marriage age may be lowered by a competent authority. It is interesting to note that the family legislation currently in force does not impose any limitation on the age to which legal marriage can be lowered in this situation.[4] Thus, if a good reason is present and the intending spouses consent, the young people may be married at any age.

The draft of the new Family Code of Ukraine includes a change to the marriage age of women – it is lowered to 16 years of age. As statistics indicate, in Ukraine a permanent increase in the number of young marriages has occurred and legislators have been forced to consider this tendency. Young marriages are the least dependable. In many cases, the marriages of young people last until the parties are no more than twenty two years of age and exist for less than five years. As already mentioned, in Ukraine cohabitation is not very widespread. That is why these marriages have the character of a so-called "trial marriage." After divorce, people who initiate a second marriage have certain experiences of family life and these subsequent marriages are more stable. In many countries there is a contrary tendency - people have a family after getting an education and attaining a solid position in life. In Ukraine, most families are created under the ages

---

4   The Decree of the Presidium of the Supreme Soviet of Ukraine, "On Amendments to Article 16 of the Code on Marriage and Family of the Ukrainian SSR". Vidomosti Verhovnoi Rady Ukrainy. No 4. St. 25. (1992).

of 30 to 35 years. Ukrainian women generally stop child-bearing by 33 years of age. The procreation rate among people 35 to 39 in Ukraine is one of the lowest in the world.[5]

Ukrainian legislation traditionally holds to the principle of monogamy. Spouses may only be in one marriage. Furthermore, a spouse's rights and obligations only arise from a marriage which was registered by the special state authority (Article 13 of the MFC of Ukraine). The State's registration allows authorities to take stock of the registered marriages and avoid the situation where the person intending to marry is in another undissolved marriage.

Cohabitation does not initiate the spouses' rights and duties. When Ukraine was a part of the structure of the USSR, the State's policy towards unmarried cohabitants changed historically. After The October Revolution in 1917, the registration of marriage was completely abolished. Later the law regulated both registered and unregistered marriages. However, after July 8, 1944, when the Decree of the Presidium of the Supreme Soviet USSR came into play (which concerned an increase in the state's help to pregnant women, families with multiple dependents, and unmarried mothers... in the USSR), only marriages which were registered were recognized.

This condition is preserved in the draft of the new Family Code of Ukraine. Cohabitation engenders only some of the possible consequences. If, for instance, one partner was a dependent of the other partner and lived with him, he may receive a certain share of inheritance. However, any dependents have the same right, not only a cohabiting partner. The religious ceremony of marriage also does not engender legal consequences and is the private affair of the intending spouses. In recent times, a lot of marriages include a wedding ceremony after the official marriage registration.

It is known that a close genetic relationship between parents may have a negative influence on their children's health. In connection with this, the family legislation includes some restrictions. According to Article 17 of the MFC of Ukraine, marriages between direct relatives in the line of ascent and

---

5   N. Lakiza-Satchyk. I demografichne vyzhyvannya. Polityka i chas. No 4. S. 18. (1994).

descent are forbidden. Apart from this, the law also prohibits marriage between full-blood and/or half-blood brothers and sisters.

The draft of the new Family Code of Ukraine extends this law to a larger range of blood-relatives who will not have the right to marry one another. At the present time, there is a proposition to prohibit marriages between first cousins and aunt-nephew and uncle-niece relationships, which are currently permitted. Marriages between such relatives are rare, but their registration does take place today.

The relationships between adoptive parents and step-parents and their respective children equate with natural parent-child relationships (Article 117 MFC of Ukraine). For moral reasons, marriages between these people are forbidden.

As already mentioned, at the time of a marriage's registration, consent of the parties is required. Proper mental capacity is one of the basic requirements for the validity of a marriage. The Ukrainian family legislation does not contain a special list of illnesses giving rise to nullity of a marriage. A person cannot marry if he is found incapable by a court to participate in a civil proceeding. There are two criteria for this: (1) the presence of a mental illness (medical criterion) and (2) the incapacity to understand the legal consequences of his own actions (juristic criterion). Other than this, a marriage may be held to be invalid in a case where a capable person intending to marry has a temporary mental disorder and is not aware of his actions.

The question about the health of the persons intending to marry is certainly very important to the spouses as well as to the children. The Family legislation of Ukraine contains a rule, which reads as follows: "The spouses should be mutually informed about one another's health conditions." (Article 18 MFC of Ukraine). Unfortunately, this rule is generally dependent on the good will of the spouses, and its violation does not engender any legal sanction. At the same time, the general health of the Ukrainian people is the subject of serious anxiety among specialists and in the community. The lifespan of people in Ukraine takes forty-seventh place in the world. The death-rate, on the other hand, is one of the highest – second place for infant mortality and seventeenth for adult deaths.[6]

A large negative factor for Ukraine is the consequences of the Chernobyl catastrophe. Officially, the number of people who suffered from the Chernobyl accident is 1.5 million, including 90,000 children, who are the future of the country. According to the opinion of specialists, the radioactive irradiation was received in some degree by about twenty percent of the Ukrainian population.[7] Certainly, family legislation cannot do anything to improve the people's health. But it can make provision to try to ensure that intending spouses are made aware of the importance of this question of health, and to defend the rights of the victims. In the draft of the new Family Code of Ukraine, there is a new mandatory requirement that intending spouses should be informed about the condition of one another's health. If one of them hides an illness from his/her spouse which could be dangerous for him/her or their future children, the other spouse has the right to require that the marriage be annulled.

The draft of the Family Code contains special rules where the state takes upon itself the obligation to require all intending spouses to pass a medical examination to make known his/her health condition. It is hard to know to what degree this rule may be realized, taking into account the difficult situation of public health in Ukraine. However, besides this rule, it is impossible to require that spouses inform one another about all health conditions, as there may be cases in which one or other may not know about an illness.

III MATRIMONIAL PROPERTY RELATIONSHIP

While the communist ideology held sway in Ukraine, only the state's property was recognized as the basis of the economy. Private property took on a secondary importance. Civil legislation included many rules restricting private individual's rights to their possessions. For instance, private property

---

6   S. Pirozhkov. N. Lakiza-Satchyk. Chy bude syn, chy bude maty? Viche. No 6. S. 40. (1993).
7   Lavrinenko N., Bydko E. Suchasna sim'ya: portret v zazhyreniyi rami. Ukraina. No 12. S. 22. (1994).

was completely prohibited as far as means of production were concerned. People could only have consumer goods as their private property. However, this situation was limited as well. The same was true in the family sphere. To each family belonged one dwelling-house measuring not more than 80 square metres (Article 101, 102 Civil Code of Ukraine). The legislation determined the maximum amount of cattle an owner could have, and included other restrictions of property (Article 108 Civil Code of Ukraine).

For many years, there existed in the theory of family law, a secondary, disdainful set of laws regarding the treatment of a spouse's property. The matrimonial property regime was regulated very strictly and could not be changed by the spouses' will. With economic reforms in Ukraine and the gradual movement to a free market economy, many important changes took place in the civil and family legislation of the country. These changes first concerned matrimonial property. At the same time, the most offensive, odious rules of the Civil Code of Ukraine were abolished. Article 13 of the Law "About Property", which came into force on February 7, 1991, reads, "The composition, number, and cost of private property are not restricted."[8] This rule applies to a spouse's property also. The operative Family Code was supplemented by a number of new dispositive rules. Intending spouses were given the right to conclude a marriage contract and independently regulate many aspects of their property relationship. Therefore, in the Ukrainian family legislation there exists two ways (legal and contractual) to regulate the spouses' matrimonial property at the same time. They define the regime of the spouses' property.

A   The legal regime of the spouses' property

The legal regime of the ownership of property by spouses is based on the following provisions. In accordance with the Ukrainian family law currently in force, property may belong to both spouses or to either of them. Family law applies a different legal regime to common as opposed to separate property of spouses. That is why this question is very important. Sometimes

---

8   The Law of Ukraine, "About Property" of February 7, 1991. Vidomosti Verhovnoi Rady Ukrainy. No 20. St. 249. (1991).

the question about whether property belongs to one or both spouses is contentious. In considering this contest, the court ascertains at what time the disputed property was acquired, from what source, and so on. Moreover, each of the spouses can produce his/her own evidence (different contracts, other documents, confirmation of their rights to the property, and so on).

In general, in Ukrainian family law, there exists the presumption of the community of the spouses' property. This means that until otherwise shown, any disputed property is considered to be in common ownership. The Courts' decisions have proceeded from this presumption while considering different cases. In the Family Code's draft, this principle is fixed as a concrete rule. The common property regime arises by operation of law. At the present time, it may be rebutted by a contrary intention as to ownership evidenced by specific provision in a marital contract.

B Common property of the spouses

According to Article 22 MFC of Ukraine, all property acquired by spouses during a marriage is their common property. This includes all personal and joint real estate, the fruits of this property, income and profits. By a court's decision, separate property may be treated as common property. This is possible in a case where, during the marriage, both spouses over a long time used property which belonged to one of them. Aside from using it as a residence, it is important to note that the non-owning spouse may have invested his/her time or money in maintaining the given property.

According to Article 23 MFC of Ukraine, spouses jointly possess, profit and dispose of their common property. Until today, spouses' disputes about the management of their common property did not interest the Court. This situation is explained by the absence of the ownership of very expensive objects by citizens of the Ukraine. However at the present time in our country, a citizen's private property may include these same objects. That is why the draft of the new Family Code includes a special rule which enables spouses contesting the management and enjoyment of their common property to apply to the Court.

Where one spouse concludes a transaction, it is considered that he/she operates with the other spouses' consent. Some transactions require an obligatory notarisation (for example: changes or alterations in the ownership or state of the house, car, boat, country-cottage, etc.). For these alterations, the consent of the other spouse must be expressed in written form. In other cases the other spouses' consent may be expressed verbally. If a spouse concludes a deal in connection with common property without the consent of the other spouse, the deal may be recognized as invalid by the Court. Other than that, it is imperative that the other party to the transaction was aware that the other spouse did not give his/her consent to the transaction.

The spouses' property is not in shares. That is why a spouse's property rights do not depend on his/her contribution to common property. The size of a spouse's income (or even a complete lack of income) does not influence his share of the property. If, for example, the wife has no salary and raised the children, this has no effect on her right to receive a share of the spousal property (Article 22 MFC of Ukraine). In this way, as long as the marriage exists, the shares of the spouses' common property are not certain. Such a necessity arises only in the case of division of the property which, as a rule, is connected with divorce. In this case, the spouses' shares in the property are recognized to be equal. Sometimes the Court may violate the equality principle, to meet the needs of minor children. In this case, the Court will increase the share of property of the spouse with whom seriously ill children will be living and so on (Article 28 MFC of Ukraine).

In some cases, concerning the division of the spouses' property, the legal importance of the size of the spousal contribution to the common property may increase. It is connected with blameworthy conduct of one spouse in the marriage. Fault of a spouse can have an effect in that, by his own actions, the spouse may have caused damage to the family property. This would be the case, for example, if a spouse spent money in a way that was not in the interests of the family or entered into financial transactions without the agreement of the other spouse, and so on. In this case, the Court may take into account the adverse behaviour of the spouse and, when dividing the property, reduce his share. The Court may take account of some other circumstances in favour of one of the spouses (Article 28 MFC of Ukraine).

The Court may divide up property in different ways. Some items may be simply split between the spouses. In some cases the Court may give property to one spouse and require him/her to compensate the other for one half of the value of the property. The draft of the new Family Code of Ukraine gives the Court the opportunity to order the sale of common property where property division proves impossible, and then to divide the proceeds as it sees fit.

C Separate property of the spouses

Separate property is property which belongs to each of the spouses. In conformity with Article 24 MFC of Ukraine regarding separate property of spouses, the following matters are considered:

a   possessions owned before the marriage;
b   property presented to one of the spouses during the marriage;
c   property inherited by a spouse during the marriage;
d   individual possessions for personal use, except jewellery;
e   According to Ukrainian legislation, the spouses are not required to live together. Presumably, property is acquired during the marriage by mutual consent, even if they are living separately. However, cases arise when the spouses have ceased to have a real marital relationship, but legally the marriage has not been dissolved. If the spouses, during the marriage, lived in separation and actually terminated marital relations, then the property acquired in this period can be, by the Court's decision, considered separate (Article 28 MFC of Ukraine).
f   According to Ukrainian legislation, Article 29 of the Family Code, the spouses may voluntarily divide their property between themselves. In this case, they would not go to court. Such a decision by the spouses must be certified by a notary. After dividing common property, it becomes separate property.

Each of the spouses may make his/her own arrangements for the use and disposition of their separate possessions (sell, grant, exchange, lease, etc. to any people including other spouses). The property owned by the spouses separately is not divided.

D   The contractual regime of the spouses' property

Until 1992, the property relations of the spouses were rigorously regulated by the Family Code. The Code determined which part of the spouses' property was common and which was separately owned by each spouse. The prescribed division could not be changed by the spouses' agreement, and substantially restricted the spouses' rights.

A significant amendment which could have a far-reaching influence on the development of spouses relations was the introduction of the marriage contract. This law, approved on June 23, 1992, Article 27-1, amends the Family Code of Ukraine, and is named "Spouses' Rights to Conclude a Marriage Contract".[9] According to this Article, spouses acquire the right to determine a matrimonial property regime different from the legal one. Thus, spouses are entitled to transfer their separate possessions to their common property. On the contrary, if according to the law, their property is considered common, they may, by mutual consent, consider it separate. Spouses are entitled to agree to voluntary division of their property. If the spouses have concluded a marriage contract, the division of property in dissolving the marriage is carried out according to the conditions of the contract.

Unfortunately, family law contains many restrictions concerning the form and conditions of the marriage contract. Thus, according to Article 27-1 MFC of Ukraine, marriage contracts can be concluded only by couples who are being married today, while a large number of those who had married before 1992 did not have this right. Besides this, there is a series of essential conditions which spouses may not include in a marriage contract. For example, no conditions may be specified for alimony payments. The manner and conditions for receiving spousal alimony payments are strictly regulated by law. Spouses may not include in the marriage contract conditions about spouses' debts, the level of child support payments and so on.

---

9   The Law of Ukraine, "On Changes and Amendments to the Code on Marriage and Family of the Ukrainian SSR" of June 23, 1992. Vidomosti Verhovnoi Rady Ukrainy. No36. St. 528. (1992).

Article 27-1 MFC of Ukraine provides that a marital contract must not contain clauses which worsen the position of one of the spouses in comparison with the Family Law of Ukraine. Realization of this rule is very difficult. According to Ukrainian legislation, a marital contract is in force only if it has been certified by a notary. Therefore, it becomes a notary's duty to verify clauses of the marital contract and to advise the spouses to remove any clauses of the contract not in accordance with the law. However, in itself, the notion of "being worse off" is quite uncertain. At present, the notary profession can not form an accurate conception of which of the contract's clauses may fall foul of this rule. The rule has been criticized by legal critics and scholars. The Family Code's draft does not contain such a rule.

The draft of the new Family Code of Ukraine significantly widens the rights of spouses to conclude marital contracts. Spouses will be able to conclude prenuptial contracts, reconciliation agreements, separation agreements and so on. This gives spouses the opportunity to specify more carefully their rights and obligations and to establish their property responsibilities. Spouses will be able to include in the marital contract requirements relating to their mutual financial maintenance. Spouses will also have the opportunity to conclude agreements about the division of property in case of a divorce and so on.

The draft of the new Family Code addresses the question of possible invalidity of the marriage contract. It provides that a marriage contract may be recognized as invalid if it contradicts any law – family law as well as civil law. Thus, the marriage contract will be invalid for reasons including fraud, duress, and any other undue influence on an intending spouse. Due to the absence of experience in this field, Ukrainians may only imagine the kind of violations of law which may arise in relation to marital contracts in the future. For this reason, how other countries deal with this issue is very important to the legal theory of the Ukraine, and theorists are working to study different cases and to learn to understand them.

IV   MAINTENANCE OF SPOUSES

According to Article 32 MFC of Ukraine, spouses are obliged to support one another. The Ukrainian family legislation proceeds from the position that spouses have equal and mutual duties in supporting one another. Disputes between spouses about support are within the jurisdiction of the Court. As practice shows, support suits arise rarely in the courts. As a rule, such a suit is brought by a wife who does not work and educates a child. This support suit is commonly decided parallel to a suit for child support.

The right of one spouse to require support from another only arises in the presence of the following conditions:

1) The spouse in need of support is disabled. Disability is considered to exist when one of the spouses is unable to provide for himself/herself the necessities of life due to illness. According to Article 32 MFC of Ukraine, women, during pregnancy and up to three years after a child's birth, have a right to receive support as a disabled person. In legal practice, there sometimes arises a question about the recovery of alimony from a wife to her husband if he nurses a child and does not work. However the legislation currently in force makes no provision for such a case. As already mentioned, the Ukrainian family legislation enunciated a principle of equality of the spouses' rights. Hence, such a condition violates this principle. That is why the draft of the new Family Code of Ukraine provides a special rule which provides that the husband has the right to require support from his wife if he does not work and takes a care of a child.

2) Spouses who require alimony should be recognized as worthy by the court. Requirements are considered to be the absence of living wages. The notion "living wage" is an estimation, and is ascertained specifically in each case. A spouse may be recognized as needy if any of the conditions (retirement, sick benefits etc.) are sufficiently evident.

3) Alimony is only given in the case where the giving spouse is able to provide it regularly, i.e. he/she has a permanent and stable income, etc.

Family legislation provides the opportunity for spouses to recover alimony not only during marriage, but even after the marriage has ended in divorce in favour of one of the former spouses. According to Article 32 MFC of Ukraine, one of the needy divorced spouses is entitled to receive support from the other spouse if he/she became disabled within one year after the final divorce.

The amount of the alimony recovered by one of the spouses in his/her favour from the other spouse is decided by the court as a fixed sum, taking into account the property entitlement of both parties. Alimony payments are made every month. The draft of the new Family Code of Ukraine provides a number of new rules with respect to the recovery of alimony. They state that the spouses' support may be expressed not only in money, but that the paying spouse may pay alimony in kind. Other than that, according to the draft Code, the spouses have a right, with mutual agreement, to pay alimony for some months in a lump sum. According to a law which is currently in force, the volume of alimony established by the court may be changed by the request of both of the spouses (Article 33 MFC of Ukraine). More often, the payer of alimony applies to the court for a reduction in alimony arising from a worsening of the condition of his/her property. Otherwise, a needy spouse may request an increase in the amount of support.

In some cases the court may free one of the spouses from support or restrict his/her duty by some term. This is possible in the following cases:

a   if the couple were only married for a short time;
b   if the needy spouse conducted his/herself unworthily in relation to the other spouse;
c   if the needy spouse abused alcohol or drugs and as a result of this became disabled (Article 35 MFC of Ukraine).

In addition, the draft of the Family Code provides two new conditions:

e   if the needy spouse purposely disabled him/herself;
f   if the disability of the needy spouse was concealed from the other spouse during the marriage's registration.

As a rule the rights of the spouse receiving support are not limited by time. Nevertheless, family legislation provides a situation where this right ceases (Article 36 MFC of Ukraine). This is:

i   if the needy spouse's health is restored and he/she may work;
ii   if the needy spouse obtains other means to live;
iii if the needy spouse marries again.

V   DIVORCE

The family legislation of Ukraine is based on the principle of freedom of divorce, though the state does have some control in this sphere. Spouses have an equal right to initiate divorce proceedings. However, this rule has one exception: the husband may not require a divorce during the period of his wife's pregnancy and for one year after the birth of a child (Article 38 MFC of Ukraine). This rule is also enforced in the case of a stillbirth.

Ukrainian family law provides for two different types of divorce: administrative and judicial. According to Article 41 MFC of Ukraine, a marriage may be dissolved by a simple administrative order if both spouses agree on divorce, have no underage children, and do not disagree on the division of property. Aside from this, an administrative order can be made in relation to "special persons," which can be any of the following:

· a person who is recognized by the court as mentally incapable to consent to marriage;
· a person who is found to be absent for more than three years; in this case the court can rule by default;
· a person who is sentenced in a court to imprisonment for more than three years.

In all other cases, a marriage may only be dissolved by a court.

In accordance with Article 40 MFC of Ukraine, a marriage is dissolved if the Court establishes that further cohabitation of the spouses has become impossible. The sole reason recognized by the law for divorce is the irretrievable breakdown of the marriage. This may take place, for example, if the spouses do not live together and both apply for a divorce petition. A marriage can also be dissolved where one or both spouses already have a separate family. Often the spouses tell a judge that they do not intend to live together for various personal reasons. Thus, the Ukrainian divorce law is not based on the principle of fault. A Court need not determine who is at fault in the breakup of the family. So guilt does not affect a divorce.

During the legal proceedings, the court may take certain measures to preserve the family unit. By its decision, the Court may give the spouses a period for trial reconciliation. This term may not be more than six months. At the end of this period, if at least one of the spouses still insists on divorce, the marriage is dissolved. Divorce must be permitted if, on the evidence, reconciliation is impossible.

Divorce is usually accompanied by a number of problems between the spouses. They may be of a personal nature or property-related. As a rule, during the divorce proceedings, questions of property division, spousal or child support, decisions on spouses' surnames after divorce, the spouses' and the child's residence, and many other subjects arise.

In all cases where the marriage is dissolved, the court should make arrangements to defend the child's interests. Legal practice shows that the prevailing situation is one where after divorce, the child is left to live with the mother. The law makes no provision giving preference to the mother regarding the child. Rather, the law emphasizes that the spouses indeed have equal rights in relation to their child after divorce (Article 59 MFC of Ukraine). Nevertheless, courts traditionally leave the children (especially those of a younger age) with the mother. In recent times, fathers/men have become more active in raising claims to their children and demanding to have an opportunity to meet with their children without difficulty. In some cases, fathers even demand that the child be handed over to them.

Questions concerning the surname of the spouses after divorce are also decided in divorce proceedings. If one of the spouses at the time of the marriage registration changed his/her surname, he/she can recover the former name or retain the new second name. The consent of the other spouse is not required.

With the end of the marriage, the legal connection of the spouses is brought to an end. With this, the personal and property rights and obligations of the spouses also terminate. After divorce, spouses may only retain obligations of alimony and support.

THE UNITED STATES

FOCUS ON ADOPTION

Marygold S. Melli *

I INTRODUCTION

Although there was a variety of family law developments in the fifty American states in 1994, two of the most important related to the adoption of children: a new Uniform Adoption Act proposed for the States and a Multiethnic Placement Act adopted by Congress. These American adoption developments followed soon after the approval in 1993 of the Hague Convention on Intercountry Adoption[1] by the Hague Conference on Private International Law and indicated a high interest around the world in improving adoption services for children. This summary of activity in the United States in 1994 focuses on these two adoption developments.

II   THE UNIFORM ADOPTION ACT

One of the most significant developments in 1994 was the approval by the Conference of Commissioners on Uniform State Laws in August 1994 of a new Uniform Adoption Act.[2] The Conference on Uniform State Laws is a prestigious organization of representatives of all the states that has drafted and proposed some of the most influential laws in the United States, including the Uniform Child Custody Jurisdiction Act and the Uniform Interstate Family Support Act. The new Uniform Adoption Act was five years in preparation and replaces the Uniform Adoption Act which was approved by the Commissioners and the American Bar Association in 1953. That act was revised in 1969 and amended in 1971, but only eight states have adopted one of these versions. The new act represents a sophisticated attempt to reflect the changing face of adoption practices in the United States

---

*   University of Wisconsin, Madison Law School.
1   The full title of the convention is "Convention on the Protection of Children and Cooperation in Respect of Intercountry Adoption".
2   The new Uniform Adoption Act was approved by the American Bar Association in February 1995.

A. Bainham (ed.), The International Survey of Family Law 1994, 483–496.
© *1996 The International Society of Family Law. Printed in the Netherlands.*

and to balance the interests of the child to be adopted, the birth parents of that child, and the family seeking to adopt the child.[3]

A   *The need for uniformity*

There is general agreement that there is a real need for uniformity in the laws governing adoption. In the Prefatory Note to the Uniform Act, the Commissioners on Uniform State Laws discuss the need for adoption laws in the states that are more uniform. They note that, although thousands of children need homes, there are so many differences and inconsistencies from one state to another that possible adoptive parents are often discouraged. Laws differ from state to state on "who may place a child for adoption, whose consent is required and when consent is final, how much money can be paid to whom and for what, how much information can or should be shared between birth and adoptive families, what makes an individual suitable as an adoptive parent, and what efforts are needed to encourage the permanent placement of minority children and other children with special needs who languish in foster care."[4] The new Act reduces this confusion. These variations in laws not only make it difficult to comply with the law in a mobile society in which interstate adoption has become more common, but they also may lead to forum shopping. One commentator has noted that adoptive parents may go where they can most easily find a child, satisfy the state parental fitness standard, and acquire speedy termination of parental rights. Birth mothers may go where they have greatest say as to who adopts their child, where "reimbursement" for expenses is highest or where the birth father's parental rights may be most easily terminated.[5]

---

3   The Uniform Adoption Act has its share of critics. See, Mark Hanson, "Fears of the Heart", 80 *A.B.A. Journal* 58 (Nov. 1994).

4   Uniform Adoption Act, Prefatory Note, p. 2 (1994).

5   M.E. Selmann, "For the Sake of the Child: Moving Toward Uniformity in Adoption Law", 69 *Wash. L. Rev.* 841 (1994).

B An overview

The Uniform Act recognizes the variety of contexts in which adoptions occur and the differing protections needed in different contexts. Therefore, there are separate Articles in the Act on the adoption of minors, the adoption of stepchildren by their stepparent,[6] and the adoption of adults and emancipated minors.[7] The Act contains a total of eight articles. The first article contains definitions and general provisions that apply to all types of adoptions. Article 2 applies to the Adoption of Minors and is divided into four parts covering placement of children, evaluation of adoptive parents, and consent to and relinquishment for adoption.

Article 3 deals with the procedures to be followed in an adoption, including the contents of the petition, the notice to be given, the disclosure of fees and charges. It applies to all types of adoptions.

Article 4 covers the adoption of a minor stepchild by a stepparent. Article 5 deals with the adoption of adults and emancipated minors. Articles 6, 7, and 8 apply to all adoptions. Article 6 contains provisions on records, confidentiality and access to confidential information. Article 7 deals with activities and payments that are prohibited and those that are allowed. Article 8 contains some miscellaneous provisions applicable to all adoptions.

The following discussion of the new Act focuses on the adoption of minors and the provisions of the act that relate to those adoptions.

C Placement of children for adoption

Part 1 of Article 2 deals with the placement of minors for adoption. The Act defines placement for adoption to include two functions: the selection of a prospective adoptive parent and the transfer of physical custody of the minor child to the prospective adoptive parent.[8] At present, all states authorize an approved agency[9] to place children for adoption. Most also

---

6   See Uniform Adoption Act, Art. 4 (1994).
7   See Uniform Adoption Act, Art. 5 (1994).
8   Uniform Adoption Act §§ 1-101 (3), 2-101 (1994).
9   Agency is defined in § 1-101 as a public or private entity authorized by the law of the State to place children for adoption.

allow a birth parent to make a direct placement with an adoptive parent chosen by the birth parent. But there is wide difference of opinion and practice as to the use of an intermediary when the birth parent places the child directly. A related issue involves the role the birth parent may play in selecting the adoptive placement when the placement is made by an agency.

The Act authorizes both agency and direct birth parent placements[10] and permits the use of an intermediary by the birth parent or the prospective adoptive parent in the direct placement. Section 2-102(b) provides that a parent who places a child directly with an adoptive parent may be assisted by another person, including a lawyer, health care provider or agency in locating or transferring legal and physical custody of the child to a prospective adoptive parent. Section 2-102(c) allows a prospective adoptive parent to be assisted by another person in locating a minor who is available for adoption. The Act is silent on the specific role of these intermediaries other than to provide in § 7-101(a)(1) that only a parent or an adoption agency may advertise knowledge of a minor available for adoption and in § 7-101(a)(2) that only an adoption agency or a prospective adoptive parent with a favorable preplacement evaluation may advertise that a person is willing to accept a child for adoption. However, the Act appears to recognize that information about prospective adoptees may be available to adoptive parents in other ways because § 2-203(d)(9) requires that the preplacement evaluation of a prospective adoptive parent contain information on whether that person has identified a parent interested in placing a minor for adoption and, if so, a brief description of the parent and child.One of the major attractions for a birth parent of direct placement has been the ability of the birth parent to pick a particular adoptive parent or to specify desirable characteristics for the adoptive parent of the child. The Act provides a parent who places a child through an agency with the same authority by providing that an agency may agree to place a child with a prospective, adoptive parent

---

10   Uniform Adoption Act §§ 2-101, 2-192, & 2-103 (1994).

selected by the birth parent[11] or with an adoptive parent having certain characteristics specified by the birth parent.[12]Unlike most adoption statutes, the Act in § 2-104 establishes an order of preference for the adoptive placement of children in the legal custody of an agency if the agency has not agreed to place the child with prospective adoptive parents chosen by the birth parents. Included in this list are persons who have cared for the child for a substantial period of time, such as foster parents. However, the section also prohibits the delay or denial of an adoption placement solely on the basis of the child's race, national origin or ethnic background.[13]

One other provision in Part 1 on placement should be noted because the Commissioners view it as a significant contribution to improving adoption practice.[14] It is the requirement in § 2-106 for the disclosure to the prospective adoptive parent of information about the child's medical, psychological and social history before the prospective adoptive parent accepts physical custody of the child. In their Comment to § 2-106 the Commissioners point out that most states require some nonidentifying background information but very few provide that the information must be furnished before placement when it can play a major role in the decision of the prospective adoptive parent on whether to proceed with the adoption.

Finally, on the placement of children for adoption the Act contains an innovative provision in Part 3 of Article 2 specifically recognizing and authorizing the transfer of a child directly from a hospital or birthing center to a prospective adoptive placement if the birth mother signs an authorization for transfer of custody.

D   Preplacement evaluation of adoptive parents

Part 2 of Article 2 deals with what the Act calls preplacement evaluation. The Act requires that all adoptive placements, whether by an agency or directly by a birth parent, be made only with a prospective adoptive parent who has had a favorable preplacement evaluation within 18 months of the

---

11   Uniform Adoption Act § 2-104(a)(1) (1994).
12   Uniform Adoption Act § 2-104(b)(2) (1994).
13   See the discussion of the Multiethnic Placement Act of 1994 later in this article.
14   See Comment to § 2-106 Uniform Adoption Act (1994).

time of the placement.[15] This requirement continues a trend in adoption law toward preplacement investigation. Agency placements have always involved a preplacement investigation as part of the agency process for approval of adoptive applicants. But a growing number of states have also required it for nonagency or independent placements made directly by the birth mother.[16] The requirement of the Act for preplacement approval of an adoptive home in the independent adoption, however, will be a change for most states. Concern has been expressed that such a requirement of preplacement approval will discourage some adoptive parents, particularly those who are interested in adopting hard to place children.[17] But evaluation of adoptive homes is a practice of long standing. All states require that adoptive placements receive a favorable evaluation in the adoption proceeding prior to the entry of a final judgement of adoption. This is a requirement of the new Uniform Act also.[18] Its purpose is to assess how the adoptive placement is functioning so that the court is able to determine whether the adoption will be in the best interest of the child. The Uniform Act treats all adoptive placements alike by requiring all to have a preplacement evaluation by an evaluator who is qualified by a state licensing board to make preplacement evaluations. The Commissioner's Comment to § 2-202 notes that the Act does not assume that the only qualified evaluators for adoptive placements are employees of child-placing agencies but envisages independent evaluators. The Act does not specify any standards for persons who wish to qualify as evaluators but the Comment suggests

---

15 The Uniform Adoption Act § 2-201(a)(1994). There are two exceptions to this re-
    quirement in the Act. (1) A court may excuse the absence of a preplacement evaluation
    for "good cause shown." The comment of the commissioners to § 2-201 gives as an
    example of a case that might constitute "good cause" to waive the requirement of a
    preplacement evaluation: a child placed with a foster parent after removal from an
    abusive or neglectful home and after termination of the parental rights of the child's
    parents, the agency wants the foster parent to adopt the child. This placement should
    not be invalid simply because the transfer of physical custody occurred before a pre-
    adoptive evaluation. (2) A preplacement evaluation is not required if the child is placed
    for adoption with a relative. Relative is defined as a grandparent, great-grandparent,
    sibling, first cousin, aunt, uncle, great-aunt, great uncle, niece, or nephew of the in-
    dividual whether by whole or half-blood, affinity, or adoption. Uniform Adoption Act
    1-101(14).
16 Joan H. Hollinger, "Adoption Law ", 3 *The Future of Children*, No. 1 43 (Spring 1993)
    at note 32.
17 Ibid at 48.
18 The Uniform Adoption Act §§ 3-601, 3-692, and 3-603 (1994).

that the individual states develop criteria for certifying individuals as qualified evaluators.

Section 2-202 of the Act provides that an agency may, in addition, require its applicants to have a preplacement evaluation under its auspices even though the parents had received a favorable report from another qualified evaluator.

Two other provisions in Part II on preplacement evaluation should be discussed. They set out in the statute matters that in the past have not been so readily available to adoption applicants. The first deals with the criteria by which a prospective adoptive placement is to be judged. Section 2-203 specifies the information that is to be obtained for the evaluation and requires a personal interview and a visit at the residence of the prospective adoptive parent. Section 2-204 spells out the standard to be used in determining suitability of an adoptive parent: whether the information obtained about the parent "raises a specific concern that placement of any minor, or a particular minor, in the home of the individual would pose a significant risk of harm to the physical or psychological well-being of the minor."

The second provision on preplacement evaluation that should be noted is in § 2-206 which gives prospective adoptive applicants whose preplacement evaluation is negative, the right to judicial review.

E   Consent by birth parents to adoption

Part 4 of Article 2 covers the consent by the birth parents to the adoption of their child. Mothers and married fathers must consent to the adoption unless they have relinquished their right to the child[19] or have had their rights terminated.[20] An unmarried father has a similar right only in the following circumstances: if he has been judicially determined to be the father or has signed a document establishing paternity and has supported and communicated with or visited the child; or (2) if he has married the mother after

---

19   Section 1-101(15) defines relinquishment as the voluntary surrender to an agency by a child's parent, for the purpose of adoption, of the rights of the parent with respect to the child, including legal and physical custody of the child.

20   Uniform Adoption Act §§ 2-401, 2-402 (1994).

the child's birth or (3) if he has received the minor into his home and openly held the minor out as his child.[21]

Other possible fathers are entitled to notice of the adoption proceeding under §§ 3-401(3) and 3-404. One purpose of this notice appears to be to protect fathers from whom the mother has withheld information about the birth of the child. The Commissioners refer to these fathers in the Comment as "thwarted fathers." If a father responds to this notice and asserts paternity, it will be necessary to terminate his parental rights in a proceeding under Part 5 of Article 3. Under § 3-504 the father must prove by a preponderance of the evidence a compelling reason for not supporting the child or being willing to assume legal and physical custody of the child. If the father is successful in proving that he had a compelling reason for not performing his parental duties, the court will deny the petition to terminate his parental rights, dismiss the adoption proceeding and determine the issue of the custody of the child in the child's best interest as provided in § 3-704.

Limiting the requirement for consent to adoption by an unmarried father to those who have undertaken parenting responsibilities will be a change for the states that now require the termination of parental rights for all fathers, particularly those for whom a paternity determination has been made. The Commissioners cite the United States Supreme Court for the position that such a limitation is constitutional and the court has never given fathers the right to veto an adoption based only on the fact of biological parenthood.[22] Sections 2-404, 2-405, and 2-406 set out very specific procedures that must be followed for a consent or a relinquishment to be valid. The purpose of the procedures in these sections is to protect birth parents from hasty and ill-informed decisions about their child. The consent or relinquishment cannot be executed before the child is born. Once it is given, the parent has eight days (192 hours) from the birth of the child in which to revoke the consent or relinquishment. If the consent or relinquishment is not sought until more than eight days after the birth, the birth parent has no basis for revoking except to have the court set aside the consent under § 2-408 or the relinquishment under § 2-409 on the ground that it was obtained by fraud or duress.

---

21 Apparently, there is no requirement in the Act for any official determination of paternity in this case. See § 2-401(a)(1)(iii).
22 See the Comment to Uniform Adoption Act § 2-401 (1994).

Section 2-404 requires that the parent be informed of the meaning and consequences of adoption, the availability of personal and legal counselling and other information related to the adoption process. Section 2-405 requires that the consent or relinquishment must be signed or confirmed in the presence of a judge of a court of record, another person designated to take consents or relinquishments, or a lawyer, who cannot represent either an adoptive parent or the agency to which the child is relinquished. The person who takes the consent or relinquishment of the parent must certify in writing that the contents of the consent or relinquishment were explained to and understood by the parent. Section 2-406 specifies the contents of the consent or relinquishment that must be in English or in the native language of the parent, if that is not English. The consent or relinquishment must state that after it is signed, it is final and may not be revoked after eight days of the birth of the child or set aside, except under §§ 2-408 or 2-409 for fraud or duress, for any other reason, including the failure of an adoptive parent to permit the birth parent to visit or communicate with the child.

F Adoption expenses

Parents of newborn infants often prefer to deal with agencies or adoptive parents who will pay for medical and living expenses and other expenses connected with the adoption. But these kinds of payments have long been the subject of strict state regulation or even prohibition because of concerns about "baby selling." The Act openly acknowledges the issue of payment for adoption related expenses. Sections 7-103 and 7-104 contain a complete list of expenses that may be paid for by adoptive parents directly to the birth parent or to a provider of a service or an adoption agency. These include medical costs related to the child's birth, living expenses of the birth mother for reasonable periods of time, legal and counselling services and travel costs incurred by the birth parents.

Control over the payments to be sure that they are not "unreasonable or unnecessary when compared with the expenses customarily incurred in connection with an adoption"[23] is exercised through a requirement in § 3-702 that (1) the petitioner file a signed and verified accounting of any

---

23   Uniform Adoption Act § 3-703(a)(9) (1994).

payments made with the amount of each payment and the name and address of the recipient and that (2) the lawyers for the petitioner and the birth parents and any agency involved file an affidavit itemizing any fee paid to the lawyer or the agency. The court then reviews the accounting from the petitioner and the affidavits from the lawyers and the agency and determines whether to deny, modify, or approve the expenses.

G Confidentiality

In spite of current interest in "open adoption," i.e., an adoption in which the birth parent knows and maintains some relationship or communication with the adoptive parents and the child, the only mention in the Act of the possibility of that type of arrangement is the Prefatory Note where the Commissioners state that "The Act permits mutually agreed-upon communication between birth and adoptive families before and after an adoption is final." This mutually agreed on communication is achieved through the provisions in Article 6 for birth parents, adoptive parents and adoptees to file statements authorizing the release of identifying information from the adoption records. However, under § 2-406(d)(1) failure of an adoptive parent to honor an agreement for communication between the child and the birth parent is not a ground to revoke consent to adoption.

In general, the confidentiality provisions of the Act are similar to those of most of the States and have as their objective the substitution of the adoptive family for the original family of the child. Adoption proceedings are confidential,[24] all records in the adoption proceedings are confidential and sealed,[25] and the adoptee's original birth certificate is sealed and a new one is issued giving the adoptive parents as the official parents.[26] However, the Act limits the closed record to 99 years.[27] In the last quarter century, recognition of the importance of family history for some medical problems has prompted most states to require that nonidentifying medical and genetic information about a child be available. The Act contains this requirement in § 2-106 which is not limited to medical and genetic information but

---

24 Uniform Adoption Act § 3-203 (1994).
25 Uniform Adoption Act § 6-102 (1994)
26 Uniform Adoption Act § 3-802 (1994).
27 Uniform Adoption Act § 6-102 (1994).

includes a broad array of nonidentifying social and other background information as well. Of even more significance, is the fact that § 2-106 requires that this information be provided to the adoptive parents prior to placement of the child with them. Section 6-103 provides for the release of this nonidentifying information to adoptive parents and to adult adoptees on request.

Section 6-104 deals with the more sensitive issue of the release of identifying information. It allows the release of such information to adoptive parents and adult adoptees if the birth parent has filed a written consent to the disclosure of identifying information, either unilaterally or subject to the requirement that the adoptee and the adoptive parent release similar identifying information. The section also allows the release of identifying information about the adoptee to the adoptee's birth parent if the adoptee has authorized disclosure in writing. Section 6-106 provides for the establishment of a statewide registry for the filing of these documents authorizing the release of identifying information.

In addition to the consensual release of identifying information, § 6-105 provides for an action by an adoptee, an adoptive parent or the birth parent of the adoptee to obtain sealed information on a showing of "good cause" and a conclusion that there is a compelling reason for disclosure and the benefit to the petitioner is greater than any harm from disclosing the information.

H Finality of adoption decree

The Act, like the Uniform Putative and Unknown Fathers Act and the Uniform Parentage Act, provides that any challenge to a final adoption decree must be brought within six months of the entry of the decree.[28] In the Comment to § 3-707 setting forth this provision, the Commissioners note that "Under current law in most States, it is not clear for how long a decree of adoption may be challenged for fraud, undue influence, duress, failure to provide notice, lack of subject matter jurisdiction, or other alleged irregularities or constitutional violations." The Commissioners conclude that six months is a sufficient period to allow for such a challenge to the adoption

---

28 Uniform Adoption Act § 3-707 (1994).

decree because that period minimizes the risks to adoptive children and their adoptive families and because there are likely to be few challenges if the procedures in the Act are followed.

III MULTIETHNIC PLACEMENT ACT OF 1994

The Multiethnic Placement Act of 1994[29] is federal legislation, enacted by Congress to promote increased adoption opportunities for children, particularly minority children, who are awaiting placement for adoption, by requiring the states to make transracial adoptions easier. Transracial adoption is the adoption of a child of one racial background by a family of a different racial background. More specifically, the term refers to the adoption of Asian, Hispanic (primarily Mexican, Central or South American), Native American or black children by white adoptive parents.[30] Transracial adoption is one of the most controversial children's issues of the latter part of the 20th Century. Although it has provided thousands of minority children with adoptive families some have questioned its desirability[31] and strong opposition to it has developed, particularly by Native Americans and blacks. The Native Americans succeeded in virtually stopping the adoption of Native American children by white parents with the passage by Congress of the

---

29 The Multiethnic Placement Act of 1994 is Part E of the Title V of Improving America's Schools Act of 1994, Pub. L. No. 103-382, 108 Stat. 3518.

30 Transracial adoptions in the United States did not occur in significant numbers until after World War II. The first transracial adoptions involved children from the war ravaged countries of Asia; first small numbers of Japanese and Chinese children were adopted by white Americans. Later at the time of the Korean War, children from South Korea were adopted; that practice has continued so that the largest number of transracial adoptions in the United States is Korean born children adopted by white Americans. In the 1950s and 1960s, increasing interest in adoption resulted in shortages of white adoptable children while at the same time changing attitudes increased the willingness of adoptive couples to participate in a transracial adoption. During this period white adoptive couples adopted Native American and black infants. Native American advocacy groups objected to the fact that most adoptions of Native American children were by white Americans. As pointed out in the main text, the enactment of the Indian Child Welfare Act of 1978 virtually ended that practice. In 1972, the National Association of Black Social Workers passed a resolution opposing transracial adoption.

31 See discussion in Arnold L. Silverman, "Outcomes of Transracial Adoption", 3 *The Future of Children*, No. 1 105 (1993). See also, background in Elizabeth Bartholet, "Where Do Black Children Belong? The Politics of Race Matching in Adoption", 139 *Penn. L. Rev.* 1163 (1991).

Indian Child Welfare Act of 1978.[32] Blacks, with leadership from the National Association of Black Social Workers, were successful at having adopted in over half the states policies or statutes that require the adoption agency to delay placement of a minority child for adoption until a search has been made for parents of the same race. As a result, Congress has found that tens of thousands of children are in foster care awaiting adoption and that the median length of time children wait to be adopted is 2 years and 8 months.[33] It is estimated that minority children spend, on average, twice as long as nonminority children awaiting adoption.[34] The Multiethnic Placement Act makes the practice of delaying adoptive placement to seek same race parents illegal. It prohibits an agency that receives federal assistance from denying to any person the opportunity to become an adoptive parent, solely on the basis of the race, color, or national origin of the adoptive parent or the child. However, it does allow the agency to consider the cultural, ethnic or racial background of the child and the capacity of the prospective adoptive parents to meet the needs of a child of this background as one of a number of factors to determine the best interest of a child.

The Act also applies to foster care placements although in discussion of the bill, congressional attention was focussed primarily on the problems of adoption of minority children.[35] The Act provides two mechanisms for enforcing the prohibition against discrimination in adoption or foster care placement. First, pursuant to § 553(b), any person who is aggrieved by an action that he or she believes constitutes discrimination in violation of the Act has the right to bring an action seeking equitable relief in a United States district court. Second, the Act provides that noncompliance with the prohibition is deemed a violation of the Civil Rights Act of 1964. Under regulations published by the Office of Civil Rights any individual may file a complaint with that office alleging that an adoption or foster care organization funded with federal funds has violated the Multiethnic Placement Act and Title VI. If the Office of Civil Rights finds that this is the case, it will move to enforce the law.

---

32 25 U.S.C. § 1901 et seq.
33 Multiethnic Placement Act § 552(a)(2)(3).
34 N.Y. Times, April 27 1995, "New Rules Try to Ease Interracial Adoption".
35 Department of Health and Human Services, *Policy Guidelines on The Use of Race, Color or National Origin as Considerations in Adoptions and Foster Care Placements*. Federal Register, April 25 1995, at 20272.

IV CONCLUSION

Providing stable loving homes for the thousands of children who are available for adoption in the United States is a highly desirable public policy objective. Adoption is a child welfare service of the highest priority. Both pieces of legislation discussed here, the Uniform Adoption Act and the Multiethnic Placement Act, are intended to expedite and improve the adoption process and thus to enhance the opportunities for children of permanent homes.